CW00552981

MCGILL-QUEEN'S STUDIES IN THE HISTORY OF RELIGION

Volumes in this series have been supported by the Jackman Foundation of Toronto.

SERIES TWO   In memory of George Rawlyk
Donald Harman Akenson, Editor

Blood Ground

Colonialism, Missions, and the Contest for Christianity in the Cape Colony and Britain, 1799–1853

ELIZABETH ELBOURNE

McGill-Queen's University Press
Montreal & Kingston · London · Ithaca

© McGill-Queen's University Press 2002
ISBN 978-0-7735-2229-9 (cloth)
ISBN 978-0-7735-3453-7 (paper)

Legal deposit second quarter 2002
Bibliothèque nationale du Québec

Printed in Canada on acid-free paper
First paperback edition 2008

This book was first published with the help of a grant
from the Humanities and Social Sciences Federation of
Canada, using funds provided by the Social Sciences
and Humanities Research Council of Canada.

McGill-Queen's University Press acknowledges the
financial support of the Government of Canada through
the Book Publishing Industry Development Program
(BPIDP) for its activities. It also acknowledges the support of the Canada Council for the Arts for its publishing program.

National Library of Canada Cataloguing in Publication Data

Elbourne, Elizabeth
    Blood ground : colonialism, missions, and the contest for
Christianity in the Cape Colony and Britain, 1799–1853

(McGill-Queen's studies in the history of religion. Series two)
Includes bibliographical references and index.
ISBN 978-0-7735-2229-9 (bnd)
ISBN 978-0-7735-3453-7 (pbk)

    1. Khoikhoi (African people)—History—19th century.
2. London Missionary Society—History—19th century.   3. Cape
of Good Hope (South Africa)—Politics and government—
1795-1872.   4. Missions, British—South Africa—Cape of
Good Hope—History—19th century.   5. Cape of Good Hope
(South Africa)—History—1795-1872.   6. Great Britain—
Colonies—Africa.   I. Title.   II. Series.

DT1768.K56E42 2002   968.7'004961   C2001-903421-0

Typeset in 10/12 Sabon by True to Type

Contents

Acknowledgments

I have accumulated manifold debts to many remarkable and generous people over the long course of this book's composition. The following list is in no sense exhaustive.

I would first like to thank the supervisor of the original thesis, Terence Ranger of Oxford University, from whose brilliance and generosity I so greatly benefited. I would also like to warmly thank John Darwin, who suggested the topic and skilfully guided me through the early days of research. My thesis examiners, Stanley Trapido and Boyd Hilton, made many perceptive and helpful comments, while Stanley's knowledge of nineteenth-century Cape history proved invaluable at other times as well. Many people helped me with the manuscript at different stages, gave suggestions, or hosted seminars at which I presented work in progress. I am particularly grateful to Tanya Abramovitch, who created the index and finalized the bibliography, as well as to Henry Bredekamp, Arthur Burns, Isabelle Caron, Robert Cookson, Archie Crail, Sandra den Otter, Catherine Desbarats, Wayne Dooling, Wilhelmina Fredericks, Joanna Innes, Jiji Jeppie (for painstaking instruction!), Shamiel Jeppie, Karl Hele, David Keen, Paul Landau, John Lonsdale, Canby Malherbe, Shula Marks, Robert Shell, Mitra Shirafi, Doug Stuart, Masarah van Eyck, Dror Wahrman, Michael Wasser, and Brian Young. Richard Elphick read and commented exhaustively on an early version of the manuscript, Robert Ross on a late. Robert has also been a constant source of unpublished material and archival resources. The generosity of both astounded me, as always: thank you. Dan Peris, historian and stockbroker extraordinaire, painstakingly edited the first four chapters at a crucial stage. Aaron Chang created the maps. Astrid Thoné helped me translate Dutch archival material. Bianca Alvarado helped with proofreading. Thank you to all. Errors that remain are, of course, my responsibility.

During research trips to South Africa, I was overwhelmed by people's kindness, often at difficult times. For hospitality, as well as invaluable advice, I wish to thank the Reverend Jacob Alberts of Bethelsdorp, Monica, Robert, and Adam Cerf and families, Rasheeda and Dawood Edross, Patrick Harries, James and Kirsten Klopper, Rachidi Molapo, Bill Nasson, Susan Newton-King, and Nigel Worden. My thanks to the Reverend October of Genadendal and Johannes Davids for the *kinderfees*. In London, Judith Elbourne and Georgia Kaufman and Richard Wolfe were unstintingly kind hosts, as well as sounding boards for ideas. I worked on some of the manuscript during a stay at the Shelby Cullom Davis Center of Princeton University as a Social Sciences and Humanities Research Council of Canada post-doctoral fellow; later, I wrote the final draft while on leave from McGill University, again visiting the Department of History of Princeton University. I would like warmly to thank Nathalie Zemon Davies for hosting my first stay and Robert Tignor my second, as well as the many generous people in the Department of History and in African Studies. I am very grateful to Amy Gutmann and the Center for Human Values for providing me with office space during the latter sojourn.

In Montreal, I have benefited from a congenial home in the Department of History of McGill University. I am grateful to my colleagues, not least for lively advice on titles. Three excellent departmental chairs and acting chairs, Gil Troy, Catherine Legrand, and Suzanne Morton, as well as one superb administrator, Georgiii Mikula, gave me invaluable assistance while I was writing the final manuscript, helping to arrange leaves and material assistance. Colleagues in British and African history, Colin Duncan, Myron Echenberg, and Brian Lewis, created an enjoyable working environment. Thank you.

Research demands extensive resources. The McGill library system does extraordinary work with a severely limited budget. My thanks to the interlibrary loan department of McLennan library as also to the staff of the entire institution. I would also like to thank the staff of the library of the School of Oriental and African Studies, University of London; Allan Bell and other staff of Rhodes House library, University of Oxford; the Bodleian Library, University of Oxford; and the archivists of the Cape Archives, South Africa.

Generous support from the Social Sciences and Humanities Council of Canada and Les Fonds FCAR du Québec made this research possible. The Rhodes Trust supported my doctoral work, while my doctoral research was further assisted by a grant from the Beit travel fund of

Oxford University. The Aid to Scholarly Publications program of the Social Sciences and Humanities Research Council of Canada supported the publication of this book. I am grateful to all these bodies.

McGill-Queen's University Press has gone the extra mile with this project, and generally been everything a press should be. My particular thanks to Roger Martin, Joan McGilvray, John Zucchi, and Don Akenson. Curtis Fahey was a perceptive and assiduous editor of the final text.

Finally, it is a great pleasure to acknowledge my debt to my family. My mother, Ann Elbourne, my father, the late Gavin Elbourne, and my father-in-law, the late Henri Weinstock, were and are a great inspiration to me. Emma and Benjamin made me laugh constantly, which must count for a great deal, and are the lights of my life. Daniel Weinstock, who supported me throughout this work, makes everything not only possible but wonderful.

Montreal, July 2002

Some of this material has already been published in other venues. I am very grateful to the following for permission to republish it here: to the University of Witswatersrand Press and *Kronos* for permission to reprint extracts from E. Elbourne, "Early Khoisan uses of mission Christianity," in H.C. Bredekamp and Robert Ross, eds, *Missions and Christianity in South African History* (Johannesburg: University of Witswatersrand Press, 1995) and in *Kronos: Journal of Cape History/ Tydskrif vir Kaaplandse Geskiedenis* 19 (1992); to David Philip and Ohio State University for permission to reprint extracts from E. Elbourne, "Who Owns the Gospel? Conflict in the LMS in the 1840s," in John de Gruchy, ed., *The London Missionary Society in Southern Africa: Historical Essays in Celebration of the Bicentenary of the LMS in Southern Africa 1799–1999* (Cape Town: David Philip, 1999 and Athens, Ohio: Ohio University Press, 1999); and to the *Journal of African Cultural Studies* for permission to reprint extracts from E. Elbourne, "Race, Warfare and Religion in Mid-Nineteenth Century Southern Africa: The Khoikhoi Rebellion against the Cape Colony and Its uses, 1850–58," *Journal of African Cultural Studies* 13, no. 1 (2000).

Leah missed being in the acknowledgments to the first edition of this book, by virtue of not yet being born, but she has added immeasurably to the author's sense of perspective ever since. My post-publication thanks to her and, as ever, to Daniel, Emma, and Benjamin.

Montreal, April 2008

Portrait of an anonymous Khoekhoe woman, engraved by
William Daniell from an original drawing by Samuel Daniell
(Daniell, *Sketches Representing the Native Tribes, Animals
and Scenery of Southern Africa*. With permission of the
Royal Ontario Museum, Toronto. Photo credit: Wanda
Dobrowlanski)

Portrait of an anonymous Gonaqua man, engraved by
William Daniell from an original drawing by Samuel Daniell
(Daniell, *Sketches Representing the Native Tribes, Animals
and Scenery of Southern Africa*. With permission of the
Royal Ontario Museum, Toronto. Photo credit: Wanda
Dobrowlanski)

Khoekhoe women dancing, from a seventeenth-century drawing by an unknown artist (National Library of South Africa, INIL 6263)

The colonial interest in classification: Samuel Daniell portrays three men he distinguishes as Khoekhoe, San, and Tswana. Engraved by William Daniell from an original drawing by Samuel Daniell (Daniell, *Sketches Representing the Native Tribes, Animals and Scenery of Southern Africa*. With permission of the Royal Ontario Museum, Toronto. Photo credit: Wanda Dobrowlanski)

A Khoekhoe family (top) and a poorer man (bottom) with their respective stock, from a seventeenth-century drawing by an unknown artist. The man on the bottom left has his head partially shaved as a sign of mourning (National Library of South Africa, INIL 6256v)

Cape Town, with workers portrayed as part of the landscape, in the late 1790s: the entrance into Cape Town from Green Point (Barrow, *Travels into the Interior of Southern Africa*)

View of Fort Frederick and Algoa Bay, engraved by L. Portman from an original drawing by W.B.E. Paravicini di Capelli (*Quatre vues d'Afrique*, published in conjunction with Ludwig Alberti, *Description physique et historique des Cafres sur la côte méridionale de l'Afrique* [Amsterdam: E. Maaskamp 1811])

Johannes Theodorus van der Kemp (*Evangelical Magazine*, April 1799)

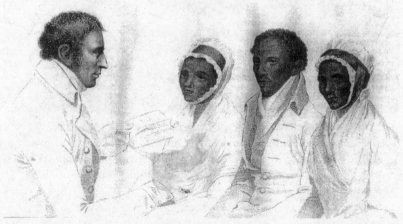

J.J. Kicherer, Sara Fortuin, Martha Arendse, and Klaas van Rooij in Amsterdam in 1803 (*Berichten van den predikant Kicherer, aangaande zijne zending tot de heidenen*. Amsterdam: 1805)

Meeting of General J.W. Janssens and Xhosa chief Ngqika, engraved by L. Portman from an original drawing by Chevalier Otto de Hawen and J.M. Smies (*Quatre vues d'Afrique*, published in conjunction with Ludwig Alberti, *Description
physique et historique des Cafres sur la côte méridionale de l'Afrique* [Amsterdam:
E. Maaskamp, 1811])

Heroic explorer in domestic guise: John Campbell with parasol and wagons, pointing to the
southern African interior. (Campbell, *Travels in
South Africa Undertaken at the Request of the
Missionary Society*)

John Campbell's view of Bethelsdorp (Campbell, *Travels in South Africa
Undertaken at the Request of the Missionary Society*)

James Read, Sr, in a portrait made during his
visit to England in 1835 (National Library of
South Africa, PHA)

John Philip, engraved by Thompson from an
original painting by Wildman, published by Westley & Davis, Stationer's Court, 1829 (Le Cordeur
and Saunders, eds., *The Kitchingman Papers*)

Andries Stoffels in London (*Evangelical Magazine and Missionary Chronicle*, vol. 15 – New Series, February 1837, frontispiece). With permission of the United Church of Canada/ Victoria University Archives, Toronto (catalogue number BV 2351 E9 1837 PS).

Dyani Tshatshu in London (*Evangelical Magazine and Missionary Chronicle*, vol. 15 – New Series, May 1837, frontispiece). With permission of the United Church of Canada/Victoria University Archives, Toronto (catalogue number BV 2351 E9 1837 PS).

Visual propaganda: an engraving entitled "The Humane and Generous Caffre," publicized in an 1836 LMS publication. The text comments that, "although the social condition of the Caffre Tribes has long been unfavourable to the development of virtuous and humane feelings, they nevertheless often exemplify valuable traits of character." (*Missionary Magazine and Chronicle* in the *Evangelical Magazine and Missionary Chronicle*, November 1836, 523)

Dyani Tshatshu, Andries Stoffels, John Philip, James Read, Jr, and James Read, Sr, giving evidence before the Committee of the House of Commons, painted by H. Room, engraved by R. Woodman; published by Fisher, Son & Co., London and Paris, 1844. The original painting is held at the Moffat Mission, Kuruman, South Africa

Mary Moffat as a young woman, drawn from
an original by Rudolph Blind (Moffat, *The
Lives of Robert and Mary Moffat*)

Robert Moffat in old age (Moffat, *The Lives of
Robert and Mary Moffat*)

Notishe, the teacher whom GAMS missionary Hepburn tried
to dismiss in the early 1840s. This engraving, made from an
early solorprint, was made when she later visited Scotland
at the age of twenty-two in the company of the GAMS
missionary Niven. The accompanying text in the *Juvenile
Missionary Magazine* states that she was a Xhosa woman
who fled to the Chumie mission rather than be married to
Xhosa chief Xoxo. My thanks to Canon A.J. Butler for
this image (*Juvenile Missionary Magazine of the United
Secession Church* [1845] 1: 97)

The joint grave of William Philip and his eleven-year-old nephew, both drowned in the Gamtoos River in 1845 just after the opening of the Hankey irrigation tunnel. Jane Philip was also later buried in this grave. (Photo credit: Robert Ross)

The grave of John Philip at Hankey (Photo credit: Robert Ross)

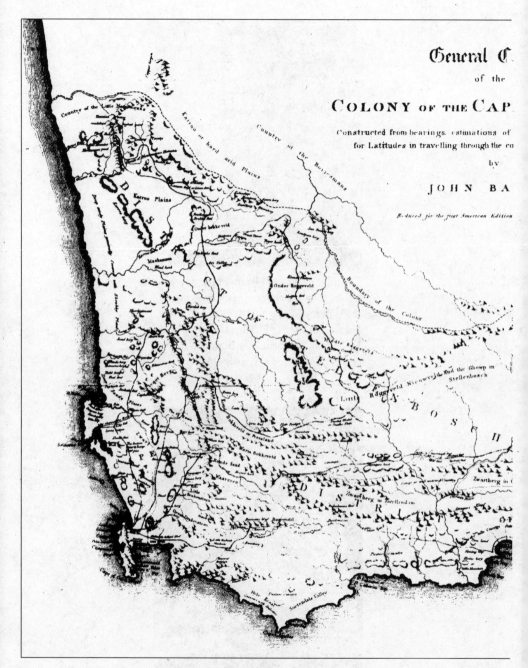

Map 1 Mapping and colonial possession: John Barrow's map of the Cape Colony in 1797–98 (Barrow, *Travels into the Interior of Southern Africa*, vol. I). This version of the map was simpli-

hart

E OF GOOD HOPE,

distances, and frequent observations
untry, during the years 1797 & 1798.

R R O W.

by Arthur Joseph Stansbury

fied and rendered more legible for the American edition of Barrow's *Account* by Arthur Joseph Stansbury. The map refers to the "Ghonaquas" as "a race now extinct."

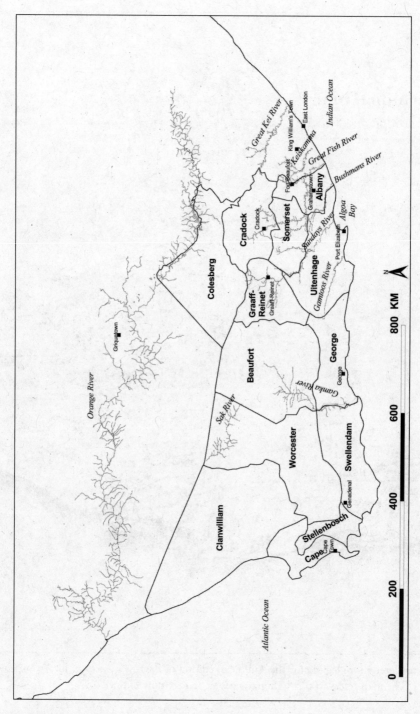

Map 2 Colonial districts in 1838

Atlantic Ocean

Indian Ocean

Orange River

Griquatown

Clanwilliam

Colesberg

Sak River

Beaufort

Graaff-
Reinet

Graaff-Reinet

Cradock

Cradock

Great Kei River

King William's Town

East London

Keiskamma

Fort Beaufort

Great Fish River

Somerset

Grahamstown

Albany

Bushmans River

Worcester

Gamka River

George

George

Uitenhage

Sundays River

Algoa
Bay

Gamtoos River

Port Elizabeth

Swellendam

Genadendal

Stellenbosch

Cape
Cape Town

N

0   200   400   600   800 KM

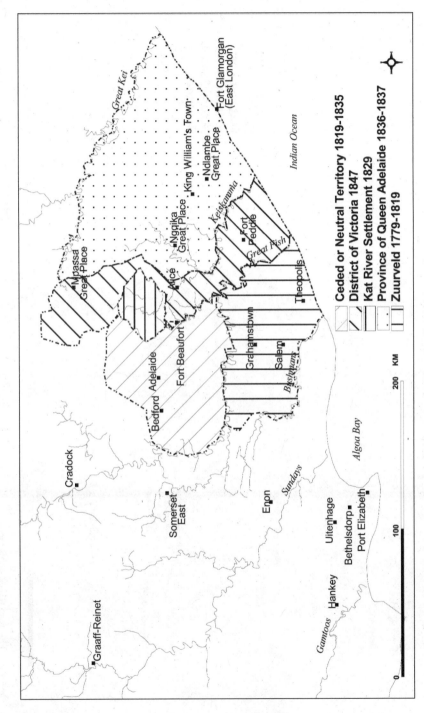

Map 3 Overlapping land claims: territorial divisions in the Eastern Cape, 1811–48.

Ceded or Neutral Territory 1819–1835
District of Victoria 1847
Kat River Settlement 1829
Province of Queen Adelaide 1836–1837
Zuurveld 1779–1819

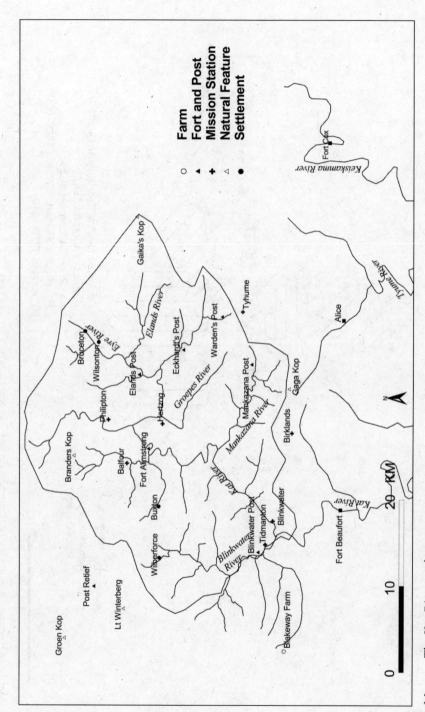

Farm
Fort and Post
Mission Station
Natural Feature
Settlement

Map 4   The Kat River settlement

Blood Ground

"Cain said to his brother Abel, 'Let us go out'; and while they were in the open country, Cain set on his brother Abel and killed him. Yahweh asked Cain, 'Where is your brother Abel?' 'I do not know,' he replied. 'Am I my brother's guardian?' 'What have you done?' Yahweh asked. 'Listen to the sound of your brother's blood, crying out to me from the ground. Now be accursed and driven from the ground that has opened its mouth to receive your brother's blood at your hands. When you till the ground it shall no longer yield you any of its produce. You shall be a fugitive and a wanderer over the earth.' Then Cain said to Yahweh, 'My punishment is greater than I can bear. See! Today you drive me from this ground. I must hide from you and be a fugitive and a wanderer over the earth. Why, whoever comes across me will kill me!' 'Very well, then,' Yahweh replied, 'if anyone kills Cain, sevenfold vengeance shall be taken for him.' So Yahweh put a mark on Cain, to prevent whoever might come across him from striking him down. Cain left the presence of Yahweh and settled in the land of Nod, east of Eden."

– Genesis 4:8–16 (*The Jerusalem Bible*)

"Hierdie grond was afgeeve door bloed.
Die bloed kom van my oupa.
Agter my oupa kom daar 'n oorlag!
Ons gee drie seuns, drie ...
....
My vader het vir 'n oorlog gestaan.
My oupa het vir 'n oorlog gestaan.
My vader het vir 'n oorlog gestaan.
My kinders, my vader se kinders, wat het vir
'n oorlog gestaan.
My oompie se kinders wat het vir 'n oorlog gestaan.
Bloed!
Van bloed!
Om dat die plek vrymaak, laat hy, laat hy
....
En vandag moet ons dit lkaat staan.
Sonder lus.
Sonder lus.
So is die ding."

"This ground was washed clean by blood.
The blood came from my grandfather.
After my grandfather there came a war!
We gave three sons, three ...
...

My father stood up for a war.
My grandfather stood up for a war.
My father stood up for a war.
My children, my father's children that stood up for a war.
My uncle's children that stood up for a war.
My auntie's children that stood up for a war.
Blood!
Of blood!
To make the place free, that it, that it …
And today we must let it go.
Without wanting.
Without wanting to.
Such is this thing."
– Piet Draghoender on the eviction of the Kat River
    community, 1984 (Jeff Peires, "Piet Draghoender's Lament,"
    Social Dynamics 14 [2] [1988]: 11.)

"Now as they were eating, Jesus took some bread, and when he had said the
blessing he broke it and gave it to the disciples. 'Take it and eat,' he said,
'this is my body.' Then he took a cup, and when he had returned thanks he
gave it to them. 'Drink all of you from this,' he said, 'for this is my blood,
the blood of the covenant, which is to be poured out for many for the forgiveness of sins."

– Matthew 26: 26–8 (*The Jerusalem Bible*)

Prelude
James Read and History

In September 1800, a twenty-two-year-old carpenter from Essex named James Read stepped ashore in the Cape Colony in the employ of the recently formed London Missionary Society (LMS), which had begun operations in southern Africa in 1799. Read would live for most of the rest of his life within the white colony in the frontier zones of the eastern Cape. He came expecting to meet exotic and "savage" African peoples beyond the reach of the Christian message; instead, he encountered Khoekhoe communities whose members had once been nomadic cattle herders but were by the late eighteenth century mostly subjugated labourers on white farms, their numbers augmented by dispossessed hunter-gatherers. They had not, however, by any means forgotten their recent days of independence. The type of Christianity borne by Read would prove an unsettling complication in a society ravaged by ethnic conflict in which race, religion, and status overlapped in complicated ways.

It had taken James Read a long time to reach Africa. The ship on which he left Plymouth in 1798, bound for Tahiti, had been captured by the French off the coast of Brazil. It had been more than a year before Read was able to return to Britain, still in pursuit of his missionary vocation, after a long voyage via Rio de Janeiro, Uruguay, and Portugal. He proved one of the few young men selected by the LMS to work in "Otaheite" (Tahiti) to remain committed after the disasters of the initial voyage. He set out again, undaunted, this time for the Cape. He arrived as ignorant of the continent of Africa he hoped to convert as he had been of the South Pacific. After a period working in Cape

Town with British soldiers, Read would travel to the eastern frontiers of the newly acquired British colony, and so into a war zone and a new life.

I imagine Read perpetually arriving, a wide-eyed young man stepping into new roles: as the husband of the young Khoekhoe woman Elizabeth Valentyn, the unexpected proponent of frontier justice, the equally unexpected adulterer and outcast. He would become committed, his life irrevocably interwoven with this ferocious place. In the beginning, his presence was an accident of history. He represented an ill-informed missionary society, stumbling despite itself into the cauldron of southern African power struggles and racial violence. Local peoples competed to use this society to their own advantage, as Christianity became a critical element in the conflicts of early-nineteenth-century South African society.

Fifty-one years later, the same James Read, now the elderly and respected pastor of the Philipton church in the Khoekhoe Kat River settlement, would ride out with his son and a small company of Khoekhoe elders to a rebel camp, once again in a time of frontier warfare. The group had come to parlay with the enraged young men of the settlement, to plead with them not to rebel against the seemingly unassailable might of the British empire. The loyalists turned back disappointed. The rebellion proceeded, and during its doomed course a number of rebels used Christianity to justify their actions. Read died several months later, on the same day that a colonial court condemned to death for treason Andries Botha, elderly *veld cornet*[1] of the Kat River settlement, on the basis of trumped-up evidence. Read's son melodramatically claimed that his father died of sadness. Whatever the truth of that, Read Sr was certainly confronted with the incompatibility of settler colonialism and the hopes of a Christianized Khoekhoe elite for economic and political parity with whites, as land-hungry colonists used the Khoekhoe rebellion as an excuse to break up much of the Kat River settlement.

History demands narrative, as many theorists have taught us.[2] Any historian creates a story from limited materials, however careful her attention to the rules of evidence – a reflection that must impose humility on the historian of colonialism. The beginnings and endings of the narrative are, of course, artificial. The past makes no clean breaks, above all in a place as haunted by memory and the suppression of memory as colonial southern Africa. Furthermore, this book is about more than missionaries – Christianity rapidly passed out of the hands of the Europeans who had brought it. Unfortunately, one of the main problems in writing about late-eighteenth and early-nineteenth-century Cape religious history is the predominance of white voices in the source material in proportion to the relative importance of white historical actors. All the more reason, then, not to present Read as a symbol of the whole. Nonetheless, these vignettes of the beginning and ending of Read's life in southern Africa might serve to frame the chronological sweep of this study of Christianity and empire, of Khoekhoe groups at the Cape and the LMS between the late eighteenth and mid-nineteenth centuries.

Read came with naive expectations, fuelled by faith, to a place of which he knew nothing. In one sense he was a witness to "success," in evangelical terms, beyond his expectations, as Christianity, already influential among at least some Khoekhoe, was taken up by many more in the early nineteenth century. Yet, although the sheer level of physical violence against the Khoekhoe diminished over the nineteenth century, the hopes of many converts were ultimately disappointed, and the equality they had hoped would be accorded by a white-dominated colony to a "civilized," Christianized society of Africans was never fully granted. Indeed, rebellion provided white colonists with the excuse they had long been seeking to entrench the economic dispossession of the Khoekhoe, in the name of the very Christianity Read espoused. Christianity twisted like a snake in the hands of those who sought to use it: millenarian prophets, authoritarian and radical missionaries alike, British abolitionists, Khoekhoe preachers, and racist settlers all sought to control its language in a climate of intense power struggles, but none was able to establish final ownership.

James Read was only one of the many players in this drama, but he was a central one and a key witness, whose life spans the period of this book. His career further suggests the impossibility of disaggregating "national" histories from one another. The limitations of an exclusively domestic focus from either the British or the South African perspective will in fact be a key theme of this book. Read and his half-white, half-Khoekhoe family also illustrate the profound interconnection of the lives (and indeed bloodlines) of "white" and "black" in the early-nineteenth-century Cape Colony, whatever a parallel rhetoric at the time about ineradicable difference and separation might have suggested.

Read was present at all the major events examined in this book. He participated in the wave of Protestant evangelical revival which swept through England in the late eighteenth century, affecting not only the movement that would become Methodism but also the Calvinist dissenters and Calvinist Anglicans who would spearhead the invention of a large-scale British missionary movement in an era of revolution and tumult. Read married into the Khoekhoe community, witnessed the Khoekhoe struggles to overcome the violent legacy of colonialism, was part of a team testifying in Britain before the Select Committee on Aborigines of the House of Commons of 1835–36, was involved in the foundation of the "free" Khoekhoe settlement of Kat River, and saw the rebellion of 1850–53. He reminds us of the stubborn role of the individual at the confluence of larger historical forces – even as the gaps in his life story, notably the experiences of Khoekhoe and so-called "mixed-race" people who refused Christianity, pose the question of what the costs might be of succumbing to the seduction of biographical narrative.

I will return throughout this book to these issues and events. In a moment I will turn to processes, debates, and introductions. I want to begin, however, with the complexity, even impenetrability, of a single person. It seems symbolically appropriate that James Read began his South African career with expectation in a climate of violence and ended with despair at a time of seeming legal amelioration. In some sense, this seems a metaphor for the endlessly destructive and violent relationships between "black" and "white" in the nineteenth-century Cape Colony, of which Christianity was an integral part. Those relationships never completely permitted either optimism or the complete and final abandonment of hope.

Introduction

This book describes the relationship between the LMS of Great Britain and the Khoekhoe of the Eastern Cape during the last years of Dutch governance and the first fifty-odd years of British colonialism in southern Africa. Over this period, Protestant Christianity proved open to a variety of interpretations in both Britain and southern Africa. Although this might seem like a truism, the fluidity with which Christianity was interpreted and debates over interpretation *within* the Protestant fold had a profound importance in both regions. The communities brought into contact through the colonial encounter, whether Dutch-speaking farmers in frontier districts, the Khoekhoe and their descendants, evangelicals in Britain, or white British settlers at the Cape, all used the language of religion, particularly Protestantism, in competing ways. Communities deployed Christianity to define their identities, to justify internal stratification in their own societies, and to frame the ways in which they interacted with other communities. The encounter between a missionary society and a colonized group in this context could never be about religious belief alone. Khoekhoe conversions to Christianity disturbed existing power relationships at the Cape, to take just one example, because they disrupted the grammar of what was "said" with the language of Christianity about "whiteness" as a religious category. Similarly, the earliest backers of the LMS were in competition with other Protestants over what kind of Christianity most appropriately represented Britain.

The worlds of evangelical Christianity in Britain and of colonial society in southern Africa were brought together not only by the missionary movement but also by a long series of political struggles throughout the nineteenth century over the destiny of the Cape Colony. Christian converts in the Cape Colony and British evangelicals took a prominent role in these conflicts. The apogee of Christian evangelical influence in the Cape Colony came in the late 1820s and early 1830s, when the abolitionist movement momentarily took up the Khoekhoe first as the victims of slavery by another name and then as a paradigmatic example of a civilized black community enjoying the benefits of liberation without ceasing to work in the wage economy. After the 1830s, the focus of the Colonial Office in its consideration of white settler colonies shifted primarily to white settlers themselves. The evangelical "friends of the aborigine" (as they sometimes called themselves) lost influence at the colonial centre, even as Christianity and civilization became ever more bound up in the popular imagination with colonialism itself. The shifting role of missionaries in the British imperial project and changing popular views in Britain itself of the role of Christianity in colonialism were part of some real changes in the relationship between Christianity and British imperialism. These changes had substantial political implications which I shall explore throughout the book.

I also argue that the Khoekhoe and their (often multi-ethnic) descendants used Christianity in a cornucopia of ways. I consider Khoekhoe preaching, the incorporation of Khoekhoe religious behaviour into the new form of Christianity, the material functions of mission stations, and Khoekhoe uses of Christianity to claim status in colonial society. Until recently, the nineteenth-century history of the Khoekhoe, on their way to becoming part of the community classified as "coloured" under apartheid, was understudied by historians and downplayed by descendants. An increasing number of scholars, however, are skilfully recreating that history, which has come to occupy a major place in the historiography of the period, particularly in light of the interest of people of Khoekhoe descent in Khoekhoe history and identity in post-apartheid South Africa.[1] The role of Christianity is a critical part of that history. The book seeks to show that, and to expand on why it mattered.

Overall, I hope that this book will illuminate the early-nineteenth-century role of Christianity in linking, constraining, and changing the lives of disparate peoples: African nomads, white settlers in Africa, the self-proclaimed members of the British "religious world," and the parliamentary and colonial officials whom all the previous groups attempted to influence. Evangelicalism had a multifaceted influence on the relationship between Britain and Africa which cannot be captured by the simplistic vision of the topee-coiffed Victorian as agent of cultural imperialism. Finally, I want to suggest that much of this influence occurred at the popular level: missionaries in the early nineteenth century tended to be drawn from the upper ranks of the working classes, while their early converts were generally those with little social status to lose by adopting a new religion. My aim is to join micro and macro narratives and to cross national boundaries: somehow to combine Khoekhoe resistance to colonialism with the ambivalent conversion of Khoekhoe spokesman Andries Stoffels, or the confusion of the young idealist James Read, setting foot in South Africa in September 1800, with the brutal imperatives of empire.

The first date of my title signals the arrival of the first LMS missionaries in the Cape Colony. The second marks the conclusion of the gruelling 1850–53 frontier war, during which many colonial Khoekhoe rebelled against the white colony. I sometimes range beyond these chronological frontiers. I also move between Britain and Africa throughout the book. As my focus shifts from one geographical area to another, I want to show the interconnectedness of Britain and the Cape Colony in the nineteenth century, despite the profound local distinctiveness of each area.

KHOEKHOE AND EUROPEAN AT THE CAPE

The relationship between Europeans and the Khoekhoe at the Cape before the nineteenth century was long-standing and generally destructive, despite the widespread European myth of the so-called "Hottentot" as an unspoiled inhabitant of the state of nature. By the late sixteenth century, European merchants were already using the Cape to refresh the ships which plied a regular long-distance sea trade between western Europe and Asia. The Vereenigde Oost-Indische Compagnie (VOC), or Dutch East India Company, the London-based East India Company (EIC), and other European trading companies all regularly sent ships on the gruelling voyage around the tip of Africa. On the way, vessels paused at the Cape of Good Hope in order to take on board the meat and scurvy-fighting fresh vegetables needed to feed their often disease-ravaged crews. This meat necessarily came from the cattle herds of the local Khoekhoe. In 1652 the VOC appropriated a small piece of land at the Cape in order to establish a refreshment station staffed by its own employees. This was the beginning of the formal European colonization of the region which would become the Cape Colony – and which in 1910 would be united with three other territories, Natal, the Orange Free State and the Transvaal, to form the British colony of South Africa. Former employees of the VOC and their descendants moved in waves of colonization farther into the interior, setting up large cattle farms themselves and competing with Africans for resources.

Hunter-gatherers, often termed San or "bushmen" by twentieth-century interlocutors, and related semi-nomadic cattle herders calling themselves Khoekhoe, or men of men, inhabited much of the Cape in the seventeenth century (see map 1).[2] Scholars have fought over what the relationship was between hunter-gatherer and pastoralist groups, and even what names the hunter-gatherers would have preferred for themselves. Controversy also rages over the processes by which these nomads were subordinated and the degree of agency remaining to particular groups at particular times. We shall come back to these issues. For now, it is enough to say that the small-scale San (or bushman) and Khoekhoe societies, often grouped together under the rubric "Khoisan," lost badly in their struggles with European settlers, traders, and sailors in possession of superior technology. Successive Khoekhoe and San groups were robbed of their land and lost the cattle which were the marker of wealth of Khoekhoe societies. Many moved farther into the interior in the face of white advance. Others became servants within the white economy, their status often analogous to that of slaves. Many were killed. By the turn of the nineteenth century, the Khoekhoe and San no longer lived independently in the Eastern Cape.[3]

I argue in this book that Christianity played an important role in that subordination. The so-called white community under the VOC defined itself as "Christian," and individuals often justified racial subordination and forced labour in the name of religious difference. The (often extramarital) children of white fathers and African mothers were accepted – even nominally – into the white community only through baptism. This required the father's recognition of his children at the baptismal font. Intense colonial opposition to a short-lived mission to the western Cape Khoekhoe from 1737 to 1744 by the Moravian Georg Schmidt reflected larger struggles between the "Moravians" (or Unitas Fratrum) and the Dutch Reformed Church, but also demonstrated just how controversial was the Christianization of the Khoekhoe, particularly baptism.[4]

The reader will need to know that the Cape Colony changed hands three times in the late eighteenth and early nineteenth centuries, as a pawn in European wars being fought out across the globe. In 1795 William of Orange ceded the Cape of Good Hope to Britain as French revolutionary armies menaced his kingdom and war engulfed Europe. The British held nominal power until 1803. In that year the Cape was granted to the Batavian republic which had ousted the house of Orange with French assistance and now ruled the Netherlands as a puppet regime of France. The republicans governed the Cape only until 1806.

Further European treaty negotiations then yielded the Cape yet again to Britain, although British possession was not finally sealed until the 1814 Treaty of Amiens as the Napoleonic Wars staggered to their close.[5] In the 1820s, the British, now confirmed in their possession of the Cape Colony, launched large-scale white immigration. Throughout the early nineteenth century, the British expanded the frontiers of the Cape Colony like the Dutch before them, but with the greater efficiency of the British military, in a series of wars with the Xhosa.

Throughout these changes of regime, inhabitants of the colony struggled to use international developments for local ends, seeking allies in local power struggles the underlying logic of which was little altered. Both Africans and Europeans tried to mobilize what they saw as the power of Christianity. The white British settler community, however, did not police its boundaries through baptism in the same manner as the eighteenth-century Dutch. I argue below that the British tended to resist the logic of the incorporation of Christian Africans into white society in part by devising new mechanisms of exclusion, framed in terms of "civilization" and to a certain extent of "race." In consequence, the very attempt to convert Africans was seen as less controversial by British settlers than it had been by many Dutch-speaking frontier farmers. Rather, Christianization was increasingly described as a benefit brought by the British to the colonized.

From the 1790s on, the presence of western missionary societies added a new dimension to local struggles over the political, economic and social uses of Christianity. In 1792 German-speaking Moravians resumed their long-interrupted mission to the Cape, and in 1799 the LMS followed. Other societies would arrive from the 1810s onward. If Christian evangelization was scant and controversial in the late eighteenth century, by the mid-nineteenth-century mark southern Africa had become one of the world's most crowded "mission fields." European societies such as the Glasgow Missionary Society, the Wesleyan Missionary Society, the Rhenish Missionary Society, the Paris Evangelical Missionary Society, and the (Anglican) Society for the Propagation of the Gospel, among others, all targeted the region; the American Board of Commissioners for Foreign Missions was active from the mid 1830s; the African Methodist Episcopal Church, also based in the United States, and the Roman Catholic Church played important roles in the late nineteenth century.[6] All this was on top of African evangelization efforts, often outside the formal structures of missionary societies, as well as the evangelical activities of local whites.

Among the European missionary societies, the LMS was, however, probably the most politically important and certainly the most controversial. The LMS was the second missionary society created in Britain and it remained the largest well into the 1810s. South Africa was the LMS's second mission, after the South Seas, and only grew in importance as the first LMS missions to Tahiti collapsed ignominiously. The actions of the LMS in Africa were therefore perceived as more paradigmatic by the early-nineteenth-century British public, and were more widely publicized, than were many subsequent missions. The Khoekhoe converted in large numbers – albeit for a much wider range of reasons than mere missionary preaching, as we shall see. Christianity had a disproportionate influence on the political and social life of Khoekhoe communities in the early nineteenth century, in contrast to the relative indifference with which the gospel was received in many other areas. LMS converts and agents influenced the overall direction of empire in the late 1820s and 1830s, most notably in persuading the imperial government to overturn the settler conquest of Xhosa land during the 1835–36 frontier war. At the mid-century point, the rebellion of a Christian peasantry under LMS patronage in southern Africa helped persuade imperial administrators that missionaries were less effective agents of the legitimization of empire and the procurement of imperial collaborators than had once been hoped. For all these reasons, a focus on the LMS remains fruitful, despite the rich vein of existing writing on the history of the society.[7]

MISSIONS AND EMPIRE: AN ARGUMENT

In the late eighteenth and early nineteenth centuries, evangelical nonconformists spearheaded missions around the British empire. Nonconformists were political outsiders in Britain itself, where they were still legally excluded from many political offices and from the two great universities, Oxford and Cambridge. Protestantism was an important element of the construction of "British" identity through the eighteenth century and as such helped to unify diverse communities.[8] Nonetheless, there was more controversy than many historians allow over exactly what type of Protestantism might represent the nation. The chosen nation proved a slippery concept in practice. Evangelicals, especially nonconformist evangelicals, were often seen by imperial administrators and domestic elites as dangerous enthusiasts, particularly as war raged with revolutionary France and later with Napoleonic France. Furthermore, early missionary activity was often organized across national boundaries and societies employed people from a range of national backgrounds, in part because of the constraints imposed by pan-European warfare on evangelicals in particular countries. Evangelicalism in the late eighteenth century had a relatively international focus and British evangelicalism was influenced by continental organizations and networks.[9]

The early nineteenth century saw a shift to a closer national focus as missions themselves became more respectable in elite eyes. The rhetoric of missions at the outset emphasized that Britain was the recipient of divine favour, as the survival of the empire demonstrated, and thus needed to act as an agent of God's will on behalf of other nations less able to do so. By the mid-nineteenth century, despite important variations across societies with different theological approaches, mission-society rhetoric tended rather to emphasize that Britain would spread through her empire specifically national virtues linked to economic progress. Britain was widely presented as the world's most economically and politically advanced nation, a status it owed to God's blessing. Missionaries became increasingly focused on making indigenous peoples into (metaphorical) virtuous Englishmen as the century developed, while, for Africans, alliances with missionaries became more tied to alliances with Britain per se.

In the early nineteenth century, missions played a critical if ambivalent role both in Britain's imperial expansion and in the local power struggles and social relations which accompanied the growth of empire. From the late 1790s onward, Christian missionary activity preceded large-scale white colonization in many areas of the empire, including South Africa. Missions did not cause white colonization, and many individual missionaries opposed settler and trader interests. Nonetheless, by the latter part of the nineteenth century, missions had come to be seen by many in Britain as emblematic of some larger national imperial project. It was, however, in the early nineteenth century, at least in southern Africa, that missionaries were most eagerly sought by African leaders as political intermediaries, before the advent of more extensive colonial networks and substantial white settler communities reduced the political importance of the missionary as diplomat.

For many of those directly colonized or living on the periphery of white colonization, missions were an important vector of contact with the British imperial centre. Missionaries could liaise with imperial and settler governments. They were also potential intermediaries in trade, including the crucial arms trade for those beyond the formal boundaries of empire. Missionaries were, as well, sources of useful information about European technology, culture, and religion. Such information could be used to protect societies against imperialist incursions, as much as to internalize the dictates of cultural colonialism. At the same time, almost all white British missionaries, whatever their political beliefs, hoped to instill loyalty to the imperial government in their converts, and many wanted to remake their converts in the image of the British. Not surprisingly, the encounter between missionary and

African was consequently often characterized by conflict.[10] Furthermore, despite the fact that missionaries were sometimes thorns in the
sides of colonial administrators and of settlers, they were also more
effective advocates of loyalty to the imperial *centre* than were the less
ostensibly altruistic settlers. Many encouraged groups that were still
independent to become part of the British empire, often supposedly to
protect themselves against worse ills, such as uncontrolled settler incursions. Converts and those engaged in diplomacy through missionaries
were not sufficiently naive to succumb to missionary enthusiasm for
imperial alliances in the absence of intense material pressures in
regions that were violent and turbulent. All the same, missions provided networks and greatly facilitated contact between Africans and imperial administrators, making alliances easier to conclude. From the very
beginning – indeed perhaps more so at the very beginning – missions
had a disproportionate political influence on the margins of empire.
They were also from the outset a double-edged sword from the perspective both of the enthusiasts of full-fledged white domination (who
were often criticized by missionaries) and of the colonized themselves
(whom missionaries often sought to dominate and to change).

Missionary societies in the early nineteenth century were one of the
main sources of information and imagery in Britain about the non-
western world, and about the British empire more broadly. Missions
were heavily publicized in Britain. The religious were interested in evidence of the activity of God on earth. Missionary societies needed a
constant flow of money; the LMS, for example, was financially
strapped throughout the entire period of this study. Annual missionary
meetings and quieter pressure groups depended on publicity, or the
threat of it, to maintain what political influence they had at the imperial centre. The respectability and social capital which accrued to
donors from their support of missions required a well-oiled publicity
machine.

In the meantime, missionary networks enabled a handful of converts
to travel to Britain to make political and religious representations and
to gather information, often in exchange for displaying themselves as
"civilized" converts and speaking at missionary meetings. Much more
often, the words of converts, heavily mediated by missionary translation and presentation, were employed by missionary societies and by
evangelical groups such as the Aborigines Protection Society (APS) to
demonstrate the feasibility of converting the heathen and sometimes to
make political arguments. The information networks associated with
missions thus facilitated a politics of display, in which dramas of civilization and savagery were acted out to a variety of political ends (and
sometimes more directly personal ones). The early-nineteenth-century

LMS missionaries were important practitioners of this type of politics, as debates raged in both Britain and South Africa about the meaning of "civilization" and its political implications.

In part through this process, missions legitimized and domesticated empire for many in Britain. Imperialism might be portrayed as altruistic, even for some as a divinely sanctioned instrument of Christianization. In the well-worn Victorian formula, empire was thought to spread Christianity, commerce, and civilization – an idea exemplified in the writings of David Livingstone, an LMS missionary before he was a well-known explorer. Partly in consequence, many early- to mid-nineteenth-century critics in Britain wanted to ameliorate empire, rather than to abolish it. Missionary propaganda denigrated the many cultures of other groups within the empire, in a manner that in itself could serve as a justification for conquest. The British could describe themselves to themselves as modern, and as agents of a rationalizing modernity in the world through the medium of Christianity: ironically, eighteenth-century evangelical eschatology ultimately came to sit at the feet of secular progressivism.[11] At the same time, some British evangelicals such as Thomas Fowell Buxton, the parliamentary leader of the abolitionist movement, thought that missionary activity was a necessary gesture of atonement that Britain needed to make to colonized peoples in order to compensate for the wrongs done to them by colonialism. Missions were not solely used to legitimize empire.

At the outset, in the absence of large white settler communities, nonconformist missionaries tended to be more likely to form kinship links with local societies and to live in greater accord with their cultural norms. Missionaries had little power to effect change in the early years of the nineteenth century and were often marginalized mavericks. In the 1820s and early 1830s the overall influence of evangelicals on foreign policy at the metropolitan centre increased, with the campaigns to abolish slavery and the key role played by the evangelical James Stephen at the Colonial Office. At this point the imperial administration still tended to look for military allies among a Christianized native population. By the 1840s, however, white colonization was in full flood in the white settler colonies after a long slowdown in the aftermath of the loss of America. The imperial government switched its support largely to white settlers and became less ready to use missionaries to broker agreements with indigenous peoples. By the 1850s, disillusion was rife among groups that had made bargains with the imperial state through missionary mediation – or more broadly, and more nebulously, had tried to exchange Christianization for the rights of citizens. It is not surprising that the 1850s and 1860s saw a wave of colonial revolts against imperial rule, including the Khoekhoe rebellion of

1850–53. There was a corresponding disillusionment in Britain with the liberal assimilationist project and a greater willingness to embrace ideas of radical difference, including racial ideas. I will argue that what happened in the Cape Colony and along its frontiers both illustrated and had an important influence on the overall course of events.

In making these broader arguments, the book will proceed as follows. Chapter 1 examines the roots of the missionary movement in Britain in the 1790s. Key influences included European evangelical revival, shifts in the nature of British nationalism, reaction to the French Revolution, the growth of empire, and the continuing development of working-class consumer culture – a complex mix of factors that reflects the peculiar intersection of the global and the local even in the formation of a "British" movement. I argue broadly that ecclesiological concerns and fears for social order in the wake of the French Revolution initially made the political and religious establishment chary of missionary activity. In the aftermath of the Napoleonic Wars, this attitude softened. The British missionary movement became increasingly anglicized and increasingly tied to Britain's understanding of its imperial role in the world.

The following chapters turn to Africa. Chapter 2 provides background to Khoekhoe attempts to use mission Christianity. Here, I discuss the politics of the Eastern Cape frontier in the late eighteenth century. I also explore eighteenth-century British visions of Africa – those stereotypes that Africans and missionaries alike would try to manipulate and that would prove so damaging to Africans. Despite epistemological problems of race and voice, I discuss the particular missionaries who came to South Africa, with particular attention to J.T. van der Kemp.

The following two chapters take up events on the early-nineteenth-century Eastern Cape frontier. The Khoekhoe uprising of 1799–1802 framed the resistance of many to the LMS missionary project, as well as the desire of others to adopt new strategies in the face of colonialism. I look at legal resistance to colonial violence, among other issues. In chapter 4 I discuss Khoisan religious, political, and economic uses of mission Christianity in the context of this close interweaving of religion and politics in the religiously and racially stratified society of the Cape. The stereotypes of sexual impurity and lack of work discipline which were attached to LMS converts, I argue in chapter 5, demonstrate the entanglement of religious and political discourse in South Africa and the depth of settler unease at the inversion of the colonial order. Sexual scandals among missionaries entrenched this discourse and vitiated the (already limited) political effectiveness of missionaries.

By the 1820s, I argue in chapter 6, the mission had begun a drive to respectability. "Intermarriage" and the adoption of certain elements of African lifestyles were in essence abandoned. Men such as John Philip focused instead on what needed to be done to gain equal rights and political influence, seeking in consequence to present converts and missionaries as "respectable" according to British norms. The LMS tried with some degree of success to work within the parameters of the economic and political liberalism which was increasingly influential in Britain itself, including among a number of imperial administrators attempting to refashion the empire. Against the background of these "politics of civilization," I re-examine the often-studied passage in South Africa and Britain of legislation requiring that laws be colour-blind. Chapter 7 analyses the warfare of 1835–36, the House of Commons Select Committee on Aborigines, and the LMS delegation of Andries Stoffels, Jan Tshatshu, John Philip, and James Read Sr and Jr that testified before this committee. An independent Khoekhoe territory designed as a buffer zone between white settlers and the Xhosa beyond colonial frontiers, the Kat River settlement, was an important innovation of this period. I also consider the seemingly inexorable pressures towards poverty and proletarianization exerted on mission communities in the 1830s. Chapter 8 explores further the economic struggles of mission-based Khoekhoe during the post-1828 period and the rethinking of missionary liberalism which took place among converts and among whites, from a variety of perspectives. Chapter 9 considers splits among LMS personnel, problems with the transformation of "missions" into "churches" in the midst of settler society, and the nascent drive of Africans to wrest control of mission churches from white missionaries. Missions became more overtly conservative in the 1840s, while at the same time many people not defined as white accumulated grievances against "white" colonists. The final chapter examines the rebellion of a number of "loyal" Khoisan in the frontier war of 1850–53, the growing entrenchment of a language of "race," and the mobilization of concepts of the "Hottentot" nation. Khoisan rebels and loyalists debated the meaning of Christianity: the theological debates with which we began had come full circle. I conclude with some speculations about conversion, nationalism, and the uses of Christianity.

POLITICS AND INTERPRETATION:
SOME METHODOLOGICAL CONCERNS

I see this book as part of a recent trend in the historiography of South Africa to incorporate the study of religion more thoroughly into the mainstream of cultural, social, and political history, broadly conceived,

after a long period in which Christianity in general and missions in particular tended to be ignored, or, if examined closely, either harshly criticized or unduly praised. Christian converts, for example, should neither be singled out as cultural traitors nor portrayed as particularly
noble: we need a historiography that does not indulge in special pleading for Christians one way or the other but tries to understand religion
in context. From fairly different perspectives, anthropologists such as
Jean and John Comaroff and historians such as Paul Landau, Johannes
du Bruyn, Nicholas Southey, Norman Etherington, Richard Elphick,
and Christopher Saunders have all called for a reintegration of Christianity into the "mainstream" of South African historiography – as
indeed have I.[12] This is not the place to remake that case in detail, but
the concerns of all these writers have influenced what follows.

This book also tries to escape from the trap of seeing Christianity as
monolithic. Christianity, as many theologians and other theorists
argue, is a religion informed by narrative and subject to interpretation.
Biblical mythology forms a template for many believers in their daily
conduct of their lives and in the way they think about politics and society more broadly. The type of evangelical Protestantism explored in
this study was, above all, a religion of "the book." Individual reading
of the Bible was seen as critically important by evangelicals, and
though many of them expected that the Bible's divine truths would
generate only one reading, I would suggest that many biblical narratives accommodate a great number of interpretations in practice. A
language can be held in common and still have different meanings for
different speakers, changing subtly over time and across cultures. This
is not to argue for the vacuity of mythical language or of parable, but
for the capacity of language and story to be constantly reinterpreted,
within certain limits, according to the needs of teller and hearer. Translation creates further possibilities for the reinterpretation of biblical
texts. Under the guise of universalism, evangelical Protestantism meant
– and means – different things across a range of cultures and subcul-
tures, and even for different individuals bringing different experiences
to the same texts.

A central methodological innovation of this study, then, is to portray
the history of Christianity in the Cape Colony not only as a dualistic
clash between cultures (as much of the existing scholarly literature
argues and as was in fact partly true) but also as a series of negotiations within the limits of shared language. My analysis differs, therefore, from such influential work as that of Jean and John Comaroff
which describes missions as a "dialectic" of modernity. This is partly
because my focus is on a colony in which Christianity already had multiple meanings. On the other hand, it is also because I think that an a

priori commitment to dialectic risks silencing the voices of Christian converts who interpreted what they heard. It may also downplay the role of nonwhite proselytizers, and more generally reify cultures. In what follows I do not ignore the brutal dichotomies of "race," culture, religion, and language bifurcating southern Africa; indeed, one of the reasons I find the study of Christianity interesting is that it helps explain the creation and maintenance of such categories. I do argue at the same time, however, that the politics of difference were mediated by the politics of interpretation.

A great advantage of such an interpretive approach is that it helps us to escape from the pitfall of dualism. There is a difficult road to walk here. On the one hand, missions helped rigidify the notions of "black" and "white" which had such a profound deleterious impact on South Africa. At their starkest, they were sites of confrontation between people claiming to represent "white" or "British" or "European" culture and religion, and Africans who were often inspired in turn to define their own experience and ways of doing things as constitutively something else, whether "black" or "African" or "Xhosa." Cultures confronted one another through missions, even as missions also helped reify cultural identities. On the other hand, the influence of Christianity in southern Africa worked in even more complicated ways. Khoisan people ended up working as important agents of the spread of Christianity. To pursue one example that this book will take up again later, Griqua, "mixed-race," and Cape Khoekhoe intermediaries played crucial roles in the foundation of the LMS mission to the Tswana, somewhat misleadingly described by Jean and John Comaroff as a prime instance of a cultural dialectic. Khoekhoe missionaries tried to develop a more liberationist understanding of the gospel than that held by many of their white counterparts and to wrest control of their own churches from the hands of European societies; not surprisingly, however, these intermediaries were rendered almost invisible in much of the published historical record under the control of missionary societies. Neither European nor African culture was monolithic, and they quickly became entwined in complicated ways.

Jean and John Comaroff are not as simplistic as my outline account suggests, and they do modify their arguments somewhat in the second volume of what will eventually be a three-part study. They stress the multiplicity of meaning systems among different African groups and among various sets of missionaries over time. Indeed, this is a central innovation of their analysis. In practice, however, their study of the fluidity of meaning conflicts with their overarching analysis. Is it possible that the Comaroffs are in fact operating with two incompatible theoretical models, the one stressing cultural variation and the fluidity of signs, and the other a dichotomous vision of capitalism interacting with pre-capitalism, and of "western" thought interacting with "African," with the conquest of signs as the loss or gain of battle positions between competing and incompatible terms? Would it be simpler to discuss power relationships as parallel to but also independent of religious relationships? The Comaroffs stress the development of new meaning systems and the phenomenon of cultural *bricolage*, the taking of bits from different cultures to form new ones, and yet can analyse these only as acts of resistance or compliance in a dichotomous world. Sometimes the actions described by the Comaroffs do not seem convincing as acts of resistance, while at other times people (such as those adopting western economic practices) seem to be sacrificing symbolic resistance in order to offer more straightforward resistance to unabashed economic aggression. I am unsure that the grids of religious meaning and of power relationships mesh as neatly as *Of Revelation and Revolution* implies, and yet the details of many of the particular discussions in the Comaroffs' work are tremendously illuminating. Do they need to be squeezed into so cramped a Procrustean bed?

Be that as it may, I find a more fluid model helpful. My own thinking about language and interpretation has been influenced by the work of Quentin Skinner, particularly his stress on ways in which the evaluative upshot of words in social contexts can change without an explicit battle over interpretation: that language is not, in other words, a guide to meaning through time in any straightforward sense.[13] Of further interest in Skinner's approach is his focus on the way in which a new ideology becomes conventional in the concrete circumstances of particular power relationships. As he has argued, the ideological success of an innovation will depend in part on how well it corresponds to existing schools of thought and on the extent to which its progenitors control instruments that will enable its dissemination. The latter point is also important to this study. The missionary movement not only controlled but also created mechanisms for the dissemination of ideology which were to have a powerful impact on both African and British societies. These mechanisms ranged from organizational networks designed for the oral transmission of religious belief to annual meetings in London, missionary magazines, travelling lantern shows, missionary maps, and all the paraphernalia of the missionary-information enterprise. Thus, we will be concerned not only with interpretation but with the mechanisms of transmission of particular interpretations and the contest to establish the ideological hegemony of one interpretation over another.[14]

A third broad methodological commitment of this book is to the crossing of regional frontiers and the interrogation of "British" and

"South African" history simultaneously. Like so many others, the story told in this book is not one that can be neatly folded within the embrace of so-called "national" history. It might rather be seen as a product of the intersection of several "local" histories and of global interaction that cut constantly through the local in unexpected ways. One of these "local" histories inextricably bound up with the "global" is that of Christianity in South Africa. It goes without saying that Christianity beyond the institutional confines of missionary stations had, and has, a profound influence on southern Africa. It obviously has a long history that is separate from that of the British empire, as also from that of missionary buildings and bureaucracies. Africans spread Christianity (often in transformed versions) more effectively than white missionaries, crossing colonial boundaries in the process. A ferment of new religious ideas greeted the political upheavals in southern Africa of the eighteenth and nineteenth centuries, and the incorporation of elements of Christianity was part of that ferment. At the same time, African Christianity was both naturally shaped by existing beliefs and practices and creatively remade to greet changing circumstances. Christianity was used by groups such as junior royals or the socially marginal struggling for power against older elites.[15] The history of reaction *against* Christianity, or more narrowly against mission Christianity, is also a crucial element in the intellectual, cultural, and political history of nineteenth-century southern Africa.

There is also, of course, a related but separate narrative to be told about the domestic impact of missionary activity in Britain itself. In the words of Jean and John Comaroff, "colonialism was as much involved in making the metropole, and the identities and ideologies of colonizers, as it was in (re)making peripheries and colonial subjects."[16] Susan Thorne has recently underscored, for example, the important role played by Congregationalist missions in the formation of a dissenting middle class in nineteenth-century Britain.[17] Christianity was mobilized in power struggles between old and new elites and between the socially marginal and the powerful in Britain as much as in Africa. The missionary movement was a critical part of such struggles. Though relatively understudied, evangelical missions were an important component of the imaginative and associational lives of millions in nineteenth-century Britain.

It is not, however, easy to separate out these diverse "local" histories and the common history which at least initially bound them. Experiences intersected and diverged at unexpected points. In keeping with recent calls for a borderless approach to imperial history, this book tries to write a transnational narrative, despite the many hazards of such a project.[18] Neither British nor African experience is reducible to the common narrative, and yet neither can be understood without a sense of shared interaction. The relationship between Khoekhoe and the LMS had ripple effects throughout British, African, and Cape colonial societies, just as it was forged in the fire of intense social and political change in both Britain and southern Africa. I want, therefore, to look at this relationship as a case study in writing a history that is about irreducibly separate experiences which nonetheless cannot be fully understood in isolation.

Finally, two caveats impose themselves on the broad points made above. The first is that I do not want to argue that "religious" language was void of meaning, nor that the faithful did not hold intense *religious* beliefs (however one defines that slippery concept "religion"). These spiritual beliefs had a dynamic of their own and deserve to be considered in their own right, not as "really" being about material issues. Spiritual experience needs to be taken seriously by the historian, no matter how hard to quantify (or indeed to grasp from the outside). The relationship between religion and other compartments of life is complicated.

A second caveat is that Christianity may have become in some senses a shared language, but Christian missions were still often sites of confrontation. Missionaries were often abusively scornful of their targets' societies, for example, and this scorn had costs. It is not surprising that, although missionaries may have become more academically respectable topics in the new South Africa, they still carry emotional freight for many. The concerns of historians with the role of missionaries in conquest have echoed the continuing struggle of black, African, and liberation theologians to reject the cultural imperialism of the missionary movement, whether to distill a liberatory *kerygma* from the gospel, freed from western accretions, or to argue for the equal validity and cultural dignity of other African beliefs.[19]

Even so, there has been a growing tendency in studies of southern African Christianity over the past few years, as opposed to studies focused more closely on missionaries, to recognize that Christianity was in fact spread largely under the aegis of Africans.[20] Christianity was domesticated sooner than may have been previously believed, and in that sense it was not a completely successful instrument of full-fledged cultural imperialism.[21] At the same time, mission Christianity was also from the start a more authoritarian instrument for the attempted control of African communities than more haigiographic accounts of missionary activity might have allowed, while Africans also used Christianity in power struggles between community members as well as across competing groups. In this, as in so many other ways, Christianity was used in ambiguous fashion in southern Africa and Britain alike.

VOICES

There are many roadblocks to a full understanding of these processes. Not the least is the distortion of the archives in favour of the voices of the Christian devout, and particularly literate white missionary voices (there are some notable exceptions). It is possible, of course, to read missionary records in a variety of ways. One can contextualize their approaches, and read between the lines, while converts themselves were certainly not wordless. Nonetheless, the following remains necessarily a partial account. Although I have gained greatly from discussions with many people descended from communities studied in this book, I would particularly have liked to have been able to live for a long period of time in South Africa, had work and family obligations in Canada permitted, in order to talk with a wider range of individuals about their family histories. Oral community histories proved hard to uncover, given our chronological distance from the early nineteenth century, the loss of the Khoekhoe language, urbanization, the multiplicity of identities of the descendants of Khoekhoe people, the suppression of memory as a product of colonial shaming, and the concrete and dramatic dislocations of apartheid. This is why a painstaking reconstruction of the past through the collation of a wide diversity of individual memories may prove helpful, even though the early 1800s are beyond the reach of precise oral memory. I remain convinced that many individuals will have family memories that would illuminate events described in this book, although they will be widely scattered. I can only hope that the following work will form part of an ongoing conversation and be a helpful starting point for others – even perhaps for my own revisiting of the subject. There are many stories still to be told.

1 "The Lord Is Seen to Ride on the Whirlwind": Protestant Evangelicalism in the 1790s

How can we place the missionary movement within the larger sweep of British social and political history? Overseas missionary activity developed as an extension of the domestic "missionary" activity carried out by evangelicals in the late eighteenth century. Any answer to this question must therefore be closely tied to the history of Protestant evangelicalism and its wider relationship to politics and to both popular and elite religious culture.

Evangelicalism was often controversial in eighteenth- and nineteenth-century Britain, even if it became to some extent a marker of Victorian middle-class identity.[1] In the eighteenth century in particular, the very forms adopted by popular evangelicalism, such as itinerant preaching by unlicensed proselytizers, as well as some evangelical theological ideas, were perceived by many in the Anglican political and ecclesiastical establishments as a threat to the status quo. On the other hand, this does not mean that the political beliefs of various evangelicals were not sometimes authoritarian, nor that evangelicals did not themselves attempt to quell political radicalism. Ecstatic religious experience outside the bounds of traditional church order could both attack and shore up authority. From this stemmed a number of paradoxes.

The fortunes, both literal and metaphorical, of evangelicals rose as the nineteenth century progressed. Furthermore, Christians less readily classifiable as "evangelicals," such as the high Anglicans of the Society for the Propagation of the Gospel, began to participate more widely in overseas missionary activity, as education and religious instruction became ever more tightly bound up with the British imperial project.

The missionary movement shifted in the aftermath of the Napoleonic Wars from being a rather marginal activity to one that could be presented as emblematic of national virtue. Claims about national virtue and who represented it were, of course, almost always about domestic power struggles rather than reflections of actual consensus. Nonetheless, there was more at stake in struggles to claim symbolic ownership of the missionary movement by the mid-nineteenth century than in the 1790s, when the supporters of missions were often seen by Anglican elites as dangerous iconoclasts and religious "enthusiasts." Similarly, nonconformity and nonconformists moved closer to the centre of political and social power through the nineteenth century. By the mid-century mark, nonconformist internal and external missionary outreach was perceived relatively widely as a useful part of the middle-class drive to civilize the unruly and the unrespectable within and without Britain. In the 1790s, in contrast, missionary activity could be portrayed in elite circles as a rearguard action by precisely the unrespectable and the marginal. So too, however, could be less "respectable" missionary efforts, such as the China Inland Mission, even in the heyday of popular support for missions. The social role of the missionary movement in Britain was thus in frequent flux, just as little consensus existed around the utility of its efforts or the respectability of its practitioners.

Missionaries in Africa often presented themselves as the bearers of Britishness, or Englishness. At home, missionary magazines, annual sermons, missionary autobiographies, and other publications similarly emphasized the national benefits of missionary activity and the national virtue embodied by its agents. Such claims did not necessarily reflect actual consensus in British society, even if historians have themselves too often accepted such claims at face value. This was all the more true in the 1790s. While Protestantism was more broadly a critical component of the British construction of national identity in the late eighteenth and early nineteenth centuries, as much recent historical work has argued, disagreement still existed about what *kind* of Protestantism most appropriately represented the nation.[2] In the first instance, what missionaries most successfully exported was not so much a reified "Britishness" as variants of evangelical Protestant religious culture about which contestation existed in Britain itself. Furthermore, this religious culture was to some extent shared across national boundaries and provoked confrontation.

EVANGELICAL REVIVAL

Many British people at the close of the eighteenth century believed, mostly on good evidence, that they were living through a period of extraordinary social and political change. On the heels of revolution in France, war engulfed much of Europe from 1792 onward. Closer to home, there was a bloody and complicated uprising in Ireland in 1798. By the early 1800s, Britain would seem to many Christians to have been providentially preserved from conquest and revolution – surely for some higher purpose – but at many points in the 1790s this outcome was far from certain. Hunger was widespread in a number of agricultural regions of the country during recurrent periods of dearth, political radicalism threatened the constitutional status quo, and the loyalties of the poorest could not be taken for granted by the richest. There were promising signs too, of course, from a British perspective. Beyond Europe, the farthest reaches of the world were open at last to British exploration, settlement, and economic development. Captain James Cook's accounts of his voyages to the South Pacific were wildly popular. Britain had even founded a penal colony on the distant shores of Botany Bay. The American empire had crumbled, but new vistas were opening.

Whatever one makes of the claim – much debated by historians and political scientists – that the eighteenth century was a crucial period of transition to "modernity," it is a fact that many evangelicals imposed their *own* universalist and teleological (and in that sense "modernist") narratives about change, history, and progress upon their historical period. This was a Protestant narrative, which described the actions of God and the response of nations and individuals to his unfolding purposes. Evangelicals – like many other Christians – struggled to explain the upheavals and new possibilities alike of the late eighteenth century in terms of a divine plan for mankind. They also used with aplomb many of the tools that had created a rapidly expanding public sphere: the press, associational culture, increasing popular literacy. Evangelicals may or may not have been "modern" (whatever one means by that much-contested word), but they did see themselves as God's agents for change and renewal in a turbulent period. They used long-standing Protestant narratives about chosen communities and God's grace. At the same time, they employed these narratives to explain change, and they exploited the communication techniques that late-eighteenth-century technology and economies of scale were making ever more widely available. For example, theologians and ministers, including the founders and patrons of the LMS, wrote widely, often for a pan-European or transatlantic audience, on millenarianism, the approaching end time, and the action of God in history. The mostly working-class early missionaries shared many of these views. Protestant evangelicals thus had their own explanations for the religious, social, and political change around them and, more narrowly, for the growth of missionary activity in the 1790s.

Historians, however, must seek in the first instance for more terrestrial explanations. There *is* clearly something to explain, since the British Protestant missionary movement to the world beyond Britain began so rapidly and on such a large scale in the 1790s, after a long period of quiescence. Particular Baptist missionaries established the first British society in 1792, the Baptist Missionary Society (BMS). Three years later, an interdenominational committee of evangelical ministers formed the more ambitious LMS, uniting Calvinist evangelicals across different denominations in an ambitious project to Christianize the world. Even the Anglican Church of England became involved in missions to non-Christians with the formation of the Church Missionary Society (CMS) in 1799 by Anglican evangelicals, though resistance from within the church itself meant that supporters would not feel free to proselytize openly until after the end of the Napoleonic Wars. In Scotland, the Scottish Missionary Society and the Glasgow Missionary Society (GMS) were both founded in 1796. The 1796 General Assembly of the Church of Scotland voted down proposals for Church of Scotland missions, but the vote of fifty-eight to forty-four signalled a significant evangelical presence and hinted at fights to come.[3] In this climate of controversy, the most important functions of the existing Scottish societies for many years would be to raise funds and personnel for the London-based societies and, of course, to pray for the conversion of the heathen. Despite resistance and unease in the established churches, Britain thus went from having almost no institutionalized overseas missionary activity to possessing a substantial organized movement in a matter of several years.

The roots of such a seemingly sudden transformation were deep and tangled. The proximate cause, however, was the explosion of a much broader popular evangelical movement, which came to a head in the 1790s. On the one hand, the Church of England dominated the institutional religious life of eighteenth-century Britain. Its institutional challengers from within the Protestant fold, the dissenting denominations such as the Baptists, Congregationalists, and Quakers, all forged in the flames of seventeenth-century religious conflict, were hobbled by restrictions on the political rights of "nonconformists." The widespread practice of "occasional conformity" (occasional partaking of Anglican communion in exchange for the right to take oaths of office) allowed some measure of compromise, but staunch non-Anglicans were broadly excluded from political office and from the universities of Oxford and Cambridge. Catholics faced much more severe restrictions on their civil liberties before Catholic Emancipation in 1829 and were a minority presence outside Ireland and the Irish diaspora. Bubbling beneath the surface were popular religious movements which many in the established church viewed with a suspicious eye, although ministers of more evangelical leanings sometimes tried to harness them. Occasionally, popular religious enthusiasm would come to a head in what contemporaries described as moments of "revival." The mid- to late 1730s, which saw the birth of Methodism, and the 1790s, during which the institutionalized missionary movement was founded, were two such periods.

"Revival" is a complicated term. Contemporaries often described the many movements of spiritual renewal in the seventeenth- and eighteenth-century Protestant world as "revivals." At the same time, "revival" also had the more specific sense of a large-scale but short-term and regionally based movement of repentance and conversion to "true" Christianity. Often such movements were inspired by the "sacred theatre" of collective, quasi-ritualistic activities. Such activities ranged from public response to the preaching of a successful clergyman to (among Primitive Methodists, for example) a several-day camp meeting. Clarke Garrett, for one, discusses the "collective sacred theater of public conversion that ... characterized Methodism's early years" and argues that this element of sacred theatre provides a link between a range of movements loosely classified as based on, or marked by, "spirit possession."[4] Despite great local variations, most of the Protestant renewal movements of the period were characterized by some use of revival in this second sense of communal conversion. Such movements were also marked by a corresponding belief in the power of God to move many people at once in particular moments of blessing and activity on earth, by resort to communal rites designed for conversion in line with a belief in justification through faith in some form, and by several other theological and organizational similarities.

Another word that demands discussion is "evangelical." This is also a slippery term, not least because its use has changed so much across time and space. "Evangelical" was an adjective appropriated by the Protestant Reformation well before it was a noun attached to party groupings within religious groups in nineteenth-century England (or indeed twenty-first century North America). Nonetheless, the term "evangelical," however malleable, was not void of content. It conveyed a constant sense of orientation towards the spread of the gospel and adherence to "true" Protestantism – whatever that might be taken to be. In late-eighteenth-century Great Britain, many British evangelicals themselves used the term in a loose, unifying sense, to suggest commonality of principle across denominational and national boundaries. The international background imparted universalist overtones to the rubric, however much the word would eventually harden into a more introspective party label.

A cluster of theological attitudes was attached to being an evangelical in Britain. David Bebbington has distinguished four characteristics in modern terms: "*conversionism*, the belief that lives need to be changed; *activism*, the expression of the gospel in effort; *biblicism*, a particular regard for the Bible; and what may be termed *crucicentrism*, a stress on the sacrifice of Christ on the cross."[5] In eighteenth-century terms, British evangelicals across denominations emphasized the depravity of man, the atonement of Christ on the cross for the sins of mankind, Christ's offer of saving grace, and the necessity for faith in Christ in order for this offer of grace to become available.

Among the founders of the leading British missionary societies in the late eighteenth century, the term "evangelical" had the dominant sense of actively seeking to "convert" other people.[6] Non-evangelicals might have considered many of the targets of evangelical proselytizing already to be Christian, however. Christianity was divided against itself, and different groups thought of "conversion" in different ways. There was a wide variety of theological disagreements even among self-confessed evangelicals about what conversion was and how it was experienced. Yet, at its heart, conversion occurred when the sinful individual accepted God's offer of grace and thereby gained forgiveness for his or her sins. Most (certainly not all) evangelicals thought that conversion occurred at a particular moment in time, despite potential backsliding. Many believed that even Christians who had not had a conversion experience were not truly saved. They lived under the law but had not experienced the spirit.

An important qualification is that branches of late eighteenth-century British evangelicalism with doctrinal differences recognized one another as evangelicals. Many felt that, regardless of denominational divides, an "evangelical" was in contact with Christ, had undergone certain life experiences including, for many, recognition of personal guilt and a moment of conversion, or rebirth, and felt compelled to proselytize. As Roger Martin observes, evangelicals were united by "experience," which was "not a matter of theological reflection, but rather a general experiential crisis, rooted in a deep-seated sense of sinfulness and spiritual insufficiency and a thirst for assurance and personal salvation."[7] The evangelical of this period thus had a set of expectations about experience. He or she expected, for example, to experience certain emotions in sequence at the time of conversion (such as indifference followed by despair, followed by joy upon recognition of God's grace and an assurance of salvation). This stress on the experiential, typical of continental Protestant evangelicals such as the German pietists and the Unitas Fratrum (or Moravians), helps explain why so many late-eighteenth and early-nineteenth-century evangelicals idealized interdenominationalism and internationalism. It was in the name of shared experience of God that the early LMS, in common with many other evangelical organizations of the period, sought to overcome barriers between different Protestant groups.[8] Late-eighteenth-century evangelical revival in particular was characterized by interdenominational cooperation, in a great wave of evangelical revulsion against what were perceived as denominational rigidities and the arid complexities of systematizing theology.[9]

In Britain, the first great movement of revival of the late 1730s and 40s had been spearheaded by the activity of so-called methodists (the lower case is used deliberately here). The term methodist had originally been applied to John Wesley and his coterie at Oxford in the 1730s; according to their critics, these people were "methodists" because they sought to govern every aspect and every minute of their lives in accordance with spiritual discipline. John Wesley became the most important revivalist leader of the eighteenth century, proselytizing throughout Britain and organizing a vast network of circuit preachers to convert sinners. "Methodist" was, however, as much a term of abuse in the early eighteenth century as it was a clear "party" label. Many methodists had unclear denominational allegiances. People might be labelled "methodist" – or might so label themselves – if they worshiped in unconventional places, saw the necessity for a "new birth," accepted the spiritual leadership of itinerants, or itinerated themselves, for example. The LMS's founder, the unconventional Anglican priest Thomas Haweis, considered that the term methodist was applied in the mid-eighteenth century as "the indiscriminate title of all those, who with awakened sensibility, and real solicitude, seek in the first place the Kingdom of God, and his righteousness, as manifested in the son of his Love Christ Jesus."[10] Methodism itself was a fluid form, sometimes spread without regard to organizational nicety. Although methodism (in this broad sense) first emerged as a movement of renewal within the established church, revivalist activity and evangelical beliefs were not confined to followers of Wesley and Whitefield or indeed to Anglicanism. Clarke Garrett considers eighteenth-century Methodism to have been "as much a style of spirituality and an affirmation of the possibility of the immediate experience of divinity as it was an organized religious body". Methodism was thus "the most visible sector of a broad movement of popular piety that affirmed that the age of miracles was not past and Christianity would regain the purity and vitality of its beginnings."[11] This characterization cannot be extended into the 1790s, when Wesleyan Methodism hardened into a separate denomination.[12] Garrett also downplays John Wesley's drive to centralization. Nonetheless, Garrett does nicely capture the sense of ambiguity that typified mid-eighteenth-century evangelicalism.

Indeed, key methodist preachers, such as John Wesley, the Calvinist George Whitefield, and the Welsh Calvinist Howel Harris, all struggled to remain within the embrace of the Church of England. By the 1790s, however, methodists would be forced out of distrustful mother church (or would remove themselves, depending on historiographical emphasis) and form new denominations.[13]

A second wave of revivals came in the 1780s and 1790s. This time, the most important impact was on so-called "old dissent," the older Protestant nonconformist denominations. "Old dissent" was much more active than was once believed in fostering revival and movements of personal piety.[14] Indeed, the most important short-term impetus behind the missionary movement was probably the late-eighteenth-century explosion of itineracy among Calvinist dissenters which directly led to the formation of the LMS.[15] Itinerant preaching within Britain, often "evangelical" rather than specifically denominational, grew exponentially in the 1790s and became more organized, although evangelical itineracy had long been a vital religious form in Britain, as on the European continent.[16] There was a great flood of people to both "old" and "new" dissenting churches outside the established Church of England, as religious revivalism seemingly filled the spiritual needs of a rapidly burgeoning population often ill-served by the establishment. Both sets of revivals were characterized by the drive to "convert" those throughout Britain who had not yet undergone a rebirth in Christ and thus had not experienced true conversion. These revival movements were thus oriented to missionary activity from the start, albeit of a domestic variety.

Despite interdenominational cooperation, there were many different strands to evangelical revival in Britain. Calvinists, who argued that salvation came only through grace, fought bitterly throughout the eighteenth century with Arminians, including John Wesley, who argued that works contributed to salvation. There was a late-eighteenth-century rapprochement between Calvinism and Arminianism as part of the move of evangelicalism away from the more abstract reaches of theology, but there was also an ironic coda. Methodist Arminians, for whom salvation was potentially available to all, had no trouble in arguing in theory for the need to evangelize the world. It was, however, Calvinists who first spearheaded overseas missionary activity. Calvinists had a difficult tradition of election with which to contend. Extreme Calvinism was not conducive to evangelization: the elect might be a small remnant, plucked by God from the fire. As Derek Lovegrove argues, the crucial theological development that enabled domestic Calvinist itineracy in the 1780s and 1790s, and by extension a vigorous missionary movement in the late 1790s, was the moderation of Calvinist theology. Moderate Calvinism had its origins in the thought of continental theologians from the early seventeenth century and beyond, but it did not become a powerful force in England until the mid-eighteenth century. Moderate Calvinists dissociated themselves from the ideas of particular redemption, limited atonement, and pre-destined reprobation; they argued instead that God's grace was suffi-cient for all even if it was efficient only for the elect. This unleashed a storm of missionary energy, for it combined a belief in damnation which could *only* be halted through faith with the creed that no one could know in advance to whom this grace through faith was offered.[17]

The overseas missionary movement sprang directly from this seedbed of local evangelical culture and vigorous debate beyond the ambit of the Anglican clergy. Many of the young men who would later be missionaries, as well as several clerical founders of the LMS, cut their teeth on preaching during the renewed explosion of local itinerancy of the 1790s. James Read would remember itinerating with Thomas Haweis: he recalled that his reception by the Xhosa compared favourably with that at Ponders End, where "a Man with a Fiddle came and played before us, and the others with old kettles shaking full of Stones."[18] John Campbell, who twice inspected the South African mission, itinerated extensively in Scotland with Robert Haldane at the turn of the century.[19] Similarly, George Burder, pioneer of numerous evangelical institutions and a secretary of the LMS, began itinerating in 1776 and continued to do so until his death in 1825. He was also the author of the much-used *Village Sermons*, designed for use on peri-patetic tours among the "dark places" of rural England. The founda-tion of the LMS itself spurred greater itinerant activity at home. LMS secretary and early editor of the *Evangelical Magazine*, John Eyre, founded the Village Itineracy Association, while LMS director Samuel Greatheed helped create interdenominational unions for the promotion of Christianity.[20] Missions to the heathen of foreign lands were very much extensions of missions to the "dark villages" and other unillu-minated places of Britain which had been the object of evangelical preachers since the methodist revivals of the 1730s.

In all these movements, both ministers and laity played critical roles. Revival movements had a direct impact on ministerial interest in mission. Many Congregationalist academies were consciously seeking to mould a mission-oriented ministerial body by the end of the eigh-teenth century, for example, while ministerial associations played a key role in fomenting overseas missions.[21] Nonetheless, it was lay enthusiasm that was the engine of the late-eighteenth-century mis-sionary movement, as it was of domestic evangelical revival. By the late eighteenth century, a popular religious culture flourished which was oriented towards indiscriminate evangelization as a primary religious duty.

LOCALISM

There is a certain irony to the rhetoric of internationalism which accompanied the development of missionary societies. Most of the earliest British missionaries came from small communities and had little previous experience of actually living overseas. They had probably garnered most of their knowledge of the world from a handful of books and from the fairly abstract precepts of the missionary societies themselves. Increased literacy rates, the wide reach of newspapers, and the growing dissemination throughout Britain of organized "knowledge" about the non-western world (whether in the form of atlases, compendia of information, or the heroic accounts of individual travellers) generated abstract information in the frequent absence of actual experience. Furthermore, it is a fair guess that, despite the healthy flavouring of British nationalism in mission-society rhetoric, many of the earliest missionaries were not well acquainted with the other constituent regions of the United Kingdom either. Rather, they were bound together in an "imagined community" of shared Protestantism.[22]

The importance of the growth of information networks for the formation of missions is illustrated by the fact that the earliest mission-society decisionmakers were aware of geography but usually had little sense of the non-Christian societies inhabiting the spaces on the maps. Here is the Edinburgh Missionary Society explaining why its directorate had decided to send a "Mission of Inquiry to Astrakhan," deep in the Russian empire: "The more we examined the map of the world, and considered the moral and religious state of its inhabitants, the more deeply did the idea impress our minds. Almost in the centrer of the Old Continent; – on the confines of several of the greatest empires in the world, having Persia on the south, Turkey on the west, Persia on the north, and Tartary on the east; – surrounded on every hand by numerous tribes of men, all sunk in the deepest ignorance and depravity ... what a wide field of usefulness here for faithful Missionaries!" The society implored potential donors to "look into the map of world, and see in what a desirable and hopeful situation Divine Providence has placed them."[23] As discussion made clear, however, the directors had no personal knowledge of the Caucasus whatsoever when they dispatched the former chaplain of the colony of Sierra Leone in company with a British "mechanic" and "an African youth" to travel 1,400 miles into the Russian interior.

Both domestic organizers and, even more so, actual missionaries were thus internationalist in theory but often parochial in terms of their direct experience. A report written on board ship as the first LMS mission headed for the South Seas attested proudly that "though there were so many men and women on board who had never before seen the sea, and some of them persons of delicate constitutions, yet they sailed over the distance of 74 degrees of latitude without suffering a single complaint but common sea-sickness."[24] The mundane sea-sickness of the first missionaries to the South Seas as they experienced the sea for the first time in their lives reminds us to look more closely at the local environments from which missionaries came.

In eighteenth-century Britain, despite important adherents from the aristocracy and upper-middle classes, people from the mobile ranks of the upper-working classes responded most vividly to itinerant evangelical preaching. They were not so much the utterly dispossessed as, in the words of Michael Crawford, "people struggling at the margins of respectability" – artisans and small tradespeople, for example.[25] Members of this group were seeing their work and lifestyles change as industrialization transformed Britain. They were also more likely than, say, agricultural day labourers to live away from the purview of the established church. Indeed, historians have fruitfully linked particular manifestations of evangelicalism in Britain and large-scale economic change. Although the reasons have long furnished a subject for vigorous debate, economic transformation helped create material conditions and intellectual needs that were conducive to the large-scale adoption of evangelical revivalist culture in newly industrializing areas of Great Britain.[26] The upper-working classes were the most susceptible of all social groups in Great Britain to evangelical revival and to the formation of new religious organizations.[27] Revival most frequently affected newly industrializing areas with limited penetration by the Church of England. The adherents of revival, typically, were young and subject to social anxiety: they tended to be poised for mobility either up or down the social scale.[28] Evangelical revival was the religious form par excellence of mobile young workers in artisanal professions with some degree, however limited, of independence and control over their own destiny, coupled with the possibility of economic failure.

Interesting trends are evident in the autobiographies and application papers of several missionaries employed by the LMS, as well as in the biographies of early directors. I do not want to be too reductive about religious experience, nor to dismiss the wide variety of personal experiences of "conversion." Nonetheless, some broad patterns do emerge. There were narrative conventions in the conversion narrative which recur in the accounts of conversion offered by prospective LMS candidates, as also in the narratives told later by converts overseas and in much evangelical literature. After a wicked life, the unsaved person gains sufficient self-knowledge to recognize his or her sinfulness and to fall into despair. God's offer of salvation is taken up. Once the person is saved, he or she can look back on past life and recognize it for what it was. Conversion permits a true narrative about the self, in other words.

The stress of evangelicalism on self-discipline, the creation of a new self, and anxiety-resolution was arguably well suited to persons facing situations of social and economic insecurity in which reputation and behaviour could make or break one's economic future (even if less tangible factors were also at work). LMS candidates who described their conversion experiences had typically been teenaged apprentices living away from home when they "lapsed" from the religion of their parents. They were also sometimes schoolboys; almost invariably in the late eighteenth and early nineteenth centuries, the prospective missionary had either received no secondary education or had received it away from home, often with a tutor, because the small towns and villages from which missionaries came did not have the appropriate local resources. "It will not, indeed, be matter of suprize to those acquainted with the wickedness of the human heart," commented the *Evangelical Magazine* in 1803, "that a young man, sanguine in his temper, of quick perception, and eager in his pursuits, unrestrained by parental authority, destitute of religious instruction, placed in a town where vital religion was but little known, and associating with companions more dissipated than himself, should, occasionally at least, exhibit affecting instances of dissipation and depravity."[29] "The vile inclinations of my wicked heart began to break out furiously," wrote Evan Evans in 1816 of his period as a schoolboy away from home, "and what with the bad example of dissolute schoolfellows, and my own wickedness, I ran a wild course for some time."[30] Thomas Haweis, haunted by the memory of an alcoholic father who had drunk away a large inheritance, never drank heavily when he was an apprentice surgeon. Nonetheless, he failed to think of hell and eternal things despite his constant attendance on the dead and dying in mine accidents and smallpox epidemics in Cornwall.[31]

Following the narrative expectations of evangelical conversion, these young people away from home were often overtaken by periods of intense anxiety. A sermon by a visiting preacher plunged Evans into depression: "I could not sleep all night and if I began to slumber, I thought that the bottomless pit was ready to receive me every moment; all the admonitions of my parents, masters and friends, rushed like a torment into my mind; and the deep guilt of conscience, the wrath I justly deserved, and the terrors of eternal punishment made me weep and groan."[32] Haweis was filled with anxiety after a young woman whom he was courting died suddenly of smallpox.[33]

After the necessary recognition of personal guilt, resolution was offered by a conversion experience – often while the young men were still in their teens and before they had become independent of master or schoolmaster. LMS missionary Robert Moffat was rigorously religious throughout his youth, assisted by a mother who (according to her grandson) "united a sternness of religious belief bordering on gloomy vindictiveness with one of the tenderest and most loving hearts that ever beat." Indeed, the mother made the son promise to read two chapters of the Bible a day for the rest of his life as he left Scotland to take up employment as an under-gardener in England at the age of sixteen. Even Moffat, however, "mingled with the gay and godless, in what were considered innocent amusements," which he renounced when, isolated and far from home on his master's estate, he had an emotional conversion experience under Methodist influence at around age nineteen or twenty.[34] Haweis became a Methodist while still young enough to be clouted by his irritated master for his pains.[35]

Although the evidence of these autobiographies and conversion narratives is necessarily anecdotal, the process of sin, guilt, and conversion during an artisanal apprenticeship away from home fits with the general social and psychological profile of groups prone to revival proffered by Michael Crawford and others. The kind of expectations LMS missionaries had about conversion and its role in their lives may also illustrate the extent to which artisans actually shaped the expected pattern of evangelical experience in line with their own life experience; for them, conversion was a sudden, life-changing event in the midst of danger. Wealthier Anglican evangelicals with gentler childhoods tended to have gentler and more gradual conversion experiences with less emphasis on anxiety resolution. The leading Cambridge evangelical of the early nineteenth century, Charles Simeon, for example, denied that "we require a *sudden* impulse of the Holy Spirit ... to convert the soul to God ... It may be so gradual that the growth of it, like the seed in the parable, shall at no time be particularly visible, either to the observation of others, or to the person's own mind ..." This type of conversion might be seen as facilitated by education and the gradual acquisition of wisdom. It contrasted with a conversion experience which immediately catapulted the less well educated and the less well-off into a position of spiritual authority. At the same time, debates about the rapidity of conversion and whether or not conversion was a process that needed to be repeated reflected theological debates among Protestants across Europe, including those between Arminians and Calvinists and between pietists and Moravians.[36]

The working-class people who adopted a new approach to religion were claiming that God might talk to whom he pleased. They were also affirming the right to choose among competing religious options. Few converts would have thought that one route to God was as good as another. Nonetheless, it is striking that converts were often actually changing religious allegiance, adopting a more intense kind of spirituality, or indeed returning to a childhood faith. Many of the men who became missionaries had relatively religious lives as children – as was broadly typical of those most responsive to revivals.[37] They did not always, however, return to the religion of their parents. Circuit preaching further reflected and entrenched the drive to individual choice. Revivalist preachers often left small groups in their wake, who would be served on a rotating basis by circuit preachers; Wesley's system of "classes" was designed, for example, for groups to help one another in the absence of a permanent pastor. Such small groups might also form independently and seek their own preachers. This gave more power to the laity than did the parochial system of the Church of England. Circuit preaching was dependent on the willingness of hearers to attend at an informal place of worship, often chosen by the community, in contrast to the view that the church itself was "holy space" to which all members of a parish were expected to repair as a matter of duty. A circuit preacher for the Congregationalist-run Village Itineracy Association could write piteously to the secretary in 1799, for example, that he had had "little encouragement from the people at Godalmin. I should have been very happy in serving them on a sabbath day but if I cannot please them it is not likely I should be a mean of profiting them – They seem to be a very dissatisfied people – One of them told me that they were High Calvinists but they did not think that I was And another that they were for strong meat and liked to hear election."[38] In some places there were no parish churches within easy reach; in others, attendance on itinerant preachers could complement parish attendance, although the non-evangelical Anglican parish clergy tended to oppose even Anglican itinerants. Several different itinerant preachers might be in competition in the same area. Itinerant "antinomian" preachers taught that since salvation was through faith alone, saved individuals could not sin and could act in ways otherwise considered transgressive. The historian receives tantalizing glimpses of eighteenth-century antinomians competing for hearers with Methodists and Anglican evangelicals, to the disgust of the latter.[39] The import of "unorthodox" preaching – circuit, itinerant, outdoor, or simply unlicensed – was, in sum, to endorse individual choice and to attack the parochial system.

A more detailed look at another autobiography by a working-class evangelical, William Carey, illustrates these broader processes at work in the life of a single man and his wider community. Carey was one of the most famous missionaries of the early nineteenth century. He was a poor shoemaker in Northamptonshire who became a Baptist minister and later worked as a schoolmaster in order to support himself. Instrumental in the foundation of the BMS in 1792, he himself went out as a missionary to Bengal and ended his life as a professor of Indian languages at India's Serampore College.

Carey's autobiography reveals a relatively literate village culture in Northamptonshire (the old stamping ground of leading Anglican evangelical Philip Doddridge in the 1840s). Several different groups were run by local people, suggesting a vibrant local religious culture, quite unhinged from the hierarchical supervision of the Church of England. "During this time," Carey affirmed, "the people at Hackleton formed themselves into a church, and I was one of the members who joined it at that time." When the church was formed there was a "considerable awakening," and many attended prayer meetings. "A sort of conference was also begun, and I was sometimes invited to speak my thoughts on a passage of scripture, which, the people, being ignorant, sometimes applauded, to my great injury."[40] Religious groups in the region competed for clients on a basis of individual choice, in opposition to the Anglican drive to sanctify the existing collective order.

Literacy facilitated a culture of religious choice. Different books gave access to a variety of theological views and could thereby encourage people to make their own minds up on religious questions. At the same time, books besides the Bible were rare and time to read them scarce. This perhaps increased the sense of awe in which they were held and their utility as a way out of as well as into the church. In his own autobiography, William Jay (in later life a secretary of the LMS) conveyed his sense of the extraordinary and wonderful when he was a boy in a much less literate village in agricultural Wiltshire in the 1770s. Jay's minister presented him with "the first two publications I ever called my own," Watt's *History of the Old and New Testament* and the great Puritan and evangelical staple, John Bunyan's *Pilgrim's Progress*. "Never shall I forget," he commented, "my feelings at the receipt of them; for books (what a change has since taken place!) were then very scarce in villages; at least few came in my way."[41] Books were clearly more widely available in the more industrial region of Northamptonshire. They were, however, no less reverenced by men such as Carey. Although William Carey had "but little leisure to read,"[42] he describes his journey through several different religious groups in terms of influential books, as well as recording the preachers whom he went to hear – underscoring the parallel importance of oral culture. When the young Carey began work as an apprentice shoemaker, he was a "churchman," or Anglican. He brought Jeremy Taylor's *Sermons* and Spinker's *Sick Man Visited* to bear as ammunition against his fellow apprentice, "who frequently engaged with me in disputes upon religious subjects, in which my master freely joined"; the latter was a "strict churchman" although he drank too much.[43] As Carey began to evolve new beliefs he was influenced by a group in a nearby village made up of "a number of people who had drunk deeply into the opinions of Law and other mystics." After a while, "and after, by reading some few books I had formed what I thought a consistent creed, one of these persons, the clerk of that parish, sent me word that he wished to have some conversation with me on religious subjects ..."[44] Later still, a gift of Hall's *Help to Zion Travellers* had a "wonderful" impact and helped push Carey to become a Baptist circuit preacher.[45]

Surely the contrast between Northamptonshire and Wiltshire underlines the greater access to books of those in relatively more industrial areas. People in more purely agricultural regions simply had less chance to encounter the written word – and arguably less access in consequence to dissenting Protestant opinions, although this is another topic. In both places, however, the book could have a striking impact.

The missionary movement at its outset was intimately linked to this local rejection of traditional structures as well as to the linked spread of literacy and of organizational forms such as circuit preaching. This is neatly encapsulated in the fact that a key pamphlet by Carey, written to encourage missionary activity, was printed and sold by a group sympathetic to radicals, as E.A. Payne's research has revealed. Carey's printer, Ann Ireland, was probably the wife of John Ireland, printer of the radical *Chronicle,* until the newspaper closed under threat of prosecution in 1791. The local advertiser of the *Enquiry* was the Leicester *Herald,* whose publisher was prosecuted eight months later for circulating Paine's *Rights of Man.* The work's London booksellers were Joseph Johnson, a friend of Paine and Blake, who had employed Mary Wollstonecraft and published her *Vindication of the Rights of Women*; one Knott, who had published a number of anti-slavery tracts; and Edward and Charles Dilly, who were friends of both Johnson and the radical politician John Wilkes.[46] This is not by any stretch of the imagination to say that most nonconformist missionaries were radicals. Nonetheless, Carey's set of contacts underscores the links between nonconformity and political radicalism in the eighteenth century.[47] John Collett Ryland is said to have told a pupil at the time of the American Revolution: "If I was George Washington, I would summon all my officers around me, and make them bleed from their arms into a basin, and dip their swords into its contents, and swear they would not sheath them till America had gained her independence."[48]

What is important here, however, is not the political allegiance of particular individuals but rather the existence of alternate networks of communication which made possible substantial challenges to the religious as much as to the political status quo. This possibility coexisted with the strong personal drive to conservatism of many evangelicals. Old dissent nonconformists tended to be more "left" leaning than Anglicans in any case – and throughout the nineteenth century, nonconformists supported first the Whig and later the Liberal Party in disproportionate numbers. In the eighteenth century, in a more fluid religious setting, evangelicals in general shared some of that radicalism for some of the same reasons: the very structure of evangelicalism was a threat to the status quo and facilitated individual choice. In fact, the early-nineteenth-century Methodist church (as it became) ironically struggled to bring disorderly local revivalism under the control of central leaders.[49] Many very similar fights would be fought in South Africa.

INTERNATIONALISM

Even as revival had many local meanings, it was also a religious form with a long history outside Britain and international antecedents, befitting Protestantism's transcendence of national frontiers.[50] Across the Protestant world of the seventeenth and eighteenth centuries there were numerous movements of spiritual renewal with broad popular appeal. Examples include surges of pietism in German-speaking areas in the seventeenth and eighteenth centuries, prophetic movements within Huguenot communities in France confronting persecution towards the end of the seventeenth century, revivalism in early-eighteenth-century Scotland, and the so-called "Great Awakening" in America in the early eighteenth century.[51] These movements were linked both in practice, as a common Protestant religious form, and in the evangelical imagination as part of an overarching history of the action of God in advancing his cause in the world through moments of religious revival as the end time drew nearer. In the late eighteenth century in Britain, many of the earliest advocates of missionary activity saw themselves as participating in this larger history.

W.R. Ward has argued convincingly that the roots of the forms and theology of evangelical revival must be sought in the reactions of continental Protestantism to the political crises of the late seventeenth and early eighteenth centuries.[52] Revival movements spread in complicated ways through the central Europe of this period in the context of substantial population movements linked both to religious persecution and to the labour needs of an area that had been depopulated by years of war.[53] There were also strong transatlantic links between Protestant Britain and American Protestants. Transatlantic influences, especially Scottish and Irish, were important for American revivalism, notably the Great Awakening of the 1730s and early 1740s.[54] Conversely, British evangelicals frequently saw themselves as fellow soldiers for Christ with evangelically minded Americans across a range of denominations, and they continued to keep in touch with events in the former colonies. In the meantime, concrete links between Protestants of different nationalities, such as those between Moravians resident in Britain and Calvinist evangelicals in the north of England, were important in the establishment of missionary organizations. Not all historians have admired the search for overarching linkage between revival movements, and not all have agreed that pietist roots were important for eighteenth-century Anglo-American revivalism.[55] Yet, although the overall picture is complicated, I would argue that the birth of international missions in late-eighteenth-century Britain was indeed part of an international Protestant revival.

The internationalism that was so key to the missionary movement's early organization found direct expression both in the personal networks maintained by prominent evangelicals, especially clergymen, and in the public world of shared texts. Such late-eighteenth-century British evangelicals as the Scottish minister John Erskine maintained an extensive correspondence with evangelical leaders in different countries, as well as publishing and publicizing their works.[56] Religious publications with an evangelical bent circulated across national frontiers and were frequently translated. The first LMS south African director, the Dutchman Johannes Theodorus van der Kemp, for example, was inspired to offer himself to the LMS after reading a translation of the society's statement of purpose, put into his hands in Holland by a Moravian from Herrnhut.[57] These networks of information exchange, both private and public, had been a feature of English-speaking revivalist Protestantism since at least the early eighteenth century.[58] Furthermore, British missionary societies used many volunteers from the continent, particularly during the war years. The CMS, for instance, could not have kept missions going in its barren early years without a steady flow of Lutheran missionaries from the Basle and Berlin academies, while the LMS in south Africa relied in its early days on German-speakers and Dutchmen.[59]

International links inspired optimism and a sense of participation in a large and powerful movement, while also restoking the fire of British domestic evangelical activity. For many, international similarities proved that God was acting on earth in a concerted manner and that the current time was one for which he had extraordinary plans. In the late 1730s and early 1740s, the simultaneous occurrence of revivals throughout Great Britain and the Great Awakening in the United States was proof for many of God's hand at work. Indeed, John Erskine believed that the coincidence of revival in Scotland and the American colonies proved the imminence of the end time.[60] As the historian John Walsh remarks, revival magazines in "London, Boston and Glasgow spread the news of worldwide conversions, giving the awakenings an international dimension as aspects of one vast outpouring of grace."[61] Similarly, divine agency was also seen in the way in which missionary societies and support groups sprang up throughout the Protestant world in the late 1790s, not only in England, Scotland, and Wales but also in the United States, Holland, Scandinavia, Switzerland, and the German states.

Evangelical leaders and societies thus considered themselves to be united in the same battle across national borders, well beyond the now well-studied Anglo-American transatlantic axis.[62] The early LMS directors were convinced that "the agency of the blessed Spirit of God" was "uniting and harmoniously animating all his children, and bringing them to concur in important public exertions."[63] The comments of the LMS directorate on early missionary activity elsewhere in Great Britain typify the attitude that God was working beyond parochial boundaries: "Nothing can more strikingly demonstrate the finger of God than such a union on both sides the Tweed; not forgetting to mention the like tokens of affection manifested by some of our brethren in Ireland. From the Orkneys to the Land's End, the people of God appear to be animated by the same mind, the same zeal, all directed to the same object."[64] Later expressions of support from beyond the British Isles, even as the war between France and Great Britain worsened, led the directors to expand their vision of cooperation and to exclaim that these were surely "blessed symptoms that the Spirit of God is moving upon the face of the troubled waters." Reassuringly, therefore, "amidst the desolations spread on every side, the horrors of war, and the overflowings of infidelity and impiety, the Lord is seen to ride on the whirlwind and direct the storm."[65] It was in such a spirit of dogged optimism that Thomas Haweis composed a *History of the Church of Christ*. The book considered the progress of Protestantism throughout the world, taking each country one by one in a systematic fashion. "Amidst the convulsions which of late have agitated the nations," commented the *Missionary Magazine* in its review, "the Kingdom of Jesus seems evidently on the increase."[66]

International prayer was a particularly powerful tool for drawing together in imagination the scattered elements of international Protestantism, as well as for fostering awareness of the non-Christian world. In the United States in 1747, Jonathan Edwards, a leading figure in the Great Awakening, issued a call for an international "concert" of public prayer for the renewal and spread of Christianity throughout the world in anticipation of the millennium.[67] For many Christians of the day, the millennium was a period of felicity or of catastrophe (depending on one's interpretation of biblical texts) which was to precede the end of the world and the last judgment; mass preaching of the gospel was a necessary precondition to the apocalypse. Edwards's call was in response to memorials circulated by Scottish ministers after a two-year trial of concerted prayer in Scotland.[68] It also had parallels with a similar summons to quarterly public prayer made by Philip Doddridge in 1742. Edwards's work inspired the Baptists to organize the "Prayer Call" of 1784, which likewise encouraged interdenominational prayer for revival and mission.[69] The premise behind these movements was that united prayer would cause God to fulfil biblical prophecies and pour out the Holy Spirit to convert the nations and thus set the final days in motion. According to Edwards's interpretation of the prophecies of Zechariah in the last days, "there shall be given much of a spirit of prayer to God's people in many places, disposing them to come into an express agreement unitedly to pray to God in an extraordinary manner, that he would appear for the help of his church, and in mercy to mankind, and pour out his Spirit, revive his work, and advance his spiritual kingdom in the world as he has promised ..."[70]

Many early missionary society supporters were convinced that the beginning of international mission was in response to this united prayer. W. Lambert wrote to LMS secretary John Eyre in 1799, for example: "In the Church and congregation I minister to, we have had monthly meetings for prayers for the revival of religion at home, and the spread of it abroad, long before the foundation of the Missionary Society. The reading of Edward's Humble Attempt to promote a union in extraordinary prayer, first led me to propose it to my people. The formation of the Missionary Society in 1795, to be present at which I shall ever esteem as one of the greatest privileges of my life, and the happy effects that have resulted from it, we have viewed as an evident answer from the Almighty."[71] The Warwickshire Independent Association for the Spread of the Gospel at Home and Abroad, a clerical society, held prayer meetings on the first Monday of every month from 1791 onwards.[72] The custom was maintained by the LMS.[73] Until at least the 1830s, converts at mission stations in south Africa continued to pray for world mission on the first Monday of the month, in a conscious gesture of international solidarity. In all these ways, Protestantism created an imagined community of the godly across national frontiers.

THE MILLENNIUM

In addition to the role of Protestantism in creating an imagined international community, Protestantism was key to the self-conception of the "British." An examination of the characteristic millenarian ideas of the early proponents of missionary activity helps illuminate the paradox. Nations might be chosen by God to play particular roles in the unfolding of the divine plan – or indeed, be singled out for particular chastening. In the turmoil of the mid-1790s, Britain's role was unclear. With victory over France and the expansion of the second British empire, however, Britain appeared to have been blessed by God.

Internationalism dovetailed with millenarian ideas to suggest that God had purposes for the world as a whole which could be assisted only through international action. International links were therefore both a proof of the action of the Holy Spirit and a means by which the Spirit could be implored to descend. In this context, missions were a sign of the imminence of the millennium, as well as a means of bringing it about. As we shall see, the characteristic millennial beliefs of LMS personnel would have an important impact in south Africa.

It is significant that many of the earliest seventeenth-century emigrants to the American colonies from Great Britain did not evangelize on a large scale among the "heathen," tending to preserve the apocalyptic attitudes of their British forebears and to seek rather to build a "city on a hill" of the spiritually pure. It was not until towards the early eighteenth century, as expectations of the immediate end of the world died down, that many latter-day Puritans in the New as in the Old World came to see themselves as obligated to act on behalf of God – rather than as more passive instruments and observers of his will – in the conversion of the non-Christian world.

This change was linked to shifts in the basic attitude to the millennium. The dominant conception of the earlier period was that an imminent apocalypse must be prepared for by withdrawal from an impure world and that catastrophes on earth signalled the beginning of the end. The idea that came to dominate Anglo-American evangelicalism of the later period was that the millennium would probably be preceded by progressive improvement and, even if not, had to be worked for through active engagement *with* the world. One might hypothesize that it was above all this intellectual shift towards activism that permitted missionary "work."[74]

Different attitudes towards the millennium and its implications for missions to the heathen recurred throughout the eighteenth century, providing fuel for debate among evangelicals. No cut-and-dried distinction is possible for this period between "pre-" and "post-millenarians"; although the area demands more research, the effort to peg a range of other views to this theological distinction is less fruitful for the eighteenth than for the nineteenth century.[75] All the same, ideas about the millennium had an important influence on ideas about mission. When Carey first proposed a Baptist missionary society at a "Ministers

Fraternal" in 1785, he was told by John Collet Ryland that God would convert the heathen in his own time and that he, Carey, should sit down.[76] However famous this incident in subsequent missionary mythology as an example of resistance to missions by soporific eighteenth-century divines, the point of it should be rather that Ryland was a fervent pre-millenarian and student of the Book of Revelation. He believed that men were currently living under the sixth trumpet and that the sounding of the seventh, which could well be imminent, would "bring on the spiritual reign of Christ over all the nations of the earth." During this "Philadelphian state", "the Jews will all be converted and brought into their own land with great honour and prosperity – the fulness of the Gentiles will take place, and the whole earth shall be filled with the knowledge of God in Christ."[77] The period of the seventh trumpet could best be brought about by fervent prayer and constant study of the Bible.[78] From such a perspective, missionary activity simply did not seem necessary. It is a telling instance of the change in views within a generation that Ryland's son would became secretary of the BMS in 1815.

The early LMS was highly "prophetic," founded in a spirit of great confidence in the Holy Spirit. "'Yet a little while, and the latter-day glory shall shine forth with a reviving splendour,'" promised "An Address to Christian Ministers and All Other Friends of Christianity, on the Subject of Missions to the Heathen" circulated in January 1795.[79] The first circular letter to corresponding members later in the same month echoed the theme. "Amidst the desolating strife of mortals," the letter reassuringly affirmed, "God has often 'appeared in his glory' to extend the kingdom of his dear Son. This remark, in the present aera [sic], is suited to afford peculiar consolation. And the recent 'shaking of nations' has led not a few pious minds to anticipate those glorious days when 'the knowledge of the Lord shall cover the whole earth.'"[80]

In evaluating such material, it is important to recognize how relatively mainstream millenarian and apocalyptic speculation was at all levels of the church in the late eighteenth century.[81] If not everyone did it, millenarian speculation nonetheless remained within the pale of respectability. In certain Christian circles, millenarianism provided a standard language to discuss the politics of the day: like any great mythological text, the Book of Revelation both formed beliefs and acted as a receptacle for existing beliefs and fears. The 1790s did, however, see a particularly strong resurgence of millennialism, much influenced by internationalist perspectives and by a conviction of the uniqueness of the current period. In this climate, apocalyptic speculations and interpretations of biblical prophecy flourished.[82] It seemed likely that this was the promised time of catastrophes which many believed would precede the last judgment. Many interpreted Napoleon as the Antichrist; others saw in the convulsions shaking Catholic France and Spain the promised fall of a different Antichrist, the pope, while still others conflated the two as the Napoleonic Wars wore on. Joseph Hardcastle, one of the founding members of the LMS, wrote to the missionary Van der Kemp in 1809 that European affairs suggested the fulfilment of biblical prophecies. "We entertain a strong persuasion that the political convulsions on the Earth, on the one hand – and the missionary exertions on the other – are both intended by divine providence to bear a relation to that object, and contribute to accomplish that great result."[83]

In such a context, LMS millenarian belief was in fact empowering. Millennial rhetoric reassured the mission supporter that, although events seemed overwhelming, they were following a plan with a good end in which the human being could participate. As an 1806 LMS sermon affirmed, "the present crisis is awful [awe-inpspiring]; a succession of unexpected events, with unexampled rapidity, have taken place. There is a great shaking; thrones are overturned, and all the foundations of the earth are out of course. 'But the Lord reigneth, let the earth rejoice,' 'Be ye not troubled, for such things *must needs* be.'[84] The final words were those of Jesus, expounding to his small group of apostles the devastation that must precede the second coming, including the destruction of the Temple. "Public affairs are darker than ever. What will the end be! Perhaps *our extremity* may be God's opportunity. However it may be, we cannot do wrong by praying," was the private comment of CMS supporter and Anglican evangelical Thomas Robinson in early 1801.[85] In 1794 another Anglican evangelical minister and key mover in the CMS, Thomas Scott, reflected to John Campbell that, although "it behoves us to be prepared for the worst," he hoped that "when the present company of pullers down have removed the rubbish, they will be removed, and the great Architect will employ others to build something on the ground they cleared."[86]

The public rhetoric of the LMS was more optimistic and more extreme. The moral drawn by the *Report of the Directors* in 1806 echoed calls repeated again and again throughout the first two decades of the LMS's existence. "The peculiar character of the Divine dispensations in the present day," the report urged," – the important changes under which a great portion of the world is passing – the rapidity with which the plans of providence appear to be advancing to a crisis; should all inspire the hearts of Christians to new energy, to improve occasions as they continually arise, and on the ruins of the kingdom of antichrist [Catholicism], as well as in heathen countries, to hasten to lay the foundations of Christian temples."[87] Had not Jesus promised that from the ruins of the temple of the Jews would arise the temples of the New Jerusalem?

A final, crucial point was that, despite economic crisis in Britain and uncertainties over the war, Britain increasingly appeared to have been preserved from the virulence of events in France. Britain's ultimate victory over France and preservation from invasion suggested to many evangelicals that the nation had been saved for the purpose of spreading the word. This was in accord with the idea that God selected certain groups at times of upheaval to spread the gospel or to preserve true Christianity. It was in a similar vein, for example, that the Moravian bishop Jan Comenius had commended to the British Puritans in 1649 the care of "our well-beloved mother, the church,"[88] after the Peace of Westphalia had confirmed the Holy Roman Empire's ownership of Moravia. The favour of God might pass from nation to nation, and this favour carried with it a particular duty to carry out the divine will. In the same letter mentioned above, Thomas Scott, writing as an Englishman to the Scotsman Campbell on the state of Britain, reflected even in 1794 that despite the gloominess of the times "I trust the Lord will preserve us, as a Nation, for the Sake of his chosen remnant; tho he may correct and humble us."[89] This theme, simultaneously internationalist and nationalist, would become stronger as victory appeared more likely in the Napoleonic Wars. It would be developed extensively by the more conservative CMS. After 1815, indeed, it would take on increasing overtones of a *mission civilisatrice*, becoming more and more intertwined in liberal evangelical circles with ideas about the commercial success of Great Britain as a divine goad to both economic and religious proselytizing. As victory seemingly approached, the 1812 CMS annual report closed on a citation from the official "Report of the Formation of the Cambridge Auxiliary Bible Society," portraying Britain's opportunity to spread the gospel, military victory, and the empire alike as providential. "Great Britain now stands alone among the nations, with the wreck of Europe scattered at her feet: and, though the dangers of war have been imminent beyond all example of former times, yet it has pleased Providence to give her strength to resist all the efforts of her enemies, and to establish an empire co-extended with the bounds of the ocean." The society hoped that Britain had been "exalted among the nations for nobler purposes; that the empire of Britain shall be an empire of mercy." Judging from the "signs of the times," surely it was not presumptuous to indulge "the humble and pious hope, that to Great Britain may be entrusted the high commission of making known the name of Jehovah to the whole earth"?[90]

This stress on God's dealing with Britain as a nation with a divinely

ordained mission underscores a key paradox at work in British Protestant beliefs about how God acted in the world. Eighteenth-century
British evangelicals, like most of their Protestant contemporaries elsewhere, emphasized the relationship of the naked and solitary individual with God. Before God no one could clothe himself or herself in
ritual or fall back on community sanction. At the same time, paradoxically, God was also believed to interact with, and act through, communities as a whole. Michael Crawford captures this central ambiguity well in his discussion of evangelical revivals in Britain and New
England. In his words, the Puritan Reformed tradition considered that
God was believed to deal with "entire communities as discrete moral
entities." Different communities thus had "covenants" with God, modelled on the covenant between Yahweh and the Jews. Communities
were judged or rewarded on earth, unlike the individual. Hence, "good
works" had an entirely different function in the lives of communities
than they had in the lives of individuals. Communities were also
composed of the saved and the damned alike. "Hence, a community's
relationship with God was not determined so much by the inner gra-
ciousness of the people as it was by their external compliance with his
law."[91] Outside the Reformed tradition, other strands of evangelicalism may have downplayed the notion of national covenants, but they
also emphasized the action of God through communities as a whole,
for which he had particular plans. Boyd Hilton has explored ways in
which what he terms "extreme evangelicals" among the political elite
of early-nineteenth-century Britain stressed, among other things, God's
chastisement of communities as a whole: the Irish famine was read
along these lines, with disastrous effect.[92] Such belief in the actions of
God through particular nations opened the door to a more implicitly
nationalist reading of missionary activity, even though eighteenth-
century advocates of mission downplayed supposed British cultural
superiority in order to emphasize God's plans for the world as a whole.

The early LMS was, then, internationalist in its rhetoric. Its leaders
were in contact with a number of Protestant groups in Europe and
America, while footsoldiers and leaders alike considered Britain as only
one among a number of Protestant nations touched by the spirit of
God.[93] In 1798 LMS directors saw signs of renewed missionary activity on the continent through an internationalist lens. These were
"blessed symptoms that the Spirit of God is moving upon the face of
the troubled waters," and the directors had "reason to hope" that
when God's "thunder and tempest shall have cleared the sky of Europe
of the noxious exhalations of superstition and atheism, his gospel will
arise and shine with more resplendent glory."[94] Nonetheless, it was
Britain that was actually free to engage in extensive missionary activi-

ty. From the beginning, Britain was portrayed in LMS rhetoric as possessing a divinely ordained mission. In more material terms, throughout the period of war, continental European missionaries would be channelled through British societies. Internationalism therefore readily coexisted with calls that "the distinguishing protection of Providence to our highly favoured country" be matched by "our vigorous and united exertions in spreading the kingdom of Immanuel over the world."[95]

Although it is clear that millenarianism played some role in this internationalist rhetoric, as it did in bolstering belief in Britain's specifically national mission, historians have differed as to the importance of millennial, or millenarian, beliefs as an incentive for missionary activity. J.A. De Jong has argued that millennialism was second only to "love" as a motive for the rise of missions.[96] Gidney's study of evangelical efforts to convert the Jews, in large part in order to hasten the millennium which could occur only once the Jews had been converted, bears out De Jong's emphasis on millennialism.[97] Alan Frederick Perry, on the other hand, believes that millennialism as a motivating force behind the LMS has been exaggerated: it constituted vague background, rather than "immediate inspiration," and by mid-Victorian times, intense millennialism was "a creed for cranks."[98]

Millenarianism might, however, be better read as a narrative myth. On the one hand, it was not a simple belief that could alone motivate the missionary movement: we have seen that millenarianism probably deterred rather than encouraged missionary activity in the seventeenth century, and we will see further the many different shapes that apocalyptic and millenarian beliefs might assume. On the other hand, at this stage, millenarianism can probably not be separated out from the complex of beliefs (such as a Christian conception of history and faith in the Holy Spirit) which both informed millenarianism and made it possible. In other words, millenarianism was part and parcel of an eighteenth-century "prophetic" outlook. As such, it was relatively motivating but cannot be singled out in a cut-and-dried manner. In addition, millenarianism was crucial for many during the period of the French Revolution and the Napoleonic Wars, in alleviating anxiety, in bolstering a sense of national mission, and in utilizing the prophetic energy generated by a period of crisis. Millenarian language bridged the gap between the internationalist outlook of Protestant networks and a more localist nationalism during a period of bitter warfare.[99] Perry is right that millenarianism died down in the mid-nineteenth century in the religious mainstream, as part of a general collapse of confidence in the validity of the Bible as a tool for precise (rather than vague) prophecy about the future. At the outset of our period, however, millenarianism, like the conviction of God's action among Protestants across national boundaries, must be seen as part of a complex tissue of beliefs urging the evangelization of the world.

THE BOOK AND THE WORLD:
LINKING THE GLOBAL AND THE LOCAL

The local and the global were linked above all by the printed word. The existence of communication networks extending down the class scale to a relatively literate upper-working class was a crucial factor in the development of an overseas missionary movement. The artisan communities from which the bulk of missionaries came were inspired to spread evangelicalism to the "heathen" as they themselves received more information about the non-Christian world. This occurred as rates of literacy increased among the elite of the working classes – especially, I hypothesize, the *evangelical* working classes with their overpowering emphasis on teaching literacy and their networks of Sunday schools.[100] At the same time, the British market for travel literature and popular geography grew tremendously towards the end of the century.[101] This encouraged people to think in global terms and opened up a new realm of imaginative possibilities.

Take, for example, the impact of the voyages of Captain Cook to the South Pacific. "Reading Cook's voyages," Carey claimed, "was the first thing that engaged my mind to think of missions."[102] Many others could make the same claim. John Hawkesworth's anthology of accounts of Cook's first voyage to the South Seas was so widely diffused that he was able to sell his copyright for the enormous sum of £6,000.[103] It was reading Cook's *Voyages* and the later accounts of Captain Bligh that led Thomas Haweis, chaplain to the Calvinist Methodist Countess of Huntingdon and future co-founder of the LMS, to become obsessed with the idea of sending a mission to the South Seas.[104] Even in Holland, J.J. Kicherer, one of the LMS's first four missionaries to south Africa, confessed his excitement at hearing of the formation of the LMS by claiming: "No information in the world could so much have gratified the ardent desires which, years before, had been excited in his heart, in consequence of reading the Voyages and Discoveries of Captain Cook."[105]

William Carey's influential missionary tract, *An Enquiry into the Obligation of Christians to Use Means for the Conversion of the Heathens*, illustrates the impact on religious communities in Britain of information about the world beyond the western hemisphere. John Ryland commented of the first draft that it needed little correction, "so much had this young man attained of the knowledge of geography and history, and several languages, in the midst of the pressures of poverty, and while obliged to support himself as a journeyman shoemaker, and afterwards as a village schoolmaster; since his people could raise him but ten or twelve pounds a year, besides five pounds from the London fund."[106] Carey used information garnered from Cook, geographic manuals, the local newspaper, the Northamptonshire *Mercury*, and possibly other sources[107] to draw up a list of all the countries in the world, their surface area, population, and number of adherents to various religions. He calculated that the inhabitants of the world amounted to "about seven hundred and thirty-one millions, four hundred and twenty million of whom are still in pagan darkness; an hundred and thirty million the followers of Mahomet; an one hundred million catholics; forty-four million protestants; thirty million of the greek and arminian churches, and perhaps seven millions of Jews." It was striking "what a vast proportion of the sons of Adam there are, who yet remain in the most deplorable state of heathen darkness, without any means of knowing the true God, except what are afforded them by the works of nature; and utterly destitute of the knowledge of the gospel of Christ, or of any means of obtaining it."[108] Such a calculus of damnation would become a staple rhetorical trope among the more extreme evangelical groups. In 1792 it was a novel, if predictable, reaction to the spread of geographical knowledge. Furthermore, according to W.R. Ward, Carey's "historical scheme" was "already a cliché, and would have been instantly recognized as such not merely by his immediate circle but by like-minded men right through the reformed world"; Carey's view of history as a panorama of the world progress of the gospel with human assistance had ultimate roots, Ward claims, in John Gillies's 1754 *Historical Collections Relating to Remarkable Periods of the Success of the Gospel*.[109] The impact of such compilations confirms the centrality of the book and the spread of a certain type of information to international reform movements. Carey's calculations neatly fused evangelical theological beliefs with the spirit of rational scientific enquiry, in a manner typical of the early missionary movement. In the same universalizing mode, the *Missionary Register*, launched in 1816, would provide information on Protestant missions around the world, regaling its readers with geographical lists and a "Missionary Map: Exhibiting the Various Stations of Protestant Missions throughout the Eastern Hemisphere."[110]

Carey's work also suggests the extent to which Britain's commercial activity was giving ordinary people a sense of the possibility of action on a global scale. "Have not English traders, for the sake of gain, surmounted all those things which have generally been counted insurmountable obstacles in the way of preaching the gospel?" Carey enquired. "Men can insinuate themselves into the favour of the most barbarous clans, and uncultivated tribes, for the sake of gain; and how different soever the circumstances of trading and preaching are, yet this will prove the possibility of ministers being introduced there."[111] The development of trade and imperial communication networks furnished both the means for foreign evangelization and the conviction, in the context of activist millenarianism, that God was making his will plain.

Information about missions themselves to the non-Christian world also circulated widely in British society. Reports from the American colonies joined Moravian publications, as well as accounts of the Lutheran missionaries supported by the Society for the Promotion of Christian Knowledge (SPCK) in Tranquebar from 1714 onwards. By the 1790s a sentimental library of missionary classics had already begun to develop: Jonathan Edwards on David Brainerd's work among the Amerindians; and *Letters on Missions* by Melvill Horne, former chaplain to the Anglican evangelical colony of Sierra Leone.[112] Such failures as the collapse of the Huntingdonian mission to the Cherokee and the internicine warfare between Methodists and Baptists which jeopardized the success of missions to Sierra Leone in the early 1790s were discretely downplayed.[113]

Evangelical leaders themselves were conscious of the social impact of new technology and eager to turn it to religious advantage. The periodical could reach farther down the social scale, and faster, than books. The implications were not lost on evangelicals. The obituarist of John Eyre, founder of the *Evangelical Magazine*, reflected: "A periodical publication exhibits a mode of instruction, with which the world was formerly unacquainted; but since it has been adopted, has produced a surprising revolution in sentiments and manners. Thousands read a Magazine, who have neither money to purchase, nor leisure to peruse larger volumes ... an engine, so capable of a destructive or salutary tendency, ought to be applied for evangelical purposes."[114]

In 1796 the *Missionary Magazine* was founded as "a repository of discussion and intelligence respecting the progress of the gospel throughout the world."[115] By 1797, its editors enthused that "never was there a greater number of religious publications carried on than at present, and never were any of them more generally read. The aggregate impression of those alone which are printed in Britain every month, considerably exceeds THIRTY THOUSAND."[116] Soon after its foundation the LMS began to publish an annual collection of *Transactions*, while the Glasgow Missionary Society published its *Reports* well before it had missions on which to report. The secretary of the CMS, Josiah Pratt, was also an early editor of the *Christian Observer*, begun in 1802.

In this sense a strawman "social control" theorist, or indeed a straw-man postmodernist looking for the birth of "modernity," would be correct in claiming that the spread of missionary activity was dependent on capitalist change within Britain itself and on the development of an imperial economy. This was, however, more because economic change facilitated the spread of an evangelical culture which was already strongly established among the British upper-working classes than because "capitalism" in the 1790s gave birth in a linearly direct fashion to international missionary activity. The artisanal classes and evangelical missionaries had an increased capacity to gain knowledge about the non-Christian world, to spread information in turn, and to travel outside Britain (particularly within the empire). In this sense, the missionary movement was the product of the growth of the "public sphere," in Jürgen Habermas's terms, and thus in unexpected ways was a child of the modern world.

AUTHORITY AND ANXIETY

Late in the day as it may seem for religious unorthodoxy to have remained a point of political tension, the political ambiguities of religious dissent were certainly not lost on contemporaries, whether ecclesiastical elites, politicians, or "church and king" mobs. Dissenters were still excluded from full participation in civic society by the requirement of occasional conformity to the Anglican communion and subscription to the Thirty-Nine Articles for the filling of civic offices and access to the universities of Oxford and Cambridge; the Test and Corporation acts were not completely repealed until 1828. More nebulously, the very culture of religious choice that had developed at a popular level was threatening to an established order which linked religious, political, and social hierarchy.[117] The mobilization of sometimes ill-educated itinerant preachers, the growth of independent congregations outside the Church of England, working-class uses of literacy to make religious choices, and perhaps even the breakdown of deference that such activity implied, all provoked anxiety in which religious and political concerns were closely mingled. Regardless of the actual links between working- and middle-class political radicalism in the early 1790s and the rapid growth of popular evangelicalism, critics were not slow to connect the two. Certainly, the metonymic identification between literacy and freedom that LMS missionaries would transport to south Africa was one upheld by both dissenting evangelicals and by activists in working-class constitutional societies. It was feared on that basis in Britain, and would meet with similar anxiety in the Cape Colony.

Ambient concern about religious unsoundness, which included

worry about evangelicalism within the Church of England, was intensified by the French Revolution and the subsequent wars with France.
The support of many dissenters, including LMS founder David Bogue,
for the early stages of the French Revolution intensified distrust of dissent in more conservative circles and by extension of evangelicalism
and missionary activity.[118] "Church and king" mobs helped generate a
climate of fear and suspicion. In fact, by the mid-1790s, French atheism and revolutionary excesses as well as fears of real revolution in
Britain had pushed many evangelicals – non-conformists and Anglicans alike – into far more conservative postures.[119] The challenge to
church hierarchy offered by the *forms* of itineracy and informal
preaching, and the intellectual challenge of the seeming rejection of
hierarchy, remained, however. One might see in this the threat that
ecstatic religious experience offers to traditional sources of authority,
across cultures and time, even as appeals to the divine from unorthodox and unauthorized sources (such as women, children, or the poor)
can ironically establish new forms of authority.[120]

The developing progress of evangelicalism among high society in
Britain was checked by the general climate of moral panic. Threats to
the ecclesiastical status quo appeared more severe than ever after the
bloodbaths of 1796, seemingly perpetrated by people who had thrown
off all political restraints along with their religious deference. Attacks
on the church made by Paine and other political radicals led the established church to draw in its horns even farther and to proclaim all the
more loudly the value of church discipline and order. It was against this
background that in 1796 the General Assembly of the Church of Scotland rejected a motion to send out missionaries and to support the burgeoning revival movement. Opponents claimed that the denizens of
uncivilized lands were not advanced enough to receive the gospel and
did not necessarily need it; the need to maintain political and social
order was also a factor in debates.[121] In the same year, the evangelical
Anglican minister Thomas Scott felt obliged to hold back from full
involvement with the newly fledged LMS. As he told a friend:

My situation ... as a minister of the establishment prevents me, by considerations of expediency, from fully uniting with a society which is looked upon
with jealousy by our staunch churchmen, especially our rulers. At the same
time I feel it incumbent on me to be cautious about how I commit myself in a
business which is under the management of persons varying in their views and
in their measure of respectability. Hence I am constrained to be considerably a
stranger to the persons selected for missionaries, and to the interior of the
management; though I am privately a steady advocate for the institution, and
contribute my mite to the cause. In my situation, I cannot make any public

collections, or take any other ostensible measures: but my few steady friends liberally support them.[122]

In addition to the inevitable association with sectarians,[123] missionary activity was particularly unrespectable in establishment eyes because it required itinerary. In 1799–1800 George Pretyman-Tomline, bishop of Lincoln and Winchester, and other high churchmen were pressing for an act of parliament to outlaw itinerary in Great Britain. Anglican evangelicals, such as the parliamentarian William Wilberforce, tried to be conciliatory and to work behind the scenes. LMS personnel, heavily committed to itinerary, were naturally less compromising. "The Devil is busy in England," wrote LMS director Matthew Wilks to the missionary Johannes Theodorus Van der Kemp in South Africa, "and has made a bold attempt to stop the spread of the gospel in England, by a member giving notice in the House of Commons of his intention of bringing in a bill to amend the toleration act [to eliminate itinerant preaching] ... but I hope and believe he who sitteth in the heavens will laugh."[124] LMS and BMS organizers made things more difficult by hailing the ways in which domestic and foreign evangelism fed off each other and by claiming much of the credit for the spectacular growth in itinerary in rural England in the mid- to late 1790s which had sparked the establishment clampdown in the first place.[125] Although Michael Angelo Taylor, MP for Durham, was persuaded to drop his bill restricting itinerary, partly under threat from his own dissenting constituents and Methodist election agent, itinerary remained under profound suspicion.[126]

In this context even the London evangelicals among the Anglicans came under attack, particularly as they were making themselves visible through election to lectureships and the occupation of purchased livings. The *Anti-Jacobin Review* lobbed a series of damaging articles in the evangelical direction in 1799 and 1800, alleging that evangelicals were probably seditious and at the least arousing unrest among the common people.[127] By 1802, the Blagdon controversy had errupted over the schools of Hannah More, as opponents criticized the efforts of this leading evangelical to teach the poor to read and, especially, to write, as politically dangerous. A former supporter of More's, William Cobbett, had launched his *Annual Register* with an all-out attack on Anglican evangelical clergy – "cool, of consummate cunning, of great industry and perseverance, and supported by men of no little wealth," akin to the "*Gospel-Preaching Ministry* so loudly clamoured for by the apprentices and chimney-sweeps of London, in their petitions to the regicide parliament."[128] The atmosphere in general was one of anti-Methodist moral panic.[129] Even at the most respectable end of the evangelical world, supporters of the evangelical parliamentary group known as the Clapham Sect were sometimes suspicious of the ecclesiastical loyalty of the very evangelical ministers they sponsored. Henry Thornton wrote to Wilberforce in 1801 that he found it "curious" that Anglican evangelical Josiah Pratt should collaborate so much with dissenters: "It tends to prove what I have often thought that the evangelical min[i]s[ters] in the Church who are warm on points of doctrine & talk much of "*seeing clearly*" & indeed most of those who are serious find themselves so naturally connected with Dissenters that consid'g human Nature it is scarcely possible for them to be very staunch friends of the Church under the present Circumstances of the Establishment."[130] In 1802 Thomas Robinson wrote to CMS secretary Thomas Scott in a state of jitters, refusing the CMS request that he give the anniversary sermon because of his "many objections and difficulties" and rebuking Scott for associating with Rowland Hill, an Anglican practitioner of itinerancy. His comments reflect the nascent formation of evangelical and high church parties within the Church of England: "The times are critical with respect to the state of religion in the Church. Evangelical Ministers are increasing around us; but they are watched with a malignant eye. They are evidently more and more hated by the Clergy of an opposite description, & I doubt not but plans are in agitation to check them or to drive them out of the establishment ... I say to all my brethren so aimed at; Be more than ever circumspect, maintain a perfect consistency of character, shew yourselves true friends of the Church by [avoiding?] everything which might weaken her interests, and then abide all consequences."[131]

If evangelicalism was attacked from the outside as politically subversive, it was also split within between worried conservatives and reluctant radicals. A number of evangelical ministers themselves, especially from the Anglican tradition, tended to worry about the political dangers of empowering the very groups on whom they themselves depended for their chief constituency. Even literacy aroused anxiety: missionary and evangelical publications from this period tend to emphasize the need for the dangerous engine of the press to be brought under the right religious control. The same Anglican evangelicals behind the CMS and the *Christian Observer*, more conservative than their nonconformist counterparts, had during the era of the French Revolution projected a secret society to "counteract the Designs of Infidels against Christianity." It would ideally control the press, "since literature is at present the great engine operating upon society." The project came to nothing more alarming than a number of pamphlets and tracts on the model of Hannah More's *Village Politics* and a series of weekly sermons on "the Signs and Duties of the Times."[132] Its very existence, however, testifies to the growth of an information culture and to the conviction of contemporaries that this culture was like an "engine," able to control readers for good or ill. The *Christian Observer* was all the more necessary, its editor contended, "at a period like this, when Dramatic Compositions, Novels, Tales, Newspapers, Magazines, and Reviews, are disseminating doctrines subversive of all morality, and propagating tenets the most hostile to piety, order and general happiness."[133]

Similar anxiety was manifest in theological objections from within the religious camp to evangelical theology and proselytizing techniques. Many high Anglicans (including a preponderance of colonial officials) had theological concerns about evangelical preaching, which often merged with their political concerns. Many late-eighteenth-century high Anglicans distrusted the low-status and ill-educated evangelical preachers whom the "Spirit" had inspired. Many were made further uneasy by the belief in the natural depravity of man which was held most vehemently by high Calvinists but was echoed across the evangelical spectrum.[134] For Calvinists, man stood necessarily condemned because of his intrinisic evil. Salvation was thus an act of free grace. It occurred *only* through personal contact with God, and since God's presence could not be doubted, the process of conversion might be rapid – some groups indeed demanded that it be so, although, as we have seen, others (including some evangelical Anglicans) allowed for a slow progression. Such an approach conflicted with high church Anglican convictions that salvation might be reached gradually through life, through learning, sacraments, and the discipline of the church. As Doreen Rosman argues, evangelicals were distinguished from non-evangelicals above all by the former's emphasis on the spirit of God. "While evangelical Anglicans by no means disregarded and in some cases highly valued the ordinances – and also the order – of the established church, they refused to limit the Spirit, believing that in the essential converting and nurturing of each individual he used other instruments alongside the discipline and sacraments of the Church of England."[135] This emphasis on the spirit over the benefit of church discipline was even more likely to typify dissenters and Methodists. The implication was that traditional church hierarchy could be bypassed in favour of spiritual individualism.

Behind all these concerns stood the spectre of the religious past. Evangelicalism was often termed "enthusiasm," the very term reminiscent of the bloody excesses of civil war in the seventeenth century. Had not the breakdown of religious order led in the past to wrenching civil war and to Oliver Cromwell's Protestant dictatorship? The weight of history and the ambiguities of popular religion in an age of hierarchy would be transported to the colonies, while new debates on different issues but on similar lines would continue to reflect the power struggles possible from within the confines of a shared Christian narrative.

INSTITUTIONS: THE FORMATION OF MISSIONARY SOCIETIES

The most influential model for the British activists who established the BMS in 1792 and the LMS in 1795 was probably that of Moravian international missionary activity. The influence of the Moravians in fact illustrates many of the themes we have been pursuing in this chapter: local interaction helped create local associations and local revivalist movements, while at the same time the Moravians were an international body based in a German principality who saw themselves as acting across national frontiers. Both personal contact and the international market in printed periodicals, pamphlets, and books created and enabled their influence on British evangelicals.

The Moravian community at Herrnhut on the estates of the German noble Count Nicolaus Ludwig Graf von Zinzendorf had been formed in the 1720s by refugees from what is today Czechoslovakia, who had termed themselves the "Unitas Fratrum" in Czechoslovakia. The best-known instance of Moravian influence on British evangelicalism is that of the personal impact of Moravians in both London and Georgia on John Wesley. The Moravian community also, however, provided a model for the late-eighteenth-century missionary movement. The Renewed Unitas Fratrum (as it preferred to be called) furnished a unique example of a Protestant missionary church. Zinzendorf presented his church in exile as a community of pilgrims, always on the lookout for spiritual opportunity and ready to send out messengers: "It is rightly said that my Society was set on Foot principally to assist so great and good a Work as the Conversion of the Heathens, and that this was its particular Calling."[136] This was in keeping with the mobility and internationalism that had been forced on the brethren through years of persecution and warfare, as they lived through the wars of religion in current-day eastern Europe and endured a period of dispersal between the 1648 Treaty of Westphalia and the reconstruction of the Moravian community in Herrnhutt.[137] The Moravians had an ongoing self-understanding as a small, disciplined, pure remnant of the apostolic church with responsibility for transmitting the flame of true Christianity. They saw themselves as a pilgrim church.

As befitted the shock troops of Protestantism, young men among the Moravians were expected to consider a missionary vocation; the community at Herrnhut even cast lots to see which members of the congregation would go out as missionaries.[138] The community first started sending missionaries in 1732. In 1736 Georg Schmidt began a short-lived mission in the Cape Colony to the Hessequa of the western Cape. By 1771, the Unitas Fratrum as a worldwide body was fielding 160 missionaries, catechists, and assistant missionaries in North and South America, the Caribbean, Africa, Asia, and Greenland. London was the jumping-off point for missions to the American colonies. This brought many prominent Moravians through England.[139] Later, when the English Moravians were better established, they founded in London a "Society for the Furtherance of the Gospel" which raised funds and received and read the reports of missionaries. From 1790 onwards, this society published a periodical journal which was a model for the later *Transactions* of the LMS. It also published extensively in English on its missionary activity.[140]

A number of the interdenominationalist, Calvinist evangelical founders of the LMS admired the Moravians. Samuel Greathead, an early proponent of interdenominational domestic itinerary, for example, admired and read Zinzendorf.[141] Thomas Haweis met at Oxford a Moravian called Brandt, a "painter by profession" who "served a little knot of people called at Stanton Harcourt." Brandt met with the "young students who assembled at my Room for improvement." Through Brandt, Haweis met the Moravian leader Benjamin Latrobe. Haweis was so impressed by Moravian missionary activity that, when seriously ill in Cornwall, he bequeathed all his money after the death of his wife to Moravian missions. Fortunately for Haweis if not for Moravian missions, Haweis recovered and had other charitable projects and two unexpected late-life children by the time he actually died; nonetheless, he entertained "the same good will" for Moravians throughout his life.[142] The example illustrates well the interchange of religious ideas in the eighteenth-century Protestant world.

In the 1740s the Moravians withdrew from London and established a series of communities in the north of England. These communities played a significant role in the religious culture of the northern counties, which were to prove a power-house of revival. LMS missionary Robert Moffat's wife Mary was educated by Moravians, for example. The Moravians also had small communities scattered through other counties. These included several in Northamptonshire in the East Midlands, near the area in which William Carey lived and worked.[143] Northamptonshire provides a particularly strong circumstantial case for Moravian influence on the development of evangelical missions. Carey both cited Moravian missionary work as an example to spur on other denominations and brandished the Moravian missionary magazine in 1792 in a public meeting as proof of the feasibility of missions.[144] John Newton, a founder of the CMS and a well-known evangelical figure, also lived in the same area of Northamptonshire and was sufficiently influenced by the Unitas Fratrum to have translated the works of Zinzendorf. It is worth adding that, as a centre for missionary activism, Northamptonshire illustrates the extent to which local evangelicals worked together despite denominational differences. In addition to Carey, Thomas Scott, first secretary of the CMS, John Ryland, a BMS founder, and John Newton, the abolitionist former slavetrader who was so key a figure for the development of late-eighteenth-century Calvinist evangelicalism, all lived in the region, corresponded with one another, and had a mutual influence.[145] In 1793 it was Scott who tried unsuccesfully to get permission from the East India Company for Carey to enter India.[146] In the rosier year of 1813, Scott wrote to Ryland: "I do most heartily rejoice in what your missionaries are doing in India ... May all India be peopled with true Christians – even though they be all baptists!"[147]

All of these links were, however, personal and small-scale. The Moravians had an important influence on key individuals, but their communities were not large in Britain. The Moravian *Periodical Accounts* do not appear to have been diffused as widely as subsequent missionary journals; Carey needed to make his Baptist colleagues aware of their existence. It would be left to British societies more fully to exploit local information networks.

In 1792 William Carey and a handful of colleagues founded the first denominational missionary society, the BMS. Circumstances around its formation underscore the centrality of literacy and information networks. We have already seen the impact on Carey of geographical knowledge, religious books, and Moravian periodicals. On the other hand, communities needed patrons to launch such efforts. They also required the expertise of the visitor from overseas, or at the least contact with overseas "experts." Carey was unexpectedly given money in Birmingham to print his pamphlet by Thomas Potts, a businessman who had met African Americans and Amerindians while in the American colonies. The BMS board began with the less than princely start-up capital of £83.2s.6d. Ryland recorded that they "knew not how to proceed, whom to send, nor where to begin our operations" but were inclined to target the "Pellow Islands" in the South Seas, of which one member had read an account. "But just at this time, Mr. John Thomas returned from Bengal. He had repeatedly written from thence to Dr. Stennett, to my father and to Mr. Booth, and given some account of his conferences with the natives." Thomas was now trying to raise funds and hire a companion to go back to Bengal as a fellow missionary; the BMS consequently merged their two efforts.[148] After further false starts, the BMS would finally establish itself firmly in India.

The BMS was basically Carey's brainchild and was run by a small group of Baptist ministers. Nonetheless, it both expressed and nurtured a growing trend. Three years later, the organizational efforts behind the LMS came to a head. Like the BMS, it was spearheaded by clergymen but depended on lay participation. Unlike the BMS, the LMS was large, ambitious, and interdenominational. Although the society was never as interdenominational as it had hoped, and by 1818 confessed itself Congregationalist, the scope of its vision demonstrated the rapidly developing optimism and self-confidence of the evangelical missionary movement.

The LMS was clearly an idea whose time had come. It grew from the confluence of small groups, albeit with many interconnections, working towards the same end. In addition to the influential "Prayer Call" movement, more tangible support was drawn from various associations with missionary aims, modelled on the evangelical voluntary bodies and collegiate gatherings which were so prominent a feature of evangelical life. These included, for example, the Glasgow Missionary Society, founded in 1795 by Scottish Congregationalists with its "sole object" being the "propagation of the pure and unadulterated gospel of Christ in the dark places of the earth." It promoted missions through "meeting together for friendly and Christian conference, by prayer to God for his blessing, and by collections, contributions and subscriptions."[149] Not until 1820 did the society attempt its own mission, at the Cape of Good Hope (not in fact begun until 1821), owing to a lack of missionary candidates and supporting funds.[150] Such small support groups were, however, important sources of funds, personnel, and validation for the larger societies.

Ministers' discussion groups, such as the Warwickshire Independent Association, the Anglican evangelical Eclectic Society, and the Independent Worcestershire Association, furnished another source of support.[151] Such groups were popular in the 1790s as a means of fostering evangelical concerns and promoting a common sense of purpose. Many of the early mission organizers were drawn from their ranks. As with the BMS, the press played an important role. Early LMS directors were also involved in 1793 in the establishment of the influential interdenominational *Evangelical Magazine*, which sought "to arouse the Christian public from its prevailing torpor, and excite [Christians] to a more close and serious consideration of their obligations to use means for advancing the Redeemer's Kingdom."[152]

In the meantime, Thomas Haweis "pityingly viewed" the "Southern savage isles," as his tombstone proclaims.[153] In 1791 he tried to send two men out as missionaries on Captain Bligh's ship. The attempt was foiled by the refusal of the bishop of London, Beilby Porteus, to ordain the men, despite the representations of William Wilberforce and the London evangelical minister William Romaine.[154] Porteus was the most pro-evangelical of the bishops and the only one who might conceivably have ordained students with Methodist links. He was a leading member of the Proclamation Society, a body formed by Church of England ministers in 1787 to combat vice, immorality, and blasphemy and to enforce Sunday observance. He also admired Hannah More, supported anti-slavery bills in the House of Lords, and argued for foreign missions, notably the establishment of the Church of England in India. In his last sermon before his death he cited "the known recorded opinion of some of the ablest and most distinguished Divines" that the Antichrist of popery and Mahomet would be extinguished and the millennium begin in fifty to sixty years, expressing the hope "which seemed to elevate his soul, that this Country might possibly be the chosen instrument in the hand of God to diffuse the light of the Gospel throughout the world, and ultimately to accomplish the great schemes of Providence."[155] The fact that he would not, however, ordain students of the Countess of Huntingdon's seminaries illustrates the depth of the rift between the Anglican establishment and its challengers, as well as the political impossibility of open support to non-Anglican missions for a prominent member of that establishment.[156] "I am sorry you have had so much anxiety," wrote Wilberforce to Haweis after the refusal, "though as to what regarded the ordination of the two missionaries, *as I had originally no hopes*, I have sustained no disappointment."[157] A subsequent attempt by Haweis to send missionaries in 1793 appears to have collapsed through a last-minute failure of nerve on the part of the prospective envoys, a smith and a carpenter, despite, interestingly enough, the apparent support of Prime Minister William Pitt himself.[158]

As an inducement to the foundation of a missionary society, in 1793 Haweis offered £500 from his private purse through the *Evangelical Magazine* for the equipment of missionaries. The Countess of Huntingdon was also generous and may have been the donor of a further £100.[159] In September 1794 the Reverend David Bogue of Gosport published an "Address to Professors of the Gospel" in the *Evangelical Magazine*. In this address he upheld an abstract vision of the miseries of the heathen, presenting a central plank of the missionary platform: that non-Christians were held captive in the land of Satan and must be rescued from their misery.[160] The Holy Spirit was urging individuals to fulfil God's ends, with the prophetic assurance of success. "The sacred Scripture," Bogue urged, "is full of promises, that the knowledge of Christ shall cover the earth as the waters cover the channel of the sea;

and every promise is a call and a motive to enter on the service without delay. It is the cause of God and will prevail."[161] Urging the Congregationalists to greater zeal, Bogue exemplified the domino effect of
missionary activity: he cited the work of the Roman Catholics ("O that
they had but conveyed Christianity *pure* to the blinded pagans!"), the
Church of England, the Kirk of Scotland, the Moravians, the
Methodists, and the Baptists.[162]

Early successes appeared to justify the optimism of the LMS's
founders. In October 1795 the editors of the *Evangelical Magazine*
informed the journal's readers of the spectacular success of a week-long
conference held in September officially to form the London Missionary
Society. The *Evangelical Magazine* was undoubtedly a biased reporter,
but its account is nonetheless striking. "It is with infinite satisfaction
and joy unspeakable, that we now inform our anxious readers that
their wishes are not only gratified, but our own expectations far, very
far exceeded."[163] Crowded morning and evening services had been
held throughout the week. At one service, "a vast congregation assembled in the evening, at the Tabernacle, an hour before the appointed
time. Thousands are said to have gone away unable to get in ..." On
the final evening, "some of the ministers present ... could not, for a
time, proceed for tears of joy."

By 25 September, the Anglican evangelical banker Henry Thornton
was able to write informally to a future leading organizer of the CMS,
John Venn, on the rapid fundraising success of the new society, which,
Haweis informed him, had already raised £10,000. "What a striking
thing it is that a Bishop of London [Beilby Porteus, responsible for the
church in the West Indies] is hardly able (as I suspect) to scrape a few
hundred Pounds together for the Missionary Plans in his hands among
all the people of the Church Establishment & that £10,000 shd be
raised in such a few days by the Irregulars who are also so much poorer a Class of People than the others ..."[164] The fledgling society quickly
attracted a sufficient number of missionary volunteers to be able to
select twenty-one to travel to the South Sea Islands, in a ship, the *Duff*,
that the society purchased itself for an outlay of £5,000 and outfitted
with "a crew of godly mariners" – a capital outlay which represented a
considerable act of faith in the success of the enterprise.[165] Some of this
optimism was to prove ill-founded: the first mission to the South Seas
collapsed, and the *Duff* was shortly thereafter captured by the French.
What is perhaps more surprising, however, is just how much of this
optimism was to appear justified by the early nineteenth century.

Nonetheless, missions would never have been able to attain a significant position of influence in nineteenth-century British society had
they remained confined to those outside the bounds of ecclesiastical

discipline. The establishment of the first evangelical Anglican missionary society, the Church Missionary Society, was a key step in the adoption of missions by the Church of England – although the foundation
was a nervous affair, in contrast to the ebullient rhetoric of the LMS,
and the first few years were not on the whole successful.[166] The early
history of the CMS reveals an interesting passage from relative failure
and distrust by fellow Anglicans to the successes of the post-1813 era,
suggesting the growing acceptability of missionary activity to the ecclesiastical establishment, its broader popularity outside the evangelical
world, and the related growth, however temporary, of the political
clout of missionary societies at the imperial centre.

In contrast to the LMS, the CMS was not founded by a relatively
broad-based, highly public coalition of disparate groups. Rather, it was
conceived by evangelicals at Oxford, in response to a bequest. It was
put into operation by a small, tightly interlinked group of Anglican
evangelical clergy in London, centred on the clerical discussion group,
the Eclectic Society.[167] Many of these clergy had benefited from the
pro-evangelical ecclesiastical patronage of the Clapham Sect; indeed,
several of the "Eclectics" had been brought to London by men who
would subsequently become lay patrons of the CMS.[168] These were
important links: we shall meet the Clapham Sect again as the so-called
"Friends of the Negro," influential at Westminster on African issues
until the late 1830s and the LMS's main source of domestic clout. Eclectics and Claphamites already collaborated on a range of associations
designed to promote Christianization and the improvement of public
morals, from the 1788 Society to Effect the Enforcement of His
Majesty's Proclamation against Vice and Immorality onwards. The
CMS was thus only one among the numerous private societies which
were so key to the Anglican evangelical Reformation of Manners
movement.[169] Nonetheless, the CMS represented a particularly apt
dovetailing of interests: the Anglican evangelical need for a respectable
missionary society, and the Claphamite imperial need for a means to
Christianize colonies without opening the back door to enthusiasm.[170]

For their part, the Eclectics welcomed, indeed depended on, the
respectability that the Claphamites were able to bring to the charged
project of a missionary society. Given their cross-denominational affil-
iations, individual Anglican evangelicals watched the beginnings of
missionary activity with great interest leavened in many cases by personal contact with the participants.[171] At the same time, many CMS
evangelicals were genuinely distrustful of the intense providentialism
of the LMS. "Many [in the LMS] are too sanguine," Thomas Scott
reflected in 1796, "do not sufficiently count their cost, have not wisdom equal to their zeal, and lean more to favourable providential

appearances, and second causes, than to the omnipotent activity of the Holy Spirit."[172] More seriously, both ecclesiastical and secular politics dictated public distance from missions.

Despite, or perhaps because of, such ubiquitous suspicion, the CMS evangelicals determinedly professed themselves loyal to church and state, and their theology was far from antinomian or dangerously enthusiastic.[173] By 1799, as the heat went out of the controversy among evangelicals between Arminianism and Calvinism, Anglican evangelicals moved to a compromise position between the two.[174] In this regard, Bernard Semmel is likely right in claiming that this doctrinal moderation allowed evangelicalism to be turned to more conservative social ends after the 1790s.[175] For example, many CMS evangelicals allowed for grace without a specific moment of new birth.[176] This affirmation of spiritual enlightenment through gradual education left the door open to arguments for the value of hierarchy, helping to explain CMS reluctance to ordain the uneducated. In a similar vein, the mostly "moderate" evangelicals of the CMS and the Clapham Sect were largely post-millenarians, in contrast to the theologically less doctrinal LMS, which harboured men of more "extreme" views[177] (although cut-and-dried distinctions would be inappropriate for this period). Both groups employed the language of national retribution in the very early 1800s,[178] but the CMS tended to place less emphasis on suffering, destruction, and punishment and certainly did not hope for national chastisement. CMS anniversary sermons employed more millenarian language as the political situation improved (since God's blessing on England was a sign of development towards the millennium), whereas the more violent aspects of LMS millenarian rhetoric languished after victory over France. Millenarianism, in other words, tended to be used by CMS propagandists to support existing authority relationships, rather than to predict their imminent overthrow.

The CMS began cautiously, at a meeting which proclaimed that God's providence must be followed not anticipated, and that "it is better that a Mission should proceed from small beginnings and advance according to circumstances."[179] Early Claphamite support was equivocal, and Wilberforce seems to have been initially nervous about taking the chair, while the necessary sanction of the archbishop of Canterbury, John Moore, was only grudgingly and ambiguously offered.[180] The CMS's very self-description, published and circulated among evangelicals, emphasized the social benefits of the spread of Christianity before it urged the spiritual, pointing out optimistically that "the husband and wife, the father and son, the master and servant, at once learn from it their respective duties, and are disposed and enabled to fulfil them ... Rulers become the fathers of their people, and subjects cheerfully yield obedience."[181]

The most serious roadblock to CMS success was, however, the unexpected dearth of missionary candidates. Conversely, this suggests the importance for the LMS of lay support and the taproots of the society in popular religious culture. One initial explanation for the dearth of CMS missionary candidates is that the ministers themselves had pre-existent notions of what a suitable candidate would look like and would ordain candidates only as catechists to the mission field and not as priests. The LMS Board of Directors had more fluid selection criteria in the early years and offered a form of ordination to its missionaries which might be read (however incorrectly) as ordination to the ministry outside the mission field. This is insufficient, however, to explain the twelve-year dry spell that followed, during which the CMS was driven to employing German Lutherans from the Berlin Academy for lack of British offers.

I have argued elsewhere that part of the answer is that evangelically minded young men seeking to become preachers were drifting to the Methodists or indeed being chased to them by local church authorities.[182] Having spent much energy stifling evangelism from below, it was not easy for Anglicans, no matter how evangelical, to re-animate it. Furthermore, there did not yet exist a cult of missions among the Anglican laity – one that would sentimentalize missions, make heroes of missionaries, and provide information about the places to which they would go in order to make the idea less terrifying.[183] The few early offers that did occur tended to be thwarted by family opposition or by last-minute cold feet. The language in which they were couched tended also to be less uniformly rhetorical and stereotypical than LMS offers or than the CMS letters of even ten years later, suggesting that there were limits to the popular rhetoric of mission. George Smith, for example, wrote to implore the Macaulay brothers to intervene with his fiancée's mother, resistant as she was to the desire "which I have had of late more fully, to go as a Missionary to the East Indies if my way could be made clear."

I have no wish but just to live and do all the good I can – I wrote to the Young Woman's Mother that if she would not consent for her Daughter to go or give us 20 pounds a year to what I have in an English Circuit, to make her Daughter comfortable, we must do violence to our own feelings and I must go alone. I only wish to do my duty to God and the Young Woman as I have real affection for her. I have had no answer but a charge from her Mother of deserting her Daughter after having gain'd her affections. I have grieved so much that with a cold I had taken and distress of mind I have been under the Doc^{rs} Hand and confined to my Room for a fortnight.

Putting his finger on one of the key problems for the CMS, and illustrating the gulf between leaders and constituency, Smith added, "I have always been of the Church of England and I should not like to go out without Episcopal Ordination – unless I went out as a Methodist Preacher."[184] Three days later, however, Smith had just received "a letter from the Young Woman – that if I see it my duty to stay at home and Labour, she will trust on the providence of God and comply with my wishes – and as I know there is real affection on both sides I think my duty and happiness to Marry her and do all the good I can in England."[185] This candour and indecision contrasts with the standardized rhetorical flourishes of a typical letter ten years later: "If you are in wants of young men to go abroad on the all important Errand of Proclaiming the unsearchable Riches of Christ to the Poor Perishing Heathen, & if after suitable inquiry and Examination I am approved of, I will thro divine grace with difidence, Sincerity and Pleasure give up myself to God & to you for the Great, Arduous and Awfully Responsible yet delightful & Honourable work of a Missionary."[186]

The difficult years between these two letters were nonetheless characterized by the growth of self-confidence through the nurturance of supportive congregations, in a process given a significant fillip by the local mobilization involved in the fight to abolish the slave trade and by the growing success, despite opposition, of the British and Foreign Scripture Society. Throughout the period, the CMS quietly employed German Lutherans to man missions in Sierra Leone and New Zealand, following the model of the SPCK in south India.[187] Nonetheless, the society remained nervous of exposure, and it felt too threatened to adopt LMS methods of domestic prosletyzing, such as fundraising tours and an open use of the press – beyond a discreet alliance with the *Christian Observer*, edited first by Josiah Pratt and then by Macaulay.

The new success and popularity of the society after 1813, when Anglican evangelicals in parliament forced a reluctant East India Company essentially to permit a colonial episcopate and the entry, albeit regulated, of missionaries to India as a condition of the renewal of its licence, illustrates the close linkage between domestic support for missionary activity and popular images of the depravity and misery of the "heathen." CMS anniversary sermons had long attacked the prevalent notion that the heathen did not in fact need saving; preachers reiterated that faith not good works alone was needed for salvation, but they also took on the Enlightenment vision of the noble savage. "Several modern travellers (who, by the help of their coadjutors the infidels, have often seemed to labour at proving that Christianity is useless or needless) have launched out in commendation of the virtuous Hindoos, Chinese, or inhabitants of the South-Sea Islands," Scott affirmed in 1801, "yet, it is undeniable, that the more these have been known the fuller has been the proof, that they are exceedingly prone to vices of every kind; as well as given up to idolatry, or sunk in total ignorance concerning God and religion."[188] It was the debate over India, however, that provided a focus for popular activism and enabled the CMS, in tackling the orientalists head on, to pass from vague generalities into confrontation over specific issues.[189] India was the great exemplar of the value of non-Christian civilization: to devalue its morality in the popular imagination was a key step in encouraging popular support for mission and in seeing God's hand in the growing success of the British empire. Since the Vellore Mutiny of 1806, missions to India had come under widespread attack in colonial circles for dangerously provoking indigenous sensibilities. The CMS, like other missionary societies, thus became involved in struggles over how to define the direction of imperialism and what its relationship would be to Christianity.[190] In 1812 the CMS organized some 800 to 900 petitions from around the country pleading the need of India, almost all modelled on a precirculated CMS petition arguing "that this Society [believes] the natives of India, both Mohammedan and Hindoo, to be in a state of mental and moral degradation ..."[191] The debate also saw the elaboration of a more complicated rhetoric of necessary linkage between Christianity and civilization, which would have ramifications in south Africa, as missionary proponents sought to counter fear of social disruption by arguments from social utility.

The success of 1813, coupled with the triumphant end of the war, combined to help make both evangelicalism and missionary activity newly respectable, particularly in Anglican circles, even if still subject to criticism and ecclesiastical internicine warfare.[192] Indeed, 1813–15 saw a pandenominational surge in mission support across Britain, enabling Bernard Semmel to term these years the *anni mirabiles* of missions.[193] From 1812 on, CMS officials were able to adopt techniques of fundraising and publicity which the dissenting societies had pioneered. They formed associations around the country, gave subscribers a voice in forming CMS policy, went on itinerant tours to promote missions, and began to publish CMS magazines, founding the *Missionary Register* in 1813 and the *Quarterly Papers* in 1816. In another move that would have been impossible during the early period, the *Quarterly Papers* were aimed at exciting missionary support among children and the working classes and were distributed to those who could raise a penny a week among friends.[194] Having put to rest the general fear of missions as a vehicle for seditious working-class enthusiasm, the CMS was now ironically enabled to adopt a "top-down" approach of soliciting working-class support on behalf of the better-off organizers of the society. This trend coincided with a rise in the class level of candidates in all the established missionary societies.[195] The CMS was also able to focus on spreading knowledge of the ignorance and miseries of the heathen. It thus contributed to a developing discourse across the different missionary societies about the "heathen" as a separate category, removed from the culture of domestic evangelical itineracy.

This survey of the foundation of the principal missionary societies has shown considerable ambiguity in the changing relationship of missions and authority relations in Britain. The original seedbed of missionary activity was evangelical revival in the 1790s, fuelled not only by ministerial linkages to the broader Reformed world but also, and most crucially, by popular religious enthusiasm and, in some cases, revolt aginst the forms of the established church. Political and religious dissenters alike promoted literacy, freedom of choice, and the overcoming of some traditional hierarchies. Particularly during the French Revolution, missionaries, especially dissenting missionaries, were deeply distrusted by many in the political and ecclesiastical elites, as were evangelicals in general. Like their domestic counterparts, many colonial officials would prove deeply averse to evangelical mission. On the other hand, evangelicals themselves were divided on the danger of empowering the working classes and showed a range of political attitudes. Furthermore, denominational differences in political posture would prove increasingly important as interdenominationalism faded in the early decades of the nineteenth century and as missionary activity ceased to be the purview mostly of Calvinist dissenters. By the end of the Napoleonic Wars, support for missions was increasingly unhinged from the debates and anxieties that had dominated the 1790s. Mission societies were from the beginning competitors in the struggle to control and define British imperialism. By the late 1810s, this competition involved broader rhetorical attacks on the "civilization" of the "heathen," in a manner that would ultimately facilitate the readier assimilation of missionary and settler approaches to empire, even as the moderation of extreme evangelical language gave the missionary movement more political and social clout. All this, however, still lay in the future in the heady and anxious days of the mid-1790s.

2 Terms of Encounter: Graaff-Reinet, the Khoekhoe, and the South African LMS at the Turn of the Nineteenth Century

The first LMS envoys to southern Africa expected to encounter "savages" who lived in wildernesses, had never heard of the "saving word" of Christ, and were in consequence damned. Whatever the moral problems of their perspectives, it was also historically inaccurate. Christianity was already being used in a wide variety of political ways in late-eighteenth-century southern Africa, and the LMS message was received in that broader context. The heroic LMS rhetoric of the journey and evangelical theology alike suggested that missionaries were about to lift the curtain on the first act of a spiritual encounter between Europeans and Africans. In reality, the LMS envoys arrived fairly late in the play. They were to prove rather more minor players than they had imagined, but they provided important weapons to the principal antagonists. A further irony is that the LMS never in fact intended to work among the colonial Khoekhoe; true to the society's foundational mandate, missionaries hoped to spread the gospel in virgin fields. Not only would LMS missionaries find their most receptive audience among the Khoekhoe, however, but Khoekhoe preachers would end up themselves pioneering missions to other African groups.

THE KHOISAN AT THE TURN OF THE NINETEENTH CENTURY

The San (or Bushman) and Khoekhoe peoples of southern Africa had once been spread throughout much of the region. European and African colonists pushed them into ever smaller areas through the

seventeenth and eighteenth centuries, just as cattle herders had themselves displaced hunter gatherers in many of the richest grazing lands of
southern Africa. The historical relationship between "Khoekhoe" and
"San" was complex and is heatedly debated by modern scholars.
Khoekhoe groups and some Khoe-speaking hunter-gatherers spoke or
speak variants of the same Khoe language. According to anthropologist
Alan Barnard, Khoe-speaking groups past and present include the
Khoekhoe of the Cape region, the Damara of Namibia, the Bushmen of
the central Kalahari and Okavango, some Bushmen in northern Namib-
ia including the Hai//om, and possibly other smaller groups in Angola.[1]
In the seventeenth century the Dutch knew of four large clusters of
groups calling themselves "Khoekhoe," and whom the Dutch called
"Hottentots," in the lands of modern-day South Africa and Namibia.
The Cape Khoekhoe lived in the modern-day Cape Province south of
the Orange River valley. Spread out from east to west, beyond the Cape
peninsula, were the Korana, the Einiqua, and the Namaqua.[2] All these
Khoekhoe groups used some variant of the term "Khoekhoe," or
Khoekhoen (or Khoikhoi/ Khoikhoin), to describe themselves. The term
meant "men of men." Khoekhoe is the contemporary Nama spelling of
the term Khoikhoi; the terms are interchangeable. In Nama, "Khoe"
requires a number-gender suffix: the plural is *Khoe-khoen*, while *khoeb*
is a man and *khoes* a woman, or *khoera* two women, for example.[3]
Julia Wells has recently proposed the variant "Kwena" as being less sex-
ist, since Khoekhoe is a male-specific term; this is an interesting suggestion although not well enshrined in the literature.[4]

Hunter-gatherer "Bushmen" groups in different areas of southern
Africa, including the !Kung of Botswana, Namibia, and Angola, the
!Xo of Botswana, and Cape Bushmen groups, notably the /Xam of the
northern Cape, spoke or speak a variety of languages. Khoe and San
languages have common roots and are all characterized by the use of
tonal clicks. Having spread out over southern Africa over a long period of time in small and isolated groups, however, San may have had
less of a sense of common identity *as* San (or Bushmen) across different smaller groups, various communities speaking mutually incompre-
hensible languages. Khoe languages in contrast are mutually comprehensible. Perhaps this facilitated the nineteenth-century sense of a
pan-Khoekhoe identity, despite the cultural diversity of Khoe-speakers.[5]

Among all these communities, the Cape Khoekhoe, like the Cape
Bushmen, no longer exist as a separate group with their own language.
In the nineteenth century, Christian missions would accelerate ongoing
Cape Khoisan cultural disintegration, although the prior loss of land,
labour servitude, the violent break-up of Khoekhoe chieftaincies and
in general the extraordinary material pressures of colonialism did the

most damage. Mission Dutch-language schooling and preaching helped push Khoisan people to shed their original languages and to adopt Dutch instead, which they would help forge into Afrikaans. Nonetheless, throughout the period of this study, even as processes of assimilation were cruelly under way, people at the Cape still identified themselves as "Hottentot" and that identity had powerful political implications. A much smaller number described themselves as "Bushman" in extant records.

As noted, a great deal of ink has been, and is still being, spilt on the contentious issue of the historical relationship between "Khoekhoe" and "Bushmen," as also on the related issue of naming. It is also debated to what extent linguistic divisions, economic divisions between hunter-gatherers and cattle-herders, and actual genetic distinctions overlapped.[6] Traditionally, the "Khoekhoe" had cattle in the seventeenth century and their preferred mode of gaining a living was pastoralism. The "San" were hunter-gatherers. Both groups were nomadic, albeit within the confines of a roughly defined territory for each subgroup. How much had ethnicities blurred and overlapped by the eighteenth century and indeed earlier? Were these two groups really distinct at the Cape? Certainly, large numbers of Cape Khoekhoe had lost their cattle by the eighteenth century. The colonists may well have called all those beyond the colony and without cattle "Bushmen." Shula Marks has suggested that those "Khoekhoe" who chose to fight colonial incursions by force were seen as "Bushmen" while colonists perceived those who worked for them as "Hottentots."[7] The colonial term "Hottentot" was therefore a labour category, and a marker of social practice, as well an ethnic signifier. Richard Elphick reminds us that colonialism and its devastations made categories increasingly fluid. He argues that "we must replace the static Khoekhoe-San classification with a dynamic model of interaction between Khoekhoe and their neighbours."[8] Susan Newton-King and Nigel Penn both stress, on the other hand, that certain San groups, such as the /Xam of the northern Cape, appear nonetheless to have been culturally distinct communities rather than amalgams of resisters as late as the late eighteenth century.[9] Pastoralism and hunting were different ways of life, and to argue that people passed easily from one to the other may be to downplay the importance of cultural difference. Newton-King indeed suggests that hunters may have resisted European incursions sooner and more implacably than herders precisely because they were hunters and, unlike pastoralists, had little possibility of shared economic interest with European stock farmers. Be that as it may, those identified by colonists as "Bushmen" were ruthlessly attacked, often by commandoes which included men of Khoekhoe descent. At the same time, Newton-King underscores that the "Hotten-

tot" labour force of the Eastern Cape was in fact relatively heteroge-
neous, given not only white and slave admixture but most crucially the
considerable presence of San war captives who appear to have been
assimilated over time into the community. The vortex of late-eighteenth-century colonialism and military conflict did indeed smash previous categories and create a subservient colonial class.[10]

The debate is less crucial for the nineteenth century than for the eighteenth, since, as we shall see, those within the ambit of the colony had
considerably remade their identities by then. Nonetheless, I am persuaded by the arguments of Penn and Newton-King that, despite overall fluidity, separate San identities persisted longer than some believe,
and "Bushman" is not simply coincidental with "resister." By the early
nineteenth century, all the same, the colonial term "Hottentot" sub-
sumed many of the deracinated of the colony, including those of /Xam
and other San descent, even as many of the descendants of the Khoisan
mobilized "Hottentot" ethnicity to political ends. This tendency
doubtless accelerated as Dutch spread as the lingua franca of the dispossessed, replacing Khoekhoe and San languages and the languages
that slaves had brought with them. Extensive sexual activity between
whites (mostly men) and Khoekhoe and San (mostly women) gave rise
to the alternate identity *baster*. At the same time, relations between
Khoisan and slaves from a wide variety of places in Africa and Asia,
more often formalized in marriage, further diluted the ethnicities
"Khoekhoe" and "San." Whatever the genetic "truth," for my purposes the nineteenth-century *uses* of the identity "Hottentot" are as
interesting as the actual origins of that identity.

All this has an impact on the controversial issue of the kind of ter-
minology one uses to describe people in the past. The widely used artificial term Khoisan admits ambiguity and is a good way to signal the
fluidity of categories, although it was not used by anyone at the
time.[11] On the other hand, whatever the reality it was labelling, the
concept of Khoekhoe or "Hottentot" identity remained significant
throughout the early nineteenth century, culminating in the mobilization of Hottentot identity by nonwhite rebels in the rebellion of
1850–53. In consequence, I will also use the more ethnically specific
term "Khoekhoe" where possible as a means of underscoring that this
concept remained significant to many who identified as such. Although
it is a difficult point to prove precisely, I think that dominant identities
within colonial boundaries were either Khoekhoe or, to a more limited
extent, "baster." At least some children of San farm labourers seem to
me to have integrated culturally into the numerically dominant
Khoekhoe group in the early nineteenth century, particularly in the
early years of the century when the Khoe language was still in regular

use, but it is hard to be certain. In any event, it would prove politically important that people of Khoekhoe descent felt attachment well into
the nineteenth century to particular pieces of land on which their
ancestors had historically lived and made, as we shall see, political
claims on the colonial state in consequence. "Khoe" and "San" thus
do not have equal historical weight in discussing the "Khoisan" of the
Eastern Cape. The alert reader will notice that in places I prevaricate
between Khoisan and Khoekhoe. I think that either term has draw-
backs. The former downplays the political importance of specifically
Khoekhoe ethnicity (whether invented or not) and land claims made
well into the nineteenth century on that basis. The latter term downplays, however, the San presence among the subjugated labour force of
the Cape. It is important to remember that naming is a necessary act
for communication to occur but in this case it cannot be precise. There
is another important issue. "Hottentot" became the identity behind
which people actually mobilized and was the word that people of
Khoekhoe descent actually used to describe themselves in the early
nineteenth century. I shall use it as well, albeit sparingly and in quota-
tion marks, to indicate contemporary usage. The problem is that "Hottentot" is a loaded term because it has insulting connotations today.
On the other hand, it is historically accurate and sidesteps the need for
an artificial ethnic precision. Furthermore, those insulting connotations are themselves a legacy of the crucial role of shaming in the imposition of colonialism.

Different Khoekhoe and San groups had a number of common features before colonial contact.[12] The societies of nomadic pastoralists
centred around cattle, a source of wealth and prestige. Particular
groups were nomadic within defined territories. Some Central Cape
Khoekhoe groups cultivated and traded *dagga* (a form of marijuana)
but otherwise the Khoisan did not practise agriculture.[13] Material
goods reflected the demands of mobility: Khoekhoe houses, for example, shaped like large beehives and made of a wooden frame and a
cover of skins and mats or dry bushes, were light and portable and
could be rapidly assembled and disassembled.[14] Primary Khoekhoe
social units were small and tended to be fissiparous given the necessity
of mobility and the difficulty for large groups of people and cattle of
living from the same patch of land. This was all the more true for
hunter-gatherers, whose need for mobility was even greater, especially
as they were pushed into less fertile lands by richer Khoekhoe groups.
Political organization was based around kinship in complicated ways
but appears to have been relatively fluid, probably in consequence of
the small size of groups and the survival value of flexibility of all kinds.
Groups of from "several hundreds to a couple of thousand," accord-

ing to Isaac Schapera, formed the core Khoekhoe political unit, known by a distinct name and headed by a chief.[15] This larger group was broken down into smaller clusters of households which camped together, the central group of which claimed descent from a common male ancestor. The temporary village formed by the houses of people camping together, arranged in a circle, was called a !âs in Khoekhoe, according to the late-nineteenth-century observer of the Nama, Theophilus Hahn; the Dutch termed a camping place a kraal.[16] Clans were headed by leaders, putatively hereditary despite flexibility in practice, whom the Dutch termed *kapteins,* or captains. Captains formed the advisory council of chiefs and limited their authority.[17] The Dutch sought to bind captains to allegiance with the VOC through granting them staffs of office. Although it is hard to know to what extent the Dutch were inventing and rigidifying Khoekhoe forms of authority, there were clearly leaders, mostly men but in at least a few cases women. Authority in this situation depended on wealth and status, and dissatisfied people could leave captains fairly easily. Some form of this loose organization persisted into the nineteenth century; Khoekhoe at the earliest mission stations of Theopolis and Bethelsdorp would continue to preserve captaincies and their own decision-making processes (in selecting men for colonial service, for example), side by side with their necessary but ambiguous acceptance of missionary authority.

Men were permitted to be polygamous in Khoekhoe societies, although it was hard for most men to accumulate sufficient wealth to practise polygamy on a large scale. The division of labour was gendered as Khoekhoe men tended cattle and hunted while women milked cattle and prepared and gathered food, including bulbs, roots, and honey. In San societies, women retained this primary responsibility for the foodstuffs that furnished the bulk of the hunter-gatherer diets, while men hunted.

Precolonial Khoekhoe religion is difficult to generalize about, given the nature of the sources. Indeed, David Chidester has gone so far as to claim that it is impossible to decode the exclusively white colonial accounts of Khoekhoe "religion" of the seventeenth and eighteenth centuries sufficiently to discern with confidence the content of Khoekhoe religious beliefs. For Chidester, white observers interpreted Khoekhoe "religion," as they did other African religions at different historical moments, as a function of the political situation; in particular, whether or nor Khoekhoe groups were even seen as having a "religion" at all (as opposed to random superstitions) was largely a function of the state of the colonial frontier and the degree of military threat posed by the Khoekhoe at a given time. In consequence, generalizations about "Hottentot" religion by various specialists demonstrate merely "the fluctuation of comparative maneuvers on a contested frontier." Certainly, Khoekhoe people have had "human experiences and expressions that could be designated as religious," but "their 'religion' was thoroughly and completely a European invention, a product that was invented and reinvented by a frontier comparative religion."[18] Paul Landau goes a step farther and claims that the very category religion is too culturally specific to be applicable across cultural and linguistic barriers; in particular, it is impossible to use the term "God" in a non-culturally specific manner. He uses this example to criticize an earlier discussion of mine of Khoekhoe belief in what I termed "the divinity."

I am mindful of these concerns. I do not accept that uncertainty is a sufficient argument for complete silence, nor (as I discuss in more detail later) that existing evidence is completely impenetrable. Nonetheless, the related issues of sources and the cultural assumptions of the contemporary scholar remain valid concerns. A further legitimate worry is that Khoekhoe groups were so small and scattered that it is hard to know to what extent there was continuity in the belief structures of particular groups across time and space and how influential other African groups were in particular areas. In the Eastern Cape, the Gonaqua had long been in contact with the Xhosa, who had dominated them and had intermarried with them; not surprisingly, their spiritual practices overlapped. Given these caveats, I will discuss in more detail, and in a fuller historical context, the question of what might be deduced about early-nineteenth-century Khoekhoe religious beliefs and actions at the Cape from missionary and other white records in a later chapter. Rather than trying to generalize here in an abstract manner about Khoekhoe "religion" as though this were a self-evident proposition, I will raise only a couple of points at this point, to which I return in detail in chapter 4.

Broadly, I agree with Alan Barnard that Khoekhoe religious structures were fairly fluid. This meant that individuals were open to new religious directions, without necessarily seeing them as incompatible with other beliefs. From a perspective that was hostile to Khoekhoe belief but probably well informed, James Read Sr commented in 1847 that before conversion to Christianity the Khoekhoe of the Eastern Cape did not have a "regular system" and were open to religious innovation. They were "neither Idolators nor Sunworshippers, but were like the Athenians highly superstitious and in the absence of any regular system they like some other nations were ready to repose in any adventitious idea that might float into their minds."[19] Leaving aside for a later chapter the question of value judgments and the further question of why Read described the Khoekhoe as "superstitious," this comment does back up Barnard's argument that Khoekhoe religious beliefs were fluid, albeit within structural constraints. A wide range of taboo beliefs were important for the nineteenth-century Namaqua and were probably meaningful in Cape Khoekhoe societies as well. A number of sacred beings populated the earth, of varying degrees of spiritual power. At the same time, there is strong evidence the Khoekhoe did believe in what one might for the sake of communication term a high god, although it is unclear whether or not they thought of this god as benevolent or responsive to prayer. The Eastern Cape Khoekhoe believed that certain human beings could acquire spiritual power, which might be used for healing, for prophecy, for rainmaking, or for leadership in battle. Khoekhoe spiritual practices included dances at night at the time of a full moon. Dreams bore important messages to the dreamer. The spirituality of Khoekhoe people would shape their reaction to Christianity and the forms that individual "conversions" would take.

COLONIALISM AND THE KHOISAN

At the same time, late-eighteenth-century Khoekhoe spirituality was already influenced by Christianity and by the colonial situation by the time of Khoekhoe contacts with LMS missionaries. As this suggests, descriptions of features common to precolonial Khoisan societies are of limited use in describing how the Khoisan lived at the turn of the nineteenth century. Colonialism was determinative.

From the seventeenth to the nineteenth centuries, despite often intense resistance, successive Khoisan communities found it impossible to preserve land and cattle before what would prove the inexorable processes of white outward expansion. Although a declining number of individuals hung on in pockets of unsurveyed land well into the nineteenth century, the Cape Khoisan as a whole had lost their political independence and much of their cattle by the 1800s.[20] Other clans migrated out of the colony altogether, such as the Amaqua of the Clanwilliam district who trekked to Great Namaqualand under the chief !Akeb.[21] The decline of the Cape Khoisan was accelerated by the diseases of cattle and men: smallpox cut a swathe through African groups from 1713 onwards, while scab and other stock diseases devastated cattle in the Western Cape in the early seventeenth century. Most individuals ended up working for whites, often as farm labourers. San groups, whatever their genetic make-up, were on the whole ruthlessly exterminated in the eighteenth and early nineteenth centuries after many decades of warfare. Various Khoekhoe and San groups were also under the control of Khoisan or other African groups at different points: the Xhosa, for example, had conquered and begun to incorporate Khoekhoe groups in the Eastern Cape in the eighteenth century.

Violence, and lack of freedom, did not necessarily characterize relations between Dutch-speaking farmers and Khoekhoe pastoralists at every stage of their historical relationship. Richard Elphick and Hermann Giliomee argue that Khoekhoe men down on their luck often entered into clientage relationships with white farmers which would have permitted them to rebuild herds in the early years of colonialism – and might indeed in the Graaff-Reinet region in the late eighteenth century have provided a way to escape Xhosa domination for some Khoekhoe men. Clientage was a long-standing feature of Khoekhoe economic organization, and clients hoped eventually to rebuild their stock of cattle and regain independence. Rich men were supposed to be generous, and their maintenance of dependants was, in Kate Crehan's phrase, "both the expression and the basis of their power."[22] Crucially, however, neither the Eastern Cape economy at the turn of the eighteenth century nor the seventeenth-century Western Cape economy described by Richard Elphick readily permitted the renewed accumulation of wealth once a Khoekhoe individual had entered white service. In the late-eighteenth-century Eastern Cape, for example, impoverished white stock farmers, dependent on an uncertain Cape Town market, did not redistribute stock on a large scale to clients. It was thus extremely difficult for either individuals or clans to complete what Elphick identifies as the traditional cycle from scarcity to plenty.[23]

Furthermore, the threat of violence was ever-present in white-Khoisan relations, even if not always realized. In the case of the Eastern Cape, as Newton-King contends, the poverty of most white stock farmers and the military insecurity of recent penetration ensured that violence would ultimately be used to keep Khoisan dependents under control, even if Khoekhoe clients initially entered into voluntary contracts with farmers. Violence was a currency of everyday exchange, as groups and individuals struggled for limited resources.[24]

Overall, the history of the Khoekhoe was in constant flux. It also cannot be separated from that of other groups in the region. Rich scholarly work on the seventeenth- and eighteenth-century Cape frontier districts, including some seminal theses, indicates the complexity of interactions, as well as the difficulty of generalizing at any one time about what were in effect a large number of small groups, however similarly affected by the same structural forces.[25]

Despite the need for constant attention to local variation, some common themes in the history of Khoisan interaction with Europeans do emerge. One critical issue is that the mobile colonial frontier was a major influence on the history of the Khoisan. The Cape Colony was in a state of almost constant outward expansion from 1652 onwards. By the early eighteenth century, the VOC's initial policy of monopoly trade in cattle with the Khoekhoe had broken down, as the Khoekhoe chieftaincies in the vicinity of the Cape settlement began to disintegrate and as pasturage in the vicinity of settlement was exhausted. From 1703 onwards, free burghers were allowed to roam beyond the limits of established settlement in the search for fresh grazing land. They were encouraged by the so-called loan-farm system which allowed a family to occupy a substantial extent of land wherever its head chose within the formal limits of colonial jurisdiction, in exchange for a putative annual rent to the company which the VOC in practice had little means to enforce.[26] Thereafter, free burghers in quest of land for themselves and their sons on which to herd stock constantly pushed back the de facto frontiers of the colony, with or without initial company sanction. In fact, the VOC had much less control over the expansion of its unruly colony than its governing council back in the distant Netherlands – or indeed the governor and his officers in Cape Town – would have liked. In the aftermath of white settlement, however, the VOC invariably moved its formal frontiers to accommodate the new reality, despite initial attempts to keep farmers within prescribed territories.

These *veeboeren*, or stock farmers, as Susan Newton-King has termed them (to replace the nineteenth-century term *trekboeren* which falsely implies constant mobility),[27] required the same resources as the pastoralist populations already in possession: breeding stock, water fountains, land with sweet grass for seasonal grazing, and labourers. Their ancestors were the impoverished of the Low Countries, modern-day Germany and modern-day eastern Europe, since to join the VOC with its extremely high death rates required desperation or coercion. The poorer farmers who trekked into the interior tended to be under-capitalized and often died in debt. They had few ways to gain land and labourers other than violence.[28] Members of this group were often termed "Boers," or farmers, by English-speaking contemporaries from the Dutch *boeren*; the term was also sometimes translated as "peasants."

The farmers' quest for new land was driven by agricultural and inheritance practices, as well as by fertility. The farming community had a very high birth rate. The system of inheritance under Roman-Dutch law ensured that property would be divided among heirs on the death of a man or woman; this led to an active land market that gave heirs some wherewithal (including access to credit) but ensured that they would be relatively under-capitalized. At least some both needed to seek new lands and had some initial credit with which to do so. Furthermore, sons tended to set themselves up to herd stock at a relatively young age on massive tracts of new land rather than working with fathers to intensify the output of existing farms (which might not remain in family hands after a parental death).[29]

These stock farmers sought extensive pieces of land, encouraged by the generosity (from the settler point of view) of the loan-farm system. They also tried to control the springs which watered the land and whose use was traditionally within the gift of the dominant African group in the vicinity.[30] Beyond the well-watered Cape region, springs were rare and precious; the success of the well-armed free burghers at monopolizing the use of fountains was critical to their takeover of land. The access of burghers and their dependants to guns and ammunition in regions not yet penetrated by the (illegal) arms trade from the colony ensured the success of relatively small groups. Stock farmers were, nonetheless, dependent on locals for labour since mobile white labour was not sufficient to fill all needs. These frontier inhabitants were seemingly tied to the colonial market, since they traded meat with Cape Town and its environs and used a variety of goods obtainable only from trade. They also depended on the colony for teachers, ministers, and spiritual sacraments, although all of these were difficult to obtain.[31] Supply routes were long and precarious, and journeys to the Cape were very expensive, however. The VOC exercised in practice little control over these frontier settlements, and farmers cherished their political independence.

Although the *veeboers* were relatively few in number, and did not establish hegemony easily, they, and the resources of the VOC, nonetheless had an enormously disruptive influence on local populations. Cycles of violent struggle for limited resources characterized all the frontier zones of southern Africa in the seventeenth and eighteenth centuries. The institution of the commando, firmly under the control of frontier farmers themselves from at least the mid-eighteenth-century onwards, became a critical tool in white control of the frontier.[32] The struggle for resources between colonizers and colonized remained unresolved in southern Africa and frontiers remained in flux throughout the nineteenth century. Indeed, this must surely furnish some part of the explanation for the extreme brutality of conflict.

It is not surprising that the frontier, or rather the more ambiguous frontier zone, has been a critical issue for debate among Cape historians, with some praising its centrality and others seeking to bury it as an illegitimate historiographical distraction from the more formative influence on the later apartheid state of the late-nineteenth-century mature capitalist state. However convincing the argument that the frontier did not in fact form twentieth-century racial attitudes among whites, the unresolved conflict over resources represented by frontier zones beyond the formal (and shifting) frontiers of the white colony itself was certainly a driving factor in intergroup relations in the eighteenth century.[33] I use here the definition of a frontier zone put forward by Martin Legassick, following American historians of the 1960s, and widely adopted by South Africanists, to mean an area of contact between two or more societies, characterized by the disputed distribution of resources, unclear political boundaries, and cultural contact. Hermann Giliomee and others distinguish between "open" and "closing" frontier zones:[34] an open frontier zone is marked by extensive cultural contact and ongoing competition for resources, while in a closing frontier zone one group is in the process of gaining a decisive advantage over others and of establishing clear-cut hegemony. A greater degree of intergroup cooperation might be expected in an open frontier zone, although I tend to see inter-ethnic competition for resources as trumping the trend to intergroup cooperation in an impoverished environment. The very concept of a frontier zone ultimately depends on the European notion of a fixed political frontier and hence might be said to contain an assumption of the inevitability of the mapped boundary.[35] I therefore do not see the notion of a frontier zone as one with clear-cut cross-cultural utility, but it is central to understanding southern Africa in the late eighteenth and early nineteenth centuries.

The Khoisan had been gradually pushed from their lands but at different times for different communities. The northern frontier zone had been the main area of colonial expansion through much of the eighteenth century. In the 1770s white pastoralists moved in large numbers for the first time to the Eastern Cape, opening the eastern frontier zone. Beyond these zones of contact, at the turn of the nineteenth century, Transorangia and Namaqualand still provided areas in which Khoisan groups could fight for survival on at least an equal footing with other inhabitants. The mobile, indeterminate nature of the south African frontier zone ensured that all those grouped there under the colonial term "Hottentot" had different recent experiences of colonialism, although the underlying structural forces were similar.

A further critical issue shaping early colonial Khoisan experience was that the line between slavery and "freedom" in the Cape colony and its frontier zones was very thinly drawn in social practice, however well defined in legal language.[36] Although the Khoekhoe were technically "free," their status in many respects at the turn of the century in the Eastern Cape approximated that of slaves, particularly in rural areas where the mobility of so-called Hottentots, as well as their ability to get out of contracts, was severely limited by local legislation, including vagrancy legislation, and by quasi-legal custom. San children taken in commando raids had long been distributed among white farmers as "apprentices." "Apprenticeship" itself was designed to attach the Khoisan "child" to the white farm well into adulthood, and indeed to compel the servitude of entire families. Local custom permitted farmers to apprentice "children" who had grown up on their farms as labourers, depriving them of the ability to leave, up to the age of twenty-five. The apprenticeship of children often kept entire families bound to particular farms. In addition, the very violence often used by farmers against Khoisan dependants on white farms, although obviously designed to ensure obedience and in part the product of long-standing warfare, was also a symbolic means of entrenching a system of dishonouring which mimicked the rituals of dishonour around slavery itself. In the cash-poor white economy, in which indebtedness was common, the Khoisan thus came to fill functions parallel to those of slaves in the wealthier wine-growing Western Cape.[37] Indeed, whites probably perceived their need for labour as great both because of their genuine inability to hire labourers for cash and because their cultural expectations about appropriate white labour had been formed in a slave society.

GRAAFF-REINET

By the late eighteenth century, white frontier settlement had reached what would become the district of Graaff-Reinet on the eastern fringes of the then colony. The veeboers were at the Sneeuwberg mountains and the Camdebo and Sundays rivers by the late 1760s. By the 1770s, they were at the Fish River, where they would come up at last against the westernmost vanguard of Xhosa settlement. In 1775 the government moved the eastern frontier again, to the Fish River in the north and to the Bushman's River in the south, in response to settler petitions to be allowed to occupy excellent grazing land beyond the Bruyntjes Hoogte. In 1786 the government formally created the administrative district of Graaff-Reinet, the better to pursue the company's ongoing war against the Khoisan.[38] Graaff-Reinet's eastern boundary of the Fish River was well within territory, known to colonists as the Zuurveld, which was claimed by several Xhosa groups. Zuurveld translates as sour grass. As the name suggests, much of the grass of the Zuurveld plains was too sour for cattle to eat year-round, although the grass of the well-watered river valleys was sweet. This meant that Xhosa groups came and went in the Zuurveld, and that whites and Africans quickly came into conflict over gazing lands.

The Graaff-Reinet district covered the entire eastern frontier area before it was subdivided in 1804 by the British into the Uitenhage and Graaf Reinet districts, both of which encompassed more land than they would in the twentieth century. Turn-of-the-century colonial estimates of the population of Graaff-Reinet (excluding the Xhosa) ranged from 14 to 30,000, including over 4,000 white farmers, about 1,000 slaves, and anywhere from 9 to 25,000 "Hottentots."[39] From the perspective of white colonists, the extensive district of Graaff-Reinet was isolated and sparsely populated, cut off from ready communication with Cape Town by a long and difficult journey by ox wagon through the semi-desert lands of the Karoo. The colonial government exercised little real authority in the region, since the *landdrost,* or local governor, was backed up by completely insufficient force and was utterly dependent on local *veldwachtmeesters* (later veldcornet), drawn from the ranks of colonists and in turn beholden to their guns and interests.[40]

Different groups jostled one another in this turbulent frontier zone with its lack of clear authority. A number of communities re-formed themselves under the pressure of the race for resources. Khoisan, Europeans, and Xhosa competed for power, in conflicts in which the weaker Khoisan groups tended to lose out.[41] There were also tensions within each of these broad groupings, and alliances across them.

Several Khoekhoe clans had retreated from the southwestern Cape in the eighteenth century to the east of the Gamtoos River. Other Khoekhoe groups had moved to the west beyond the Fish River in the face of pressure from the Xhosa. Between the Fish and Gamtoos in the eighteenth century, various Khoekhoe clans had combined to form larger chieftaincies, the most important of which were the Gonaqua (with considerable Xhosa admixture) and the Hoengeiqua (formed from various fragmented groups by a man named Ruyter, himself flee-ing his earlier murder of a fellow Khoekhoe man in the Roggeveld). These chieftaincies were, however, themselves disintegrating by the late eighteenth century, in the face of combined white and Xhosa pressure on the lands they occupied.[42] In the meantime, the Xhosa had incor-porated a number of Khoekhoe groups into their own society, follow-ing the traditional mode of expansion of the southern Nguni peoples.[43] Despite the collapse of loose Xhosa hegemony over several Khoekhoe and San groups as a result of white competition, the legacy of Xhosa domination remained in the considerable mixing of Xhosa and Khoisan culture and bloodlines, especially in the groupings nearest the colony.[44] Despite their Xhosa admixture, the Gonaqua identified them-selves as Khoekhoe, while members of the westernmost Xhosa clan, the Gqunukhwebe, which had likewise intermarried extensively and possessed numerous Khoekhoe clients, identified themselves as Xhosa. The Khoisan diaspora had a wider regional impact.

To the north, in "Bosjesman's Land" as contemporaries termed it, /Xam groups, augmented by dispossessed Khoekhoe, continued to maintain a desperate guerilla struggle with the Cape Colony, launching cattle raids and receiving in return commandoes with a mandate for extermination. The Bushman campaigns against frontier farmers were highly destructive and expensive; in the nine years after the Drostdy of Graaff-Reinet was set up in 1786, farmers lost an estimated 19,161 cattle and 84,094 sheep.[45] In addition to revenge killings, the settler commandoes also captured people, usually children and women who were not perceived as an immediate military threat. They were brought back to the colony to work as captive labour. They were not legally slaves but often were in effect enslaved by a complex and arbitrarily applied net of customary labour legislation. Newton-King estimates that by 1795 there were more than 1,000 war captives among a farm labour force in Graaff-Reinet, whose numbers were officially put at 8,635 in 1798. White farmers continued to fear what Newton-King tellingly terms "the enemy within."[46]

To the far northwest, independent groups such as the Nama in contemporary Namibia continued to exist relatively unmolested by white farmers. They were, however, threatened by armed Khoisan and "baster" (mixed white/Khoisan) intruders who fled from the ambit of the Cape to Little and Great Namaqualand. Other dispossessed Khoisan and so-called mixed-race groups moved northeast, beyond the Orange River, where they would form the core of Griqua communities.

In the Eastern Cape, there were also political tensions among the Xhosa themselves. The several Xhosa groups who lived west of the Kei River by the mid-eighteenth century, including the Ntinde, Gwali, Mbalu, Dange, and Gqunukhwebe, had split from the core political unit at the end of the seventeenth century. By the late eighteenth century, these groups lived some or all of the time in the Zuurveld. In the mid-eighteenth century, the core Xhosa polity split again between the followers of the chiefs Gcaleka and Rharhabe. The Rharhabe Xhosa moved west towards the Fish River, where subsequent Rharhabe chiefs would claim hegemony over the chieftaincies in the vicinity who had split earlier from the main polity. As Hermann Giliomee puts it, the actual relationship of the Ciskei chiefs with Rharhabe and his successors was, however, "vague and shifting," dependent on the shifting regional balance of power. In the early 1790s, Rharhabe Xhosa allied temporarily with white colonists in the southeast to try to subordinate the Zuurveld Xhosa, who in turn incorporated Khoekhoe and escaped slaves to bolster their own numbers.[47]

The complicated late-eighteenth-century situation in the Zuurveld was made even more complicated as some additional Xhosa moved into the region, seeking, again to cite Giliomee, "pasture and opportunities for barter, labour and begging."[48] After the First Frontier War between whites and the Xhosa in 1779–81, largely fought over cattle,

Ntinde, Gwali, Mbalu, and Dange chiefs supposedly recognized the Fish River as the boundary between themselves and the colonists (however much this proved to be ignored in practice), but the Gqunukhwebe refused to make a boundary settlement. In the late 1780s, Xhosa came back in large numbers into the Zuurveld in the wake, on the one hand, of the severe drought of 1786 and, on the other, of the rise of the aggressive Rharhabe chief, Ndlambe, regent for the heir Ngqika during Ngqika's minority, who was determined to consolidate authority over both the Rharhabe Xhosa and the "rebel" chieftaincies. In 1793 the Second Frontier War broke out after several years of escalating tension between Xhosa and whites. Despite their superior firepower, the outnumbered Europeans could not chase all the Xhosa from the Zuurveld. They drove many into the arms of Ndlambe, whose forces killed the Gqunukhwebe chief Tshaka. Nonetheless, many colonists themselves panicked and fled the region during the war. Many farm servants deserted their masters, and a number stole stock, at least according to Landdrost Maynier.[49] The Xhosa sacked many white settler homesteads and began returning after the end of hostilities to newly emptied land.

In the meantime, hostilities mounted among Europeans themselves. Frontier farmers had long felt that the VOC tried to govern them with too heavy a hand. Colony-wide economic depression made life difficult for stock farmers in the mid-1790s, as the price of sheep and cattle tumbled. Furthermore, the farmers of Graff-Reinet felt betrayed in 1793 because they believed that the VOC had not backed them adequately. Colonists particularly resented the landdrost, Honoratus Christiaan David Maynier, who had refused to call out another general commando against the Xhosa in the wake of the 1793 war, did not try to drive all the Xhosa from the Zuurveld, and did not fight for the return of all colonists' cattle. He tried to restrain colonists' raids into Xhosa territory and gave Khoisan and Xhosa farm servants a degree of court protection to which colonists passionately objected. In 1795 rebel farmers expelled Maynier and other officials and rejected VOC rule. Styling themselves "Patriots" after the Cape Patriot movement against the VOC of the 1770s onwards, the rebels adopted the iconography of Jacobinism and the trappings of international revolution, proclaiming sympathy with the pro-French Batavian regime in Holland.[50]

Meanwhile, the British invaded the Cape Colony in that same year of 1795. In the first instance, Britain took temporary custodial possession in the name of William of Orange in order to prevent the colony falling into the hands of revolutionary France, through the Batavian government which had overthrown the Orangist regime in the Netherlands. A new British-appointed landdrost in Graaff-Reinet, Frans

Bresler, was in turn expelled by the Patriots in 1796, but the rebel republic proved short-lived when the government cut off trade in ammunition. In Xhosaland, intra-Xhosa political tensions continued as the young Ngqika tried unsuccessfully to compel Ndlambe to step down completely; instead, Ndlambe and some councillors of Ngqika moved over the Fish where Ndlambe established regional hegemony.

By this point, the position of Khoisan had deteriorated further. Regions of the Graaff-Reinet district which within the memory of adults had contained many independent Khoekhoe homesteads now held almost nothing except vast Dutch farms. Here the Khoekhoe, despite outnumbering the Dutch, were either client labour or lived precariously, and for the most part "illegally" according to Dutch law, on the margins between white homesteads.[51] At the turn of century, British official John Barrow recorded: "Twenty years ago, if we may credit the travelers of that day, the country beyond the Gamtoos river, which was then the eastern limit of the colony, abounded with kraals or villages of Hottentots, out of which the inhabitants came to meet them by hundreds in a group. Some of these villages might still have been expected to remain in this remote and not very populous part of the colony. Not one, however, was to be found."[52] The Khoekhoe themselves claimed that their numbers were shrinking in the late eighteenth century. In response to admittedly very pointed questions before the House of Commons Select Committee on Aborigines of 1836, Andries Stoffel attested that the "Hottentots" were in a "bad condition" at the turn of the century. They had much diminished in number since the advent of the Europeans: "the missionaries picked up a few, and they are increasing now [in 1836]."[53] The Third Frontier War of 1799–1802 was just one in a long series of struggles across these frontier lands. It was, however, of unique importance for the battered remnant of Eastern Cape Khoekhoe for whom this represented a serious but unsuccessful throw at regaining lost land in a desperate situation.

In January 1799 the British arrested Adriaan van Jaarsveld, a ring leader of the previous farmers' revolt, on unrelated charges of fraud. As Van Jaarsveld was being taken to Cape Town, rebels led by the former leader of the 1795 rebellion attacked his escort and freed the prisoner. This incident sparked a further settler revolt, which has come to be known as the "van Jaarsveld rebellion." A force of British and Khoekhoe troops was dispatched from Cape Town to the frontier to suppress the rebellion. Seizing the opportunity provided by an incoming British force hostile to their oppressors, a number of Khoekhoe attempted to form a delegation to parlay with the British before they left the region, despite settler opposition. In what V.C. Malherbe has described as an "inevitable" escalation of violence, farmers tried to prevent their Khoisan servants from leaving, often by violent means.[54] In tandem, a growing number of Khoekhoe deserted their Dutch masters. The ranks of the deserters included women, children, and the elderly, although, as we shall see, male rebels would be hampered by the fact that many of their dependants remained with the settlers.

John Barrow, then secretary to the British governor Lord Macartney, later recalled meeting one delegation to the British led by Klaas Stuurman. Stuurman's group intercepted the party of the British general Thomas Pakenham Vandeleur after the latter had suppressed the Boer rebellion. The "large party of Hottentots" was "so disguised, and dressed out in such a whimsical and fantastical manner, that we were totally at a loss to conjecture what to make of them. Some wore large three cornered hats, with green or blue breeches, the rest of the body naked; some had jackets of cloth over their sheep-skin covering, and others had sheep-skins thrown over linen shirts." The group had taken weapons as well as clothing and other goods from the Dutch – in lieu of unpaid wages, according to Stuurman.[55] At a subsequent meeting, Stuurman articulated the overarching grievances of the Khoekhoe, in a striking (and widely quoted) speech, albeit one inevitably filtered through Barrow's translation and memory: "'Restore', he said, 'the country of which our fathers were despoiled by the Dutch and we have nothing more to ask'... 'We have lived very contentedly,' said he, 'before these Dutch plunderers molested us, and why should we not do so again if left to ourselves? Has not the Groot Baas given plenty of grass roots, and berries and grasshoppers for our use; and, till the Dutch destroyed them, abundance of wild animals to hunt? And will they not return and multiply when these destroyers are gone?'"[56]

Struggle proved contagious. By May 1799, as Malherbe and Newton-King have convincingly argued, the Khoekhoe were engaged in a self-conscious fight to regain their land and to expel the Dutch.[57] Some came to the British standard to seek alliances, while still more united with Xhosa groups resisting white settler incursions, particularly as disillusion set in over British intentions.

In the meantime, in 1799 the incoming British force ill-advisedly pushed the Gqunukhwebe out of their own territory and into that of Ndlambe. The British general Vandeleur then began to plan his return to Cape Town, leaving his new-found Khoekhoe allies unprotected. Many more Khoekhoe rebels went to the Zuurveld. There they made common cause with the Gqunukhwebe Xhosa and shared with them the spoils of joint attacks on their mutual enemy the Dutch. "The Caffres and Hottentots have found out that Englishmen are not Invulnerable, they have likewise tasted the sweets of Plunder, and learnt to

Despise the Dutch Boors who formerly kept them in Subjection," com- mented British official Andrew Barnard.[58]

The Dutch settlers fled in the face of Khoekhoe and Xhosa aggres- sion, leaving the Gonaqua Khoekhoe under Klaas Stuurman temporar- ily in command of the Algoa Bay area. British reinforcements under General Francis Dundas readily defeated the rebel Dutch in 1799, while the former landdrost, Honoratus Christiaan Maynier, who had returned under British sponsorship, persuaded some Khoekhoe to go back to their farms in exchange for promises of better working condi- tions, contracts, and legal protection against maltreatment. Others remained in the Zuurveld, where they lived by raiding. After a brief negotiated truce, however, the frontier once again exploded in 1801. It was in this turbulent context that the elderly Dutchman Johannes Theodorus van der Kemp and the young British carpenter James Read began the work of the LMS among the Khoisan.

THE FIRST SOUTH AFRICAN MISSIONARIES

To move away from large-scale movements to the particularity of indi- vidual missionaries who went to southern Africa at the turn of the eigh- teenth century is both risky and liberating. It is liberating to acknowl- edge the quirkiness of individuals, who messily refuse to be confined within the abstract admonitions of the historian's patterns. Indeed, one would hardly expect complete conventionality from those undertaking what were, from a late-eighteenth-century European perspective, such dangerous voyages into the unknown for such quixotic ends. To acknowledge the individual seems in some ways more faithful to the complex vagaries of the past than an agentless account. At the same time, it is perhaps particularly risky in a history of missions to introduce the traditional figure of the individual missionary, whether in virtuous or villainous guise. As Doug Stuart and Jean and John Comaroff have reminded us forcefully, European missionaries depended for their financ- ing, and on some deeper level for their internal self-justification, on a heroic model: again and again in missionary-society publications, the individual missionary was described as a hero, venturing into the lands of Satan in the name of Christ, able to transform entire societies because he (or she) worked as an agent of God. A certain subgenre of writing about missions has indeed tended to perpetuate that stereotype. A more intractable problem stems from the nature of the sources. Before the early nineteenth century, it was the missionaries who documented their own voyages and lives, often to feed (however reluctantly in some cases) the insatiable appetite for publicity of the missionary fundraising machine. And the private papers that have survived are for the most part those of the missionaries. Consequently, the written record reveals more about the self-understanding of particular missionaries, mostly white, and more about the missionary's perception of those he or she was trying to convert, than about the self-understandings of hearers. It would be foolish to refuse to discuss the individual biographies of missionaries. Nor do I want to minimize the epistemological problems of biography even in relatively well-documented cases – and nor in fact do I think that the agency of converts is irrecoverable. I do, however, want to stress that, if I can say more about the personal lives of most missionaries than the personal lives of most early-nineteenth-century converts, this is not because I consider the former more important than the latter. Secondly, understanding as much as possible the preoccupations of our primary observers increases the chance of being able to decipher their texts, and to read against the grain of self-presentation.

With these caveats in mind, who then were the first LMS missionaries to the Cape? In general, the LMS had a relatively open recruiting policy in its earliest days. It was willing to hire from the ranks of the literate working classes, believing that the inspiration of God was more important than the degree of education of candidates.[59] Thomas Hawies called, for example, in his 1798 anniversary sermon for "the smiths, the carpenters that smooth the planes, as well as the architects that plan the fabric" – a literal as well as metaphorical call for all types of men "whom the Lord hath furnished with ability and zeal to build up the ark of his church."[60] The social composition of the earliest LMS missionary cohorts in southern Africa as elsewhere thus reflected that of the British population that had been most touched by evangelical revival. Two of the most important British missionaries in early-nineteenth-century southern Africa, James Read and Robert Moffat, had been a carpenter and a gardener respectively in Britain.

The first four LMS recruits to southern Africa were nonetheless not entirely representative of this trend. Two of the four, Johannes Theodorus van der Kemp and J.J. Kicherer, were Dutchmen, and two were British, William Edwards and John Edmond. William Edwards probably fit the profile of the young artisan missionary the most closely of the four. He was about twenty-six years old on his arrival in Africa, and was a craftsman. According to Karel Schoeman, he had been married and therefore was probably a widower.[61] He was not as well educated as the other missionaries, if one can judge from the fact that Haweis wrote to Van der Kemp from London imploring him to "exhort our Brother Edwards to improve himself in spelling, in which he is very defective."[62]

It is hard to tell what John Edmond's earlier background was. He was certainly a better speller, although his spelling of his own name fluctuated.[63] Edmond (or Edmonds) had initially approached the LMS directors with the proposal that the LMS translate the Bible into the "Indostan tongue." He had earlier lived in Bengal and spent time in Benares, before returning to England and experiencing conversion in Manchester. It seems a reasonable assumption that he had been a trader of some kind. In any case, the LMS directors had proposed instead that Edmond return to Bengal as a missionary, despite East India Company restrictions on the free entry of Britons to their Indian territories. Tellingly, Edmond had resisted before agreeing to become a missionary, in terms that reveal his sense of social distance from Indians: "Perhaps I should be left without any support to Beg my Rice and water of the people I had formerly looked upon with Contempt." Edmond would later leave south Africa for Bengal, finding himself unable to bear either the Xhosa or the tumult of frontier warfare. In an earlier letter he nonetheless praised the "Rohillas" of India, among whom he also proposed working: "A people very much like ourselves they are a brave, industrious and inoffensive people, if not provoked." In addition to his symptomatic unease with extremely foreign peoples, Edmond's account of his decision to become a missionary also underscores the importance for many missionaries of the non-material realm of visions, dreams, and prayers. Edmond had sought to know the will of God "by a Dream, or some evident way by his word being applied with energy to my soul." But instead, "one morning as I was putting on my Cloths thinking on what took up almost all my thoughts – 'I wish I knew what I ought to do' – these words came into my mind – 'Lo I am with you alway, even unto the end of the world' – This did not come with the energetick force to the soul that I had formerly experienced (I used to compare it to what an electrical shock is to the body) But with a gentle heart reviving influence ..."[64] Although Edmond was to have little influence on southern Africa, his biography reflects existing trends.

The two Dutchmen, Johannes Jacobus Kicherer and Johannes Theodorus van der Kemp, were to prove far more significant figures in the LMS. Their presence attests to the importance of Dutch evangelicalism to the British missionary movement. It also reminds us, as Doug Stuart underlines in his doctoral thesis, of the centrality of continental pietism as a formative influence in the early LMS.[65] Kicherer had heard of the formation of the LMS from the minister of family friends.[66] He was then recruited by Van der Kemp through the Netherlands Missionary Society founded by Van der Kemp in late 1797 to work in conjunction with the LMS. Kicherer was a theology student who had studied at the universities of Leyden and Utrecht. He was the son of a German Lutheran father from the pietist stronghold of Wurttemburg and a half-Dutch, half-German mother, and was twenty-four years old when he offered himself to the LMS.[67] He was formally set aside to preach to the heathen in Utrecht by Gerhard Masman, before his departure for London and thence to the Cape Colony. Although it is somewhat unclear whether this was a full-fledged ordination, Kicherer was probably better educated than the majority of LMS envoys of this period, and he was able to present himself once in the Cape Colony as a respectable minister of the Reformed Church.[68] Another Dutch recruit, who changed his mind before leaving, Jacob van der Pauw, was more typical in being a shoemakers' apprentice.[69]

It was Johannes Theodorus van der Kemp, however, who most obviously defied the generalizations made in an earlier chapter about the social backgrounds of missionaries, in many respects ranging from his age to his high degree of education. He also left more information about himself than the average missionary, in part precisely because of his education and high social status. Given both the impact of Van der Kemp on early-nineteenth-century southern Africa and the relative rarity of the kind of private information contained in the spiritual autobiography he left among his private papers, I want to pause to look in some detail at Van der Kemp's life and intellectual preoccupations before he arrived at the Cape Colony.[70]

JOHANNES THEODORUS VAN DER KEMP

Johannes Theodorus van der Kemp was a scion of two well-placed Rotterdam families. He was heir to family traditions of public involvement and of education. Johannes Theodorus's father, Cornelius van der Kemp, was, like his own father Johannes, a well-known minister in the Reformed Church. By the time of the birth of Johannes Theodorus in 1747, Cornelius had been a professor in practical theology for the past four years. Johannes Theodorus's mother, Anna Maria Van Teylingen, was the daughter of a mayor of Rotterdam.[71] Van der Kemp's older brother, Didericus, who was sixteen years older than he, became a prominent Reformed Church minister of conservative leanings and a professor of theology in his own right.

Van der Kemp's cousin on the paternal side, François Adriaan van der Kemp, took a less conventional path: he was a Mennonite minister, and one who saw no contradiction between the Bible and the sword.[72] François Adriaan was a passionate Patriot leader and critic of the Reformed church during the 1780s. He was imprisoned in 1787 for his role in the failed Patriot uprisings put down by Prussian invasion, and was banished from Holland in 1788.[73] He took refuge in the United States, where he settled in western New York State and became the correspondent and friend of a number of prominent players in the American Revolution; he saw many parallels between what he thought of as the American and Dutch struggles for liberty.[74] The early travails of François Adriaan in student poverty, once his religious positions had cut him off from patronage, suggest a relative decline in family fortunes. Still, his sense of family glory, and his own feelings of self-importance in consequence, doubtless had echoes for Johannes Theodorus. As François Adriaan, close to Johannes Theodorus in age, recalled in his autobiographical memoir: "Even when a boy, I felt an exquisite delight, that I could, that I might call loudly my ancestors by name; that I could celebrate their virtues, their prowess in arms, their great renown in literature, without apprehension of meeting with obloquy or contradiction. From my father's side, the *van der Kemps*, the *Bax*, the *van Drongelens'* – from my mother's, the *Leydekkers*, the *de Huyberts*, the *de Witts*, Lords of Hamsteede, with their numerous alliances, – were so many spurs to him, in whose breast the last spark of glory was not extinguished for their emulation."[75] Indeed, the two cousins seem quite similar in the assurance with which they played public roles, bolstered by a deep conviction of God's approval. Although the two took opposing political positions, since Johannes Theodorus was a partisan of the Prince of Orange and an opponent of the Patriots, François Adriaan nonetheless recognized common patterns in their lives: "I knew him well. He was a man of vast learning and profound mind ... and surprising talents ... by which I often have benefitted. I cannot say I envy the situation of his last years ... There has been a striking ... coincidence in many respects of our lives, and we may at length arrive at the same goal by a different course."[76]

In his early fifties by the time he came to the Cape, with relatives and contacts playing prominent roles on both sides of the fratricidal Dutch conflicts of the 1780s, Van der Kemp was not a man to be pushed around, whether by local farmers or by government dignitaries. The LMS began its south African operations in the wake of the British takeover of the colony from the Dutch EIC. Van der Kemp would have little respect for the vestiges of the VOC system. Indeed, he had earlier been offered a job as a commandant of a corps of soldiers at the Cape by the VOC but had refused, since "the aversion which I had always had of the object and manner of acting of that Body would not permit me to give myself as an instrument to support its measures, and urged me to reject the proposition."[77] When the British regime temporarily gave way to the Batavian, after the French Revolution brought the Patriots to power in Holland, Van der Kemp was similarly not overawed.

Van der Kemp's self-confidence was doubtless reinforced both by his relatively high degree of education and by his previous professional experience as a military officer, as a doctor, and as an adminstrator. By his fifties, Van der Kemp spoke thirteen languages (including a "light touch of the Ethiopian Dialect")[78] and had published books of philosophy and theology. His early education reflected the resources available to a bourgeois Dutch family of the period. He was tutored at home until the age of ten in writing, reading, French, English, and religion. At school first in Rotterdam and then in Dordrecht, he continued his study of classical languages. At sixteen he registered at the University of Leyden, where he attended lectures in science and philosophy in anticipation of later studying medicine. At the beginning of his fourth year, however, he abruptly dropped out of university, partly because his older brother Didericus had just been appointed professor of ecclesiastical history at the University of Leyden and the younger Van der Kemp was unable to bear being in a junior role at the same university, and partly because he no longer thought of medicine as an honourable profession.[79] Like his cousin François Adriaan at a similar stage of life, Van der Kemp joined the military instead, entering the Dragoon Guards. He rose through the ranks for sixteen years before resigning his captaincy in 1780 in the wake of Prince William V's disapproval of Van der Kemp's relationship with a spinning woman, Christina Helena Frank.

After marrying Frank in the same year, Van der Kemp moved with her and his daughter by a previous relationship to Edinburgh. There he qualified as a doctor and as an obstetrician, carrying out signficant medical research in the process, including investigating "bodily symptoms upon drowning" with his friend Edmund Goodwyn. The work seems to have involved drowning cats.[80] Van der Kemp then worked for nine years as a doctor in Middleburg, where he became head of the local hospital for the poor. He also carried out research in chemistry and anatomy, gave public lectures on scientific subjects, and published some of his work in chemistry. By 1790, however, Van der Kemp felt compelled by bad health to leave Middleburg. After so many years as a doctor, on the cutting edge of medical research of the period, he carried out another of his characteristic renunciations. He had become convinced, he later wrote, of the "vanity of Physick." Accordingly he abandoned medicine: "experience had abundantly taught me how little good, in comparison of the inexpressible evil which it was to the credulous world."[81]

Van der Kemp attempted to devote himself to the study of philosophy and oriental languages, but he was interrupted by the outbreak of war with revolutionary France. Still a staunch Orangist, Van der Kemp accepted a call to work as a doctor in the Dutch army in Flanders and became a staff doctor at the allied military hospital in Ghent. He subsequently worked as superintendent of a field hospital, in constant retreat from the French army, and then as superintendent of a military hospital at Feyenoord, near Rotterdam. In early 1795 Rotterdam capitulated to the French. Van der Kemp continued for some months to run the hospital under French direction, but he resigned his post rather than accept a further position. In 1797 he received a copy of the address of the LMS on the formation of the new society, from the Moravian community at Zeist via Herrnhut. Shortly thereafter, he offered himself to the LMS as a missionary.

Given this history, it is not surprising that the early LMS directors seem to have been somewhat overawed by Van der Kemp and supported his unexpectedly radical activities. In the charged context of the 1790s, a well-educated and well-born Orangist was conceived of literally as a godsend. Indeed, the LMS was reluctant to send Van der Kemp to Africa. "This appointment was made in compliance with the earnest wish of the Doctor himself," the society's official memoir of Van der Kemp would later proclaim. "The Directors would have preferred a station among the more polished nations of the East, for which his superior talents so eminently qualified him."[82]

Although this brief sketch of Van der Kemp's education and professional career helps explain his surprising degree of influence on the LMS directors and his self-assurance in intervening in southern African politics, it does not do justice to the complicated currents of his autobiography. God, guilt, redemption, sexuality, and the quest to escape society and the self are all key themes in the spiritual autobiography that runs parallel to Van der Kemp's account of the events of his life. Van der Kemp's struggles with deism, his attempts to master his own voracious sexuality, and what might be read as attempts to escape his own social background were all part of a lifelong quest for redemption, marked above all, it seems to me, by a struggle to find purity and to escape guilt through a series of renunciations.

If this is correct, then Van der Kemp was not alone in the quest for purity through renunciation. Simon Schama has an intriguing analysis of the ideology of the pro-republican Patriots in the 1780s and 1790s. He contends that the late eighteenth century was a time of declining economic fortune in the Netherlands, in which a small group of the rich grew richer and the poor grew poorer. The Patriots, in common with moral reformers elsewhere in Europe and America, saw the restoration of national moral virtue as the necessary concomitant of political reform. Extravagant luxury was to be curbed, social equality was to be restored, and national virtue would ensure that the providential dispensation would once again favour the Netherlands, from which God had withdrawn his approval. The concerns of the Patriots echoed a tradition among late-eighteenth-century Dutch essayists of calls for a return to the fabled Dutch sobriety, for a rejection of foreign influences, for a rediscovery of the virtue of the common people. According to Schama, the vast armies of servants in major cities were portrayed as a free people enslaved, while the works of Samuel Richardson, including *Pamela*, the tale of a servant girl who reforms her immoral master and marries him for her pains, were wildly popular.[83] Although religious reformers, including such Patriot clergymen as François Adriaan van der Kemp, bitterly attacked the luxury and self-satisfaction of the Reformed church establishment, those on all sides of political debate used intensely religious language. As Schama observes, "it was ironic that Groen van Prinsterer, the Calvinist historian, should, like the abbé Barruel, suppose that revolution is by definition the work of the godless. The truth of the matter in the Netherlands was exactly the reverse. Even the language of its politics was saturated in deep religious conviction, *especially* when directed against the clerical establishment."[84]

If nationalist Patriots such as François Adriaan van der Kemp sought for national redemption through a communal return to simplicity and virtue, in accordance with a purified Christianity, Johannes Theodorus looked for personal redemption through a return to religious first principles and, in a project with overtones of the Romantics, through communion with those beneath him in social status. At the age of thirty, J.T. van der Kemp walked through Germany, France, and England in disguise to observe the military techniques of those country's armies. He cut his hair and took only what he wore, a "rough grey coat," a comb, two shirts, and a pocketbook. I take this journey as a metaphor for Van der Kemp's lifelong effort to wrestle with God through the negation of the self and the world and through dramatic changes of lifestyle. His voyage to south Africa was surely part of the same quest.

In describing what he was trying to escape, Van der Kemp painted himself as a slave to his physical desires, in an account that recalls *Les confessions* of Rousseau in its mingling of sexual and intellectual detail. Van der Kemp's sexual activity before his marriage might not have been atypical for a Dutch soldier of the time but does perhaps argue for some self-destructiveness in an only partially lapsed Calvinist. Son, grandson, and brother of prominent Reformed ministers, Van der Kemp was conscious that he was transgressing the expectations of his family. During his teenage years as a student at the University of Leyden, Van der Kemp said that he often observed to his "bossom friend" J.L. Versten that he saw "with open eyes" that he was "hastening on to destruction" but was powerless to stop himself.[85] Later, in the Dragoon Guards, Van der Kemp claimed that his conduct became "more and more base" and many "decent people" dropped his

acquaintanceship. In an inverted version of his later quest to find purity in working-class simplicity, Van der Kemp stated that he made up
for the loss of these respectable acquaintanceships by "connexion"
with the "lowest sort" of women. He picked up women in the Leyden
poorhouse through the mediation of the matron. In Rotterdam he took
the pseudonym Corporal Jack and dressed as a non-commissioned officer while he had affairs with two women recently released from prison,
one of whom had been accused of murdering her child. In the Hague
he slept with the wife of the hangman.

Van der Kemp also began what would prove a long-standing affair
with a wig-maker's wife. After this affair had progressed, Van der
Kemp gave up most of his other women. In his words, he "stole" the
woman from her husband and took her to Leyden, where he lived with
her publicly. Van der Kemp's father cut off his son's allowance and
pleaded with him to abandon vice; his brother Didericus likewise urged
him to reconcile with his father and to accept God's grace. Van der
Kemp told his father: "I have deeply insulted you, but ... I am ruled by
lust, and I believe that I deserve some pity, if only because I carry my
almost unbearable punishment with me in my heart." To his brother
he wrote: "My ailment is irredeemable ... Verily I am embondaged ...
and the feeling that you and my father love me and that I wrong you
both, make up the greater part of my unhappiness."[81] He asked the
woman to go and live at the Hague, and his father died shortly thereafter. Van der Kemp was convinced that his own conduct had hastened
his father's death and struggled with a lifelong sense of guilt. Others
agreed: Cornelius Boem, an old family friend, in a letter of reference
for Van der Kemp to the LMS, conflated sexual and theological improprieties and stated that Van der Kemp's "worthy father had died of the
grief" occasioned by his son's "infidel conduct."[87] At the time, however, Van der Kemp was furious at his father's will, which left money to
Van der Kemp on condition that he give up his lover. This had the
opposite effect on Van der Kemp, who brought her back to Leyden and
lived with her openly again. In 1773 the former wig-maker's wife gave
birth to a baby girl, Joanna. Van der Kemp was terrified that his sins
would lead God to punish the child: "My love and care for this child
were [beyond?] all conception, and my prayers to God, that he would
be gracious to it, and not let it bear the consequences of my unrighteousness, were continual and abundant from the moment of its birth.
Nothing hurt me more than the consideration of the injury I had done
to this innocent child, through my disgraceful conduct, and [I] sought
to redress it by a redoubled zeal for its welfare."[88]

If Van der Kemp found joy with the wig-maker's wife, or saw his other
women as anything other than battlegrounds for the war within him

between lust and duty, he did not say so. Of course, the perspective he presents is that of the elderly penitent. Even from that point of view, however, he stresses more than he might need to his constant sense of slavery and his self-degradation. Instead, Van der Kemp seems to have seen his lust as a theological as well as a moral problem. "Blind to my depravity I embraced with eagerness the prevailing idea, that the will always inclined to what the understanding considered to be good, and that therefore when the will shewed itself adverse to good, this was alone to be ascribed to an error in the understanding, by which it conceived things to be good, which in reality were evil ..."[89] Van der Kemp's main subject here was his quest to know the attributes of God through reason, but the underlying theme was also key: how could it be that he did not love God enough to refrain from sin, even if his understanding willed this?

In 1777 Van der Kemp finally separated from his lover, whose husband was still alive and whom he therefore could not marry. According to Van der Kemp, she gave up Joanna to him "with ease." She then vanishes from his autobiography. Van der Kemp continued to see various women, as he had while he still lived with the wig-maker's wife, but he was perturbed by the return of religious conscience after being dragged to church by a certain General van Goens. Later in the same year, he met a young wool-spinner in the streets of Leyden, Christina Frank, whose stepmother's ill-treatment had forced her to find temporary lodgings and to toil at the bleach-works. Van der Kemp records that he was immediately in love with her. He offered to help her and the next day hired a house for the two of them, promising her that he would not offend her. Shortly thereafter he proposed to her and asked her to be a mother to his child; she apparently replied that she wanted to meet the child first. In any case, no marriage took place until a year and a half later. In the meantime, Van der Kemp gave up all other women and embraced Frank's lifestyle with enthusiasm. The stadtholder, the Prince of Orange, let it be known to Van der Kemp that he disapproved of this relationship. As a result, Van der Kemp left the military in 1780 (although he seems to have hoped that his projected resignation would shock the prince into rescinding his censure, and he was then too proud to recant once it was clear this would not happen). Despite the disapproval of most of Van der Kemp's family and friends, Van der Kemp and Frank were married on 29 May 1778. François van der Kemp appeared as witness for his cousin.[90] Van der Kemp found a purified community in Frank's world: "I took such pleasure in the low circle in which she moved, that I was inclined immediately after marriage actually to stoop to the same conditions, and to exchange my manner of living to that of a common macanick or journeyman." Frank continued to dress as a spinner and acquired a double spinning-wheel which Van der Kemp sometimes used. He would bring her pails of water while she was scrubbing the street. Much later, in south Africa, Van der Kemp would follow a similar pattern by marrying a thirteen-year-old slave girl from Madagascar, whose father was a Muslim priest and whose liberty Van der Kemp purchased, along with that of several of her relatives. In both cases, of course, the power imbalance between Van der Kemp and his wives was striking.

Van der Kemp also sought purification through suffering. This was an intellectual move typical of the pre-millenarian, for whom, in Boyd Hilton's words, "temporal misfortunes were always 'special' or 'particular' judgements on men and nations" and might be taken as a sign of God's grace in seeking to rescue his erring people.[91] Shortly before his late-life "conversion," Van der Kemp "prayed to the Lord (more earnestly than for virtue) that he would bless me, as I expressed myself, with chastisements," in the hope of gaining emotional as well as intellectual conviction of God's existence and somehow freeing himself from guilt. After an intellectual passage into deism around the time of his marriage, Van der Kemp struggled with God's distance from him. "I was convinced that the internal source of my voluntary actions were in their nature unclean, so that sin originally belonged to the essence of my soul so that I therefore could not be released from sin or become virtuous except God by a properly speaking new creation changed my soul in an essence of quite a other nature, for I had now learned that 'twas not to be ascribed to any misunderstanding in my judgement that I chose evil, but that from nature I loved sin, known as such, and desired it above all what was good." Therefore he wanted God to punish him gently, so that "I should learn with more earnestness, to plead with him for a new heart."[92]

On Monday, 27 June 1791, Van der Kemp and his first wife and daughter took a boat out sailing before teatime. A sudden storm arose and overturned the boat. Twice Van der Kemp pulled Christina from the bottom and lost her; both she and Joanna drowned in front of him. "Being brought back to my dwelling I thanked God for what had happened with a stoical hardness, and going to bed, I deliberately thought of the dreadful circumstance." Shortly thereafter in church, psalm 42, verse 3 was sung, which his wife had sung almost every day: "I have no food but tears day and night; and all day long men say to me, 'Where is your God?'" "Sitting down I imagined that I had my wife and daughter present, and that imagination was so strong that besides them I scarcely saw or heard any thing." At communion, which the deist Van der Kemp normally never took, he heard Jesus speaking to him, telling him that grace was freely given and not earned – only grace could expiate his guilt. Van der Kemp returned to Christianity from an anguished and unsatisfactory form of deism. Even while a deist he had never lost his central conviction of "God's justice in imparting Adam's transgression to his posterity."[93] He was able at last to feel that God offered grace through Jesus to escape this central dilemma.

Despite his conviction of God's grace, Van der Kemp retained as a key element of his theology this conviction that God might make his creatures suffer and still be gracious. When he fell ill in a military hospital after his conversion, for example, he complained to Jesus, and felt that Jesus replied: "Do you think, that reversing my promise I could not on account of your pretension suffer you to die? You complain of the vermin in which you lay! but, I have not suffered them as *Philip* the Second, to gnaw you through. You complain of the Rot, and the ulcering that exists by you, but I have not suffered, as I did with him the flesh in pieces to fall from your face, because it might not be said in this [Catholic] country, that this happened to you on account of your stubborn heresy, but take care, that it does not happen to you hereafter![94]

Van der Kemp thus came to south Africa expecting to find evil and suffering. He would find Satan lodged, however, not only in the hearts of the heathen but in the breasts of Dutch peasants. He would became a self-confident and ferocious, if completely isolated, critic of colonial regimes at the Cape between 1799 and his death in 1811. His critique was consistent with his conviction that the nominal Christian was more evil than the non-Christian, and needs, I think, to be seen in theological as well as political terms. For example, Van der Kemp's hatred of natural man, and the dislike of the non-religious world which led him to say, in Enklaar's words, that he "loathed civilized society,"[95] would enable him to transfer a critique of postlapsarian man to most of white society at the Cape and to uphold a contrasting, and subversive, vision of the purified and redeemed Khoekhoe.

Van der Kemp's autobiography furnishes interesting evidence on the relationship between evangelicalism and Enlightenment thought. Before his final conversion, Van der Kemp attempted consciously to mould his life according to the precepts of the great rationalist, systematizing thinkers of the period. Following Descartes, he tried to deduce knowledge of God and the good through reasoning from first principles: "I thought that a well grounded knowledge of the being and properties of created substances depended in a great measure upon a knowledge of God. This induced me to apply with diligence to the pursuit of this knowledge and I endeavoured to deduce it from first principles in imitation of Des Cartes ...[96] Indeed, Van der Kemp's efforts to pursue truth through a variety of renunciations are reminiscent in form of the intellectual projects of Descartes or Spinoza.[97] They may have been in the air. François Adriaan van der Kemp records that he, too, "endeavoured to lay aside all preconceived prejudices" in order to inquire alone into "the truth and nature of the Christian Revelation." François was more fortunate than Johannes: "I remained in my study and continued my studies night and day, taking no more rest than was imperiously required, and was within a short period of time fully convinced of the historical truth of the Christian revelation."[98] For his part, possibly following Spinoza, Johannes considered that his "depravity" was due to an insufficient "love of God," defined, in terms that sound like those of Spinoza, as knowledge of the whole, attainable only through a long process of intellectual striving. Therefore, if Van der Kemp sinned, this must be because he did not love God enough, which in turn was because he did not know him. Since knowledge of God was knowledge of the whole, the route to virtue lay via the acquisition of knowledge.[99] Consequently, Van der Kemp took up philosophy in order to become virtuous and happy through reason – only to be failed by it, and frustrated by his inability to become either chaste or happy.

From this perspective, Van der Kemp's conversion is symptomatic of eighteenth-century religious revival as a response to the perceived emotional inadequacies of deism and the stress on reason at the expense of feeling. This makes aspects of early evangelicalism more explicable: the emphasis on the futility of intellectual approaches to God, and the intense stress on God's active intervention in human affairs. As Van der Kemp put it in his second letter of application to the LMS directors, "faith in Jesus is an Act of the *Will*, rather than of the *Intellect*, as no involuntary Act can be the Object of a moral law." This, for Van der Kemp, was "the form and essence of Christianity; it is simply resting on Jesus."[100] In this he echoed a critical theme in late-eighteenth and early-nineteenth-century evangelicalism across denominational and national boundaries.

The cumulative impact of these tendencies among the earliest missionaries was a more *potentially* socially egalitarian message than has been recognized – although this potential was, of course, not necessarily fulfilled. The poor and uneducated were believed to have as much access to truth as the leisured (and therefore wealthy) intellectuals of the rationalist model espoused by Descartes and Spinoza, because God, and hence knowledge, was experienced rather than attained through ratiocination. In this sense, evangelicalism came into direct conflict with so-called Enlightenment thought (to borrow a contentious shorthand term) in a contest over the relationship between reason and knowledge of "God." It was a dramatic reversal of assumptions when Van der Kemp decided after his conversion that "I found that I could agree better with those, who were most simple and untaught with respect to the World, than by those by whom the simple truths of Christ were suppressed under a weight of less holy wisdom and through their own witty argument [of?] systematical piety." Transferring this debate to south Africa, Van der Kemp believed that the Khoisan were better Christians than the Dutch – a disturbing claim in a society in which oppression was often justified by the claim that the Khoisan were constitutively incapable of becoming Christians. In no sense did all missionaries share this assumption. And later missionary liberals like John Philip, a subsequent LMS superintendent in southern Africa, would harness the political and economic thought of the Scottish Enlightenment to political ends in southern Africa. There was no simple relationship, in other words, between evangelicalism and eighteenth-century rationalism and deism – nor, indeed, between evangelicalism and romanticism. All these currents were mingled in complicated and unexpected ways.

IMAGES OF THE KHOEKHOE: MISSIONARY PRECONCEPTIONS

Missionaries and missions-society propagandists would propound powerful narrative myths about the people and areas of the world to which they went. They also traveled before arrival with strong preconceptions which in turn shaped how and what they saw. As Edward Said and many others have taught us, "seeing" is by no means a transparent process.[101] There was also not one way of seeing, and the Khoekhoe themselves struggled to influence and manipulate missionary visions. Indeed, an important component of politics around missions in the early nineteenth century was competition over what discourse would dominate, and who would control that discourse. Yet, all that said, the range of ideological choice available to missionary visitors was relatively narrow.

What, then, did the earliest missionaries expect to "see"? Missionaries going to southern Africa, particularly those of British origins, had little concrete knowledge of the Khoekhoe in particular, or of Africans in general, but they did have a wide variety of accumulated prejudices. As Dutchmen, Van der Kemp and Kicherer almost certainly had more extensive access to information on south Africa and its inhabitants than did the British. There was a long-established tradition of ethnographic accounts by Dutch-speaking travellers at the Cape, however doubtful the veracity of some.[102] Popular knowledge of some sort was doubtless in circulation. Van der Kemp, for example, was unusually precise in proposing to LMS directors that he be sent to work among the Namaqua, and, as we have seen, he had already been approached to work for the VOC.[103] Nonetheless, general stereotypes were what were available to most missionaries, before the LMS had itself had the chance to generate a powerful set of narratives about the Khoekhoe and the Cape Dutch. The British were probably less well informed than the Dutch, drawing the bulk of their information from popular compendia of information and a bastardized and truncated version of Peter Kolb's magisterial writings.

At the turn of the eighteenth century, material about Africa read by evangelicals fell into three broad categories: abolitionist material, ethnographic and travel literature, and the religious accounts of earlier missionaries. The fight to abolish the slave trade was generating a flood of publications on Africa.[104] Much abolitionist literature portrayed a fairly undifferentiated injured Africa, to whom Europe owed compensation. In announcing their intentions to launch several missions to Africa, LMS directors indeed drew on this language, claiming that Christian missions were a means for Europe to make atonement to Africa for the slave trade. "The injuries which that unfortunate quarter of the globe has sustained, by the avarice and cruelty of Europeans, appeal to the justice and compassion of Christians, and call for their efforts, for the enlightening and salvation of its wretched nations."[105]

The Cape Colony was not recognized as a slave-supplying nation on international markets, although there was a strong covert regional trade in Khoisan captives.[106] Nonetheless, the colony utilized slaves and as such was liable to the rhetoric turned by abolitionists against other slave-holding societies. Several of the earliest missionaries came to south Africa predisposed to condemn its white inhabitants – and to apply the language of abolition to their treatment of indigenous peoples as well as of those who had been formally enslaved. Van der Kemp ended his autobiography with a condemnation of the lot of slaves in the Cape Colony: "those unfortunate creatures, which according to the rights of this miserable country are sold as beasts, and which with their posterity are kept in an endless slavery by those monsters who call themselves Christians, and of which some in reality are."

He testified to the custom of having slave women raped until they produced offspring:

Of all this inhumanity a stranger arriving at the Cape seldom hears anything, the slave owners themselves taking care continually to bawl in his ears how kindly and paternally they treat their slaves and endeavouring to prevent the slave from saying anything of the conduct of their masters ... I will not speak of these murders which these unfortunate persons commit in order to release their relatives from that state of slavery in which they know they will be kept if their lives should be spared: yet I cannot conceal what a female slave told me after I had gained her confidence, how mothers were accustomed to run pins into the brains of their newly born children that they might speedily and without fear of detection deprive them of their lives and deliver from a state of wretched and cruel slavery.[107]

This account was clearly the product of Van der Kemp's personal experience, since he purchased the liberty of several slaves and married one. Against Van der Kemp's outrage, one must counterbalance the fact that at least one director of the LMS held slaves through a family estate in the West Indies; he was forced to resign but it clearly was possible to be an evangelical and to accept slavery. Nonetheless, abolitionist debates and assumptions had a deep impact on evangelicals between the 1790s and the final abolition of slavery, and many of the same people promoted both missions and abolition. Abolitionist literature also, however, tended to portray Africans in general as passive victims, awaiting the saving work of Europeans. This fit well with missionaries' perceptions of themselves as heroic saviours of helpless Africans from the slavery of sin and Satan.

A second body of literature discussed the Cape Colony and its environs, mostly for the amusement of readers. Prior to the first British occupation of 1795, few British had spent significant time at the Cape and fewer still had had the chance to observe the Khoisan outside the confines of the Dutch settlement. Nonetheless, many sailors had had brief contact at least with the relatively impoverished Khoisan around the port of Cape Town. Additional information came from a variety of continental accounts, mostly Dutch. The most prominent of these were synthesized in such popular English-language compendia as the *New General Collection of Voyages and Travels*, published by Thomas Astley in 1745–47, or the *Universal History*, which appeared between 1736 and 1765 in sixty-five octavo volumes.[108] The accounts in these two anthologies were favourable, especially in Astley's work which drew heavily on the relatively sympathetic (if unreliably translated) Peter Kolbe;[109] both, however, were self-consciously written against the grain of popular prejudice. The editor of Astley's section on the "Hottentots" anticipated that the reader would "be both surprised and pleased with the agreeable Variety he finds in the Manners and Customs of these people; whom the Ignorance or Malice of most former Authors had represented as Creatures but one Degree removed from Beasts, and with scarce any Thing human about them except the Shape."[110]

Many superficial physical differences encouraged this derogatory European view: Europeans found the Khoekhoe language almost impossible to master, were immediately repulsed by the grease with

which Khoekhoe smeared themselves as protection against the sun, and
disliked habits such as eating lice from their own bodies (the early
Khoekhoe, apparently, were equally disgusted by the European taste
for green vegetables, which they considered cattle food).[111] As the *Universal History* put it bluntly, "our English seamen who have touched at
the Cape, could never be reconciled to the Hottentots, but always considered them as the nastiest and most brutal people in the world. This
is chiefly owing to their ill smell, occasioned by their greasing themselves continually ..."[112] The revisionist *New General Collection of
Voyages* attempted to enrol the Khoekhoe in the ranks of noble savages, after offering a detailed and sympathetic account of Khoekhoe
political groupings which tried to correct the impression of animalism:
"In short, the Integrity of the Hottentots, their Strictness and Celerity
in the Execution of Justice, and their Chastity, are equaled by few
Nations. An amiable and charming simplicity of Manners adorns all
their Actions. Numbers of them have given it as a Reason for their not
harkening to Christianity, that they were hindered by the Envy,
Avarice, Lust and Injustice, which they saw so prevalent amongst those
who professed it."[113] Rousseau, in fact, incorporated the Khoekhoe
into a lengthy footnote drawn from Kolbe in the *Discours sur l'origine
de l'inégalité* (1754) in which he discussed their physical superiority to
civilized man.[114]

Nonetheless, the Khoekhoe failed to be accepted as potentially noble
savages with the same enthusiasm as the Amerindian or the distant
Tahitian.[115] Accumulated prejudices were too strong, as the well-established use of the term "Hottentot" as a blank emblem of savagery
attests. The eighteenth-century attitude is perhaps better summed up
by Lord Chesterton's description of Samuel Johnson as no more than
a "respectable Hottentot."[116] Indeed, as Nigel Penn has observed, it
was a "time-honoured tradition" for Europeans to perceive "those
beyond the margins of Christian Europe as being, simultaneously, both
more 'savage' and more innocent than Europeans."[117] The idea that
the Khoekhoe (or other supposedly "primitive" people) were savages
was the mirror image of the idea that they were innocent: both categories removed them from the domain of the ordinary and remade the
Khoekhoe as the exotic "other," functioning to provide symbols to illuminate the nature of the observer's society.

The vogue in the second half of the eighteenth century for categorizing and ranking societies according to their level of economic
progress – an intellectual trend emanating above all from the Scottish Enlightenment and writers such as David Hume, Adam Smith,
and Adam Ferguson – did further damage to the reputation of the

Khoekhoe. As pastoralists who did not appear to have "advanced" economically at all through history, the "Hottentots" were almost invariably placed at the bottom of the different ladders of societies worked out by a number of social theorists. William Marsden, for example, in his 1783 *History of Sumatra*, seems to have been typical in placing at the top of his fivefold division of peoples "the refined nations of Europe," and at the bottom the Hottentots, "who exhibit a picture of mankind in its rudest and most humiliating aspect."[118]

An idea that persisted in both favourable and unfavourable accounts was that the Khoekhoe were somehow wilder even than other "primitive" peoples and therefore resistant to westernization. "They are so fond of their own country, and the sweets of a vagabond life, that there is no getting the better of their invincible reluctance to adopt the European manners and customs," avowed the *Universal History*. The author went on to tell the story of an infant who was adopted by a governor of the Cape, richly clothed, taught several languages, brought up as a Christian, and sent to work as an imperial bureaucrat at the "Indies." On his employer's death, the boy returned to the Cape in a sheepskin. Visiting his white relatives, he gave back his European clothes, and said: "'Be so kind, sir, as to take notice, that I for ever renounce this apparel. I likewise for ever renounce the Christian religion. It is my firm resolution to live and die in the religion, manners, and customs of my ancestors. All the favour I ask from you, is to leave me the collar and the hanger I wear; I shall keep them for your sake.' These words were scarce out of his mouth, when he took to his heels, and was out of sight, nor did he ever appear among the Europeans again."[119] This fable, with its overtones of the fairy child returning to fairyland, is remarkable both for its assumption of the equal intellect of the Khoekhoe (an idea that was to weaken as the century progressed) and for its analysis of "savagery" as a somehow ontologically separate state from that of European culture: the Khoekhoe were to be neither despised nor lived with.

A second persistent stereotype, closely linked to that of wildness, was that the Khoekhoe were lazy and therefore preferred idleness to self-improvement. The "prevailing Passion" of laziness, wrote Kolbe, "rules equally their Minds and Bodies. Reasoning with them is Working, and Working is the Capital Plague of Life. Though they are daily Witnesses of the Benefits and Pleasures arising from Industry, nothing but the utmost Necessity can reduce them to work. Their Love of Indolence and Liberty is their All; Compulsion is Death to them."[120] As Scottish Enlightenment notions gained ground, an older sense of the impossibility of westernizing Khoekhoe, owing to their laziness and wildness, remained. The implication, in a colonial setting, was that if the

Khoekhoe could not advance and assimilate, then the tide of history not only justifiably might, but almost inevitably would, sweep them aside.

A subgenre of travel literature was that of the scientific-exploration narrative. Urged on, and often sponsored, by scientific or geographical societies, such as Sir Joseph Banks's African Association in Britain, men such as Anders Sparrman, William Paterson, François Le Vaillant, and William Burchell studied the botany and zoology of the Cape. Local peoples were often described as part of the flora. The genre encouraged the author to take the position of all-knowing scientific commentator. Nonetheless, the works of John Barrow and of Le Vaillant, at least, did include relatively sympathetic accounts of the sufferings of the Khoisan under white colonization.

At the same time, such accounts often reinforced with the weight of science the notion of the intellectual vacuity of the savage. Neither "Boshies-men" nor "Hottentots" were "sensible of the existence of any Being, who is the origin and ruler of all things," although they gullibly entertained superstitions about magic and the power of "conjurers." "We are poor stupid creatures," Sparrman reported Khoekhoe as saying. "There is no doubt," Sparrman nevertheless believed, "that the Hottentots might be easily converted to the Christian faith: but it is much to be doubted, whether any body will ever trouble themselves with the conversion of these plain, honest people, unless it should appear to have more connexion than it seems at present with political advantages."[121] The "scientific travellers," in sum, did not ignore the political situation of the Khoekhoe but portrayed them as intellectually unformed.

A third source of information and beliefs about southern Africa was the developing library of missionary accounts, whose assumptions tended to overlap with those of abolitionist material. The Unitas Fratrum preceded the LMS in south Africa. The first mission was founded in 1737 by the German-speaking butcher Georg Schmidt among the Hessequa of the Western Cape, He was forced to abandon the mission in 1743, because of colonial objections to his baptizing converts and to aspects of his theology.[122] In 1792 three Moravian missionaries recommenced Schmidt's abandoned mission; Schmidt's station of Baviaanskloof would be renamed Genadendal. An LMS missionary reading the Moravian *Periodical Accounts* before arriving would have received descriptions such as this one of the Western Cape Hessequa, drawing on an earlier account by Schmidt:

The Hottentots are of a phlegmatic disposition, and sleep much in the daytime. In a moonlight night they amuse themselves with dancing, caper-cutting, and singing, and at the same time watch over their flocks ... They neither plant, sow, nor cultivate the ground, but move with their cattle from place to place wherever they can find the greatest quantity of provender. There they set up five or six tents under the control of a captain. They have neither divine worship nor any ceremonies, and seem to believe nothing but that there is a great Lord of all, whom they call *Tui hqua*, and a devil called *Ghauna*, of whom however they do not seem afraid. The Hottentot word for heaven is *chuma*.[123]

Moravian accounts almost fifty years later revealed considerable decay in the position of the Hessequa – prophetically enough for later LMS missionaries. Farmers had taken all the good land, and the Khoekhoe were largely obliged to work for the Dutch; they also now seem to have been able to speak Dutch. Vehettge Tikkuie, baptized Magdalena by Schmidt, described the change in her people's circumstances: "At that time the Hottentots were not so poverty-struck, as at present; they had much cattle and meat, and milk in abundance. The country was likewise better inhabited. Upon inquiry, from what so great a change could have originated, she answered, that as soon as George Schmidt returned to Europe, the Hottentots went to work with the peasants, and entirely forsook this place."[124]

In conclusion, missionaries probably had a loose conception of the "Hottentots" as the particularly savage inhabitants of a miserable continent. LMS propaganda emphasized how misguided a belief in "noble savages" was, so missionaries were probably prepared to side with the more derogatory accounts of Africans. As Van der Kemp pushed past the boundaries of the colony towards the Xhosa, LMS directors John Eyre and Joseph Hardcastle tried to strengthen his resolve: "He hath placed you amidst Dens of Lions and Mountains of Leopards, and what is more to be feared, among Men more savage many of them, and brutish than the beasts of the field, but Daniel was as safe in the Den, as in the Palace."[125] A few accounts emphasized the deleterious impact of white colonization, but these accounts were less widely diffused than the popular stereotype of primitive savagery.

JOURNEYS

A final set of stereotypical expectations arose from evangelical theology itself, as well as from the related narrative myths of evangelical popular culture. One of the most powerful of these narrative myths, which reflected many evangelical ideas about the "savage," was that of the journey. Missionary journeys fired the imagination of missionaries and mission supporters alike.

There were imaginative and concrete links between explorers and missionaries. For example, Sir Joseph Banks, first secretary of the

Association for Promoting the Discovery of the Interior Parts of Africa, founded in 1788,[126] a companion of James Cook, and the president of the Royal Society, was an early patron of missions. It was he who wrote to the acting governor of the Cape Colony, Major-General Francis Dundas, on behalf of the LMS.[127] Not surprisingly, therefore, LMS directors Hardcastle and Eyre thought of Van der Kemp as an explorer and eagerly asked him to send home information concerning the African interior: "Animals, Birds or fishes, described accurately – Trees, fruit, flowers. Bark either medicinal, tinctorial or if of unknown quality, possessing some strong tokens of Energy. The Habits and Manners of the natives you have conversed with – what intelligence you have received of the Nations around you ... Is there any animal resembling the imagined Unicorn ..."[128] Van der Kemp obliged, writing a preliminary grammar and vocabulary of the Xhosa language by August 1799 and making observations of the longitudes until the mission's pocket watch broke and had to be sent home for repairs.[129]

At the same time, the missionary journey had transcendent significance. The voyage by which the missionary passed from his former life to the status of emissary to the heathen was a vital stage in his spiritual journey through the testing ground of life to heaven: it was not insignificant that Bunyan's *Pilgrim's Progress*, the archetypal pilgrimage narrative, was one of the books most widely read by eighteenth-century working-class evangelicals, after the Bible itself.[130] The missionary journey was part of humanity's journey through divinely ordained time to the end of time: movement through space echoed and enabled the transcendent trajectory through time.

The journey was also a daring military raid into enemy territory, staged to rescue Satan's captives. From the beginning it was thus powerfully associated with metaphors of liberty and release from bondage. "From Greenland's icy mountains,/ From India's coral strand," began one 1820 missionary hymn. "Where Afric's sunny fountain/ Roll down their golden sand;/ From many an ancient river,/ From many a palmy plain, /They call us to deliver /Their land from Error's chain."[131] Van der Kemp looked on the wars that greeted him as the "strugglings of Satan with a view to exclude us and the gospel of Christ from Caffraria, and on the side of the Lord as a trial of our faith in him."[132] The secretary of the LMS echoed the military metaphor, hoping that Van der Kemp had "experienced the faithful and powerful protection and guidance of the Great head of the Church under whose auspices and benediction you have gone forth – and whose precious and saving name you will make known to those miserable Captives of Satan who are in the chains of darkness among the shades of Death."[133]

The moment of departure as well as the voyage itself were often romanticized in missionary literature. "About five o'clock the next morning the missionaries embarked at Blackwall, multitudes flocking around them to take their leave," stated the LMS in describing the departure of its first group of missionaries to the South Seas. The missiosnaries themselves reported that, "and as we sailed down the river, singing the praises of God, the scene became still more deeply affecting. The sailors in the different ships as we passed viewed us with silent surprise, and the serious people on both sides the river, waving their hats, bid these holy servants of God a lasting farewell." As expectations about what a missionary should feel and do became more entrenched, with the ever wider diffusion of missionary texts such as sermons, journals, and popular biographies, missionaries echoed the conventions of the genre in their own diaries and memoirs. The grandiose rhetoric with which they tended to record their journeys to the mission field doubtless reflected the eagerness with which the mission diary was begun, however soon to be superseded by terser and wearier daily comments. At the same time, such rhetoric was considered suitable for a sacred passage from one form of life to another, from the kingdom of God to that of Satan. George Burder lapsed into apostrophe as he boarded ship for south Africa in 1815: "Farewell all friends in that town and on my native land. I do not leave you with regret but with joy. I go to proclaim a Saviour's love to the heathen who reside in the interior of Africa." And as the ship pulled away he proclaimed: "Farewell ye happy shores, blest with the light of the gospel. May the shores of Africa soon be favoured with the same and followers of Jesus adorn that benighted country."[134]

Such rhetoric around the missionary journey entrenched the central idea, underscored by Doug Stuart in his doctoral thesis, that the heathen remained in the grip of original sin. More, the very lands of the heathen were in the hands of the devil. LMS sermons of the 1790s and early 1800s stressed again and again that the romantic view of the savage as noble was false. In practice, a number of missionaries would prove to have ambiguous views on this very point, particularly in the heat of political battle. The rhetoric of departure, however, demanded that the captives of Satan be miserable and their territory a testing ground for the missionary himself, who came to offer salvation even as he earned his own in this most extreme of confrontations.

By the turn of the century, the Khoisan of the Eastern Cape were in a seemingly permanent state of crisis. They were ready to try new strategies. LMS envoys, on the other hand, were to be confounded in their original expectations but were to prove flexible enough to find Satan in a colonial setting as well as in a savage wilderness. The stage was set for an opening encounter.

3 War, Conversion, and the
Politics of Interpretation

CONVERSION AND STATUS

At the turn of the nineteenth century in southern Africa, the question of who could be a Christian was politically explosive. Christianity was an important token of belonging to the "white" community.[1] This mattered in particular in the frontier districts as ethnic tensions flared in struggles over land. The colony itself was widely called the land of the Christians, and both colonial inhabitants and at least some Africans beyond the colony thought of "the Christians" as a political entity. For example, in 1801 the Xhosa chief Ngqika tried to avoid disciplining cattle raiders from other chieftaincies by questioning why a great nation ("eene magtige Natie") such as the "Christenen" needed his help to chase out cattle raiders.[2]

At the same time, however, the very permeability of ethnic boundaries, whether through sex, baptism, or through shifting political alliances in a politically chaotic open frontier zone, exacerbated tension over existing markers of identity. The lines of ethnicity blurred in practice. "Christian" farmers depended on "Hottentots" for many things, from herding their cattle to providing sexual partners to killing for them on commandoes against the San. This state of colonial dependence on a servile class, indeed the very need to create and maintain a servile class, doubtless in itself deepened the need of colonists to maintain social distinctions.

In the 1790s, many white frontier farmers felt insecure about how little access they themselves and their children had to schoolteachers and, especially, priests, guardians of the gates to membership in the "Christian" community. On Van der Kemp's initial arduous journey through the eastern frontier districts of the colony as he tried to discover a way to reach the Xhosa of Ngqika, sometimes travelling with Dutch farmers, the missionary found that frontier settlers had an "incredibly great" desire to hear the gospel. Many came seven or nine hours on horseback to hear him preach. There was an evident field of labour for five or six itinerant preachers from Holland in this land without priests, he reported; the farming families would readily support them.[3] In the same year, J.J. Kicherer and William Edwards similarly found that settlers flocked to hear them as they travelled to Sak River through the Karoo in the northern reaches of the colony. According to Kicherer, some colonists came "four days journey to hear the word of God, and to partake of the Lord's supper; for many of these people have no church which they can attend nearer than Rodesand, which though eight days journey distant they sometimes attend."[4]

In a 1779 petition to the VOC, early Patriots from the Western Cape region bitterly complained that poverty drove their sons to live with the Khoekhoe if they wanted wives. Even without this, the children of the inhabitants of the interior were, the Patriots worried, "effectively deprived of all proper education, because poverty prevents many parents from employing a schoolmaster, and the schoolmasters who are to be found there are mostly persons who, through their incompetence or bad conduct, could not manage nearer to the capital and have to teach at a place far away from there."[5] The impoverished farmers "look with compassion to the fate of their children," urged a subsequent Patriot petition in 1784 (written substantially by the Cape-born Dutchman Hendrik Swellengrebel, son of a former governor): they must see "the approach of a complete bastardization of morals from so primitive a life-style in the veld, and this in their own beloved progeny," and the rise, through the union of impoverished whites and Khoekhoe, of a "completely degenerate nation, which might become just as dangerous for the colony as the Bushman-Hottentots now are."[6] Whether or not these petitions fully reflected the views of Eastern Cape frontier settlers at the time, a number of Dutch speakers clearly felt anxiety about the lack of education and religious instruction among more distant settlers. They also worried about what they saw as the related phenomenon of sexual relationships between whites and Khoisan, which does indeed appear to have been widespread.[7] In a climate of social anxiety, at a time of economic difficulty and ethnic warfare, few white farmers in the late 1790s and early 1800s proved in a mood to forego their own chances for priests and schoolteachers in exchange for missionaries to the "heathen."

Popular anxiety over the simultaneous flexibility and necessity of ethnic boundaries in a "white" society dependent on "nonwhite" labour was reflected in attitudes to the baptism of children of unions in which at least one parent was not Christian. Robert Shell has shown that the last international meeting of the Reformed churches, the 1618 Synod of Dort, was not able to issue a canonical opinion on the issue of "whether children, born of heathen parents, who had become members of Christian households, ought to be baptised, when the householder promised to bring the child up in the Christian faith?"[8] Nonetheless, the eighteen diverse opinions issued by Reformed authorities clearly indicated that baptism was a household responsibility (and therefore a choice of the household head). Statements included, *inter alia,* the key opinion of Swiss theologian Giovanni Deodatus, which would become orthodoxy at the Cape and be confirmed in the 1770 revision of the Statutes of India by the Council of Batavia: baptized slaves could no longer be sold. Although the VOC baptized company slaves, this prohibition was a significant block to the baptism of slaves by private owners. Shell further shows that the already low rate of slave baptism fell at the Cape throughout the eighteenth century, and that objections against slave baptism were extended by farmers to objections to baptism of the Khoisan as well. At the same time, there was a split between patrician urban circles and rural areas: some support for slave baptism was found in Cape Town, while rural settlers tended fiercely to oppose the baptism of the "heathen," whether slave or Khoisan. In Shell's view, the settlement came to be divided between "a religious patrician minority in the towns and a recusant patriarchal rump in the rural areas."[9] In my opinion, rural settlers at the turn of the century were also "religious," even if their form of Calvinism was a popular reinvention. They were also affected by the late-eighteenth-century and early-nineteenth-century religious revival. Nonetheless, favourable attitudes to the baptism of nonwhites were indeed mostly found among urban patricians and rarely among rural settlers.

As we shall shortly see, the issue was further complicated by the willingness of some rural settlers to look to nonwhite ministers and preachers in the absence of white. Perhaps this reflected a conviction that Christianity was powerful. Christian settlers wanted to deny *power* to their dependants but once a "nonwhite" person had acquired spiritual authority and power, "whites" were willing to appropriate some in return – just as they also used Khoekhoe medicines, snake healers, and midwifery techniques. In other words, the resistance of the farming community to the conversion and baptism of their nonwhite dependents and military enemies did not necessarily spring from a *lack* of "religion" so much as a different conception of Christianity. Their resistance may have been paradoxically a sign that they took the power of Christianity seriously.

Be that as it may, there was, less ambiguously, an important religious revival in certain Dutch-speaking circles in the 1780s and 1790s, centred initially at Cape Town. Two key figures in this revival were the evangelical Calvinist ministers Helperus Ritzema van Lier and Michiel Christiaan Vos; a number of women also played important roles.[10] Van Lier's sister, Catharina Allegonda van Lier, was an important pietist, whose diary and letters, published posthumously in 1804, were widely read at the Cape. She was engaged to be married to J.J. Kicherer at the time of her early death – although Christina Landman questions (albeit without positive evidence) whether the ambitious young missionary did not trump up a supposed engagement after Catharina's death in order to justify his publication of her papers.[11] The Cape revival reflected European trends and is evidence of intellectual linkages between the Netherlands and the Cape. The Van Liers were Dutch, while Vos was Cape-born but had been educated in the Netherlands. They had all been deeply affected themselves by the late-eighteenth-century evangelical revival in Europe. Indeed, the minister John Newton, that key figure in the early British missionary movement, corresponded with van Lier and, according to Landman, "strongly influenced" him.[12] Both Vos and van Lier adhered to the Dutch "Continuing Reformation," or *Nadere Reformatie*, tradition, which stressed that true conversion was necessary before an individual was saved and decried the mere following of church forms without a changed heart. The Continuing Reformation tradition urged missionary activity among both the heathen and the nominally Christian, and a number of the pious at the Cape enthusiastically supported missions, including Vos and the formidable widow Machtelt Smit (known to the British as Matilda Smith). Indeed, Vos rushed to Cape Town from Roodezand in order to greet the first incoming LMS missionaries.[13]

Vos had both European and Asian ancestry and thus was presumably of partial slave descent. Similarly, one of Machtelt Smit's grandmothers was a freed slave. The widespread religious influence of both among the white Dutch and their clear incorporation into the "white" community underscores that racial lines could be crossed and that Christianity was not perceived as exclusively white.[14] On the contrary, the examples of Vos and Smit reinforce my argument that the fact that baptism permitted entry into the "white" community helps explain the deep anxiety which a movement aimed at mass conversion aroused among frontier farmers dependent for their livelihood on a distinction between heathen servants and Christian masters. The boundaries had to be policed precisely because they were, at moments, permeable.

Interestingly, both Vos and Smit worked to educate and convert slaves, and both were slave-owners themselves: on Van der Kemp's urging, the LMS would lend "Maart," a slave of Vos's who changed his name to Verhoogd, the money for his emancipation, while Van der Kemp would require Smit to abandon her sewing school at Bethelsdorp because she was unwilling to emancipate her slave, Daniel. In 1812 Vos successfully petitioned British governor Sir John Cradock to repeal the 1770 ruling that baptized slaves become inalienable. Evangelical enthusiasm at the Cape did not preclude slave ownership, but the converted descendants of manumitted slaves were nonetheless accepted into the ranks of evangelicals, at least in Cape Town, just as they were incorporated into Cape society more broadly.

The 1799 foundation of the South African Missionary Society (SAMS) gave proof of local evangelical enthusiasm. Shortly after his arrival at the Cape, Van der Kemp read a letter of exhortation from the LMS to local Christians urging the formation of a missionary society. Vos had already been thinking along similar lines, and he and others responded enthusiastically. The new missionary society was run mostly by better-off local notables among the pious from Cape Town and Stellenbosch, including Bartholemeus Schonken and V.A. Schoonberg.[15] At the very beginning of the LMS mission, SAMS, the LMS, and the Netherlands Missionary Society all cooperated closely. Van der Kemp would, however, later quarrel fiercely with SAMS for what he saw as its focus on whites at the expense of the "heathen."

These various controversies about the social implications of baptism and the desirability of missionary activity had concrete material implications for the children of unions between white men and Khoekhoe or "free black" women. Reformed clergymen at the Cape would not baptize an infant were the father not present to acknowledge the child.[16] In both rural and urban areas, white men who refused to present for baptism their own illegitimate offspring by slave or Khoisan women were denying their children full kinship with them and equal civic rights. In particular, not having been baptized and thus publically acknowledged precluded nonwhite offspring from the equal share in their father's estate which was theirs under Roman-Dutch law.[17] As Robert Shell argues, there was a four-tier hierarchy of religious identity in colonial Cape society: "Christians, Muslims, pagan slaves, and unbaptized bastards."[18] Such "unbaptized bastards" furnished an eager market for full Christian conversion by means other than paternal acknowledgment.

Regardless of divisions among whites over the conversion of the "heathen," many colonial Khoisan, especially the children of the "degenerate nation" of white fathers and Khoisan mothers, proved eager to gain the status associated with Christianity. Meanwhile, in Britain itself, these colonial Khoisan were considered to be archetypal primitives. The existence of a "baster" community was widely ignored. The very fact that Khoisan *could* be converted to Christianity was a source of wonder, not to mention a political symbol that the missionary societies were eager to deploy against their many opponents. In all these contexts, conversion had political connotations.

THE FIRST YEARS OF THE LMS

The four LMS missionaries who disembarked in Cape in March 1799 quickly split into two teams the better to confront the massive task before them. It was decided that one team was to travel through the Eastern Cape frontier districts to try to settle among the Xhosa. It was originally hoped that the other would travel to Klein Namaqualand. The news of fierce fighting in the region threw doubt on this proposal, however. Unexpectedly, three San captains from the northern frontier district of the Roggeveld then arrived in Cape Town.

These captains were known to Van der Kemp by their Dutch names, Vigiland, Orlam, and Slaparm.[19] One, Orlam, was in fact of Korana background. As Nigel Penn suggests, the names Orlam and Slaparm imply a degree of exposure to western culture.[20] The captains had travelled this long distance as a result of peace talks between some San groups just beyond the frontier and local white colonists. The talks had been initiated by the frontier farmer Floris Visser, with government support, after a long period of debilitating warfare and cattle raiding. The pious Visser had proposed that the San cease cattle raiding, that in exchange local colonists halt commando raids against them, and that the San accept a Christian mission in their midst.[21] Colonists and the mission together were to persuade the San to become pastoralists, and colonists were to help the process by giving the San livestock. Accordingly, the three captains expressed to the recently arrived missionaries "their ardent desire to leave off all acts of criminal violence for ever, and to be instructed in the knowledge and service of the God of the Christians." They stayed at least briefly with the missionaries, "and adhere so close to us," Van der Kemp reported, "that we find it difficult to separate ourselves from them."[22] One of the captains visited Lady Anne Barnard, the wife of the colonial secretary. She reported that Captain "Philan" had a "countenance" which was "good-humoured to the greatest degree, with more character in it than the Hottentot face, which rarely has more than gentleness to boast of" and that his "wrist was as delicate as that of a ladys, yet when he bent his bow, it seemed to be strong, and the wildness of his figure was striking."[23]

The missionaries saw the arrival of the captains as a "providential call," downplaying the politics involved. Edwards quickly determined to respond to providence. Although the precise details are unclear, the missionaries cast lots to determine his companion. The use of lots recalled the practices of the Moravians, who also deployed lots to allocate mission fields and to make important decisions. The lot chose Kicherer.[24] Accordingly, the entire group left Cape Town on 22 May, to divide later on the road. The LMS *Transactions* reported that "on the morning of their departure, their lodgings were crowded with friends to take leave of them, and many of the slaves to whom they had ministered with blessings came with little presents of fruit, handkerchiefs &c., expressing their grateful sense of their labours during their residence at the Cape; with all these, and the Directors of the South African Missionary Society, they bowed their knees to the God and Father of our Lord Jesus Christ, and they reluctantly parted."[25]

The group travelled together to Roodezand. They stayed there until the end of June with Vos, who ordained Edwards and Edmond. They also visited the Moravians at Baviaan's Kloof, later Genadendal. As Nigel Penn puts it, the missionaries were thereby "paying their respects to the pioneers in the field."[26] Once the group split up, Kicherer and Edwards headed for the northwestern frontier of the colony, while Edmond and Van der Kemp crossed a zone of sporadic and undeclared warfare to try to reach Ngqika beyond the eastern frontier.[27] The latter two were guided by a Moravian Khoekhoe man, Bruntjee, "a famous elephant hunter."[28] Kicherer and Edwards were later to quarrel so badly that Edwards, who soon left his and Kicherer's first station, Blydevooruitzigt, to establish an English-language mission farther into the interior, would by early 1801 be trying unsuccessfully to get Kicherer dismissed from the LMS for immoral behaviour.[29] Instead, Edwards was himself dismissed for illegal trading.[30] The Sak River mission at Sak River became closely identified with Kicherer, in consequence. Nonetheless, Kicherer had crucial assistance at various points from others, probably including Floris Visser's /Xam-speaking son Gerrit (as Penn plausibly speculates), Cornelis Kramer, a colonist sponsored by SAMS as a teacher in the Roodezand district and allowed by his sponsors to help the mission, and, especially, the Dutch-speaking Khoekhoe man Willam Fortuin and his San wife, Catharina Dorothea.[31] Meanwhile in Xhosaland, Edmond, traumatized by the violence around him would soon abandon the mission. The leadership of the Xhosa mission is therefore (more fairly) identified with Van der Kemp alone.

Despite the rhetoric of the missionary journey – ideally heroic and solitary – none of these missionaries travelled alone. Quite the opposite. They moved through dangerous territory in the company of large groups. It is an apt symbol for the fact that, from the start, missionaries were dependent on Khoisan assistants and local patrons, both black and white, and embedded in networks of power.

Kicherer and Edwards travelled to the Sak River region from Floris Visser's farm at the outermost edge of the Karoo, "accompanied by their generous host Mr. Fischer, with several other Farmers and their servants, to the number of about fifty, having in their train six waggons full of provisions, sixty oxen, and near two hundred sheep, the kind presents of the Dutch settlers."[32] Van der Kemp and Edmond moved towards Xhosaland through the contested territory of the Zuurveld, as they sought permission from Ngqika to approach further. Conflict raged on all sides, although the details escaped the often bewildered missionaries, who did not understand Xhosa politics. The followers of Ndlambe and Ngqika were at war; Xhosa in the Zuurveld, including the followers of Ndlambe, were "exasperated against the English and Dutch colonists"[33] and attacked the white Zuurveld colonists, many of whom fled; Khoisan servants had begun an uprising against their former masters and mistresses at the beginning of the year and many remained allied with the Xhosa; the 1799 Patriot rebellion had only recently been put down by the British, and another rebellion by local Dutch-speaking settlers was on the verge of breaking out. In this turbulent, and confused, environment, Van der Kemp and Edmond initially travelled for protection with a large group of white colonists and their Khoisan servants looking for new places to live, the farmers having fled before joint Xhosa-Khoisan incursions into their previous territory. Van der Kemp does not specify numbers, but the group included more than fifty Boer families and was large enough to hold off thousands of Xhosa assailants by arranging their waggons into a laager and using their guns. Since Van der Kemp further records that on the entire journey the group lost "2,700 oxen and more than 20,000 sheep," this was almost certainly a very substantial migration of people moving with vast quantities of stock.[34] Van der Kemp described them as "volks planters." Van der Kemp and Edmond left the large group at the Sneeuwberg mountains. Still needing protection, the two missionaries temporarily attached themselves to Johannes van der Walt before proceeding farther. Van der Walt was a frontier farmer who had an entourage of seventy-four San and had recently supported a more conciliatory policy towards the San.[35] He was also, ironically, to be one of the commanders of a large group of rebels who would, as we shall see, two years later attack Van der Kemp and his patron Maynier in the town of Graaff-Reinet. In early 1801, after his mission had faltered, Van der Kemp fled Xhosaland without Ngqika's knowledge in the motley company of "4 so-called Christians, 2 women, 2 children. 13 bastard children, 1 Xhosa man and a woman, three young Xhosa girls, 4 Hottentots, 6 Hottentot women, about 15 Hottentot children, a young man of the Tambookie nation, 5 English deserters, a German and a slave." The group travelled with three waggons and had, in addition to sheep and goats, 300 head of horned cattle and about 25 horses.[36] In all of these movements one notes how important it was for men who wanted influence, as for travellers who wanted protection, to accumulate as large a number as possible of allies and dependants, whether temporary or permanent. Solitary heroism was almost impossible.

Neither Kicherer's mission to the San nor that of Van der Kemp to the Xhosa would last more than a few years. Both missions have been well chronicled by historians and I will not reproduce their work here.[37] Some significant patterns, however, characterized these abortive early missions which would recur in later, more enduring efforts. Both missions began because African patrons were at least to some extent interested in political alliances with white colonists. At Blydevooruitzigt, San leaders used the mission to explore peace with the colony. When this alliance began to fall apart, San fell away from the mission. Vigiland, for one, became actively hostile. He killed his fellow captain Orlam, incited other San against the mission, and later tried to stab Kramer. At one point in the ensuing conflict, Kicherer managed to get Vigiland arrested by a commando raised by Visser's political rivals; Vigiland escaped but not before exclaiming (in Penn's translation), "What are the missionaries doing in his country why don't they stay with the other Dutch people he could not endure the Dutch living in his country."[38] The mission remained only because other San continued to support it and because of the power of the colonial state behind Kicherer.

In the case of the Xhosa, the Rharhabe chief Ngqika sporadically pursued alliances with white colonists in the 1790s as he struggled with the breakaway chiefdoms of the Zuurveld and with the rebel Ndlambe and his followers. Ngqika's desire for a mission was doubtless linked to diplomatic hopes. For example, in August 1799 Ngqika delivered a message to Van der Kemp affirming that he wished to protect the Cape settlement against the rebellious Xhosa; Van der Kemp jubilantly, and correctly, took this as a signal that his way was clear to establish a mission.[39]

African leaders were not solely interested in missions for diplomatic purposes, even if they were far from predisposed to Christianity. The relationship between Ngqika and Van der Kemp seems to have been marked by wariness on both sides, especially as the missionary suspected the chief of wanting to have him killed at an early point in the mission.[40] Nonetheless, once Van der Kemp was finally living near

Ngqika's great place, the chief saw the missionary as a possible source of earthly power through his contact with unseen forces. This was in keeping with the Xhosa conception that spiritual power resided in many different places, pervading a world in which there was no distinction between "natural" and supernatural." At a time of drought, the chief and other key advisers frequently asked the missionary to pray for rain, probably reflecting the Xhosa practice of employing liminal outsiders such as the San as rainmakers in addition to Xhosa specialists. Among others, Ngqika's mother, described by Van der Kemp as "the chief witch for procuring rain in this country," told Van der Kemp that "she could not make it rain in ye land as ye hole from which it was procured, was stopped by some malevolent people, and requested that I would make it rain."[41] At the end of October 1800, Van der Kemp finally yielded to a delegation from Ngqika bearing payment of two cows and some calves (which Van der Kemp refused). The Dutchman's prayers were rewarded the following day by a great downpour which eventually flooded the king's house, accompanied by such thunder that the chief "let me know, that I should pray God that he never might hear more such tremendous thunder claps."[42] When Ngqika fell sick, he both had a witch put to death and asked Van der Kemp to pray for his recovery.[43] The chief also studied the alphabet with Van der Kemp. None of this meant that Ngqika saw Van der Kemp as a purveyor of a truth which excluded all others. At the same time, competition over rainmaking presaged later conflicts over access to sacred power between missionaries and African spiritual specialists in which the stakes would be higher as the exclusivity of Christian claims to truth became more widely recognized.[44]

Intermediaries maintained both missions. In the case of Kicherer's mission to the San, local and central colonial governments supported the mission, at least in the first instance. Governor Dundas thought that the missionaries might pacify the San and end regional warfare. Local colonists for a while lent their support with the same aim, hoping for a pliable labour force rather then enemies. They therefore gave the donations of livestock without which the mission could not have continued. On the other hand, Visser's political competitors tried to undermine the mission and Visser's policies in general. Other colonists tired of making donations of livestock and game as drought afflicted the area, game increasingly seemed to be hunted out, and the ecological crisis of the region generally worsened. In the case of Van der Kemp's mission to the Xhosa of Ngqika's community, Khoekhoe interpreters played a crucial role as religious mediators. There were also several white refugees from the colony, former rebels who had fled to Ngqika's court and hoped to create military alliances with him, includ-

ing Coenraad du Buys. At various points, these refugees were important as political intermediaries with the chief, although they were also
suspicious of Van der Kemp.

Another important sign for the future was that Khoekhoe (or, rather,
those defined as "Hottentots" by the colonists), so-called mixed-race
individuals, and the enslaved all proved more interested in Christianity than either the Sak River San or the Xhosa. Van der Kemp's few
early converts were for the most part female Khoisan dependants of
Xhosa and white men. They included Sarah, the wife of a Xhosa man,
and Maria, consort of a white refugee. At the Sak River, Khoisan and
"mixed-race" people gradually replaced the San for whom the mission
had originally been intended.

A further significant point is that Van der Kemp's early mission to
the Xhosa of Ngqika was as affected by the politics of colonialism as
was that of Kicherer and his colleagues to the San – although at this
point the Xhosa beyond the Zuurveld had far more room to manoeu-
vre than the San of the northern frontier zone. At the same time, Van
der Kemp, albeit on occasion a sharp observer of political struggle,
read his experiences primarily through the lens of his theology. For
example, he saw the violence of war all around him in 1799 as the
struggles of Satan to exclude the gospel from his kingdom. "Satan
seems therefore to be violently contesting our entry into Xhosaland,"
he observed to his nephew after a lengthy description of conflicts with
Xhosa groups and anxiety among Afrikaner refugees, "but we have a
more powerful master ..."[45] God and Satan clashed, devastating the
landscape in their fight over the christianization of Africa. Similarly,
Van der Kemp would reflect in 1801 that the further destruction of
Afrikaner homesteads by Xhosa and Khoisan insurgents came from the
hand of God, raised to punish those who opposed the Christianization
of the heathen.[46]

Edmond appears to have had a less sanguine view of the several
occasions on which the missionaries' lives were in danger. After some
vacillation, he ultimately left Van der Kemp in Xhosaland because, he
said, of "great horror and trouble of mind from the time that we fled
before the Caffers from Bavian's River till I came to a resolution that I
will not stay in Caffreland as my heart is in Bengal." He found himself
unable to love the Xhosa.[47] The LMS directors saw this as a failure of
faith. "Poor Edmond's name is not mentioned in the letter perhaps they
have done with me before I have done with them," wrote Edmond
plaintively to a friend (probably Edwards) from the Cape when the
directors stopped writing to him. He added sadly that "Mrs. Jaffories
was married soon after we left London to Mr. Bowen your friend they
courted but a few days – I must now give up all thoughts of these

things."[48] And to the LMS directors he pleaded as he awaited a ship for India, "Dearly beloved Brethren pray for a poor wanderer."[49] Van der Kemp was made of sterner stuff. He believed that God protected him through multiple trials since he was the instrument of the introduction of Christianity to the heathen. From the very beginning, passionate evangelicals such as Van der Kemp imposed a theological narrative on a devastated landscape.

DISPLAY AND POWER: THREE CONVERTS IN LONDON

A thoroughly unexpected side-effect of J.J. Kicherer's Sak River mission and its problems was that in 1802 the ambitious young missionary decided to return to Europe, taking with him the converts Sara Fortuin, Martha Arendse, and Klaas van Rooij as living examples of the efficacy of missionary activity. These converts testified – one might say were displayed – in churches in Holland and Britain. Their experience underscores the power disparities in missions, as well as the crucial role of the politics of display in missionary activity.

The British press knew this trio as Martha Arendse and Mary and John van Rooy, the latter two being baptismal names.[50] Arendse was about fifty years old and a widow.[51] She had been born in Graaff-Reinet, of partial slave and partial Khoekhoe descent. According to Kicherer, she had worked earlier as a servant to a farmer's wife. The farmer's wife had taken Arendse with her on a trip to hear Kicherer, but the employer had forbidden the servant to listen, "as Christianity, she said, was not for Hottentots." Arendse nonetheless used to go and hear the singing at Kicherer's station and much wished to be able to understand the preaching. "This her mistress so resented that she beat her unmercifully with a large stick till the blood flowed from her head." Once Arendse's term of service expired, she accordingly left her mistress and went to live at Kicherer's station, where she was converted to Christianity. She later accompanied Kicherer from Sak River to the outskirts of Cape Town and worked there as his housekeeper.[52] The younger Sara Fortuin (or van Rooij) was described by Kicherer as "a very sprightly woman, loquacious and very lively in religion."[53] She had previously been married to another man, with whom she had a child before the man left her; she was now married to Van Rooij with whom she also had a child. Her mother was Khoekhoe while her father was of South East Asian slave descent.[54] She had agreed to come to Europe only after friends and relatives had been found to take care of her children. According to Karel Schoeman, she had at least five children and still had not seen three of them again by 1807.[55] Nonetheless,

Kicherer affirmed that she missed her children deeply.[56] Fortuin had earlier lived on a tobacco plantation from which Kicherer sometimes obtained the tobacco which undergirded his mission; she was told of his preaching by messengers from the station and travelled the 105 miles from the plantation to hear him.[57] Kicherer was at pains to point out that Klaas van Rooij was of entirely "Hottentot" descent, "geheel Van Hottentotse afkomst," although some other sources described him as a "Bastaard Hottentot" of partial slave background.[58] Both Klaas and Sara were from the Bokkeveld, a remote region of the Cape Colony renowned for its farmers' ill-treatment of slaves.[59] Despite these thoroughly colonial backgrounds, the group would be presented to British audiences as paradigmatic children of the wild whose Christianity proved the very possibility of converting the uncivilized primitive.

Why Kicherer decided to return to Europe at this juncture is somewhat unclear. Possibly he felt that his reputation had been besmirched by his bitter public quarrel with Edwards, including Edwards's accusations of sexual impropriety, even though Edwards was dismissed before Kicherer's departure.[60] Furthermore, Kicherer seems to have been depressed at some of the difficulties encountered in the mission. Kicherer himself claimed that, in the wake of his father's recent death, he wanted to care for his mother (with whom he had earlier lived in Holland), as well as to rebuild his shattered health after the vicissitudes of missionary work on a remote station and to discuss missionary affairs with the LMS.[61] The arrival of the group was in any case upsetting news for Kicherer's cash-strapped superiors. As Doug Stuart reminds us, by this juncture the LMS was struggling with such difficulties as travel problems during the Napoleonic Wars, the recent loss of the expensive missionary ship, the *Duff*, and the closure of the Otaheite (or Tahitian) mission in the South Seas.[62] The society did not provide home leave for its missionaries; indeed, as late as 1835, Kicherer's visit was recalled by embittered fellow missionaries unable to obtain home furloughs from the LMS.[63] Although both the Netherlands and the London missionary societies ultimately embraced the publicity opportunities offered by Kicherer's visit, their directors required considerable persuasion to accept Kicherer's return.

Whatever Kicherer's motives, reputable or otherwise, in coming to Europe, he brought "his" converts with him as a way of showing his work and establishing his good reputation among both Europeans and his own congregation. He had earlier introduced Arendse and the Van Rooijs to the Stellenbosch Missionary Society with similar aims. As T. Desch (secretary of the Stellenbosch Missionary Society after its split from the South African Missionary Society) observed, Kicherer "wished also that we should be eyewitnesses of the blessing, which he has upon his Labour, therefore he brought with him, three heathens natives of that land where he preaches the gospel of the cross, to which converted persons out of the heathens, he also would give occasion that they should be convinced, that the Christians here were united with them in the great main thing of Christianity, in order that they when they return might give witness to their countrymen."[64] Kicherer was using the Khoekhoe to further his own ends, and he did so through an act of display.

Unsurprisingly, Kicherer himself ascribed more agency to his converts. As he pleaded from Holland for the LMS directors to receive him, Kicherer argued that for three years the Khoisan had insisted on coming to Europe "in order to converse personally with the Society and others of the Lord's people on the subject of Salvation, and thus to be convinced, that they likewise held the same language I did." He further argued that "the poor creatures [his converts] are in constant danger to get entangled in errors and doubts thro' the great depravity of many of the white settlers that constantly aim at seducing my congregation by suggestions, that we do not preach unto them such a religion as the Europeans chose to believe." Kicherer's objections on the economic grounds of the expense of the trip to Europe were, he claimed, finally worn down.[65]

Doug Stuart has criticized an earlier account of mine concerning the motivation of the converts, claiming that I exaggerate their degree of agency in the face of Kicherer's overwhelming need to prove himself.[66] Stuart's thoughtful comments are a useful contribution to a larger debate about the agency and relative power of missionaries and converts, and his views have modified my own reading of these events. Obviously, there were huge power disparities between Kicherer and those who were essentially his dependants. Nonetheless, one might still seek to disentangle Kicherer's motivations from the much harder-to-recapture aims of his companions; the overwhelming imperatives of white power did not completely preclude the agency of Christian converts, even in this distasteful display. For example, Kicherer's claim that at least some among those to whom he preached wished to be convinced that European Christians "likewise held the same language I did" is not entirely implausible, given debates on the frontier about the meaning and ownership of Christianity, even though the main impetus for this voyage certainly came from Kicherer. Whatever the degree of agency on the part of Kicherer's south African hearers in planning this particular voyage, it was incontestably to their advantage to garner proof that Christianity was not the exclusive prerogative of local farmers. The challenge to missionary authority posed by this questioning is significant: clearly, those to whom Kicherer preached were unwilling to accept his testimony at face value. There were also status gains to be made from the chance of becoming a preacher; it may be significant that at least one member of SAMS commented that Kicherer had gone to Europe "to have his baptized Bastard ... taught how to win more souls with the view to his being employed in that work among the Heathen."[67] Kicherer's own discussion of the process of choosing companions for the voyage to Europe lends potential support both to the hypothesis that the Khoisan were powerless and to the alternate hypothesis that they had motivations of their own. On the one hand, Kicherer describes choosing people to come with him; on the other hand, he underscores that some were unwilling. He also demonstrates considerable concern to change the minds of his converts about Europeans, of whom, he suggested, they had profoundly negative opinions in the wake of European actions in Africa: this, too, does not bespeak a man completely in control of "his" congregation.[68]

Whatever the truth of the matter, the LMS directors were initially sceptical. They refused at first to meet with Kicherer, and the Dutch missionary was allowed to visit England only after the LMS's Netherlands contact, one Ledboer, had intervened on his behalf.[69] In the meantime, Kicherer wrote plaintively to the LMS board from Holland to ask permission to bring the trio with him to London. "The three Hottentots live in my mother's house without being chargeable to the Society," he attested. "They are well pleased with all they meet with, desire their cordial salutations to you, and would be glad to accompany me."

Once the group was finally in London, however, the same directors were quick to make use of the possibilities. No hint of controversy was allowed to sully in public Kicherer's representation of early successes among the supposed savages of Africa. Despite the partial slave background of Arendse and Sara Fortuin and the long experience of all in labouring for white settlers, the converts were presented as paradigmatic "wild" Hottentots who had now become "tame" through Christian influence. Kicherer did tell the Netherlands Missionary Society that all three had worked in their youth in conditions akin to slavery.[70] Nonetheless, at public meetings in Britain, Kicherer also stressed that his work at Sak River was among "wild Hottentots, called Boschemen; a place where no Christians, no farmers, no Dutchmen live; only wild waste land, where wild people live in the holes like beasts."[71] "Mark them, savage once and wild," "Aliquis" exhorted readers of the *Evangelical Magazine* in lengthy verse: "Now adorned with smiles serene, / Gentle, teachable, and mild, / Decent look and pious mean. / Hark! Religion joy doth bring ..."

Arendse and the Van Rooijs were further displayed as paradigmatic converted sinners. As such, they spoke in London churches before thousands, the proceedings being widely reported in the *Evangelical Magazine* and in pamphlet literature. Their sins were, however, displayed as those of their society as much as the product of individual choice. Their conversions were extraordinary because they furnished proof of the very possibility of converting "primitive" peoples. In that sense, the converts were inserted into a traditional evangelical narrative, at the cost of portraying their societies as profoundly other.

Whether or not the Van Rooijs and Arendse were in Europe for their own purposes, they were clearly objects of display. Their very names were forms of evangelical display. They had all been baptized by Kicherer, who had renamed Sara as Maria (Mary) and Klaas as Johannes Jacobus (John); one wonders if Martha was also a baptismal name. It is possible that the converts chose their own baptismal names. Yet it is striking that Johannes Jacobus was, of course, Kicherer's own name. Mary and Martha are a suspiciously well-matched duo. Since Martha Arendse was Kicherer's housekeeper, was her name deliberately reminiscent of the biblical Martha who kept house while her more spiritually inclined sister Mary sat at the feet of Jesus? Be that as it may, Kicherer had certainly "named" inquirers at his station. As Kicherer's biography put it: "Business increasing every day and the Boschemen flocking to them in considerable numbers, he was obliged for the sake of distinguishing them one from another, to give them names, which he wrote with chalk on their backs; accordingly when any one of them approached him, the first thing he did was to shew his shoulders."[72] The practice of converts receiving new names on baptism had become, as it were, commercialized by the 1830s: large-scale donors to the LMS could have their own names, or names of their relatives, given to the particular "native agents" whom their donations sponsored. A final complication in this issue of naming is that slaves were given names by their purchasers usually based on the month of their disembarkation at Cape Town. In at least one case a converted slave at the Cape station of Bethelsdorp abandoned his slave name, Maart, for a Christian name meaning "uplifted," as a gesture of defiance and rejection of the past. All this is to say that, whether or not Kicherer actually named Mary, Martha, and John, or whether they chose new names for themselves, their very array of "Christian" names underlines a range of colonial ambiguities. The process of naming symbolized the way in which missionaries saw themselves as writing on an African tabula rasa.

The Khoisan were further on display as converted primitives, furnishing, as the *Evangelical Magazine* boasted, "ocular proofs of the power of Divine Grace on some of the most abject of the human race" and removing thereby "the scruples of many persons, who doubted of the practicability of converting the heathen."[73] At several London churches, the group was examined by the minister, with Kicherer serving as translator from English to Dutch and back again. These dialogues have been preserved since they were recorded and published in the evangelical press. Their authenticity is obviously problematic, particularly given Kicherer's interest in presenting convincing converts, but they are the most extended direct speech recorded by the converts.

Whatever the flaws of the converts' replies as historical evidence, the impact on the British audience of the dialogue seems to have been great. The public theological catechisms were designed to demonstrate the validity of the "Hottentots'" conversion, and were triumphantly taken to have done so in both public and private comments by LMS personnel.[74] At Surry Chapel, for example, "Mr. Hill" (doubtless the controversial leading dissenting minister, the Independent Rowland Hill) began his grilling by asking the leading question, "What quantity of good works is sufficient to merit heaven?" Mary van Rooij gave the correct answer from a Calvinist perspective, in Kicherer's reported speech: "She say, by nature we can do no good work, and when by spirit do good work, then we no think to merit heaven thereby. She say, she merit only go to hell, but through merit of Christ she go to heaven: her best work merit eternal death." She also successfully identified the difference between a real Christian and a sham Christian, namely the power of Christ upon the soul.

Mary van Rooij went beyond the question-and-answer format, however, to preach to the congregations. She exhorted sinners to turn to Christ: "She say, she trust there be many here, who have pity for themselves, and for others, compassion for own soul, and soul of others; but wish it was all, but perhaps it was not all; perhaps some here have not compassion on own soul. O that they would take counsel of poor Hottentot ... Tell to them that no people go to Christ! but Christ save them, when they like to be saved! That Christ never say 'I won't save them.'" Van Rooij also drew on her experience as a mother: "And she hope, people here, who have children, she feel what is parent; she hope they would bring children to feet of Christ ... She say, she feel it on her heart; O what is it, she go to heaven and her children go to hell."[75] This certainly constituted unconventional preaching, even if Mary van Rooij was not in a position of authority. For a Khoisan person to suggest to a white audience that they might not be saved was a considerable inversion of southern African racial and religious politics. In a period when female preaching was controversial, if not unheard of among the more radical dissenting sects,[76] it was also unusual for a woman to testify in an Independent church.

Despite its profound inequalities, the "encounter" was in some limited sense a two-way one, with both parties attempting to gain from the transaction. In addition to presenting public testimony, the "converted Hottentots" were introduced to Sir Joseph Banks, president of the Royal Society. They were then presented to the king by Banks. Given this range of contacts, the visiting Khoisan clearly gained prestige from their visit. It is not surprising to find at least one of them attempting to capitalize on this prestige in later life in otherwise degrading circumstances.

In 1812 the British botanist William Burchell engaged as servants on his travels into the south African interior two Christian Khoisan men, Cornelius Goieman and Jan (or Klaas) van Rooij, on the recommendation of Kicherer. Kicherer had by now moved to the colonial village of Graaff-Reinet with his slave-owning wife, Clara, having abandoned his Sak River station fairly soon after his return to south Africa. The Van Rooijs and Arendse had accompanied him as domestic servants. Some time after Kicherer's removal to Graaff-Reinet, however, according to Burchell, "Jan and his wife, giving way to their propensity to that ruinous vice, inebriety, and proving in other respects immoral and undeserving, their protector found himself compelled to put them out of his house, although he still continued, with benevolent feelings towards them, to watch over their conduct."[77] Both Van Rooij and Goieman resisted being treated as "Hottentots," claiming superior status by virtue of their Christianity. Both were described by Burchell as "too fond of brandy"; alcoholism was, in fact, a serious problem for the demoralized and colonized Khoisan of this period. By baptism, Christian Khoisan were supposedly allowed the same privileges as Dutch colonists and might purchase alcohol at will. Kicherer and the landdrost had, however, forbidden the local shopkeeper to sell Goieman brandy unless he had a paper from one of them specifying the amount. Burchell recorded: "In this state, the man, finding his demands for more brandy resisted by the *pagter*, flew to the landdrost; and with violent and impertinent language, insisted in having his right. That step not availing him, he came to the minister, and in a turbulent tone, asked what right any one had to restrain him as if he were a Hottentot: Was he not a Christian! and could he not have as much brandy as he pleased, without being obliged to ask leave of any man!"[78]

Goieman, according to Burchell, pretended to speak less "Hottentot" than he really could and affected to command the others "in right of his being a Christemensch." Van Rooij made the same linkage between language and status: he saw his son at the mission station of

Klaarwater, where the latter was living, and was "ashamed and displeased" that the son knew much more of the "Hottentot language" than of Dutch.[79] Both Goieman and Van Rooij proved recalcitrant servants, reluctant to surrender status. After Goieman had three times persuaded someone else to watch Burchell's oxen, Burchell called the people together and held a trial. When the witnesses proved uncooperative, Burchell brought out a Bible. "I therefore, after repeating to him the substance of several passages in the New testament, desired him to lay his hand on the book, and say, whether, in his own conscience, he really thought that his conduct towards me was influenced by the spirit of obedience which that book taught and commanded a servant to show to his master. Self-conviction instaneously operated on his mind, and he answered, No. I then asked him, in a tone which might encourage him to *give* the answer I wished, if he now felt disposed to conduct himself in future as his duty demanded, to which he readily replied, Yes."[80] This small and unpleasant fable might be taken to illustrate many things about the Christianization of the Khoisan, not least perhaps the malleability of the biblical text and the complicated politics of Christianity in a racially charged situation. It also demonstrates just how ambiguous was the 1803 evangelical display of "converted Hottentots," in ways that doubtless escaped the European evangelical audiences of this religious theatre. If the converts were presenting themselves as saved savages, in a rhetorical move that depended on their denigration of their previous state, they clearly expected substantial gains from this shift in status. These gains were, however, contingent on a dichotomy between, at its most extreme, "Christemensch" and "Hottentot."

It would appear in any event that all the Khoisan who visited Europe did indeed have difficulties in later life. They are remembered as getting drunk too often, although it is hard to distinguish between colonial stereotypes and reality on this issue.[81] Jan van Rooij had a particularly unpleasant end. In 1818 LMS director John Campbell, on a mission of inspection to south Africa, recorded in his diary that "John, one of the three Hottentots who was in London a few years ago, husband to Mary was lately murdered by the Caffres [Xhosa] near Winter mountain. A boy who was with him ran and concealed himself among bushes and thereby escaped."[82] Van Rooij was killed in the course of frontier warfare with the Xhosa. There was considerable tension between Khoekhoe in the Eastern Cape districts and Xhosa, given both previous Xhosa conquest and partial incorporation of Khoekhoe groups and the status of Khoekhoe within the colony as servants and clients of whites who had dispossessed the Xhosa. Colonial Khoekhoe were thus sometimes attacked by Xhosa as part of their attempts to regain land The very Christianity that was a basis for status claims within the colony might have been taken as a challenge by extra-colonial Xhosa during a bitter period of frontier warfare. In the end, van Rooij died as he had lived, enmeshed in the ambiguities of colonialism.

REVOLT AND MISSION CHRISTIANITY

By the time Van der Kemp had begun to make his way to Ngqika, the Khoekhoe revolt of 1799–1803 against the Dutch had already been under way for several months. By 1801, even before the LMS officially began its work among the Khoekhoe, the fortunes of the Khoekhoe rebellion and of the LMS mission would become to a certain degree intertwined, in part because of diplomatic circumstance and in part because of the wider relationship between Christianity and politics in the Eastern Cape. Van der Kemp would also be caught up in the ongoing, and related, white settler revolts of the period.

Van der Kemp's first contact with the rebel Khoisan came in July and August 1799 as he travelled with the fugitive farmers of Agter Bruins Hoogte. As Newton-King points out, the fact that these farmers still had Khoisan servants with them suggests that the desertion of their masters by the Khoisan could be described as "wholesale" at this point only in the southern coastal areas, and not in De Bruins Hoogte and the Sneeuwberg.[83] Relationships were obviously tense between masters and servants. Before a fight with an imiDange Xhosa group, many Khoisan deserted to the Xhosa with horses and rifles.[84] At J.P. van der Waldt's farm, Van der Kemp continued to preach to those Khoisan who remained. They proved reluctant to worship with their masters at the evening service, and so Van der Kemp held separate meetings with them in his room. Every night they sang psalm 118: "They compassed me about like bees; they are quenched as the fire of thorns: for in the name of the Lord will I destroy them. Thou hast thrust sore at me that I might fall: but the Lord helped me ... I shall not die but live, and declare the works of the Lord ... The stone which the builders refused is become the head stone of the corner ..."[85]

Despite the early enthusiasm of the white settlers to hear Van der Kemp preach, there is considerable evidence of tension between Van der Kemp and the settlers over access to Christianity by the time of Van der Kemp's return from Xhosaland. As we have seen, and as was typical of so many evangelicals, Van der Kemp believed that church ceremonies were useless in and of themselves; the evidence of salvation was a relationship with God, not Christian birth or the mere following of church practice. Jonathan Gerstner has argued in a carefully documented study that most settlers at the eighteenth-century Cape had slid into what he regards as the theological error of assuming that infant baptism into the Reformed community conferred salvation, and thus that the community of the elect was coincidental with the church itself – and by extension, in southern Africa, with the community of Christian whites.[86] Whether or not Gerstner is right about the racial implications of this theological posture, Van der Kemp's refusal to baptize either children or adults on demand was both religiously and politically offensive to the white Reformed community and became a *causa belli* in the Patriot revolt against the established authorities.

During the terrifying voyage back from Ngqika's territory, Van der Kemp and one of the white rebels who had taken refuge at Ngqika's court paused for a theological quarrel. The deserter, the consort of the Khoekhoe woman Maria, interrupted Van der Kemp's attempt to baptize the converted Maria and her small children. He felt that the baptism should take place in the manner of the Reformed Church of the Cape Colony, according to known custom. In opposition to Van der Kemp's use of partial immersion and sprinkling, the man argued that baptism should occur on a Sunday, after a sermon, only through sprinkling and only after the reading of a prescribed formula. He further wanted his eldest daughter baptized, as well as his children by his second wife, a Xhosa woman. Van der Kemp did not object to changing baptism ritual but he vehemently refused to baptize either the adult daughter, "as she herself was showing no fruit worthy of conversion," or the other children, since "the young children born of religious parents had likewise no right to seal the bond." Van der Kemp then took the opportunity to deliver a sermon from Romans 2:28–9, to the effect that a Christian was not one who merely was a Christian in public, nor was baptism done in public to the flesh; rather, a Christian was one who had been vouched for and baptism was of hearts through the spirit. Fate was not determined by men but by God.[87] This is an interesting quarrel on a number of counts. Christianity mattered to the tough men of the frontier. It is clear in this particular debate that the issue was not whether blacks might have access to Christian baptism; indeed, this case provides evidence for relatively stable sexual unions across ethnic lines in a frontier zone. On the other hand, the protagonists divided sharply over whether baptism could occur because the parents wanted it. This was the issue behind the splits identified by Gerstner: was admission to the Christian community automatic because of birth, or did it have to be earned by a "true" conversion experience? Van der Kemp was here undercutting the central identity claim of the "white" Christian community.

On 14 May 1801, five and a half months after leaving Ngqika's court, Van der Kemp crossed a mountain and arrived at last in Graaff-Reinet to meet his new colleagues, the young English carpenter James Read and the Dutchman A.A. van der Lingen, two of four further missionaries sent to Africa under the auspices of the LMS.[88] The town was in a state of upheaval. It was the seat of the Landdrost H. Maynier, whose government had already been the target of settler rebellion and would be challenged again in the months to come.

During the first fragile period of peace in the 1799–1803 conflict, the conciliatory Maynier tried both to persuade Khoisan rebels to return to work under the Dutch and to compel the resistant white farmers to treat them better by force of law. In June 1801 a group of some 200 farmers marched on Graff-Reinet and demanded renewed supplies of ammunition and the right to launch commando raids into Khoekhoe territory. The village already contained about 200 Khoisan refugees under Maynier's protection. With the prospect of renewed hostilities, more refugees poured into Graaff-Reinet under the leadership of their captains, while many other farm labourers flocked to the independent Khoisan captains living with the Xhosa over the Sundays River. By late 1801 there were some 300 Khoisan families, comprising nearly 800 individuals, in the village, as well as a large force of Dutch settlers encamped outside.[89]

When Van der Kemp first arrived in Graaff-Reinet, he was sought out by an eager Reformed church community which was then without a pastor. Van der Lingen and Van der Kemp alternated preaching at the Reformed church, while Read evangelized English soldiers. The white congregation offered Van der Kemp the permanent pastorate of their church. Van der Kemp refused, however, because he felt that it would be a deviation from his calling to the heathen, because he disagreed with the congregation on points of doctrine (although he thought this issue was surmountable with mutual tolerance), and because he thought that the community had a scandalous lack of church discipline, Most hurtfully, perhaps, he refused to baptize the children of believers, arguing that these children had shown insufficient signs of repentance and a changed heart. This was a significant issue, given the difficulty frontier farmers had in finding ministers to baptize their children; when the Reverend Michiel Vos visited Graaff-Reinet in November 1801 and was dispatched to preach to the rebels as a peace gesture, he baptized over 100 children.[90]

When Dutch rebels began to move against the drostdy shortly thereafter, they complained that the Graaff-Reinet church was without a minister while the "Hottentots" had three for themselves. In the meantime, about 200 Khoisan were attending Van der Kemp's meetings at

Graaff-Reinet. At the monthly missionary prayer meeting on 1 June, Khoisan in attendance sang psalm 134, which proclaimed (in the King James version), "Lift up your hands in the sanctuary and bless the Lord." Colonists in the congregation responded by singing verses 4 to 10 of psalm 74, beginning "thine enemies roar in the midst of thy congregation," and concluding with "O God, how long shall the adversary reproach? shall the enemy blaspheme thy name for ever?"[91] On 3 July the Boer rebels, now closer to Graaff-Reinet, sent an ambassador to request that Khoisan who had committed murder be surrendered to them and that the Khoisan be refused access to the Graaff-Reinet church. Soon afterwards, rebels added the requests that the seats and walls of the church be scrubbed clean, the churchyard fenced with a stone wall, and a black cloth be hung over the pulpit as a sign of mourning for the absence of a regular minister.[92] To calm nerves, Van der Kemp stopped using the church and held meetings at his own house. This particular crisis was averted, partly through Van der Kemp's own work as a negotiator, but the underlying issues were unresolved.

Van der Kemp became convinced that the white farmers had incurred God's anger. In August, he was part of a delegation requested by Ngqika. After an inconclusive parlay with the king and many of the leading figures of his court at the edge of the colony, the group returned to Graaff-Reinet by a different route than they had come, via Bruins Hoogte and the Vogel River. The former dwelling places of the settlers were devastated: wolves wandered through the houses, wildebeests grazed in the corn fields, and the Khoisan in the party filled their knapsacks with fruit from the deserted orchards. Van der Kemp saw this as God's punishment against the settlers for their mistreatment of the "heathen" and their refusal to teach them Christianity. His sermon at the first inhabited homestead to which he came, that of den Graaven Naude, warned of the terrible consequences should the settlers not turn away from wickedness. He warned the farmers that they must include their servants at household prayer; the assembled whites agreed to this with the greatest reluctance, according to Van der Kemp. The type of popular attitudes behind such reluctance are hinted at in the 1802 report by Van der Lingen that, as he carried out his pastoral duties, a number of farmers "prepossessed with hate against the Heathen Nation" troubled him by asking "whether it became Heathen to be instructed in the doctrine of the Gospel? whether it was possible they could be converted? if they were not damned? and such like questions, where with they vexed me much, as I was asked these same questions at so many different places ..."[93] Despite Van der Kemp's warning about divine retributions against settlers, he was in fact deeply shaken when den Graaven Naude, whom Van der Kemp considered a good man, was murdered in 1801 by Xhosa from Ngqika's court known to the missionary.[94]

When he preached to the household of den Graaven Naude, Van der Kemp chose as the text for his sermon Romans 11:20–2. The provocative choice suggests that Van der Kemp thought that God punished those peoples who rejected their covenant with God and that new peoples might be chosen for his blessing. The verses concern Paul's discussion of whether God had rejected his chosen people, the Jews, and what the relationship of the converted gentiles was to Jews. Paul says that God has cut off some Jews from the olive tree and that some gentiles have been grafted on to the tree in their place, but God can still reject these gentiles and the new converts should not be proud. Once the pagans have been converted, they will re-convert the remaining Jews who have erred; the Jews are still God's beloved chosen people. Van der Kemp's appropriation of a biblical text typified the way in which evangelicals of the period, across international boundaries, used the Bible to lend transcendent significance to events as they occurred – to sacralize them, in effect. Particularly frequent use of the Bible was made in the public culture of Calvinist Holland, where the stories of the Pentateuch furnished metaphors for national progress.[95] Here Van der Kemp reversed this rhetoric to describe national regress.

Van der Kemp's entire understanding of the Third Frontier War was in fact shot through with theological assumptions which conflicted with those of white settlers while sharing some fundamental features. In a telling 1802 letter to Fiscaal Van Ryneveld which deserves a digression, Van der Kemp argued that the farmers fled like Cain from their homesteads because they possessed a presentiment of the judgment of God and were pursued by guilt. "God's word declares," he argued, "that 'the wicked fleeth when no man pursueth'. The judgment of the Almighty is plainly marked upon these wretched wanderers, who find no rest, because He allows them none. Their unpunished outrages, and their murders of the Hottentots, equal the crimes of their prototype Cain, and a like judgment to his is pronounced upon them." In essence, the settlers externalized their guilt and transformed it into fear of the African. "The fear of vengeance allows them no rest ... Night brings with it the dread of attack instead of its wonted repose, and they consider their own domestics to be leagued against them." They therefore ran into the open countryside and huddled together with others. They tried to escape vengeance and indeed to escape themselves by killing all those whom they had injured: "although the motive be concealed, still it is openly professed as the belief of the whole class, that 'the utter extermination of these villains' (meaning all heathens not in their service) 'is the sole means of peace to the good burghers upon their farms.'" And yet commandos brought no peace. "When the delight he has felt in hunting down human beings is past, and he calmly reflects upon his gains, then is disappointment felt." The cycle began again.[96] This is a powerful analysis of any community caught up in cycles of guilt, fear, and inter-ethnic violence.

Van der Kemp was a millenarian who believed in the particular judgments of God to punish or warn the guilty, and who was convinced that God would soon intervene on the side of the oppressed in south Africa. As we have seen, Van der Kemp, like many of his evangelical colleagues, also believed in the action of God through *nations* and in collective judgment on erring communities. Van der Kemp was firmly within this tradition when he informed the fiscal (prosecuter) that the war was God's judgment on the Dutch nation, and anticipated "that the desolation will go further, and that God will make the natives, irritated as they are by the acts of the commando now out, the instruments of his wrath." In illustration, he referred to Isiah 5:25: "So, Yahweh aflame with anger against his people / has raised his hand to strike them; / he has killed the princes, their corpses lie / like dung in the streets. / Yet his anger is not spent, / still his hand is raised to strike." It was characteristic that James Read and Van der Kemp believed that the earthquakes that afflicted Cape Town in 1810 were the result of the white oppression of the indigenous people. "The Judgements of God threaten this country continually," wrote Read, "but the inhabitants don't learn righteousness. None are aware of the sins that are the cause and this gives us to fear a heavier stroke."[97] It is unsurprising that most white settlers so disliked Van der Kemp.

Shortly after the Ngqika delegation's return to Graaff-Reinet, the settler rebels around the town renewed their threats against the drostdy in the run-up to an armed attack. This time, the "crowd called out" against Van der Kemp, as he put it. They circulated a statement of grievances among the inhabitants of the Sneeuberg which described the missionaries as corrupters of Christianity, and accused Van der Kemp specifically of trying to incite the Xhosa against the Dutch and of having tried to lure Boer leaders into the Graaff-Reinet church in order to have them assassinated.[98] Even the exasperated Maynier, who seems to have seen Van der Kemp as well intentioned but dangerous, told the missionary that the land would not have fallen "in rep en roer" had he stayed in Xhosa land. In the day-long melée that ultimately ensued, Van der Kemp was shot at several times. He thought of Acts 21:28. The verse describes how some Jews from Asia caught sight of Paul in the Temple and stirred up the crowd against him "shouting, "Men of Israel, help! This is the man who preaches to everyone everywhere against our people, against the Law and against this place.

Now he has profaned this Holy Place by bringing Greeks into the Temple."[99] Van der Kemp clearly drew parallels between Paul's mission to the gentiles and his own to the non-Christians of Africa. Despite historiographical controversy over the extent to which the frontier Afrikaners saw themselves as a "chosen people," the prevalence of covenant theology in Reformed Holland and the widespread identification of the political community (whether Dutch or settler) with Israel ensured that these would be charged and painful debates. Van der Kemp did not make things easier by quarrelling vigorously with SAMS, calling the organization a "synagogue of Satan" destined for destruction when he learned that the society had detained one of the newly arrived LMS missionaries, Bastiaan Tromp, and dispatched him to work among whites in Wagenmakers valley.[100]

In contrast to the bitter animosity between Van der Kemp and the veeboers, many Khoisan people and at least a few slaves demonstrated an unexpected interest in Christianity. Some 200 came regularly to be instructed by Van der Kemp, including thirty-two who enrolled themselves as "catechumens." Unfortunately, the records are relatively silent on the religious experiences of these people. The movement was, however, too substantial and too rapid to have been prompted by the preaching of the missionaries alone. The example of Cupido, "an African slave" from the Sneeuberge, is instructive. In the middle of the attacks on Graaff-Reinet, Van der Kemp preached to the "heathen." Cupido attended this meeting and testified "with great freedom" about the truth of the doctrine taught; he defined prayer as a rope "tossed to a poor sinner, and by means of which he fastens himself to heaven."[101] Cupido reported that, despite great opposition, he held a meeting every evening at his master's farm "with various heathen, in order to speak with them about the way to live and to pray."[102]

Another slave also fought with her master in order to become Christian. A Zezuru-speaking Shona woman named Puwatier, more commonly known in Graaff-Reinet as Suzanna, had long "sought the Lord Jesus in prayer night and day, yearning that he might discover himself to her." After a long dry spell, the Holy Ghost assured her that she was now the property of Jesus. Using the imagery of motherhood, she told Van der Kemp: "A child when scarcely born, comes into a new life, and likewise into a new world, before it was in the dark but now in the light, However as long as it is not washed, it is covered with filth from its former living place and it seems disgusting. I have been born but not washed! But Christ can cleanse me of my filth through his Holy Spirit and melt my stony-rock heart [*klip steenen hart*]."[103] Puwatier/Suzanna wanted to be baptized. Although her master was a deacon of the church, he forbade her baptism, since he did not want to be deprived of the right to sell her. The master later said that he would allow her to be baptized if Van der Kemp paid him the equivalent of her purchase price; Van der Kemp refused, however, on the ground that this would incite others to follow the example.[104] The family prevented Puwatier from going to church and incited a fellow slave to bring a false accusation of theft against her. Undaunted, Puwatier compared herself to the biblical figure of the Samaritan woman, another outcast to whom Jesus revealed himself. In an important move in his politico-theological conflict with settlers, Van der Kemp then gave Puwatier communion without prior baptism. This move, doubtless shocking to many, undercut the necessity of the central rite of entry to the "white" community.

In the meantime, some at least of the Khoisan beyond Graaff-Reinet were also interested in Christianity. In late 1801 the "famous Captain Stuurman" (in Van der Kemp's words), who had already heard Van der Kemp preach and was then on the Zwartkops River near Algoa Bay, invited Van der Kemp several times to instruct himself and his people in religion.[105] Despite, as would later become clear, the strenuous objections of other captains, Stuurman and his fellow captain Ourson even offered to pull back from the country outside Graaff-Reinet if they could be granted land in a region other than Graaff-Reinet to which Van der Kemp would come to offer instruction. With these contacts, Van der Kemp began to act as a mediator between Stuurman and the British.

In all of this, I think that there was an underlying struggle over who should have access to the power which many appear to have believed was conferred by Christianity. Van der Kemp was convinced that God intervened actively in the world and gave power to his converts. Nothing suggests that the major players in the dramas outlined above felt otherwise. It would be a mistake to think of Christianity as being perceived at this point as a tool to teach passivity and acceptance of fate; on the contrary, divine power was a force to be harnessed and therefore worth struggle. The anxiety felt by white settlers over their own lack of access to ministers and, more profoundly, over the conversion of the "heathen" probably reinforced the apparent conviction of many of the oppressed of the Cape Colony that there was indeed power in Christianity.

Throughout 1801, stock-raiding and fighting between the Khoisan and the colonists increased. Newton-King argues that the combined Khoisan-Xhosa raids were designed to drive the colonists westward.[106] Through Willem Bruintje, Van der Kemp's interpreter and guide, and through the visits to Graaff-Reinet of the Khoekhoe Captain Ruiter, Van der Kemp was put in touch with several Khoisan groups, sheltering themselves among the Xhosa, as he put it, "against the barbarities of the Colonists."[107] Van der Kemp himself believed that the raids were motivated primarily by hunger, and he wrote frequently to the British administration urging that they grant Khoisan captains vacant land in Graaff-Reinet where they could settle with their people.

At the end of November a Khoisan group led by Stuurman, Hans Trompeter, and Boevesak shot the veldcornet C.J. van Rooyen in the left eye and killed him on his doorstep, probably in revenge for previous murders. The tradition of the blood feud was probably still strong among the Khoekhoe. In the same month, Maynier was recalled to answer charges laid by local settlers that he had encouraged unrest and disloyalty among the Khoisan gathered around him in Graaff-Reinet. Khoisan raids against the Dutch intensified. In the meantime, the Khoisan at Graaff-Reinet who were still trying to obtain peaceful redress from the government chafed at the lack of progress. The hands of the men seem to have been tied by the fact that the wives, children, and cattle of many were still trapped by the farmers. Nonetheless, by the end of December they were threatening violence.[108]

Van der Kemp and Dundas concurred in the conviction that a mission station for Khoisan might be a way out of the conflict, Dundas because he wanted to defuse the military situation, and Van der Kemp because he was eager to remove the Khoisan from the influence of the Dutch and set about the business of conversion. The governor also wanted to use the mission as a tool of cultural change. Van der Kemp would later report that in correspondence Dundas had asked the missionary to share his thoughts concerning the best way to lead the "Nation" to Christianity and "a more orderly and hard-working way of life, outside a slavish servitude."[109] Both hoped that the missionaries would be able to persuade the Khoisan living in the Zuurveld peacefully to return to the colony. Dundas promised every assistance to the mission and immediately sent a ship with rice and other provisions from the Cape.[110] From the beginning, the government tried to use the mission as a political tool to pacify the Khoisan. In the early debates around the LMS mission, one might indeed see a template for debates which would occur among administrators across the colonial world about how to incorporate conquered aboriginal peoples into white settler colonies. In any case, although it was not clear at the time, the grant of land for a mission was perceived by Dundas as a war concession to the Khoisan. It would be their only lasting territorial gain from the conflict.

In late 1802 the British would withdraw from the Cape Colony and hand over control to the Batavian Republic of the Netherlands, a puppet state of the French republic, as part of the Treaty of Amiens. The terms of the treaty became known at the Cape in late December 1801.

Although Dundas tried to dissuade Read and Van der Kemp from going ahead, as settler control broke down completely in the interior,[111] the missionaries nonetheless trekked towards Algoa Bay on 20 February 1802, confirmed in their decision by the "disgraceful conduct" of English soldiers towards the Khoisan.[112] According to Van der Kemp, about 300 of the 463 Khoisan people living at Graaff-Reinet who were not already in government service (out of a total of 799) decided to leave with the European missionaries. Some 190 would vanish just after departure; Van der Kemp claimed that they were deterred by widespread rumours of a planned settler attack, but they may have simply wanted to leave Graaff-Reinet without going to a missionary station.[113] Numbers would change further en route, as another forty left with the Khoisan Captain Wildeman, while over a hundred others came out of hiding places in the mountains and woods to join the group. Obviously many of those who trekked towards the Bay had their own agendas. Indeed, it is striking that Khoisan leaders at Graaff-Reinet had resisted Van der Kemp's initial suggestion of trekking to the north, to the headwaters of the Tarka River, because most yearned for "een Land waarin, in oude tyden hunne voor vaders waarin" – a land in which their forefathers had lived in olden times.[114]

Once again, Van der Kemp put a biblical text to pointed use. Before leaving Graaf- Reinet, he gathered the people together and read Genesis 35: "Then Jacob said unto his household, and to all that were with him, 'put away the strange Gods that are among you, and be clean and change your garments, and let us arise, and go to Bethel, and I will make there an Altar unto God, who answered me in the day of my distress, and was with me in the ways which I went.'"[115] Here Van der Kemp again appropriated existing Dutch rhetoric about the nation as the new Israel and applied it the Khoekhoe. In the verses preceding this passage, God had told Jacob to move to Bethel to escape their enemies, the Shechemites, At Bethel, God spoke once more to Jacob: "Your name is Jacob, but from now on you shall be named not Jacob but Israel ... I give you this land, the land I gave to Abraham and Isaac; and I will give this land to your descendants after you."[116] When the community was finally permanently granted land for a mission in 1804, following provisional arrangements, Van der Kemp named the station Bethelsdorp, after the place of consecration of the children of Israel. This was probably a tribute to the Moravians, one of whose villages in Hernhut was named Bethel. It also, however, made an implicit comparison between the Khoekhoe and the Israelites. This metaphor was maintained in the first years of LMS activity. In 1803, in a letter to the new Batavian governor, Jan Willem Janssens, Van der Kemp compared the Hottentots to the "children of Israel under Pharaoh," while in

1812 James Read, arguing for civic justice for the Khoisan, would publicly recall the covenant between God and the Israelites.[117]

On 3 March the small group saw the Indian Ocean at last, and two
days later, at the Zwartkops River, they met again with "the famous
Hottentot Captain Klaas Stuurman," who was by this point "master,
from Bosjesman's River to the Zwartkops."[118] He was surrounded by
"Gonaka Hottentoten," or Gonaqua Khoekhoe. Both Read and Van
der Kemp have left reports of Stuurman's words, although the existence of slightly discrepant multiple accounts only highlights the difficulty of reconstructing Stuurman's thought. Clearly, however, Stuurman saw the land as his. He complained bitterly about the barbarity
with which the colonists had treated his "nation" and expressed his
disappointment at the failure of the British to live up to their promises. "I see that this was only words, and it appears they are too weak or
unwilling to protect us." In the context of that failure, men had duties
to their dependants. According to Van der Kemp's annual account to
the LMS, Stuurman continued: "I and my friends [the Gonaqua Hottentots who were with him] are obliged to protect ourselves and our
households ourselves, it is a duty owed by every son, husband and
father to his elders, wives and children."[119] Stuurman's comments were
also, however, a form of surrender. He pointed out that his people were
reasonable and would not cause problems in "this *my* land." He
desired to live in submission to the government and asked only for
equal treatment under the law, and a piece of land where his people
might live under their own protection and where "we should have the
opportunity of hearing God's word without running the risk of our
life."[120] According to Read's version of events, Stuurman said "his present steps were to revenge himself on the Boers of their barbarous conduct to his people, and that he was determined to do till Government
could or would do justice although, he wished for nothing more than
to live a peaceable life, but especially to hear the word of God, for said
he 'we are blind Heathens, we know nothing and in this state the Boers
wish to keep us!'"[121] After this parlay, Klaas and his people had lunch
with the missionaries and the group from Graaff-Reinet. According to
Van der Kemp, rumours had spread among the Graaff-Reinet
Khoekhoe that farmers were waiting in ambush at Thomas Ferreira's
farm to kill them; a hundred or so accordingly left with Stuurman.

Later that same day, Read, Van der Kemp, and about 160 remaining
fellow travellers arrived at Fort Frederick where they were welcomed
by Lieutenant-Colonel Lemoyne and other British officers. On 7
March they took possession of Botha's abandoned farm in a region
from which most settlers had fled. There they found an abundance of
grass, timber, and limestone as well as three deserted residences, of

which Read and Van der Kemp commandeered one to use as a church and schoolhouse and another to house a printing press. The appearance of bounty proved, however, deceptive. A nearby source of water was stagnant, and fevers and diarrhoea would follow. Van der Kemp himself would be afflicted with severe rheumatism and what he said was locally called the "paralysing sickness." For eleven months he would be unable to leave his sick bed.[122]

Over the next two years, in the midst of great political turbulence, the station would establish a rhythm of institutional life, framed by frequent religious services and instruction in reading and writing. A ship wrecked in the Bay yielded a bell, which the missionaries used to call the people together for school and divine service. It seems an apt symbol for the colonization of time demanded by the Protestant missionary project; the missionaries' sense that the days and weeks should be divided into regulated and prearranged pieces of time contrasted sharply with what Van der Kemp saw as the supposed indolence and unsettled nature of the Khoekhoe. Almost two hundred years later, the Reverend Jacob Albert of the modern Bethelsdorp Congregationalist community commented to me that the community still remembered the bell calling people to work picking aloes, which he felt disproved the widespread allegations of laziness made against the early settlement. The bell was a powerful sign.[123]

The community had its own internal government, but Van der Kemp and Read selected at least some community officials in the early days. Seven men were chosen by them as judges, to deal with small issues as they came up without reference to the missionaries.[124] In 1804 Van der Kemp made reference in his diary to an unnamed woman, "whom we had named as head of the women."[125] In 1803 Jan Stoffels was selected (by whom is unclear) as deacon, with control over the money designated for the poor.[126] At later points in the history of the LMS Eastern Cape missions it is clear that mission communities themselves selected "captains" to oversee things like work details, while the deaconate of the church was a potentially powerful pole of authority, elected from among congregational members. The result was a hybrid institution, theocratic but with room to dispute the lines of authority. The missionaries attempted to impose time discipline and work discipline, as they perceived them, while also attempting to select leaders, but, as we shall see, a great deal of ancillary evidence suggests that such attempts at cultural and political control were only ambiguously successful.

In March 1802, however, all this lay in the future. In the aftermath of his meeting with Klaas Stuurman, Van der Kemp became a go-between in negotiations between the Khoekhoe captain and Governor Dundas. Through the missionary, the captain conveyed his desire to abandon the war in exchange for land for his people and an end to ill-treatment by settlers. Governor Dundas and the fiscaal, Willem Stephanus Van Ryneveld, agreed to this, but they first demanded that Stuurman restore all the cattle stolen from the colonists and currently held in Xhosaland, although Stuurman had no jurisdiction over the separate rebel bands. Several of Stuurman's allies resented and resisted his separate peace. Van der Kemp reported that "Boezak and his men entertain the deepest animosity against me, as having seduced Klaas in order to ruin the other Hottentots."[127] Resentment was particularly deep because Stuurman attempted to return to the colony all the cattle which the Khoisan had stolen from the colonists. Boezak and other chiefs attacked Klaas, stripped him of his weapons, cattle, and people, and threatened to treat the mission in the same manner, "looking upon us as the cause of the resolution which he had taken."[128] To save his life, Stuurman fled to the Xhosa chief Cungwa, who took him under his protection.

In the meantime, the British treacherously organized a new and much larger commando of some three hundred men, again led by J.P. Van der Walt's brother Tjart Van der Walt, to attack the Khoisan across the Sundays River. Despite the governor's promise of protection to neutral Africans, the commando attacked all Xhosa without distinction. The governor forbade the missionaries to accept further applicants. The Khoekhoe-Xhosa alliance attacked the commando, forced it across the Gamtoos River, killed the leader Tjart Van der Walt, and dispersed the armed group.

The European political situation continued to change. In September 1803, following the Treaty of Amiens, Governor Dundas withdrew his troops from the interior and fled to Cape Town to hand over power to the new rulers. Before his departure, Dundas tried in vain to persuade the missionaries to withdraw to the safety of the Cape, fearing for their lives in the absence of British military protection.[129] Read and Van der Kemp believed that it was the will of God that they stay with "our people" (one notes already the possessiveness of the language).

The Botha's Farm community was indeed vulnerable to plunder and attack. Not only were the missionaries blamed by at least some rebels for having weakened the war effort, but the farm was well supplied with cattle and goods, having received substantial parting gifts from the stores of the departing British. The first attack came at night, eight days after the departure of the troops. It took the form of an armed cattle raid with deadly intent. One of the station inhabitants approached the attackers and spoke in a friendly manner. They cried in response, "Daar koomt een vredemaker! Steek hem dood! Schiet hem" – "There comes a peacemaker! Kill him! Shoot him." A mêlée ensued, during which a bullet pierced the thigh of an attacker, cutting an artery so that he bled to death. In the morning light the corpse proved to be that of Klaas Stuurman's brother, Andries.[130] Two subsequent attacks were larger and bolder, and the last included Xhosa reinforcements.

After the third attack, the group at Botha's Farm reluctantly moved to Fort Frederick. The colonists sheltering at the fort expected Read and Van der Kemp to make common cause with them, but they were disappointed by Van der Kemp's declaration that they "kept a strict neutrality in the war with the Savages, and that we did not make use of arms, but only for unavoidable self-defence, nor opposed the disorders of the Savages, but by Christian admonitions and examples of which they could see the effect on our Hottentots." In the meantime, the Xhosa punished Andries Stuurman's band for the attack on the mission and killed three members on their return – suggesting both that there were mixed attitudes to the missionaries among the allies and that the Khoisan in the Zuurveld were under Xhosa jurisdiction. Klaas Stuurman himself fell under suspicion and with difficulty preserved his life; Van der Kemp gives no indication that he believed these accusations, but they do complicate further our picture of this Khoekhoe leader

In the tense period before the arrival of the Batavians at Algoa Bay, there was a great deal of overt hostility, coloured by fear, between the Dutch farmers and the Khoekhoe at Fort Frederick. Armed bands plundered in the area and no central authority placed any limits on ethnic conflict. According to Van der Kemp, the farmers now murdered Khoekhoe with impunity, stole their belongings, and even spirited away children and sent them far away, presumably as slave labour.[131] This last comment lends support to the arguments of Susan Newton-King and others that an important trade existed in captive children; it also suggests that farmers were blurring the lines, unclear as they may have been, between Bushman captives taken in war and "apprentices" taken from the community of "free" Khoekhoe. Van der Kemp further claimed that the settlers tried to "seduce" the Khoekhoe to "drunkenness, prostitution and other crimes" and to turn their minds against Christianity. Although Van der Kemp read this social interaction as a form of spiritual violence, it does nonetheless underscore how closely connected were the lives of Africans and settlers, even in this climate of hate. Overall, Van der Kemp concluded, "nothing less" would satisfy the settlers than "to wash their hands in the blood of the poor people." In this emotional climate, religious conversion accelerated, especially among the children. Many others fled Fort Frederick.[132]

Van der Kemp received no answer to letters he had written to the incoming Batavian government; later the community would learn that on two occasions messengers bearing letters in reply had been intercepted by colonists and killed. At last, however, a small contingent of Batavian troops arrived to take over Fort Frederick on 18 April 1805. On 8 May General Janssens himself followed. He would stay in the Bay area for a month, attempting to negotiate peace with the various warring parties, including Klaas Stuurman. Janssens's aide-de-campe, Willem Bartholome Eduard Paravicini di Capelli, left a compelling description of Van der Kemp as an old man lying under a sheepskin covering in a room with almost no furniture in a mud and reed hut, wearing a coarse blue-striped linen shirt, who said in response to questions about his living conditions that he was nauseated by human society and that God had given him a task of bringing to salvation his lost fellow human beings for which he was prepared to abandon all material comfort forever.[133]

In the aftermath of the arrival of the Batavians, the rebel effort visibly fell apart. In light of the destructive British commando attack, the Xhosa of Chungwa appear to have wavered in their support for their Khoisan allies. All the same, the full reasons for the collapse of the war effort on the arrival of the Batavians are obscure, and Newton-King finds it "astonishing" that the Khoisan did not seek to gain more advantage from their position of strength.[134] Factors playing against them included the greater hostility of the Batavians to the Khoisan and their greater sympathy for the Dutch settlers, heavy losses and shortage of ammunition among the Khoisan, and disunity among both the rebels and among the Khoisan as a whole.[135] It is possible that the Khoisan perceived the Batavians simply as allies of the Dutch settlers and reasoned that there were limited political gains to be made by further resistance. Most of the captains gave up, although Boezak was irreconcilable and remained in the Zuurveld until he was murdered by some of Ndlambe's Xhosa in 1804.[136] The rebel leader Hans Trompetter eventually joined Bethelsdorp, as did descendants of the murdered leader Ourson, members of the Boezak clan who appear to have been active on both sides of the war, Jan Kaffer, and a further Stuurman, Windvogel Stuurman.

It is unclear how powerful the Khoisan rebels were at this stage of the rebellion. Newton-King suggests that the rebels were in control of the situation and abandoned a winning hand, in part because of Van der Kemp's blandishments. Although, as both Newton-King and Malherbe stress, we have insufficient knowledge of conditions in the rebel camps to come to definitive judgments, there is some evidence that their situation was in fact quite precarious. Stuurman's band worried about women and children who essentially remained hostages under farmer control. There was also hunger. Van der Kemp contended that much of the raiding by rebel bands was to get food. In the final year of war, Van der Kemp described people, principally women and children, fleeing through the war zone to reach him, emaciated with hunger and devoid of possessions. According to the missionary, when he was forced by government fiat to turn them away, they chose rather "to maintain themselves in the woods amongst the Brutes, than to return to their tribes."[137] It is also not clear how independent the Khoisan in the Zuurveld were from the Xhosa. This was not a relationship of equality, despite extensive intermarriage.[138] The critical question, difficult to answer, is whether the Eastern Cape Khoekhoe were truly in a position to withstand British (or Batavian) armed might and settler revenge over more than a short period and regain their country by force of arms. Khoisan who resisted more ruthlessly in the Western Cape were also killed more ruthlessly. This is a particularly pertinent issue given the small size of the Khoisan groups involved in the fighting; when in 1804 Dawid Stuurman finally led his people to the farm that had been promised his brother, he had with him only nine men with thirty-two women and children.[139] If the rebels were relatively weak, Van der Kemp, with his extensive knowledge of the Dutch and British military, may have had less of a class-determined ulterior motive in trying to make peace than Newton-King concludes. Furthermore, although Newton-King's analysis of Van der Kemp is penetrating for the most part, I disagree with her depiction of Van der Kemp as a "liberal": this is anachronistic and perhaps reflects the historiographical debates of the 1970s and 1980s between "liberals" and "radicals" in South Africa more than it does the theologically determined outlook of the iconoclastic Van der Kemp.[140] Be that as it may, I am more persuaded by Malherbe's summation that "the missionary's purpose was to save colonists and Khoi from mutual destruction,"[141] as well as by her argument that he found himself in an impossible, and unwelcome, situation once the commando attack had been launched, but struggled to keep the two parties talking.

Despite this, it is still the case that Van der Kemp encouraged Stuurman to make a separate peace with the colony and provided the means for him to do so. This weakened the rebels and promoted divisions between them. A central dilemma in the relationship between Christianity and empire was thus present from the very beginning. The divergent fates of Andries, Klaas, and Dawid Stuurman symbolize the early divisiveness of the Christian mission among the Khoekhoe. Klaas tried to make alliances with the British through missionaries to improve his lot; Andries died fighting the British, the settlers, and the mission; Dawid was finally granted a small farm but would continue to resist and in 1809 would be transported by the British to Botany

Bay.[142] Similarly divergent choices were made by the Boezak family –
either brothers or close clansmen (the Khoekhoe word for "brother"
also meant a close male relative). One Boezak, as we have seen, was
one of the fiercest captains during the war and opposed the nascent
mission settlement. The elephant hunter Hendrik Boezak struggled
between his "two hearts" before becoming a leading Khoe evangelist.
A third Boezak kinsman, Jan, again took a different route. When he
joined Bethelsdorp in 1807 he was an alcoholic, who had been
"famous with the Farmers on their commandos against the Caffras,
Boschesmans and Hottentots" and had fought on the Boer side in the
war. He soon left the station, in part because he could not "bear the
faithful admonitions of his Brother," but, "like the poor prodigal son,"
he "waisted his cattle for brandy at a neighbouring farm house, and
after finding no succor or even safety by the farmers returned to us."
He eventually converted and was "baptized and received as a brother
among us."[143] From the beginning, the war and mission split families.
Different opinions existed at the start about whether the new mission
station offered a good way out of an untenable situation, or whether it
was in fact an agent of the colonial state. This ambiguity would continue throughout the early history of the missionary project.

THE AFTERMATH OF WAR

The war continued to have an impact on relationships in the Graaff-
Reinet area for many years: it was remembered, resented, and mythologized by Khoisan, missionary, and Boer alike, and it determined the
way in which Bethelsdorp was seen by the Dutch. The British, however, remained only dimly aware of these dynamics, not least because
they were compelled to leave the Cape in 1802 before the conclusion
of hostilities. The strongest impression made on the British imagination
by the war was through the work of John Barrow, whose portrayal of
the Dutch farmers as inadequate moral agents in part because they
were also inadequate *economic* agents presaged later liberal attacks on
the Dutch.

The impact in the Eastern Cape was, however, profound and bitter.
Many of those who sought refuge at Bethelsdorp would otherwise have
suffered revenge killings or maltreatment at the hands of the farmers.
Farmers complained that the missionaries "stood with the plundering
Hottentots and Cafferians in a connection, which was dangerous to the
safety of the good inhabitants, and that we caused our institution to be
a place of refuge for robbers and Murderers."[144] Frontier memories
were long. As late as 1812, the report of the Commission of Circuit
(a circuit court established in 1811 to serve the frontier districts)

commented that, although it was true that some Hottentots had suffered injuries from farmers in the past, there were also many "Hottentots" at Bethelsdorp "who have had a considerable part in plundering,
robbing, setting fire to the places, and even murdering the Inhabitants;
and as the Hottentots as well as the missionaries, who at present exercise the immediate control over them, do not wish to see those things
brought to light, but that they should be considered as forgotten and
forgiven, the same forgiveness therefore should extend to those by
whom they have been injured."[145]

The missionaries and the Khoisan themselves mythologized the war
well into the nineteenth century. James Read and his son, James Read
Jr, attempting to act as spokespeople for the Eastern Cape "Hottentot"
community, stressed on several occasions that the missionaries had
made peace with the rebels on behalf of the colony, and that a contractual relationship of good treatment in exchange for political peace
still obtained. In 1811, in a letter to the LMS directors pleading the need
for a judicial break on violence against the Khoisan, Read Sr claimed
that the uprising had been provoked by colonists' ill-treatment of the
indigenous people and had been arrested by the missionaries: "'Twas
after this scheme of wretchedness began that the Hottentots began to
rise to try to procure themselves justice, happily for the country that
our Institution was at this moment formed, and was a means of putting
a stop to the proceedings of these rebels (if they may be so called) most
of whom joined our Institution as soon as they heard that they could
find an Asylum in it, and have become from that time the most peaceable subjects in the country."[146] In a petition of January 1812 to the
newly arrived governor, Sir John Craddock, Read, struggling to re-
establish the credibility of Bethelsdorp in the face of colonial criticism,
pointed out that the missionaries had persuaded many rebels to come
to Bethelsdorp and that in exchange the British government had
promised land and justice.[147] Some forty years later, Read's son, pleading for sympathy for the Khoisan rebels of Kat River, also recalled that
Dundas had offered the rebels "every legal and political protection
against their oppressors." Despite the commando immediately called
out by Dundas, "from that time to the present unhappy period, the
Hottentots have been loyal and faithful subjects of the British Crown,
attached to its laws and political institutions, and grateful to the Christian public of Britain for the blessings of the Gospel."[148] As Read Sr
summarized the political stance of the Bethelsdorp Khoisan in 1821,
"the Hottentots of Bethelsdorp have always shewn themselves loyal to
the British Government, and the greatest readiness to exert themselves
to the utmost, at the time of the insurrections of the Boors, and in the
late [1818–19] war with the Kaffers."[149]

This understanding was shared by the Dutch settlers and by the subsequent Batavian administration. "The almost universal clamour" among the Dutch, Van der Kemp reported in 1804, was that Bethelsdorp was English and therefore dangerous to the public peace, although he believed that "our relation to English benefactors was only a pretext to give vent to a deep rooted enmity against God, his Christ, and the extension of his kingdom of love and grace among the Heathen."[150] Governor Janssens protested in a letter to Van der Kemp that when the English held the Cape they "did not act like the sovereigns of the whole country, who were desirous of steadily, but mildly checking the barbarities suffered by one class of its inhabitants, the Hottentots, from the Europeans, another class; and at the same time compelling each to discharge its duty to the other." Rather, they had "looked at large bodies of these inhabitants as at open war with each other, and took part with the Hottentots like allies."[151]

It is important in other ways that many of the inhabitants of Bethelsdorp had been rebels. This group was politicized and probably nurtured a strong sense of recent grievance. Nonetheless, as the contrast between James Read Sr's comments before the Select Committee on Aborigines in 1836 and his son's in 1851 suggests, the missionaries downplayed the active role taken by the Khoisan in the Third Frontier War, and played up their role as passive victims for a British audience. In reality, settlers and colonial administrations at the Cape remained afraid of the Bethelsdorp Khoisan and expected for some fifty years that they might rebel again.

THE MISSIONARY AND THE GOVERNOR: COMPETING VIEWS OF "CIVILIZATION"

The new Batavian governor, rationalist representative of a republican regime, and Van der Kemp, the evangelical missionary, had a rocky relationship. Enlightenment and evangelicalism confronted one another in the shape of two strong-willed personalities.

Despite Van der Kemp's early – and mistaken – belief that he had allayed Janssens's suspicions of the supposed allegiance of the LMS missionaries to Britain, the relationship between the missionary and the governor was coloured throughout by Janssens's conviction that Van der Kemp was a dangerous man who had "perverted" the Khoisan.[157] Janssens's suspicion of the LMS missionaries came partly from his fear that they were allied with the British and influenced the Khoisan in the same direction. The charter by which Janssens granted land for Bethelsdorp to Van der Kemp, for example, included in its long list of preconditions that the institution should know no authority or political influence other than the Batavian government.[153] When in 1805 Janssens finally moved to prevent Van der Kemp from working as a missionary outside Cape Town, he justified banning Van der Kemp from Bethelsdorp on the grounds of his "English-mindedness."[154] At the same time, Janssens was suspicious of the Orangist Van der Kemp personally. He complained of the unrest aroused by soldiers from Bethelsdorp in the Cape Corps, into which Khoisan were impressed as soldiers. Although in the past the men from Bethelsdorp had behaved themselves particularly well, more recently, he wrote in 1805, "it is just some of those who as ringleaders have misled others to disorder, who nearly altogether have their homes in the Drosdy and some in or near Bethelsdorp – in practising their irregularity, in the obstinate persever-ence in the same, they called out the name of Mr. Vanderkemp not in the way of lamentation but of provocation."[155] At the root of the extended and vigorous quarrel between the two men were irreconcil-able visions of "civilization." When Janssens left the Cape, his written assessment, studded with headlines such as "Missionaries Harmful" and "Many Enemies of the State," noted that the sending societies were ignorant of the fact that "since 1795 these missionaries have enjoyed much protection – for political reasons – to the detriment of Holland and only to the advantage of our enemies, the English." It was painful, he continued, "to be obliged to provide protection and to grant favours to people who do their best to corrupt the minds of the natives, in order to turn them into enemies of the State."[156]

The entire Batavian interlude thus saw increasingly bitter confronta-tion between the LMS missionaries and the colonial administration.[157] Arguably, Van der Kemp was accepted as a de facto captain of sorts by the inhabitants of Bethelsdorp because he was an inveterate enemy of their enemies, the Dutch, and because he possessed the means of communicating with the authorities which the illiterate and scattered Khoisan lacked. In April 1804 Van der Kemp refused to cooperate any longer with the government in sending labour from Bethelsdorp to the neighbouring farmers as a "voluntary" goodwill gesture, on the ground that the farmers' treatment of the Khoekhoe was inhumane. He also refused to compel Bethelsdorp inhabitants to join the Cape Corps.

In 1805 Janssens summoned Read and Van der Kemp to Cape Town and forced Van der Kemp effectively to face charges of fomenting sedi-tion against the Dutch among the Khoekhoe. Read believed that Van der Kemp had in fact been "exiled" to the Cape for urging the punish-ment of crimes against the indigeneous people,[158] although this cannot be proved from the surviving correspondence between Janssens and Van der Kemp. "I have been obliged, at least so long as the war with England continues, in a discreet but [definite?] way to keep Mr. Van der Kemp away from Bethelsdorp," Janssens reported to the Netherlands. "He is a highly intelligent man who reasons very well about almost everything, but on the point of the conversion of heathens, he has such strange notions and behaved so strangely, that it threatened great danger."[159] To Landdrost Ludwig Alberti of Uitenhage, he confessed that "with Mr. Van der Kemp I am very much at a loss, as one so easily is with men of his type. I judge his return to Bethelsdorp to be impolitic but still do not know how, without according him the honour of martyrhood, I can manage this."[160] For the moment, Janssens simply detained Van der Kemp, Read and their Khoekhoe entourage in Cape Town.

At issue in the ensuing debate was the contrast between, on the one hand, Janssens's pragmatic desire for political compromise leading to peace, and, on the other, Van der Kemp's more purist sense of the demands of a vengeful God. Van der Kemp wanted murderers brought to justice; Janssens was in the delicate position of trying to negotiate peace between warring factions, and in particular to calm discontented settlers whose military support might prove essential in the event of a British invasion. According to Van der Kemp, the governor felt that it was currently politically essential to placate the settlers in the context of recent local conflict and of European war, until the time came that good could be accomplished.[161] Janssens felt that Van der Kemp should have sought to win the affection of the settlers as well as of the Hottentots, "for love had good and hate nothing but bad results." Certainly Janssens would have been conscious, following his tour in the interior, of reciprocal atrocities visited against settlers during the recent conflict as he met many refugees.[162] Van der Kemp, in contrast, affirmed that he was happy to be hated by "crooks and murderers."[163] At the same time, Janssens did acknowledge and deplore the wrongs done to the Khoekhoe, as did other officials of the Batavian regime. Indeed, Read would later claim that Janssens had declared that, given the many cases brought to his attention between Cape Town and Algoa Bay, if he did full justice more than a third of the colonists "must be punished by death."[164] Janssens affirmed, and Van der Kemp agreed, that the settlers held the land solely by the "right of the strongest," presumably with the implication that this could not be changed. For Van der Kemp, however, the biblical notion of blood guilt overrode the need for political realism. He argued that the uncompromising protection of the mistreated was the only means to avert the "revenge of God for the bloodshed of this godless country." The missionary informed his colleagues in the Netherlands that he felt Janssens was personally convinced that he was not in fact seditious or criminally pro-English but, like Pontius Pilate in his treatment of Jesus, Janssens refused to release him because of the "cry of the people." This does suggest, of course, that Van der Kemp's view of his own role was scarcely modest.

Another leitmotif of the debate between the governor and the missionary was the civilization of nomads and their proper role in a well-ordered society. For both Janssens and Alberti, who oversaw Bethelsdorp in his capacity as commanding officer at Fort Frederick, the process of civilizing "savages" was fraught with problems. "Civilized people – Europeans, with whom I reckon the colonists – never mix with the uncivilized but to their destruction," observed Janssens.[165] In his later book on the Xhosa, Alberti professed himself uncertain whether or not "the true happiness of a savage, or rather a semi-savage people is really promoted by civilization or not"; the cultured person has more gratifications but the uncultured does not long for them. Should the process be undertaken, it must be done with the greatest care,

and that at all events, no European Missionary Society whose efforts are aimed at the so-called conversion of heathens, be entrusted with it. These are mostly ignorant people belonging to the lower classes and are usually religious visionaries. They cause confusion in the minds of their disciples, who are unable to assimilate these religious concepts. They pay little or no attention to the instruction in useful handicrafts and other accomplishments which their apprentices are capable of, and have no adequate understanding of the intrinsic meaning of the civilizing process. They are spiteful enough, intentionally to thwart the ultimate objective, and consequently are more often dangerous than useful.[166]

The Batavians, heirs of the French Revolution, were religious rationalists, opposed to the charismatic religion of the missionary "religious visionaries"; they also saw "civilization" as being about imparting technology. On the verge of departure, Janssens had been planning to start civilizing the Xhosa, Alberti commented, by bringing youths, especially the sons of chiefs, to Cape Town to learn "the use of various manual occupations, and especially those relating to agriculture, apart from moral upbringing." They were then to be sent back home with the technology to put what they had learnt into practise; "in this way they were to introduce and spread their really useful knowledge."[167]

In contrast, as the enthusiastic reception accorded the visit of Martha Arendse and the Van Rooijs to London underscored, many British and Dutch evangelicals at the turn of the century equated civilizational "backwardness" with lack of knowledge of God, and held that conversion led instantly to the acquisition of the moral traits of a civilized person. As A. Albrecht wrote in the course of an account of the customs of the Nama: "Such are the manners of this poor unenlightened people! who would not feel for them! and humbly hope that an attempt to call them to the light of the love-breathing gospel to soften their manners, and to enlarge their conceptions, will be pleasing to our God and their God, to our Father and their Father."[168] The Albrecht brothers in the future Namibia were more zealous than the Eastern Cape missionaries in promoting technological change and in equating this with conversion; they tried to persuade their converts to abandon a "wandering life," for example, which was held to be a barrier to morality. Both groups of missionaries, however, thought that religious conversion preceded a separate thing called "civilization." Read and later J.G. Ulbricht, Georg Messer and F.G. Hooper at the Cape thought of civilization as essentially technological and in that sense a desirable but optional extra; the Albrecht brothers, and most of the domestic popularizers of mission in Britain, thought that civilization was associated with all the economic virtues such as docility, hard work, perseverence, self-consciousness, and contemplative ability which had propelled their own rise up the class ladder. All tended to believe that imparting "civilization" was not in itself problematic or disruptive, and that there were no limits on the immediate capacities of the converted person. Civilization was the product, in a varying combination, of environment and the application of evangelical virtues. This early LMS worldview was flexible enough to accommodate internal differences largely because it was not based on a well-entrenched "scientific" model of race. It rested on more haphazardly accumulated prejudices and beliefs among the missionaries themselves, who were not particularly well educated. These prejudices tended to be filtered more through the lens of class than of race: Africans were perceived in much the same way as were those at the very bottom of the class ladder in England, with similar duties as long as they remained working class but with parallel opportunities for self-advancement. Both African and working-class culture were thought of as *absences* (of "cultivation" or self-discipline, for example) rather than full-fledged and valid alternatives to some other culture.

Janssens's responses to Van der Kemp were based on the premise that the LMS did not understand the civilizing process. In contrast, Van der Kemp, who is the exception to many generalizations about missionaries, did not particularly care for or talk much about civilization, although he upheld the virtues ascribed to in the evangelical model described above. He did not even believe that abandoning nomadism was essential to civilization, as most of the other LMS missionaries did. In June 1802, reacting to news of Van der Walt's commando attack, he wrote angrily to Ross that he and Read had never expected "an universal instantaneous return of all the different Hottentot hordes." On the contrary, he thought, "some of them will prefer to live away from civilized society. Nor must all these be called rogues and plunderers. Some are men of respectability and of the strictest integrity."[169]

In an effort to curb missionary activity, the Batavians made it illegal to teach a "Hottentot" to write. Van der Kemp, on the other hand, wanted to establish an "Academy for Young Hottentots and missionaries" at Bethelsdorp, and he wrote to England once the Batavians had left in quest of "Geographical and travels, especially through Asia and Africa, – descriptions of arts and manufactures, Grammars and dictionaries for instruction in the Latin, Greek and oriental languages, classic authors in Greek and Latin; we want especially a good General map of the world, particularly maps, and a celestial planisphorium and a pair of Globes."[170]

In contrast, Janssens believed: "In regard to the Hottentots learning to write, that may be deferred until they are so far advanced that it can be useful to them. But I cannot understand how it will benefit people who have neither knowledge to build a house to live in, nor a desire to wear clothes, nor the least share of civilization."[171] The identification made by many of the Kat River settlers between literacy and economic advance on a specific western model may possibly be dated from this Batavian edict. In 1806, when the British lifted the prohibition, "our poor people rejoiced with us" at the lifting of a Batavian ban on Khoekhoe entry to Bethelsdorp and of the "inhumane and scandalous interdiction" against teaching their children to write.[172]

Janssens's comments on a further proposal of Van der Kemp's to establish a Khoekhoe officer corps in the Cape Regiment exhibited not so much cruelty as incredulity: "Were your expressions less bitter, I should think you were jesting, in the ridiculous proposal to place the Hottentots under officers of their nation; but if their abilities admitted such a measure, I would adopt it, since they are unquestionably free as we are, and joint inhabitants of the land with us."[173] These arguments ultimately rested on differential assessments of the capacity of the Khoekhoe, rather than on political claims about their conquest.

The LMS and the Batavian regime were engaged in a dialogue of the deaf. Janssens continued to insist that the Khoisan did not possess major reasons for discontent and that Van der Kemp was stirring up an otherwise docile group for treacherous political purposes. Towards the end of Janssens's tenure, he forebade English missionaries to preach, and the LMS filled its south African posts with Germans and Dutchmen. Proving that German missionaries could also be troublesome, the young Ulbricht, who was left in charge of Bethesldorp, shared Van der Kemp's views of the oppression of the Khoisan, although he was often ill and lacked Van der Kemp's forcefulness in arguing with the local authorities. In 1805 he wrote that he thought often of Isaiah 9:1–3 ("The people that walked in darkness has seen a great light")

as I consider the Hottentot nation as particularly the oppression and mighty bondage under which they are brought and though it is their country they are deprived of it by violence and force ... And it is impossible to live in peace here with the inhabitants of this country if one takes the cause of Christianity to heart and that state of such an unfortunate nation. If one would help to oppress that poor unfortunate nation then should one be respected and live in peace, but rather bear pain and contempt, than be friends with those who seek only to exercise wickedness. Never could I have believed that beasts come out of men, they are like unto a beast who are of such ignorance in the world.[174]

By late 1805, Janssens was threatening to shut down the LMS mission altogether. Van der Kemp found his faith in God's promises wavering and "quarrelled not a little with the Lord." Could it be that he was too sinful to find mercy in God's eyes? That God would not in fact support his endeavours? At that moment of crisis, however, Van der Kemp found himself in the presence of God himself, in a way he had never previously experienced. God asked him (so Van der Kemp recorded), "Do you now believe that you will find mercy in my eyes?"[175]

Instead of the closure of the mission, ships arrived from Britain as the Napoleonic Wars broke out again. On January 1806 Sir David Baird retook the Cape, this time to hold it in earnest. Read and Van der Kemp saw the arrival of the British as the providential intervention of God. Indeed, Van der Kemp characteristically thought that the British re-conquest of the Cape was God's vengeance on the Dutch.[176] As it transpired, however, before the 1820s the British were to do little but codify the local custom which kept the Khoisan in bondage.

4 Khoisan Uses of Christianity

Despite its inauspicious beginnings, Bethelsdorp would become an important resource for Khoisan in the Cape Colony at a time of difficulty and oppression under both the Dutch and the British. In 1834 Hendrik Smit of Theopolis said that, before the abolition of vagrancy legislation in 1828, "we were like a man enclosed in a cask full of nails, which cask was rolled downhill, and because it was downhill there was no cessation of suffering, it was always rolling." Andries Jaeger recalled in the same year that the old time had been a "time of sorrow," under the evils and oppression of which "I have often wished I was dead (God forgive me) to be eased of my burden."[1]

In the early nineteenth century, the options available to people of Khoisan descent who did not choose, or were unable, to emigrate were limited. Men might join the Cape Corps, the Khoisan regiment based in Cape Town. All might work as servants in white households, mostly farms. Residence at a mission station was a third option. To pursue an independent existence within colonial territory was difficult, given the web of local custom and vagrancy legislation which immobilized Khoisan labourers and kept them tied to white employers. Bethelsdorp, and later other LMS Eastern Cape mission stations including Theopolis (1814) and Hankey (1822) provided a weapon in the ongoing struggle of the Khoisan with settlers and with the colonial administration. It was, however, a weapon selected at a time of great duress and limited choice. At the same time, widespread Khoisan conversions to Christianity were not solely instrumental, and one must take seriously the evidence, however faint its traces, of the spiritual and intellectual issues at stake for those who interacted with Christianity. Furthermore, there were, as we have seen, different ways of thinking about Christianity at the Cape and its political implications: Khoisan converts were using one form of Christianity against the versions of settlers and administrators in order to assert their own fundamental humanity. Why, and how, did Khoisan people try to use both Christianity and the mission stations themselves in the early nineteenth century? This chapter examines some possible answers, looking in turn at the inextricably linked issues of violence and social breakdown, material conflicts between settlers and Khoisan, linkages between Christian and earlier Khoekhoe religious ideas and practices, and the politics of text and status.

VIOLENCE

It is in extreme circumstances that groups become peculiarly open to radical cultural and intellectual change – and in need of an intellectual explanation for suffering. The scale of the social and personal disruption being experienced by the Khoisan, particularly the type of violence which confronted individuals in their day-to-day lives and in which they themselves participated, must be a large – if certainly not sufficient – part of the explanation for the early utility of missions stations to the Khoisan of the Eastern Cape and the initial appeal of Christianity to many.

Violence was the glue that held the frontier world together, affecting all groups of society. In the north, settlers and San continued to wage war. Commando after commando of white farmers accompanied by Khoisan servants shot people, sometimes hundreds at a time, except for young children who were captured to be brought up as client labour. When Maynier was appointed landdrost of Graaff-Reinet in 1792, he learnt from the reports of commandos that "that generally many hundred of Bosjesmen were killed by them, amongst which number there were perhaps not more than 6 or 10 men (they generally contriving to save themselves by flight), and that the greatest part of the killed comprised helpless women and innocent children. I was also made acquainted with the most horrible atrocities committed on those occasions; such as ordering the Hottentots to dash out against the rocks the brains of infants (too young to be carried off by the farmers for the purpose to use them as bondmen), in order to save powder and shot."[2] Many of the so-called San, if Shula Marks is correct, were impoverished Khoekhoe and fugitives from the colony, in which case the commando system needs to be seen as equally as devastating to the Khoekhoe as to the San.[3] Even if Marks overestimates levels of Khoekhoe presence in San bands, there was also a psychological cost to those on the other side of commandos. Although some Khoisan servants of white farmers presumably served voluntarily on commandos, many Khoisan in service were forced to participate in these commandos. Indeed, the propensity of reluctant farmers, eager to avoid commando duty, to send their Khoisan dependants in their stead was an ongoing source of tension between local adminstrators and their subjects.[4] Andries Stoffels, whose biography James Read wrote after his death, "had been an *agter ryder* to a Dutch Boor [a boy riding behind the master with his large gun upon his shoulder, especially on commandos] and had witnessed many scenes that affected him through life."[5] Others took the techniques of commandos outside the colony and used them themselves to subdue indigenous Khoekhoe in Namaqualand and Transorangia.

The ferocity of the war between San and settlers escalated significantly in the last quarter of the eighteenth century, partly as a result of increased pressure on the San from the other direction from Xhosa and early Griqua communities, as well as the white invasion of San heartlands.[6] Numerous small groups participated in violence and theft against one another in a struggle for survival. San incursions were organized resistance against white land theft. At the same time, large numbers of the San were frequently hungry by this time, and cattle theft may have been the only way to stay alive.[7] The overall atmosphere is suggested by the animosity of the so-called "Bushmen" against "Hottentots" in the service of farmers attested to by Barrow in 1797: "Should they seize a Hottentot guarding his master's castle, not contented with putting him to immediate death, they torture him by every means of cruelty that their invention can frame, as drawing out his bowels, tearing off his nails, scalping, and committing other acts of violence equally savage."[8]

Violence within the colony was as pervasive in Graaff-Reinet in the 1790s and first years of the 1800s as it was in the contested border areas. This violence of at least some settlers was not only disciplinary violence required to maintain labourers in a state of de facto slavery, but also extreme and dysfunctional, as is typical of slave societies. This violence was also in some measure known to the Cape Town authorities, both Dutch and British. Two examples may be cited. The private secretary of Governor Janssens of the Batavian period reported that, when the English left, a colonist named Ferreira took possession of the fort in Graaff-Reinet. The Xhosa, thinking that all war was over, sent him an animal to kill as a gesture of friendship, led by a Xhosa messenger and a Khoekhoe guide. "Ferreira, as a return gesture, seized the Caffre, burnt him alive; attached the poor Hottentot to a tree, cut out a piece of flesh from his thigh, made him eat it raw, and then let him

go."[9] More routinely, since the above might have been an isolated incident, the type of violence later described by Read and Van der Kemp
went well beyond the needs of labour discipline. Normative theorizing,
furthermore, must not blind the scholar to the particular – the particular sadism, the particular gesture. Read wrote in what would prove to
be an influential letter to the LMS board in 1808:

The poor Hottentots continue to be a suffering and an oppressed people ... A
poor Hottentot came to us a little time back who had been kept in service
twenty-five years, without being hired, and was now obliged to run away to
get free and leave his property behind. When asked if he had Children, he said
he had left a daughter behind pickled – that is, she had been flogged to pieces
with a sambok or whip made of the skin of the rhinoceros or seacow and then
a vast quantity of salt rubbed into the wounds, (sometimes gunpowder and
vinegar is mixed with the salt) this had not however been sufficient to preserve
her from putrefaction, for the worms were crawling from her body, and he
expected she would be now dead.

The first name of this woman was Catrijn.[10] Read then described the
murder of a man called Ourson, a former waggoner to Colonel
Lemoyne, and his wife and baby.

We have likewise been informed of the murder of a Hottentot girl by a farmer's
wife who might be considered a Monster, but is in this Country, considered a
worthy Inhabitant ... A farmer in her neighbourhood told me, he saw her stab
a Hottentot woman with an iron craw that the Child with which she was pregnant fell from her body, and expired with the mother ... An other poor old
slave woman came here naked about a fortnight ago who had been so horrid-
ly beaten that she could scarce walk. She had come about six miles upon her
hands and knees; her child likewise had been murdered – we recommended her
likewise to go to the landdrost but she said she should only be given into the
hands of her master, who she was sure would kill her immediately – Her Master and Mistress are well known here as famous for cruelty and murder – the
latter has been known to throw Hottentot women in the oven and burn them
alive, and tear out slaves' eyes while alive with the thumb and finger as if she
had a dead sheep's head.[11]

The late-eighteenth- and early-nineteenth-century Eastern Cape witnessed a widespread culture of violence with grave implications for all
its inhabitants.[12]
    Under these brutal conditions, and deprived of the land upon which
their traditional cultures depended, the colonial Khoisan in the early
1800s continued to be enmeshed in a process of widespread social

breakdown, characterized by alcoholism, a declining birth rate possibly linked to malnutrition, much heavier use of *daccha* (marijuana) than in the past,[13] heavy death rates from western diseases,[14] and crushing poverty. James Read and his eldest son believed that, at the turn of the century, the Khoekhoe suffered from contingent "mental weakness" produced in large part by their "political depression" and the "mental apathy" which it invariably created.[15] Be that as it may, mission history must be read against the background of conquest, violence, and related social crisis.

It is arguable that in this atmosphere Calvinist evangelical mission Christianity provided a theology of evil that furnished an explanation for the apparently meaningless oppression of the Khoisan, as well as a means for individuals to expiate their own guilt and anxiety. Bethelsdorp Christianity not only attacked white Christianity but also explained it: settlers were only nominal Christians, had never experienced rebirth, and were still sunk in original sin. The purification of the rebirth experience may furthermore have provided an outlet for the anxieties pervading Khoisan communities. There is a tremendously high level of outward emotion described in services, revivals, and conversions at Bethelsdorp, with floods of tears drenching missionary reports. Many individuals felt traumatized by their pasts, and there was a strong Khoisan response to the ideas of hell and of personal guilt on which the evangelical missionaries placed so much emphasis.[16] Hendrik Boezak, for example, was said to have "a peculiar address, great boldness, and a heart burning with zeal for the salvation of sinners, and when surrounded with a body of hearers he rests not till most or all are in tears, which he calls laying down the weapons."[17] One Kruisman, a preacher and a shoemaker, had lived with a farmer before coming to Bethelsdorp. He had been treated badly when he expressed a desire to come to Bethelsdorp but persisted because he was concerned about his soul and because he conceived "that what he saw daily, Murder, drunkenness, adultery, swearing, &c &c could not be pleasing in the eyes of God – and wished to know if there were no remedy." The magistrate finally released Kruisman from service to his masters and allowed him to come to Bethelsdorp. Once there, however, he "began to see that the sins which he had seen in others, were his own, and he began to be almost in dispair that of such a monster could be saved."[18]

Other individuals expressed a similar sense of looking for change before they encountered the LMS – again, a sign of culture under severe stress. Accounts, of course, play up the evil of the sinner before conversion; this was a necessary element of conversion narratives, and it is problematic to rely for evidence on a genre with such stylized conventions. On the other hand, the element of search *before* meeting the

agent of religious change is more evident in early accounts of the
Khoisan than in parallel British narratives; it is also counter-intuitive
that missionaries reporting for an administration hungry for news of
their effectiveness would downgrade their own contributions.

Cupido Kakkerlak, for example, had been "famous for swearing,
lieing, fighting, but more perticular for drunkenness, which often
brought him upon a sick bed, being naturally weak." He was anxious
to stop drinking but found it difficult.

He inquired by all he met for means to deliver him from the sin of drunkenness, supposing that to leave the rest would be easy – some directed him to
Witches and Wizards, to whom he addressed himself, but these were miserable
comforters, for they told him, that his life was not worth a farthing, for when
people began to make such enquiries it was a sure sign of speedy death, others
presented various kinds of medicines, which he eagerly took, but all proved in
vain – His feet were providentially led to Graaff-Reinet where he heard, in a
discourse from Brother Van der Lingen, that Jesus Christ, the son of God,
could save sinners from their sins. He cried out to himself "that is what I want!
that is what I want!" He immediately left business, to come to us, to get
acquainted with this Jesus, and told all he met, that he had at last found one,
who could save him from his sins.[19]

MATERIAL STRUGGLES AND MISSIONS
STATIONS: LABOUR AND MOBILITY

At the same time, this atmosphere of violence and coercion meant that
mission stations became foci of material struggles between Khoisan,
farmers, and administrators over the control of nonwhite labour and
mobility. Whether looking for shelter against violence, greater economic independence, literacy, or indeed salvation, many more individuals tried to come to Bethelsdorp, and later to other LMS stations, than
local settlers, through their control of the local administrative appara-
tus, would readily allow. Van der Kemp claimed in 1804 that "our
labours, and present Institution have from its first origin been a stumbling block in the eyes of the Unchristian inhabitants of this country,
and an object of their hatred."[20] The resulting struggles echoed earlier
conflicts over access to the Western Cape Moravian station of
Genadendal in the early 1790s.[21] In the 1790s and early 1800s, farmers from the Uitenhage district also resented and tried to curtail
Khoisan and slave preachers, and more broadly to limit the access of
their nonwhite dependants to Christianity. They saw this as a means of
maintaining power over the "heathen." To take just one example – and
we will see more instances of conflict later – when Michiel Vos was on

the road to meet with the first four LMS missionaries at Cape Town, he stayed at the house of a farmer who was infuriated by the prospect of missions among the "heathen" and in a temper asked, "Staat er niet geschreven ... 'gij zult de Heidenen hebben tot uw erfdeel, en de einden der aarde tot uwe bezitting'?" ("Is it not written ... 'I shall give the Heathen to you as a possession, and the ends of the earth as your possession'?"). The citation is from psalm 2; Vos contended that God was speaking here to Jesus rather than to Christians as a whole.[22]

More materially, Bethelsdorp was a threat to farmers because it seemed to jeopardize a supply of labour to white farms – labour that was conceived of as being slave-like and bonded to particular places or people. By 1807, the new landdrost of Uitenhage, the American-born Jacob Cuyler, was complaining bitterly to his superiors at the Castle that few of the white inhabitants had "Hottentots" resident since most of them had been "enticed" to Bethelsdorp "through the arts and insinuations of Mr. Vanderkemp."[23] White missionaries and farmers alike were part of the African calculus of power, albeit for different reasons: to accumulate people was to accumulate power and wealth, whether of the spiritual or material variety, and missions and farms were in direct competition.

There were strong economic reasons for Khoisan adherence to a mission station and for white opposition. In the early years there were many people living at LMS mission stations who were not converts or even attending church. At the most basic level, the community function of the station ran parallel to that filled by missionary institutions in less damaged societies: at the beginning people tended to come to it if they were marginal or outcast or in need of concrete protection, rather than because they necessarily wanted to convert. In the same way, early LMS and Glasgow Missionary Society stations among the Xhosa furnished a refuge for people in trouble, especially women, such as those accused of witchcraft killings.[24] Bethelsdorp functioned as a political asylum in the immediate aftermath of war. It continued to fulfil the role of haven for people escaping difficult situations with the farmers. The Khoisan man whose actions precipitated the Afrikaner rebellion of Slagter's Nek tried to escape to Bethelsdorp in 1816, for example.[25] A mission station might also be used as a base from which to seek legal redress in a crisis situation (however small the chances of obtaining justice). Just over two weeks after the above case, the missionary George Barker witnessed the arrival at Bethelsdorp of a "Hottentot" woman: "She had resided a long time with a certain Boer and had co-habited with a slave of his, by whom she had several children. The Boer had driven her away & deprived her of the man with whom she had so long lived that he might take a slave woman to wife, that the Boer might gain slaves (the children of the Hottentot being free). Her children were obtained by the Boer and apprenticed after the usual manner." Four days later this woman travelled to the landdrost to complain, in company with another woman "who had been shamefully beaten having large wounds on her back from the sambok." When, however, "these poor creatures arrived at the drosdy, the Landrost ordered the people who had accompanied them from Bethelsdorp to return and put the women into prison without giving them a hearing."[26]

In addition to being short-term shelters, mission stations also had long-term attractions as a means to improve economic and social status.[27] Bethelsdorp, Theopolis, and Hankey provided economic bases from which a Khoisan labourer in the Eastern Cape could hire him or herself out if financially pressed (as almost all the inhabitants of mission stations were forced to do in the early years), with the chance of escaping serfdom. The nub of the problem was the assumed incapacity of a "Hottentot" to own land, which was enshrined in colonial custom if not in law.[28] In theory, all the land of the Uitenhage and Graaff-Reinet districts had been divided up among white farmers. In practice, farmers' "places" were so large that small groups of Khoisan, castigated as bandits, might with difficulty survive in the interstices of white property. All such independent existence, however, theoretically constituted trespass and vagrancy. The LMS was the nominal owner of all mission station land; inhabitants might have custodial use but could not alienate land. Thus, if a person defined as a "Hottentot" were nominally registered at a mission station, even if rarely living there, he or she had a place to which legally to return on the expiry of a contract, rather than being given a maximum of three days in which to find a new employer and place of residence. Without an attested residence under the direction of a white person, and a pass signed by a white indicating the destination and purpose of his journey, a Khoisan person or free black on the road could be arrested by any white, thrown into jail, and hired out to a white employer at the whim of local officialdom.

In addition, having a legal base meant that a farm worker could leave his family and any cattle he might have at the mission station while he was away doing long-term contract labour. He was also enabled to take short-term contracts. Both of these capacities lessened the master's leverage. We have already seen how many male rebels during 1799–1803 were constrained by the fact that their former masters still had control of their women, children, and cattle. Cattle might also be impounded for debts of food and drink incurred by the farm worker, while children born and brought up on a farm became "apprenticed" to the farmer until the age of eighteen or twenty-five. Consequently, an entire family could become immobilized on a farm. On the other hand, a farm worker's hire usually included maintenance for his family if his wages were insufficiently high to buy them food;[29] it was therefore an ideal situation for the family to receive the maintenance without the legal ramifications of a long term stay on a farm. In the 1810s and 1820s, Bethelsdorp always had a much higher percentage of women, children, and elderly people actually living at the institution, while the bulk of young men went out to work at a distance in a small-scale precursor of the migrant labour system of the so-called "home-lands." In a further parallel with the bantustans (the overcrowded territories to which many Africans were confined under the apartheid regime), the dependent population left at the station experienced immiseration because the land was relatively infertile and the station had few productive resources. This group was heavily dependent on the earnings of the male household head; when men were conscripted into public labour at low wages or forced into the army for no pay during wartime, their families starved.[30] Nonetheless, these families clearly chose the uncertain economic situation of the missionary station, which offered a greater shot at economic well-being accompanied by greater risk, to the loss of independence as de facto bonded farm labour.

For those who were in a situation to grasp economic opportunities, especially those who believed in material accumulation, mission stations could offer a certain prosperity, however precarious. The San convert Andries Pretorius told LMS inspector John Campbell in 1813 that

when he came to Bethelsdorp he had four oxen, and has now ten and a waggon, and one horse, besides four stolen by the Caffres. He stated, that from childhood until he joined the Institution in 1806, his thirty-third year, he had served a boor, for which long service he had received one heifer and six ewes. Being asked how he had four oxen when he came to the settlement, since he had received only one heifer from the boor; these oxen, he said, he procured by making iron rings at leisure hours in the evening. In one year at the Institution he earned two hundred dollars, with which he purchased a waggon from his former master. He has large fields and a plough; and provides for a wife and eight children of his own, and two orphans.[31]

In the same year, Campbell investigated the economic situation of Bethelsdorp, in response to colonial charges that inhabitants were "idle, lazy – that they did no thing," and that individuals had brought some 6,000 head of cattle to the station and had reduced them, through improvidence and idleness (that is, consuming and selling their stock), to 2,000. Presenting the colonial Khoisan as, on the contrary, effective economic and, therefore, moral agents, Campbell pointed out that Bethelsdorp had extensive cultivated fields hidden from the eye of the visitor, and that cattle ownership had risen over the past few years from 218 to 2,206, of which very few were slaughtered for food.[32] People were therefore coming to Bethelsdorp in a state of poverty and using it as a base to acquire stock. For the most part, mission-station inhabitants were nonetheless poor. All the same, however, residence at Bethelsdorp offered a better economic bet than permanent residence on a white farm, as also, probably, than a hand-to-mouth existence as a fugitive. It also provided some guarantee of independence, particularly for men made vulnerable by the possession of families and stock. In addition, mission stations permitted some individuals to struggle to pursue a traditional economic existence, since they provided a place to leave stock and allowed individuals to travel off the station extensively and to gather food in a traditional manner. The early LMS institutions were thus used in a variety of ways for economic ends by inhabitants.

Before 1812, an informal system of coercion limited access to Bethelsdorp. Slave-owners and employers often prevented Khoisan and slaves from coming to the station.[33] In the meantime, local officials, who frequently refused passes and manipulated contracts in order to keep Khoekhoe labour immobile, blocked access in a more spuriously legitimate fashion.

Khoisan disillusionment with the British was at first alleviated and then entrenched at the prospect of substantial legal change under Lord Caledon in 1809. Caledon sent Colonel Richard Collins to investigate the eastern frontier region, in anticipation of regularizing the situation of the Khoisan. Collins's report was critical of Bethelsdorp and castigated its inhabitants for laziness; it, too, echoed Boer complaints about the shortage of labour, which had swelled since the abolition of slavery in 1807. It described Bethelsdorp as "the cause of the greatest embarrassment to the inhabitants of the neighbouring districts, whose servants leave them on the slightest pretext to repair to Bethelsdorp ..."[34] The institution ought to be broken up and its inhabitants sent either to work for farmers or to the Moravian stations, where, as Collins had remarked in an earlier report, the "greatest regularity and industry" prevailed.[35]

Caledon did not attempt to break up Bethelsdorp, but he did try to tackle the problem of labour shortages. The resulting Caledon Code represented a stab at reform but in fact codified existing coercive labour practices without ensuring that the code's enshrinement of work contracts and limits on their duration could be enforced.[36] Regulations concerning work contracts were in practice widely ignored, while the pass laws that the Code formalized were (even on their own terms) thoroughly abused in order to press Khoisan into service.[37] The code ordained that every "Hottentot" was to have a fixed place of abode. A "Hottentot" required a pass issued by his master or a local official to move within a district, and a certificate signed by the landdrost to move between districts. Any white person had the right to stop a Hottentot, demand to see his or her pass, and deliver him or her to local officialdom in its absence.[38] In practice, local officials tended to compel Khoisan to enter into a contract with a white farmer in need of labour. As Newton-King has demonstrated, these measures had two important effects. First, they made it legal for colonists to compel a nonwhite person not on government service to work for farmers. This gave local officials, the landdrosts, and veldcornets, total control over Khoisan mobility. Second, local officials gained substantial opportunities for patronage in the distribution of Khoisan labour.[39] Furthermore, the many Khoisan living outside the purview either of mission stations or white farms, whom Van der Kemp termed "Woodmen,"[40] were at once turned into outlaws. Residence in Bethelsdorp became both more desirable and harder to obtain. The local veldcornets, the 1810 Bethelsdorp annual report attests, "against the weight of justice hinder them [the Khoisan] from going out of their cornetships, from fear they should go to Bethelsdorp, and force them to serve the boors."[41]

After 1812, the landdrost was effectively granted the right to screen admissions in the wake of a quarrel between Cuyler and the then acting head of Bethesldorp, James Read. In that turbulent year, the Uitenhage landdrost ordered Read to deliver up from the station two "girls" of (he claimed) twelve and eleven years who had been apprenticed in their early childhoods. Cuyler charged that they had been illegitimately admitted to Bethelsdorp. Because they were under eighteen and so had not yet served out their apprenticeships, they must be returned to their masters. Read protested that the young women were manifestly over eighteen, both being about twenty-four years old, and that one, at least, had been born and brought up at the Moravian station of Genadendal and had no knowledge of ever having been registered as an apprentice. As the age of the women was indisputable, the demand was eventually dropped. In response, however, Cuyler insisted "to prevent impositions, disputes and troubles, I request that you do not receive any Hottentots of what ever description at your Institution (those already enregistered excepted) without their having been with me and obtained a permit for that purpose." Read's protest to Governor Cradock proved futile, at a time at which, as we shall see in a later chapter, the mission was in disgrace with the British elite and Craddock was eager to see the station kept on a tighter official leash. The records of Bethelsdorp, and after 1814 its sister station Theopolis, are henceforward studded with references to outright refusals by the land-drosts of Uitenhage and Graaff-Reinet to endorse applications for admission. Most frequently, able-bodied men were ordered to find long-term contract work with the farmers rather than being allowed to join a mission station. Dragoönder Anagerman, for example, honourably discharged from the Cape Regiment in 1821 after ten years service and heading for Bethelsdorp, was intercepted by Cuyler, who wrote on the back of the pass which a missionary had issued for him: "This Hotten-tot named in the within pass must find a master within three days with whom he must come to the Landdrost to hire."[42] In 1821 the Theopo-lis missionary George Barker lamented the "base ingratitude" of Saart-je Bezuidenhout, who wanted to leave his home after he had reproved her for misconduct. "After having done so much for Saartje to get her admitted and for that very purpose took her into our house when we had two more, my mind was very much hurt and my temper ruffled."[43] This latter example suggests that women as well as men encountered registration problems, and that employment with a white missionary was seen as a sufficient substitute for farm work. It also, incidentally, emphasizes the growing wealth and "social distance" by the 1820s of LMS missionaries, some of whom were as eager as their lay counterparts to use Khoisan labour. Such quarrels were as much about the control of Khoisan labour and mobility as about spirituality.

The function of the mission station as a means for some to develop economic independence from farm labour became more important in the 1810s and 1820s as the village of Algoa Bay grew into a small port town, renamed Port Elizabeth in 1820. In that year, as Britain decided at last to develop South Africa as a British settler colony rather than simply using the country as a trade depot and refuelling station run on the ground by the Dutch population, groups of British settlers arrived in the Eastern Cape and were settled along the frontier with the Xhosa. In the short run, the economic impact of the 1820 settlers was benefi-cial for the Khoisan, however deleterious white competition in a racist society was ultimately to prove.[44] The settlers boosted the population of Algoa Bay, founded the town of Grahamstown, and expanded local economic possibilities by hastening the monetization of the economy and providing a market for artisanal skills, food, and wood products and such skilled labour as transport riding. Bethelsdorp had been known as the "school" since its inception; now there was an increas-ingly evident point to the instruction in trades and crafts which the sta-tions struggled to offer alongside academic and religious instruction. In 1817 LMS missionary J. Georg Messer reported that one man received six rixdollars for a year's work as a farm labourer.[45] In 1821 a Bethels-dorp missionary, presumably James Read, attested that an inhabitant had made 270 rixdollars in ten days "by his waggon."[46] The colonial officials to whom Philip mentioned this in a statement of grievances denied that it was possible; at the very least, however, their own investigation showed that a waggon driver customarily made seventy rixdollars for the nine-day journey to Grahamstown and back.[47]

Yet these expanded economic possibilities were not accompanied by any lessening of settler desire to use the Khoisan as cheap manual labour. As the colonial secretary, Colonel Christopher Bird, no particular friend to Bethelsdorp, commented in 1823 in the course of conversation with the commissioners of inquiry (sent out from Britain primarily to investigate settler problems and Cape politics), "the British settlers that first arrived seemed to expect that they would be allowed to make drudges of the Hottentots although they were restricted from holding slaves."[48]

At the same time, as some mission Khoisan became more prosperous, the "Hottentots" began to be perceived not only as recalcitrant manual labour but also as a potential economic threat. One Dutch settler, for example, testified to the commission in 1823 that inhabitants of Bethelsdorp had been awarded the Commissariat's waggon-hire contract "against a large competition of the Boors in the same district, and hence arises the aversion of the latter to the Missionary Institution, and the attempts of the Landrosts to oppress them by heavy demands upon their Labour for Government Services."[49]

This sense of threat was particularly characteristic of the British settlers, who had been thrust onto farms for a statutory period but had for the most part been artisans themselves back in Britain. Many of them were anxious to abandon an unprofitable and unfamiliar farming life and return to being independent craftsmen. Therefore they resented skilled nonwhite labour. By the end of the 1820s, when the immigrants and their sons were no longer required to stay on their farms, the Khoisan were being squeezed out of the white market through economic discrimination. As Jane Sales observes, "in the long run, this economic competition with the whites meant that the possibility for success in the artisan class ... could only be achieved in two ways: either by 'passing' into the white group if skin colour and the nature of their hair made this possible, or working for wages so much lower than the whites were willing to do that one still got some trade." The obvious result was that "even skill did not lift one out of poverty."[50]

The growing scarcity and expense of slaves from 1807 onwards contributed to the pressure on Khoisan labourers. The colonial administration had hoped that the labour shortage of the colony could be resolved by white immigration. This policy proved unsuccessful, on the whole. The immigrants themselves were reluctant to remain in their

menial jobs as farm workers or servants, since such jobs were not con-
sonant with the new-found status accorded to them in a slave colony
by virtue of their skin colour.[51] There was also resistance from employers. One disgruntled British farmer alleged to the commissioners that
European labourers were encouraged to make frivolous complaints in
the law courts at the expense of employers, because the judges and
magistrates were all slave-owners who wanted "to discourage the
employment of free Labourers and apprentices or any species of labour
that might have a tendency to diminish the profit of that of their own
slaves."[52] Another witness, a Mr. Buckenroder, testified: "In allusion to
the present eager disposition to appropriate the labour of Hottentots ...
the desire to obtain labourers had increased with the augmented value
of slaves, which formerly might be purchased for two hundred and are
now scarcely to be had for two thousand rixdollars and even so far as
five thousand rixdollars."[53] The white community, in effect, was reluctant to see white labour filling the jobs of slaves and "Hottentots,"
while white workers were unwilling to put up with the conditions and
wages of nonwhites. They were also resistance to the Khoisan taking
better-paid and higher-status employment away from whites. The mission station seemed to represent these processes.

In a more tightly regulated environment under the British, settler and
state opposition to unfettered Khoisan freedom of economic action at
mission stations was expressed through legal control of the stations
rather than through the more violent and decentralized coercion of the
earliest years. Mission-station inhabitants were subject to a heavy burden of "public" work. The conservative governor Sir Rufane Donkin
justified the policy in 1821 by arguing that "these institutions are protected by Government and have lands assigned to them – in return
Government has a right to a reasonable priority of service at a fair
rate."[54] The rate of pay was, however, derisory and demands were so
frequent and so protracted as to menace the independence of Khoi
labourers.[55] A man was paid about two shillings a day for public work,
whereas an average daily wage for an independent worker based at
Bethelsdorp was one and a half to two dollars,[56] even leaving aside the
much larger payoffs possible for transport work by men with access to
a waggon and oxen. Since public work was organized by local officials,
the Khoisan were also called out to work for the local community as
well as (illegally) for individuals with influence with the drostdy
administration.[57] Demands were made in an arbitrary fashion; the
landdrost would write to the missionary in charge of an institution and
order, say, twenty men to present themselves at his office within a couple of days to carry out several weeks' worth of road repair.[58] The missionary would then pass on the demand to the Khoisan corporals,

elected annually by the people, who were responsible for administrative detail and organized the work parties.[59] The whole process was obviously highly disruptive. Corvée labour demands were met with difficulty in an institution with such a low percentage of able-bodied people resident at any given moment; in 1821, for example, there were about 1,200 people resident at Bethelsdorp, of whom some 900 were generally absent at work (these statistics appear to exclude children).[60] Between January and October of the same year, demands placed on work parties included, among other things, providing unspecified labour under the direction of local farmer L.M. van Rooyen, repairing the road from Bethelsdorp to the bay, clearing stones from the road from the Swartkops River to Port Elizabeth, clearing the road from Port Elizabeth to Bethelsdorp, hauling powder for a private individual, clearing water courses, carrying out unspecified public work, and repairing the roads leading to Ada's Drift. Many of these demands were evaded by inhabitants, however, who were either genuinely absent or unwilling to report.[61] Time limits were often unspecified: at the beginning of March 1821, for instance, men sent to Somerset to cut corn in December 1820 had still not been released and their families at the station were in great distress.[62]

The return given to the commissioners of inquiry in 1823 showed a total of 21 "Europeans" and 2,221 "Hottentots" attached to Bethelsdorp; of the "Hottentots" 648 were men, 704 were women, and 859 were children. At the time of the return, 514 of the men, 517 of the women, and 501 of the children were listed as "absent," leaving 679 in residence (the high absentee figures for women may suggest new work possibilities as servants).[63] Labour requisitions principally affected those who were not away as servants or registered at farms on long-term contracts, primarily independent labourers such as woodcutters, elephant hunters, transport workers, or craftsmen, who were trying to make Bethelsdorp or Theopolis a home base. The notice was too short to call people away from contract work, and in any case the head of a missionary institution had, as Read and Philip put it, "legally no power to call individuals away from the service of the Inhabitants."[64] The primary group targetted was precisely that beloved of the missionaries: people who were seeking to change their economic lifestyle in accordance with missionary strictures. Read and Philip tellingly complained that the families of those called out to work were deprived of their principal wage-earner "upon whose earnings most assuredly rests every hope they have of procuring the decencies and ordinary comforts of life and without which it is quite clear they can never have it in their power to raise themselves above the degraded conditions in which they are unfortunately generally to be found, that of being able to command only a scanty subsistence from day to day and nothing beyond it."[65]

White settlers were required to perform some public work but were well remunerated and tended to send out their Khoisan servants to do it for them, without passing on the wages. The inhabitants of Bethelsdorp, for example, were required to take letters on journeys which sometimes amounted to a day's round trip, with no remuneration. Afrikaner "post boers" were in charge of organizing the system. In 1809 Colonel Cuyler could not "say otherwise than that the Post Boors should be paid at the rate of Three Rixdollars per hour per month. The Government expect prompt and speedy conveyance of their orders, which they have a right to demand when its servants are fully compensated for their labour, but on the contrary when an inadequate pay is given we cannot expect nor compel with justice an individual to injure himself."[6] Wages during public works were insufficient to feed the worker's family, whereas adequate food was given to farm workers for their entire families. As public-works projects often continued for several months at a time, this was a serious problem. The overall punitive element of public works requisitions is brought out by the fact that demands upon the Caledon Institution, run by the dissident, slave-owning missionary Johannes Seidenfaden who had been disowned by the LMS but kept on by the colonial government, were far lower, and Seidenfaden was paid 800 rixdollars per annum as a postmaster.[67]

A further legal means by which the local administration tried to undermine the independence of mission-station inhabitants was through the *opgaaf*. This head tax was levied on every person in the colony, including children. At the time it was seen by those sympathetic to missions as "a direct attack upon the missions and an attempt to force the mission Khoi into the service of farmers," in the words of historians Christopher Saunders and Basil LeCordeur.[68] It was many times higher for a Khoisan person at a mission station than for a farm worker. In addition, employers generally paid the opgaaf of employees attached to their household on a long-term basis. People had to scramble to find the cash, in an economy which was still not fully monetized and in which so many obstacles existed to Khoisan employment in cash-yielding jobs; many hired themselves to farmers in the weeks before the tax fell due. This was a precursor of later, wider British colonial attempts to use taxation policy to force labour from Africans. Both corvée labour demands and the opgaaf were also clearly punitive moves. So, too, was Cuyler's sudden refusal in 1822 to allow Bethelsdorp sawyers to continue cutting wood at the Tsitsikamma forest, about one hundred miles west of Bethelsdorp, on which they depended for certain types of wood. The decision was overturned by the governor in 1824, but in the meantime the Bethelsdorp men had been forced to sacrifice a valuable contract with the whaling station and (so Philip alleged) white colonists had picked up much of the business which had been an important component of the growing prosperity of Bethelsdorp.[69] The main goal of such interference was not, at this stage, to "proletarianize" the so-called "coloured" people by pushing them into wage labour; the aim was more to maintain them in a state of essentially unwaged personal servitude and to keep them from competing in the white job market.

It makes sense that this more or less British model of legal regulation (albeit put into practice mostly by Dutch officials) was accompanied by a theological language of social order which came increasingly to be shared by British and Dutch elites. Van der Kemp was convinced that he saw the process in motion by 1806, as the missionary society at the Cape which he had founded was taken over by men with whom he disagreed: "The Ecclesiastics of this country are exasperated against the Cape [Missionary] Society. In the beginning they would have nothing to do with it, in hope, that it soon would dwindle in to nothing. But seeing that it is in some measure protected by Government, and themselves disappointed in their expectation, they now as an alternative seem to [aspire?] at the direction, and by degrees to model the evangelisation of the Heathen after the principles of a tyrannical Hierarchy.[70] The Khoekhoe were constitutively capable of becoming Christian, according to this model of "social order," since they did share the same order of humanity as whites, but this Christianity ought to teach them to become faithful labourers and to overcome their supposed innate laziness and obstreperousness.

An incident recorded by the missionary James Kitchingman in the late 1820s illuminates some assumptions of colonial reformers operating within this paradigm. On LMS superintendent John Philip's request, Kitchingman had sent two young girls from Bethelsdorp to act as temporary servants to the wife of Major William Colebrooke while the latter visited Cape Town for the commission of inquiry; the girls were the only daughter of Andries Stoffels and Joanna, an orphan girl living with the Kitchingmans. The girls returned to Bethelsdorp after Mrs Colebrooke went back to England. Some time later, an irate Colebrooke summoned Kitchingman in order to complain that the girls had gone home. Stoffels's daughter, whom "he supposed to be his drudge," was "lazy at first" but could improve, "and he thought it wrong that parents should manifest such a desire of taking their children from situations where they were doing well, that he knew it often proceeded from mere selfish motives." Joanna, on the other hand, was a good servant whom "two or three of the most respectable families" had asked to employ after Mrs Colebrooke's departure. For Colebrooke, the putative reformer, "it seemed to prove what the boers said that you may keep a Hottentot for a time and learn him but he returns to his old state – that he wondered Dr. Philip had not done some thing for the Hottentots in Cape Town for we had most awful specimens of their character in the beer shops &c."[71]

The advocates of a "social order" model of Christianity placed great pressure on Khoisan individuals to be "respectable" according to white expectations. In contrast, many farmers denied to their Khoisan dependants the material means to be respectable, such as adequate clothing by western norms, instruction in Christianity (as we have seen), substantial wages, solidly constructed houses, or control over their own bodies. Both approaches were related to work. Colebrooke wanted respectable servants for respectable households, whereas many farm employers, probably in practice closer to their employees through lifestyle and kinship links, needed to dishonour them. In both cases, shame became a mechanism of coercion. Many converts responded by asserting their own respectability through their adherence to Christianity and such things as temperance, monogamy, and literacy. This would become an increasingly important strategy, particularly for the mission elite, as the century developed.[72]

Nonetheless, many Khoisan inhabitants of mission stations, particularly in the early years, often resisted the strictures of officials and missionaries alike to be "respectable" on white terms. Drinking was a very serious social problem, opposed by Khoekhoe prophets of temperance and national rejuvenation such as Andries Stoffels, but it also symbolized the evasion of missionary attempts at social control or of the calls of officials such as Major Colebrooke for a sober workforce dedicated solely to the interests of potential employers. Missionary-society records are a good deal less revealing about resistance to missionaries by mission-station inhabitants than about the behaviour of supposedly ideal converts, but sufficient comment exists to make it plain that even church members resisted the hegemonic control of their lives by missions. The constantly self-doubting LMS missionary James Kitchingman worried in his private diaries in the 1820s about his inability to control the private behaviour of Bethelsdorp inhabitants, especially that of young women out of missionary control in Algoa Bay. "This evening we had three young girls before us, who have been living in lewdness in the Bay, what to do with them I know not. May God change their hearts!" he lamented on 4 January 1825.[73]

Inhabitants also resisted related missionary calls for obedience. In theory, missionaries were supposed to be able to report to the state on the whereabouts of "their" people at all times; in practice, inhabitants clearly took care that this be impossible.[74] The unpopular George Barker, a more authoritarian and conservative man than Read who worked at Bethelsdorp and Theopolis, clashed with many residents. Aggrieved by the constant departure of nursemaids and servants from his Bethelsdorp household, he lashed out in an unusually revealing letter to Cuyler which "after mature consideration" he decided not to send: "The ingratitude & unreasonableness of those people among whom Providence has cast my lot is a source of poignant grief every day of my life." He even went so far, in this unsent letter, as to suggest that the Bethelsdorp community be obliged to furnish their teachers with two girls and a boy, to serve a year for wages. F.G. Hooper, a more liberal missionary who served at Bethelsdorp until 1819, complained in that year about the many people who wanted the South African missionary effort to be more "useful." He found too many laws and regulations deleterious. "The Brethren find it hard to agree in dictating rules; the People have their habits quite opposed to them; and the unbelieving around are jealous of those who are resolute enough to differ from them."[75] There clearly was tension at the station about missionary efforts at civilization, against the background of all the stereotypes that we have been outlining. "The people appear to get worse day on day," wrote the unpopular J. Georg Messer at around the same time. "Last week some were so impudent as to say to me, You may give smooth or sharp words, however, we will not behave otherwise than we are used to do. – These were even baptized people."[76] On his second journey of inspection to the South African missions, John Campbell noted that several Christian Khoisan from Bethelsdorp who had served some years in the Cape Regiment and had been "consequently obliged to attend to cleanliness," on their discharge "almost immediately relapsed into their old habits."[77] When one reads between the lines of more varnished accounts, it is clear that many Khoisan resented and resisted missionary control and the attempts of some missionaries (particularly after the 1820s) to tie down labour for themselves. This did not, however, prevent people from trying to make use of the resources of mission stations, and even of converting in large numbers to Christianity.

CONVERSION

Many Khoisan, both on and off mission stations, converted to Christianity. Although numbers are hard to come by, by the late 1840s at any rate missionaries were confidently asserting that most of the descendants of the Khoisan at the Cape owed at least nominal allegiance to Christianity.[78] Despite the centrality of material concerns, it would be a mistake to assume that all conversion to Christianity was solely instrumental. At the same time, the concept of "conversion" needs to be analysed critically, as an extensive scholarly literature on conversion in Africa suggests.[79] To reconstruct why and how Khoisan people converted in increasing numbers is an impossible task, particularly given the inevitable diversity among individuals. Nonetheless, in what follows I will try to provide some clues.

Early Khoisan interaction with Christianity was shaped by existing Khoisan and, particularly, Khoekhoe beliefs. The contours of interaction were also formed by the fact of many years of contact among Khoekhoe, San, and white settlers, although the exact extent of existing Christian influence is hard to determine. What is important is that Khoisan converts did not receive the gospel in exactly the way in which European missionaries intended; rather, they "heard" the message in accordance with their own needs and existing situations. At least some converts, for example, seem to have seen missionary activity not as a rejection of all their old beliefs but as a response by a God, in whom they already believed, to a crisis situation.

In fact, Christianity was spread well beyond the boundaries of the stations among the Khoisan, largely by those identified in the colony as "Hottentots." This Christianity was largely oral, since its spread antedated large-scale literacy among the Khoisan. It must have contained a number of Khoekhoe assumptions and interpretations from the outset. When a delegation from Bethelsdorp came to George in order to testify before the Commission of Circuit in 1812, for example, many Hessequa Khoekhoe from Hooge Kraal flocked to religious meetings, and Read observed existing allegiance to Christianity. "The first we heard was that a Hottentot woman who had been for some time at Bethelsdorp, but now living at the Hooge Kraal was so influenced that she could not refrain from admonishing her fellow creatures and this she did morning and evening much to the benefit of many."[80] Many people wanted to come to Bethelsdorp. Read felt that this would be impractical, and so a group of inhabitants requested their own missionary instead. The initial impetus, then, behind the mission station Pacaltsdorp which was established the following year at Hooge's Kraal was local interest in Christianity – whatever the eventual ominous implications of the station for the remnants of Hessequa culture, and despite the fact that the government itself saw the station as a labour reserve.[81]

Requests for missionaries were also initiated by many Khoekhoe groups outside the Cape, particularly in Transorangia, where fugitives from the colony and the Orange River area were in the process of establishing regional hegemony. This had a great deal to do with the power balance of open frontier zones: among other things, missionaries were seen as agents of communication with the colony, as protectors in some minimal sense in ongoing power struggles among small groups, and as potential gun-runners.[82] The missionary was thus a power-broker far more outside the colony than he was within. Individuals also opposed the acquisition of a missionary by a particular group. The point is, however, that the debates were internal to the groups in question, sometimes preceded the arrival of missionaries themselves, and took a wide range of factors into account.

The most startling element in the relatively rapid, early growth of the Moravian station of Baviaans Kloof (later Genadendal) and the LMS station of Bethelsdorp was that individuals came and asked to join from quite wide areas. News about the missionaries was spread largely by Khoekhoe individuals, in other words. At Genadendal, earlier converts of Georg Schmidt, such as Vehettge Tikuie, had kept alive Christian teaching after Schmidt's departure.[83] Even on the mission stations themselves, conversions appear to have been made more often by Khoekhoe than by missionaries. In his private diary, George Barker of the LMS recorded, in 1816, that at Bethelsdorp he heard "five women examined previous to baptism not one of them attributed the beginning of the work of grace in their hearts to the preaching of the Missionaries but to their own people (Hottentots) speaking to them."[84] He made similar observations at Theopolis and remarked with surprise that a convert, Klaas Windvogel, ascribed his first conviction to the preaching of the gospel by a missionary, "a thing not common among the Hottentots ... This is a singular instance of one of them laying so much stress upon preaching as a means of their being brought to conviction."[85]

Early on, Bethelsdorp developed a small but devoted core of lay evangelists, including Gerrit Sampson, Cupido Kakkerlak, Hendrik Boezak, and Jan Goeyman (or Cornelius Goieman), as well as Dyani (or Jan) Tshatshu, the son of a minor Xhosa chief who was brought up at Bethelsdorp. These men would itinerate in the neighbouring areas or as they carried out jobs which took them far from home; Boezak, for example, was an elephant hunter who would preach at farms which he visited while on hunting expeditions. Such itinerant evangelization by lay people was typical of the culture developed by the domestic wing of the LMS at the same time as it was first sending foreign missionaries. Tshatshu helped found and run Joseph Williams's mission to the Xhosa at Kat River (begun in 1817 and cut short by Williams's death). Khoekhoe missionaries established an outpost in Algoa Bay, itinerated in Xhosaland as well as inside the colony, and co-founded the LMS mission to the Tswana. A mixed-gender group of Khoekhoe from

Bethelsdorp helped run the Tswana station of Kuruman until Robert Moffat arrived, got rid of the Khoisan evangelists, and turned Kuruman into the station of Lattakoo which became a household name among the Victorian pious with no knowledge of its indigenous origins.[86] Khoekhoe evangelists from Bethelsdorp, including Goeyman, also played key roles at the short-lived LMS missions to the San at Toornberg and Hephzibah from 1814 to 1818. In an interesting expression of the range of possibilities within the early LMS, as well as of ethnic diversity within early-nineteenth-century Dutch-speaking communities, the former station was supervised by a white man, Erasmus Smit, and the latter by a black man, William Corner. In later years Smit would be predikant to the voortrekkers, dissident Afrikaners who trekked away from the British Cape Colony in the late 1830s to establish new political communities which imposed harsh legal distinctions by "race"; William Corner was a former slave from the West Indies. In about 1816, a Khoisan convert Piet Sabba started teaching the San at Ramah, north of the Orange River, while the teachers, identified in missionary records as Kruisman and David worked at Konnah to the south, all under the nominal supervision of LMS missionaries at Griquatown. Jan Goeyman later taught at Philippolis from 1822, before the hamlet was taken over by Adam Kok II and his followers in 1826 to become the capital of this Griqua faction.[87]

Indigenous evangelization was all the more important because, given the large number of Dutch-speakers among the Khoisan, and given the difficulty of tonal-click languages for Westerners, European missionaries notoriously failed to master Khoisan languages. Although the linguistically gifted Van der Kemp apparently transliterated Cape Khoekhoe and wrote a catechism in the language, now lost, the Bible was never translated into the language of the Cape Khoekhoe. Dutch was used as a lingua franca instead. When talking to the less acculturated, European missionaries relied on interpreters. Even when a supervising missionary was present, in the early days, far more of the actual work of evangelization would have been carried out by African assistant missionaries and less formally sanctioned advocates than would be the case later on.[88]

In South Africa, as in Britain, it is hard to know what messages were spread by oral processes which, in many ways, were out of the control of European missionaries from the beginning. Indeed, the early history of mission Christianity is one of missionaries slowly struggling to bring indigenous versions of Christianity, and indigenous preachers, back under white control, after an early period of expansion fuelled by African preachers and bearers of news. Missionary-society reports are one-sided and lay undue emphasis on missionary successes; nonetheless, mission papers do provide useful insights into the process.

On the basis of parallels with the rapid spread of prophetic movements in better documented neighbouring communities, it is not surprising to find evidence of at least one previous movement of religious innovation, spread through oral transmission, among the Khoekhoe. In the Western Cape, a few years before the second advent of the Moravian Brethren, "a rumour spread among them – they heard it from the Christians – that the end of the world was at hand, so none of them wanted to work for the farmers anymore ... They killed their cattle and wandered about and told all their people about it."[89] The Khoekhoe leader Jan Parel attempted to lead a revolt against the colonists, persuading his followers that the world would come to an end on 25 October 1788 and that all Christians must be killed by that date. As Russel Viljoen has argued, participants expressed the desire to become "*omme een tijd wederom meesters van het Land te worden*" – once again to become rulers of their land. This seemingly millenarian cattle-killing movement presaged the great cattle sacrifices made by the Xhosa in the 1850s in a similar effort to reverse colonial conquest.[90] Without further investigation, it is hard to tell whether the earlier Khoekhoe movement was influenced by contact with Xhosa prophets, or whether, indeed, the Khoekhoe later influenced the Xhosa. It also seems possible, however, that the mission diarists were correct that the movement betrayed some Christian influence. The apparent permeability of Khoekhoe religiosity at the Cape is striking, as also is the readiness to turn outside influences to "national" ends. One also notes the *structure* of the spread of religious innovation by rapid oral transmission, spearheaded by people who "wandered about" to bring news.

We have two reports, at least, in Moravian records of Khoekhoe converts who retroactively incorporated the advent of missionaries into an indigenous prophetic tradition. These moves may well reflect traditions of earlier converts, such as Tikkuie. They might also, however, be taken as symbolic ways in which to make the Christian missions part of the religion of the ancestors after the fact. Here are the two relevant passages in full. Caffer Magerman commented in 1806 that "when I was quite young my father used often to address us thus: 'Children, I have a kind of presentiment, as if some time hence good people would come to us heathen from a great distance, who will tell us, that after this life our souls will go either to a bad or a good place. Now if you should hear that such people are come, do not stay here, but go and hear them.' Many years after this, therefore, when we heard of Bavianskloof we remembered the words of our father, and determined not to rest until we came hither."[91] Catherine Pick's recollections at Genadendal in 1808 give an even more powerful sense of Khoekhoe conviction of a particular communication from the high god Tsuni-*I*Goam to the Khoekhoe: "I remember what my late father used to say, exhorting us children to take notice and follow those people who would once come from a distant country, and show us Hottentots a narrow way, by which we might escape from the fire, and the true Toi-qua [Tsuni-*I*Goam]... When the first teachers came to show us the way, the farmers were very angry, and told us, that they meant to sell us as slaves. But I remembered my father's words, and would not be prevented from moving to Baviaans Kloof."[92]

As these comments suggest, Cape Khoekhoe groups at the turn of the century appear to have possessed independent ideas about a powerful deity who under certain circumstances could intervene in human affairs, although it is unclear whether this being was considered benevolent. According to the two James Reads, in a retrospective account written in 1847, the early-nineteenth-century Cape Khoekhoe "had a name for the great first cause, but they appear only to have conceived of him as possessed of the natural attributes of power and greatness but had no distinct conception of his goodness, benevolence, much less of his love to a lost world."[93] On the other hand, some evidence that I will discuss shortly suggests benevolence. Cape Khoekhoe seemingly further believed in forces of evil, sometimes enshrined in the form of a destroyer deity. They also believed in a multitude of unseen forces. Again according to the Reads, "they had cherished ideas of [illegible] spirits under various names and affects."[94] Note here that I am cognizant of the concern that "belief" is an inappropriate term in this context since, as Paul Landau has pointed out, it contains the implicit notion of the possibility of unbelief and hence is itself a product of western ideas about "religion." In the end, however, I am using the term to describe the action of belief from an outside perspective, rather than making a statement about the attitude of the believer towards the action of belief, in much the same way as one says of someone that he or she "perceives" a colour or an object, whether or not that person is an epistemologist analytically committed to doubt about the shared nature of perception. Furthermore, since Khoekhoe at the turn of the century were exposed to different religious systems, the notions of religious difference and the related one of "belief" may not have been so foreign as Landau assumes. However one describes them, the "beliefs" of the early-nineteenth-century Khoekhoe dovetailed with a certain number of Christian beliefs.

More evidence can be adduced for this claim if one supplements the relatively meagre accounts of early missionaries with later accounts, particularly from Namaqualand, and the earlier comments of travellers and observers. This is, of course, problematic. As David Chidester has argued, early white commentators on Khoekhoe religion were embedded in colonial relationships and often simply ill-informed about Khoekhoe religion. Different groups, furthermore, doubtless had somewhat different ideas across time and space: continuity needs to be demonstrated, not assumed. Observations from Namaqualand come mostly from the late nineteenth century onward, after extensive contact between Khoekhoe and Christians. On the other hand, significant eighteenth- and nineteenth-century Khoekhoe emigration from the Cape colony to Namaqualand increases the odds of continuity. Indeed, late-nineteenth-century ethnographer and fluent Nama speaker Theophilus Hahn (the son of a missionary) went so far as to affirm that "all Khoi-Khoi tribes have one and the same language ... As they have the same language they have the same *religion* and *mythology*."[95] Hahn himself knew well the station of Bethanie, which had been settled, according to him, by "Amaqua" who were originally from the Clanwilliam district and had migrated to Great Namaqualand in the early years of the century under the chief !Akeb. Hahn's own father had founded a station at Windhoek settled by the Eixa*l*ais ("the 'savage, furious Gang'"), or Jonker Afrikaner's people, who were originally from Tulbagh before their extensive wanderings in the interior.[96] Hahn's own influential description of Khoekhoe religion was therefore based at least partly on his experience growing up among groups with roots in the Cape and ties across a wide geographical range. On the other hand, late-nineteenth-century Nama evidence about Tsuni-*l*/Goam as a being able to receive prayer and intervene in human affairs cannot be assumed at this late date *not* to have been influenced by Christianity.

Alan Barnard makes two pertinent contentions. The first is that Khoisan religious systems tend to conform to different patterns across different groups. The second is that the particularities of belief are nonetheless notably fluid – leading historically "to cross-cultural uniformity and, at the same time, to intra-cultural diversity." Barnard speculates, however, that the Khoekhoe may have been more susceptible than the San to the "structural transformation" of their religious systems, precisely because Khoekhoe systems were more rigid; there was a limit to how far they could bend.[97] One could go further and suggest that the very fact of fluidity and openness to new ideas may have made individuals likely to listen to religious innovators – thus giving European missionaries, for example, an initial opening.

The most widely used name for a high god (however one defines that) by the Khoekhoe is some form of Tsuni-*l*/Goam, "the name by which the Redmen called the infinite," in Hahn's formulation.[98] Even many commentators such as Schmidt who denied that the Khoekhoe had a religion per se acknowledged the existence of belief in such a figure. The Ngqika Xhosa name for "God" when Van der Kemp first encountered them was Thixo, an adaptation of the Khoekhoe word that indicates the extent of Khoekhoe influence on the Xhosa in religious matters.[99] Van der Kemp claimed that he could not see that the Xhosa had any systematic "idea of the existence of God," although many individuals had "some notion of his existence, which they have received from adjacent nations." Van der Kemp clearly included the Khoekhoe among "adjacent nations," since he went on to write that the "individuals just mentioned" called God "*Thiko*, which is a corruption of *Thuike*, the name by which God is called in the language of the Hottentots, literally signifying *one who induces pain*."[100]

The etymology of Tsuni-//Goam has been much debated. A leading theory, however, is that the term contains the sense "wounded knee": Tsuni-//Goam was believed to have fought against and vanquished the destroyer deity, //Gaunab, who nonetheless wounded Tsuni-//Goam in the knee.[101] He was "essentially the rain God," according to anthropologist Isaac Schapera,[102] who was considered to be the giver of all good things. Hahn's account seems to me, however, to suggest a broader conception of Tsuni-//Goam founded in his role as rain-maker but more broadly akin to an abstract monotheistic notion. Beliefs concerning //Gaunab, on the other hand, were more ambiguous. Alan Barnard cites a variety of possible roles, all connected with evil: "//Gâuab, G//auba, G//amama, etc. is almost universally among Khoisan peoples a term for the evil god, the evil aspect of the good god, the evil spirits, or the spirits of the dead." Barnard also cites Schapera with approval: "The beliefs regarding //Gaua ... are not crystallized into clear-cut conceptions, but are vague, inconsistent, and ambiguous."[103] Under missionary influence //Gaunab became identified with the devil.[104]

The pre-Christian Nama told tales of at least two figures who were akin to Tsuni-//Goam and //Gaunab but operated within the secular sphere, namely the hero figure Haitsi-aibib (or Heitsi-eibib in Hahns' formulation), and the evil ≠Gama-≠gorib.[105] Hahn believed that Heitsi-eibib and several other figures must all be taken as identical with Tsuni-//Goab. "All ... come from the East, and this is why the doors of the huts and the graves are found in that direction. The bodies of the deceased are also placed towards the East, so that their faces may look towards sunrise."[106] Schapera, however, convincingly disagrees with Hahn's identification of these figures of divinity, arguing that Heitsi-eibib was the central figure in a cycle of myths, often assuming a trickster role with a not altogether blameless character, whereas Tsuni-//Goam had creative powers and was "looked upon with far more respect and reverence."[107] Heitsi-eibib "died in many places, was buried and always came back to life again."[108] The Khoekhoe would throw pieces of clothing, skin, dung, twigs, or stones on the many 'graves' of Heitsi-eibib dotted about South Africa, accompanied by a prayer; they would also throw material on the graves of the recently dead and on some occasions at least, such as a period of crisis recorded by Hahn, would pray to their ancestors.[109] In 1815 John Campbell commented on the many "great Hottentot captains" buried in the interior, observing that, if a Khoekhoe person passing a grave neglected to throw a stone or branch on it, he believed he would be drowned in the next river he tried to cross.[110] Among other beliefs and practices, Khoekhoe peoples ascribed sacred powers to people white outsiders termed "conjurers" or "magicians." They believed that //Gaunab killed people, that his power was accessible to human individuals, and that such individuals could both nullify this power and detect and punish the wrongdoers. Like other African sacred specialists, Khoekhoe healers cured bodily diseases; Khoekhoe snake doctors, according to a late-nineteenth century ethnographic account, were so widely employed to cure snake bites at the Cape that "the rich Boers generally keep a Hottentot snake doctor to be treated by him in any emergency."[111] Rainmakers also played an important part in Khoekhoe society. Hahn believed that the rainmaking role and the healing role were usually filled by different people. These indigenous figures preserved authority throughout the early period of evangelization.

Moravian missionaries encountered belief in Tsuni-//Goam. Dorothy of Genadendal, a "skilful midwife" well known for "prudent and orderly behaviour," informed Genadendal missionaries, in 1808, that European travellers were incorrect that the Khoekhoe did not believe in a "Divine Being." On the contrary, "Hottentots" as well as other "Heathen nations" "believe on [sic] a Supreme Being as the Creator of all things. She said: 'We have known that a God exists before we came to the land of the Christians' (by which she meant the snow-mountains on Fish River). 'We call him *Sita*, which means the God and Father above. If we were in distress, we always called upon him. Only those Hottentots, who have been born and bred among the Christians, know little or nothing of him.'"[112] This suggests that many Khoekhoe, brought up as de facto bonded labour in the Western Cape, may have been in the position of being cut off form the religion of their forefathers and yet barred from access to any worship available to, or generated by, the farmers to whose households they were tied. Christian missions may have filled the gap.

In 1739 the first Moravian missionary Georg Schmidt recorded that he asked his interpreter Africo "whether they knew that a great Spirit dwelt above, who had given them their cattle and all that they had. He answered, 'Yes we know him. He is called *Tui hqua*.' I added, 'This good Spirit is he alone who can save you, and I am come hither with no other view, than to make you acquainted with him.'"[113] This passage in the Moravian *Periodical Accounts* is probably based on a discussion Schmidt had with Africo while Schmidt and his newly hired interpreter were smoking tobacco together on the evening of 14 September 1737, shortly after Schmidt's arrival at the Cape. The two men spoke in (possibly rather fractured) Dutch, but Schmidt recorded the conversation in his own first language, German. Africo had just called Schmidt "Baas." The German text reads: "Ich fragte ihn auch, ob sie wohl wusten, dass ein grosser Baas sei, welcher ihnen ihr Vieh und alles, was sie habben, gegeben hätte. Er sagte: Ja. Wie nennt ihr denselben? Er sagte: Tui'qua. Ich sagte: Ihr lieben Menschen, der Tui'qua, das ist der Heiland, der Seligmacher. Der ist einmal ein Mensch geworden und fur uns Menschen am Kreuz gestorben, und der will euch auch zu seligen Leuten machen. Dazu sagten sie nichts."[114]

Paul Landau has voiced an important concern about my use of this particular passage. Landau queries whether "die groot Baas" (as the Afrikaans version has it) can be taken as the equivalent of a high god figure, and whether I do not assume a Judeo-Christian concept of "God." While acknowledging the complexity and indeed intractability of these issues, I nonetheless want to make two comments. The first is that Klaas Stuurman (who did convert to Christianity) also used the term "Groot Baas" for some kind of overarching divinity. As Stuurman famously asked John Barrow, "Has not the Groot Baas given plenty of grass roots, and berries and grasshoppers for our use; and, till the Dutch destroyed them, abundance of wild animals to hunt?"[115] Although the broader issue of translation is of enormous importance, the use of this particular phrase does not in itself necessarily prove much one way or the other, especially given the pidgin level of Dutch communication between the German-speaking Schmidt and his Khoekhoe-speaking interpreter, or the English-speaking Barrow and the Khoekhoe-speaking Stuurman. The second comment is that the question of what Khoekhoe actually meant by "God" or "die groot Baas" or "ein grosser Baas" or "Tsuni-//Goam" and whether this was the same as whatever the missionaries meant, or indeed whatever I mean, is probably unanswerable. On the other hand, the concept of "God" is an infinitely varied one, the meaning of which has been a subject of tremendous controversy even within the limited confines of the Judeo-Christian tradition. There is a difference between observing that a term meant something to speakers and knowing what the full content of that meaning was. My points here are three in number: the Khoekhoe had a term for a being which evidence suggests was considered to be above all other beings and which subsequently became identified by some at least with a Christian God filling a similar role; some Khoekhoe and some missionary observers alike saw continuity between Khoekhoe and Christian beliefs; some saw instead radical discontinuity, but this very perception drew on dichotomous concepts of good and evil which appear to have been present in Khoekhoe religious ideas. Late eighteenth- and early-nineteenth-century Khoekhoe religious ideas had doubtless been influenced by interaction with various groups, including Xhosa, Christians, and San. Nonetheless, I am primarily interested in interactions in the 1790s and 1800s, rather than looking for a "pure" Khoekhoe religion which, I would agree, is impossible to recapture, if it ever existed. It is more helpful to look for structural continuities.

Other comments also suggest a sense of continuity between old and new religious systems. Martha Arendse testified in London that she was unwilling to believe what the missionary Kicherer told her about Christ until she had consulted God. Kicherer translated her narrative (and certainly translation poses a significant epistemological issue here) as follows: "Then she go try. She fall down in the field; she cry, 'O God! what your servant say to me, I don't believe it. O tell me if it be your truth.'"[116] Similarly, in 1792 Moravians recorded: "The report has spread far and near, and it is become a common saying among the Hottentots, that God has sent men to teach them the way of salvation, and that whoever now refuses to hear and believe, must expect a heavy punishment from God."[117] Forms of religious worship remained similar to older customs. Khoekhoe converts would pray in the bushes at dawn, facing east. This was characteristic of the worship of Tsuni-//Goam, considered to be present in the eastern dawn.[118] Evidence exists for a preexisting Khoekhoe custom of direct prayer to God. Hahn, for example, records a hymn to Tsuni-//Goam in the late nineteenth century, a version of which was sung by many different groups when the Pleiades first appeared on the eastern horizon. The invocation begins: "Thou, oh *Tsui-//goa*! / Thou Father of the Fathers / Thou our Father / Let stream [let rain] the thunder cloud! / Let please live [our] flocks! / Let us [also] live please!"[119] The intense personal prayer of many Khoekhoe converts thus seems to have had deep antecedent roots.

Dreams provided another point of continuity between old and new religious beliefs. In common with many other African groups – and indeed many European Christians – Khoekhoe and San communities believed that dreams and omens imparted messages from the supernatural to the natural world.[120] Many British and American evangelicals of the period, especially Methodists, also believed in dreams as a means of divine communication, even if more cautious theological leaders urged adherents to trust rather in the written word.[121] LMS missionaries thus enthusiastically chronicled the dreams of their converts, whereas the Moravians were more sceptical. "The Hottentots are great dreamers," complained J.P. Kohrhammer of Genadendal testily in 1799, "and we have much trouble to direct their minds from any deepseated prejudices, which they have imbibed concerning the interpretation of dreams and visions."[122]

In many cases, however, dreams and omens were clearly used to validate the adoption of Christianity. I noted two cases, above, of the advent of missionaries being incorporated "backwards" into an indigenous prophetic tradition. The first Genadendal missionaries also recorded the testimony of a man who "dreamt that three would come to teach them ... They [the Khoekhoe] say that they spoke about it often because they very much wished for it to happen."[123]

Often, the dreams recorded by missionaries pertained to personal life crises. To offer just one example among many possibilities, a Bethelsdorp woman, whom Ven der Kemp calls Margaret "Langoe" in his English annual report and "Griet Luangô" in his Dutch diary, dreamed in 1804, a few days after her baptism, that she followed Jesus through a desert: "He conducted her to a river, and then said, 'what a privilege is it now, that thou hast taken thy refuge with me?' and then helped her through the river. This moment she started out of her sleep, awaked by a violent pungent pain, she felt in her breast, which soon after proved to be excited by a peripneumony, which in four days [reduced?] her on the brink of the grave." During Langoe's illness she saw a black spider climbing up by a thread towards the roof: "She asked the Lord What this meaned? and he answered, that she in the same manner was to be taken up to him! This determined her to reflect upon the vileness of her heart, but found herself assured that Christ would give her strength to ascend to him by the thread of her faith fixed in heaven. She then ordered her arm rings to be taken from her wrist, and after they were made narrower, to put them on the arms of her three little children." She said she was not worried about her children because God had told her he would give them to Van der Kemp to take care of. Having previously said she wanted to go to Christ, she then decided that she did not want to die after all, and miraculously recovered.[124] It is suggestive that a spider brings news of Langoe's death: in both Khoekhoe and San cosmology, animals brought information of the death of relatives and friends, as well as of one's own death. Here, a Christian message, brought through "traditional" structures, eases 'Langoe through a time of crisis.

It is further noteworthy that Langoe interpreted her own dreams and visions rather than taking them to an intermediary. One would want to know more about whether or not Khoekhoe culture accorded authority to interpreters of dreams in an organized fashion: in other words, were dreams a personal experience, however open to public discussion, or were they embedded in a power network? Knowing this would help one to understand what roles missionaries were taking over. My hunch is that dream interpretation was only weakly linked to existing authority networks, such as those formed by healers: dreams seem to have been perceived as a means of direct communication between the individual and the supernatural world. Consequently, they were available as a spiritual technique which could be used across what a western missionary would have perceived as doctrinal lines. Certainly, missionary accounts of the dreams of converts frequently suggest that converts saw these dreams as comprehensible messages from God or Jesus, or as predictions of the future, which did not require further interpretation by designated experts. On the other hand, it must be added that converts obviously reported at least some dreams to missionaries, and sometimes asked advice about how best to fill their prescriptions. It is also striking that converts sometimes dreamed that *missionaries* were giving them messages. One woman at Genadendal "dreamed that when she died – which she believes won't be long now – we were going to give her a letter which would be bound underneath her head, and when she came to heaven she should give this letter to her child. This child was buried four days ago and was still feeding at her breast. Her child would take the letter to the Father in heaven." The diarists added that "they dream about us everywhere and tell us strange things. But in their dreams we usually direct them to the dear Saviour."[125] There are many levels of mediation at work in a dream such as this one about a letter written to God and delivered by the spirit of a dead child. Even here, however, the authority roles are relatively ambiguous and the lines between Christianity and earlier Khoekhoe beliefs are blurred. The missionaries provide the power of the written word, but it is the dead Khoekhoe child who takes the letter to God, possibly illustrating the persistence of the Khoekhoe belief in the mediation of the recently dead between visible and invisible realms.

Other dreams touched directly on conversion experiences and thus served an overtly integrative function. As late as 1975, Jane Sales remarked that she knew of so-called "coloured" churches where young people in catechism classes were asked if they had had a vision or dream to authenticate their conversions, sometimes even being encouraged by the old deacons to "stand near a particular bush until they have had such a vision." Old people talked of the days in which the church was strong as the time when dreams were commonly part of people's Christian experience.[126]

Side by side with continuities such as the spiritual use of dreams and omens, dualism, prayer, and worship techniques must be placed examples of converts abjuring elements of their old religion. The missionary James Read's Khoekhoe wife, Elizabeth Valentyn, may have deliberately violated taboos associated with birth, without the observer, Van der Kemp, understanding the implications of her actions: she did not undergo purification rituals or observe a period of seclusion, but ran to the river immediately after giving birth, possibly proving that she was not !nau (in Nama terms, subject to certain taboos as a result of being in a state of transition) and could safely have contact with cold water.[127] Cupido Kakkerlak used to scatter twigs and stones placed by believers on the graves of Heitsi-eibib (or possibly of great chiefs, as Campbell believed), again openly carrying out a dangerous and forbidden practice.[128] Moravian missionaries noticed, without understanding why, that early arrivals at Baviaans Kloof refrained from dancing at night – although certainly at Bethelsdorp, and probably elsewhere, all-night sessions of communal hymn singing and mutual exhortation would become an integral part of Christian worship at times of revival.[129] In one case Read records that, when he was on a missionary journey with Khoekhoe assistants, he went to bed while the Khoekhoe moved among the people and sang hymns with them all night. Both types of behaviour reflect Khoekhoe ceremonies of dancing at night before the full and new moon, seen by Alan Barnard as not worship of the moon per se but as akin to the worship of God through the adoration of one of his attributes. Various ceremonies of transition and cyclical festivals also demanded dancing and singing at night, including the annual welcoming of the Pleiades accompanied by prayers for prosperity.

In the case of the Moravians refusing to dance, as of Valentyn and Kakkerlak, converts symbolically rejected older beliefs without missionary direction; many missionaries were simply too ignorant of Khoekhoe and San customs to know how to instruct their disciples. An internal set of distinctions was clearly being made, however. An elderly "Bushman," Jacob Adams of Genadendal, was quite clear about distinctions between Christian customs and those of his boyhood. After relating, through an interpreter, several San and Khoekhoe beliefs, Adams refused a missionary request for more information, saying that "he did not like to remember and relate such bad things, having at his baptism renounced the devil and all his works, and therefore wished to have nothing more to do with his old customs."[130]

The picture that emerges overall is of an ambivalent relationship between early Christianity and "traditional" Khoekhoe religion, which indicates the vitality of the latter. On the one hand, some concepts such as Tsuni-//Goam and modes of prayer appear to have been transformed rather than negated by Christianity, especially since the first missionaries used Khoekhoe terms for God and the devil and much proslytizing in the first twenty years of mission was done by Khoisan preachers themselves. On the other hand, there are examples of individuals deliberately rejecting more specific and perhaps more mechanical older beliefs.

Debate over music and dance, which were central to Khoekhoe and San culture and ritual,[131] gives insight into the complexity of interaction. Before his conversion, Hendrik Boezak had said that he had two warring hearts: "'The one Heart' (said he) 'will do nothing but sing all kinds of Hottentots and Bushemans songs, and all that is bad – and the one Heart strives to sing the praises of Christ; tells me to go to Christ, to pray to him, &c &c.'"[132] Having chosen the Christian heart and become a preacher, Boezak found himself one day speaking at a farm on the "necessity of regeneration." The colonists listened attentively, but the Khoisan mocked him. "Being sorry for it," Boezak lay down in a hut, but the farm workers came and "played on the violin and danced about him." Enraged, Boezak "was not satisfied until he had broken the violin to pieces and dispersed these disturbers of his rest." When Read requested a donation of musical instruments from LMS supporters for a Khoisan orchestra, he suggested French horns, clarinets, a bassoon, and two flutes but on no account a violin. "The Hottentots are great singers and lovers of musick except the violin (against which those among us whose hearts have been changed by the grace of God seem to be much prejudiced on account of their former attachment to it)."[133] In 1814 in the Western Cape, a fight over a violin symbolized a larger clash between the Moravian missionaries of Groene Kloof and a Khoekhoe healer. Station inhabitant Klaas Trompetter would "entice women and children, and others, to come to his house and join in a dance, connected with the most superstitious and indecent practices." The affair being betrayed by some school children, Trompetter eventually came to ask forgiveness from the missionaries. They granted it on the condition that Trompetter deliver into their custody "his violin, with which he had set his wicked dance a-going"; at this, Trompetter "got up, ran home, took the old violin down, and exclaimed 'Get out of the house, thou instrument of the devil!.'"[134]

It is risky to generalize about very different groups and individuals, especially given that these people came from fairly diverse ethnic backgrounds. There does, however, seem to be a general pattern to testimony about the relationship between Christianity and previous religious beliefs among mission converts. In contrast to the mostly sceptical Nguni, many Khoekhoe who were attracted to Christianity at the turn of the century tended to see Christianity as a revelation from a god in whom they already believed and who many thought could, and did, intervene in the affairs of humanity. What was new was a set of ideas about Jesus. These beliefs were clearly expressed, particularly by Western Cape converts. This raises the possibility that beliefs about a high god were influenced by long contact with European settlers, and possibly even by earlier contact with Schmidt. It also suggests, however, that the Khoekhoe may have held religious beliefs, such as those in a creator and a destroyer divinity, which dovetailed with evangelical Christian beliefs more readily than did Nguni systems.

On the other hand, a number of converts, particularly those who became most active in the new religion, applied Christian dualism to their own old customs, classifying some as evil and as the work of the devil. The missionaries established the dualist distinction, but converts supplied the content. How far older beliefs in //Gaunab themselves permitted this dualism remains to be determined.

TEXT AND STATUS

In the early nineteenth century, before the full-fledged attempts of the British to turn Christianity to the ends of labour discipline, religious change and political struggle came together in conflict over the ownership of biblical texts and the social implications of allegiance to Christianity. I have argued that many rural settlers saw the access of non-whites to Christianity as a threat to relationships based on status and thus as threatening to their own conceptions of labour discipline. The result was that some farmers would go to considerable lengths to prevent their farm workers from preaching, or from becoming Christians. Despite the subsequent mythology of hierarchical and paternalistic farmer incorporation of nonwhite dependants within the Christian "family" of the household, the doors to family prayer were more often than not firmly barred against slaves and Khoisan in the 1790s and early 1800s.[135] In the household of Diana, a Khoekhoe woman illegally held as a slave near Tulbagh in the early nineteenth century, the Bible was sometimes read "but never in the presence of the coloured people." Diana contrived to hear some of the Bible by carrying in water to wash the feet of family members just as the reading was taking place. This being discovered, she was forbidden to enter the room while the Bible was being read and driven to the expedient of listening at a place where the threshold of the door was worn down.[136] In the Eastern Cape in 1803 or 1804, a "licentious" man called Jocham, for whom the missionaries feared when he went into service at Graaff-Reinet, instead "assembled the Heathen together residing there and made known unto them the Gospel of Christ." The "Christians" were very displeased and had Jocham and his assistant Abraham thrown into "the cage," where Abraham was flogged. Both were forbidden to preach. The district veldcornet, however, refused to countenance this and ordered the two released, whereupon they began again and "numbers attend them."[137] At some point in the intervening years before 1809, Jocham was deliberately given a false pass by a farmer at Olifants River. He was arrested as a vagrant, given several floggings for preaching to the "Hottentots" of the farmers, and thrown into gaol for two years. He was finally released by the landdrost of Swellendam and found his way back to Bethelsdorp – where he regretted the spiritual decline which he thought had taken place while he had been imprisoned.[138] Some Khoisan converts were explicit about their rejection of an exclusive vision of Christianity. As Esau Prins put it bluntly in 1834: "I am a Boor's child, although I had to sit behind the chairs and stools, as my Mother was a Hottentot woman, and therefore I consider myself a Hottentot also. Men say I have Christian blood in me, but I know only of one blood that God has made. The so-called 'Christeman' steals the name."[139]

At the same time, initial opposition by farmers to black preaching or access to services might be overcome. Sometimes, Khoisan preachers at the turn of the century found themselves filling the void created by the lack of regular priests, while others were invited to serve as schoolmasters to white children. On a journey in or shortly before 1809, for example, Cupido Kakkerlak attracted large numbers of both "Hottentots" and whites, "from whom he gets continual invitations to return, especially from the latter to act as schoolmaster."[140] While travelling, the black LMS missionary John Corner met several white farmers who insisted on his preaching to them, including one between Bethelsdorp and Graaff-Reinet who rode out in the morning to be instructed on his daughter's advice despite being "blindly intoxicated."[141] On one occasion, Hendrik Boezak was on a tour of farms where he had previously evangelized. "He found great opposition, and in one place in particular ... it was told him that it was the intention of the farmers to kill him, accusing him of persuading their people to go away. No sooner did he hear this than he entered the house, against the persuasion of mother and wife who advised him to run away. He attacked his enemies in the name of the Lord, and continued till he had gained the victory. They confessed their guilt, and acquiesced in his words as truth, and gave him full liberty to instruct the people. He gained such an influence that they were afterwards afraid to drink a dram in his presence."[142] Gerrit Sampson did not "ever fail to tell the

Colonists of their neglect in keeping him and the rest of his Nation ignorant of the contents of the Bible."[143] A Mozambican slave named Sapphire held prayer meetings on the farm of a white settler. Initially furious, the man's wife was convinced by his speaking and invited him to hold regular meetings in the house. Read reported that she "told me with many tears in her eyes what the Lord had done for her, and begged to be informed by me if there was that difference between them and the Heathens as the Christians insisted upon for that she was convinced from the conversion of Sapphire that God were no respecter of the person." After sending letters inviting people to come and hear Sapphire, the women had to clear the barn to accommodate the large numbers.[144] As these incidents imply, Khoekhoe converts and preachers contested both explicitly and implicitly a settler model of the racial exclusivity of Christianity – and sometimes broached the defences of resistant white settlers.

This missionary activity by Khoekhoe and slave preachers implicitly opposed an alternate discourse of Christianity to that upheld by many white settlers. Khoekhoe preachers upheld a Christianity of equality, arguing for access to the moral community through grace alone rather than skin colour. By becoming missionaries among dependants of the patriarchal household, Khoekhoe preachers were also establishing an alternate source of authority to that of the white patriarch. They were writing themselves into a narrative which had previously excluded them, and asserting authority through one of the few avenues left open to them.

Conflict over the meaning of Christianity sometimes involved explicit debate over the meaning of texts. To illustrate this, I want to look at a final example of the activity of Khoekhoe preachers. Barnabas Shaw of the Wesleyan Methodist Missionary Society recorded a conversation in the 1810s between three Nama Christians and a Dutch settler, at whose farm the four had been proselytizing. Jacob Links, cited in this narrative (also quoted at length by Richard Elphick)[145] was a member of a leading political family and an early Nama preacher who claimed that he was attracted to Christianity because it affirmed racial equality. He would later be murdered by San in company with another Khoekhoe preacher and a Methodist missionary with whom he was travelling to establish a new mission station.[146]

Boer: What kind of singing and praying is this that you have had? I never heard any thing like it, and cannot understand.

Jacob Links: I think, master, you only come to mock us, as many of the farmers say we ought not to have the gospel; – but here is a chapter (John iii) pray who are the persons that must be born again? (Handing the Testament).

Boer: Myne oogen [sic] zyn niet goed ... so that I cannot see very well, but I suppose Jesus Christ.

Jacob: No, master, no such thing; – Jesus Christ says we are all sinners, and that we must be born again in the Spirit, or we cannot enter the kingdom of heaven.

Jan Links: But, master, you once told me that our names did not stand in the book, and that the gospel did not, therefore, belong to us Namaquas. Will you now tell me master, whether the name of Dutchman, or Englishman is to be found in it? (No answer).

Jacob: Master, you who are called Christi mensche (Christians), call us heathens. That is our name. Now I find the book says, that Jesus came as light to lighten the Heidenen (Gentiles). So we read our names in the book. (Farmer silent).

Hendrik Smit: That master cannot understand many things in the book, is not strange; Paul says, "The natural man receiveth not the things of the Spirit of God," 1 Cor.ii, 14.

Boer: Who is then the natural man?

Hendrik: All men in their sinful and unregenerate state, so that we can only understand spiritual things by the help of the Spirit of God, &c.

Boer: Ik ben geen zendeling (I am no missionary), therefore cannot explain scripture passages.

Jacob: But, master, do you ever teach your slaves and servants anything of the gospel?

Boer: Neen, volstrekt niets (No, certainly nothing at all), for were they taught, it would make them equally as wise as myself.[147]

This passage was doubtless framed and manipulated by the missionary translator and transcriber. It is nonetheless fascinating not only for its explicit debate over access to Christianity but also for the conflict it illustrates between an oral and a written religion – with, ironically, the African preachers relying on the written word and the settler of European origin calling on folk understanding. As Elphick points out, the Dutch farmer is almost certainly trying to conceal his illiteracy.[148] The farmer's belief that the names of the Khoekhoe "did not stand in the book" may be an echo of the popular millenarian belief, derived from the Book of Revelation, that the names of the elect were sealed in a book by God; it was a common feature of British millenarian movements, for example, that followers be "sealed" by a messianic leader. The farmer cannot, however, present the biblical evidence for the claim that the Nama are not "in the book," while Jacob Links can illustrate from the Bible that Christ came for the conversion of the "heathen," and thus that conversion is possible.

Hendrik Smit goes even farther and argues in effect that the Nama are real Christians while the Dutchman has not had a true conversion

experience and so remains a "natural man." The language of evangelical Christianity could thus be turned against white settlers to the
extent of arguing that they were not true Christians, just as many evangelicals in England claimed that the placeholders of the established
church were only "nominal" Christians.

Another striking feature of this conversation is that it revolves
around interpretation of the Bible. The lesson that Christianity was
based on interpretation of the Bible may have been one of the greatest gifts of the early nonconformist missionaries to their converts.
Read, for example, was extremely eager that the Khoekhoe become
literate in order to read the Bible for themselves and check their own
interpretations against those of the missionaries. Other missionaries
were less willing to put their own authority at risk. Nonetheless, they
almost invariably believed that converts must become literate and
that the Bible was the touchstone of truth. By the 1820s, knowledge
of the Bible had become widespread among the Khoisan, although
the text was often memorized rather than read. At Bethelsdorp in
·1828, for example, Read attested that the desire to read had become
intense and that from two to three hundred attended his classes in
adult literacy. Many had the Bible in their hands, he affirmed, and
committed much of it to memory, repeating text at the church's
quarterly examinations as well as before class superintendents and
monitors.[149]

The result was a Bible-oriented religion which was potentially open
to subversion through alternate interpretations of the sacred text from
which authority was considered to flow. The unpopular George Barker found his authority undermined at Theopolis in 1820, for example,
through debate over the appropriate biblical text for the administration of justice. He had enquired in a public meeting into the rape of
Elizabeth Zeeland by Willem Rondanger. When Rondanger confessed,
the people present decided to exile him from the institution. Two days
later Barker complained:

Willem Rondanger should have been sent yesterday to the Landdrost, but was
neglected. This morning ordered him away. Several of the people came to plead
for him, even of those who had sentenced him to be excluded the Institution. I
set before them the nature of his crime, read to them the 22nd chapter of
Deuteronomy: Told them I was fully determined to make an example of him
& go he should. One of them, Samson Tivor, brought his Bible and pointed out
Galatians: 6-1, saying that according to that he thought Willem ought not to
be entirely excluded the place. Asked him if Paul spoke of rape & then brought
him the big bible and besought him to read the notes and compare the
references.[150]

The role of the Bible as source of authority meant that converts with access to it claimed increased social status. The role of Christianity as creed merged with the role of Christianity as a social symbol and marker of boundaries. The Griqua state founded its claim to political equality on the Christianity of its members, for example.[151] The Eastern Cape records indicate that some converts aggregated to themselves the right to dominate nonconverts. "If a man is rich," remarked "Mr. Hendrick" bitterly at a meeting at Kat River in 1834, "although he is short in stature as I am then he is great, and if a man is baptized then he becomes a 'Baas.'"[152]

Textual interpretation could prove a double-edged sword, however. It could also be turned by whites, especially those operating within a duty-oriented understanding of Christianity, against Khoisan converts to soften this claim to social status. The encounter of Cornelius Goeyman with the British botanist William Burchell, discussed in chapter 3, is illuminating in this regard. What Burchell's attempt to use the bible to instil obedience perhaps illustrates above all is the malleability of the biblical text and consequent conflict over its implications in social practice. In addition to the lesson that travellers should not believe all they hear, the story demonstrates how much more vulnerable the Bethelsdorp model of Christianity was to competition with the high Anglican model of social order than it was to the exclusionary settler model.

NARRATIVE AND CONVERSION

Let me conclude by suggesting the importance of narrative in weaving together the political and the religious. Even religious myth can be seen to be political, without being reducible to politics. Rather, stories can hold many meanings in them at once: they can be about self-worth or self-abnegation, for example, as well as being about God.

Conversion narratives, for example, were both a literary genre with rhetorical conventions and stereotypical storyline and a form replete with individual variation. Some Khoekhoe converts adopted the missionary evaluation of their old economic lifestyle as worthless and empty, while others, as we have seen, resisted such categorization and interference. Those in the 1830s who would argue that the "Hottentot" nation was rejuvenating itself often drew on the conventions of a conversion narrative: the sinner underwent a passage from evil to good via the acquisition of self-knowledge through God's intervention. The convention of an evil early life – that is, of individual guilt – characteristic of English conversion narratives as much as those of South African converts would be all too easily transposed into an affirmation of *collective* guilt. Nonetheless, such narratives also provided a means for the expiation of anxiety and of personal guilt at a time of violence and crisis. The evangelical conversion narrative offered a language about overcoming guilt and adversity, at the expense of acknowledging guilt and "accepting" it as constitutive of one's being and even of one's society. Thus the paradox of evangelical salvation: it creates a climate of shame while offering an immediate way out. People whose cultural vocabulary has no place for evangelical conversion, and who thus do not experience guilt as, in a sense, the necessary precursor to the overcoming of the emotion, are perhaps susceptible to evangelical conversion only if they want change badly enough to generate shame about their past. If this is true, it does not mean, however, that such people are solely passive victims of forces beyond their control.

Consider the life story of one convert, Andries Stoffels, who travelled to London in 1835 to testify before the Select Committee on Aborigines. Stoffels was a Gonaqua Khoekhoe, born, as he put it, "at the Bushman's River among shep and cattle," in or around the 1770s. Stoffels witnessed the Dutch rise to regional hegemony: "We soon lost all our property and our land and water."[153] He entered service with Dutch farmers and participated in violent Dutch attacks against San groups, an experience that affected him throughout his life.[154] At some stage, presumably while in a clientage relationship with a farmer, Stoffels was able to accumulate cattle, the marker of wealth in Khoekhoe society. He was, however, "obliged to leave the service of the farmer and my 130 sheep and 30 cattle to this day in his hand."[155] Following the British invasion, Stoffels fought in the Third Frontier War on the Khoekhoe side and was injured in the battle against Van der Walt's commando. He was later taken prisoner by the Xhosa and brought to Xhosaland, where he learnt Xhosa and acted as an interpreter. All of these experiences marked Stoffels: "Like Moses," commented Read, he "felt severely the degraded state of his countrymen as having lost their country, their property, and their liberty."[156]

Stoffel first came into direct contact with mission Christianity while acting as an interpreter for a Xhosa chief visiting Bethelsdorp. According to Read, Stoffels experienced missionary preaching as an effort to instil guilt and responded because of his own existing guilt and anxiety. "The Missionary came in and began to read, then to talk to the people, then to scold. He concluded that some of them had done something very bad, and had been called forward to receive a public reprimanding, and that the book contained a list of their crimes." Suddenly becoming convinced that the preacher was addressing him directly, Stoffels accused his cousin, who lived at Bethelsdorp, of having denounced him. The cousin claimed, however, that "the word of God always appeared so that it exposed the actions and the very thoughts of men." Stoffels was perturbed and, seeking purity, spent time alone. He could find "no rest" in his old life. "He then went among the farmers, where there was dancing and merriment; but was pursued by his conscience; he returned to Bethelsdorp; but his convictions were deepened by the word of God, and often had he to rise from his seat and run out of the chapel to the bushes and thickets, weeping aloud, and spending hours and even days from men, praying to God for mercy." This continued for two or three years, until "light broke in upon his mind, that he understood the way of salvation through a crucified Saviour."[157] On the heels of the failure of violent resistance, Stoffels turned to Christianity.

Stoffels eventually became an enthusiastic advocate of western education for the Khoekhoe and of national salvation through Christianization. He was one of the first Kat River settlers and became a church deacon. In the 1830s he was a strong advocate of temperance. In this, too, he was preoccupied by the collapse of older Khoekhoe society. As he pessimistically told the Kat River Temperance Society in 1834: "Every nation on earth still exists; but the Hottentot nation is done; there is only a small remnant of two or three left; and what, you might ask, has swallowed up the Hottentot nation? I answer brandy! brandy! Before the white man came and introduced brandy among the Hottentots they were a healthy, brave, and honourable nation, but the Hottentot nation is now good for nothing ... Great medicine can't cure the Hottentots now, their lives are in such a state that medicine has no effect on them."[158] Christianity provided a rhetoric of rejuvenation but at a high cost. In London, at least, Stoffels wielded this language at the expense of typecasting the Khoekhoe as degraded and their culture as a void. He testified to the parliamentary committee that the English were wearing down the "Hottentots" through racially based economic discrimination: "It is not now murder, they do not murder, but it is like a newspaper that you put in the press and wear down." The "Hottentot" has "no water; he has not a blade of grass; he has no lands; he has no wood; he has no place where he can sleep; all that he now has is the missionary and the Bible."[159] Speaking before the annual meeting of the London Missionary Society at Exeter Hall, at a time when the missionary lobby was tying cultural assimilation to political rights, Stoffels put forth his vision of the harmonious interation of white and "Hottentot" communities under the influence of Christianity, and presumably, the Khoekhoe adoption of white material culture: "My nation is poor and degraded, but the word of God is their stay and their hope. The word of God has brought my nation so far, that if a Hottentot young lady and an English young lady were walking with their faces from me, I would take them both to be English ladies ... We are coming on, we are improving; we will soon all be one. The Bible makes all nations one. The Bible brings wild man and civilized together. The Bible is our light. The Hottentot nation was almost exterminated, but the Bible has brought the nations together, and here I am before you."[160] The terrible ambiguity of even the most well-meaning mission station is inherent in these words: Stoffels inadvertently underscores the problem of any culture relying on another for all its positive images and self-respect.

Despite this situation, conversion nonetheless served a reintegrative function for Stoffels. On the most mundane level, it permitted him to accumulate wealth and prestige at Bethelsdorp and Kat River certainly more than he had as a farm worker and probably as a Xhosa dependant. More profoundly, it permitted him to work for the "rejuvenation" of his people and to remain politically active. Whatever the effectiveness of his activity, it provided a sense of purpose.

In many ways, then, Khoisan individuals used mission stations and mission Christianity, even in situations that did not appear overtly political. Many of these uses are not recoverable by the historian, but some can be glimpsed. Whatever the profound ambiguities and pain of that usage, it is important for the historian to try to untangle this complex process. Above all, it is useful to look for complex relationships between religion and politics, and not to write off complicted individual responses under excessively broad rubrics. In truth, it is easier on the pen to celebrate resistance to westernization than to understand the partial incorporation of western myths and technologies, but this natural tendency cannot do justice to the ambiguity, pain, and partial accommodation that are the stuff of everyday life.

5 The Rise and Fall of Bethelsdorp Radicalism under the British, 1806–17

Any hopes that the Khoekhoe might have entertained of rapid political reforms under the new British administration of 1806 were quickly dashed. Van der Kemp immediately presented the incoming acting governor, Major-General David Baird, with typically imperious letters of advice. He urged that the Khoekhoe be granted representation before the governor. "As the Hottentots on account of their local situation have no free access to the courts of justice, it seems advisable that five or six of the most accredited Hottentots, as deputies of their nation, may have access to the acting Governor, immediately to lay before him from time to time the state and complaints of their [nation?]." He further contended that the Cape Khoekhoe should be given "one or more pieces of land, which they may call their own home," where people who were currently "dispersed and vagabonding" might establish a "more or less civilized society."[1]

Read and Van der Kemp were permitted to return home to Bethelsdorp. Nonetheless, Baird's initially warm feelings changed once he received a "sinistre report" from Janssens about the missionaries, warning him "to be on his guard against the machinations of two dangerous persons viz. Hendrik Rensburg and Vanderkemp"[2] (Van Rensburg was a fractious Zuurveld farmer). By 1807, the minds of the Bethelsdorp inhabitants were "not a little alienated from the British Government, to which they were formerly so much attached."[3] Read similarly reported in 1806 that Bethelsdorp residents complained that "it were not the same English as there had been under the Gov't of Lord Dundas."[4]

Critical points of tension included struggles over corvée labour, over access to Bethelsdorp, and more broadly over the system of pass laws and restrictions on Khoisan mobility and choice of workplace, formalized, despite reformist rhetoric, in the Caledon Code of 1809. A further flashpoint was the question of Khoisan military service. The British determined to make military allies of the Khoisan and pestered Bethelsdorp for recruits to the Cape Corps. Furthermore, Uitenhage landdrost Jacob Cuyler insisted that Bethelsdorp inhabitants serve on settler commandos against the Xhosa, with whom the frontier Dutch skirmished regularly before the explosion of the Fourth Frontier War of 1811. On the other hand, Van der Kemp allowed deserters from the Cape Corps to enter Bethelsdorp, refused to coerce men into joining, and urged the government to improve the working conditions and pension arrangements of soldiers. Van der Kemp claimed that Janssens had exempted Bethelsdorp from being commanded by local officials and from serving on expeditions against the Xhosa or their own countrymen.[5] With the rejection of these arguments by the British, Van der Kemp was compelled to abandon his vision of Bethelsdorp as an independent theocratic domain excluded from the politics of the frontier, and the Khoisan were forced, reluctantly, into the role of full-fledged military allies of the British – the very outcome Dundas had hoped for.

The relationship among Van der Kemp, Read, and Cuyler quickly degenerated to the point of vitriolic hatred, as wider political struggles rapidly acquired a personal dimension for the white protagonists. In addition to his other roles, Cuyler as landdrost was also the judge for the district and did not do justice often enough in cases of Khoisan complaints against settlers, according to Read and Van der Kemp and the Khoisan witnesses whose testimony the archives have preserved. When two men travelled to Cuyler to testify that their wives and children had been swept off a public road and forcibly detained by a former master and mistress, Van der Kemp added in his accompanying letter that he hoped for justice to correct "these and other excesses, which being left unpunished daily increase in number, and atrocity, and render this country an exsecration [sic] to every stranger, in whom the last spark of humanity is not yet entirely extinguished."[6] In his turn, Cuyler complained to the Castle that it was impossible for him to be answerable for the tranquillity of the area "while so lawless and turbulent a character who has so much influence with the savage nations, is suffered to act as he pleases."[7]

LAW AND LABOUR: LEGAL STRUGGLES

It was against this background of oppressive labour legislation, continued judicial abuse, and conflict with landdrost Cuyler that the

Bethelsdorp missionaries tried to play their trump card, namely, the political influence in Britain of their evangelical connections. The events that followed provide a case study of the advantages and limitations of the imperial networks provided by missionaries, into which autochthonous people tried to tap. Throughout the period under discussion, the LMS gave extensive publicity to Read and Van der Kemp, particularly in the early years of the 1800s when the society had had only a handful of missions on which to report. The *Transactions of the London Missionary Society*, an LMS occasional publication, printed Van der Kemp's lengthy reports with little editing, while the *Evangelical Magazine* and the Scottish *Missionary Magazine* both provided regular capsule summaries of LMS activities in South Africa. The Anglican evangelical *Christian Observer*, in contrast, was very subdued in its early coverage of missions in general, despite the fact that it was edited by leading CMS organizer Josiah Pratt for many years. This reflected the Anglican evangelical public discomfort over missions, for the reasons outlined earlier. The audience for Van der Kemp's reports was therefore probably large among the moderate Calvinist interdenomonationalist wing of the evangelical movement and far smaller among Arminian Methodists and the Anglican Evangelical "regulars" with ecclesiological concerns about church order.

Readers in Britain received reports from the mission field with tremendous fervour, believing that they were indicative of the action of God in the world as the millennium approached. "Every eye displayed wonder and astonishment, and every heart seemed to overflow with gratitude and praise,"[8] said W. Lambert in describing the reception accorded his reading aloud the most recent account of Van der Kemp's activities to a prayer group of four different congregations. The LMS focused on Van der Kemp in particular and built him into an early missionary hero. As one disgruntled missionary to South Africa, George Thom (whom we shall meet again) wrote in exasperation in 1814: "A cordial approval of a man's talents and labours is enough without making him next thing to a Catholic Saint ... Many good and zealous Brethren in this colony have been lost sight of because *one* who was of respectable Parents, of age, Education &c was a missionary in Africa. I wonder how Dr. Vanderkemp felt when he read in the first volume of the Transactions that he was 'as great an Evangelist as had been since the Days of the apostles' (I think that is the expression)."[9]

These eulogistic reports certainly filtered the spiritual experiences of Africans through a web of European theological preconceptions, but they also reproduced Van der Kemp's political understanding of South Africa in a fairly straightforward fashion. In essence, the LMS directors seem to have been too much in awe of Van der Kemp to modify his strong language, just as they invariably took his side in more minor administrative disputes among the missionaries themselves.

Despite the enthusiasm with which these reports were read, and despite a certain Afrikaner mythology persisting well into the twentieth century that, from the beginning, the LMS missionaries were in the pocket of a powerful English enemy, the society's audience had little direct political clout in Westminster in the early 1800s. During the Batavian administration, clout in Westminster was immaterial, of course, and between 1806 and 1811, the LMS was too much in the shadow of "irrespectability" and of dissenting support for the French Revolution to aim for it. It was not until 1811, as relationships warmed again between evangelical dissent and evangelical Anglicanism,[10] that George Burder felt confident enough to approach William Wilberforce with a list compiled by James Read of atrocities committed against the Khoisan.

Read's complaints came first in the course of the letter to the LMS of August 1808 which I cited in chapter 4. The document reads more like a despairing *cri de coeur* than a call for action: "We are in the way of hearing more of this thing than any other persons and could multiply the account of such as I have mentioned and of a more horrid nature, but should be perhaps as little believed as Valliant [Vaillant] and Mr. Barrow."[11] Edited selections were published in the 1809 *Transactions*. Thanking the directors for this effort, Read sent them a further account of the difficulty for a Khoisan person of obtaining justice or even of presenting a complaint before the appropriate official. The legal system was administered by white local officials, and no white person would testify against another in a case involving a "Hottentot," Read attested. Using the ammunition of the pass-law system, Khoisan were often illegally prevented from travelling to the magistrates to make depositions.

When a Hottentot makes his escape to complain to the Magistrate, letters are immediately circulated, commandos formed, the roads and bypaths taken possession of, and 'tis a thousand to one if he escapes, if taken is cruelly treated, if not killed; if he has the fortune to arrive he is treated very cooly, if heard, is sent back sometimes three or four days journey with a letter to fetch his master, here he is at once put in the hands of his enemies, the letter of the Magistrate treated with disdain, or burnt and if the Hottentot is missing and never returns no enquiry is made after him, if he escapes death and returns he is sent the same road again, till he meets his fate, or gives up the business, and chuses to sacrifice his wife, children, and property to the farmers ...[12]

According to Van der Kemp's subsequent account, Lord Caledon saw a copy of the *Transactions* in 1809 and ordered Cuyler to summon

Read to investigate the complaints. The power of information networks is amply demonstrated in this event. Cuyler predictably claimed that there was little in the complaints; Read felt that witnesses were afraid, although he acknowledged that there were some small discrepancies between stories. Read gave Cuyler further accounts of murders to forward to Caledon, including some by government office-holders, "besides numerous lesser complaints of misusage of all kinds, and which increase from time to time."[13] He asked the colonial government that the cases be considered by a judge other than Cuyler, "recalling that Major Cuyler was, on account of his marriage, related to several of the malefactors, and could of course not be considered, neither as a competent judge, nor even an impartial informer in the affair." Read requested rather to be allowed to present information in Cape Town.[14] On 19 October 1810 he added a personal appeal to Caledon. His letter called on abolitionist stereotypes of injured Africa and of the missionary as the protector of the hapless and oppressed African:

The poor Hottentot in vain turns his eye to any person to whom he comes to unbossum his wounded spirit, and lay open his sore complaints: he has sought for redress perhaps at the hazard of his life, at last he finds in a Missionary a friend, whom he afterwards begins to experience, is more or less concerned for their temporal and spiritual welfare, then and not without some degree of fear, he tells his pityable story, and a heart of stone must bleed to hear the father relate the loss of his child, that of the child of the father, the tender husband of the wife, and the wife of the husband &c &c, and the survivors forced into an almost endless bondage, and the orphans made worse than slaves.

The missionaries had been placed in a position to hear of this by providence, Read informed the governor, and providence had chosen Caledon as the Africans' "instrument of deliverance."[15] By January 1811, however, Read was complaining that crimes were still occurring almost daily and that justice was being sacrificed to policy. He used the metaphor, often employed by Van der Kemp, of blood which had impregnated the very land and itself called out for divine revenge: "If we take the whole upon an average what a dreadfull pool of blood must present itself, and which must cry to God for vengeance."

In early January 1811 Van der Kemp wrote again to Governor Caledon.[16] Contrasting with the polite and humble tone of Read's letter, this was another of Van der Kemp's imperious missives in which he lectured doubtless irritated colonial officials on their moral duty. "With confidence," he wrote, "I expected that your Excellency would have taken effectual measures to put a stop to the current of barbarities to which this unhappy people is exposed: I find myself disappointed."[17]

The letter went beyond criminal cases to criticize the systematic abuse of pass laws and labour legislation by local officials in the interior. In spite of Caledon's 1809 proclamation, the Dutch continued to "take and keep Hottentots into service by force." The veld-cornets used the legal system to enslave the Khoisan, by unjust use of pass laws, for example, by forcing people to sign forged hire contracts, or by compelling people to stay at work past the expiry of their contracts until replacements were found. The flawed administration of justice by the landdrost allowed no protection against the subsequent murder of Khoisan plaintiffs, even if individuals managed to circumvent great obstacles to have a complaint heard and received a favourable judgment. Van der Kemp therefore called for a thorough and impartial investigation, and for adequate means to verify and register hire contracts. In sum, Read and Van der Kemp demanded a complete overhaul of the labour system.

On 28 February 1811 Colonel Bird informed Bethelsdorp that the whole question was under Caledon's consideration and that fourteen of the complaints in particular had been placed in the hands of the Cape fiscal.[18] In March, Read and Van der Kemp were called to Cape Town in order to testify before an "extraordinary commission" appointed by Caledon to investigate their complaints, consisting of the fiscal, two members of the Court of Justice, and the secretary.[19] This had a further deleterious impact on relationships in Uitenhage and Graaff-Reinet between the Dutch and the Khoisan. In the convoluted English of LMS missionary Michael Wimmer, LMS preaching within the colony to mixed audiences "is now by the Anger of Satan, and his Instruments put a stop to; when hearing, that Br. Read through a Letter written to England about the Oppression of the Farmers of this Land upon the Hottentots, their character were made stinking." Despite the dangers of travelling without passes, many people rushed to get information to Read and Van der Kemp on the verge of their departure.[20] Bethelsdorp inhabitants strongly demonstrated their support for the complaints. "We left our dear Bethelsdorp the 28th of March with many cries and tears on both sides and the whole institution lead us out about a quarter of a mile from the village and with allmost broken hearts we parted," wrote Read.

Read and Van der Kemp arrived at Cape Town on 27 April and were received cordially by the governor and other leading officials. Through May and June they presented 113 cases before the commission of "Hottentots being murdered by Christians, almost all during our residence in this country, of which we have been informed accidentally by our people at Bethelsdorp." In response to Van der Kemp's call for a comprehensive investigation to uncover the full extent of abuse,

Caledon appointed a special commission to travel to the districts in which the crimes were committed. Van der Kemp's concern, however, was that "though the contents of the proclamation appeared to me extremely well calculated to counteract oppression, they would be of little use, unless the members of the intended deputation were characters of the strictest integrity and firm resolution." He informed the LMS directorship that, should efforts to procure justice for the "innocent sufferers" prove unsuccessful, he would consider it his duty to publish the cases which he had laid before the Court of Justice – "though it may be perhaps more advisable to communicate them previously in private to the Minister in the Colonial department."[21]

As Van der Kemp had apparently feared, events then came to a standstill. In June, Cape Town was shaken by earthquakes. In keeping with his stern theology of retribution, Read believed that these were warnings from God: "Indeed this is a guilty country the blood of the innocent cries for vengiance."[22] Other inhabitants thought so also, and both Read and the South African Missionary Society were caught up in a general religious revival.[23] Nonetheless, no concrete advance was made concerning the administration of justice. Read fell into a depression, originating, Van der Kemp believed, in "nostalgia." He became "ill of a bilious fever, which though it went off again, left him in a state of melancholy, in which he complains of various, and alternating symptoms, oppression in his brain, pains in his breast, stomach, belly, tremor, loss of appetite, restlessness, and a constant, universal depression of mind."[24] In July 1811 Caledon was recalled from the Cape, and there was a two-month lull before the arrival of his replacement during which neither Read nor Van der Kemp felt that they could leave Cape Town. In the eastern frontier districts, fighting between farmers and Xhosa intensified in the run-up to the outbreak of war at the end of the year. Meanwhile, Van der Kemp himself became increasingly ill.

Actions in London were always out of step with events in south Africa. Therefore it is unclear how much the LMS directorate knew when they sought at last to enlist support from their Claphamite connections. It is clear, however, that the inquiry at the Cape had already been instituted by the time that the LMS turned to William Wilberforce. It is in fact probable that the LMS directors turned privately to the British government because they were highly alarmed at the prospect of Van der Kemp publishing an all-out attack on the colonial administration of south Africa if the governor should fail to take sufficient action. As the directors wrote to Van der Kemp, they feared that such a step would be "fraught with danger." "We should entertain most serious Apprehensions for the Safety of our Missionaries by the publication of any thing on the subject in the colony."[25] The sentiment doubtless arose from a mixture of genuine fear for the safety of the south African missionaries and from a sense of the society's own relatively precarious position in English society. The year 1812 was in any case a bad time to be launching public assaults on Britain's conduct of its empire. Evangelicals were lobbying intensively for the lifting of restrictions on the entry of missionaries to India under the terms of the upcoming renewal of the EIC charter, and at the same time they were struggling to refute the damaging implications of the Vellore Mutiny that missionaries were imperial troublemakers. Dissenters, meanwhile, were endeavouring to get the political disabilities of nonconformists lifted.

The common assumption that the Circuit Court was instituted as a direct result of Colonial Office pressure is thus incorrect,[26] as Caledon had adopted and adapted Van der Kemp's suggestion of a perambulatory commission by early 1811. What does seem right is that metropolitan pressure necessitated an investigation which would be seen to be comprehensive and would produce conclusive results. Regardless of Caledon's intentions, colonial government policy in 1812 over the Circuit Court would in fact prove an exercise in damage limitation which would permit the claim of a visible victory for the rule of law without full justice being done; even here, however, the investigation was probably on a larger scale than would have occurred without pressure from London.

In the late summer of 1811, LMS secretary George Burder sent William Wilberforce a copy of Read's letter to Caledon, with an appeal for backing and the claim that Caledon had been prevented by his ill-intentioned advisers from hearing the extent of missionary complaints. Wilberforce, the "uniform friend of injured Africa,"[27] was a natural target: he was the leader of the parliamentary abolitionist movement, had been discreetly active in the CMS, was a personal friend of the LMS Treasurer Hardcastle, and had a strong if carefully private working relationship with leading LMS figures. In gaining Wilberforce's attention, it cannot have hurt that it was to Wilberforce's advantage for Burder and Hardcastle to owe him a favour, as he tried to keep his dissenting allies out of the fray over the EIC charter renewal and to postpone for a year their effort to repeal the Coventicle Act in order to facilitate passage of the EIC bill.[28]

The statesman's reaction was all that could be hoped for. As the LMS directorate had clearly hoped, he considered abuse of the Khoisan to be a product of the same set of assumptions about black labour which permitted slavery, and he was quite willing to class the "savage" Dutch farmer with the West Indian planter. He immediately sent a warm reply expressing "not only my strongest abhorrence of such detestable proceedings, but the willing Assurance of my firm determination to use my utmost Endeavours to put a stop to such a System of Abominations, for Systematic they really appear to be." He, too, recognized the importance of debates about the civilization and humanity of the "Hottentots": "I am ... of opinion, that the execution of one or two of ye Boers, after a formal trial, for ye murder of one or more Hottentots, would do more towards vindicating the Claim of the poor injured Beings to the name and Rights of ye Human Species, and towards obtaining for them the better treatment which would naturally follow from thus raising them in ye Scale of Beings – ye Capital punishment of two or three of ye most powerful and savage of the Boors wld. do more I say for ye accomplishment of these valuable purposes, than all the Publications, all the Proclamations in ye World."[29] Wilberforce immediately waited upon Lord Liverpool, then minister for the Colonial Office. He also wrote at length to Lord Wellesley, citing Barrow as proof of Read's assertions.[30] This action was taken more quietly than Wilberforce would have wished. He regretted that he had not had the information before the prorogation of parliament: "In cases of this kind, proceedings of ye nature of those which we may have to institute, are smoothed and quickened in their progress, by the probability of a speedy public discussion if an appeal to ye Legislature shld. be required."[31] In consequence, the issue made no waves even in British antislavery circles, and the "Hottentots" did not yet enter the abolitionist consciousness as an important cause. All the same, the Colonial Office quietly issued orders to the Cape colonial government for a thorough investigation of abuses. When the new governor, Sir John Cradock, arrived at the Cape in September 1811, he had a mandate from Liverpool "to secure the exemplary punishment of such atrocious crimes, and to shield the injured natives from the barbarity of their oppressors in the future."[32]

Although Van der Kemp immediately presented Cradock with a list of requests, including the prosecution of the cases brought before the government, Cradock proved more preoccupied with the colony's relationship with the Xhosa.[33] Unlike Caledon, Cradock was a military man who decided to deal in a ruthless fashion with the Xhosa "problem," exacerbated by mutual raiding in the Zuurveld. Between October 1811 and March 1812, the British sent the entire Cape Regiment with a few European troops to the Eastern Cape, where the force joined a commando of about 1,500 farmers, according to James Read.[34] Under the efficient leadership of Lieutenant-Colonel John Graham, this force drove some 8,000 Xhosa across the Fish River by virtue of superior British military technology.[35] The army has been remembered as a British force by many; J.B. Peires, for example, states that

"British regular troops, backed by Boer militia, systematically and ruthlessly drove the Xhosa beyond the Fish."[36] The troops were, however, almost entirely Khoisan rather than "regulars." In addition, men resident at Bethelsdorp between the summer of 1811 and the conclusion of operations were forced to participate as conscripts to local burgher commandos and defence groups. In the summer of 1811, for example, the station was compelled to send an eighth of its inhabitants to keep watch with the veldcornets against Xhosa raids.[37] In large part, the Khoekhoe had no choice about their participation. Is it not also possible, however, that their desire for a favourable verdict in upcoming court cases led them to cooperate with the British at this crucial moment?

This was the first of four frontier wars in the first half of the nineteenth century in which the Khoisan fought on the side of the colony, struggling to make a trade-off between influence and loyalty. It also may have been one of the most difficult. The Gonaqua and the Gqunukhwebe were both mixed Khoekhoe-Xhosa groups. Gqunukhwebe came often to visit Bethelsdorp while Bethelsdorp people travelled into the interior to visit and evangelize among neighbouring Xhosa. In 1810, in pursuance of the recommendations of Colonel Richard Collins, Caledon had ordered that all Xhosa leave the colony, principally owing to Collins's fear of "an improper connexion existing between the Kaffres and the members of the institution at Bethelsdorp."[38] After considerable difficulty deciding who was or was not a Xhosa, Bethelsdorp was forced to expel a large number of its residents. Most went to live with Chungwa's people. Later they would form the nucleus of the first LMS mission among the Xhosa at Kat River. Consequently, the Khoisan were fighting old acquaintances, and in some cases relatives.

Between the departure of Read and Van der Kemp for Cape Town and the return home of Read on 12 December 1811, farmers murdered another four Bethelsdorp inhabitants. In the meantime, Cuyler launched an abortive attempt to have Ulbricht, Wimmer, and Smith charged as "Backbiters" in the drosdty court – illustrating the peculiar mixture of the putative rule of law and arbitrary government which characterized the frontier districts and made redress so difficult.[39] Just before the commando departed, the commission appointed by Caledon to administer justice in the country districts made its first appearance at Bethelsdorp.

This initial investigation was fairly cursory, and no criminal charges were actually heard. Indeed, the presiding officer had once (according to frontier rumour) been involved in an assassination plot against Read and Van der Kemp themselves. Read had rushed to Bethelsdorp in order to be there when the commission arrived. He reached the institution on the very day of the commissioners' visit and was granted an interview of only a few minutes with Commissioner Rijneveld before the commission departed at once. This haste suggests a cursory examination, at best, of witnesses, as well as what looks like a deliberate unwillingness to allow Read to coordinate evidence.[40] Four days later, Van der Kemp died in Cape Town.[41]

By late 1812, Read was writing with resignation that he was grateful to Wilberforce and Liverpool for their intervention but they would scarcely believe that, as far as he knew, not one step had been taken to punish any of the crimes which had been laid before the government. "Even the poor girl pickled or salted is yet (if alive) in the hand of her monsterous Master and Mistress and may have been pickled ten times more by this for what any person seems to care." The commission set up by Caledon might be productive of some good but was flawed by being partly made up of people who had been long in office and who would thus themselves be thrown into a poor light by a critical report. "The fact is, as long as the country Magistrates and courts are not cleansed, and misdemeanours taken notice of, and example made of them, all commissions appointed, and proclamations issued will have no effect."[42]

Shortly after this letter, Colonial Secretary Bird informed Read that the fiscal had at last made a full report to the governor. The cases reported had been divided into three classes: those concerning "murder and other cruelties during present English government," requiring criminal prosecution; those concerning criminal events before the previous surrender or of uncertain date; and those describing "arbitrary conduct or real injustice" but not requiring criminal prosecution. Information was still being collected on those cases in the second category. Those in the first would be examined by the next Commission of Circuit, which had been lamentably held up by the frontier war. Those in the last category were dismissed.

By this latter ruling, Cradock removed the issue of the systematic abuse of Khoisan labour from the agenda of the inquiry. This was in keeping with the Cradock administration's recent passage of the Apprenticeship of Servants Law. The apprenticeship law formalized the existing system by which Khoekhoe children who had been brought up on a white farm to the age of eight were "apprenticed" to the farmer as labourers between the ages of eight and eighteen, theoretically in order to discharge the expenses of their upbringing.[43] This system was open to numerous abuses, in addition to its intrinsic injustice.[44] The 1812 legislation in theory provided legal redress for Khoekhoe kept apprenticed past their time, and it also reduced the end of the apprenticeship from age twenty-five, as it had been in some areas, to age eighteen. Nonetheless, it enshrined a practice akin to serf-dom, and signalled the incoming governor's perhaps unsurprising intention to believe his own bureaucrats rather than missionaries on the subject of labour relations. Well-entrenched abuses of the apprenticeship system were thus permitted to continue.[45]

The Caledon and Cradock administrations brought the Khoekhoe within a legal framework and thus putatively enshrined the rule of law. They did not, however, replace the administrative personnel of the outlying districts, who had remained in place through successive Batavian and British gubernatorial regimes, nor did they seek fundamentally to revamp the customary laws regulating labour relations. The substantial legal advance that did fit into this schema was the establishment of the circuit court system, which furnished a court of appeal and guaranteed the enforcement of the existing criminal law.

On 23 August 1812 a summons finally came to Read through Cuyler that he and a number of witnesses were required at once to travel to George to meet the Commission of Circuit, which would go down in settler memory as the "black circuit" at which farmers were compelled to answer the charges of Khoisan plaintiffs. It is impossible to know whether Cuyler maliciously misinformed Read; the possibility cannot be discounted. The group from Bethelsdorp travelled laboriously to George, only to find that the commission had taken the opposite route and gone first to Graaff-Reinet. Not only did the group have to make its way back home but, one assumes, the testimony at Graaff-Reinet was heard without input from Bethelsdorp. Back at Bethelsdorp on 2 November, Read had to set off immediately to Uitenhage. At the beginning of December, Read, Wimmer, and the group of Khoisan plaintiffs toiled back to George.

These journeyings of the plaintiffs were overladen with religious symbolism – or at least became so in the report subsequently filed by James Read. The first journey to George, with five waggons and about sixty people, was long and dangerous because it was the rainy season and the rivers were overflowing their banks. The farmers en route were extremely hostile and refused to supply the party with provisions or fresh oxen. Religious exhortations, prayer meetings, and hymn singing characterized the pilgrimage. Before a particularly swollen river, the people were inspired to cross by a text on which Read had preached: "When thou goest through the waters I will be with thee, and through the rivers they shall not over flow thee." The "Hottentots" passed a notoriously cruel farmer travelling with his wife to appear before the landdrost, and twice helped his waggon out of the mud. This was in conscious fulfilment of the Christian injunction to "love thy enemy" and was thus also an affirmation of their Christian, and equal, status.

During the second visit to George, crowds of Khoekhoe arrived from the neighbouring Khoekhoe settlement known to Read as "Hooge Kraal" (later to become the mission station Pacaltsdorp) to hold religious meetings with the people of Bethelsdorp. One's strong impression is that Christianity was identified with the demand for national redress. Read certainly preached in this fashion. He held services that were attended by the commission, the landdrost, and all the government servants, as well as by the inhabitants of Hooge Kraal and Bethelsdorp. His last sermon before the opening of the court session was on psalm 74, verse 20, "Have regard for thy covenant." Verses 18 to 21 of this psalm read: "Remember this, O Lord, how the enemy scoffs, and an impious people reviles thy name / Do not deliver the soul of thy dove to the wild beasts, do not forget the life of thy poor for ever / Have regard for thy covenant; for the dark places of the land are full of the habitations of violence / Let not the downtrodden be put to shame; let the poor and needy praise thy name." Read drove the point home, appropriating the Calvinist language of God's covenant with the people of Israel to the ends of the Khoekhoe cause: "He considered of the state of parts of the Earth, *Dark*, 2ly the consequence *cruelty*, 3ly the remedy the *covenant*. Referred to this country, to the circumstances that had brought us here to the Drosdy, observed the appointment of God in ordering the sword of Justice to punish in this life what the Gospel does not restrain, acknowledging the goodness of God, the care of Government and the happy prospect of liberty to proceed from the present circumstances."[46] The sermon was in a sense a high point of the Bethelsdorp model of evangelical radicalism – even as a series of court rulings were about to illustrate the impossibility of its fulfilment.

"AN OVERSTRAINED PRINCIPLE OF LIBERTY": THE VERDICT OF THE BLACK CIRCUIT

Surely it is unsurprising that the Black Circuit of 1812 returned no verdicts which were favourable to Khoekhoe plaintiffs in criminal cases. "I find myself at a loss to say anything upon the result of Lord Caledon's Commission," complained Read at the beginning of 1813, adding that it had turned out as he had always expected. "Only a few cases reported to have been committed under the present government have been investigated and few have been wholy proved but much less proved to be false, not a Hottentot was permitted to an oath whether baptised or not, not one accused was arrested except he or she confessed his crime viz. when 'tis a Christian [white person] that accused. In civil cases however many of the Hottentots got justice done them and I hope the commission will be of importance in the long run. I wish we had a few judges from England."[47]

Some historians have tended to repeat the judgments of the court as though they indicated the legal weakness of the Khoi cases, but in fact one could argue that the verdicts were fairly predetermined. One might also note the discrepancy between the investigation Read and Van der Kemp proposed and the one they actually got.[48] According to colonial custom, the evidence of non-baptized witnesses could not be accepted as legally binding, because non-Christians could not give evidence under (Christian) oath. As Read stated in the letter cited above, the Circuit Court of 1812 invoked the popular identification of Christians with whites to refuse legal weight to the evidence of all nonwhite witnesses in the trials, even the considerable number who were baptized. Therefore it was de facto impossible for any white accused to be convicted unless there were white witnesses who were willing to testify against him. According to LMS inspector John Campbell, "most of the cases which came before the court could not be substantiated by *legal* evidence; for, according to the Dutch law, the oath of a Hottentot is inadmissable." The upcoming 1813 circuit would not have much business to transact, "nor can they have much, till some law be made to admit instructed Hottentots to give evidence on oath; because, in the present state of the colony, it would be one of the most difficult things imaginable, to get one white man to witness against another, if it referred to any injury sustained by a Hottentot."[49]

The judges were local officials with long track records which were being called into question, and with long-standing links with many of the families whose members were now on trial. Bethelsdorp plaintiffs missed the Graaff-Reinet trials altogether. Furthermore, plaintiffs believed that only recent crimes would be considered. At Uitenhage, Cuyler demanded the investigation of cases relating to the earlier period at the last minute, presumably once it became clear that the other criminal charges would be dismissed. In contrast to the confidence of white contemporaries that charges were unfounded, historian Hermann Giliomee underscores that the records of Graff-Reinet do in fact contain approximately twenty cases of unnatural deaths of Khoekhoe between 1786 and 1800, in most of which "a *prima facie* case of murder or homicide could be made out against colonists.[50]

The published report of the commission nonetheless was an implicit defence of frontier labour policy and an explicit rejection of the charges under consideration, claiming that Van der Kemp and Read had simply not taken the trouble to investigate the complaints made to them in an impartial manner. At the same time, the commissioners adopted an idealistic rhetoric of the rule of law. They felt they had made clear to the landdrosts the principle of the "maintenance of *equal right* and *equal protection* to all classes of society." The innovation of public trials was particularly valuable, they argued; it "carries with it a certain dignity," disseminates knowledge about justice and injustice, and imprints in hearers' minds "a perfect confidence in the administration of justice and the measures of Government as every one can now see and feel conviction in himself that the whole art of government consists *in doing justice to all*."[51] Justice had been visibly seen to be done, in a ritual designed to impress the populace with the even-handedness of the law and thus instil "self generated" compliance with political power among those at the bottom of the heap. This is a charge that Douglas Hay had some difficulty in making stick to the British eighteenth-century legal system as a whole, but Hay's analysis of the public administration of criminal justice in eighteenth-century England is pertinent to the early circuit courts in South Africa – a society in which racial and class divisions reinforced one another sufficiently to exclude the black working class from the moral universe of the white upper-class lawgiver perhaps more thoroughly than happened in England itself.[52]

The commissioners threw into doubt the right of the contemporary Khoekhoe and San to be considered as peoples and therefore implicitly to exist independently of the white labour market. The "Hottentots" were "this people that one can scarcely more consider as such, because that excepting the kraals at the Slange River in the district of George, they have not anywhere an independent subsistence," while the "Bosjesmen," several pages later, were "this people, which one can scarcely consider as such, because that they have not the smallest idea of social order, of Government, or of a head."[53] Gathering and hunting were not perceived as an "independent subsistence." The Khoisan were thus signalled as available for absorption into "organized" society as labourers. "Hottentots" ought to work for the farmers. The farmers would necessarily treat them well out of "self interest, this great spring of all human action," in the context of the increasing cost of slaves and recent government legislation, presumably including the 1809 proclamation of the Caledon code regulating labour and the 1812 Apprenticeship of Servants Law.[54] Smithian beliefs about the overall social harmony generated by the pursuit of individual economic self-interest were adopted and turned against the Khoisan.

To complete the humiliation, the commissioners drew a damning comparison between the more quietist Moravian mission station of Genadenthal, and Bethelsdorp. In the "very useful" institution of Genadendal, "the principle adopted there by the teachers seems to be to encourage those people to industry, order and subordination, and to practise those social virtues as essential religious duties"; in consequence, the Moravian Khoekhoe had neat English gardens, were unusually clean, and gladly went out to work at ploughing and harvest time. In Bethelsdorp, in contrast, Van der Kemp had "established such an overstrained principle of liberty as the ground work, that the natural state of barbarism appears there to supersede civilization and social order ... Laziness and idleness, and consequently dirt and filth, grow there in perfection, and an inimical partiality against the Inhabitants reigns in such manner that not only the Hottentots belonging to the Institution, are not to be induced to hire themselves to the Inhabitants, but even frequently the other Hottentots are drawn away from the service of the farmers and seduced to encrease the number of the idle and lazy."[55] The implication was that the "failure" of the court cases was linked to the laziness, idleness, and dirt of the institution, and that those who would not work were insufficiently adequate moral agents to testify truly.

PURITY AND DUTY:
SETTLER STEREOTYPES OF BETHELSDORP

This type of rhetoric about Bethelsdorp was widespread within the colony. It parodied and annulled that of the early LMS. It portrayed the Khoekhoe and San as poor moral agents, just as British commentators such as Barrow and Wilberforce had themselves stigmatized the Dutch farmers, because they failed to fulfil criteria of "civilization." This alternate "rhetoric of civilization" was part of an ongoing way of talking about the indigenous people of the Cape, practised by both Dutch- and English-speaking colonists. It equated the lack of civilization with *impurity* and quasi-slave status – in Mary Douglas's terms, using pollution taboos to impose order on the social world.[56] The Khoekhoe were also described as sexually deviant, whether unduly lascivious or indeed averse to sexual activity, as "purebred" "Hottentots" were often thought to be.[57] This was conflated with the supposedly "deviant" genitalia of the Khoekhoe and San groups.[58] A set of characteristics thus came to be associated with Bethelsdorp, well summarized in the last-quoted extract from the commissioners' report. As late as 1970, the *Standard Encyclopedia of South Africa* fumed under "Bethelsdorp": "Van der Kemp and Read had failed to teach their converts to do manual work so as to be self-supporting, and consequently the farmers in the vicinity were much troubled by the people of 'Bedelaarsdorp' (beggars' village)."[59] V.A. February has illustrated the persistence of stereotypes of laziness, fecklessness, and impurity, from their application to the Khoekhoe in the early nineteenth century to present-day attitudes about the so-called "coloured" people in South Africa.[60] The chief difference between stereotypes from the 1830s onwards and earlier images was that the Khoekhoe came to be portrayed as comical, whereas in 1812, when the rebellion was still remembered clearly and the colony was more militarily dependent on Khoisan soldiers, there was a sharper element of fear lurking behind settler rhetoric.

The customary settler appeal to "civilization" was not disinterested. Judgments about material customs were informed by the agenda of preserving existing race and labour relationships. Bethelsdorp had a hard time defending itself against this second-order agenda, because the settlement was peculiarly vulnerable to criticism at the material level. The settlement had few outward signs of civilization, for example, by which critics usually meant square stone houses, ordered streets, cleanliness according to western standards, and western clothes.[61]

All of this was made worse by the fact that some missionaries in the early years of the century adopted elements of Khoekhoe culture, rather than the other way round. To some extent, poverty left them with little choice. By the mid-1810s, the standard base missionary salary of 245 rixdollars, or about 20 pounds sterling, was completely inadequate to maintain a white standard of living, particularly in remote and expensive areas, while the allowance for housing was insufficient and no provisions were made for widows and orphans.[62] The impoverished I.G. Hooper lived in a windowless "straw hut ... about 9 feet square (form of a sentry box)," which the people had helped him build. "The daylight may be seen through all sides of the roof," he added, "consequently abundance of rain comes through; but I can sleep comfortably in a sheepskin blanket in the worst weather on a bed or a board, and am as pleased with a fare chiefly of dry bread as with the best provisions when in my native land."[63] Read wrote that he could not always afford shoes. William F. Corner, after his marriage to a sister of Jan Goeyman, found himself so short of money in 1816 that he had spent his annual allowance by June. "I went out of the Colony, without a single article, not so much as a grain of Tea, and without provision!" he complained. His "cloath" became so worn out journeying unexpectedly to Toornberg from Graaff-Reinet "that I was obliged to buy more cloathe and when I returned I had hardly a shirt or Trousers to put on and as to shoes I had none a man lent me a pair to take me home."[64] Van der Kemp had private money but chose voluntary poverty. Henry Lichtenstein, tutor to Governor Janssens's young son, reported seeing Van der Kemp "without a hat, his venerable bald head exposed to the burning rays of the sun ... dressed in a threadbare black coat, waistcoat and breeches, without shirt, neck-cloth, or stockings, and leather sandals bound upon his feet, the same as are worn by the Hottentots."[65] Read wrote approvingly of the ini-tial efforts of Anderson and Kramer in Namaqualand, who followed the nomadic Nama: "For three years they travelled from place to place without any of the comforts of life, no bread, no vigitables, no Tea, coffee &c &c and almost naked, when the people saw them ready to persevere in suffering to communicate that they were the servants of the living God, and this seems to have been the means of bringing some souls to Christ and the respect they still retain on this account is very great."[66]

"Your missionaries, when they came to us, suffered with us, and they wept with us," said Andries Stoffels in 1836 to the LMS annual meeting in London, extolling the early Bethelsdorp missionaries.[67] This ideal was not always lived up to; it was, however, a dominant one in the days of the ascendancy of the "Bethelsdorp" model, whether from necessity or conviction. It differed in important ways from the ideology of social distance which quite quickly came to characterize the later missionary movement and now filters the way we perceive nineteenth-century missions.[68] Perhaps the greater initial poverty of the earlier missionaries, in European terms, made them more willing to live in some ways like the Khoekhoe; perhaps also they perceived this as sharing poverty rather than culture. Read was quite cheerful about his lifestyle and observed that missionary hard-ship was greatly exaggerated. In the meantime, he lived shoeless in a clay hut with a Khoekhoe wife, learned to like Xhosa sour milk, gave up bread, tea, and coffee when he could not afford them,[69] and attracted white opprobrium as an inadequate civilizing agent. "Dr. Van der Kemp and Mr. Read, I believe is still of his opinion, never did think civilization or order as part of their system but if the Heathen just had enough to support animal life it was enough," wrote one missionary critic angrily.[70]

Lichtenstein's condemnatory account is well known and perfectly illustrates the colonial elite's assumption of coincidence between mate-rial order, Christianity, and a docile labour force. Lichtenstein com-plained that, however "plausible and meritorious" the original plan of the LMS mission to the Khoekhoe appeared, the "over-pious spirit and proud humility" of its head undercut any utility. The Khoekhoe were certainly instructed for some hours a day in Christianity, "but these instructions made much more impression upon their memory than upon their understanding ... No attention was paid to giving them proper occupations, and, excepting in the hours of prayer, they might be as indolent as they chose." The physical appearance of Bethelsdorp (in contrast to the relative prosperity of the well-run Moravian station) reflected the degredation of its inhabitants:

It is scarcely possible to describe the wretched situation in which this establishment appeared to us, especially after having seen the one of Bavianskloof [Genadendal]. On a wide plain, without a tree, almost without water fit to drink, are scattered forty or fifty little huts so low that a man cannot stand upright in them. In the midst is a small clay-hut thatched with straw, which goes by the name of a church, and close by, some smaller huts of the same material for the missionaries. All are so wretchedly built, and are kept with so little care and attention, that they have a perfectly ruinous appearance ... the ground all about is perfectly naked and hard trodden down, nowhere the least trace of human industry: wherever the eye is cast, nothing is presented but lean, ragged or naked figures, with indolent sleepy countenances.[71]

Lichtenstein's book was published in two volumes in English in 1812–13 and had a sensational negative impact, reinforcing colonial criticism of Bethelsdorp. It was in vain that Read protested that the Bethelsdorp people had extensive cultivated fields and a cattle place which were out of sight of the casual observer, and that many inhabitants hired themselves out to white farmers.

A more sympathetic observer, the British Moravian leader C.I. Latrobe, attested to the damage done to the reputation of the LMS by the aspect of Bethelsdorp when he travelled through the colony on a voyage of inspection of Moravian missions. "We had been willing to believe," he commented, "that the very unfavourable accounts, given by travellers of Bethelsdorp, were greatly exaggerated, if not altogether false" and that it was unlikely such a wealthy society as the LMS would permit such conditions, to be constantly used as an argument against missionaries. Latrobe was obliged to confess, however, that externally at least, "nothing can be more miserable and discouraging."[72] He also remarked on the seeming indifference with which the inhabitants greeted the arrival of his waggon, in contrast to the eager welcome of the Genadendal Khoekhoe: "towards evening, a few old men approached the waggon, in the shade of which our people were resting, and entered into conversation with them, but from *us* they seemed to stand aloof." Mrs Read refused to meet with the party and was visited separately by one of the missionary wives.[73] This was entirely explicable, however, although Latrobe could not have known it, by the fact that Cuyler was escorting his party, and is a testament to the state of hostility existing between the settlers and the Bethelsdorp inhabitants.

In defence of Bethelsdorp, apologists urged that the site had been designated as temporary, and so there had been no incentive for individuals to improve their houses or to cultivate extensively.[74] What was more important, surely, was that the inhabitants themselves had little desire to alter their own culture and preserved many Khoekhoe characteristics such as digging for roots and picking berries rather than planting grain and wearing sheepskins.

The minutes of the first missionary synod for southern Africa, held at Graaff-Reinet in 1814, are revealing precisely because they are so defensive about the level of civilization at Bethelsdorp in the wake of extensive colonial criticism.[75] Read, Kicherer, Ulbricht, Erasmus Smit, and William Corner were present, joined shortly thereafter by William Anderson of Klaarwater. As chair, James Read strived for a vindication of Bethelsdorp and an affirmation that the institution did indeed pay due attention to civilization. Kicherer acknowledged that he "had heard from Sir John Craddock ... Cuyler, Reyneveld and others that the houses were very bad, people idle &c &c," and others present agreed. Read then asked, first, "if the two Brethren conceived that the place had been permanent Brothers Van Der Kemp and Read would have given occasion not to build better houses," to which Corner and Ulbricht said no, while the Dutchman Smit understandably said that he did not understand the question. Next, were Van der Kemp and Read "against decent clothing"? The conclusion was no: Van der Kemp, "anxious that the people should be well cloathed," had first written to Holland for clothing, and that failing, had ordered clothes from the Cape and sold them at cost to the people; he had likewise got skins tanned, had purchased Spanish sheep with the aim of spinning and weaving, and in 1810 had proposed ordering clothing from England (presumably charitable donations).

Third, were Van der Kemp and Read against cleanliness? Here the meeting started to get slightly out of hand: "Brother Ulbricht answered that Brother Van der Kemp never insisted upon it, and that once he had opposed him when he said to a child 'why don't you wash yourself,' the Doctor had said 'you must not pleg them.' Brother Smit said that the Doctor once said 'I never wish to see them better dressed than in their greasy karosses, all civilization is from the Divil.'" Finally, Read asked "if the Brethren Van Der Kemp and Read were against activity and labour?" Everyone answered no. After this, "a Debate took place which lasted three days, the particulars of which we have agreed for the present not to lay before the Directors."[76] One might guess that even at this stage the Bethelsdorp mission was controversial among LMS missionaries themselves.

In the end, it seems to me that what Van der Kemp in fact did, through his focus on spirituality over "civilization," was to enable the Khoekhoe to maintain tattered remnants of their previous lifestyle. The complaints of outsiders (and of some fellow missionaries) that Bethelsdorp inhabitants were lazy were in large part the product of cultural bias. They might also be used, however, to illustrate the extent to which the Khoekhoe and San were still hunter-gatherers and pastoralists. They gathered roots and berries in the traditional fashion, and the primary economic concern of many was for pasturage for their cattle. San traditionally conserved energy or socialized when they did not need to be finding food: the hunter-gatherer lifestyle usually left more leisure time than an agriculturalist one, and even today San societies devote much time to social "exchange" activity.[77] Must not malnutrition and social despair, on the one hand, and a lack of desire to work for the invading whites, on the other, also have played a role in Khoisan "idleness"?

These stereotypes of laziness, material disorder, and "filth" went hand in hand with stereotypes of sexual disorder. The most visible symbol of this, conflating sexual and racial issues, was the intermarriage of a number of early LMS missionaries with black women. These marriages were perceived as problematic even before a series of accusations of sexual misconduct at an "alternate" missionary synod in Cape Town in 1817 blew apart the LMS mission to south Africa.[78] Despite the prevalence of sexual unions across ethnic lines, by the early nineteenth century actual marriage caused increasing unease. "'To take a black Hothonton is a great Scandal among all the People here and coloured people themselves," claimed the German missionary Karl Pacalt in 1809.[79]

The most disordered marriage of all was that of Van der Kemp with a thirteen-year-old slave girl from Madagascar called Sara Janse, whose father was a Muslim priest, and who was not herself a convert to Christianity at the time of her marriage.[80] Van der Kemp purchased her freedom from V.A. Schoonberg, a member of SAMS, who corresponded with Rotterdam about it indignantly.[81] Van der Kemp also bought her mother's freedom and that of five other slaves, some of whom were his wife's relatives. John Campbell records meeting Van der Kemp's mother-in-law at Bethelsdorp: an old woman who sat in a hut alone and turned her head to the wall, weeping for her three dead sons, Abraham, Moses, and Jacob. (Was it Van der Kemp who named them upon their baptism? And did he also rename his wife, after Abraham's wife Sarah, the mother of the people of Israel?)

For much of her married life with Johannes, Sara van der Kemp was ill, having frequent epileptic fits. Between 1806 and 1811, the couple had four children, Cornelius Johannes Theodorus (1807–59), Didericus (born 1808), Africanus, who died in infancy in 1811, and a girl born after Van der Kemp's death, Sara Theodora.[82] It is difficult to tell from the sparse existing evidence whether or not Van der Kemp's marriage to Sara represented for the husband a further effort to escape the world and the self, or whether it was a conscious political gesture, an act of lust, or a genuine love-match.[81] One of Van der Kemp's reasons for the marriage may have been instrumental: he had always hoped to evangelize Madagascar. Conversely, Sara may have interested him because of the attraction exerted by her country. There is, however, a glimpse of affection in Van der Kemp's agonizing over whether or not he ought to leave for Madagascar after all, six weeks before his death in Cape Town. Concern over his own "advanced years, and my dear wife's desorder" weighed heavily with him, "especially when I reflect upon the various dangers and distresses, to which my wife and my dear little ones might be exposed both during my life, and after my decease by this enterprise." Characteristically, however, these concerns did not ultimately have sufficient force to deter him: "The only question with me is, if the present state of Bethelsdorp ... permits me to absent myself from that Institution, especially as we lately have been warned by a Gentleman of distinction, that the clamour against Bethelsdorp was at this time so loud, that that Institution would be suppressed, as soon as I should be removed from it."[84] Sara van der Kemp's motives in the marriage are even harder to discern, especially given the power disparities intrinsic to the relationship. Years after Johannes's death, however, Walter Hooper found Sara reluctant to surrender his papers, for she liked to look them over to remind her of him.[85]

Van der Kemp was also instrumental in arranging for the LMS finally to obtain the full liberty of a slave of Mozambican origin whose slave name was Maart. Maart had originally belonged to the Dutch Reformed minister Michiel Vos. When Vos left for England and a subsequent career himself as an LMS missionary in Ceylon (modern-day Sri Lanka), the LMS arranged through SAMS to purchase Maart. Maart changed his name to Andries Verhoogd (or "uplifted") to throw off the shackles of a slave name indicating only the month of purchase. Apparently inadvertently, his status remained ambiguous; Van der Kemp pushed the LMS to make the final arrangements for his liberation and seemingly incurred some of his outstanding purchase price personally. Verhoogd then agreed to work for the LMS at Bethelsdorp for six years in order to pay off his purchase price.[86] When Vos passed back through the Cape in 1804, Van der Kemp recorded with some concern Verhoogd's need to avoid meeting Vos, suggesting unresolved transactions and quarrels. Indeed, one wonders whether Van der Kemp's opposition to slavery was a factor in his decision to sever all ties with the "synagogue of Satan," SAMS.

Van der Kemp's marriage furnished a flash point for colonial criticism of his inversion of the natural order of slavery, as well as causing shock among the "pious" of Cape Town. "Now he [Van der Kemp] has bought a young girl, left with her, and has declared her his wife. What a sensation this caused, what gasps this has resulted in amongst the pious, I need not explain," wrote one correspondent of Henry Lichtenstein.[87] Nonetheless, the pious tried to keep the news as quiet as possible. The marriage was widely assumed to be itself disordered. LMS internal dissident George Thom (who tended to exaggerate sexual misdemeanours) claimed in 1814: "Dr. Vanderkemp's marriage with a slave girl of 16 [an overestimate] was thought at the time exceedingly disgraceful and it has proved so. *Two* missionaries told me that when the Doctor was alive she was a Pharaoh's [Pottifer's?] wife with them. She now lives almost as a prostitute. One of the Doctor's children is thought to be a man's in Cape Town."[88] The LMS directorate was also uneasy about this marriage. Sara van der Kemp's age has been scored out in several letters in the LMS files.[89] The official LMS memoir of Van der Kemp, published immediately after his death, did not mention his second marriage, although it did record that he had emancipated several slaves, at a cost of "many hundred pounds."[90]

Other missionaries married Khoisan women, including Read, Ulbricht, John Bartlett, and the West Indian William Corner, all originally based at Bethelsdorp; Lammert Jansen (or Jansz) at Klaar Water; Michael Wimmer (in a manner of speaking) at the Caledon Institute; and Johann Heinrich Schmelen in Namacqualand.[91] The circumstances surrounding these marriages varied considerably. In 1815 John Bartlett and William Corner married sisters of the LMS assistant missionary Jan Goeyman in a double ceremony. These may have been fairly instrumental alliances. Both Corner and Bartlett had committed adultery with other Khoisan women just before the joint marriage, and Bartlett had already had an illegitimate child. Bartlett had also jilted a young white woman, the daughter of a Mr Roos, to whom he had earlier promised marriage. For his part, Corner had repented passionately of his extramarital relationship in 1814 with his housekeeper. Nonetheless, Corner's marriage proved unhappy. As Doug Stuart points out, John Campbell claimed that Corner's light-skinned wife despised him because of his darker skin. Later, Corner would again commit adultery with a different woman; unlike his housekeeper, she was young enough to bear a child and accordingly did. Corner would be privately dismissed by the LMS in 1818.[92]

Other marriages were seemingly happier. James Read painted Jansen's marriage in a warm light, informing the LMS directors in 1813 that Jansen had recently married a "young woman of colour," a pious member of the church. She spoke seTswana "and may be of great service to that Mission if Brother Jennzen be disposed [to] give himself up to that Mission to it, which we hope he will."[93] Ulbricht's marriage to Elizabeth Windvogel excited little colonial comment although it took place only after a long delay in obtaining official permission. From the report of this delay, it appears that Van der Kemp had been banned from performing interracial marriages except among inhabitants of Bethelsdorp.[94]

James Read married an impecunious woman from Bethelsdorp named Elizabeth Valentyn, who was about his age. Read's letters to the LMS contain a number of references to his love for his wife and family. "I have no reason whatever to repent of my marriage [to] a Native," he confided in 1806, "but on the contrary experience teaches me what reason I have to bless the Lord in this respect."[95] Before the marriage it was a struggle to remain chaste, Read confessed much later. James had wanted Elizabeth to wear her kaross at the marriage, "to please my fancy," although she insisted on wearing instead "another Petticoat (as is and was then still more a custom) on her shoulders."[96] The genuineness of James's love for Elizabeth is suggested in the poetry he wrote in Cape Town, while waiting with an increasing sense of desolation upon lords Caledon and Cradock to give evidence in the Black Circuit investigations. Two poems, in the style of hymns, were sent by Michael Wimmer to the LMS directorate without Read's knowledge, so one can assume that they were not written for public consumption. Although it can hardly be called great poetry, I shall reproduce in its entirety the poem in which Read mentions his family – one of the first surviving written love poems, of a strange sort, from a white man to a black woman in south African history.

I

Lord! God of Host whose sovereign way
Whose eyes pierce both night and day
Saints, sinners, Divil, life and Death
Sickness and health in hand He hath

2

Lord I've begun another day
An other week began to pray
My poor imperfect breathings hear
When I poar out my heart in prayer

3

Think on my partner infants dear
In all their trials be thou near
A present help in time of need
A sure and steadfast friend indeed

4

But Lord my prayers and theirs unite
Each others eyes to have a sight
Our joys and sorrows to relate
And of thy mercies wondrous great

5

Art thou not he that Rahab slew
That dreadfull monster Dragon too
The sea in twain thou didst divide
And the poor waves of Jordan chide

6

Is this too wonderful for thee
This blessing to bestow to me
Me with my wife and children dear
To reunite our Souls to cheer

7

No! Dearest Lord with thee is power
With thee is wisdom, love and grace
Help me to trust thee now and ever
Until I see thee face to face.[97]

In 1815 Read committed adultery with Sabina Pretorius, the daughter of Andries Pretorius, a "Bushman" and a deacon of the Bethelsdorp church. This act of adultery was, he later swore, "the very first and only one in my life."[98] When Elizabeth Read learned that Sabina Pretorius had confessed that she was pregnant with Read's child, she was "like an insane woman, running about the place in such a passion that cannot be described."[99] Sabina later gave birth to an illegitimate son, Isaac Johannes Pretorius. Although the adulterous couple sought to avoid further meetings (or so Read claimed), they did so by accident and the child was therefore born while the Read family were travelling together with Sabina and her parents on an extensive mission tour in the interior.[100] Despite these troubling events, James Read and Elizabeth Valentyn seem to have been genuinely in love when they married, ultimately had seven children, and remained married for almost half a century.

Like Van der Kemp's, Read's marriage was assumed to be even more disordered than it actually was. Doug Stuart has demonstrated that the charge against Read at the infamous Cape Town synod of 1817 was not only that of adultery but also that of having lived in concubinage with Pretorius while sleeping with his wife, and thus of having adopted an African mode of polygamous marriage.[101] Although Read was able to refute these particular charges, they hint at the depth of colonial feeling against him. After Read's exposure, Colonel Cuyler told an anti-Read missionary, Evan Evans, that "with Mr. Read it is no new thing he hath been a rake since his youth up, this is not the first Hottentot girl *by many* that hath been of child of him." When Evans repeated this to another unsympathetic missionary, J. Georg Messer, the latter replied, "It is very *true* when he was married to Mrs. Read she was so big with child she was [*ashamed?*] to stand in the church without her caross." Read denied these additional allegations, and was in particular able to show that his first child had been born eleven months after his marriage.[102]

The case of Michael Wimmer and his bride Susanna (or Sabina) Adams was controversial from the outset. By 1815, the actual legality of marriages between LMS missionaries and local women had become an issue, as hostile local administrations seemingly tried to limit such marriages. A critical issue was that of baptism: local bureaucracy and a dissident wing of the LMS alike insisted that marriage could not be contracted either legally or within the bounds of church order between "heathen" and Christian partners.[103] Marriages had to be approved by the Matrimonial Court and by the local landdrost and carried out by an approved minister. In 1815 Wimmer, a missionary at the Caledon Institution, declared that he was in love with Caledon resident Adams and that they were engaged to be married. The head missionary, Seidenfaden, reacted with horror: this seemed to confirm the earlier ugly rumours of fornication which had been flying around the station and which Wimmer had already denied from the pulpit. As Seidenfaden had said on an earlier occasion, when the rumours began, such a marriage under such circumstances would undermine the respect of government, colonists, and mission-station inhabitants alike for the missionaries, would spoil "good order," "and will be a cause of grief to you forever."[104] Worst of all, Adams was not baptized. Seidenfaden nonetheless agreed to perform the marriage if the Matrimonial Court approved and the landdrost provided a licence. The landdrost refused to do so, since Adams was not baptized, and Wimmer needed in addition special permission from government. On 22 August, Seidenfaden baptized Sabina, and she took the baptismal name Susanna. By early March, Wimmer had returned disconsolate from another visit to the landdrost at Swellendam. The landdrost had told Wimmer that Susanna's baptism was not lawful, and that as a matter of fact the marriages of Read and Van der Kemp had not been lawful either and their children were bastards. "I have now used all the means in my power to be lawfully married, but I cannot," said Wimmer to Seidenfaden.

"Therefore I declare before you that from this day forth Susanna is my wife [...] I am married to her before God and I shall never leave her."[105] The couple then lived together openly. In August 1816, some six months after their final unsuccessful application for a marriage licence, they had a child. Read seemed quite happy with this and applied for a married couple's allowance on their behalf, much to the disgust of some of his more conservative colleagues.[106]

Regular or irregular, these marriages and liaisons all attracted criticism from the white community as well as, increasingly, disquiet from some missionaries themselves as the LMS grew more "respectable." All the same, it is interesting that the focus of criticism was more the assumed greater irregularity that accompanied black-white marriages than the marriages per se. This reflected a society which was becoming less tolerant of "intermarriage" but in which it was still not unheard of. The tragedy for the more radical wing of the LMS was that some of these rumours were accurate. The eventual scandals would provide potent political weapons to opponents: in a sense, however, the veracity of the rumours was almost incidental to the function they fulfilled in white south African society.

A further example of sexual disorder cited by critics of Bethelsdorp was the undeniable presence of venereal disease on the station. Venereal disease conflated fears of disease, moral laxity, and racial impurity, especially as it was passed largely between white soldiers and farmers and women of colour from Bethelsdorp. John Campbell found that everywhere he travelled, "especially in Cape Town and there chiefly among the great," three charges against Bethelsdorp met him "in the teeth": "viz 1 that it reduced the Hottentots to beggary, for they had brought with them 6,000 head of Cattle, which number was now reduced to 2,000. 2 That it was the seat of illness. 3 That it was a fountain of debauchery, and the venereal."[107] Whites blamed Bethelsdorp as the source of VD, whereas the inhabitants claimed that the disease came from the whites. Campbell was predisposed to blame the soldiers of the neighbouring British regiment at Algoa Bay. There had been some soldiers at Fort Frederick throughout the British occupations, and then a large influx to the frontier area during and after the Fourth Frontier War of 1811–12. These soldiers seem to have been readier to be drinking partners and sexual partners of the Khoisan than were the farmers of the area, if missionary complaints about "irregularities" are any indication. Some Khoisan women worked casually as prostitutes in Algoa Bay. Others simply slept with soldiers when away from home doing farm work. Campbell reported home that he had not yet held a formal inquiry but believed that when he did he would find that some young Bethelsdorp women had been seduced while working for farmers and had returned "ruined and diseased." "They tempt them with fine handkerchiefs &c. So that instead of these girls being the ruin of the soldiers, the soldiers are the ruin of them."[108] The problem was sufficiently serious for a locally stationed army surgeon, William Wolfe Milton, to have proposed establishing a hospital for the treatment of VD at Bethelsdorp. Van der Kemp refused, however, since he wanted to discourage "vice" and did not want the settlement to be stigmatized in this fashion. He also argued that the disease was imported into rather than exported from Bethelsdorp. Sufferers were instead quarantined from the main settlement and compelled to live at a distance.

The problem persisted. In 1812, missionaries informed London of their uncertainty over what to do about sexually transmitted diseases. Farmers were clearly complaining about servants with VD. If the missionaries kept sufferers at Bethelsdorp, however, the 1812 Bethelsdorp annual report contended, farmers would be outraged at the loss of servants. On the other hand, "to drive them away after they have fallen into their misfortunes would be to shut them out from the means of grace, and be dangerous to others." Nonetheless, the instances were "not numerous, nor can we complain of the irregularity of the younger part of our community as in some former reports."[109]

In 1813 Campbell investigated accusations against Bethelsdorp, including the prevalence of VD, through interviewing "eight or nine of the most sensible people" at separate meetings. He concluded that venereal diseases were indeed exogenous and that women came to Bethelsdorp *because* they had contracted diseases. He had made "some countenances assume a paleness," he claimed afterwards, when he said "that I could lay before government the names of the places where each girl had been seduced, caught the disease, and when diseased had been driven away, and took refuge at Bethelsdorp, from whence they were not driven, but kept as the lepers of old at a suitable distance from its precincts."[110] This implies that farmers were also implicated in the spread of VD – which is not inconsistent with the contention that soldiers were the original source. Again, the veracity of colonial rumours about the source and spread of VD is, of course, important, but it is not the whole story: the Khoisan were clearly assumed on an a priori basis to be sexually deviant, whereas similar complaints were not laid against white soldiers or farmers. There clearly was a great deal of sexual activity between white men and Khoisan women, and yet this activity was accompanied by stereotypes of Khoekhoe filth, disease, and danger.

The LMS employment of black missionaries broke further purity taboos. It is possible that Corner, as a "native of Demerara," was an emancipated slave. In 1811 Corner had been on the verge of travelling to Madagascar with Van der Kemp, had that ill-fated mission not been cut short by Van der Kemp's death.[111] He would have been accompanied by Andries Verhoogd, who certainly was a former slave even if not yet completely free. If this mission had taken place it would have been a striking testament to internationalism: the founding party would have consisted of the Dutchman Van der Kemp, the German missionary Carl August Pacalt, the West Indian Corner, the Madagscan Sara van der Kemp, the Mozambiquan Verhoogd, several Khoisan people, and Johannes's and Sara's "mixed-race" children.

This commitment to nonracialism was in keeping with the initial LMS policy of establishing indigenous, self-governing churches around the world, which could cease to rely on missionaries sent by European societies – albeit at an unspecified distant date. As Campbell wrote on the training of Khoisan missionaries, this would eventually make it unnecessary to send further missionaries from Europe. "When Titus was itinerating among the Islanders of Crete, he received an Apostolic letter from Paul, desiring him to ordain elders (or pastors) in every City," Campbell commented. "I do not observe it mentioned in the letter, that Paul dispatch from Rome a number of Missionaries, or that he had written to Judea for such men, no, they were to be looked for among the churches."[112] This insistence on African self-governance in part reflected the basic Congregationalist (or Independent) belief in the independence of individual congregations from any hierarchical church structure. It was an important tenet of Independency, for example, that congregations should "call" their own ministers. This was put into practice at Bethelsdorp when James Read was ordained only after having been first called by the church. The Congregationalists became increasingly dominant in the LMS directorship, until the society officially became a Congregationalist organ in 1818. It is therefore unsurprising to find a stress on indigenous church government rather than, as happened in the Anglican missionary societies, an effort to establish daughter churches attached to the Church of England.

A related issue was that of the ordination of Africans as missionaries, a move that was strongly encouraged by James Read when he became African director upon the death of Van der Kemp. The 1814 Graaff-Reinet missionary conference ordained five Khoekhoe men as assistant missionaries, with the understanding that they might become full-fledged missionaries (that is, entitled to head stations in their own right) after a year. Jan Goeyman was designated to accompany Erasmus Smit in his work among the "Bushmen," even though Smit asked to have a European assistant. Having had Goeyman foisted on him as his assistant and another Khoekhoe man, Kootje de Kries, as "particular friend," Smit plaintively asked at the least for some more "Bastard Hottentots" "for the civilization of the uncultivated Bushmen." He was sent Martha, who had formerly been in England, her aged husband, Adrian Deerling, and their son.

Following John Campbell's wishes, William Anderson of Griquatown had "made a trial" of Jan Hendricks, Pieter Davids, Berend Berends, and Andries Waterboer. The latter two were later to become Griqua leaders and powerful regional players – Berends to break completely with the LMS, Waterboer to consolidate his power through canny alliance with the society. The meeting agreed that the group should continue and be paid 100 rixdollars a year. It then devised a ceremony of "setting apart," by which the five became assistant missionaries. This ceremony included a talk by Anderson on "the abilities of the persons to be set apart, their zeal to labour, and success they have already met with ... the urgentcy of the business, the fields were ripe, and the Coranas [the Korana of Transorangia] and Bushmen had requested that if there were no European missionaries that these might be sent to them." Kicherer conducted a question-and-answer session and then gave each candidate a Bible, saying, "Go now into all the World, preach the Gospel to every creature," before leading a prayer. Read concluded with a sermon.[113]

The invention of this ceremony reflected the flexibility of an essentially dissenting mission: Anglicans, for example, would not have been able to invent ceremonies with such fluidity, nor to institute missionaries without prior training and formal episcopal ordination. Indeed, we have seen that the CMS ran into early domestic recruitment difficulties through its efforts to placate a hostile ecclesiastical hierarchy by refusing to ordain missionary candidates. These LMS ordinations represented precisely the types of evasions of ecclesiastical order that got the evangelicals into hot water at home; they would therefore have been unacceptable to Anglican officials on ecclesiological grounds, in addition to being offensive to settlers for racial reasons. On both counts, they were disordered.

In sum, there were a multitude of ways in which Bethesldorp violated purity taboos widespread in the early-nineteenth-century Cape Colony. The station did not exhibit outward signs of civilization; its head married a thirteen-year-old slave girl; other missionaries married Khoisan women; some had missionaries had adulterous affairs and illegitimate children; the station was infested with venereal disease; "ill educated" former slaves and Khoisan worked as assistant missionaries and de facto ministers. These criticisms furnish a substratum to the overriding complaint of settlers against the station, which, as we have seen, was that it removed "Hottentots" from the colonial labour market. Against this background, concerns about labour deficiencies can be seen as *also* concerns about impurity and the inversion of the natural racial order.

"THE RED ROSES OF HIS BLOODY MARTYRDOM": THE 1817 MISSIONARY SYNOD

By the 1810s, British officials shared the Batavian assessment that the LMS was an agent of disorder. The Castle refused to allow more LMS missionaries to work outside the colony. Indeed, in 1816 the colonial administration shut down William Corner's mission to the San at Hepzibah; the governor in person ordered Corner back to the colony. After the governor's departure, Landdrost Andries Stockenstrom (father of the well-known son of the same name who will feature later in our narrative) charged Corner, were he to start another colonial station as the governor had offered, "not to establish a second Bethelsdorp or Theopolis." If so (presumably with some hyperbole) "he should be obliged to write to Government not only to abolish the Mission but to root out by its root (as it seems to the degree of impiety) and take every Man bound to Graaf Reinet that if Government was not willing to abolish such a mission that assimilates Bethelsdorp and Theopolis that he (the Landdrost) would immediately resign his office altho Government should offer him twice as much the salary." In a bitter letter to the LMS, Corner pointed out that government was tacitly upholding settler complaints that San left their service to go to the mission, and he wondered whether the British government had abolished slavery only to substitute the unacknowledged bondage of the Bushmen.[114]

The southern African LMS was not united in the face of social opprobrium, administrative opposition, and genuine internal problems, including low salaries and a growing tally of missionary improprieties. Once Van der Kemp had died and the Black Circuit commissioners had delivered their damning report, dissident LMS missionaries felt freer to voice their fury at Bethelsdorp in general and Read in particular. "Cape Town has been full of these things for years," wrote the most vehement internal critic. "Now the subject is revived because the Commissioners of Justice have seen things as they are."[115] This was the voice of George Thom, one of a new breed of missionary with very definite ideas about the instillation of social order through Christianity.

The Scotsman Thom had been a parishioner of the Congregationalist minister John Philip (who would himself later become LMS African superintendent). Thom arrived at the Cape in 1812. He established himself in Cape Town where he accumulated sexual gossip and passed it on to London on gilt-edged writing paper. He was flattered to be paid attention to by the great, who relayed to him their concerns about the LMS. "I am just removing from my lodging to a House of one of the first men of the place which will introduce me more into the higher circles of the Dutch ... thus I shall be able to be more useful," he wrote shortly after his arrival. With some plausibility, however, he argued that more was to be gained by conciliating the colonial elite than by the ferocious and outspoken opposition of a Van der Kemp. "We are to be meek and prudent but at the same time we are to be as bold as lions," he commented. "Government are as afraid of us as we are of them."[116]

Thom soon abandoned political opposition to government, however, in order to attack the morality of missionaries from his own society, particularly at Bethelsdorp. He was not alone in his discontent. J. Georg Messer, a German Lutheran stationed at Bethelsdorp, and his colleague Pacalt both shared Thom's beliefs about the need for greater order at the institution.[117] The Welshman Evan Evans knew a lot about his colleagues' sexual sins and wanted to see discipline imposed. Later arrivals would strengthen Thom's party. Most important, fellow Scotsman Robert Moffat, who arrived in 1817, would become an important supporter of Thom and a key voice for political conservatism and moral order from within the LMS citadel.

By late 1813, Thom was writing in worried tones that the governor had received very bad reports about Bethelsdorp, even from some of its missionaries. In fact, it would not be surprising if the government were to close down the institution. Thom's revealing concerns are worth quoting at length:

Could things be otherwise? If equality both in the World and Religion is taught Hottentots? if indolence is indulged what can we effect? ... The Hottentots are stated by the missionaries themselves to be worse now than before. One writes me "The Brethren and I have conversed about the miserable state of Bethelsdorp concerning the bad behaviour of the Baptised, because some of them are Harlots, Drunkard, Swearers, liars &c. all is confusion and encreases daily" ... I cannot but declare that Dr. Vanderkemp's system is unworthy of the protection of Government and will never advance the evil state of these tribes; but with some religion will engender sloth, disorder, and what belongs to an uncivilized state. The missionary character is not to be brought down to a Hottentot's; but his character raised to the missionary's.

"How painful is it thus to write of one who is now in Heaven, and how unpleasant thus to reflect on the living!" added Thom, rather unconvincingly.[118]

Van der Kemp's autocratic treatment of his fellow missionaries had clearly raised hackles and created divisions which continued to fester. Van der Kemp himself had complained about "a spirit of licentiousness and independency [which] prevails in some of my fellow missionaries."[119] He judged harshly anyone who deviated from what he considered the appropriate level of support for slaves and the Khoisan and of opposition to the farming community. He placed great pressure on his missionaries to accept the opprobrium of white society, and to side with him in his political quarrels with authority. If so many recently arrived missionaries cracked in the "wrong" direction, one can only imagine what the climate must have been like for Khoisan, unprotected by a white skin. Van der Kemp also insisted on low salaries for missionaries, ready obedience, and lives of relative deprivation In 1811 Pacalt wrote bitterly:

In respect of baptising the People we are not permited, because the Pope is remoofed from Rome to Bethelsdorp as the Brethren here express it ... If a Brother Missionary spans the Oxes in the waggon which are of the Society to fetch wood in the forest and he is not pleased with [it, then he says ...] span out the oxes I will not have it, and many other things took place which de dear Directors know nothing of, for every thing which he doth not approve of, [he] counts it as coming from the Divil. If then one mus be silent because Dr. Vanderkemp is old ... My poor two brothers Ulbricht and Smith, being in such slavery so long, I trust but their prayers and my will come before God's Remembrance who shall break the slavish Bonds and bring them out of this Babel.[120]

The various strains which Van der Kemp had managed to keep in check during his lifetime ironically became unsupportable on his death, even though Read was an infinitely milder man who disliked being pushed into a position of leadership. In the end, it was an internal missionary lobby, egged on by a colonial elite that no longer shared the old British disdain for the farmers of the interior, which brought down Read and with him the more egalitarian approach to Khoekhoe culture of Bethelsdorp in its early days.

In 1817 Thom and his supporters called a dissident synod at Cape Town to investigate a series of charges against fellow missionaries. Synods were used in Scotland as church courts, so this was effectively a trial of one faction of the south African LMS by another. The synod found plenty to condemn. An anguished Corner had told many people about his adultery. The less repentant Bartlett had openly insulted a white woman who considered herself his fiancée, as well as giving his own name to an illegitimate child. Andries Verhoogd was unbaptized and ill-educated and, some said, an adulterer and a thief, and yet he was still kept on as a missionary assistant at Bethelsdorp. Wimmer had openly lived in sin. Another missionary, Schmelen, had married himself to a young Khoisan woman after having been forced by circumstances beyond his control to spend a night alone in a wagon with her; the woman herself, according to Doug Stuart's reconstruction, was taken aback by the marriage proposal. F.G. Hooper lived a disgracefully slovenly lifestyle, according to the synod, was incompetent, and should be given passage money back to Europe; there was a complicated quarrel between Hooper and Thom in the background. Most glaringly of all, there was Read's adultery, his illegitimate son, and the widespread colonial belief that Read continued to live polygamously out of the white eye at the station for the Tswana which he had founded at Lattakoo (later Kuruman).

The synod addressed other issues as well, although sex was clearly the main agenda item. Salaries were far too low, and provision should be made for widows and orphans. Indeed, the synod charged that Van der Kemp's own children had been reduced to beggary. The regulations established by Van der Kemp were Draconian and should be repealed. Most important, a council of missionaries should replace the hierarchical system of mission-station heads, overseen by an overall superintendent. The synod also discussed what missionaries should do if they married women who owned slaves or were themselves given slaves as gifts. There was consensus only that missionaries should not buy or sell such slaves. Several thought that the slaves should be liberated altogether. Thom, whose own wife was a slave-owner, argued nonetheless that adults should be freed but children kept enslaved until the age of twenty-five or the decease of their owners. The core business of the meeting was, however, to call for the dismissal of Verhoogd, Bartlett, Hooper, Wimmer, and Read, and to threaten mass resignation if these dismissals did not occur; and to demand higher salaries and provision for widows and orphans.[121]

Corner was pardoned by the synod, since his offence was in the past, while Schmelen's marriage was considered highly irregular but not a dismissable offence. Read was formally and publicly dismissed by the LMS as a missionary and as south African supervisor and was recalled from his current work with the Tswana. Read would remain in the country nonetheless as an artisanal and educational mission assistant until being called by the Kat River community as their independent pastor in 1830. Similarly, Bartlett and Wimmer were quietly sent to Namaqualand – a "Botany Bay" for "fallen missionaries," in Moffat's memorable phrase.[122] Hooper resigned, while Verhoogd's ultimate fate is unclear. Evan Evans and George Thom did indeed leave the LMS to work as pastors in the Dutch community; other dissidents, notably Moffat, remained to nurse resentments which would continue to erupt over the next thirty years.

John Philip and John Campbell, two doughty pillars of Scottish Independency, were summoned to the Cape to try to pick up the pieces. In keeping with Congregationalist practice, Campbell insisted that the

Bethelsdorp church itself must dismiss its own pastor and discipline its own members. As Campbell's biographer, John Philip's own son, described the situation, Campbell had to persuade the community to discipline "some offenders who, in other respects, were general favourites with the people" – which one must assume meant Read.

This was no easy task. The church did not dispute nor palliate the guilt of the culprits. Indeed they bewailed and condemned it, but they shrunk from punishing it. They wept, and wavered, and resolved, and repented. But Mr. Campbell was firm. He reasoned, and explained and had patience with them; but still threw them upon the New Testament. This had the desired effect at length, and he had the satisfaction to see an African church of Hottentots yield more obedience to the laws to the Christ, than either the authority or eloquence of Cyprian could win from the church at Carthage, or than his memory could command, even when (to use his own language), "the red roses of his bloody martyrdom were blended with the white lilies of his virtues." [123]

The debates of 1817 were a key turning point in the history of the LMS in southern Africa. The synod's unveiling of sexual irregularity seemed to confirm the settlers' conflation of political radicalism with dirt and disorder. The most influential scandal was that around Read, at once the most prominent radical voice in the LMS in 1817 and the most evidently guilty of a sexual sin about the gravity of which there could be little dispute. Later on, Read claimed that he had been overcome with passion, had not slept with Sabrina Pretorius many times, and was overwhelmed by guilt. Nonetheless, there was little that he could say in self-defence beyond requesting forgiveness. His fall seemed to invalidate at least some of the political arguments he had been making about the need to abolish vagrancy legislation and the injustice of corvée labour demands upon the Khoisan. Read tried to intervene politically again in 1821, when he thrust a statement of grievances with corroborating evidence from Bethelsdorp cupboards into the hands of incoming acting governor Sir Rufane Donkin. Read was scarcely a credible spokesperson, however, even had Donkin been predisposed to attend to the issue of Khoisan mobility. The scorn with which Read was treated on this occasion underscored the continuing linkage between respectability and influence. Henceforward, the LMS would discourage "racial" intermarriage, would urge envoys to "civilize" as well as Christianize the Khoisan, and would attempt to project an image of respectability.

The scandals also influenced a wider move on the part of the directors to control emissaries more tightly, to try to educate them more extensively, and to look for applicants from a higher class level.

Similar sexual scandals had engulfed the mission at Tahiti, as well as, in that case, severe organizational problems and the resignation of several missionaries. The directors felt that more careful selection and education of candidates might overcome these problems, as they moved away from their initial support for the enthusiastic uneducated; they also tried from the 1810s onward to persuade missionaries to acquire wives before departure. Both in Britain and in southern Africa, LMS personnel tended to move closer to settler perspectives as they adopted ideologies of social and sexual distance between "black" and "white." The 1817 synod thus represented a major blow to such political clout as the "Bethelsdorp" missionaries possessed, and called into question in a damning manner the closer social interaction between white missionaries and Khoisan converts which a number of its residents espoused. This was, however, only part of a broader move towards the hegemony of British settler ideals of social distance and ideas about "blackness" and "whiteness" which would gain increasing prominence with the growth of the white British settler community.

6 The Political Uses of Africa Remade: The Passage of Ordinance 50

In the aftermath of 1817, the LMS in southern Africa struggled to reinvent itself as respectable. In 1819 the Congregationalist Scottish minister John Philip, who had originally come to southern Africa as an inspector in company with John Campbell to help clean up the mess, was appointed African superintendent by the London board. Philip had strong liberal views. He would prove an important figure in a new wave of humanitarian liberalism at the Cape Colony of the 1820s and 1830s, which would have a much more significant political impact than previous reformist movements largely because it dovetailed, however temporarily, with wider ideological and economic shifts at the metropolitan centre of empire.[1]

Philip was an appropriate prophet for a more liberal age. Born in 1785, he was the largely self-educated son of a handloom weaver from Kirkcaldy. Like those other key Scottish missionaries, Robert Moffat and David Livingstone, Philip believed that economic progress was possible and could and would morally transform society. Had he not witnessed in his own life the growing prosperity of the "wild" Scottish highlands and increased chances for upward mobility among his fellow artisans? Philip was passionately convinced of the value of education, which he saw as a means to social transformation, and had been much influenced by the tenets of Scottish Enlightenment political economists: in both these things he was deeply Scottish. As a Congregationalist, Philip had also in his youth been part of a broad Scottish religious movement against the established Presbyterian elite.[2]

In the course of liberal political campaigns, Philip would urge new strategies to gain political rights for the Khoekhoe, including encouraging them to become more assimilated in order to appear worthy of political freedom. Part of the LMS drive to respectability involved presenting the society and its converts as potential allies of the imperial government, at a time when the imperial government was itself more influenced by liberal evangelicalism than it had been in the early nineteenth century. The results were surprising: under the activist direction of Philip, the LMS made unexpected gains at the imperial centre. At the same time, however, converts were under increased pressure to submit themselves to a "civilizing" regime. For some, at least, in the 1820s and 1830s, the game seemed worth the candle, as the LMS for a while successfully manipulated the symbolism of "civilization" to wring real political concessions to the Khoekhoe from the British parliament.

By the 1820s and 1830s, leading LMS personnel held ideas about Christianity as a source of civilization and social order which were closer than those of their predecessors to the approach of the governing elite. At the same time, evangelical tenets in general exercised a greater hold upon a broader spectrum of British society while evangelicals enjoyed an unusual degree of influence at the Colonial Office and in parliament more broadly. The Whig alliance with nonconformity in the 1830s created political opportunities,[3] even as the power of the popular antislavery movement lent influence, if only briefly, to its chief parliamentary proponents. Therefore, new opportunities for political influence were offered to nonconformist missionaries in Africa and to their converts and African interlocutors, using missionary and evangelical information networks. The "price of admission" to such networks was, however, placed higher.

ECONOMIC TRANSFORMATIONS AND CONTINUITIES

From the early 1820s to the 1830s an upheaval occurred in British imperial politics concerning south Africa which has been characterized by Stanley Trapido as a passage from "paternalism" to "liberalism".[4] This was part of a wider economic reorganization of the empire effected in the aftermath of the Napoleonic Wars. In 1823 a three-man Commission of Inquiry (consisting of John Thomas Bigge, W. Blair, and William Colebrooke) arrived in Cape Town as part of a broader Eastern Commission of Inquiry instituted by London to advise on economic and political reforms within the empire. By the early 1830s, the metropolitan government had imposed legislation on a reluctant Dutch farming community, seeking to liberalize trade and to further monetize the economy, and had put labour relations on a new footing through the abolition of slavery and vagrancy legislation and the granting of equal civil rights to all regardless of colour. The 1828 reorganization of the colonial administration, on the heels of the Commission of Inquiry, was "a kind of revolution," in the words of Lieutenant Governor Richard Bourke, enabling the colony to shed its "old skin" and to "appear on 1st January next as bright as Virgil's snake."[5] A second "revolution" was the introduction of state-organized immigration from Britain to south Africa in 1820.[6]

The 1820 British settlers proved instrumental in wresting relative freedom of the press from a reluctant governor, Lord Charles Somerset, and in persuading the metropolitan government to impose an advisory council on the governor as a first step – so agitators hoped – towards more fully representative institutions in the Cape Colony. To cite J.B.Peires's comments on the transformation of the Cape which began under the rule of the autocratic Somerset:

It was his [Somerset's] misfortune to govern the Cape at the time when the new social forces generated in a rapidly industrialising Great Britain engulfed the colony, sweeping aside not only Somerset but the entrenched power of the local oligarchy and the established rhythms of the local economy. The double explosion of the 1820 settlers at the periphery of the colony and the "revolution in government" at its centre reverberated far beyond the borders of the Cape, exposing the peoples of the interior to a dual invasion by British settlers, apostles of free enterprise and free trade, and Afrikaner Voortrekkers, bearers of a racial ideology predicated on a system of coerced labour.[7]

In order to take advantage of these metropolitan reform initiatives, activist LMS missionaries had to present their converts as more economically progressive than the Afrikaner farmers, and thus as an interest group deserving of government support. This presentation, however, required some manipulation of the truth. The "traditional" Khoekhoe nomadic lifestyle had by no means vanished from the Eastern Cape by the 1820s, even though a number of Khoekhoe-descended people, especially mission elites and members of "baster" communities, were also trying to establish themselves as honourable and respectable by white norms for their own ends.

Competing white factions proposed two broad options to the Khoisan: to become farm labourers or to become independent artisans. Both models, however, required that the remnants of various nomadic groups settle down, and, even at this stage, a sedentary lifestyle was not particularly attractive for many. Settlers played up this reluctance as a justification for the use of coercion; missionary propagandists played it down in public in order to argue in favour of equal civil rights, and privately attempted to extirpate Khoekhoe cultural traits connected with a nomadic pastoralist lifestyle.

On this issue, the evidence of Van der Kemp's oldest son is clearly slanted. The young Cornelius van der Kemp had been sent away to Scotland for an education. His sick mother had summoned him back to the Cape Colony in 1827 before the end of his program, erroneously believing she was dying.[8] The younger Van der Kemp, marked by his black skin in a racist colony despite an education superior to that of many settlers, clung desperately to his dignity. He was remarkably purist, even for the missionary community, concerning the application of "white" standards of "respectability." While a schoolmaster at Bethelsdorp, Van der Kemp complained about the laziness of inhabitants and looked forward to the establishment of pass laws. Nominal residents of the station "prefer to live wherever they can get a footing and I can enumerate four different kraals where they bring their time through in laziness and are a great disgrace to our Institution." Others hired themselves out to white settlers for low wages or were "wanderers" on and off the station despite putatively living there. They had no "permanent dwellings." "Their wants are few and being able to subsist any where on wild fruits and roots they are lazy, filthy, wretched I cannot say as they are entirely indifferent and ignorant ... Their children are suffered to go where they have inclinations."[9] It may have been partly because of Van der Kemp's unseasonable complaints that Philip would later write coolly to the directors that "Cornelius van der Kemp was taken up and placed in the school at Bethelsdorp merely on trial, and more out of respect to the memory of his Father than from any expectation I formed of his ultimately proving an efficient labourer at a Missionary station."[10] Nonetheless, Van der Kemp's comments do inadvertently underscore that inhabitants preserved aspects of an older lifestyle.

Philip himself wrote more sympathetically about Khoekhoe nomadism in 1834, possibly as an exercise in damage limitation: "There are still lingering on the out skirts [sic] of many of the farms in the interior, the ancient possessors of the soil, herding a few sheep and goats in the most barren places in a state of independence. These as you may suppose are the last of the Hottentot nation not at a missionary institution [untrue, since Philip is ignoring farm labourers]. This class of people is in point of character above the farmers in the eyes of every humane traveller.[11]

On the stations themselves, many people retained pastoralist and nomadic propensities. Of course, it is impossible ever truly to separate reality from stereotype in the ideologically loaded comments of missionaries and settlers about the "Hottentots" as a whole. It does seem clear, however that many people of Khoekhoe descent were still pastoralists by choice, or, rather, would have been if circumstances permitted. Adam Robson commented in 1828 that he found it difficult to persuade the people of Bethelsdorp to farm, despite food shortages, because "they have generally been brought up a pastoral people accustomed to follow their flocks, and consequently averse to manual labour and much exertion ... [They] dread the thought of working their corn &c day and night or of being at, for them, the immense trouble of making a fence or ever finishing that which nature has left incomplete."[12] Missionaries also commented on the Khoisan need to be able to travel at any moment, the frequent journeys they liked to take, and their dislike of daily constraints. William Foster advised against trying to set up a self-enclosed boarding school with strict visiting restrictions, since the Khoisan were "accustomed from their infancy to great freedom of action and to indiscriminate association with each other"; restrictions on socializing would be particularly resented, for, "being incapable yet of appreciating fully the advantage of a good education, they would in many cases consider the Society the obliged party."[13]

Some Khoisan continued to dig for roots and to gather wild honey and fruit and to feed themselves in this way while travelling. The proposed Cape vagrancy legislation of 1834 proclaimed that "the searching for, and digging or gathering roots or fruits the natural produce of the earth, or wild honey, or the searching for, taking and killing any game, or any other wild animal of what kind soever on any ground not being the property of the person so doing,[14] or on which such person has not previously obtained the permission so to do from the proprietor of such ground, shall not be deemed or taken to be lawful employment, by which any person can honestly earn the means of subsistence."[15] Under the strictures of the 1828 order-in-council concerning the Cape Colony, the vagrancy legislation was framed in race-neutral terms – but, as John Philip pointed out, "no one acquainted with this colony can be at a loss to determine against whom the provisions of this act were intended."[16]

One also notes the continued economic dependence of the Khoisan on their cattle. At Bethelsdorp, for example, a near-famine situation was precipitated in 1828 when the inhabitants were called out on commando against a rumoured Zulu invasion.[17] The harvest was left uncultivated, and no wages were received for the time the men were away. In the following months, inhabitants had to slaughter most of their cattle and transport oxen for food, thus undermining their most productive economic resource. Widespread hunger followed.[18] At this stage the Khoisan economy was a fragile and complicated balance of various survival strategies – a small amount of farming, freelance artisanal or transport work for colonists, farm labour, aloe gathering, older-style gathering of the "fruits of the field," a little precarious hunting, reliance on their own cattle. Mission Khoisan had a virtual monopoly of commercial transport by ox wagon between the emerging towns of Algoa Bay (later Port Elizabeth) and Grahamstown and

Cape Town; this economic niche permitted the maintenance of herds and, perhaps, some characteristics of a nomadic lifestyle. Pastoralism was still the survival method of choice, however, and people still valued their animals above all other resources. Ironically, labour as herdsmen on white farms in a clientage relationship sometimes allowed Khoisan to pursue some semblance of a pastoralist lifestyle, despite the high risk of maltreatment – a factor played down by humanitarian publicists of the plight of the Khoisan, most of whom preferred the Khoisan to become sedentary agriculturalists. The importance of cattle suggests the predominance of herder culture in this group.

Throughout this period, missionaries and farmers were in competition over who should bring Khoisan nomadism under control and in what fashion. This struggle resulted in a further competition to define the nature of the Khoekhoe. For the Afrikaner farmers, and later their more vocal allies the British settlers, the Khoekhoe were feckless wanderers who needed to be restrained (that is, compelled to work as labourers) through vagrancy legislation. For Philip and his allies, the Khoekhoe were small-scale peasants and craftsmen in embyro, prevented from fulfilling their potential by the lack of knowledge which was assumed to characterize nomadism.

As Andrew Bank has argued, the language of liberalism was in no sense the preserve of evangelical "humanitarian liberals." In the early 1820s, British settlers and their later liberal foes such as Philip and the influential editor of the *South African Commercial Advertiser*, John Fairbairn, made common cause over such liberal issues as freedom of the press, the expansion of the franchise, opposition to the importation of convict labour at the Cape, and the need for financial help to distressed settlers.[19] The debates over labour legislation in the late 1820s and, in particular, the Sixth Frontier War of 1834–35 and its bitter aftermath, marked, however, a parting of the ways.[20] By the late 1820s, the LMS found that its domestic opponents now also included a settler lobby speaking for the white south African British, with their British connections and awareness of the right channels for propaganda campaigns, even as the LMS's own evangelical lobby reached the apogee of its influence in Britain in the early 1830s.[21] The period thus saw the spread of missionary-settler warfare onto an ever more public metropolitan stage. The habits of the Khoekhoe were writ larger than ever. In the fray of battle, however, there was not much room to take into account the "Hottentots'" own vision of their past and future.

CHANGES IN MISSIONARY SOCIAL THEORY

In contrast to the earliest envoys, missionaries by the mid-1820s were on average better educated and from a higher social class, as evangelicalism itself underwent a metamorphosis from working-class to middle-class religion.[22] In the south African mission, the year 1817 was an important break; the scandals solidified the society's desire for better educated, more "respectable" candidates. As early as 1818, the then LMS secretary George Burder was able to write reassuringly to Wilberforce that "we have always had offers of service in abundance from uneducated persons; but of late God has inclined the hearts of several to this work whose talents have been proved, and who have acquired some learning."[23] The process accelerated in the late 1820s and 1830s.

This slightly better-educated, slightly higher-class, and more consistently British-origin generation of recruits tended to uphold more elaborate social theories and to perceive the "civilizing" process as long and arduous, reliant as much on human example as on the Holy Spirit. Missionaries in the 1820s also began to call on a more specifically British vision of civilization. This was in part because the LMS finally became a thoroughly "British" institution in the 1820s, after two decades of reliance on German and Dutch missionaries. These overall intellectual moves surely also reflected the evolution of somewhat modified, more nationalistic theories of civilization in Britain itself, as well as the particular political demands of the south African situation.

The debates that took place over the establishment of a Khoekhoe "seminary" typify these processes. As early as 1806, Van der Kemp had mooted an institution of higher learning at Bethelsdorp which would focus on classics, science, and medicine as well as theology – and would in fact be the only university in the country. The project apparently fell through for sheer lack of funding and of books (which would have had to be sent from Europe). The idea was taken up again in a less ambitious form in the 1820s. William Foster, missionary at Bethelsdorp, felt that it would be disastrous to locate the institution at Hankey, a station far from any towns:

It is obvious in England that education consists not only in direct instruction but perhaps more in the influence which the conduct of others in a refined state of society and the various Institutions and improvements of social life unconsciously exert upon the mind. In few places is it more manifest than in South Africa where those who have spent their lives in the interior display a deplorable inferiority to those of the more populous parts. The children of the Boers may without exaggeration be considered inferior to the Hottentot children who have been brought up at Graham's town and familiarized with the Spectacle of English activity and enterprise, at least with respect to the extent and accuracy of their ideas; and it cannot be questioned that as far as the civilization of the latter is concerned, intercourse with Europeans especially the English, will promote it as much if not more than anything else, though at first as is the case now, it may in some respects prove prejudicial.

Foster went on to argue that no Khoekhoe were yet ready to become full-fledged missionaries (that is, mission station heads) – in contrast to the model enshrined in the 1814 first missionary synod. "Hottentots" possessed a capacity for the "acquisition of knowledge" equal to that of Europeans but were not yet civilized enough to cope with the peculiar stresses of mission leadership in south Africa. "As the Institutions furnish a refuge to the Hottentots from the oppressions of the Boers and other colonists, all of whom consider that they have a right to their service, they are looked on with a very evil eye and assiduously misrepresented to the Government in furnishing only means and motives to indolence." Consequently, the burden of the missionary's daily work was become the improvement of the "Hottentots" in "industry and civilization"; if there were any backsliding, the stations would be closed. Given the peculiar position of the stations as artificially constructed communities, the missionary also had to function as something of a magistrate and something of a superintendent. All of this required "an extent and familiarity of knowledge which it would be impossible for them to acquire and such a deep conviction of the necessity of civilization as those only can feel who have been brought up in Europe or in the towns of Africa."[24]

John Philip's own ideas about "civilization" were complicated and indeed, as Bank well emphasizes, caught ambiguously between utilitarianism and evangelicalism. Philip sought to unite economic liberalism with evangelical views of the self and the self's relationship to God. His views of "civilization" also reflected environmentalist ideas about the malleability of human nature and society which were galvanizing evangelical and utilitarian domestic social reformers in such seemingly disparate areas as penal reform, abolitionism, and the movement for educational reform. He was deeply influenced by Scottish Enlightenment political economists and social theorists such as Smith, Hume, and Ferguson, even though he never fully reconciled the environmental determinism intrinsic to Scottish Enlightenment theories of the progress of societies through time with his own evangelical stress on original sin.[25] Let me take the example of Philip's attitude to housing.

In preparation for the visit of the Commission of Inquiry, Philip persuaded mission inhabitants to engage in a theatre of rationalist renewal, focused on the rebuilding of their homes. In his great 1828 work of propaganda on behalf of the Khoisan, *Researches in South Africa*, Philip described how he held town meetings at Theopolis and Bethelsdorp. He persuaded the people not only to adopt a program of economic reforms but also to rebuild their villages under the slogan "fit to be free." He stated that "it was vain to attempt to plead their cause, while their enemies could point to Bethelsdorp in its present state; that the world and the church of Christ looked for civilization and industry as proofs of their capacity for improvement, and of the utility of our labours."[26] Indeed, Philip went so far as to develop a plan for the rebuilding of Bethelsdorp with straight streets converging on a village square and new square houses built from stone and brick, rather than matting. The overall effect was to be that of an idealized Scottish village. The straight line was to dominate, suggesting, in the words of Peter Anderson considering similar plans at Kat River in 1829, "Renaissance harmonic principles" and the triumph of reason and order over the disorder of "barbarism" so strongly associated with Bethelsdorp.[27]

There was even more at stake for Philip. One of the fascinating aspects of the *Researches* is the stress it lays on the transformation of the household both as an indicator of change and as a spur itself to further advancement. As Philip put it, "one of the first steps in attempting the elevation of a savage people, in connexion with religious and moral instruction, is, to endeavour to impart to them a relish for the decencies and comforts of life. Little can be done towards their general improvement, till you can get them to exchange their straw cabins for decent houses."[28]

Philip had a fairly complicated set of ideas about why the transformation from hut to "decent house" was essential to the transformation of the Khoekhoe. First, "miserable reed huts" were unfavourable to health, since, he argued, sleeping on filth-covered earth floors and constantly inhaling smoke promoted high rates of "consumption" (tuberculosis) and an early age of death. There were also less tangible reasons. Huts were unfavourable to industry: since many people were crowded together in small huts without elbow room, inhabitants had no space to do anything and became indolent. This was particularly problematic as far as women were concerned: "The work of the men being chiefly out of doors, when they retire to their hut, it is for rest; but the women, from the nature of their employment, not requiring rest at the same time, require to be employed at needlework, or other domestic employment."[29] In huts, materials and needles were lost, making female domestic industry doubly impossible.

As this suggests, female domesticity was closely linked for Philip to the supposed civilizational progress of a group. His next example in the *Researches* illustrates this further, albeit in an ambiguous fashion. The destruction of clothing under the poor conditions of Khoekhoe huts had, he considered, "a tendency to prevent the formation of domestic habits, and to generate the opposite vices." The very possibility of purchasing clothes was a spur to female industry. Indeed, the "taste for good clothing" acquired by women at LMS stations had given rise to "exertions never witnessed among them before." Nonetheless, women were unable to preserve their dresses for long owing to the poor conditions of their houses; consequently, they extravagantly picked aloes in "printed cotton gowns and expensive shawls," knowing that their clothes would soon wear out. The desire for material goods was of greatest benefit, it would appear, if it led to property accumulation rather than the simple fact of consumption. Here there was a fine line between extravagant display and virtuous property accumulation; the difference perhaps lay in the fact that the first undercut female virtue while the other developed it. One notes, incidentally, Philip's tacit acceptance of female work outside the domestic sphere, since he lauds renewed exertions at aloe picking: female morality is tied to industriousness but not yet to total immersion in the domestic sphere. It is also worth noting (as Natasha Erlank observes) that Philip's own strong-willed wife, Jane, carried out critical administrative work, including keeping the LMS accounts, that went well beyond the ambit of expected behaviour for Victorian British women.[30]

There was a further gendered moral dimension to the issue of housing. Huts in which men and women were huddled together were "unfavourable to decency" and impeded the development of female modesty, that "outwork of virtue." This was a particularly significant issue for Philip since women's modesty was critical to the virtue of the community as a whole: "We can do little for a people in the scale of morals, if we do not succeed in imparting this virtue to the females." A final problem with huts was that their denizens could not keep books safe in the absence of shelves.

The remade Khoekhoe home thus housed an acceptably evangelical host of British Victorian virtues: cleanliness, individual privacy, female modesty, and female industriousness. At the same time, however, Philip was outlining factors needed to escape the state of nature and pass on to a higher stage of commercial society, according to the precepts of several Scottish Enlightenment theorists. Elsewhere Philip argues that the introduction of shops was a critical feature of the civilizing process on mission stations because they introduced money and "artificial wants." Here, as in his discussion of the promotion of female industriousness by the desire for clothes, Philip was echoing Locke's argument that the introduction of money permitted the large-scale accumulation of property and thus provided an incentive for people to leave the state of nature in order to protect property rights. It was essential that the Khoekhoe leave a primitive state of equality if they wished to progress economically. They had to *want* material possessions, or they would remain in Locke's primordial America.

Philip was also building on the views of Scottish Enlightenment economists that human beings were essentially creatures of appetite.

For Philip, it was the role of the missionary, agent of civilization, to *introduce* appetite if none existed – even as he (in a tension reflected in his analysis of the female desire for money, and which I do not think he ever resolved) taught the overcoming of greed, lust and other sinful desires. The introduction of shops and the increased monetization of mission-station economies were thus crucial to Philip's program.[31] It was, even more basically, the function of the missionary to persuade nomadic and semi-nomadic peoples to settle down, as a critical pre-requisite to moving through Smith's stages from hunting to pasturage to agriculture to commerce. The cozy home, rooted in the soil and impossible to move easily, was a symbol of this process.

Philip put his ideas into practice as energetically as he wrote propaganda. His private letters to missionaries on the verge of the commissioners' arrival underscore the intensity with which he put the rebuilding program into operation, as well as suggesting that it may not have been as voluntary on the part of inhabitants as he suggested in the *Researches*:

Is your kraal finished? Would it not be desirable to enclose your burying ground? These are hints merely. I do not dictate. You must be guided by circumstances. Can the houses be immediately whitewashed? ... Tell the wives to have their houses and everything about them clean. Could not something be done to get aprons for the children? ... Have a meeting with your Brethren [fellow missionaries] instantly. Having consulted with the Brethren, you should if approved fix your plan, call the people together next morning, inform them that I may be expected with some great men from England (not mentioning the Commissioners) and that everything relating to the Hottentots depends upon the way in which we find things.[32]

THE PAY-OFF: PHILIP AND THE PASSAGE OF CIVIL-RIGHTS LEGISLATION

When the three commissioners arrived in 1823, Philip bombarded them with information, in addition to stage-managing visits to "civilized" mission stations. In the meantime, he kept up a propaganda campaign to influence colonial officials. In 1825, for example, he went on an extended inland tour and consulted with, in W.M. MacMillan's words, "by no means unsympathetic frontier officials," including Andries Stockenstrom, "more successfully than he perhaps realized."[33]

It is not clear why Philip then sailed for England almost immediately afterwards in early 1826, and neither of his biographers, MacMillan or Andrew Ross, explains this episode satisfactorily. Philip claimed in his 1828 *Researches* that he left for London because the Commission of Inquiry had produced nothing for the Khoisan. In fact, the commission had simply not yet produced a report. It was divided over the issue of pass laws; Bigge was in favour of them for nonwhites under contracts of service, whereas Colebrooke and Blair supported colour-blind labour legislation.[34] Presumably Philip did not trust them to come to the right decision. He may also have anticipated the length of time their final report would take (it was not issued until 1830). Nonetheless, missionary papers make it clear that the abolition of pass laws was in the wind by mid-1826 at the latest.[35] One possibility is that Philip was less in contact with colonial official opinion than he liked to make out; another is that he did not believe pass-law abolition was sufficient and wanted full-scale equality under the law, but his case would have been weakened had he admitted in public that he knew the pass law system was to be abolished or modified.

Be that as it may, Philip arrived in London in mid-1826 with a plethora of papers from the mission stations and minimal political contacts. He was, after all, a Scottish evangelical preacher of good artisanal stock; his only way "in" to the English political elite was through the evangelical party in parliament, flexing its muscle at the time over the issue of abolition. Even there, it was not easy to get anyone's attention. Since 1823, the LMS directors had been sending polite annual missives to the Colonial Office, attempting to secure "to the Aborigines the exercise of their constitutional rights – so necessary to the success of the Society's Christian labours among them,"[36] and had been as politely ignored.

Some on the LMS board were doubtful at first about throwing their full weight behind Philip. They hesitated over the advisability of a collective approach to the colonial secretary of Wellington's Tory government, Lord Bathurst, who was known to be opposed to Philip's views. The treasurer of the society, William Hankey (after whom the Khoekhoe mission station Hankey was named), was in fact a slave-holder through, it would appear, family estates in the West Indies. In 1832 he would be forced out of the society after thirteen years at the helm, under pressure from anti-slavery societies linked to the LMS.[37] Although I have found no documentary evidence, Hankey may have been more reluctant than some to deliver a memorial calling for the abolition of de facto slavery at the Cape. Whatever the case, Philip prevailed with his own board. In January the society presented a more extensive memorial than previously, "in which many other cases of oppression were stated, not enumerated in the first Memorials, together with papers containing ample documentary evidence in support of various facts stated in the Memorials."[38] Predictably, R.W. Hay, the permanent under-secretary at the Colonial Office, returned a brief note that Bathurst would consider the condition of the Khoekhoe once he had received the results of the Commission of Inquiry.[39] It was becoming clear how badly Philip needed a parliamentary patron.

Philip's initial approaches to evangelical MPs had been unproductive. In December 1826, however, he had begun to forge the alliance with Sir Thomas Buxton which in the end would prove decisive. Buxton was a prominent evangelical Anglican and the president of the Anti-Slavery Society. He was a member of parliament with Whig sympathies but no party affiliation, in a period when the "Saints" deliberately attempted to be a cross-party grouping. He was one of that group of reforming evangelical MPs who claimed to represent the opinions of the "religious world" to parliament. He had a prominent role among them, having inherited Wilberforce's mantle as the parliamentary leader of the abolitionists. He was to be Philip's main source of influence in London between 1827 and 1837.

According to Buxton's daughter Priscilla, Buxton resisted Philip's overtures for months in 1826, preoccupied as he was with the status of nonwhites in Mauritius: "He was overladen and *would not* hear even the story – Mamma fought off Dr. Philip as much as ever she could, he was always coming however, and at length in the winter came to Cromer. He had tried everybody else and was resolute in his determination to make my Father take up the case. He was at length obliged to yield, devoted himself to it and went through with Dr. P. all his case. For a week they were shut up over it …"[40] According to Philip's own account, he finally captured Buxton's attention by persuading him that the case of the Khoekhoe was akin to that of West Indian slaves – and that their example illustrated the danger of de facto re-enslavement of the West Indians, despite the formal ending of the institution. Philip wrote later to Buxton:

That first evening I spent alone with you at Cromer Hall, a scene occurred which I shall not soon forget – After unfolding to you the condition of the Hottentots, you mentioned that Canning had proposed that you should visit Jamaica, that a frigate should be sent out for the purpose, and that he was willing to have slavery abolished, provided that you would consent that the slaves should be placed in the condition of the Hottentots of the Cape of Good Hope. Before the above details were given you started to your feet and thanked God, that you had been preserved from that snare – that but for the details you had heard from me you would have consented to the invidious proposal – and that when you should have come to know what you had done, you should have died of a broken heart.[41]

Once the "Hottentot" issue had been taken on board as an antislavery concern, other "Saints" came forward to support Philip. The 1827 session saw, however, a fruitless quest for backroom influence with the cabinet. "I found few of his Majesty's Ministers who understood the question or cared about it," as Philip later recalled. William Huskisson proved an exception, but he quarrelled with Wellington and left office before he could act.[42] Priscilla Buxton, five years after the event, recorded only her father's conversation with Sir George Murray, then colonial secretary. She claimed that Buxton went to Murray with Philip's evidence. The Colonial Office almost at once offered "amelioration," whereupon Buxton said "'I will have no amelioration at all. I must have equal rights with the Whites' – 'Oh, that's all nonsense we can't do any such thing' – 'Well then we must have a fight'."

However accurate this report is, it is certainly correct that the Saints decided Philip must "have a fight." Stephen Lushington, Buxton, and their allies urged Philip to appeal to public opinion and to provide his parliamentary supporters with a weapon, since the Tories were not readily moveable. Philip consequently wrote his famous *Researches in South Africa* at breakneck speed, dictating sections and sending each portion to the press as soon as it was completed. The book was part of an LMS series of missionary reports on various places – *Researches in the South Sea Islands* and so forth – and so fit into existing distribution networks and possessed a ready-made evangelical audience. It played, however, on missionary rhetorical norms to make an intensely political statement, and thus furnishes an interesting example of the fusion of two types of rhetoric in an attempt to reach as wide an audience as possible. Although it is not clear that the *Researches* did indeed have a large contemporary audience, the fear of negative publicity that it generated does in fact seem to have tipped the scales in Philip's direction in the "Saints'" negotiations with the Colonial Office.

THE RESEARCHES

Before pursuing this narrative further, I want to pause to look in more detail at Philip's *Researches*. The book has been well analysed as the *locus classicus* of missionary capitalism, relatively sympathetically by Stanley Trapido and Robert Ross and less so by John Comaroff and Kate Crehan. An initial caveat: the book was a political document, aimed at an intransigent Tory government, and Philip was a good politician. Consequently, the statements about the contributions of missionary enterprise to empire which have been so often quoted, from the introduction, however genuinely believed in by Philip, were also a way of countering the argument of colonial administrators such as Somerset that missionaries were a dangerous threat to empire. Philip was trying to counter the view of an Anglican elite that nonconformism per se was potentially subversive of the established order, as well as local tensions around Bethelsdorp. He was contributing an initially defensive line of argument to discourse about mission and empire which would later, in different hands, transmute into an aggressive argument in favour of the extension of empire.[43] There was evolution over time in these discussions, and the debates of the 1820s and 1830s contributed to the *construction* of ideology, as well as passively illustrating it.

Nevertheless, the *Researches* is both a passionate plea for civil equality for nonwhites in south Africa and a claim that such equality could only be beneficial to British trade and the maintenance of order within the British empire. Philip first attempts to show that the Khoekhoe have been brutally oppressed in the past. In the present, they are in a position of effective enslavement through unjust laws and the desire of colonists to maintain a captive labour force. Philip then draws on contemporary economic theory, notably Adam Smith and David Ricardo, to argue that unfree labour is in fact disadvantageous to an economy as a whole, as well as degrading to both labourer and employer. He wishes rather to remove all distinctions between different races; his ideal is a community in which race will make no difference, and labour roles will not be assigned on the basis of nationality. This ideal community, however, looks very much like contemporary Britain (without Ireland) recast as a liberal-capitalist utopia. In it, the laws of the free market will have created self-conscious and self-regulating individuals who choose to become Christian and to adopt western technology, to fashion themselves through labour, and to become "civilized." Nomadism will have been eliminated, and individuals will live in ordered, settled groups, wearing western clothes and living in western-style houses. Relationships will be regulated by affection and free will, rather than group-based economic imperatives; and the overall result will be economically advantageous to all. The Khoekhoe desire such a model, and the considerable advances they have already made towards civilization, illustrate, first, that this is what the truly self-conscious individual *must* want, because it expresses his or her true nature according to universal norms, and second, that the Khoekhoe consequently participate in the common order of humanity, sharing in the same divinely ordained nature.

What I want to do here is not to duplicate the work of others on Philip's economic theory, but rather to focus on less evident junctures between evangelical and liberal economic thought as they come together in Philip's conceptions of the self-conscious individual and of the just economy. Jean and John Comaroff have recognized the centrality of a particular vision of the self to missionary thought. John Comaroff, in an article on early-nineteenth-century missionaries in south Africa, for example, argues that the "rise of capitalism" in Britain inculcated a particular vision of the essence of the person.

Classic liberalism posited a world consisting of self-contained, right-bearing individuals who created society by the sum of their actions ... In its popular form, this philosophical individualism saw people less as products of a social context than as autonomous beings – Daltonian "atoms," says Halévy (1924:505) – with the capacity to construct themselves if they set their minds and bodies to the task. Further, the self was viewed as a divided entity (Foucault 1975:197). On one hand, it was the core of subjectivity: "I," the center from which a person looked out and acted on the world. On the other hand, it was an object: "me, myself," something of which "I" could become (self-)conscious and subject to (self-)restraint or indulgence ... The immediate corollary of such a conception of self was that the social values of bourgeois ideology could be internalized as qualities of individual *personality*. Thus the virtues of discipline and self-possession; conversely, hedonism and indolence were, literally, self-destructive.[44]

I am not happy glibly assigning the liberal conception of the self, which, after all, had a long pedigree in continental eighteenth-century thought, to the "rise of industrial capitalism" in Britain. I also would not want to argue that one idea of the "self" ruled unchallenged in British nineteenth-century society, whether on a popular or elite intellectual level. Nonetheless, Comaroff's insight that a liberal concept of the self was key to LMS thought is helpful – albeit with the necessary caveat that LMS "thought" was never uniform.

The atoning death of Christ on the cross dominated evangelical theology in the late eighteenth and early nineteenth century.[45] Consequently, the central evangelical trope in this period of intellectual compromise between Calvinism and Arminianism was that of the repentant sinner saved through the grace of God. The process of conversion, the perfectibility of the converted individual, and the possibility of backsliding were viewed differently by different evangelical groups. Nonetheless, the idea of coming to self-consciousness and self-knowledge was key across a range of theologies of conversion. The individual must become aware of his own wretchedness and insufficiency before God could extend his grace in a miraculous process (often a miraculous moment) of transformation. The saved person then acquired full self-knowledge and the ability to reflect on his past, recognizing it for what it was.

The conversion narrative was, as I have argued above, a genre with its own rhetorical conventions. One of these was the coming to self-consciousness of the individual who had undergone a conversion experience. Typically, a recognition of guilt breaks in to arrest the sinner in his heedless course: he becomes convinced both of his wickedness and that he is beyond salvation. The recognition of guilt is in itself an act of atonement, however, which enables Christ to enter the heart of the despairing sinner. At the moment of the sinner's acceptance of Christ, he becomes able correctly to retell the story of his past life, often with a new knowledge of how God had been acting in his life all along – how he had saved him from accidental death, for example, or provided him with a pious master at the right time. "At this moment," wrote Van der Kemp in his autobiography, "there sprang up a new light in my heart. I saw my former unbelief, neglect, aversion to the way of reconciliation, blindness, inconstancy, unfaithfulness, unrighteousness, &c."[46]

Philip and other LMS missionaries applied this model to the Khoekhoe as a people. They presented the "Hottentots" to the British public and, I would argue, to themselves, as a saved nation who had been rescued by their own assumption of self-consciousness – although, in Philip's case, savagery (a state of lack of knowledge) stood in for original sin and civilization (assumption of self-knowledge and self-transformation) went hand in hand with salvation.

These ideas about the saving function of self-knowledge were common in evangelical and utilitarian reforming circles. For example, penal reform provides an interesting point of comparison. John Beattie, and from an extremely different direction Michel Foucault, among others, have illustrated the evolution of secondary forms of punishment from the eighteenth to early nineteenth century: those designed publicly to humiliate the criminal, offering him up as an awful warning to others and inflicting bodily pain, were followed by those that used imprisonment as a means to allow the prisoner to effect his own reformation through a coming to self-consciousness and repentance. These moves were accompanied by a broad individualizing of punishment – by a more precisely worked-out notion that the punishment should fit the crime, rather than functioning to warn the multitude off the path of vice. Michael Ignatieff has made more perhaps of the social control-function of the rise of the penitentiary than Beattie would wish, but he is certainly correct in pointing out the importance of such schemes as Jeremy Bentham's rather extreme plan for an ideal prison designed to effect interior transformation of the prisoner through solitary confinement, external surveillance, and the manipulation of his environment.[47]

Among evangelicals, consider, for example, the fact that Buxton himself had worked earlier on prison reform – which became a "Saints'" issue in parliament in the 1810s. In an 1818 polemic against the current prison system, he argued that its core problem was that it forbade the prisoner to "reflect and repent," by taking away every opportunity to do so. "Seclusion from the world has been only a closer intercourse with its very worst miscreants; his mind has lain waste and barren for every weed to take root in it; he is habituated to idleness, reconciled to filth and familiarized with crime."[48] At the same time, the work of Elizabeth Fry, sister of one of Buxton's sons-in-law, in the women's prison of Newgate illustrated the possibility of regeneration even among the most abandoned people in terrible conditions – a possibility expressed through the imposition of order on chaos. H.G. Bennett, also writing in 1818, described in telling terms a visit from a city of London delegation to Newgate after Fry had begun her work: "Riot, licentiousness, and filth, exchanged for order, sobriety and comparative neatness in the chamber, the apparel, the persons of the prisoners ... The prison no more resounded to obscenity and imprecations, and licentious songs; and, to use the coarse, but just, expression of one who knew the prison well, 'this hell upon earth' exhibited the appearance of an industrious manufactory, or a well regulated family."[49]

In the *Researches,* Philip argued that civilization in some cases occurred rapidly through an immediate recognition of the principles of Christianity. In most cases, however, it was necessary to proceed slowly. The first step to civilizing the person in a state of barbarism was to "rouse the thinking principle." This could be done only by "proposing to his mind considerations of sufficient force to overcome his native indolence."[50] The most readily understood of such considerations were those of religion. The "thinking principle" having been "roused," however, the former barbarian became capable of adopting all the attributes of the civilized person: art, industry, the pursuit of learning and self-improvement, and the love of God. Philip referred to the Khoekhoe to illustrate this. Unjust laws and oppression in south Africa, however, prevented most Khoekhoe from embarking on the path to civilization, because no motive or opportunity was ever provided for self-transformation.

Informing this and similar missionary discussions of "civilization" were two leading ideas about the "savage," although such is the untidy nature of ideas in real life that I do not believe they were always consciously articulated by missionaries on the ground or indeed recognized as being in competition. On the one hand, strict evangelical Calvinist principles argued for the natural depravity of all men prior to the saving act of divine grace. The heathen were considered wicked as an extension of the idea of the natural wickedness of man after the Fall. On the other hand, some LMS missionaries, at least, operated with a different model in practice: of the heathen as a blank slate. The nomad, in particular, was believed to have an empty life and consequently an empty mind. For example, John Campbell, recalled of his 1813 tour of inspection for the LMS that the nomadic Korana beyond the colony seemed to have nothing to do "but, like their dogs, to lie squat upon the grass enjoying the sunshine until the next meal." He found it "heartrending to see so many clever looking young people having nothing either to do or to learn; their parents having no more to inform them of than the cattle have to tell their young." Their language "cannot be a copious language as they have so few things to talk of, but must be a pastoral language, only having words adapted to the pastoral life."[51] Indeed, the very desert landscape was empty of distinguishing features. "This constant sameness has a tendency to bring the mind into a kind of torpid state, which it is distressing even to witness. The gospel is remarkably fitted for raising such sleeping, inactive minds, by placing before them the majesty and glory of the infinite Jehovah, the endless unbounded felicity of the blessed, and the unspeakable misery of the wicked in the world to come – subjects which in all ages have produced wonderful effects on the human mind."[52] Such an implicit view of the mind as tabula rasa opened the door for the early-nineteenth-century evangelicals, distancing themselves as they were from extreme Calvinism, to stress the corrupting or elevating influence of environment on a human being who had not yet accepted God. Apparently "uncivilized" traits might then be seen as the result of the environment, rather than of original sin; in either case, such traits could be overcome by the moral activity of the individual.

In practice, political activism and personal contact pushed a few missionaries into views of the non-Christian "savage" which their home societies would almost certainly have disavowed and which tended either to lean towards the "blank slate" theory of pre-Christian man or to abandon theories of savagery altogether. In 1833 James Read Sr thought that the language used by the "Zuid Afrikaan" about the "many civilized [settlers] and barbarous few [Xhosa]" ought to have been reversed: "It should have been, the few civilized and barbarous many." Furthermore, the Grahamstown Methodist missionaries were wrong to represent the Xhosa as "the most depraved of the human race." "They believe in witchcraft and so do thousands in England – Polygamy is established among them but what is this compared with the scenes of many Towns in England."[53] A similarly frustrated John Ross of the Glasgow Missionary Society, commented in 1833 that "Savage and Savages are very common terms here. We protest against them, still they are used not only in common conversation, but in grave debate by Christians and Infidels, Ministers (only some of them I hope) & People."[54]

John Philip, author as he was of such an extended theory of "uncivilized" man, nonetheless illustrated the same ambiguity about the meaning of "civilization." In the *Researches* he had to fight, for political reasons, against the idea that aborigines and slaves were happier under white tutelage and domination than in their previous independent state. He therefore argued that, before colonial contact, the

"Hottentots" had been close to nature, passionately attached to their independence, and possessed of moral restraints. The Dutch, however, not only robbed but *corrupted* the original owners of the land. If the British government would liberate the "Hottentots" physically, then with missionary help the "Hottentots" could liberate themselves mentally and spiritually. This argument stands in interesting contrast to Philip's position as a rigid young minister, when he inveighed against the idea of the noble savage in a private letter to his fiancée:

Our missionaries have dispelled the darkness and to the confusion and no small [grief?] of the infidels, have shown [...] these moral and amiable beings to be the most depraved and [vicious?] of mortals. The human heart in every country and in every clime of the known world, is deceitful above all things and [— ?] wicked, and we should carefully guard against those descriptions and sentiments which [— ?] to lessen our gratitude for the Bible, the best gift of God to fallen man; and the only instrument in the hand of the Eternal Spirit that can restore him to holiness and happiness.[55]

Given this family of ideas about the self, despite the tensions and variations within it, Governor Benjamin D'Urban would thus make a fatal mistake when he sought to justify his frontier policy in 1835 by describing the Xhosa as "irreclaimable savages." The idea that *any* human being was irreclaimable was profoundly offensive to those influenced by evangelicalism across the ideological spectrum – including, as we shall see, Leslie Stephen at the Colonial Office, Lord Grey, and Lord Glenelg himself.

Before leaving this look at the *Researches,* I want to emphasize another important point. This is that Philip and his LMS supporters viewed the economy primarily in terms of its *moral* impact on individuals. Boyd Hilton has convincingly argued that evangelical beliefs had a powerful impact on politicians' economic creeds and economic policy making during this period.[56] His argument may be extended to a lower strata of society: to the lower-class missionaries who were, after all, the "shock troops" of evangelicalism. John Philip has been described as prophet and product of British capitalism in its mature industrial phase.[57] While the argument is substantially correct that Philip echoed the liberal-capitalist beliefs of the Whigs and liberal Tories in the 1820s and early 1830s, it is important not to miss the extent to which LMS missionaries judged economic action primarily by its capacity *morally* to transform and to mould the economic actor. Untrammelled greed, unrestrained by law, was destructive, in part because human nature could not be trusted. The labour needs of the colony kept the "Hottentots" in effect enslaved for Philip, and slavery

led to the moral degeneration of the slave. Thus, in 1834 Philip included comments on the impact of the old system on the morality and civilizational level of bonded labourers in a memorial sent to Governor
D'Urban against the reintroduction of vagrancy law:

That your memorialist in the year 1825 visited a good proportion of the districts of Graaf Reinet and Beaufort, and in these two districts, particularly on
the farther side of the village of Graaf Reinet and Beaufort, he found the Hottentots, Boschmen and other people of colour in the service of the farmers
under the system of *forced labour*, in the most deplorable condition in which
it is possible to imagine any class of labourers to exist. They were for the most
part without any clothing but the filthy sheepskin caross – in their appearance
indecent -- in their habits filthy in the extreme – often without any food but the
offals of sheep killed for the use of the families by their master. With no stim-
ulus to labour but fear, and coercion, their countenances exhibited every mark
of the deepest degradation and wretchedness.[58]

It was also an evangelical commonplace in this period that slavery corrupted the slave-owner even more than it corrupted the unfree labourer. An 1826 discussion of slavery at the Cape of Good Hope in the *Anti-
Slavery Reporter* concluded, for example: "Who, indeed, but must be
sensible that the ruling classes in every slave colony, are (and must necessarily be) depraved to an appalling extent by the early and uncontrolled indulgence of almost all the worst propensities of our nature? –
by sensuality, unfeeling selfishness, arrogance, rage, revenge!"[59]
   Philip's attack was thus a coherent critique of the white population of
south Africa, drawing on aspects of the abolitionist and economic
debates of the day, but with a strong evangelical interpretation. He was
writing against a long tradition which stereotyped the "Hottentot" as
the lowest of the human race, with no prospects for "improvement"
and destined to die out before the superior advance of the European.
Had not Patrick Colquhoun, in an 1815 treatise on the British empire,
damned the Khoekhoe as "a poor dejected harmless race, evidently defi-
cient in intellect, and almost devoid of memory," and had he not coolly concluded, "It is believed that the race is rapidly decreasing"?[60] Did
not Gibbon see the San as the "connecting link between the rational and
irrational creature"?[61] Before John Campbell toured south Africa in
1812, he recalled later, "I had been accustomed from youth to hear,
even from the pulpit, the expression 'As savage as a Hottentot.'"[62]
Philip, then, was arguing against this construction of the "Hottentot"
as dying savage by counterposing the possibility of reconstructing the
"Hottentot" as an evangelical subject. "The history of a people," he
argued, "ignorant of letters and possessing no monuments of art, com-

mences at the period when they are first visited by travellers or adventurers from more civilized communities, whose accounts have in most instances been coloured by their prejudices or their interests."[63] This false history, and the false visions of the "Hottentot" it engendered, must be rooted out and "Truth" must be revealed to the world.

ORDINANCE 50

In the end, the publication of the *Researches* appears to have been decisive, because it furnished a tool with which the "Saints" could embarrass the government in a time of gathering debate over slavery and the overall status of blacks in British colonies. Philip subsequently recounted:

It was agreed that Mr. Buxton should bring forth the motion, whilst Sir James Mackintosh, Charles Grant, Esq (afterwards Lord Glenelg), Dr.Lushington and Mr. Huskisson were expected to support it. In the meantime two copies of the *Researches* had found their way to the Colonial Office in Downing Street. Mr. Buxton was immediately sent for. At the office he found Sir George Murray with a copy open before him. Sir George informed Mr. Buxton that he had sent for him to ascertain whether he would not postpone his motion for six months. "Not an hour, Sir George. On Tuesday next at 7 o'clock I shall bring forward my motion." "You are not an opposition man" said Sir George. You take and you give; and if you promise me no speeches on the subject I will allow you and Dr. Philip to draw up your motion. We shall make it a Cabinet question and it will get through the House by acclamation."[64]

As Philip wrote to a fellow missionary at the time, he believed that Wellington and his cabinet "dreaded the impression the discussion was likely to produce on the country."[65]

The motion, passed on 19 August 1828, simply stated that the original natives of south Africa "have always been recognized by the British government as a free people," deserving of protection to their property; that the government at the Cape of Good Hope should receive such instructions as to secure the same "freedom and protection" to all natives of south Africa; and that copies of the report of the Commission of Inquiry and of papers given to the Colonial Office by Philip and by the LMS directors were to be laid before the House of Commons.[66]

For these actions Philip was immediately hailed in missionary circles as the liberator of the "Hottentots," and a heroic rhetoric began to be built up around him – albeit rather more cautiously than for less politically controversial and personally prickly characters. As Philip was at last safely back on his way to south Africa in September 1829, the *Missionary Chronicle* published "Lines on the Departure of Dr. PHILIP and the missionaries of England, France, and Germany, for South Africa, on 18th July, 1829." These began, "Let Afric's sable sons rejoice / And to the Lord lift up their voice," and continued some lines later with:

> Go, PHILIP, go – may high renown
> Thyself and thy companions crown;
> Th'eternal God thy refuge be,
> His spirit ever rest on thee.
> Thou Liberator of the slave,
> Thou Christian model of the brave;
> May grateful tribes thy advent bless,
> Be thy reward – their happiness![67]

The attention focused on Philip, despite his accomplishments, was to some extent missionary mythologizing. Just two days after the domestic passage of this legislation, acting governor Richard Bourke, lieutenant governor of the Eastern Cape, had ushered in the celebrated Ordinance 50, which granted substantially the same privileges as the British ruling. Bourke was himself sympathetic to Khoisan concerns before coming to the Cape, and while there had been further influenced by the proposals of Andries Stockenstrom for the reform of Khoisan status.[68] Ordinance 50 was passed in conjunction with Ordinance 49, which permitted extra-colonial Africans, hitherto barred from the colony, to enter into work contracts with colonists under certain specified conditions. I would disagree with the judgment of J.B. Peires that Ordinance 49 was "merely a convenient fiction to disguise the fact that the colonial government could not control the black immigration which it had permitted" (from 1825 onward, as the Mfecane began to send refugees flooding into the colony).[69] While there is truth in this observation, it also seems important that Ordinances 49 and 50 taken together freed up labour flows: although immigrant labourers still required passes, the cumulative effect was still the abolition of de facto vagrancy legislation, whether it affected labourers trying to enter the colony or farmers attempting to tie their labourers to themselves in perpetuity. This was very much in line with the metropolitan drive to abolish vagrancy legislation in England itself. Peires is closer to the mark in arguing that Bourke and the commissioners condemned forced labour not only for moral reasons but because they thought it economically inefficient. They hoped, as Peires says, that Ordinance 50 and other measures "would stimulate the Cape's feeble economy by increasing the productivity of both the labouring classes (now given the incentive of the profit motive) and the former master class (now deprived of indolence-inducing coerced labour)."[70]

Philip's own role in the passage of Ordinance 50 has been debated by historians, who are generally split along the lines of how much influence they wish to accord to missionaries in Cape politics of the period. Andrew Ross and W.M. MacMillan point out that Ordinance 50 was substantially Andries Stockenstom's idea, and that he had come under Philip's influence following the LMS's superintendent's intensive lobbying of colonial officials and the development of a personal relationship between the two men. John S. Galbraith argues that the legislation was arrived at independently, albeit using the advice of Stockenstrom, and does not grant Philip much influence over Stockenstrom.[71] Both are arguing against a background of myth: whatever the true impetus behind Ordinance 50, the legislation became associated indelibly with Philip in the minds of his few ardent supporters and many violent detractors, in ways that until recently have obscured the contributions of other policy makers.

There is a sense, however, in which the extent of Philip's personal influence with the Cape colonial government is a less interesting question than why there was convergence, however temporary, between missionary and official viewpoints. Galbraith's distaste for the missionaries of the period, whom he describes as for the most part mentally unstable,[72] leads him to downplay Philip's role in colonial politics to an unjustifiable extent. On the other hand, MacMillan's almost exclusive emphasis on Philip cannot be justified by subsequent research both into the impact of the Commission of Inquiry on colonial labour policy and into the political thought of Bourke himself. Stanley Trapido is much closer to the mark in indicating the growing attraction of free trade and associated liberal economic ideas to a certain segment of the English mercantile community at the Cape, no matter how limited, while Peires, Elphick, and Malherbe have emphasized the wide-ranging economic project of the Commission of Inquiry. Hazel King, in a 1971 study of Richard Bourke, has persuasively argued that Bourke had in fact conceived of some ameliorative legislation for the Khoisan shortly after taking office. She also makes the convincing point that Bourke believed that colonial labour problems could be overcome by an influx of *British* immigrants and thus that the colony could do without bonded African labour.[73]

The significance of Philip in this context is surely that he seized on an existing line of thought, pushed it to a radical conclusion, and coaxed out of London a more extensive statement of the equal rights of nonwhites than the commissioners, with their primarily economic focus, had been willing to concede. Thus, Stockenstrom, one of the most active proponents of Ordinance 50, was dismayed at the broader implications of the London ruling, which (as a slave-holder) he felt threatened the very principle of slavery itself.[74] The cabinet instructions were to prove important, then, because Philip and Buxton used them to persuade the metropolitan government to entrench the provisions of Ordinance 50, in such a way that legislation distinguishing between people on the basis of race had to be referred to London. When Bourke left, having earned the opprobrium of settlers for Ordinance 50, his successor, the more traditionalist Sir Lowry Cole, tried to mitigate its effect by broaching a vagrancy law. Stockenstrom, Fairbairn of the *Commercial Advertiser*, Read, and Philip were instrumental in lobbying council to abandon the idea, on the grounds of its illegality. Similar arguments would be used when in 1834 the Cape Legislative Council managed to get a Vagrancy Act as far as the statute books.

The "resolutions" that the council issued to accompany the Vagrancy Act on its way to London were an explicit debate with Wilberforce, Philip, and Van der Kemp (all named) on the best way to civilize the "Hottentots." The council struggled to take up the language of the English humanitarians and, clearly, to talk to London in a way it was assumed London would understand, in the wake of the abolition of slavery. If subsequent historians have been doubtful about the actual influence of Philip at the Colonial Office, the Cape Legislative Council was perhaps less so. The council agreed that "the communication of Christian instruction to the coloured population of the colony in general is a paramount act of duty." They thus welcomed the 1834 resolution of the House of Commons to defray expenses for the education of newly emancipated "negro populations," and recommended also the case of "the Hottentots and free people of colour of every denomination" in the hope that "by the gradual diffusion of the blessings of civilization and of moral and religious knowledge amongst them, they will be rendered not only useful members of the colonial community, but valuable members of the British empire." They further recommended that any available land be returned to the "Hottentots" as an "imperative act of justice" (although there was no actual effort to implement this). On the other hand, they requested the extension of stipendiary magistracies throughout the colony, and that "such alterations will be effected in the public gaols throughout the colony as will permit of the classification of prisoners, the use of 'solitary confinement,' and of 'tread-mills,' or some equally efficacious mode of punishment." Finally, and most interestingly, the council concurred fully in the sentiments of Wilberforce that distinctions between European and coloured races impeded goodwill and the growth of civilization, and agreed with Philip that the Khoekhoe "'have a right to

consider themselves, and expect to be treated, as a free people.'"
Therefore, free people of colour should not be excluded from vagrancy
legislation which currently affected whites alone. Most crucially,
exemption from vagrancy law actually discouraged the overcoming of
the indolence of the Khoekhoe and ensured that they would never
become civilized. The resolutions concluded, drawing heavily on the
idea of the "reconstructibility" of man:

That the Hottentots are, moreover, of an unsettled roaming disposition, fondly attached to the savage pleasures of nomadic life, averse from fixed or orderly habits and employments, and by far the greater proportion of them utterly
unacquainted with, and regardless of, even the most ordinary artificial wants
and comforts of civilized life.

That we concur with Dr. Philip, viz.: "the first step towards the civilization
of a savage, is to arouse the thinking principle. This can only be done by
proposing to his mind considerations of sufficient force to overcome his native
indolence ..." But we submit that no considerations of sufficient force to overcome his "native indolence" can with any prospect of success be proposed to
those who are permitted to roam throughout the colony in a state of vagrancy.

That with the habits and disposition above ascribed to the free people of
colour, the unhappy gift that has been conferred on them of unrestricted liberty, is powerfully calculated to impede their progress in civilization, and to
counteract that industry which should form the best means of their improvement ... Their present anomalous position in the colony is altogether incompatible with social order, subversive of the rights and security of the property
of others, and a direct infringement on that "civil liberty of every class of their
fellow-subjects," which consists "not," as we fear the coloured classes are too
prone to believe it does, "in a mere absence of restraint," but in the undis-
turbed enjoyment of legal rights, alone to be derived from the efficient protection of civil government.[75]

With this agreement on language and intellectual categories among
London and colonial authorities, however hypocritical, it is not surprising that some Afrikaner farmers wedded to an older labour model
and not particularly interested in transforming African culture were
beginning to trek on a large scale out of the colony, claiming that they
wished "to preserve the proper relations between master and servant."[76] For the moment at least, the debate over colonial labour policy had shifted onto ground which two sides claimed was common,
and which quite excluded the preconceptions of a third.

7 "On Probation As Free Citizens": Poverty and Politics in the 1830s

The years from 1828 to the late 1830s proved to be the apogee of LMS influence in London regarding south African affairs. On the heels of Ordinance 50 in 1828, the colonial state allocated the Kat River settlement for "Hottentot" colonization in 1829. During the 1830s, Khoisan agitated successfully against the renewal of vagrancy legislation; the Sixth Frontier War of 1834–35 broke out between the Xhosa and the colony; the dramatic "Glenelg dispatch" from London repealed Governor D'Urban's annexation of much of Xhosaland in the aftermath of British victory and recalled D'Urban himself; and the House of Commons sponsored a Select Committee on Aborigines, designed by its progenitors to expose abuses in the government of South Africa. Despite these highly public successes, the period nonetheless included devastating, and unrecompensed, war losses for the colonial Khoekhoe. These reflected the frustrating economic struggles of the Khoekhoe with the colony and presaged the increasingly explosive tensions of the 1840s.

KHOISAN POVERTY AND LAND CLAIMS

Ordinance 50 was not received with unmixed jubilation by the colonial Khoekhoe. From Bethelsdorp, James Read wrote privately to his fellow missionary James Kitchingman that, although the ordinance was "a great work, and a great point gained," the inhabitants of Bethelsdorp "have not been much elated by hearing of the liberty; in fact, it will not so much effect them, except in the pass system, which is now done with.[1] In a recent magisterial study, V.C. Malherbe has established that

Ordinance 50 did not in fact make a large economic difference to the majority of Khoekhoe in the Eastern Cape. The Khoekhoe mission insti-tutions were faced with crippling poverty at this juncture, caused partly by the growing overcrowding on mission stations and the barrenness of the land, in a situation echoing the problems of subsequent "native reserves" and "homelands." The aftermath of Ordinance 50, like the later emancipation of former slaves, increased overcrowding, as the landless flocked to mission stations.[2] For example, Pacaltsdorp, outside the town of George, supported some 516 people in 1834, and yet its land had originally been granted as two "half places" – the entire institution, in other words, was the size of one tract of land habitually granted to a single white farmer.[3] Mission-station inhabitants thus had little ground on which to pasture stock, severely hindering their ability to accumulate wealth. Meanwhile, Tswana and other refugees had begun to flood into the colony, fleeing disturbances in the interior. After 1828, these refugees were able legally to find work. Adam Robson believed that the colonists deliberately hired Tswana labour over Khoekhoe because they were so "annoyed" about Ordinance 50. Be that as it may, the Khoekhoe cer-tainly suffered from the downward pressure on wages exerted by refugees. Mission inhabitants also suffered greatly after having been called out on commando and consequently forced both to sacrifice a crop and to slaughter their cattle for food. "I shall never forget the condition in which I found a worthy woman with a helpless babe in her arms & five fine little boys surrounding her with tears, entreating her for some-thing to eat," continued Robson, "but alas she had naught to give them. There were too many instances of mothers being similarly situated."[4]

Alcoholism rates appear to have been rising rapidly, suggesting social despair. The burgeoning towns of the Eastern Cape brought new economic opportunities for the Khoisan, but also more opportunities for self-destruction when economic openings began to close. Wages were often paid in drink.[5] "I have opened my eyes and see how we have lost our country and what the Brandy has done for us," proclaimed Valentyn Jacobs in a public meeting in 1834. "The loss of our country reduced us to poverty, then came the brandy and made us work a whole year for a Cow or a Heiffer."[6] Indebtedness was a significant problem in the 1820s, as earlier.[7] Potential and actual employers encouraged indebtedness for their own ends. The case of several inhab-itants of Pacaltsdorp provides just one striking example: the *pachter* (storekeeper) of George, a man named Steiz, persuaded the Pacaltsdorp residents to ring up huge debts in drink and then attempted to hold them as bond servants to pay off the debts.[8]

When Jacob Jacobs and Wildschut Platje charged local white farmers with assault in 1828 and lost, their cases were taken up by the Cape administration only because of the coincidence of the presence in the area of Saxe Bannister, humanitarian gadfly and former attorney general of New South Wales. As Malherbe argues in her trenchant analysis of this case, although the subsequent firing of court officers at Uitenhage marked a victory for reformism, in fact the ease with which charges were initially dismissed, despite Jacobs's extensive injuries, demonstrates how fragile and shallowly rooted the top-down legal reform of 1828 actually was.[9] Malherbe's analysis also underscores that white farmers were trying to prevent the Khoisan use of crown land. This interfered with the ability of Khoisan to graze their stock outside the inadequate grounds of the mission stations, and affected the capacity of nonmission Khoisan to eke out an independent living, despite the abolition of vagrancy laws. Furthermore, de facto restrictions on Khoisan use of crown land made it hard for Khoisan woodcutters to carry out their work. As Andries Stoffels put it bitterly in an interview with Donald Moodie, "the Boors wished to have all the shooting as well as all the land to themselves."[10] In all of these examples, the pressing, overarching need of the Khoisan was for adequate land, without which none of these structural problems could be addressed.

In early 1829 Sir Lowry Cole received a petition for land signed by twenty-eight men from Bethelsdorp, who styled themselves "divers inhabitants of the district of Uitenhage, sprung principally from the Gona and other Hottentot tribes." This petition provides evidence for the political centrality to Eastern Cape Khoekhoe of an ongoing sense of "Hottentot" ethnicity and related land claims in the Eastern Cape – issues that would explode in the rebellion of 1850–53. The memorialists presented themselves as respectable and faithful servants of the public good, many of whom had served as soldiers. They adopted the language of economic liberalism: "Hitherto want of land has checked the natural increase of their cattle; and deprived memorialists of the just reward of industry." Most crucially, they claimed that, now that Ordinance 50 had recognized the "ancient right" of the "Hottentots" to hold land, they ought to be granted all the remaining unallocated land in the Eastern Cape, as rightfully theirs. "They do not seek to intermeddle with what is given to others of His majesty's subjects; – altho they cannot forget that it belonged to their fathers; and was lately rescued from the Caffres by their help; but they submit it to be just to reserve all that is left for them and their children." To this end, petitioners requested surveyors' plans of the district of Uitenhage in order to identify all vacant land. They also asked for the remittance of quit-rents for ten years, as was allowed to (white) settlers in the Zuurveld in 1817. The petition closed with the observation that the memorialists represented many more than themselves: they also spoke for many of the members of Bethelsdorp absent cutting wood, hunting elephants, or doing other work, and indeed "such inhabitants of the Colony as are entitled to the benefit of the late law." Sixteen of the signatories had their names signed for them by relatives, mostly children; all the signatories were male but half of those who signed for others were women. The fact that so many were "signed for" suggests one of two things: either that they were not literate, or that they were not present. I would incline to the former argument, which suggests generational differences in literacy rates. In either case, the further implication is that older heads of families were the main signatories and presumably spoke for others in the family, including women. The first three signatories were Wensel Heemro, David Scheepers, and Hendrick Hatha; others included Andries Stoffels, Hendrick Heyn, and five members of the Vincent family.[11]

The petition reflects the fact that many in Khoekhoe communities tied the benefits of Ordinance 50 to the restitution of land. The tone of the memorial is quite defiant, despite its reminders of the signatories' military service and respectability. Did anyone seriously expect the government to surrender maps of vacant land to permit immediate and unregulated Khoekhoe possession? Although the answer is probably not, the petition underlines the deep sense of collective grievance over the loss of land which would remain a political issue through the 1850s. As an anonymous Khoekhoe correspondent from Kat River put it in the columns of the *South African Commercial Advertiser* in 1834 in a letter protesting against the proposed reimposition of vagrancy legislation: "After the promulgation of the 50th Ordinance we asked that the remainder of the land still in the Colony might be granted to the Hottentots, but this was not acceded to ... It is true Government has granted the Hottentots a small parcel of land at Kat River, for which we are always grateful: but it is calculated that the Hottentot nation counts 30,000 souls and there are only 5,000 at Kat River. What becomes of the other 25,000? Must they all become vagrants?"[12]

THE KAT RIVER SETTLEMENT

In mid-1829 the picture changed somewhat, if not as dramatically as the Bethelsdorp petitioners had doubtless hoped. The Xhosa chief Maqoma had been living in the so-called Neutral Territory near the Kat River. This land had been "ceded" by Ngqika in 1819, on the understanding that it should be occupied by neither Xhosa nor colonist. Ngqika did not have the authority to make such commitments on behalf of other Xhosa chiefs, however, and does not appear to have intended to surrender as much as the colony later claimed he had. The other chiefs never acknowledged the validity of the transaction.[13] Equally inevitably, the land slid from being "Neutral" to "Ceded" Territory.[14] In the meantime, both Dutch colonists and Xhosa moved, or returned, to the area and came to occupy adjacent territories in a state of uneasy compromise.

Maqoma was the most easterly of the Xhosa chiefs, a son of Ngqika and regent of the Ngqika Xhosa until the younger but dynastically more senior Sandile came to manhood. He occupied the Kat River basin, at the juncture of the Kat and the Keiskamma – where Sir Rufane Donkin had originally planned, without success, to "plant" Scottish Highlanders. The colony saw Maqoma as living there on sufferance. Maqoma, however, clearly believed that he was continuing to occupy land which his father had conquered. In 1829 the commissioner general of the eastern frontier, Andries Stockenstrom, seized on Maqoma's military intervention in a leadership dispute among neighbouring Tembu (in which Maqoma's people captured some 3,000 cattle and pushed refugees into the colony) to recommend successfully to the Legislative Council that Maqoma be expelled from the land.[15] Although Stockenstrom always claimed that the expulsion was on legitimate grounds, the balance of probability is that the area was too strategically crucial for it to be occupied by a Xhosa group: Stockenstrom did not conceal that he had considered allowing Maqoma to remain in 1822 "a most injurious measure."[16]

The Glasgow Missionary Society had recently begun a mission station, Balfour, among the Kat River Xhosa, about ten miles from Maqoma's homestead. The fact that their eye-witness accounts and their corroboration of Maqoma's story went unheeded testifies to the relative powerlessness of missionaries per se in the absence of well-organized domestic support.[17] According to the missionaries, Maqoma told the commando: "I am glad I have heard there is a God. The teacher has told me God will judge all men according to their deeds. You have overcome me by the weapons that are in your hands. But you must answer for this. You and I must stand before God. He will judge us. I am a man who does not know God. Yet I rejoice to know he will be judge."[18]

Stockenstrom proposed to the colonial government that the territory taken from the Xhosa be turned immediately into a "Hottentot" settlement. His arguments reveal the extent of Khoekhoe land hunger and hint at Khoekhoe resistance to incorporation into white society as a servant class. There were, Stockenstrom said, "numerous Hottentot families all over the country, without fixed abodes, who lose or neglect nothing by being sent to any part of the frontier." In addition, many at the mission institutions "complain that they cannot live there, as their flocks are perishing from want of pasturage." Among servants to white inhabitants "there must also be a number remaining, too prudent to leave service before they know where to settle, and yet anxious to better their condition." Former soldiers furnished another source of respectable potential inhabitants; Noel Mostert, indeed, underscores that Stockenstrom saw the soldiers as particularly important, given the military role of the projected settlement. Overall, among "these unfortunate people," there must be "many who have stock to begin farming with" but presumably no land.[19]

From a colonial perspective, the political benefit of the Kat River settlement was apparent. As Stockenstrom himself put it, "no other class of people in the colony can be brought together in the above proposed manner, and no other set of men can be rendered efficient auxiliaries towards the object in view. The white inhabitants have their home and business to leave, and must often be dismissed when their cooperation is most wanted; the Hottentots above alluded to could, and would gladly, take their all with them; be at home on the spot where their services are required, and constitute a permanent barrier against the Kafirs."[20] Twenty-five years later, in the aftermath of the Kat River Rebellion, Stockenstrom would be harsher on himself. "It was for the selfish purpose of turning the better and more efficient part of the Hottentots into a breastwork against an exasperated powerful enemy in the most vulnerable and dangerous part of our frontier, that I decoyed them from those retreats where many of them were certainly not very comfortable, but where they were, at least, safe and legally their own masters," he claimed. "By the bait of a speck in the vast territories of their fathers, I drew them into the slavery of constant watching, patrolling, half-starving upon 'veld kost,' and the chance of any day getting their throats cut."[21] George Barker, missionary at Theopolis, rightly commented that, however humanitarian his presentation, Stockenstrom was still "a Politician." "The Military Posts are all to be removed on the extreme border, there will be two or three on the line from which Mr. Macombo has been driven, fill up the space with Hottentots and your frontier is defended, especially if you have 20 stands of arms at a place. This then I believe to be the Policy wrapped up in the Boon."[22] Barker went on to add that there was "no greater defence against the Caffres than the Hottentots": the colonial Khoekhoe had no interest in making trouble with the Xhosa, whereas white colonists and Xhosa became embroiled in endless territorial disputes and mutually destructive cattle raids, the whites believing themselves to be protected by the colony from the consequences of their actions. Stockenstrom was thus extremely anxious that Khoisan move quickly to Kat River to keep out both drought-stricken Dutch farmers and other Xhosa chiefs on good terms with the government.[23] An additional factor, according to a later memorandum by J. Rose Innes, was that white settlers would not accept farms as small as those offered to the Khoisan, "and that if they accepted of a grant at all it would be in the hope, by persevering industry and superior energy, of adding others to it, thereby defeating the main object of the settlement, and leaving the Kat River as open to inroads as any other part of the eastern frontier."[24] As this foreshadows, the Kat River settlement would be relatively protected and Khoekhoe land rights upheld as long as it was at a vital point of the frontier; once the frontier moved on, there would prove to be no a priori government objection (despite Stockenstrom's ongoing passionate commitment to the settlement) to alienation of Khoekhoe land and land speculation by whites.

The removal of Maqoma from the Kat River valley and the installation of Khoisan "settlers" reveal the facility with which the colonial government moved populations around – a facility reflected, of course, on a larger scale in government-assisted European emigration to the Cape Colony. The Khoekhoe did not see their possession of Kat River as a further shuffling of the pieces of the colonial chess board, however, so much as the partial restitution of land that was rightfully theirs. According to James Read Sr, people remembered that thirty years ago the area "was in possession of a tribe of Hottentots called *Heintemas*, it never was considered part of Caffreland."[25] After the Xhosa occupation of the area, "the remnants of the Gonaqua Hottentots or Gonas" lived under the Kat River Xhosa as clients, keeping alive the memory that this had once been Khoekhoe rather than Xhosa or white land.[26] In 1834 one elderly inhabitant of Kat River recalled "going through this part of country along with some Boors that went out to shoot 'Zeekosi' and then there was only Gona Hottentots here to be found."[27] In an 1833 discussion of land ownership, Read again underscored that the Khoekhoe of Kat River remembered vividly that the land had been taken from them by the Xhosa, although Read did recognize the claims of the Xhosa. "The idea that the country was never the property of the Caffres is laughable, it is much more so than ever the colony belonged to the Dutch – all was Hottentots land ... It is well known that the country between the Kay and Keiskamma Rivers was gained from the Hottentots by conquest, the [next?] the Hottentots receded and the caffres took possession."[28] For the Eastern Cape Khoekhoe, the "gift" of Kat River represented the legitimate return of a fragment of the land which had once been in their possession. Colonial and Khoekhoe perspectives on the Kat River settlement thus differed sharply from the very beginning. And both naturally conflicted with the ownership claims of Maqoma, who never ceased to regard the settlement with great bitterness.[29]

Once Maqoma had been removed and the government had approved setting aside part of the area for a "Hottentot" settlement, Stockenstrom personally rode to Khoisan mission stations offering the chance to take up land at Kat River. He also sent letters to all districts inviting applications from people of colour. Many responded with enthusiasm. Unlike the barren mission stations, the land was among the finest in the colony.[30]

An anonymous female observer writing around 1851, probably a white woman, conveys, despite her political agenda of attacking supposed Khoisan ingratitude, the sense of excitement with which the first "settlers" arrived at the Kat River:

At last all was ready and the "trek" began. It was a most exciting spectacle; – the old, – the young, – the decently-clad family, with a respectable little clump of cattle, and a tolerable wagon, the father mounted on an old mare with a foal at her foot and yearling trotting after her; – the old worn-down Hottentot drudge and his wife, bent and travel-worn, with a few goats; – the steady couple, with a flock of children and a little of everything, a pack-ox included, on which were seated two or three dusky urchins, and some old "*Motje*" unable to walk; – in short, all sorts, shades and sizes, for weeks were flocking up to the land of promise, and Sir A [Andries Stockenstrom] – night and day amongst them, arranging every thing for their welfare. An expression of content and cheerfulness sat on every countenance, and great gratitude was *then* expressed for the boon.[31]

The determination with which the new settlers of Kat River set out to build a successful settlement took even Stockenstrom by surprise. By 1834, there were some 5,000 inhabitants, settled in villages throughout the area. Some thirty of these villages, or three-quarters of the population, claimed allegiance to the London Missionary Society.[32] The LMS-affiliated congregations "called" James Read to be their minister, despite the opposition of Stockenstrom and other officials.[33] They would develop vigorous evangelical missions beyond the Kat River area. The settlement attracted many hundreds of mission inhabitants, driven by the desire to escape the precarious economic conditions of the stations. The majority of settlers, however, had previously been scattered throughout the colony. Many hundreds also moved to Kat River from Xhosaland, mostly Gonaqua who had been living among the Xhosa, and Xhosa who had been connected with a previous LMS mission station.[34] There were also a number of people from refugee groups, forced into the colony from surrounding areas. A large group of *basters*, about eighty heads of families, settled separately in the area under the leadership of Christian Groepe, with the Reverend W. Thomson as their minister. The *basters* quickly clashed with those who defined themselves as "Hottentots," since the *basters* tended to claim social superiority.[35] Overall, the main groups settled in clusters

of villages included former inhabitants of Bethelsdorp, former inhabitants of Theopolis, a group of *basters* from the Somerset and Graaff-
Reinet districts, a predominantly Gonaqua group from Xhosaland, a
party from Enon in Uitenhage, and a mixed group of mostly penniless
applicants from throughout the colony.[36]

The initial project had been to give land only to those Khoisan who
already possessed a certain amount of property. Stockenstrom gave in,
however, to the flood of demands from the propertyless throughout the
colony, on the urging of James Read Sr.[37] Thus, about 4,000 of this het-
erogeneous population came to Kat River "without any money or
utensils of any kind."[38] Nonetheless, they received almost no material
assistance from the government. "They have cost the government nothing beyond the salary of their minister [Thompson], from fifteen to
twenty mudes of Indian corn, and a few more of oats given them for
seed the first year 1829, and the loan of muskets, together with a little
ammunition given them for their own protection as well as that of the
country in general," remarked Stockenstrom approvingly in 1836.[39]
Hendrick Joseph of Kat River had commented on government policy
with more bitterness in the previous year: "I have been here 4 years,
and got my ground lately – but we have had no assistance – why did
not the Government give us spade, and pickaxes, as General Craig did
to Genadendal? – I was obliged to get into debt with the 'Cold French-
man' to procure these."[40]

During the first year, as the settlers were carving out their land and
digging irrigation courses, the poor had "nothing to eat while they cultivated their ground, except wild fruits of the earth, Caffre melon,
nooysboom roots, wild berries, &c, or what they might get from their
friends who were better off. Many of them had no implements of husbandry; some made ploughs altogether of wood, without an ounce of
iron upon them, and hired oxen to plough, and gave their labour in
return as pay; they were badly off for seed the first year."[41] In addition,
government prevaricated for several years before handing over the title
deeds to land. Indeed, only a few actually received these deeds – with disastrous consequences in the wake of rebellion, as we shall see. Many of
the landless – newly arrived or not yet assigned land – perpetuated traditional patterns of clientage by living on the land of others, contributing to problems of overcrowding which would become acute in the
1840s. The Gonaqua in particular were attached to the system of accumulating *bijwoner* clients, frequently from outside the colony, to herd
their cattle and help with the harvest. These clients tended to accumulate
their own cattle and ultimately to add to the squeeze on land.[42]

Despite such obstacles, many at Kat River fought to succeed. "They
had to form dams across the river and watercourses, sometimes to the

depth of 10, 12 and 14 feet, and that sometimes through solid rock, and that with very sorry pickaxes, iron crows and spades, and few of them ... They had to cut roads also on the sides of mountains of considerable height."[43] "I have a piece of land at last," said a Mr. Hendrik in 1835, "and I have brought out my water courses, and if they let me alone I will cultivate my ground, as well as I have brought out my water courses – We have come from the shambok and must I go back again to it, or to work for *one* goat in the year ...?"[44]

The settlement quickly gained a precarious prosperity; white visitors in the early years, including the antagonistic acting governor Colonel Thomas Francis Wade, commented on successes in what they saw as the linked areas of education and economic advance.[45] By 1833, a population of 2,114 owned 250 horses, 2,444 head of cattle, and 4,996 sheep and had reaped 2,300 muids (or 6,900 imperial bushels) of wheat and barley. Rose Innes reported solemnly, using the English administrator's calculus of "civilization," that "besides temporary cottages of wattle and daub, they had built twelve substantial stone houses, planted thirteen orchards and completed fifty-five canals for irrigating their allotments, of which forty-four measured 41,750 feet in length, or in round numbers twenty-four miles."[46] During a period of dearth before the 1835 war, Kat River kept Graham'stown supplied with food.[47] On the verge of war, in December 1834, stock holdings had risen to 5,406 black cattle and 8,925 sheep and goats; in the war itself the Kat River settlers would lose an estimated £30–40,000 worth of property, including two-thirds of this stock.[48] In 1845, despite these great losses, the value of fixed property, livestock, and annual produce of Kat River was estimated at over £65,000.[49] "I was much struck with the simple, but neat, appearance of many of their cottages, surrounded with their gardens and cultivated fields," attested Innes in 1839. He praised the settlement's intensive cultivation and use of irrigation. "Really, at present, the Kat River is one of the most interesting sights in South Africa."[50]

Despite these glowing encomiums, many Khoisan did not wholeheartedly adopt western lifestyles at Kat River. Housing provides a telling example. It is hard to know what Khoisan housing at Kat River really looked like, because the settlement was portrayed by its missionary supporters, and some Khoisan spokespeople, as a centre whose domestic virtue was expressed in its western-style housing, while the settlement's many critics, particularly the labour-hungry wool farmers of the region, attacked in parallel supposedly slovenly housing and domestic habits to argue that the Khoekhoe were incapable of improvement and therefore not deserving of land. There are few statements about housing at Kat River which do not hide political agendas. Nonetheless, it is telling that accounts of rebel housing in 1858 would reveal very few dwellings with more than two rooms, and most with only one for entire families.[51] Of course, the lack of "respectable" housing among rebels points to the greater propensity of the poor to rebel – and, as we shall see, government tried retroactively to justify the dispossession of rebels by pointing to their inadequate building and development of the land. That said, the uniformity of reports suggests that in practice many inhabitants had not created private domestic space in the manner so beloved of missionaries, nor had they arranged their family life in consequence.

The same anonymous and relatively hostile observer of the foundation of the settlement, cited above, commented that those of "mixed race" at Kat River built "tolerable huts" and adopted European farming methods but many among the "Hottentots" preserved their old modes of dwelling.[52] Indeed, the writer observed, those who came from Theopolis had earlier built furnished, western-style houses on their plots of land at Theopolis on missionary urging and at personal expense, but in fact they continued to live in "some conical kafir hut, or 'pondok' at the rear, that was the real domicile, where, seated on a mat or skin spread on the floor, the proprietors eat [ate], drank, and slept, comfortably in the smoke with which such miserable tenements are generally filled, never interfering with the fine sitting and bed rooms in the front." When the inhabitants left Theopolis for Kat River and wanted to be reimbursed for their expenses in building houses, the LMS refused, to the fury of those who felt that they had wasted their capital.[53] This account has overtones of the colonial obsession with the duplicity of the Khoisan, their supposedly ability to appear one thing and yet to be another, which would be particularly intense in the wake of the rebellion. It is hard to know how much to take at face value, and yet the writer's account of Theopolis builders realizing that western-style houses were a poor capital investment rings true. Since so many houses would be burnt down by the Xhosa in both 1836 and 1846, any conviction that fine houses at Kat River were a risky use of scarce resources was doubtless correct. The writer may also have been right that, for many, living communally in one room was a preference, as well as a product of poverty and economic caution.

Despite class differences at Kat River and differing attitudes to "European" cultural attributes, at least some of the inhabitants of the Kat River settlement (or at least those whose opinions missionaries liked to record) accepted to some extent the contract held out to them. That is to say, they agreed to become "civilized" – more like white people in material culture and more like evangelical Christians in religion – and to receive in return justice and, if not prosperity, then at least equal access to the white economy. Underlying such acceptance were, however, ideas that had appeal even to those outside the missionary ambit. Many stressed the need to restore stolen land and thought of the Kat River settlement, only thirty miles by two in size, as the beginning of a wider process of land restoration. Also important was the concept of "national" regeneration. Certainly, white liberals such as Read and Pringle had made a great deal rhetorically of the idea of regeneration and the passage from "savagery" to "civilization." Many of those, like Andries Stoffels, who agitated for temperance or literacy were also, however, calling for the healing and recreation of a community broken by colonialism. Although the point is hard to prove, it further seems likely that older divisions into clans, now all smashed, were being replaced by a sense of a pan-"Hottentot" nation, stretching even beyond the boundaries of the Cape Colony.

The idea of regeneration was particularly potently expressed through the struggle to establish schools and educate the "rising generation" for a more hopeful future. The great symbol of "national" redress and renewal was thus the acquisition of literacy. Since Christianity was frequently known as "the Word" among both Khoisan and Xhosa, and the "Hottentots" were termed the "people of the word," the coming of the Bible as a trigger of national regeneration could be mixed in a neat metaphor with the coming of literacy. This was a powerful trope even before the foundation of Kat River. "Before the word of God came among us," said one speaker at an LMS Auxiliary Missionary Society meeting in 1826, "we were despised and oppressed by all men, but now we have liberty to go where [we?] choose, now we are a church of God, and assem[bled?] for the extension of Christ's kingdom."[54] "I was surprised when the Bible came among us and asked the reason but no one could tell me; the reason was the oppression of the Hottentots which God saw," said Hendrik Smit in 1834.[55] This metonymic identification of the Bible with relief from oppression helps explain why so many became eager to read it; one also notes, however, that many people actually memorized portions of the Bible and were able to repeat them aloud, in keeping with an essentially oral culture.[56] The 1828 report of the committee of the Bethelsdorp Adult Sunday School, headed by James Read, reflects both Read's urgent sense that literacy and knowledge of the Bible would "leaven" the Khoekhoe and the nonetheless limited spread of literacy: "Although your committee rejoices at what has already been done, for 'tis a pleasant consideration that from time to time 500 Adult Hottentots are receiving instruction, that aged Hottentots can be taught to read the Bible, yet what is this 500 compared with the great number of those belonging to Bethelsdorp and still less compared with the whole nation of the Hottentots; greater part of which are destitute of such privileges. We must therefore encourage all the Monitors and Scholars to more vigilance and zeal in this great work till the small Leaven has leavened the whole Lump."[57]

Literacy was linked with political gain by many on the mission stations and at Kat River. At the Philipton anti-vagrancy meeting of 1834, speakers exulted in the fact that young men were writing down the speeches. "Mr. Bergman (a Bushman)" said, "I always saw pen and paper with my Master – but now I see them used by my friends the Hottentots"; another speaker thanked God that the "Hottentots" were now able to write and defend themselves.[58] In the Theopolis public meeting against the Vagrancy Act, Philip Campher exulted: "Since our king, the king of England, has ruled us, we are become men, and the missionaries have done that for us that our forefathers never thought of. In olden times no Hottentot could have read this resolution [holding it out in his hand] and hence the old men should have been here to have described to you their former condition."[59]

By 1834, there were seventeen schools among the LMS-affiliated section of the population, in addition to four infant schools, all staffed by local people under the supervision of James Read Jr, eldest son of James Read and Elizabeth (née Valentyn). "Their unwearied activity directed by the younger Mr. Read is the soul of the system," testified Rose Innes, "and I cannot but admire the efforts they have made for personal improvement under considerable difficulties."[60] A total of 700 children attended school.[61] Exiled from Kat River in 1835 and concerned about the state of its schools during the war, James Read Jr recalled the "greatest anxiety" expressed by "the people" to have their children well educated. "Every time that they returned from the market, every time they came home from taking out contracts to supply to troops with barley and oats, they would come into the schoolroom and say 'Mr. Read, you must teach our children well'"[62] Conflating the desire for education with the escape from slavery, the same letter from Read expressed cogently the theme of national regeneration from a liberal evangelical perspective: "The improvement of the Hottentots was such that their friends supposed them now to be taking their final exit from that state to which slavery naturally reduces a people. Their enemies stood aghast. It was quite pleasing to a contemplative observer to see how gradually the people threw off the shackles which their circumstances had put on them, to see ignorance fall from the eye of the mind as it had been scales and they receiving sight; the sunken eye of despondency brightened at the hope of a better day."[63]

AFRICA REMADE AND BRITISH
ABOLITIONISTS

This type of idealized vision of the Kat River settlement as a regener-
ated community was vigorously upheld by white evangelical humanitarians in south Africa and in Britain itself. British uses of the settlement need to be placed in the context of the debates around the abolition of slavery and its aftermath. The year 1833 saw the abolition of
slavery in the British empire, in the midst of great white anxiety about
the capacity of freed blacks in the West Indies to function in economically viable and orderly communities. As noted earlier, Thomas Fowell
Buxton had become the parliamentary leader of the abolitionist forces
by this stage, inheriting the mantle from William Wilberforce. A comment from one of Buxton's own constituency supporters epitomized
the public-relations problem confronting abolitionists: "He [the sup-
porter] differed from him [Buxton] in this respect, that you must
change the nature of Africans before you can make them different from
that which he had always considered them, an indolent race and prone
to idleness."[64] In particular, the anti-slavery camp was worried about
the lengthy apprenticeship period which was to accompany the end of
slavery, and anticipated a West Indian effort to pass local vagrancy legislation which would perpetuate slavery under another name.[65] All
these factors made the south African example, as Robert Ross has sur-
mized, of more importance to the anti-slavery lobby than the number
of Khoisan or their political importance actually warranted.[66]

In the early 1830s, John Philip kept the Buxton family, still his chief
political contacts in England, regaled with a stream of information
about the success of the Kat River settlement. "The day before yesterday at breakfast you were, as you very often are, the subject of our
conversation," wrote Buxton's daughter Priscilla to Philip, "and I
inwardly resolved I would begin my letter to you that very day – I am
glad however I was prevented ... for *at night* to our very great delight
arrived your two most interesting and I may say precious letters ... I
read the whole dispatch aloud to our little party and we did indeed
receive them with heartfelt joy and I hope thankfulness. My Father
walked up and down the room, almost shedding tears of joy to hear of
the prosperity and well-being of these dear people."[67] Buxton used
such information in parliament and in missionary meetings. During the
apprenticeship debate in the House of Commons, for example, to cite
again Priscilla Buxton to John Philip, Buxton urged "the safety and
advantage of entire liberty, on which he brought in your Hottentot case
and read several pieces from your letters – It told very well. Stanley
answered most cleverly but weakly and the Debate was hot for sever-

al hours."[68] The liberal *Edinburgh Review*, making similar arguments in 1834, upheld Kat River as "a still more remarkable and unexpected proof of the advantages of freedom and free labour over servitude."[69]

In 1835 Thomas Pringle, for fourteen years a prominent liberal activist at the Cape, and later secretary to the Anti-Slavery Society, clearly had a double agenda in describing the Kat River settlement at length in his 1835 memoir, *Narrative of a Residence in South Africa*. Pringle's comments directly tackle contemporary arguments that recently freed slaves were natively indolent, not "ready" for full freedom, and in need of a lengthy period of apprenticeship followed by restrictive legislation. One notices how thoroughly the Khoekhoe before Ordinance 50 might, as propaganda needs warranted, be portrayed to the British public as degraded and brutalized by previous legal restrictions, in order to contrast with their morally and economically redeemed state in independence. For Pringle, the Khoekhoe were "a people, debased by oppression and contumely, till they had sunk below the level even of the negro slaves, their brothers in misfortune; a people for generations made a byword to the civilized world for stupidity, indolence, improvidence, intemperance." This "nation of African helots, to the number of 30,000 souls" had, however, "been raised from the dust, at once and without any preparation (except what a *few* had received at the missionary institutions), to the full rights of free men." Despite the suddenness of the change, akin to the abolition of slavery, their "quiet and orderly demeanour" was notable. Pringle remarked that "above all the astonishing progress of the colonists of the Kat River, during the five years they have been placed on probation as free citizens – the entire change of character in many formerly considered vagabonds, as soon as they were enabled to emerge from conscious degradation, and the door of manly ambition was flung open to them – their self-government, their docility, their singular temperance,[70] their industry, their ardour for religious and general instruction, and their steady good conduct – are facts which speak volumes ..."[71] The language of manliness is particularly striking: the Khoekhoe – an implicitly male group – had been emasculated by oppression but were now free to assume "manly ambition."

It was during the investigations held by Buxton's so-called Aborigines Committee, however, that Kat River really came into its own as a community of the imagination. Here, for example, is Buxton coaxing answers from Andries Stockenstrom: "[Chairman] 2230. Can you conceive any contrast more decisive than that between the degraded and low and miserable condition of the Hottentots before the passing of the ordinance [50] and the improved condition and industry and the moral advancement of these people settled at the Kat River? – It astonished me. I am supported in that by very good authority, whose opinions are on record."[72].Kat River, and the Khoekhoe as a whole, thus became exemplars both of the benefits of a free market to Africans and, for abolitionists and liberals in Britain, of freedom.

VAGRANCY LEGISLATION
AND THE MEANING OF FREEDOM

In 1833 acting governor Colonel Wade proposed a Vagrancy Ordinance at the Cape. The draft legislation was drawn up after his departure by the newly formed Legislative Council in 1834, the year in which slavery was formally abolished at the Cape Colony. The attempt echoed that of former slave colonies elsewhere in the empire to bind former slaves back into the web of labour servitude. Meanwhile, in Britain itself, the issue of domestic vagrancy legislation and the need to revamp the poor laws had already been a topic of vigorous discussion in the early 1830s in the run-up to the New Poor Law of 1834. Indeed, leading British evangelical abolitionists Zachary Macaulay and James Stephen were among the candidates considered for posts as commissioners under the Law of 1834, while British evangelicals tended to support the Poor Law's abolition of the paternalist structure of outdoor parish relief and its attempts to increase labour mobility.[73] For liberal economists and evangelicals alike, it was, in David Brion Davis's phrase, the "very essence of emancipation" for both paupers and free people of colour "to remove the arbitrary constraints that stifled responsibility and concealed individual worth."[74] Freedom was a double-edged sword and included the freedom to fail economically as a result of individual choice.

None of this was in itself a guarantee that restrictive vagrancy legislation would not be passed by the Whig government under the different circumstances of the colonies, as the very real worries of Buxton and his fellow abolitionists attest. Nevertheless, it was an intellectually incoherent step which demanded particular justification. In these circumstances, the south African example was seen by anti-slavery activists as an easier test case to win in the Colonial Office than a West Indian one opposed by the still-powerful planter interest. In the meantime, the administration, which had enough on its plate maintaining apprenticeship for freed slaves and overseeing controversial compensation payments to West Indian planters, was quite anxious not to wave a red flag in front of the anti-slavery lobby by allowing blatantly "proslavery" legislation in a relatively unimportant colony. In such a context, Colonel Wade's parting shot was far less likely to be ratified by London than white south Africans realized at the time.

At the Cape Colony itself, debate around the proposed vagrancy ordinance was necessarily passionate. The draft ordinance permitted the arrest as a vagrant of any person on the road who was unable to provide an account of how he or she had subsisted for the past three days. It re-entrenched the provision that all people must have a legal place of abode. A person found guilty of being a vagrant by a local official could either be set to work upon the roads or compelled to find a master and a legal place of settlement. As in the Caledon Code, there was no distinction between the genuinely destitute and a person with, for example, cattle but no master. Although putatively colour-blind, the act clearly aimed at expelling Khoekhoe from land in the margins of white property on which they had been eking out a living, particularly in the wake of Ordinance 50: the proposed ordinance criminalized traditional Khoisan subsistence strategies such as digging for roots and redefined unallocated crown land as implicitly the collective property of whites rather than that of Khoekhoe. The act further sought to compel nonwhite labour.[75]

While the issue was being discussed by the colonial legislature, white agitators lobbied Cape Town vigorously for the passage of the legislation. In opposition, the colonial Khoisan were the chief lobbyists against the act. This was the first instance in their history of a widespread petitioning movement. Khoisan commentators reinterpreted and radicalized the meaning of "freedom," which they tied closely to the restitution of land.

Khoisan people organized meetings to oppose the Vagrancy Act and to draw up memorials to the colonial and British governments. In terms of formal structure, these occasions were modelled on the anniversary meetings of local mission-support groups, such as auxiliary missionary societies or educational fundraising groups – themselves ultimately modelled on the annual May meetings of the LMS at Exeter Hall. Resolutions in tune with the purpose of the meeting were proposed and seconded from the floor, and each was addressed through a series of speeches; detailed minutes were recorded, as happened at the LMS's own annual meetings. In the case of British meetings, accounts of the speeches and resolutions would be published in society journals and sent, among other destinations, to African mission stations. Experience with the LMS, in other words, had made the Khoisan aware of the benefit of a particular type of publicity. The theatre of a public meeting, in addition, was congenial to both Xhosa and Khoekhoe culture, since both societies in the days of their independence held large public gatherings to discuss important issues. As well as a number of petitions and letters to the newspapers, two detailed accounts of meetings survive from the mission station Theopolis and from Philipton, Kat River, which, despite the problem of being in translation, are valuable sources given the paucity of material written by the Khoisan themselves at this stage. Even in translation, the speeches reflect a particular style of oratory with the use of blank verse and striking metaphors.[76] Apparently all the speakers were male.

A number of speakers used a self-consciously liberal language (in an 1830s' rather than modern sense of the term "liberal"), making reference to rights and liberty. The speeches were also characterized by what Stanley Trapido has termed "Hottentot nationalism." "I stand here my nation to advocate your cause," declared Philip Campher, "and if it should be that I must die for my nation, I could almost do it, provided that would secure your liberty."[77] Ordinance 50 was hailed again and again, although speeches breathed a conviction that the problems of crushing poverty could be resolved only through further land grants and truly equal economic treatment, such as equal assistance to white and nonwhite smallholders. The point of the vagrancy law was clearly seen to be the economic oppression and enslavement of the Khoekhoe, in a system from which nonwhites were more excluded than missionary propaganda acknowledged:

That as far as the Hottentots are concerned, whatever may be the sentiments of his Excellency the Governor and the honourable council, it is impossible for memorialists to look at the spirit of the letters published in favour of the new law, the arguments used at public meetings convened to petition in favour of it, and to recollect how often some of us have already been taunted by being told we have been long enough our own masters, that in a little time we shall find ourselves in other hands, and not to feel that it is for cheap servants, "the compulsory service," the compulsory service of memorialists, that the whole of this clamour about a Vagrant Act has been raised. "It is a law in place of the old law" that is wanted; a law that will tame the "restlessness" of the Hottentots; a law to punish the Hottentots as felons before a felony has been committed; a law for the "prevention of crime"; a law that will encourage proprietors and capitalists to engage in extensive "improvements and speculations." Hottentots are to be obliged to enter into contract for more than one month, and their "restlessness" is to be subdued for the sole benefit of their masters.

Some speakers were even more blunt. "The law now proposed is a law the effects of which I have seen. It is a SCREW, and the same SCREW that we had before and you must all petition against it." Others commented on the racial nature of the legislation: as Slinger Booy said, "the vagrant law is for black men."[78]

Reports of both the Philipton and the Theopolis meetings convey a sense that the oppression of the "nation," whatever was meant by that term, had begun to be alleviated, but that this would be halted by the return of pass laws and forced labour. Winvogel Smit said, for example, that "when he was very young he saw his Father going with bow and arrows – he saw his Mother tied to a Window and branded by a Boor, and after she got loose she had to flee through the wilderness among the wild beasts and I had alone to take care of the Boor's sheep – but today am I here where I see one of my own Nation sitting and writing in the Chair and the children reporting behind, for which I thank God."[79] "Today we sit in the shade," said one Magerman, "and you know if you go out of the Sun into the shade, and go back into the Sun again then you feel the Sun still more – and if this law passes then we will feel it more than ever – for then we must stand the heat of the Sun, and the 'Baas' above all."[80]

Not all nonwhite people in the colony agitated against the imposition of vagrancy legislation, although most seem to have been united in opposition. Nonetheless, a group of eighty mostly baster men from the Kat River settlement who worshipped at the church of government agent William Ritchie Thomson signed a petition in support. An organizer of the anti-vagrancy Kat River petition wrote an anonymous letter, signed *Niet een van de tagtig* (not one of the eighty), to the *South African Commercial Advertiser*. He claimed that many of the signatories of the other petition did not comprehend what they had signed, and had in any case been led astray by a misguided sense of identity politics:

I know not whether it is because they belong to the Government Church, or that it is, as many of them say, that they are not Hottentots, or that it is, as some of them have said, that they belong to the Government, and therefore cannot contradict the Government, even though it should do wrong; – but further I cannot find one that knows what he has signed. They say that no paper was brought forward and explained, and it seems they had no Dutch copy as we had. Thus some say that they have signed for more money for the nation, others say they were told it was the Governor's letter, which was to be signed; and others of the people seem to be greatly at a loss.[81]

This is a particularly interesting letter, whether or not it is a completely accurate portrayal of the motivations of the opposition, not least for the author's claim that the petitioners did not consider themselves "Hottentots." This implies that a "Hottentot" identity was to a certain extent a matter of choice. It also suggests that a "Hottentot" identity claim might carry with it certain oppositional politics – as might not worshipping at the "Government Church." In any case, the views of the nonwhite community were evidently not uniform, fissured as communities were by differences of ethnicity and class.

The overall trend, however, was one of strong Khoisan opposition to the ordinance. This "forms a new era in the politics of the Colony," commented the missionary at Theopolis, George Barker, to the LMS

director, "the Hottentots as a nation petitioning for their Civil rights."
The patriotic Barker felt the issue to be a peculiarly English one, pointing out that those of the Legislative Council who opposed the act were
all English. The great shock to him was that the English settlers were
unanimously against Khoekhoe rights; he seemed to expect no better
of the Dutch. Barker was thus left to appeal to a vague higher moral
authority in England, and to muse "how soon a man forgets his British
birth-right in a slave colony."[82] Nonetheless, as he wrote to a friend,
"we are in the minority, but our side is the most respectable, the most
reasonable, and the only liberal part of the community."[83]

For the Khoekhoe, also, these events marked a public break in their
relationships with the English settler community. From the beginning
of LMS activity in south Africa, even the Dutch missionary Van der
Kemp had upheld the benevolence of England in contrast to the moral
depravity of the Dutch farmers. The very villages of the Khoekhoe
were named after English reformers and LMS officials – Buxton,
Wilberforce, Hankey – although the vast majority of the Khoisan
spoke Dutch (or Afrikaans, as it was coming to be) far more fluently
than English. By the 1820s, as we have seen, the English missionary critique of the Dutch echoed that of the Commission of Inquiry, namely,
that the Dutch peasants were corrupted by their sloth and by their
reliance on slave labour. Great things were at least rhetorically expected of the 1820 English settlers, supposedly energetic products of an
economic system which promoted morality. By the 1830s, however, the
myth of the just nation had to revert to the homeland alone. "The
British nation is our friend," said Platje Jonker, "but some Englishmen
are turned upside down, they stand on their head, they see things
wrong and want a new law." Andries Stoffels told the Select Committee on Aborigines, "When the English settlers first came, the Hottentots said 'our friends have come'; and they used to work together, to
assist each other; but I do not know what to say of them now."[84] James
Read Jr claimed in 1851: "The first event which shocked the moral
sense of the Kat River Settlement, and the native population generally
in the colony, and which affected their confidence in the Colonial Government, was the framing of a Vagrant Act ... an act which contained
the essence of despotism, which exhibited the strong prejudice entertained against the natives by the colonists, as well as indicated a want
of proper regard to the rights of men and fellow-subjects ..."[85]

In the end, Lord Aberdeen of the Colonial Office disallowed the Cape
Vagrancy Act. The imperial centre could still be portrayed as more just
than the local state. Even the Kat River Rebellion of 1851 bore a complicated relationship to this conviction. While a significant number of
rebels had lost all faith in the righteousness of the distant British admin-

istration, others were furious over the creation of a democratic colonial legislature, from which they were convinced they would be excluded, and which they construed as Britain handing them over to the mercy of the white settlers. This, however, is matter for a later chapter.

WAR WITH THE XHOSA AND ITS AFTERMATH: EVANGELICAL INFORMATION NETWORKS

Even as the Khoisan were agitating against vagrancy legislation, other colonial crises were coming to a head. Organized groups of Afrikaner settlers began to leave the Cape Colony in search of lands beyond British control in 1834. Between 1834 and 1840, several thousand Africaners, almost all from the eastern districts, trekked away from British control; historians have estimated their number as anywhere from 6,000 to 15,000. Even the lower figure would have been one-tenth of the white population of the Cape Colony. They settled in areas that would eventually, after much conflict and migration, become the twentieth-century districts of Natal, the Orange Free State, and the Transvaal.[86] In the colony itself, tension was building yet again between white colonists and the Xhosa. For years, colonial settlers and the Xhosa had been jostling against one another, and indulging in mutual cattle theft, on frontier lands which had once been Xhosa territory. Under the acting governorship of Lowry Cole, attempts were made to drive the last remaining Xhosa back over the Keiskamma: the British launched brutal organized attacks in 1831 and 1833, in which soldiers burnt houses and crops at a time of drought.[87] Flashpoints came from the commando system which was used by the colony to regulate cattle theft. A colonist had the right to summon a commando to pursue the spoor of his cattle into Xhosaland, should he find that they had been stolen. The Xhosa complained that these commandos often simply took substitute cattle from the first homestead they came to, and even killed people who tried to defend their property. Cattle thefts could spell death for a family, since milk was the main food source for the Xhosa.

In December 1834 the Ngqika Xhosa invaded their old territory and war erupted. Although many of the issues were the same as in previous frontier wars, this war had to be fought in the glare of publicity and public comment beyond south African borders: in that sense it was a modern war. The colonial Khoisan were compelled to fight on the side of the colony, in part in order to preserve their own position as allies of the British. Their actions, too, were magnified in the British public sphere. The aftermath of this war, during which the British humanitarian lobby was able to engineer the restitution of land to the Xhosa conquered during the war, marked a highpoint of liberal humanitarian influence on south African politics. This influence was the product of a confluence of circumstances which would never again be so favourably aligned. Nevertheless, the myth of humanitarian influence would continue to have an impact on south African politics through the collective memories of groups involved in all sides of the 1834–35 conflict.

In the run-up to the war, some Xhosa chiefs and some LMS missionaries tried to exploit evangelical and colonial information networks. These contacts did not prevent war, but they did affect its aftermath. In the 1820s and early 1830s, Xhosa chiefs had few reliable means to be in steady contact with colonial officials on the chiefs' own terms, despite the profound mutual influence of colonial and Xhosa societies. Missionaries were the most effective pre-war channel for correspondence, and indeed several chiefs maintained missionaries of the LMS and the Glasgow Missionary Society largely in order to use them as diplomatic agents. Relationships were not always good enough, however, for Xhosa chiefs to trust their missionaries, as Maqoma's travails first with the Reverend Kayser, who had a short temper and poor communication skills, and then with the condescending and domineering Henry Calderwood suggest. The example of W.R. Thomson's failure to be accepted as both imposed government agent and missionary at Chumie between 1821 and 1828 further illustrates the pitfalls confronting Xhosa chiefs who wished to keep lines of communication with the colony open.[88]

From 1829 onward, Xhosa leaders and other individuals also channelled occasional complaints through James Read owing to his strategic location at Kat River. Indeed, the anonymous account of the Kat River settlement written around 1851 and cited above claimed that Ngqika had wished Maqoma to be fostered as a boy with Read in order to cement diplomatic relations. According to this source, the Xhosa had compromised by sending a younger son, who had then been ignominiously expelled by colonial authorities.[89] Be this as it may, Read had found his undertaking at the Kat River at first "very dark," but by 1834 he was consoling himself by the thought that he was nonetheless diplomatically beneficial to the Xhosa. Although moving to Kat River had been "like occupying a stolen country," God had been "pleased to clear up the black Cloud by causing this settlement to prove a blessing to the caffres thus their minds have been reconciled to the Hottentots occupying this land ... We have [become] acquainted with their true situation with the colony and the abominable commando and Patrole system carried on and which threatened annihilation of the station but we have been able to give such information in a direct and indirect way so as ultimately we hope to check the evil and save the Nation and even make it a blessing to the colony."[90] Such hopes proved naively optimistic. Nonetheless, Read's information networks, including contacts and family ties between local Xhosa and Kat River inhabitants, provided material which ultimately accumulated in Colonial Office files.

As early as 1831, a case in favour of the Xhosa as good, rather than bad, "savages" was being painstakingly built up in London through Philip's correspondence with Buxton. Philip's key contacts included Read, F.G. Kayser of the LMS, and members of the Glasgow Missionary Society, active in Xhosaland since 1820. Philip also took extensive personal tours of the frontier districts; John Fairbairn, his son-in-law and editor of the *South African Commercial Advertiser*, and Alexander Bruce both accompanied him on trips.

James Read was probably Philip's most important informant – indeed, if Andrew Ross is correct, Read was in fact responsible for awakening Philip to the depth of the problems confronting the Xhosa of the eastern frontier.[91] Read had sporadic contacts with chiefs such as Maqomo, Tyali, and Botmane (who called the missionaries "our bush," according to Read Jr[92]), as well as having access to the Gonaqua from Xhosaland who, of course, maintained links with the Xhosa. Read had a particularly close relationship with Dyani Tshatshu, a Christianized small-scale chief who had been left at Bethelsdorp for education by his father while a boy.[93] Tshatshu had long worked as an occasional assistant missionary for both the LMS and the Glasgow Missionary Society.

In addition to relaying Xhosa complaints to Philip, Read also kept information flowing in the opposite direction. In 1834, for instance, Read wrote to Philip that he had "had the pleasure" of meeting with Maqomo, Botmane, Tyalie, and Tshatshu. "I read Mr. Fairbairn's proposed plan for the future management of the colonial intercourse with them, with which they likewise seemed highly pleased, and they requested me to express their heartfelt gratitude to Mr. Fairbairn and yourself for your indefatigable and continued service for them, and they hope you will not get tired of them."[94]

After 1833, when the Xhosa were forbidden to cross into the colony, the missionaries became the frontier Xhosa's only means of communication with the colonial authorities, to the great frustration of the chiefs. In 1834 the chiefs indicated their desire to Read to have a "person who can write and act for them who is not a Missionary but they said he must be a person recommended by Dr. Philip, yourself [Fairbairn] and me," since the Xhosa had numerous reasons for complaint against the colony and against the traders living in their country but no channel for redress.[95]

Maqoma suffered even more than the other chiefs from the apparently arbitrary whims of a distant colonial government. In 1833 Wade, then Cole's military secretary, expelled Maqoma and Tyhali from their last grazing grounds beyond the Tyhume, at a time of drought. A local official allowed Maqoma back for a time; the governor then overrode his permission. By this point, Maqoma thought the Europeans were making fun of him. In the same year, Maqoma was ignominiously dragged by a drunken and abusive colonial patrol from the Kat River settlement, where he had come to attend a missionary meeting and to make a speech.[96] This speech was translated by Read Jr into English for the House of Commons Select Committee on Aborigines from a Dutch translation made at the time, and is worth noticing in the context of the arguments I have been making above about Xhosa contacts with missionaries and about the Khoekhoe language of national regeneration. The speech may simply indicate that Maqoma was good at buttering up missionaries; nonetheless, the choice of words is interesting (even through the double translation), as is the tone of grievance at English downgrading of Xhosa dignity:

My friends, I am very glad to meet you on an occasion like the present; the Word of God has done great things for you; the Word of God has brought you to life again. It was only the other day that you were like dogs, and oppressed; it is the Word of God that has given you these churches and the lands you have ... Ye sons of Gayahe Kakobul, I have brought you here to behold what the Word of God hath wrought; the Hottentots were but yesterday despised and oppressed, as to-day are we, the Caffres. But see what the Word of God has done for them: they were dead; they are now alive; they are men once more. Go and tell my people what you have seen and heard; I hope we long to witness in our own land such scenes as the present. God is great who hath said it, and will surely bring it to pass ... The time is coming when Caffreland will be covered with missionaries: I have done.[97]

From the banks of the Keiskamma, Maqoma shortly afterwards attempted to get in touch with Philip, whom he had met on several occasions, in an effort to have his grievances presented to the colonial government. He dictated a letter to the LMS missionary F.G. Kayser, who translated it aloud into Dutch; the "mechanic" James Clarke then wrote it down in English and transmitted a copy to Philip.[98] It read: "Sir – As I and my people have been driven back over the Chumie River without being informed why – I should be glad to know from the Government what evil we have done ... Good Sir, I do not know why it is that so many Commandoes come into this country without sufficient reason. We do no injury to the Colony, and yet I remain under the foot of the English. I would beg the favour of your inquiring at the Government for me the reason of all these things, and I will thank you."[99]

Philip forwarded Maqoma's letter to Buxton, and through Buxton, he hoped, to the Colonial Office, as part of the mission superinten-dent's numerous packages containing exhaustive summaries of evidence and warnings of the danger of renewed war – into which Philip believed the colonists were trying to provoke the Xhosa in order to take their land. Buxton was preoccupied by the abolition issue until 1833. In late 1833, however, Priscilla Buxton was able to report that her father "is now beginning to turn his mind a little to your Part of the world and your horrid commandoes. He has been with Mr. Stanley several times about them but begins to fear that little will be done without open war and public opinion."[100]

The issue was thus downplayed but on the agenda for two years before the actual outbreak of war on the frontier. Sir Benjamin D'Urban arrived as the new Cape governor on January 1834 with LMS-influenced instructions from Lord Stanley to make alliances through treaty with independent chiefs who would control their own subjects in exchange for recognition of their independent authority and annual gifts.[101] Philip initially had influence over D'Urban but rapidly lost it. The information he continued to send Buxton nonetheless provided a formidable backlog of evidence which, in the aftermath of the war, the Colonial Office would have to admit it largely ignored. This information also helps explain why the Colonial Office was so impatient with D'Urban's extraordinary slowness to provide his own justification for the annexation of Queen Adelaide's Land.

The issue could not have been kept on the boil without the tireless work of Buxton's female relatives, notably Priscilla Buxton, his daughter, and, above all, Anna Gurney, cousin of Buxton's wife and "beloved partner" of his sister Sarah Maria. Indeed, the women of Buxton's family played a remarkable, and largely unnoticed, role in the political activities of himself and his son-in-law Andrew Johnston, including the great anti-slavery campaigns. Anna Gurney collected Philip's papers and wrote speeches for Buxton on the basis of them. It was her idea to press for a wide-ranging committee to consider the issue of the treatment of aborigines in British settler colonies as a whole, and to provide a means to investigate specific abuses in south Africa, without obtaining the prior consent of ministers. She also wrote much of the south African section of the committee's final report.

In December 1834 war broke out on the Eastern Cape frontier as the frustrated followers of Maqoma and the other frontier chiefs at last poured into the colony in the wake of attacks on members of Xhosa "royalty" and other insulting incidents which would have been taken as in themselves declarations of war by the Xhosa.[102] D'Urban quickly removed the Reads from Kat River as dangerous agitators. On 15 July

1835 Buxton moved in parliament for the establishment of a House of Commons select committee to investigate the status of "aborigines" in British settlements, claiming that four to five million lives were in the balance. Buxton was surely granted what at once became known as the "Aborigines Committee" not because of concern over south Africa but because three days earlier he had unsuccessfully pressed for the temporary suspension of compensation payments to ex-slave-holders in Jamaica and for a committee to investigate abuses against ex-slaves by the planter community. Lord Grey had been instrumental in ensuring the motion's downfall. The Anti-Slavery Society and the British and Foreign Society for the Universal Abolition of Slavery had already sent out circulars, appealing to the troops to stand prepared to re-enter the battle on behalf of blacks who were free only in name. In this charged context, it may well have seemed safest to fob Buxton off with what sounded like a much more innocuous committee.

On 26 July, Buxton drew up in rough a series of "heads of resolutions to be presented at the Aborigine Committee meeting." These summarized what would become the evangelical humanitarian gospel concerning "savage" nations. Being a "civilized" Christian did not confer "a right to rob and murder the Inhabitants of barbarous Countries." Furthermore, "– In making settlements in barbarous countries we must necessarily inflict various evils on the inhabitants – for these inevitable evils we ought to give them all the compensation in our power." The British had a duty to diffuse the "knowledge – Law – Religion" which providence had given them, "to a population standing with much need of them." In sum, "the population of barbarous countries occupied or visited by us amounts to many millions upon whom our influence may be for the greatest of blessings – Has hitherto been the heaviest of calamities!!" [103]

On the committee itself, Buxton's men outweighed the pro-colonial forces headed by Sir Rufane Donkin, William Gladstone (in his earlier more conservative incarnation), and one Bagshaw. The future governor of the Cape Colony, Sir George Grey, also sat on this committee. The whole thrust of the committee's information gathering was to illustrate these tenets: that colonial occupation had had a disastrous impact on "barbarous nations," and that now England must atone through bringing these communities Christianity, civilization, and a moral commerce which would lead to economic prosperity for all. From the outset, this was a project charged with Christian narrative, not only in its prescriptions but in its very structure. Atonement was a central evangelical notion. Indeed, the whole committee might be seen as leading to a kind of confession followed by atonement, some hope of salvation, and the averting of God's just wrath.

In late 1835 the Colonial Office's attention began at last to be drawn in earnest to the Cape Colony with D'Urban's announcement that he had concluded the frontier war by annexing some 7,000 square miles of Nguni territory which were later to be known as Queen Adelaide's Land. In the meantime, Philip had forwarded to Buxton a sensational document, namely Campbell's record of his interview with a certain Mr Glass, Colonel Harry Smith's interpreter. Glass had been present at the murder of Hintsa, when the Xhosa chief had been invited to the British camp for talks, even though he had not been directly involved in the war. In the official version, Hintsa had agreed to a wide-ranging treaty surrendering the Xhosa cattle which he had been keeping safe during the war and permitting the annexation of a huge swathe of territory; he had then, however, panicked at the last minute, treacherously tried to flee in order to avoid handing over the cattle, and in the confusion had been tragically shot. This was bad enough. Glass's testimony, however, was that Smith had forced Hintsa into the treaty through threats to shoot him and his family; that Hintsa had not in any case understood the treaty properly; that he tried to flee on realizing what Smith's version of the treaty was and after having received death threats; that Hintsa was trying to surrender when he was shot; that two "Hottentot" soldiers had refused to hurt him; that a young member of the British army's Guides, William Southey, had come up behind them and blown the top of Hintsa's head off at point blank range before hacking off his ears as souvenirs; and that Smith had watched the whole thing in a state of apparent immobile depression. The evidence was crucial not only for the sensational manner of Hintsa's death but for the fact that it seemed to invalidate the treaties with the Xhosa by which the war had been concluded and the land ceded. Anna Gurney included this information in a pamphlet which she drew up for the Colonial Office, then very much under the control of the permanent under-secretary, the evangelical and abolitionist James Stephen.

There is a letter from Buxton to Anna Gurney in the Buxton papers which I shall quote at considerable length because it sheds unexpected light on the passage of the Glenelg dispatch.[104]

You remember how cold used to be my reception at the Colonial Office when I talked about South Africa – Kaffirs – aborigines ... I went there yesterday – saw Glenelg, Gray – and Stephen – I found the atmosphere changed to blood – almost to fever heat. They talked of Hintza – Southey – Philip – Somerset – D'Urban with absolute familiarity – knew more about – and spoke more indignantly against Commandoes than you or I ever did – intimated that they would revoke D'Urban – restore the country to its owners – acknowledge error and the national disgrace – place Stockenstroom as Deputy Governor at the frontier, in an independent office – prohibit the entry of an armed man into Kaffirland – in short take the most extravagant of our whimsies – and they talked of them as sober sense – bare [justice?] – and the least which could be done for a race whom we have so grievously oppressed – Stephen said "here have I spent my life in this office – I never knew that we had received a line from Stockenstroom – I only knew that you were crack-brained about aborigines – I have now dived into all this neglected correspondence – I have read every word of the evidence before the Committee – and I am lost in astonishment, indignation, shame, and repentance – It gave me a fever said he ... It is already agreed, that you shall have protection of aborigines in every Colony where we get into contact with them" and fifty other things equally surprising and delightful ... and what has worked this mighty revolution? It was done in a cottage ... by a statement signed by T.F. Buxton but written by one Anna Gurney. What effect this may have on the latter I know not – but I can answer for it – that the former – little as is his share of it – laid awake almost all last night from an exuberance of gratification and thankfulness – The images rising – of the hunted people restored to the land – of Macomo now so dejected – soon amazed with unlooked for relief – The "irreclaimable savage" – the "just and necessary war" ... "The gratification with which I inform your Excellency that your humane orders have been executed and I this day destroyed 400 cottages, laid waste the soil tilled like a Garden – killed some and drove away the rest of these ungrateful Barbarians" – "the annexation for ever of the rich and fertile province of Adelaide to his Majesty's Dominions" – These and a thousand other impudent and damnable lies – detected, repudiated and exploded positively.[105]

There was, of course, a great deal of political horse-trading to be done, much of which John S. Galbraith brings out well in his book *Reluctant Empire*. It should also be borne in mind that Buxton had a mercurial, highly excitable temperament. Nonetheless, this incident underlines some key factors: the small size of the Colonial Office and the arbitrariness of the information that reached it, in an age of retrenchment when it had insufficient staff to cope with the ever-growing number of colonial dispatches; and the personal nature of the decision-making process, albeit within broad policy guidelines accepted by the government as a whole. Thus, Thomas Pringle could write to Philip, in reference to the appointment of Spring Rice, a quondam abolitionist, to the post of colonial secretary in 1834, that he doubted whether he and Philip would be much better off with Spring Rice than with his predecessors, since Spring Rice was "woefully ignorant of facts as regards the Cape, and consequently is far too much in the hands of Hay and such like." Hay was the under-secretary who feuded incessantly with Stephen; this again underscores the role of personality politics in the Colonial Office. Pringle planned to write at length to Spring Rice, "but the difficulty is to get those people to read any thing either in print or MS."[106] Under such circumstances, the Colonial Office might well ignore critical issues such as the build-up to hostilities in the Eastern Cape through sheer lack of time and man-power, or even of political will. On the other hand, a few determined people with only one or two valuable contacts, such as Philip and Pringle, could make a dent on a single-issue campaign, if they could attract the right person's attention and, preferably, back up requests with the threat of public embarrassment. The role of the powerful James Stephen was particularly crucial for evangelical networks. In this context, the LMS was able to function as a powerful political actor, however briefly and in a way unduly dependent on the energy of a small group of people.

Influence was also dependent on the power of what was perceived as a "pro-negro" lobby, in a period when black labour issues around the world were being grouped together by politicians on all sides.[107] This is underscored by the seeming coherence accorded by the Select Committee on Aborigines to "primitive" societies around the world in contact with white settler communities. Umbrella organizations such as the Aborigines Protection Society (founded 1837), the Africa Insti-tution (a legacy of the foundation of Sierra Leone by Clapham Sect evangelicals in the 1790s), the powerful anti-slavery societies, includ-ing the Agency Society (headed by James Stephen's brother George Stephen) and the Society for the Abolition of Slavery (founded by, among others, Stephen's father), and the "Saints" lobby in parliament headed by Buxton added to the potential clout of an individual politi-cian. In such a climate, Buxton could reasonably say that, if Spring Rice was not "friendly" over south African vagrancy legislation, then "to war with him we must go – and sooner than submit to have the Hottentot again virtually enslaved by a pretended Vagrant Act I would once more raise up the body of the religious people of England and Scotland."[108]

This was not, however, a climate that would long endure past the loss of abolition as a mobilizing issue, nor could it survive the growing conservatism and more narrowly "religious" focus of the evangelical parliamentary lobby in the 1840s and 1850s even as, ironically, evan-gelical tenets became increasingly accepted by the social mainstream. Not seeing the political process at first hand, however, the Khoisan and Xhosa peoples of the colony were left with a strong sense of the fair-dealing of the British home government of the day, which would con-tribute to their growing sense of anger and frustration through the 1840s as seeming promises failed to materialize.

THE THEATRE OF RENEWAL: THE SOUTH AFRICAN DELEGATION TO THE HOUSE OF COMMONS SELECT COMMITTEE ON ABORIGINES

In 1836 John Philip sailed again for Britain, this time to testify before the Select Committee at Buxton's instigation. He was accompanied by a political delegation consisting of Andries Stoffels, Dyani Tshatshu, James Read Sr, and James Read Jr. This group all testified before the committee. They travelled throughout England giving speeches, including particularly crucial ones at the May meeting of the LMS at Exeter Hall.

Throughout all this, the Africans were generally presented as tangible incarnations of the remade Africans. John Philip showed off Stoffels and Tshatshu at evangelical gatherings as "ocular proof" of the feasibility of remaking primitive man, in opposition to D'Urban's cutting phrase "irreclaimable savages." At one London dinner party, the Africans answered questions, offered speeches of thanks to Buxton, received the good wishes of Buxton, and sang hymns "most melodiously." "When they sat down, Dr. Philip well said, 'These are the irreclaimable savages!'" An eye-witness report of the same dinner party rather chillingly suggests the extent to which Philip demanded the denial of African identity. Mrs. Upcher wrote with enthusiasm to her friend Sarah Gurney: "Enter Dr. Philip with his tail, *such* a tail! – The Caffre chief a fine personable man – handsomely dressed in a military coat blue & gold, he has a good forehead & more – I will go no lower, lest I should affront you as I have affronted myself for fancying (I will just whisper in Sarah's ear) that his mouth caricatured a Negro's! Oh! for shame to breathe it especially as their champion protests there is *nothing African* in his countenance." [109]

At the same time, the LMS-sponsored publication the *Missionary Chronicle* (attached until 1837 to the *Evangelical Magazine*) contributed to the propaganda effort. Engravings of Stoffels and Tshatshu were published as frontpieces to different issues of the *Evangelical Magazine*. These frontpieces were usually given over to leading evangelical clerics; readers often cut them out and put them on their walls. [110] Tshatshu was presented in as regal a manner as possible, with the above-mentioned blue and gold military coat giving him an appropriately western air. Stoffels, on the other hand, was portrayed as the honest worker in a sturdy overcoat. In the meantime, the *Evangelical Magazine* printed a woodcut of a "humane and generous caffre" rescuing a white child during the war of 1835, with an affecting text that explicitly attacked the appellation "irreclaimable savages" and stressed the virtue that existed even in primitive conditions. This was a long intellectual journey for men who began with a fervent commitment to the hegemony of original sin over non-Christian societies. One notes that the Xhosa warrior is not wearing anything that looks like a Xhosa kaross, but rather a garment that suspiciously resembles a Roman toga, with delicate sandals and what might be mistaken for wings protruding from his right shoulder. The overall effect is very much that of the god Mercury. Implicitly, the print recalls the Greeks and Romans – a universally acknowledged example of virtuous heathen, who also provided better propaganda value than Africans qua Africans.

The culmination of the Africans' visit to England, from the LMS's point of view, was their starring role at the May annual meeting of the missionary society at Exeter Hall. At this meeting, the LMS directors finally delivered the stinging critique of colonialism and endorsement of his south African policies for which Philip had been angling for years; it also seems to me that the south African experience had radicalized a number of key figures. The LMS secretary, William Ellis, attacked the "secular colonialists," in a veiled attack on the British conduct of the 1834–35 war, including references to the murder of Hintsa: "They have threatened mothers that they would shoot their boys; the mothers have stood before them, and said, 'You will not fire now.' They have fired! They have shot men through women and children through their parents. They have mutilated and mangled the corpses of their enemies. They have cut off their ears and brought them away as trophies, and the individuals who have done this have been celebrated in poetry, and that poetry has been exhibited on the doors of a Christian church." Secular colonists, then, sought territory and the extension of commerce. Missionaries, in contrast, did not want to colonize territory but to colonize the mind. "No – what they want is men. They want places where there are inhabitants and not the territory; and their object therefore is to go and colonize the mind. To bring down, as it were, the ideas and principles of Heaven; those holy sentiments which we have from God's word; and to deposit them in the understandings and hearts of the inhabitants; and thus to elevate and to save them."[111]

One wonders what Tshatshu and Stoffels made of this call. Tshatshu, who had lost his land in the aftermath of the war despite his neutrality during it, and many of whose followers deserted him because of that neutrality, attempted to call his audience to fight for justice in south Africa in the name of the Bible. He also made comments about the treaty concluding the war, suggesting that he saw the voyage to England as a political mission:

When we signed the treaty with the British Government at the Buffalo River, a paper was read, which told us that we then became the children of England,

and if one with yourselves, let us enjoy the privileges of Britons. Many Englishmen in the colonies are bad, but I will hardly believe that these Englishmen
belong to you. You are a different race of men – they are South Africans – they
are not Englishmen ... Some people are afraid to stand out for the truth; other
people won't stand out for the truth; and others are ashamed of the truth; truth
is the most important thing in the world. It is honest. Where there is no truth
there is no true honour. We must all adore the truth – every man. The word of
God is truth. The word of God tells us to do good; and the word of God tells
us to stand on the truth. We ought to adhere to the truth, and to stand by the
truth. I will not say more.[112]

The long speech of Andries Stoffels (known among the Khoisan for
his skill in oratory) was an extraordinary statement of Khoekhoe
dependence on missionaries. Stoffels's aim in part was to overturn
D'Urban banishment of Read and his family. His speech was also, in
my opinion, an attempt to call in the bargain which the Khoisan felt
they had made with the British: justice for "civilization." According to
Stoffels, "the Bible charmed us out of the caves and from the tops of
the mountains. The Bible made us throw away all our old customs and
practices, and we lived among civilized men. We are tame men now.
Now we know there is a God; now we know we are accountable creatures before God." The liberation of Ordinance 50, the "charter of our
liberties," was metonymically identified with the coming of literacy:
"When the fiftieth ordinance was published, we were then brought to
the light. Then did the young men begin to write and read. Through
that ordinance we got infant schools, and our little infants have been
instructed, and they are making progress in learning." Stoffels
launched an appeal to the British which eradicated cultural difference
and called on British cultural superiority:

You, the posterity of the old Englishmen, I address you on this occasion; I am
standing on the bones of your ancestors, and I call upon you, their children,
today, to come over and help us. Do you know what we want? We want
schools and schoolmasters – we want to be like yourselves ... We are coming
on; we are improving; we will soon all be one. The Bible makes all nations one.
The Bible brings wild man and civilized together. The Bible is our light. The
Hottentot nation was almost exterminated, but the Bible has brought the
nations together, and here am I before you. You have the honour, I claim nothing. You gave us your pence and your farthings, and here am I; I am yours.[113]

There can be few clearer statements of what it was, and cost, to be
remade in the evangelical image.

The final report of the 1835–36 Select Committee represented the
British apogee of Africanist evangelical radicalism. It was also the

product of the last parliamentary session in which the middle and upper-class "Saints" remained committed to an Africanist parliamentary platform in alliance with broadly based popular pressure groups out of doors. These "pro-Negro" pressure groups dissipated after the abolition of the slave trade removed their primary focus, while parliamentary evangelicals in the 1840s became more conservative, less united, and more concerned with domestic religious issues. The settler lobby continued to gain importance. African missionaries accordingly lost a great deal of their immediate domestic political clout. The "Aborigines Report," passed in haste as the king died, was rushed through on the cusp of an election in which key abolitionist leaders lost their seats or stood down. No equivalent pressure group would arise in the mid-nineteenth century to ensure that the ideals expressed by the report, undergirded by Buxton's private opposition to much white colonization, could be put into legislative practice.

On the other hand, the report developed the idea of Britain's national mission towards the "savage races" of the world as a gesture of atonement for her past sins towards aboriginal peoples. Buxton's arguments that Britain had a duty to spread Christianity and commerce proved more enduring than his opposition to the further acquisition of white territory in Africa. The debates of the 1830s fed into Victorian theories of empire and civilizing mission, although the roots of Buxton's beliefs were in an eighteenth-century evangelical Protestantism which was far from upholding worldly empire.

The Aborigines Committee failed to have a substantial impact on south African politics in the long run; in the 1840s, the LMS ceased to have much clout in London on south African issues. Furthermore, the harsh language of the committee was eviscerated before the report was released: saliently, the material on the death of Hintsa was suppressed as a condition of getting the report published before the close of a session after which Buxton knew he would lose his seat.

In the short term, however, the committee had an important influence on south African affairs – and behind the scenes the issue of Hintsa was politically important. The testimony of Andries Stockenstrom, who was commissioner general for the eastern districts until 1833 and who agreed with the missionary critique of militarist frontier policy, was particularly telling. The reputations of the settlers were blackened, and D'Urban thoroughly discredited. On 26 December 1835 the new secretary of state, Lord Glenelg, signed a dispatch which ringingly endorsed the committee's conclusions, blamed the settlers rather than the unjustly treated Xhosa for the outbreak of war, ordered the abandonment of Queen Adelaide's Land, instituted a treaty system which would become known as the Glenelg system, and recalled Sir Benjamin D'Urban. "I know not that a greater real calamity could befall Great Britain, than that of adding Southern Africa to the list of the Regions which have seen their aboriginal Inhabitants disappear under the withering influence of European neighbourhoods," Glenelg averred.[114]

The Glenelg treaty system proved, however, relatively ineffectual at containing the tensions within the colony and its neighbouring territories. War raged again in earnest through the late 1840s and early 1850s. At the conclusion of hostilities, Sir Harry Smith was called back as governor of precisely those territories which had been returned to the Xhosa in 1836. This time, the settler version of events would prevail.

At Kat River and Theopolis in 1851, many of the religious beliefs we have been examining would fuel rebellion. Christianity would also contribute powerfully to the terrible Xhosa cattle-killing, when in 1857 Maqoma led his people and those of neighbouring groups in slaughtering all their cattle and burning all their corn in the sure expectation that a young girl had correctly prophesized that these sacrifices would bring the return of the Xhosa dead and the return of peace to the land. In a sense, the Aborigines Committee was an ironic marker of joint identity between British and south African evangelicals. Such evangelical ideas as God's providential judgment on nations, atonement, millenarianism, and the conviction of God's action in history would influence both mid-Victorian ideas of empire and African political movements with millenarian overtones such as the Kat River Rebellion and the Xhosa Cattle Killing.

Andries Stoffels was already ill with tuberculosis when he spoke at Exeter Hall. A few months later he would die in Portsmouth harbour on a boat waiting to sail for the Cape. James Read would write Stoffels's biography: a short account of the life and conversion of a perfect evangelical.[115] Dyani Tshatshu would return to south Africa, to occupy the lands which the government had returned to him. In 1848 he would join the Xhosa in their second-to-last uprising against the colony, and in 1851 he would fight on the side of the united Xhosa and Kat River rebels. In 1857, however, he would refuse to burn his corn and would ride with missionary envoys around Xhosaland, attempting in vain to persuade the desperate chiefs that God spoke through missionaries, and not through the mouth of a nine-year-old prophetess.

8 Rethinking Liberalism

The successes of the 1820s and 1830s were real. They gave many Khoekhoe and, after 1838, many formerly enslaved people increased freedom of movement and liberated the Khoekhoe from the worst abuses of the "old system" while permitting a few to hold land. Larger urban communities of Khoisan and the formerly enslaved grew up in towns such as Grahamstown. The attachment of the Khosian community to Ordinance 50 as a prophylactic against vagrancy legislation ran deep, as the public meetings of 1834 indicate. The civil rights of nonwhites were far better entrenched in 1840 than in 1800 and people experienced much less direct personal violence than in the early years of the nineteenth century.

Nonetheless, the late 1830s and 1840s saw political and economic trends that would culminate in the rebellion of 1851, so surprising to all but the best-informed of white colonial observers. Despite the complacency of many British administrators, many Khoisan did not get what they had wanted from their attempted bargain with the colonial state. The costs of military collaboration with the colony proved high, given the economically devastating aftermaths of the wars between the Xhosa and the colonial state in 1834–35 and 1846–47. This was particularly true for those living at the Kat River settlement, parts of which were burnt down in both wars. Perhaps most important, throughout the 1830s and 1840s, the colonial state allocated crown land, including much land previously used by Khoisan without formal title, to an ever-growing influx of British settlers in the Eastern Cape. It was soon clear in the aftermath of Ordinance 50 that, despite Khoisan hopes for collective restitution, the colonial government did not plan to give much land to the Khoisan as a community beyond the Kat River settlement and possibly some former mission lands, while the costs of entry to the individual market in land were prohibitive.[1] Insufficient land and the sale of remaining crown lands, especially to white farmers engaged in large-scale capitalist agriculture, squeezed those Khoisan trying to survive on the margins of white "property" and led to overcrowding in the Kat River settlement and at mission stations. This was all the more so as land-intensive stock farming remained the economic survival method of choice for many Khoisan, who had few other means to invest capital. The growing movement of Khoisan into the towns of the Eastern Cape such as Grahamstown, Port Elizabeth, Cradock, and Uitenhage was doubtless also linked to the land squeeze.[2] The labour-hungry white English settlers of the frontier districts of the Eastern Cape, led by conservative wool farmers such as Robert Godlonton and Mitford Bowker, abused their nonwhite fellow citizens both economically and in the more nebulous form of a flood of negative comment in such outlets as the *Grahamstown Journal.* The "free" market proved, in sum, neither as free nor as beneficial as its most ardent advocates had hoped, however little individuals wished to return to the "old system" of physical coercion and pass laws.

A second significant trend of the 1840s was that tensions between white missionaries and Khoisan church communities became more evident, even though the political alliance between Khoisan and the LMS remained relatively firm. It may simply be, of course, that tensions are more apparent in the archival record – but it does seem to me that Khoisan church communities as a whole, rather than individuals in isolation, challenged white missionary control of the church in a way that was novel. Like other Africans elsewhere, many in the "Hottentot" communities sought to make an independent use of Christianity and to have greater local control over their churches and ministers. At the same time, the protection of mission stations was less essential, and missionaries themselves were losing political clout on the imperial stage. Christian converts therefore had fewer ties of dependency to white missionaries. A number of missionaries showed an increasing tendency to distance themselves socially from their congregations as the local white English-speaking settler community became larger and more entrenched, and as missionary activity became more respectable overall in the eyes of the white community. This trend may also have contributed to struggles over the control of the church.

This chapter focuses on the material issues of the land question and the economic conditions of mission stations, with particular attention to the example of the rural LMS station of Hankey. I turn in the next chapter to contests over the control of Christianity in this querulous decade and to ideological shifts within the LMS itself. The vicious struggle between James Read Sr and many of his fellow missionaries in the mid-1840s provides a springboard into the larger issue of contestation among various white and black groups over ownership of the gospel. In the book's final chapter I examine the roots of rebellion and the mobilization of religion to different ends in that military conflict.

MISSION-STATION ECONOMICS IN THE 1830s AND 1840s: THE EXAMPLE OF HANKEY

Throughout the 1830s and 1840s, competition for land in the vicinity of mission stations, coupled with the widespread use of cattle pounds by white settlers to prevent cattle pasturage on "private" property, put growing economic pressure on mission Khoisan. Many Khoisan found themselves losing stock and being forced to work as farm labourers. With increased pressure on grazing land, the mission station could no longer function as a place on which people seeking to work as independent stock farmers might protect cattle and other resources.

The example of Hankey in the 1830s and early 1840s, illuminated by some frank family letters and the indiscretion of quarrelling parties, is instructive. A brief history of the station's troubles sheds light on the interrelated themes of Khoisan struggles to obtain property rights in land, tensions within Khoisan communities themselves, and the economic problems of mission stations with limited access to resources.

The station of Hankey, established in 1822, was originally seen by John Philip as a place at which members of Bethelsdorp could grow grain, since this was impossible at Bethelsdorp.[3] Doubtless he saw this as a way to promote civilization through agriculture. The station was set up on a farm on the Gamtoos River bought by the LMS directors for the use of the Khoisan inhabitants of Bethelsdorp and for the establishment of a seminary. It was partially paid for by members of Bethelsdorp. Many of Hankey's early inhabitants (such as Paul Keteldas, whose struggles for land are detailed by V.C. Malherbe) in fact used the station as a base for woodcutting, since the farm was closer than Bethelsdorp to the Tzitzikama forest.[4] Bethelsdorp residents contributed 6,035 rixdollars out of the total purchase price of 16,000 rixdollars. Those contributing money would later be termed "subscribers." Years later, subscribers affirmed "that they were given to understand that the farm was to be bona fide their property with the exception only of a small portion of it to be reserved for a seminary."[5] The 1822 deed of transfer, however, in fact made the farm out legally to Dr. Philip and to several directors of the LMS, although it did affirm (according to the missionary John Melvill in 1839) that the place was bought "for a Corn farm for the Hottentots of Bethelsdorp and for a seminary for the children of Missionaries."[6] As Jane Sales argues, there was probably never any clear and mutually agreed-upon understanding between all parties about whether all Bethelsdorp people or only financial contributors would be able to use land at Hankey, nor indeed exactly what the property rights of the LMS were relative to those of the Khoisan.[7] The stage was set for bitter conflicts over land use.

The first missionary, J. Georg Messer, was resented, according to John Melvill, for removing people from the missionary dwelling house and other buildings which he considered LMS possessions but which the people, who thought they owned the farm, saw as their own property. A series of missionaries then proceeded throughout the 1820s and 1830s to admit people to the station who had not been "subscribers."[8] Before 1831, Messer found the situation of the station so bad that he asked to be transferred. In early 1831, however, on the verge of his departure, there was a religious revival at Hankey which led to an influx of newcomers. By 29 April 1831, Messer was reporting that "Sunday last the chapel was far too small, [so] that even a great number of the auditors were sitting on the ground and there was such a movement that I almost was not heard when preaching." Few eyes were dry, he testified. Slaves came from adjacent farms, some of whom would go into the bushes to pray after service. "Almost all night long we can hear them singing and praying by whale lamps." Jubilantly, Messer added on 9 May that "daily we see newcomers from all quarters, wishing to live on the place." The enthusiastic Messer, who thought when he first came that the "most part of the inhabitants lived almost like brutes," now (unsuccessfully) rescinded his request to leave and admitted many newcomers.[9] However real the religious revival, movement to the station was also prompted, as other missionaries recognized, by the completion in 1831 of a watercourse to irrigate the station, making agriculture viable. The fact that existing inhabitants had paid fifty cows to have this work done was to prove another source of friction in the future.[10]

Over the following decade, membership fluctuated. The new missionary in charge after Messer, John Melvill, admitted 100 new families in 1834. Several years of drought thereafter and the war caused severe hardships and forced many to seek work away from the station. After 1838, former slaves released from their apprenticeship bonds provided a further source of newcomers to both Hankey and, in greater numbers, to Hankey's outstation, Kruisfontein. There were approximately six hundred inhabitants on the station's books in 1838, but the land was unable to support them, particularly given the fallibility of the irrigation system and its frequent need for repairs.[11]

In the 1820s, when Hankey's population was relatively sparse, conflicts were contained, according to Jane Sales. Once a viable irrigation system had been established and new land acquired in 1834, quarrels among an enlarged population over access to irrigated land became pressing.[12] John Melvill attested in 1839 that nonsubscribers and subscribers deeply resented one another. Subscribers said that their land was being taken from them and seem to have thought of nonsubscribers as their clients and dependants, while nonsubscribers resented the labour demands made on them by subscribers. As one old man told nonsubscribers who were seeking to build new irrigation channels on land that subscribers saw as theirs, "the ground belongs to us and would not have been obtained from Government had we not bought Hanky. We wish to keep it for our children."[13]

By the late 1830s, the large majority of the original subscribers were no longer living at Hankey, most being based at Bethelsdorp. LMS attempts to mediate failed: an apparent compromise in 1833 whereby anyone who paid 100 rixdollars could purchase in freehold one of sixty plots of land (representing the original 6000 rixdollars) was accepted at a public meeting at Bethelsdorp but thereafter vehemently rejected by subscribers.[14] "I received you under my wings," complained one subscriber to non-subscribers in a bitter public meeting in 1838, spreading his arms wide, "and now you have rebelled I will shake my wings and drive you away."[15] A nonsubscriber attested, "I was a slave among the farmers I came here in the hopes of being free but I now find I am still a slave."[16] Such comments suggest that subscribers saw themselves as landowners with the capacity to acquire clients to whom they offered protection, in accordance with long-standing Khoekhoe models of clientage. Nonsubscribers, in contrast, described by Melvill in 1838 as the "most respectable class belonging to the institution," seem to have appealed to a more typical missionary model of economic individualism to explain why they did not owe labour for land.

Be that as it may, the quarrel underscored, on the one hand, the power of the white missionary to distribute land and, on the other, the limits placed on his authority by the mission community itself. Subscribers were furious with Melvill and in consequence subverted his authority. "For several years," the missionary complained in 1838, they did "everything in their power to injure my usefulness and have privately misrepresented my conduct in a manner that prevented me from defending myself."[17] He ultimately gave up and fled to a position in the Western Cape community of Paarl. The conflict also suggests that some at least of the mission Khoisan did want to own land, rather than holding it communally through the missionary society. In the wake of quarrels, and ongoing poverty, many left the station in 1838, some to work for farmers, others to cut wood, and a few to go to other mission stations. Most who had a little property left, including all craftsmen except one carpenter, departed.[18] This suggests that those with the fewest resources chose to remain.

Other conflicts appear to have arisen over whether or not the missionary could impose his vision of a moralized and moralizing economy on inhabitants. It has been a constant theme of this book, as of the work of Jean and John Comaroff among others, that missionary views of appropriate work for converts were profoundly shaped by ideological factors other than economic rationality.[19] Like so many other missionaries, John Melvill and James Kitchingman (who briefly ran the station jointly) thought that the inhabitants of Hankey would be more moral if they farmed. Their 1831 annual report cited an early American missionary to the Amerindians, David Brainerd, on the moral necessity of "husbandry" and affirmed that "we are most anxious to give any assistance and encouragement in cultivating the soil, for experience teaches that no employment can be more beneficial to them in promoting their temporal as well as spiritual welfare, being the means of preserving them from manifold temptations to which they are constantly exposed in procuring a livelihood at a distance from the Institution."[20] Woodcutters were a particular source of anxiety, as Sales underlines. Out of missionary control, woodcutters pursued "disorderly" lives, often "lived together without the sanctions of marriage," and supposedly traded timber for brandy.[21] One can imagine that such attempts to exert control over the lives of inhabitants were resented by some and may well have contributed to tensions between subscribing Bethelsdorp woodcutters and the nonsubscribing farmers who arrived later.

There is more concrete evidence, marshalled by Sales, that the efforts of Melvill's successor, Edward Williams, to introduce weaving for almost entirely moral reasons were resisted. Just before his return to England in 1843 for reasons of ill health, Williams defended his attempted introduction of weaving against charges that local handicrafts could not compete against machine-manufactured goods from England. He never intended competition, he claimed: "It was introduced simply to occupy time which the young people spent in gossiping and sleeping ... If I had continued at Hankey I should have continued it even at a pecuniary loss for the sake of its moral effects." He felt that weaving and spinning would fill the "leisure hours" of "young women" in particular.[22] Here, from the perspective of inhabitants, was an almost pointless disciplinary regime. Comments by Williams's successor from 1842 onwards, John Philip's eldest son William, suggest that residents successfully resisted it: weaving failed, Philip reported, "because the people could not endure the confinement, became spirit-less in the work, and could not compete with a European market."[23]

By the time of Philip's tenure, from 1842 to 1845, Hankey was plunged into seemingly permanent crisis, as problems with the irrigation system persisted. Struggles over land were a major contributing factor. There remained little grazing land in the vicinity of the station. White farmers had established a pound to which they sent inhabitants' cattle whenever beasts strayed onto "private" land. As William Philip informed his father in 1842, "the People are suffering under much poverty and the farmers around are very oppressive upon them in sending their cattle to the Pound, and I really see very little prospect of the advancement of this People in civilization while they cannot accumulate property; and, instead of accumulating property on our Institution, there is not one I can safely say from personal enquiry, who came on this place possessed of a few cattle, who has not lost two-thirds and in many cases all."[24] Between 1841 and 1843, many more people left the station to look for work, most going in family groups to live with local white farmers. Some left part of their family at the station; the wages farmworkers received were, however, barely sufficient to supply their families with food.[25] By 1843, in the wake of renewed drought and a plague of locusts, there was little to eat on the station, and Philip was describing being interrupted in his letter-writing by people asking for food.[26] Another telling feature of Hankey, reflecting the flood of former slaves into mission stations, was that in the early 1840s there were "almost as many slaves as Hottentots" living at the station.[27] Despite, or perhaps because of, great poverty, religious revival rocked the station again in 1841, particularly affecting young people. "They had a most awful sense of their guilt and the wrath of God against sin," according to Williams. "Several were bordering on insanity and we found it difficult to keep them from utter despair."[28]

The rural areas around the station may have been even worse off materially than Hankey. Before he arrived at Hankey, William Philip visited Cambria, an outstation of Hankey. There he saw two people with smallpox. Given his medical training, Philip decided it was his moral duty to stay in order to try to prevent an epidemic, despite a lack of medicines and the fact that his wife was about to give birth. It proved an education in poverty. "I have seen sickness & misery in the underground dwellings of our manufacturing towns; but I never saw starvation and nakedness staring disease in the countenance as it did here," wrote Philip. "Many had not even a mat to prevent the contact of their ulcerated bodies with the ground, and he was fortunate that had an old blanket or sheep skin or a [gunny?] bag to cover him from the cold at night & from the rain – while in all the houses scarcely a

morsel of food was to be found."[29] Some 18 per cent of the inhabitants
of Cambria, or 25 people, died. Philip was convinced that at least five
of them died of starvation after recovering from smallpox, and he
pointed out that the weakened state of the inhabitants left them unable
to resist even the mildest attack of the illness. Philip himself developed
the disease but survived, while his wife gave birth unscathed.

At Hankey itself, Philip reported, inhabitants were forced to hire out
their children or to send them into the forest to collect roots and
berries.[30] Consequently, school attendance fell off dramatically. In any
case, the schoolhouse was "an old ruined building, most miserable,"
the equally miserable schoolmaster's house let in the rain, the school
had no books, and the putative infant school teacher, the wife of the
schoolmaster Kelly, had by 1843 "given up entirely attending it and, I
might also say, everything else."[31] By that point, Philip and Kelly were
trying to keep the few remaining children in school by "employing
them in making plaits for straw hats," as so many poor rural women
and children did in Britain itself. "They might earn sufficient to feed
and clothe themselves if they worked constantly at it and had a little
more practice."[32] William's young Scottish wife, Alison, oversaw the
straw plaiting while looking after her own two small children, supervising the hatmaking of inhabitants, running an evening school, and
attending prayer meetings – as Philip explained in order to justify her
not taking over the infant school as well.[33]

Despite the poverty which meant that the station could offer few
resources, the church remained an important centre for the community – at least according to William Philip, who, of course, was scarcely
a neutral observer. Many of those who were living at a distance with
farmers returned to Hankey or went to its outstation of Kruisfontein
to hear preaching on Sundays, some travelling up to thirty miles to do
so; almost all came when communion was offered.[34] Philip, who disapproved of facile adherence to Christianity, said that mission-station
inhabitants continued to press for church membership, "religion being
honourable and fashionable among them." This type of comment
dovetails with the ambivalent attitude of earlier missionaries Kitchingman and Melvill to the "very violent" religious feelings, expressed
through "cries and tears," of those affected by the revival of 1830–31.
Kitchingman and Melvill worried that expressions of repentance and a
change of heart, not always valid even at times of the worst persecution of the church, were all the more to be distrusted "among a people
who all assent to the truths preached and among whom a profession of
Christianity is honourable."[35] William Philip thought that south
Africans were more enthusiastic about church membership than those
"at home" (presumably Scotland), and he worried about hypocrisy.[36]

Overall, this type of evidence, in which missionaries expressed ambivalence about Khoisan religious enthusiasm, suggests that many people based at Hankey probably did see Christianity and the church as an important part of community life.

The station was not entirely devoid of resources. William Philip was considered a source of healing by blacks and by Afrikaners alike and thus in that sense a material resource. He was continuing the tradition of his predecessor Williams, who had visited the hospital at Cape Town for a while to get some medical knowledge, and had then become a local doctor, to whom "both Europeans and natives" came for medicine "from all quarters." Williams charged "Europeans" but urgently requested the LMS to send out supplies of medicine from England so that he could give free medicine to the impoverished "natives."[37] In contrast to his predecessor, William Philip had actually taken courses in medicine as an undergraduate, and subsequently become an enthusiastic apostle of homeopathic medicine.[38] He had brought a large supply of homeopathic powders and pills from Europe and treated people within a wide radius of the station, thus presumably changing the regimes of those previously treated by the more orthodox Williams, although it is not recorded whether anyone noticed. It is unclear whether Philip's mother, Jane, was being tactful when she averred that William's advice to take arsenic and sulphuric mercury for "erruptions" on her hands had come too late to be useful,[39] but William in any case bombarded his family with medical information. Many locals in the vicinity of Hankey thought that his healing powers went beyond his pills. "The People [inhabitants of Hankey] have most implicit belief in my globules," Philip affirmed, "and the Boers send from all quarters. These latter affirm among themselves that I cure from 'Sympathie,' as they call it, in other words 'Jugglery.'"[40]

The fortunes of Hankey took a dramatic turn for the better in mid-1843 when Philip was able to raise a loan from the LMS (which he soon overspent) to enable the people of Hankey to construct an 250-foot tunnel to irrigate their lands, supposedly resolving once and for all the irrigation question. This was to be Philip's life work in some quite literal sense, as this one-time sailor with the South Seas Company ironically drowned at home with his nephew in 1845 in the very river which he was in the process of harnessing. The urgency with which Philip promoted the project before his death at the age of thirty is revealing. The people were extremely eager to complete the tunnel, he claimed, because it would mean that they could finally hold usable land at a station that had previously had almost nothing but dry land. The ownership of land remained ambiguous under Philip's plan: erf-holders (*erf* is Dutch for an allotted plot of land) would have had to pay three

pounds within a specified period after taking occupation but did not
become outright proprietors. They would have had to sacrifice the land
if dismissed from the station, and would have to have agreed to build
a cottage "according to our model determined on."[41]

According to Jane Sales's discussion of the later years of Hankey, the
station became relatively more prosperous, if still poor, once the tunnel was completed, although the spectre of starvation did not recede
for many years; in 1849 drought once again created mass hunger and
caused many to leave the station. There were also floods: after a terrible flood in 1847, the entire village was relocated on higher ground
with money raised from mission supporters in Britain, and the irrigation works were once again rebuilt. The issue of land ownership
recurred. In 1855 William Ellis reported that the people still wanted to
be "the bona fide holders of the land, not simply tenants."[42] It was not
until the last decades of the nineteenth century, however, that the LMS
finally sold the land to inhabitants, not all of whom wished to buy.
According to Sales, "within a very few years after this was accomplished, the majority of the land was in the hands of whites, who used
the capital and the credit which they had at their disposal to turn Hankey into irrigated citrus plantations."[43]

This brief overview of the fortunes of Hankey underscores themes
that would recur elsewhere: struggles over land ownership within mission confines as well as outside, the slippage of "Khoekhoe" land into
white hands, the incursions of the pound on the capacity of Africans to
accumulate stock, the flight to underpaid wage labour in towns as well
as on white-owned farms, and the seeming entrenchment of Christianity as the dominant religion of mission communities and as a marker
of respectability. At Theopolis, Thomas Philipps, justice of the peace
and leader of a party of British settlers, established a cattle pound at
nearby Rietfontein in order to target the cattle of the people of
Theopolis in the wake of Ordinance 50. Since 1825, Phillips and the
inhabitants of Theopolis had been embroiled in a long, complicated
dispute with the colonial government over the boundaries of the station. Theopolis lost the argument, although debate dragged on into the
early 1830s. In the same period, not only were the inhabitants' requests
for more land refused, but pasturage that the mission Khoisan regarded as their own was formally distributed by the government to white
settlers. Overall, as V.C. Malherbe argues in her close examination of
the Theopolis economy in the wake of Ordinance 50, venal pound-
keepers and the loss of pasturage bled the mission Khoisan of their cattle, with a particularly strong impact on those families, like the Valen-
tyns, which had previously owned the most.[44] By 1850, Theopolis was
in a "parlous state," in the words of W.M. MacMillan, with neglected

buildings and few inhabitants.[45] Furthermore, Sotho and Tswana speakers came to be in the majority on the station in the 1840s, but no missionary there ever spoke either seTswana or Sotho, while Sales describes the activities of the "worn-out" elderly head missionary Christopher Sass in the mid- to late 1840s as "feeble at best."[46] Bethelsdorp did better. Nonetheless, as Clifton Crais has observed, taxation, poor wages, competition from Mfengu labourers after the war of 1834–35, and the 1838 drought combined to depress the economy and to drive increasing numbers of inhabitants into wage labour with local whites. Aloe-gathering and the salt pans provided cash with which to pay the opgaaf but could not create substantial wealth.[47] Once again the issue of land was central: Crais cites the 1844 observation of head missionary James Kitchingman that "'many Hottentots possess waggons & cattle, but have no lands on which to graze their cattle.'"[48] There were acrimonious disputes for many years over the piece of land known as Gorah which Bethelsdorp people used as a cattle post. In 1835 Grahamstown merchants convinced the governor to let them use the cattle post to feed their own oxen, and to expel Bethelsdorp people who had settled there. In early 1846 the government sold Gorah for good to a white settler.[49]

The local white economy squeezed rural blacks, with their minimal access to credit and capital, in unmerciful ways. Above all, without more land, the accumulation of cattle was difficult, and the promise of comfortable economic independence held out by the abolition of vagrancy legislation remained elusive. Rural mission stations suffered accordingly, even though their inhabitants were not subject to the same type of violence and servitude sanctioned under the "old system."

There was a corresponding movement of rural Khoisan to towns, where they often lived on the outskirts on crown lands in impoverished informal settlements and were perceived as squatters by white burghers.[50] "All the town is surrounded with huts inhabited by these poor creatures," wrote J.G. Messer about George in 1843. The movement to the towns seems to have outpaced missionary activity: Messer said that the "poor creatures" seemed to be "like sheep going astray without a shepherd and no proper care was hitherto taken for them," and that he had found similar conditions in Uitenhage when he first started working there.[51] By the 1840s, nonetheless, the majority of LMS missionaries in the Cape Colony were in fact working as priests in towns, ministering for the most part to "coloured" congregations which were segregated in practice, if not in theory, from wealthier white congregations. Some missionaries indeed ministered to both black and white, but often at separate services, held in different languages (English for British Congregationalists and Dutch for "coloured") and even in different buildings.[52] It was difficult for Khoisan to maintain stock in towns as well: new municipalities often tried to withdraw the right of Khoisan and former slaves to pasture stock on municipal commons.[53] The overall drift was towards prole-tarianization and wage labour in towns and away from missionary surveillance.

The Kat River settlement remained an exception to these generaliza-tions about the difficulties of capital accumulation in rural areas. Social stratification at Kat River, which partly echoed splits between wealthier "basters" such as the Groepe and Arend families and those who self-identified as "Hottentots," was also a testimony to the possi-bility of individuals accumulating stock and surviving as independent farmers.[54] Even the Kat River settlement was increasingly burdened by overcrowding, however, and suffered from the lack of new land.

Some of the increase in population in the Kat River settlement in the late 1830s and 1840s was due to the typically strong sense of obliga-tion felt by many residents to their extended networks of kin. Indeed, the 1834 memorial from Kat River against vagrancy legislation implic-itly affirmed the moral obligation of inhabitants to shelter others. It stated that "memorialists cannot contemplate the immediate effects that this Act will have on the prosperity of this Settlement, in driving multitudes to this place for refuge, as it has done to the Missionary Institutions, by which they may be eaten up and oppressed, and whom in their unfortunate circumstances, humanity will not allow them to turn away, without alarm."[55] Clientage relationships, and the general sharing of limited resources, contributed to overcrowding, but stemmed from a sense of communal obligation.[56]

Furthermore, Khoisan kinship networks were much wider than a narrow focus on "Hottentot" ethnicity or on the Cape Colony as units of analysis would suggest. Many "Hottentot" settlers had blood ties to former slaves and to whites (the latter frequently unacknowledged by whites, as we have seen). They also had strong links with Griqua com-munities on the highveld, and individuals moved from one area to another for economic or personal reasons. Andries Pretorius Sr went to Philippolis in 1835, for example, after his original erf had been appro-priated to build Fort Armstrong in the 1834–35 war and the erf he was reassigned at Blinkwater (modern-day Tidmanton) proved too close for comfort to the unpopular settlement of future rebel leader Her-manus Matroos.[57] He had earlier worked as a "native agent" in Philip-polis where, according to Martin Legassick and Timothy Keegan, he and other native agents had played a major role in the trade of con-traband articles, including ammunition, from the colony to the north.[58] Jan Pretorius, who may have been Andries Pretorius Sr's son, also left for Philippolis in 1835 "not to take up residence but to seek for work, having lost everything in the war of 1835, viz 8 oxen & 7 cows besides my crops being destroyed."[59] Bet Marcus's stepmother, in contrast, moved to the Orange River sometime in the late 1830s or 1840s to accompany her new husband after her partner at Kat River, Isaac Marcus, died.[60] Such links illuminate the sense of pan-Hottentot identity which would be so important a factor in the rebellion of 1850.

Of more immediate economic significance for the Kat River settlement were the family ties between Khoekhoe and Xhosa, particularly among Gonaqua and Gqunukhwebe. Colonial administrators typically sought to undercut these and to categorize people as one ethnicity or the other. As early as 1809, however, as Malherbe points out, Uitenhage magistrate Jacob Cuyler had confessed himself unable to "unscramble the omelet" and determine who was a "Ghonnan."[61] Only "Hottentots" and "basters" were eligible for formal land grants at Kat River. Nonetheless, many Kat River Gona, notably the settlers at Blinkwater under Andries Botha, had family and friends in Xhosaland to whom they offered shelter, often as clients, despite official prohibitions. The most disruptive of the magistrate Mitford Bowker's actions in his much-resented administration of the Kat River settlement was his burning-out and expulsion of the Gqunukhwebe and Mfengu clients of the mostly Gonaqua proprietors of the Lower and Upper Blinkwater, in a direct assault on the *bijwoner* system of clientage.[62] This system, by which landless labourers tended cattle in exchange for living space, had flourished on the overcrowded Kat River lands. The bijwoner system was of particular economic importance to the Gonaqua, who were relatively recent immigrants from Xhosaland and were still pastoralists by choice. The system was opposed by Bowker, as Kirk has pointed out, on the ground that people ought to be agriculturalists rather than pastoralists.[63] The Xhosa and Mfengu clients of the Gonaqua were expelled by the "Kafir Police" and driven back to Xhosaland, where these ex-Kat River colonists were hated for their participation on the colonial side in the last frontier war.

The land problems at Kat River were due to more than clientage relationships and assistance afforded to kin and friends, however. Despite a brief and abortive experiment at the Fish River with new Khoisan settlements, no new land was offered to Khoisan in addition to Kat River. The Fish River settlements were established by Sir Andries Stockenstrom in along the Fish River in the aftermath of the 1834–35 war in order to entrench the Fish River as a boundary between the colony and the Xhosa. Native agents from Kat River, including Dirk Hartha, evangelized there, while John Monro worked as missionary. According to Jane Sales, the new settlers, former soldiers or Gonaqua who had been living off the land, did not have property and the settlements were not well-watered. She contends that the Fish River settlements did not prove economically viable; Monro left to take up a position at Cradock after a year or so, and the settlers "drifted away."[64]

The children of erf holders at Kat River thus had few options to obtain new land, while newcomers to the settlement did not have access to an equitable market in land.[65] Families thus often stayed together on an erf; parents and grown children or brothers and sisters commonly cultivated their land together, for example.[66] The land market was theoretically open to Khoisan applicants. But in reality, white sellers of land would not grant adequate credit to Khoisan for them to purchase land in the years immediately after Ordinance 50.[67] By the 1840s, there was little further land available as the region was developed by capitalist wool farmers, and as speculation in land and immigration drove up land prices to a level that must surely have been out of reach of Khoisan and the formerly enslaved.

The failure of the state to allocate more land to Khoisan applicants was resented by many, since Kat River was perceived as inadequate. During the 1850–53 rebellion, the rebel Malau Karabana exclaimed during a visit of Kat River loyalists to the rebel camp in early 1851, "'This land is our land; but what portion of it is in the possession of the Hottentots? Strangers inhabit it, while the real owners have only this ostrich nest, the Kat River; and this is called giving a nation land.'"[68]

Not only was more crown land not granted to Khoisan, but the existing territory of Kat River was cut into by the state and the region was increasingly used as a dumping ground for imperial loyalists. The government granted land on the western banks of the Blinkwater River after the 1834–35 war to the interpreter Hermanus Matroos and a small group of his followers, for example. Matroos, once a slave who had escaped into Xhosaland before working for the British and to be in the future a key rebel leader, had gathered around him a large number of impoverished clients, mostly Xhosa and Mfengu, including forty-eight men and their families by 1842; nonetheless, Stockenstrom, who claims that he was disliked and feared by local Khoekhoe, had reduced his territory in 1836.[69] Recall that Andries Pretorius claimed to have fled the colony in 1836 because of tensions between himself and Matroos.

Some Mfengu were settled by the government in the Mancazana valley, while other Mfengu entered the settlement informally. Indeed, government officials later tried to reduce Mfengu numbers, but in a heavy-handed way which alienated most Kat River residents. There was tension, nonetheless, between Khoisan and Mfengu, presaging the divisions of the 1850–53 war during which the Mfengu would fight on the government side and taunt Khoekhoe rebels, and after which conflict between Mfengu and Khoekhoe would be a critical issue at the treason trial of Andries Botha. In 1842 the justice of the peace of Beaufort, N.J. Borcherds, investigating on behalf of government, claimed that there were about 1,584 Mfengu at the Kat River settlement. This was a substantial percentage of a total population estimated by Clifton Crais at about 6,200 in 1845.[70] Many worked as cattle herders for "Hottentot" employers in exchange only for the right to cultivate the commons attached to each location and to graze their stock there – to the detriment, Borcherds claimed, of other Khoekhoe with stock. Although the missionary James Read Sr and the Blinkwater veldcornet Andries Botha supported the Mfengu presence and claimed that they were "improving," the veldcornets Lodewyck Peffer, David Jantjes, and Andries Pretorius, the "baster" leader C.J. Groepe, and Cobus Fourie all attested (at least according to Borcherds) that the Mfengu were disruptive and wanted more land: "The Fingoes who are in service are extremely insubordinate & all whether in service or not consider themselves as much entitled to the ground of the settlement as the proprietors of the land – This feeling induces them to keep a number of idlers & hangers on of their own nation who bring cattle from various directions to be grazed on the commonage of the location to which their masters belong – These cattle graze off the whole of the pasturage so much that those who possess cattle suffer material injury, from the poor state to which their stock is reduced." These "idlers and hangers-on" also, according to this statement, traded cattle and horses illegally across the colonial boundary with the Xhosa, including stolen stock belonging to Khoekhoe "proprietors."[71] Whatever the strict accuracy of this testimony, there clearly was conflict between Khoekhoe and Mfengu, exacerbated by competition for land and labour, including access to scarce pasturage. Read wanted to Christianize the Mfengu and found in them a rewarding field for evangelization: he complained bitterly that Borcherds and his colleagues were "using every means to get the Fingo with us driven away, who are swallowing the bait of the gospel one after another and are the flower of our church."[72] Many other Kat River Christians, however, preferred not to compete for grazing lands.

By the early 1840s, there were also many "squatter" communities of the recently dispossessed in and around the Kat River settlement. The population mix was further complicated by the Xhosa communities of the followers of Botomani and Maqoma who reinhabited the area south of the original settlement in the wake of the reversal of

D'Urban's settlement.[73] In the eloquent words of Clifton Crais, "from the prosperous peasant to the impoverished squatter, the Kat River Settlement and environs emerged as a chain of communities embodying a range of sensibilities."[74] The settlement was one of the few places in the Cape Colony at which the missionary dream of a prosperous Khoisan peasantry was in some respects realized. At the same time, limited resources exacerbated tensions between a growing number of inhabitants who were increasingly socially stratified and ethnically diverse.

Beyond the Kat River settlement, the Eastern Cape was becoming increasingly an area of large-scale capitalist farming, particularly wool production, by the 1840s.[75] White settlers had been introduced in large numbers by the British government from 1820 onward. By the 1840s, crown land was virtually exhausted in the Eastern Cape, but leading men in the area, heavily involved in land speculation, continued to sell the region to potential British settlers, and a high level of land-hungry immigration continued.[76] The Kat River region was now surrounded by British settlers, as Dutch-speaking farmers were increasingly bought out by the better-capitalized British.[77] Two key conflicts flowed from this: over white access to fertile and well-watered Khoekhoe lands in the Kat River valley, and over the mobilization of African labour on white farms, particularly those devoted to the labour-intensive process of wool production. It is not surprising that white Grahamstown capitalist farmers and land speculators were the most virulent in proclaiming that the Kat River settlers were lazy and inadequate agents of civilization, who did not understand the modern market, who did not deserve the land they had been granted, and who ought to be compelled to work for their own moral good. Surrounded by land-hungry white farmers and pressured for resources within the Kat River settlement, the independent Christian Khoisan peasantry was a fragile innovation.

If the rewards of colonial collaboration seemed less secure by the 1840s, despite the successes of the Kat River settlement, the costs of military service were starkly apparent. The Kat River settlers, for example, were conscripted into the colonial forces in 1835–36 and again in 1846–47. This was despite the fact that the Khoekhoe-staffed Cape Corps already made up the bulk of the troops stationed at the Cape Colony. First to be summoned and last to be released, the entire male population of Kat River between the ages of sixteen and sixty was called into service in the war of 1835–36. The settlement was thus deprived of income from agriculture, woodcutting, and industrial labour for over a year. The men of Hankey contemplated mass desertion when they were detained after the war of 1835–36, despite the parlous condition of their families.[78]

In the 1846 war, some 3 per cent of whites but 90 per cent of Khoekhoe men of appropriate age served in the army at any given time. In 1846–47 white conscripts were given clothes and adequate food, whilst Khoekhoe soldiers were accorded worse rations and no wages and not supplied with clothes or even soap. Many of them were reduced to wearing rags – at the conclusion of the war, in what was widely interpreted as a gesture of contempt, the army took back the blankets it had issued to Khoekhoe soldiers.[79] In explaining in 1851 his reasons for rebellion, the Gonaqua Hendrik Noeka pointed out that the Khoisan had been "faithful subjects to the Queen of England" who had fought several wars over the past twenty years on behalf of the government. They had, however, been shamefully treated:

They had received not even thanks from Government after the last war, although they had served for more than two years, only receiving rations for themselves and families, without any pay, – that they were sent away from the military posts, where they had been stationed, like dogs by Mr. Biddulph, who said you may now go serve the settlers and boers, or go to the d—l. That the proclamations under which cattle were taken in time of war, as prize property, were said in times of peace to be superseded by the civil law; and that by virtue of this, M. Bowker had taken many cattle the people acquired in war, and given to those who afterwards claimed them ...[80]

During the same meeting between rebels and loyalists, Hendrik Noeka's kinsman Manel Noeka "pointed to his nose, which had been partly shot off in the Amatola, in 1846" and stated "that no notice had been taken of the wounded and maimed, or of the widows and orphans of the men who had fallen in the war; but on the contrary, that everything had been done to annoy them by unjust functionaries, and by putting a heavy tax on the forests, when the people of Kat River were struggling against the deepest poverty."[81]

Furthermore, the "concentration camps" of the South African War (using the term in its nineteenth-century military sense) were pioneered by the British at the Cape and imposed on their Khoisan allies in wartime. In both wars, the civilians of the Kat River settlement were required under martial law to congregate at camps. In the words of the Kat River Loyal Burghers Association, settlers were compelled "to abandon their home and farms with all the furniture and property which they could not carry [with?] them [into?] the small corner of a miserable camp and to congregate during 1835 and 36, and during 1846–7 at that post and those of Eland's River and Blinkwater where cattle died for want of food, and where without accommodation for health or decency, they sustained an enormous sacrifice of comfort, of property, of morality and of life."[82] In both instances, the Kat River settlement was sacked by the invading Xhosa in the absence of its inhabitants, and large amounts of property were carried off. At least half of those rebels who reclaimed their land in 1858 had had their houses burnt down during at least one of these two wars, and many had had their property burnt twice.[83] Overall, the concept of a citizen army masked the reality of a racially stratified fighting force, in which Khoekhoe men alone were to be full-time soldiers; the masculinist rhetoric of colonial self-defence also concealed the fact that the Cape Colony was utterly dependent on nonwhite troops for its self-defence.

In sum, the nature of the mission stations had changed considerably by the late 1840s, despite the fact that similar structural issues of competition for labour and land confronted the colonial Khoisan as had been the case at the turn of the century. Khoisan labour could no longer be compelled under vagrancy legislation, oppressive apprenticeship laws, and other mechanisms. Rural mission stations, in consequence, no longer fulfilled the role of shelters against de facto enslavement. On the other hand, white encroachments onto former crown land, restriction of access to municipal commonage, white land speculation, and the privatization of property in land squeezed those Khoisan who were trying to accumulate or simply protect stock. Without land, as cattle pounds and white farms surrounded rural mission stations and the Kat River settlement alike, many Khoisan were being forced into wage labour by economic pressure rather than physical coercion. Communities in towns grew more substantial. Social stratification accompanied these shifts; some managed to do relatively well as peasant farmers, while many others swelled the ranks of the landless rural proletariat.

Under these circumstances of mission impotence in the face of proletarianization, coupled with the greater political freedom, despite all obstacles, of the colonial Khoisan, it is perhaps not surprising that church communities actively chafed under the yoke of missionary paternalism. It is to this topic, and to the related issue of splits within the LMS itself, that we will now turn. Who, in essence, owned the gospel?

9 "Our Church for Ourselves"

By the 1840s, a number of African congregations felt empowered to demand more control over church life, including the right to reject and even select ministers. Congregations were less financially and politically dependent on the missionaries themselves than they had been in the early nineteenth century. Furthermore, a growing corps of African schoolteachers and "native agents" were developing career paths within the church, even if they themselves might not have thought of their evangelical activity in such instrumentalist terms.

At the same time, there were strong social reasons for white missionary unease over the lessening of missionary control, including resistance to the rapid creation of an African clergy. Such reasons may well have included the growing, if still precarious, respectability of missionary activity in both Britain itself and among the often openly racist white British settler community in south Africa: having potentially more to lose, and smarting under the sting of social exclusion in the wake of the quarrels of the 1830s, a number of white missionaries wanted to see all ministers be better "qualified" and better perceived by the white community. LMS missionaries were increasingly embedded in settler life as the white British settler community expanded. Some worried more in consequence about admitting Africans to the clergy or giving the power to local congregations to dismiss their missionaries. More charitably, perhaps, one could also point to the greater stress placed by mission societies themselves on education as a prerequisite for ordination, whether of missionaries or ministers. This reflected the "embourgeoisement" of evangelicalism itself. In either case, despite the changes in Khoisan lifestyle, many missionaries argued that the churches were not ready for full community control, nor individuals for full-fledged ordination. The stage was set for confrontation.

Conflict within the LMS was not only between black congregations and white missionaries but also between white missionaries from different factions. The two types of conflict were inextricably intertwined, especially since divisions among missionaries themselves were closely related to competing attitudes to African politics. Internecine warfare among whites seems at first glance a less edifying topic than the struggle of African churches to be self-directed. Nonetheless, it mattered. The LMS ceased functioning as an effective imperial broker for Africans in the 1840s and 1850s. In large part, this was because the imperial centre itself acted increasingly in the direct interest of white settlers. The Colonial Office looked to Europeans to act as intermediaries and ultimately moved away from experiments with using Khoisan groups, including the Griqua, as allies. The metropole wanted settlers to assume more financial responsibility for frontier warfare, and as a trade-off it needed to give them more local autonomy. At the same time, however, the political will to play the role of broker in African interests (at least as evangelicals perceived them) no longer existed to the same extent in the LMS, although LMS opposition to Afrikaner incursion into the African interior and to the Sand River and Bloemfontein conventions would revitalize political activism in the mid-1850s.[1]

This had an impact on African politics, including the politics of groups beyond so-called coloured communities. Indeed, the ambiguity of lines of authority in evangelical Christianity, and the slipperiness of Christianity as a political tool, may help explain why creative Xhosa chiefs such as Jongamsobokmvu Maqoma ultimately turned away from missionaries as potentially useful political agents and became willing to experiment with innovative millenarian prophecy with Christian elements instead.[2] Be that as it may, internecine quarrels in the LMS in the 1840s are obviously only one part of a large puzzle. Nonetheless, understanding issues such as the vitriolic local conflicts among missionaries, the pullback of the LMS from political interventionism, intellectual debates about the nature of religious authority and the relationship between church and state, and the growing gulf between many white ministers and their congregations is essential to piecing together a larger picture of the 1840s and of the entrenchment of racial division, including the development of a more united "white" front, throughout that bitter decade.

RESPECTABILITY AND WHITE MISSIONS

By the 1840s, missionary activity, like evangelicalism itself, was far more institutionalized and respectable in Britain itself than it had been

at the turn of the century. Even the venerable Society for the Propagation of the Gospel by now ran an extensive networks of missions, providing an outlet for high Anglican missions that paralleled those of the
more evangelical and lower-church Church Missionary Society. Overall,
the character of the British missionary movement as a whole was shifting in significant ways with the rapid growth of settler colonialism, the
institutionalization of missionary activity, the growing respectability of
evangelicalism in Britain itself, and the entwining of missions with the
imperial project more broadly. Although individual missionaries
remained relatively marginal figures in British society, missionaries were
nonetheless coming to be seen by a broader public as more emblematic
of the "British" as a whole than had been the potentially seditious evangelical dissenters of the 1790s. Charlotte Bronte was the daughter of an
impoverished evangelical clergyman and thus a child of the evangelical
world. Nevertheless, the romantic figure of the would-be missionary St
John Rivers in *Jane Eyre* resonated beyond the evangelical community
alone: Jane Eyre refused the missionary's hand, ultimately choosing love
over evangelical duty alone, but St John River's plan to be a missionary
was a clear cultural marker of selfless nobility.

Many British at the mid-century point had their imaginations
gripped by such men as Robert Moffat's son-in-law David Livingstone
who, rightly or wrongly, came to be seen as emblematic of the British
civilizing mission and thus in some sense a symbol of national and
imperial identity.[3] Livingstone, who went out to southern Africa as an
LMS missionary in 1840 and became an explorer instead, was every bit
as maverick a figure as James Read in his own way. Unlike Read, however, Livingstone became famous. This was not least because of Stanley's high-profile and media-friendly "rescue" expedition, but also
because of different political imperatives. Livingstone "discovered"
vast tracts of Africa in the name of Christianity and commerce; his
anti-slavery writings provided a subsequent justification for the British
takeover of many of these lands. Livingstone was seen by many of his
contemporaries as an apostle of a peculiarly British, heroically muscu-
lar liberalism. His fame partly reflected the nationalization of a missionary movement that was now taken by many to be spreading British
virtues as much as pan-European Protestant revivalism. The political
uses made of Livingstone's writings and explorations also reflect the
fact that by the 1850s there was a closer alliance between settler colonialism and missions than had been the case earlier. Philip was a passionate imperialist, but he thought the imperial centre would protect
Africans against the incursions of settlers. By the late nineteenth century, many proponents of empire were claiming that settler colonialism
offered the same benefits to Africans as did mission-sponsored imperialism in Philip's earlier vision.

In southern Africa itself, although men like Livingstone and the theologically innovative Anglican bishop of Natal, John William Colenso, were certainly unusual figures, socially unconventional behaviour on a large scale such as the intermarriage of many early LMS envoys into African communities with local black women did not easily survive the greater regulation and increasing institutionalization of the missionary movement of the 1820s onward.[4] The mobilization of Khoekhoe communities in the 1820s and 1830s to obtain civil rights was also the story of a drive to respectability by the African LMS, as Philip and converts sought to harness the politics of "civilization" to the advantage of Khoekhoe communities and of the British empire alike. Yet, if there were, as we have seen, considerable social pressures on individual converts and missionaries to be more "respectable," the direct rewards of the politics of civilization appeared to be shrinking for converts. Despite the successes of the 1820s and 1830s, for example, Philip failed in the 1840s to persuade imperial officials to follow through in his grand designs for a ring of Christian African communities around the Cape Colony under the suzerainty of the British empire, which would provide real military protection to Griqua and Sotho-Tswana groups against voortrekker incursions.[5]

Missionaries themselves, however, increasingly embraced the drive to respectability. Upholding respectability often included the creation of more social distance between white and black, or even the establishment of separate congregations. Consider the subtext to the Reverend William Elliot's plaintive complaint that he had not been allowed to put auxiliary missionary society funds, raised by his own congregation in Uitenhage, to use in building a new church:

The dense crowd that fills the chapel on Sabbath Evenings is insupportable. Several of the most respectable European families who used to attend, have discontinued their attendance, merely because they cannot endure the suffocation to which they would be exposed. I am obliged to prohibit the attendance of my own children in consideration of their health. My own health has suffered materially from the impure air which I am obliged to breathe & the debilitating perspirations to which I am subjected, so much so indeed as to have led to a correspondence with Dr. Philip on the advisableness of my removal to a more salubrious sphere of labour.[6]

Money was at the heart of much tension. Whatever their aspirations, missionaries themselves still did not have adequate salaries on which to be "respectable" – particularly those with large families or in expensive areas. Indeed, LMS archival records from the 1830s and 1840s are filled with a litany of complaints about low wages, even if missionaries were by no means as ill-paid as they had been in the 1800s and 1810s. In the same letter quoted above, Elliot cited low LMS salaries to explain why he could not fund church expansion himself. "I cannot," he claimed, "even with the most rigid economy, support my family on my salary, and were it not for the kindness of family connexions, I should soon be plunged into those harassing difficulties with which some of my Missionary Brethren have to contend in regard to accumulating debt, or be obliged to follow the example of others, who for the support of their families are driven to the adoption of measures which however honourable in themselves they feel to be inconsistent with the proprieties of the Missionary's character & the duties of the Missionary's calling."[7]

As well as being hard-pressed to live comfortably by white standards, LMS missionaries were also widely attacked in the settler community. J.G. Messer exulted in 1843, for example, that at his new home of George both white and black were willing to listen to him preach. At his previous station of Wellfound, he attested, whites had refused to attend his services. "Some of them are going a step further in their malignity and say, that the first Missionary who ever saw South Africa, ought to have been burnt to ashes."[8] Under such circumstances, missionaries tended either to identify altogether with their African congregations or to seek to distance themselves more from Africans and to mollify the white community.

A further subtext was that money problems were forcing the LMS to make the transition from an externally funded missionary society in southern Africa to a largely self-funded institutionalized church. Like other missionary societies, it often handled this transition badly. The metropolitan drive to devolve more expenses to individual "mission fields" could work both for and against the proponents of greater autonomy for African churches. On the one hand, financial self-sufficiency was a powerful argument for corresponding congregational autonomy. On the other hand, some local missionaries, spearheaded by Henry Calderwood and Robert Moffat, thought that local missionaries themselves should be the beneficiaries of decentralization, not their congregations.

Related to these questions of the devolution of both expenses and authority, and of the ambient respectability of missions, was the implicit issue of whether LMS envoys were more ministers of settled communities or peripatetic agents of evangelicalism. As the respectability of missionary activity increased, and as power devolved to local agents, a growing number of men came over to Africa thinking of themselves as ministers. In the Scottish Presbyterian tradition, in particular, ministers also had powerful control over their congregations (this was true of the English established church as well, but Anglicans did not tend to join the LMS). More missionaries were thus coming expecting a certain level of social status. Unfair as it may be to judge a man by his luggage, Henry Calderwood did not travel lightly, nor indeed did he arrive in Africa planning to live like his African congregations. "Calderwood has got a great deal of furniture," commented James Kitchingman as he helped Calderwood move from Cape Town in 1843. "3 waggon loads were sent from this place & one remaining to go up with his own waggon which John [Kitchingman's son] is to repair for him. Where he will put all I have seen I know not."[9] In sum, the white missionary drive to respectability and ministerial status was intensifying even as African churches increasingly wanted white missionaries to evangelize other Africans and in some cases (especially beyond the colony) to act as intermediaries for them with the state, rather than to control existing churches which were also sources of power for their African adherents.

THE GRAHAMSTOWN SCHISM

Overall, the balance of power in the LMS in southern Africa itself shifted decisively in the 1840s away from the Read-Philip wing and to the faction represented by men such as Robert Moffat of Kuruman, seen by a number of historians as more conservative (although Steven de Gruchy has recently provided an eloquent case to the contrary[10]). Throughout a long series of quarrels, different views of church government and church-state relations were mobilized in order to bolster competing claims to authority. Theological debates with European roots were reinterpreted at the Cape through the prism of racial and imperial politics and struggles over the ownership of the gospel.

There were a number of practical quarrels simmering in the LMS in the early 1840s. The most immediate cause of conflict was the issue of whether African congregations could "call" their own ministers and veto the choice of missionaries to their communities made by the parent missionary society. The question exploded in debate over the so-called Grahamstown church schism in 1842 and 1843.

In a detailed and convincing analysis of the Grahamstown schism, Robert Ross describes how Grahamstown congregationalists had come to be served by two pastors by the early 1840s.[11] The elder and longer-established John Locke had replaced John Monro in 1838 and had devoted himself largely to the white congregation.[12] It was for whites alone that Locke spearheaded a fundraising drive to build a new church on Bathurst Street, "of the Grecian Doric order & exceedingly chaste and commodious." In the same period at which William Philip found people dying of starvation in Cambria, the Grahamstown congregation was able to raise some £1,700 towards the total cost of over £2,500, despite Locke's concern that "we have no wealthy men among us." The remaining £800 were taken as a loan at a worryingly high rate of interest.[13] In the words of the *Grahamstown Journal*, cited by Ross, the opening of this church in 1840 permitted "the chapel hitherto used by the Independent congregation" to be "in future appropriated for the Coloured Classes connected with that denomination."[14]

In the meantime, the bulk of work among the much poorer "coloured" community was carried out by the hard-working Nicolas Smit, who imposed less social distance than Locke between himself and Africans.[15] Smit was ordained a minister on 27 August 1842. Locke refused to recognize Smit as a co-pastor, however, and would not allow him control over the administration of the church's ordinances. Matters came to a head when Smit was called to marry a Khoisan couple in Long Bush, some fifty miles away, who had been living together for a long time. Locke refused to allow Smit to have the marriage register necessary for the ceremony. As Ross and I have pointed out, different approaches to marriage and its regulation, by Locke, by Smit, and by Khoisan congregants themselves, may well have been at stake.[16] Be that as it may, Smit could not accept Locke's viewpoint that Smit was not to administer the Christian ordinances on his own authority.[17] After a period of acrimonious dispute, Smit left Grahamstown for Kat River.

As Ross puts it, matters might have stayed there had a majority of the congregation not protested the departure of Smit and insisted that they rejected Locke as their minister and wished to call Smit, with full authority to administer sacraments. "We never did understand that Mr Lock was our Minister no more than other Servants of God who might occationally preach to us," the deacons and church members of the Grahamstown church asserted in 1843, in a letter signed by Piet Vandervent and eleven others.[18] The letter implicitly insisted that this was not merely a quarrel between white men, but rather that the congregation had made an active choice among pastors. "We are aware that it was Mr Smit's own request to have us but this originated as above stated that we would not acknowledge Mr. Lock as our Pastor he Mr. Lock thinking that Mr. Smit was the cause of our disaffecion which is not true." Locke's focus on a separate white congregation had clearly aroused resentment: "Since Mr. Lock began to build his Church for the English People we began to talk together that we will have Mr. Smit for our own Minister for then we will have our Church for ourselves." Some 100 of 130 congregants separated themselves from Locke's church and "called" Smit in accordance with Congregationalist protocol. They insisted that they were exercising the core right of a Congregationalist congregation to select its own ministers.

Smit did not return to Grahamstown until 1846. In the meantime, the missionary establishment split on the issue. When a trio of investigating missionaries failed to negotiate a settlement, the matter went to the newly formed Eastern District committee of the LMS which ruled that only completely self-supporting congregations could call their own ministers. James Read Sr and his son James Jr were passionately opposed to this position. So, too, were the Khoisan members of the churches at Philipton in Kat River and at Grahamstown – and probably elsewhere, although information is scanty.[17]

Ironically, the debate mirrored Scottish developments. In the Scottish Presbyterian Kirk in which a few Scottish missionaries of the (dominantly Congregationalist) LMS and probably all of those of the (Presbyterian) Glasgow Missionary Society had been brought up, the issue of a congregational veto over the choice of ministers was a topic of virulent debate by the 1830s and 1840s between "moderates" and "evangelicals." In fact, as good evangelicals, most Scottish missionaries ought in fact to have been more firmly on the side of the Grahamstown seceders than they were.[20] In any case, throughout the 1840s, the unresolved underlying disputes over authority that had ignited the conflict continued to fester.

DISTRICT COMMITTEES
AND AFRICAN POLITICS

If one source of conflict in the LMS was debate about congregational control over the selection and rejection of ministers, a second and related cause of deep-seated tension was, as Robert Ross also underscores, disagreement over how the LMS itself should be run in Africa. Should the system of having an LMS superintendent for Africa who oversaw relatively autonomous stations be replaced by one of district committees on which only ordained missionaries would be represented, and through which missionaries would come to majority decisions and discipline one another? No final decision had been reached on this issue by the LMS directors in the early 1840s, but a large number of LMS missionaries in southern Africa were pushing for it. In June 1843, on his return from Britain, LMS missionary Moffat helped organize a committee for the eastern frontier in conjunction with his colleague Henry Calderwood, before proceeding north to organize another committee to run his home region of Transorangia beyond the northern frontier of the colony, encompassing the Griqua and Tswana missions.[21]

Deeply committed to the principle of congregational autonomy, the Reads saw a committee system as a covert form of oppression. Read Sr was convinced that men such as Robert Moffat, missionary to Tswana groups at Kuruman, and Henry Calderwood, initially stationed among Xhosa groups at Blinkwater near the Kat River settlement, wanted a committee system in order to centralize power in the hands of white missionaries and to minimize African influence. In particular, Read felt that missionary committees would bypass the local church government of deacons and elders. This was important given the centrality of church officials to the running of churches within both the Congregationalist and Presbyterian traditions. Deacons and elders were selected by congregations themselves. Not only was this an important instance of local democracy, particularly given the considerable power wielded by churches in Khoekhoe communities, it was also a vehicle for proclaiming the respectability of those chosen for the office and thus more broadly of the community itself. In contrast, Robert Moffat and several other Kuruman missionaries had been involved for years in power struggles with neighbouring Griqua communities on whom, ironically, the station had depended for military protection throughout the turbulent 1820s if not beyond.[22] Griqua chiefs, who had an instrumentalist attitude to the many LMS missionaries whom they compelled over the years to leave their own communities, saw Moffat as a threat to their local political hegemony, including their own attempts to evangelize the Tswana. Some had even attempted to get Moffat dismissed on the time-honoured grounds of adultery.[23] Read believed that Moffat fought for a district-committee system beyond the northern frontier of the colony in order finally to get the Griqua church, its outstations, officials, and extensive network of evangelizing preachers firmly under his control. "Moffat did not know how to get the Griequa out-stations under him but by a majority in that committee and by shutting out native teachers," Read Sr observed bitterly to his friend James Kitchingman.[24] For its defenders, however, the committee system was more democratic than the potentially despotic rule of one man.[25]

Behind these debates, not surprisingly, loomed intense conflict over the role of the actual superintendent, John Philip, and the political actions of himself and his allies, including support for the post-war treaty system along the eastern frontier. Debate over Philip's role was also closely linked, as the example of Moffat's desire to control Griqua outstations suggests, to the relationship of various missionaries to competing African factions in Transorangia beyond the northern frontier of the colony. In this turbulent region between the 1810s and 1840s, missionaries, with their potential capacity to confer legitimacy in the eyes of the Cape Colony and British empire, to broker diplomatic relations with neighbouring powers, to purvey literacy, and to provide access to the arms trade and trade links to the Cape Colony, were both pawns and kingmakers. Philip tried to be a kingmaker, although Moffat saw him as a pawn. Philip had long championed the cause of Andries Waterboer as chief of the Griqua statelet centred at Griquatown and as regional hegemon, and had opposed such competitors as the Bergenaars and the captaincies of Berend Berends and (at least initially) of the Kok family. Most important, Philip and such allies as Waterboer's missionary Peter Wright fought hard to make the Griqua polities of Andries Waterboer and Adam Kok III protectorates of the British crown as protection against voortrekker incursions from the late 1830s on.[26] Waterboer's Griqua in turn used Christianity to try to bring neighbouring groups within their ambit and to assert a self-confident sense of collective identity.[27] In Transorangia, Christianity was a currency of power, but whether or not missionaries would control that currency was, as elsewhere, a matter for political struggle.

Ideological quarrels between missionaries were lent further piquancy by long-standing personal divisions among men who had fought for many years. James Read, tainted by adultery and politically a more vulnerable figure than Philip, had long borne the brunt of attacks from his colleagues and other whites for what were perceived to be both his and Philip's naive and dangerous political stances.[28] The mutual dislike of Read and Moffat dated back many years to Moffat's disapproval of Read's adultery and Moffat's takeover of the Lattakoo mission founded by Read and Khoekhoe evangelists from Bethelsdorp, without due acknowledgment.[29] Moffat's romantic 1842 account of his missionary career had been full of significant silences. As James Kitchingman observed ironically of Moffat's *Missionary Labours and Scenes in Southern Africa*, "it is a very interesting book, and if perils among Lions and beasts of savage name will make a book go down in England then I would say there never was a book like it." Nonetheless, "he passes many of his former friends without noticing them at all or mentioning their names," while it was easy for "those acquainted with circumstances ... to see he neither admires Mr. Read nor Mr. Wright."[30] *Missionary Labours*, in which Moffat presented himself as a solitary hero of the wilderness, was equally silent on the vexed topic of African evangelists.[31]

The split between Philip and Moffat was also long-standing, and equally acrimonious. By the 1830s, Moffat's strained relationships with Waterboer's Griqua had destroyed any ability he and Philip might have had to work together. Moffat saw Philip as a political controversialist who neglected spiritual issues and unduly favoured the Griqua in general and Waterboer in particular. Moffat opposed Griqua evangelization among the Tswana, which he and several of his Kuruman colleagues saw as a covert form of imperialism. During his stay in Britain between 1839 and 1842, Moffat worked hard and successfully to undermine Philip's standing with the majority of the LMS board in London.[32] For his part, by 1838 Philip was privately describing Moffat to LMS director William Ellis as the most imperious man he had ever known, a man of naturally "despotic" temper, driven by his furious passions. "The defect he labours under is not in his head but in his heart." Despite the fact that Waterboer alone had protected Lattakoo from the Ndebele, and remained the station's military protector, Moffat's "passions" drove him to do everything he could to grieve Waterboer "and involve the country and the missions in one promiscuous ruin."[33]

Consider two examples from the 1830s of the complicated connections between missionary and African politics, both revolving around the Griqua captain Cornelis Kok who was unpopular with the Philip wing of the LMS as the missionaries struggled to unite the Griqua. The LMS missionary John Bartlett was closely associated with Cornelis Kok at the settlement of Campbell. Bartlett, who was one of the missionaries censured in 1817 by the dissident missionary synod for adultery, had worked beyond the Orange River since 1816. Unusually, Moffat had forgiven Bartlett his earlier sexual lapses and, as early as 1818, saw him as an effective agent of civilization.[34] Philip and Wright strongly disapproved of Cornelis Kok, whom they considered an immoral and feared local strongman who had alienated his own followers. In 1833 Philip dismissed Bartlett from the society with the approbation of the LMS directors as a result of the state of Campbell. Philip later claimed that Bartlett was hated and feared by the local people; "the natives are more afraid of him than they are of a lion." Almost everyone had left Campbell in consequence and refused to return as long as Bartlett was there.[35] Robert Moffat, on the other hand, strongly supported Bartlett, as did J.A. Kolbe and the other Kuruman missionaries, Robert Hamilton and Roger Edwards.[36] It is unclear whether or not the LMS upheld Bartlett's final dismissal in the wake of the protests of other missionaries, or whether Bartlett simply continued working for Kok on his own initiative. In any case, Bartlett refused to leave Campbell or to accept the society's proffered compensation package.[37] His dismissal clearly remained controversial for a long time, as Moffat and Bartlett's brother and others were still agitating against it in 1838. In that year, as a prophylactic measure should the society need to defend itself in public, Philip forwarded to London the transcripts of an investigation held by Donald Moodie in 1836 into the death of a young man called Goegumip at Campbell, saying that this was necessary in order to counter Moffat's misrepresentations.

The case was as follows. In January 1836 Cornelis Kok went on a visit to Philippolis. He left instructions for the apprehension of Goegumip, a Bushman in his late teens, for theft. Goegumip was a former

servant of Bartlett. He had stolen many things from the station, including from Bartlett at various times two loaves of bread, a tablecloth, a
leg of mutton, a side of mutton, meal, milk, corn, several ewes, and a
number of lambs.[38] On the orders of veldcornet Arie Samuel, a party
of men apprehended Goegumip. He refused to come, so they shot at
him, wounding him in the finger, and threw stones at him hard until he
was overcome.[39] He was flogged, as was usual at Campbell. Bartlett, a
smith by profession, put handcuffs on Goegumip. Samuel then
whipped Goegumip with a doubled-over ox whip while four men held
him down. Witnesses gave contradictory evidence at a subsequent
inquiry as to how many lashes Goegumip had received but estimates
varied from 50 to 150 on an extremely hot day. It was undisputed that
Bartlett had been in his house 120 yards away during the beating but
had not intervened. Hannah Goodman, who lived with Bartlett (presumably as his servant), had never seen a person punished before. She
went up to Arie Samuel "and taking hold of his arm said 'he has got
enough.'"[40] The beating was stopped shortly afterwards. After the
punishment, Goegumip was brought to Bartlett, who soldered leg irons
onto him. An hour later the boy died.

This tragic case highlights a number of issues. In the context of my
overall argument, it points to the long-standing nature of power struggles between the Philip and Moffat wings of the LMS, suggesting that
one might better talk of factional rifts than personal conflicts. The
boy's death is also a window into the violence of Transorangia as warring groups maintained authority through personal violence: fifty lashes was the "usual" punishment for Kok's group. Despite anti-flogging
campaigns spearheaded by evangelicals and utilitarians in the British
parliament, flogging was, of course, still routine in the British army (in
which some at least of Kok's followers may have served had they earlier lived in the Cape Colony). The case further points to the subordination of San to the armed Griqua in the region. It is also significant
that Cornelis Kok wrote to Moodie on 30 May 1834 that Bartlett did
not interfere in the secular affairs of his government: "Mr. Bartlett is
placed on my farm as a Missionary at the request of all my people and
he has not conducted himself otherwise than consistently with the
Bible he has never interfered with private concerns and has never
requested to come into my council house because I know that is no
place for a minister besides I have never heard from any of my people
neither Bushmen Corannas nor Bechuanas any complaint against Mr.
Bartlett either great or small of any ill treatment but I have seen sick
Bushmen and Bechuanas come into this house for medicine or food."[41]
Although Kok was trying to get Bartlett cleared, and to resist an
implicit challenge to his own authority, his testimony provides yet

another example of the relative subordination of the solitary mission-
ary to African leaders, outside the context of colonial power structures.
Indeed, implicit in Philip's criticisms of Bartlett was the conviction that
Bartlett had not acted as a sufficiently independent moral guide.

There was a sequel. In 1838 Peter Wright, government agent and
Waterboer's missionary, wrote to the LMS that Cornelis Kok had left
the mission station at Philippolis during the early stages of Waterboer's
treaty negotiations with the British, had joined with local "banditti,"
and had attacked Ndebele leader Mzilikatse in a conflict which led to
"dreadful carnage." According to Wright, Kok had been encouraged to
leave the station by another missionary of whom Wright disapproved,
J.A. Kolbe. Cornelis Kok's younger brother Adam, "a man of good
principle & talent," accordingly deposed Cornelis in a fit of shame
and, being "called" by "a large majority of the people," took over the
reins of power himself. Waterboer supported the more reliable Adam
Kok and signed a treaty with him. Meanwhile, Cornelis and his followers turned to banditry. Kolbe remained with Cornelis as his missionary, as the elder brother plundered and skirmished with the
younger. Wright's comment on this doubtless exaggerates the role of
missionaries but underscores the entanglement of missionary and
African politics: "Mr. Atkinson informs me it is well known that Kolbe
is the instigator of the whole – that he is doing his best to strengthen
the interests of the ex chief in order if possible to have Mr. A[tkinson]
driven away from Philippolis & himself placed there again."[42] Kolbe's
role in Griqua politics was, however, curtailed when the LMS directors
were given sufficiently damning information "to deliver the sacred
cause in which we are engaged from such a burden and disgrace."[43]

These were not meaningless quarrels. Waterboer needed a treaty of
friendship with the Kok captaincy, for example, as he sought to show
the British empire that he could bring peace to the area – and Cornelis
Kok seems to have been a bad advertisement for missionary enterprise
and Waterboer's peacemaking ability alike. Since the major players
remained stable over time and missionaries were generally attached to
their stations for life, short of dismissal, debates became intertwined
and power struggles festered. The district-committee system provided
a means for the anti-Philip majority among missionaries on the ground
to impose themselves in both Transorangia and the Eastern Cape after
many years of being on the losing side of most arguments.

In 1843 Henry Calderwood, Scottish LMS missionary to the Xhosa,
Richard Birt, and several other missionaries in the district committee
for the Eastern Cape censured Philip for his role in the Grahamstown
affair. They continued to censure Philip late into 1844, even as they
tried to depose Philip's closest allies the Reads on other grounds, as we

shall see.[44] In the face of conflict and the imposition of a committee system against his wishes, his distemper possibly compounded by the failure of his northern policy, the elderly and disillusioned Philip tendered his resignation in 1844. Read, Peter Wright of Griquatown, W.Y. Thomson, Theophilus Atkinson, and others begged the LMS board not to accept Philip's resignation. The board accordingly refused it, but Philip's continuation as superintendent was reluctant on his part and resented by his many internal opponents.[45]

THE BLOCK DRIFT AFFAIR[46]

In 1843 and 1844 Henry Calderwood and a number of allies also launched an all-out attempt to get James Read Sr dismissed and more broadly to discredit the Reads and their work. Missionaries termed this the "Block Drift Affair" after the location of a key meeting which triggered the dismissal attempt. Calderwood was a Scotsman who arrived in the Cape Colony in 1839. He left the LMS to become a government agent in 1846.[47] Ultimately, he would become a prime mover in efforts at the forcible "civilization" and Christianization of the Xhosa in the wake of the War of the Axe (1846–47). Read was, as we have seen, a symbol for whites of unwarranted metropolitan interference in colonial affairs and one of the men most hated by the white colony. The two men thus represented different interpretations of the relationship among missionaries, Africans, the imperial administration, and white settler society. Calderwood's attempt to destroy Read and his son James in 1843 is a useful way into the complicated tensions of the early 1840s – and is in some ways a microcosm of the ambiguous role of missions in imperialism.

The actual affair that triggered a final split between factions of missionaries in both the LMS and the former Glasgow Missionary Society, as well as an attempt to oust James Read Sr, was, all the same, as James Read Jr put it in May 1844, "in itself a very silly one, and scarcely worth noticing."[48] One needs to know before considering it that, by 1842, political and theological conflicts in Scotland over church-state relations had divided the Glasgow Missionary Society in southern Africa – although, tellingly, the split had been concealed from Xhosa congregations in order to avoid "imprudent excitement."[49] The "voluntarists" who formed the new Glasgow African Missionary Society (GAMS) argued for the complete disestablishment of the state-supported Church of Scotland, and felt that religious allegiance should be voluntary and churches financially independent of the state. Their rivals in the Glasgow Missionary Society Adhering to the Principles of the Church of Scotland continued to believe in and to belong to a tax-supported Scottish national church, even if Scottish evangelicals in general did not feel that the state should have any control over doctrine and ecclesiastical discipline.[50] Although the two societies had initially continued to hold common presbytery meetings, the presbyteries split during the conflicts of 1842. The passion involved reflected the disputatious, even venomous, nature of Scottish religious culture in the 1830s and 1840s, in the run-up to the final split of the Church of Scotland itself in 1843. What this suggests more broadly is that disputes over spiritual authority and its relationship to temporal authority were occurring in parallel in Scotland and the Cape Colony, both industrializing countries with an expanding potential electorate in which debates about political citizenship interacted with debates about the relationship of church and state.

The immediate dispute involving the Reads was more mundane. After a tangled series of disputes, GAMS had dismissed one of its missionaries, a man named Hepburn, from a position which had been meant to be on John Pringle's farm of Glen Thorn in the Mancazana valley.[51] Among other things, Hepburn had sought to dismiss the female "native teacher" Notishe who had been teaching at the outstation before his arrival. He had complained that his house was "not fit for a Minister" and had moved himself to a more salubrious location twenty miles away on Baviaans River where he focused on his white congregation. Hepburn also mobilized existing disputes between white power-brokers in the neighbourhood, as he exploited divisions between John Pringle and his brother to get up a "party."[52] When, after extended quarrels, accusations of falsehood, and furious exchanges of documents, the GAMS finally dismissed Hepburn, Henry Calderwood of the LMS and a number of other missionaries to the Xhosa from the other Glasgow Missionary Society branch opposed the GAMS board decision and called a missionary conclave at Block Drift to urge the directors to reconsider.

The Reads later attested that they assumed this meeting would include representatives from both the quarrelling parties. They were shocked to discover on their arrival that only the supporters of Hepburn were present, all from the opposing wing of the former GMS, and that his opponents had absented themselves, considering the meeting as "a piece of unjustifiable interference with the private affairs of a kindred society, and as setting a bad precedent in future cases."[53] Read Sr in particular felt that the meeting was illegitimate and that it was wrong to read the documents of another society and to meddle in its affairs.[54] His objections were, however, overturned. Ultimately, the meeting voted unanimously to urge the GAMS board to review the case of Hepburn. After the meeting, Read wrote privately to his friend

Dr Gavin Struthers, GAMS secretary, to explain his participation in the meeting and to express his discomfort at interfering in the affairs of another society.[55]

Calderwood heard that someone in the meeting had written to GAMS through a convoluted chain of rumour which in itself points to the strained relations among the frontier missionaries and the fervour with which some were looking for any excuse to bring down the Reads.[56] Calderwood required each participant in the original meeting to sign a document attesting that he had not written to GAMS to "controvert" the resolution passed by the meeting; he took Read's initial refusal to sign as an admission of guilt. On 30 April 1844 Calderwood located, supposedly through a fortuitous accident, a letter awaiting delivery at the Fort Beaufort post office, addressed to Struthers in James Read's handwriting. This at last was the proof for which he had been hunting to condemn Read.

The following day, eleven missionaries led by Calderwood circulated a statement of censure of Read Sr, accusing him of acting "dishonestly" and "insidiously" and of "dishonorable" conduct. They attested that, unless Read could explain himself, they would be "obviously under the necessity of withholding their confidence from him in future"[57] – a "wretched exhibition of animosity and uncharitableness," according to Read supporter and GAMS missionary Robert Niven.[58] "Eleven," lamented Read, "just the number that sold Joseph for an Egyptian slave ... The Doctor [Philip] pities *them* and other Brethren consider that I have not acted wrong, but a broken, shivered *reed* against eleven *cedars* is, as the Caffres say, *no joke*."[59] With the exception of the German Kayser, all the signatories were Scots; four worked for the LMS and six for the old GMS, while W.R. Thomson was a Scottish Presbyterian minister and government agent at Kat River who opposed Read's frontier policy.

Although Read transmitted the gist of his letter to Struthers, Calderwood and his allies accused Read of lying. In the meantime, Cumming and Campbell, key links in the transmission chain, denied that their evidence about the letter was as conclusive as Calderwood claimed. Campbell in particular furiously attacked F.G. Kayser, who had passed on his comments, for having abused the privacy of the family dinner table.[60] With increasing anger over the next few months, the missionary committee tried to compel Cumming and Campbell to rescind their testimonies. "Unless you adopt measures to clear yourself we will be compelled to regard you as deliberately abetting falsehood and calumny," wrote William Govan in fury to Cumming in December 1844.[61] This, responded Cumming, echoing Scotland's past history of political violence around church-state relations, was "the language of one holding the Bible in one hand and a sword in the other saying – if you do not acknowledge the truth of this Book you shall feel the power of the destructive weapon. Is it possible think you that any Christian man should succumb so far to the sword *in terrorem* as to comply unconditionally with your request?"[62] By the end of January 1845, the missionary committee was meeting on the issue of Cumming and Campbell, hinting at censure should they not change their stories. Despite these background quarrels and mitigating circumstances, the anti-Read group persisted.[63]

A further piece in the case against the Reads fell into place seven months after the original Block Drift meeting, in September 1844, when the indefatigable Calderwood intercepted another envelope, addressed, as he put it, in a woman's handwriting, to two Khoekhoe church officials, Arie van Rooyen and Valentyn Jacobs, of Calderwood's own church at Blinkwater. Through the thin paper he saw that the handwriting of the letter itself was that of James Read Jr, and he assumed immediately that an attempt at deception was under way. Calderwood therefore violated his policy of not discussing missionary politics with nonwhites, and called together "the Hottentot portion of his Deacons and Elders." In Calderwood's words (note the status distinctions of naming):

Mr C asked Arie & Valentyn if Mr Read had informed them of what had happened between him & the Missionaries – Arie said, *Mr. Read* had said nothing – Valentyn said he had heard something. – Mr C did not like to press them further on this point – He then related to them what had occurred & knowing Messr Read had acted secretly in the Grahamstown affair, he related also what the three Brothers appointed by the Directors had done in Grahamstown. – And this statement respecting the conduct of the Reads should never have been made to any of the Natives had not, in connection with other circumstances, J Read's letter had been put into Mr C's hands, which excited suspicions that have proved too well founded. Mr C then produced the letter addressed to Arie Van Rooyen and as Arie was proceeding to open it Mr C said "I feel strongly impressed with the conviction that there is something improper in that letter. I see through the paper that it is James Read's hand and the address is disguised & after what has happened I have a right to suspect that there is something more in that letter. I therefore as your Friend & Pastor beg a sight of that letter." After much hesitation Arie allowed Mr C to read it, & after Mr C read it he stated that "such a letter could not be *fairly* considered as private property." Mr C therefore begged the letter in order if possible to check the dishonourable & serious conduct of Mr Read towards the people & his Brethren ...[62]

The letter included an informal discussion of Read's joint plans with van Rooyen and Jacobs, and referred to "the suspicious C.," for whose opinion Read affirmed he did not give tuppence: "Ik geef geen dubbeltjie." Read threatened that the missionary committee should "feel it" if their upcoming meeting mentioned his name or that of his father. He discussed the injustice of the Grahamstown case. He concluded the letter by instructing van Rooyen and Jacobs to burn it after reading.[65]

This second letter, and an angry subsequent exchange of letters between Read Jr and Calderwood on one another's sins, furnished sufficient grounds for Calderwood and his associates to forward all the relevant documents concerning the events of that year to London on 26 September 1844 and to call for the dismissal of the Reads from the service of the LMS. The attempt failed, since neither John Philip nor John Fairbairn, when asked by the LMS directors to adjudicate the affair, could find anything reprehensible in the conduct of either of the Reads. The 1846 War of the Axe between the Xhosa and the Cape Colony eventually overrode these more parochial concerns. By the end of 1846, Calderwood had left the service of the LMS and had accepted a post as government agent in newly conquered Xhosa territory, at a lucrative annual salary of £500.[66]

AUTHORITY AND THE GOSPEL

The issue of authority lay at the heart of these debates: who had it and how was it to be enforced? This occurred at a number of levels. The first was a dispute over church government. The meetings that condemned the Reads were presented as acts of collective will representing the district-committee system in action. As minutes and letters frequently attested, meetings opened with prayer, in which God was invoked as speaking through the acts of the community. The Block Drift meeting initially condemned Read for seeming to concur with and then supposedly seeking to undermine a majority decision: "We learned that a member of our meeting had violated the confidence which we are bound to repose in one another and had done a previous injury in the cause of truth and to his Brethren by attempting to controvert a decision in which he himself had fully concurred," as Govan put it in a bitter letter to Cumming.[67] Calderwood wrote in the first person plural, representing himself as the simple conduit of the meeting's opinion, even discussing himself as "Mr. C." An underlying trope in this approach was that of God moving a group to action: the rhetoric of group solidarity permitted an intrinsic appeal to divine authority.

Calderwood and his allies were obviously using this dispute to attack Philip and to entrench the committee system of which Read was such a passionate opponent. Read was essentially accused of being a maverick who worked in secret to undermine the decisions of the majority of his brethren; this paralleled his position against the district-committee system. It was no coincidence that, two days before the Calderwood faction sent its documents back to London to obtain Read's dismissal, the Reads were the first signatories of an appeal against committee government. Not only, this document claimed, was such a system absurd in a country in which missionaries were too remote to function effectively as a collectivity, but a committee permit-ted the suspension of individual moral conscience: "It may commit the most egregious blunders, or the most flagrant injustice, and there is no one to bear the blame and individual character is often merged in the movements of associated bodies, so that the wisdom and uprightness of the persons forming such associations are no guarantee for the wisdom and equity of their corporate acts."[68] Three weeks later, Calderwood and others wrote a lengthy document attacking Read's arguments: only those guilty of ungentlemanly and dishonourable conduct truly had to fear the so-called tyranny of the majority. To prefer a superintendancy was worthy only of an Episcopalian: "For Dissenters and *congregational Dissenters too*, to argue that they must have Bishops or mock-bishops placed over them *because* an associa-tion of Brethren is an irresponsible and dangerous thing, is surely like a new thing under the Sun." A superintendent was potentially tyranni-cal; he might, for example, gain information from "improper quar-ters," while a "missionary who may be so dishonourably inclined, has *peculiar facilities* for acting in an underhanded manner against his Brethren."[69]

Debates over church government had inescapable echoes in Euro-pean history and contemporary politics for their European partici-pants. On the most basic level, they reflected splits between Episco-palians, Presbyterians, who supported self-government through presbyteries of ministers rather than bishops, and Independents or Congregationalists, who favoured self-government by each congrega-tion alone. All these groups had been involved in civil war in England or Scotland in the seventeenth century. Read Sr commented to a friend that the district-committee system "strikes at the very root of the fun-damental principle of our Society. It is establishing Presbyterianism ... The thing is worse than Presbyterianism, because in their synods and presbyteries there are always laymen to represent the churches. In the system proposed the churches are entirely at the mercy of the reverends."[70]

In the Scottish Disruption of 1843, the national church split into two as evangelicals left the established church to form the Free Church of

Scotland, in a dispute with wide-ranging political implications. Although there were many underlying tensions, the issue on which the church split was precisely that of state control over the appointment of ministers over the objections of a majority of male heads of family in a given congregation.[71] Read considered that the "fatal" struggle in the Scottish church had arisen precisely because "to force a pastor upon a church without in any way to consider its judgement or feelings would be to hand over God's heritage," and he used the example to illustrate the need for south African churches to choose their own ministers.[72] The GMS as a whole, like most missionaries, voted in 1843 to join the Free Church, as did other Scottish ministers at the Cape.[73] To support the free choice of congregations in 1843 in south Africa was thus a politically charged act which proclaimed the independence of the church from secular authority. Read was riling fellow evangelicals by implicitly comparing the missionary society to the intrusive state and equating the rights of black (or mostly black) congregations to choose ministers with the right of the church to be free from secular interference. Scottish missionaries, even fervent voluntarists such as Richard Birt (who eagerly requested the LMS to dispatch his deceased wife's sister to the Cape Colony so he could marry her despite such a marriage's technical illegality), failed to see the parallel. The LMS, as a corporate whole, argued that only congregations that paid for their own minister had veto rights – and indeed in Scottish Presbyterianism the right of veto was vested only in the male "heads of families." As was the case in debates over democracy, the notion of political rights founded on property could be used to limit that of universality, with particular application in a racially diverse community.

In societies – mission stations and Scottish parishes alike – in which ministers and elders had great authority over the members of congregations, including wide-ranging powers of discipline for moral offences, these disputes over church government were important for community life. Note, too, that ministers in the established Church of Scotland by the early nineteenth century tended to be at an educational, financial, and social remove from their poorer parishioners.[74] Debates over church government mattered particularly for a Scottish tradition in which synods acted as powerful church courts. Like the Scottish-dominated synod of 1817, the Block Drift meeting and its successors were essentially trying to act like Scottish church courts, exerting legal as well as moral control over the community of the faithful. At the same time, vigorous Scottish reformers in the 1840s, like their reforming counterparts in England, tended to want the tightening up of church control, in parallel with extending the church's presence in poor areas (often seen as deChristianized and "savage"). Thomas

Chalmers, leader of the Free Church forces, called for a more disciplined parish system which would give churches and church officers much extended social control over their parishioners in poor areas; he saw this as a solution to the immiseration and moral decay occasioned by industrialization, and opposed demoralizing state "charity." The implications were for the most part conservative, as Chalmers recommended tighter social control over the poor rather than the alleviation of their material misery.[75] The confrontation between the older Read and the younger Calderwood was also, then, a confrontation between different evangelical cultures. In south Africa, race complemented class, but similar issues were at stake in the drive to Christianize, or reChristianize, the "masses": after conversion, was the church an institution for moral police directed by accredited agents, or was its primary aim the continued spread of Christianity by the newly converted themselves, whatever the loss of institutional control this involved?

The debate over church government also echoed the debate over the role of the imperial government in white settler colonies. By the 1840s, white British settlers across the political spectrum were pushing for a legislative assembly in south Africa and a greater degree of local autonomy from imperial rule. Philip's role in the aftermath of the 1834–35 frontier war was taken by many as a prime example of problems both with imperial government and with the LMS. Both committee government and settler self-government were presented as inherently more democratic, although in both cases opponents might argue that democracy permitted the hegemony of white men. Many Khoekhoe rebelled during the 1850–53 war in part because they disliked the advent of settler government and the loss of the potential for the imperial government to act as a referee in local power disputes; Griqua leaders in the 1840s, keen to mobilize the right missionaries as diplomatic agents, opposed the district-committee system on similar grounds.[76]

Authority relations were also at stake in less tangible ways. Underlying the complaints of fellow missionaries against Read in 1843–44, as indeed against Smit and Philip in the Grahamstown case, was the sense that they had crossed over the line between missionaries and "the people" and owed their allegiance to converts rather than to fellow missionaries. This came out with particular acuity in Calderwood's attack on James Read Jr in the wake of the incident of Read's letter to van Rooyen and Jacobs. As the child of a white missionary and an African mother, Read Jr had a foot in two camps and as a consequence clearly troubled Calderwood. He was indubitably a missionary, but could he be trusted? In a lengthy attack on Read Jr, Calderwood complained:

Considering the circumstances and natural disposition of the Natives generally, all who know this country will admit that a more serious offence against the
souls of the people and the comfort and confidence of Miss[ionary] Brethren
could scarcely be committed than that which Mr Read has many a time committed in speaking and writing to the Natives in the manner of which this letter is a sample. It should also be here considered that there is an important difference between Missionaries conversing however freely amongst themselves,
about their fellow missionaries, and this *kind* of intercourse which the Mssrs
Read have with the Native people. To speak or write of his Brethren secretly,
in this manner to any one even the most intelligent Europeans would be highly dishonourable & [wicked to do?], but to do so to the Natives is *cruel* to
them & unfairness towards his Brethren in no common degree. It is also worthy of remark on this point that while Mr. J.R. speaks with the greatest disrespect & *affected* scorn & that [too?] in the *lowest terms* of the Missionaries,
he speaks to & of the people in terms of marked respect and affection.[77]

To this Read Jr responded tartly: "That I wrote a letter to Arie and
Valentyn is true: but that I wrote to the one *as an elder* and the other
as a deacon is not correct but *friends* with whom I was on terms of inti-
macy long before you thought of coming to this country: and with
whom I was in the habit of corresponding before you knew anything
of them, or they of you ..."[78] Read conveyed a keen sense of the missionary as an outsider, without the roots in a given community to claim
the kind of respect men such as Calderwood expected to command as
ministers. Calderwood, on the other hand, clearly wanted to build up
a brotherhood of missionaries bound together to one another above all
and separated from their congregations by complex etiquettes of racial
and professional exclusion. Indeed, he and others inadvertently conveyed a sense of their own loneliness and isolation as they stressed, as
part of their plea for a committee system, that "missionaries are necessarily removed from many of those social, moral and religious
advantages which are continually operating for good on Brethren at
home. It is therefore a most serious evil to keep up any system the natural tendency of which is to diminish our dependence upon and
responsibility to one another."[79]
    Locke cast his complaint against Nicolas Smit in similar terms of the
violation of boundaries in a letter to the LMS board on 25 September
1844, a day before the district committee called for Read's dismissal.
Smit had illegitimately shared private information with the Grahamstown congregation, Locke contended. In a striking denial of
Khoekhoe agency, Locke continued to claim that Smit and "some other
parties" had "acted upon" the Grahamstown seceders, and that Smit
had "countenanced and encouraged them in the manifestation of a

most improper spirit towards me and their fellow members." In injured tones, Locke described a violated relationship, undercut by a skilful competitor: "Until the period of the unpleasant occurrence I had always been on the best of terms with the people & had every reason to believe that I had a place in their affections."[78] Similarly, even the accusation of 26 September brought against Philip by the district committee was, as Birt and Calderwood put it, precisely "not that he had removed Mr. Smit but that he had written to Mr. Smit to inform him (Dr. P.) as to the feelings of Mr. Locke's people on certain points, and that too without first communicating with Mr. Locke. Dr. Philip may blame Mr. Smit, as he does, for having communicated with the people *as he did*, but how could Mr. Smit possibly answer *with truth*, the questions of Dr. Philip without communicating with the people, and which communication we must still think could produce *only* evil in the Church."[81]

In all these cases, it was the crossing of boundaries between the missionary brotherhood and the missionaries' congregations that was the heart of the problem. This reflected a preoccupation with drawing lines between the private and the public: communications between missionaries were private, while the missionary's relationship with his congregation was in the public sphere. James Read straddled the division between private and public, as did his entire "mixed-race" family. He thus became a spy within the ranks. Cumming's attack on Kayser for his betrayal of a "private" conversation reflected a similar anxiety about the need to keep private and public separate.

The distinction between minister and people, the private world of white equals and the public world of work with unequal blacks, that Calderwood was so anxious to mobilize was surely reflected in the social stratification of Cape society by race: worlds coexisted and overlapped, but the majority of whites did not for the most part accord nonwhites the social status of equals. An anecdote in passing told by James Read Sr about Tys Jurie, who had recently died at the Kat River settlement, is revealing: "... Altho a man of colour he was in his dress and address the Gentleman. He had once to call at a house in Grahams Town, the servant opening the door and not taking notice of the face, ran and said there was a gentleman at the door – he was ordered to the Parlour, but when the Lady came she was surprised to find that it was a gentleman with a brown face."[82] "In a similar play on notions of gentility and of race, James McKay, even though he criticized racial prejudice and struggled to persuade rural Dutch-speaking whites to attend school with blacks in the 1860s, told the following anecdote about the Khoekhoe rebellion of 1850–53, during which he was a sergeant in the British army. A man and his wife escaped from Willem Uithaalder's rebel encampment, which was in a state of starvation. "The vrouw said that it was pitiful to see so many fine *young ladies* going about perfectly naked and half starved. On enquiring what ladies she meant, she replied bastard and Hottentot 'ladies.' Of course I and others laughed heartily at the expression, and wondered what the ladies of Britain would think when they heard of the miserable plight their sisters were in."[83] It is telling that Calderwood's complaints against James Read and his son dwelt so extensively both on gentility and on false appearances. The Reads posed as gentlemen, but in reality they were dishonourable, acting in secret an "ungentlemanly" role. The missionaries would therefore be compelled to "withdraw the right hand of fellowship." Handshaking had an important role in dissenting churches, since it was a sign of community inclusion. There was also, as Robert Ross has written, a complicated "etiquette of race" around the shaking of hands at the Cape. As Nicholas Pos, cited by Ross, put it bluntly in 1868, "no white inhabitant of the Cape gives a coloured his hand."[84] While it would be unfair to suggest without further evidence that the signatories of the letters against the Reads upheld these colonial prejudices, it is still noteworthy that to withdraw the right hand of fellowship was a racially and socially charged gesture.

English-speakers had strong prejudices about race, respectability, and "civilization" which permitted even those who deplored Afrikaner and English settler behaviour towards Africans nonetheless to distance themselves socially from nonwhites and to elaborate a code of honour which still categorized nonwhites as intrinsically less honourable than whites. In this one can see the emergence of a newly dominant form of white missionary liberalism which defended black rights from a careful social distance, while assuming white superiority.

Despite these racial expectations about a white community of the honourable and respectable, worthy of black esteem, it does not seem far-fetched to suggest that many missionaries actually felt very insecure about their personal relationships to their congregations (and thus all the more likely to rely on their colleagues emotionally). Furthermore, this insecurity was justified. Calderwood was much disliked by most in Kat River, as James Read Jr stressed when he rehashed old incidents and reminded Calderwood that he and his father had in fact fought to "reconcile" the people to Calderwood.[85] According to the Reads, they had given Calderwood "a portion of their Missionary sphere (Blinkwater) with a good Kaffre and Hottentot congregation many members and inquirers with two schools and Schoolmasters," and had then struggled to "heal breaches caused by his (Mr. C's) temper abrupt manners and ignorance of native character."[86] The work of Donavan Williams and others on Xhosa reactions to missionaries before the cataclysmic events of the 1850s has long suggested that the bulk of white missionaries in Xhosaland were relatively ineffectual.[87] I myself suspect, in common with Natasha Erlank,[88] that many Xhosa were more influenced by Christianity before the cattle-killing than is commonly thought, but that this influence came via Khoisan and Xhosa preachers and that the only really influential white missionary in Xhosaland was, ironically, James Read. Be that as it may, even a laudatory and quasi-official 1873 history of Free Church missions commented gloomily that in the early days "the [Xhosa] men, as a rule, treated their preaching with indifference, and the women with bitter hostility," while in the late 1840s a cash-strapped Free Church contemplated abandoning its south African missions altogether. By the mid-1840s, many missionaries to the Xhosa, with the exception of Ross and Niven of GAMS, were perceived by Xhosa chiefs as working against their political interests in supporting changes to the treaty system.[89] In March 1845 Philip stated baldly to the LMS, "You must know that the Caffreland missionaries have lost the confidence of the chiefs ... The Reads form the only party among our missionaries in whom the chiefs have confidence and this is one cause of the hostile feelings manifested against the Reads and the reason why they find it necessary to give up holding intercourse with the chiefs."[90] To take just one example, despite Calderwood's stated admiration for Maqoma's intelligence and ready wit, the relationship between the two men was very strained by the early 1840s: a substantial part of Calderwood's 1858 memoir *Caffres and Caffre Missions* was devoted to a vindication of his side of quarrels with Maqoma, including lengthy discussions of Maqoma's drinking and (in a key debate over the control of women) of the fact that the chief had compelled one of his wives to put to death the child born of an adulterous affair.[91] Maqoma's quarrels with Calderwood came on the heels of his disaffection with Kayser, from whose influence Maqoma had moved away in 1838. Indeed, H.C. Hummel contends that Kayser's "fierce partisanship" in the 1844 controversy was probably greater than it would have been had Kayser "not felt acutely the loss of Maqoma's removal from his purview."[92]

A further underlying issue related to these questions of racial distinction and of social insecurity was that of whether the missionary should work with "white" congregations, particularly given the growing tendency among urban churches to segment into white and black congregations. Kat River congregations were mixed. Read felt strongly that missionaries should not work at all with white congregations, because they inevitably absorbed most of the missionary's time and effort. On the other hand, Calderwood's *Caffres and Caffre Missions* called for missionaries to minister to both whites and blacks. Ironically, one particular anecdote he cited in support of his view underscored the status anxieties that afflicted Calderwood: the minister, by then employed as government agent, recounted that he had helped spiritually a white colonel's wife on her sickbed, despite the fact that the colonel himself had earlier treated Calderwood with a "marked disrespect," owing to his "enmity to my religious views and character," such that Calderwood requested the Governor to "cause him to understand the respect that was due at least to my official position." The colonel's wife recovered but the colonel unexpectedly died in a most satisfactory manner after being seized with a cold following Calderwood's spiritual ministrations. "All this rose out of the circumstance, under the Divine blessing, of Mr.Laing and myself being led to keep up an English service every Sabbath ..."[93] It does not seem far-fetched to detect here Calderwood's considerable anxiety that he be included in the community of the respected and the respectable. Similarly, one of the underlying criticisms of Locke in the Grahamstown affair was that he focused too much on his white congregation. This was also one of the issues at stake in the Hepburn case that started the entire attempt to oust Read. Commenting on the Hepburn affair, Read criticized the whole policy of having missionaries work with whites in his infamous letter to Struthers.

White missionaries arguably felt all the more insecure because people of African backgrounds, particularly Khoekhoe, were carrying out evangelization in a way that threatened white control. The paradigm case was the extensive native agency employed by the Griqua churches. In theory (and in practice for some), the LMS was committed to creating an African priesthood and phasing itself out. As LMS director J.J. Freeman put it in 1851, "the great desideratum in all Christian missions, next to the conversion of men to the Christian faith itself, is *the preparation of a Native Ministry*."[94] In practice, by the mid-nineteenth century in south Africa, the concept of missionary tutelage for an indefinite period seemed firmly entrenched.

Several parallel developments were taking place. In Britain itself, as I argued above, evangelicalism had become more institutionally dominant and dissenting denominations more politically conservative. The missionary enterprise was tied more specifically to British nationalism and less widely seen as an offshoot of a shared revivalist culture. In the meantime, in southern Africa itself, African networks were actually becoming more professionalized and more extensive – a reality that it was often hard for the newly arrived missionary operating with a romantic self-image to grasp. Equally, whatever central administrators wanted, the local LMS was for the most part in retreat from the concept of an African priesthood. Many missionaries claimed that

Africans were insufficiently civilized, while more advanced training for native agency and eventual ordination of blacks were becoming topics for acrimonious debate.

It had not escaped missionary notice, furthermore, that Christianity was often used as part of a subversive spiritual *bricolage*: had not Nxele, war prophet in 1819 and Xhosa national hero, initially preached a version of Christianity, to be transformed into the idea of separate gods for whites and for blacks? What was Christianity if its boundaries could not be policed by its accredited agents? In this context, native agency, which both exemplified the successes of Christianity and yet threatened to take it in worryingly uncontrolled directions, evoked ambiguous reactions for many. For some, Griqua evangelization projects, and the supposed moral laxity of earlier native agents to the region from Bethelsdorp, exemplified everything that could go wrong with native agency. Calderwood unwittingly expressed some of that ambiguity well in his memoirs, extolling several Xhosa "native agents" and stressing the importance of native agency by Xhosa and Mfengu (not, one notes, Khoekhoe) in Xhosaland. Nonetheless, "they require ... constant superintendence and assistance ... There is a certain inertia in the native mind that requires continual pressure from without, with judicious instruction and superintendence. But with such instruction and supervision, native agency is of the very highest importance."[95]

One might contrast to this the views of Caledon missionary Henry Helm, who responded in 1843 to the requests of LMS directors for missionary views on native agency and the advisability of a seminary by claiming that, generally speaking, "the capacities of the youths of S. Africa, whether they be black or white, are not, as far as I know, inferior to those of Europe." Helm clearly interpreted this debate as being about relative racial intelligence. Interestingly, he reversed the emerging racial hierarchies of the day: "In conversing one day with Mr. Halbeck on this subject, he said that he had taught children in Germany, England, Ireland and South Africa, and he had found the Irish to be the first in learning and the hottentots the second." Helm went on to say: "That hottentot children do not make in general more progress in schools than they do, is not for the want of capability, but their being so frequently absent, either through the negligence of the parents or through poverty, so as it is at present the case at this place. I must however add that their progress is more in learning to read, write etc, than in other exercises in which they have to exercise more their own thoughts for instance in cyphering etc. Perhaps this arrives not from incapability but from a dislike to exercise their capabilities and if so they may cured of this by training and exercise."[96] These views were all part of the same conversation, as the LMS mooted but never brought to fruition in the 1840s the project of a seminary for the training of an African "native agency" and, ultimately, clergy; the same debate would eventually lead to the much later foundation of Lovedale, aimed at Xhosa rather than "coloured" students. Calderwood implied, without saying so directly, that the "native mind" was intrinsically inferior, whereas Helm, a supporter of the seminary project and an opponent of the district-committee system, clearly thought that poverty slanted an otherwise level playing field.[97] It is significant, however, that both opponents and proponents of a "native seminary" assumed that they needed to argue about race and intelligence, underlying the growing racialization of white discourse in both Britain and south Africa.

By the 1840s, there were well-organized networks of "native agents," based at the Kat River settlement. Participants in these networks ran a number of outstations and de facto mission stations, under the putative leadership of James Read Sr and his sons but certainly without the "constant superintendence and assistance" advised by Calderwood. Kat River native agents were partially financed by Kat River inhabitants. The auxiliary missionary society, for example, held annual meetings and publicized the names of donors and the size of their contributions, like its sister organizations elsewhere, in a way that doubtless also publicized the respectability of contributors. In 1844 Read was able to report that "we had a good meeting. Our income was then [three weeks ago] about £220; 'tis now upwards of £250, and daily more coming in; 'twill reach at least £260, if not £270."[98] Agents were also funded by private donors in Britain. Like the schoolteachers who were important intermediaries in the Kat River settlement (some of whom resigned in the 1840s because they were not being paid enough), a number of these "native agents" were essentially employees – although contractually of whom is not entirely clear – in the sense that they were working full-time in exchange for a small salary. Read was able to mobilize monetary support for these agents and schoolteachers, particularly after his 1836–37 visit to Britain. Extensive speaking tours by the south Africans publicized the Kat River settlement. In 1839 Read had over £100 in private donations from Britain to support eight "native teachers,"[99] while in 1844 he had over £100 from England for the Kat River mission to the Thembu.[100] In 1843 Read sent reports on five native agents to financial backers in Britain; he seems to have been paying these agents between £15 and £28 per annum, varying according to the size of their families.[101]

These agents included men such as Matroos Jaris, a smith. Jaris was brought up at Bethelsdorp. There he was a playfellow of Dyani Tshatshu, with whom Jaris made itinerant preaching trips. In 1815 Jaris helped Joseph Williams and Tshatshu found a short-lived mission to the Xhosa. Many years later, he accompanied Tshatshu and the new LMS agent John Brownlee to found another Xhosa mission station at the Buffalo River. After that he went to the people of the Thembu chief known to Read as "Kagalla," replacing the Khoekhoe agent Boosman Stuurman at a station which continued after Kagalla's removal and death. In 1843 Matroos was struggling unsuccessfully to irrigate the station and contending with the results of the previous year's crop failure, which had created serious problems for his large family.

Another agent, Andries Jager, supported by a Miss Hewitt, had likewise been an early inhabitant of Bethelsdorp. He had then moved to Theopolis after the creation of that station. He had done well at school there, and John Philip had sponsored him to attend the LMS English school at Salem. About 1822, according to Read, " it pleased God to change his heart," and he "became a decided follower of Christ," so esteemed by missionary and church alike that he was chosen deacon and held the office seemingly continuously until he left Theopolis around 1838 to come to Blinkwater in the Kat River settlement. Throughout this period, Jager "had likewise been employed to exhort at different times and different places." After his arrival at Blinkwater (where Calderwood's station would be established in 1839), Jager went as a native teacher to the new settlements on the Fish River, founded by the government for new Khoekhoe settlement although shortly thereafter abandoned. There, Jager had a school, taught people to read, held services on Sundays and twice during the week, and was responsible for several conversions. Once the Fish River settlements were disbanded, Jager went to work as a native teacher at the Philipton church's outstation of Bruceton, originally set up in order to serve local San and people living with them. In this place he maintained in 1843 a Sunday school and a "good day school," in addition to holding religious worship. Jager also acted as an agent of the LMS civilizing project, trying to teach agricultural techniques and encouraging the acquisition of material goods: when the station was first founded, the inhabitants of Bruceton "were in fact living upon wild geese, Qwuagga's meat and wild Roots they were almost in a state of nudity, and living in miserable habitations ...[and] seen ploughing with ploughs without an ounce of Iron." Now they were "living in comfortable dwellings are well dressed and have good ploughs and are in most comfortable circumstances and above all very many are members of [the] christian church – and enjoying the benefits of christian ministry."[102] Men such as Matroos Jaris and Andries Jager were indubitably motivated by profound Christian belief; they also had career paths. There was not much difference between what the unordained Jager was doing at Bruceton, including holding divine services, and what the ordained Calderwood, for example, was doing at Blinkwater – and it was Calderwood who was perceived as the unwelcome interloper into a functioning system.

The relative autonomy of Khoekhoe native agents is suggested by the fact that there had even been a theological schism at Bruceton some eight years previously, well before the trouble at Grahamstown – not, of course, that Read saw parallels between the cases. As he recorded, "the first native Teacher they had – was afflicted about 8 years ago with the brain fever. He has never been right since and has taken up with strange notions – as not to believe in original sin – not to believe in the Deluge not to credit the Epistles as part of the word of God &c and tis to be regretted that several of those to whom we had reason to hope he had been usefull to adhere to him, and they have their separate worship. But some of them are getting tired of the poor man's nonsense and we hope will soon leave him."[103]

The Kat River community ran an important if troubled mission to the people of the San chief Madola. Despite some tension between Khoekhoe and Mfengu, native agents also worked among the Mfengu who were rushing into the colony and in particular into the Kat River region. Khoekhoe agents also worked among Thembu groups to the north, as well as in Kat River outstations.[104] Such activity, which continued in a more formal manner the evangelization work of earlier Khoekhoe converts to Christianity, reflected broader regional patterns – as Khoekhoe-descended groups elsewhere tried to take over the missionary mantle of spiritual authority with important political implications. In areas of considerable ethnic diversity, such as Kat River was becoming in the 1830s and 1840s, Christianity also furnished a means (however fragile) of integration and the possibility of an imagined common community. Khoekhoe evangelization posed, however, a threat to a number of white missionaries, insecure as they were in both black and white communities. It is telling that one of the main bones of contention between the Read and Moffat-Calderwood factions in the district-committee debate was that the committee system deliberately excluded the unordained; Read thought that this was clearly designed to exclude native agents.

Beyond the Cape Colony, native agency was already being used by some African societies to shore up the power of particular interest groups. Missionary attempts to exert their own control over the selection and maintenance of preachers and other agents and officials interfered with the political uses being made of Christianity by groups involved in local power relations. We have already briefly considered the example of the Griqua. Paul Landau has shown this process in operation with particular force in the kingdom of Khama, among the

Ngwato Sotho-Tswana of modern-day Botswana, where younger royals mobilized Christianity to establish a new form of regional hegemony. As Landau argues, in GammaNgwato "African preachers and teachers, *baruti*, were far more important in restructuring 'missionary' Christian life than a handful of missionaries."[105] Throughout the late nineteenth century and early twentieth century, Tswana converts ousted unpopular missionaries as they ceased to serve their purposes, and Africans and white missionaries tended to compete for the management of missions. Read Sr's evidence would suggest that similar processes may have been at work even earlier.

Consider the example of conflicts between the entourage of the chief Mothibi (with whom LMS missionaries had first settled in 1816) and the LMS missionary Holloway Helmore. On an extended visit with Philip to the interior, Read acted for three days in 1842 as an interpreter between Philip and Tswana men, all, as the proletarian Read respectfully noted, "young Princes, most intelligent pious Men," who were attempting to get rid of the unpopular Helmore. The dispute came at a time at which African groups were manoeuvring to avoid voortrekker hegemony. The initial complainants included Tabe, son of the "well known chief Tyso," Mothibi's two sons "Jantze (or John) and James," and Mothibi's son-in-law and his nephew "Koka," "all office Bears [Bearers], or managers or had been so at Sekatlong, they had been my school children from 1816 to 1820." They wanted to be rid of Helmore because, among other things, he had deposed Tabe as schoolmaster and native teacher and had fired Jantze, Mothibi's son, as a deacon of the church, "both for a frivolous act, and both without consulting or the Sanction of the Church." He had barred a woman from communion against the wishes of the congregation. Furthermore, Helmore had broken his agreement, sanctioned by the LMS directors, with Griqua Town missionaries that Sekatlong was to be considered an outpost of Griqua Town: "He had broken off all friendship with those Missionaries, and all the regulations established by them had been dispensed with, and without consulting those missionaries, or the office Bearers of the Church." Running through all these complaints was the critical issue of the relative authority of the local church, particularly its officials, and of the missionary.[106] As missionaries and Christian chiefs negotiated with the British government, these were important political issues.

Philip insisted that a meeting be called with Helmore in attendance to answer the charges. At this meeting, other members of the male elite attended, including Mothibi, Tyso, and "several others of the most respectable, and influential members of the church and community." Philip indeed dismissed Helmore from his post at Sekatlong, although the LMS directors in London would overturn this decision. Wright and Read were later attacked for their role in this affair (Wright posthumously; his widow was much distressed by the letter of censure from the LMS directors, according to Read). Read, however, defended the right of native agents as employees of the LMS to appeal directly to Philip as the superintendent of the LMS in southern Africa, over the head of local missionaries – in a debate that arguably again echoed that occurring over settler democracy.

In his discussion of this earlier rift with the LMS, Read stressed that native agents and churches would increasingly demand autonomy in the future in southern Africa, and that directors and missionaries alike essentially needed to work out how to deal with a fact that they were powerless to change. The churches in "heathen lands" were beginning to understand the nature of church membership and the constitution of a Christian church, not only regarding the "duties" of members (above all to spread the gospel – a very evangelical conception) but also regarding their "privileges": namely, to admit and exclude members, to elect deacons, and to assist in the choice of pastor. This last issue had lain dormant because missions churches had not hitherto paid their own ministers, but it was now coming to the fore as a cash-strapped home society tried to shift costs to locals: "The people have asked, and have been told that if they support their own Pastor, or Missionaries they have a right in their choice – this is a new state of things for which the Directors & the Churches of England must be prepared. Tho I have been 42 years in the missionary work in Africa, I never spoke to the people upon this subject or preached upon it till the thing has been forced upon us by the natural course of events; our people know well now not only what is their duty but what is their privilege."[107]

This wider framework brings us back to the question of whether such disputes actually mattered in some sense beyond that of the injured careers and egos of the missionaries involved. I would argue that they did. It made some difference to Cape politics that the Philip/Read party ultimately lost influence so extensively both in southern Africa and in Britain, among both the LMS directors and the staff of the Colonial Office. This is evident, for example, in the ultimate failure of Philip's efforts in the 1840s to act as broker between the Griqua, Moshweshwe, and imperial government in opposing voortrekker expansion to the north. In the short term, Calderwood lost his fight with Read and left the LMS to work directly for the government. Internecine strife within the LMS was, however, a symptom of much broader problems with LMS radicalism by the 1840s. The brief promise of direct relationships between the imperial government and African groups which seemed enticing in the 1830s was essentially broken by the 1840s, although the hope of a return would remain powerful. The attacks on Read in 1843 and 1844, followed by more serious attacks on the Kat River settlement and on the vestiges of LMS radicalism as a whole in the wake of the 1850–53 rebellion of many Christians of Khoekhoe background, helped put paid to the notion of the LMS in particular as a useful conduit of African opinion. It is telling that the Kat River rebel leader, Willem Uithaalder, justified Khoekhoe rebellion in 1851 with the assertion that missionaries had grown old fighting oppression which had not ceased. "The Missionaries have for years written, and their writings won't help."[108] Other young rebels clearly shared this view at the time. Conversely, Calderwood was an important figure in the government's later program to "civilize" and Christianize conquered Xhosa groups, and he functioned as an "expert" on the Xhosa. It is scarcely surprising that his authoritarian brand of Christianity under such circumstances was profoundly resented as tensions built towards renewed warfare and the cataclysm of the cattle-killing.

Furthermore, the example of Mothibi's counsellors manoeuvring to get Helmore dismissed hints at the political issues at stake behind the theological and organizational disputes of the early 1840s. Who controlled the church, and how much control ministers and elders actually had over community life, could have implications for broader African uses of Christianity for the consolidation of control by particular social groups (as the example of Mothibi's people suggests); it also affected the degree of self-control over their communities of more embattled groups such as the Kat River settlers. Not surprisingly, African leaders tried to choose missionaries in pursuit of their own interests and rejected those both wedded to strong ministerial control and unwilling to cede the ministry to Africans.

In 1849 visiting LMS director John Joseph Freeman acceded to a request by leading male church officials at Blinkwater to ordain Arie van Rooyen, one of the two recipients of the letter from Read Jr intercepted by Calderwood, thus making him "co-pastor" with James Read. At the ordination service, a member of the congregation rose to read, "with an audible voice and suitable expression," a letter signed by the elder Cornelius Magerman and six deacons. It stated that Van Rooyen had for "many years" ministered "as an elder and unordained preacher of the Word." Most important, the signatories affirmed that the church had unanimously resolved to appoint Van Rooyen "as we understand from the Word of God, that each church shall act for itself, and may choose its own teachers."[109] This public statement in a sacral format was highly political. Two years later, in fact, many from Tidmanton became rebels in the wake of colonial injustices against the settlement. Whatever the linkage, the insistence of the Tidmanton congregation on appointing Van Rooyen, and on publicly affirming its right to do so, was politically charged.

There were real theological and intellectual issues at stake for all concerned in the quarrels of the 1840s – and there is no reason to think that at least some in the Kat River settlement did not keep abreast of theological debates in Scotland, given that the Reads were well informed. Theological debates were, however, mediated through political conflict, and in particular through the larger question of authority and spirituality. Most important, perhaps, racial conflict at the Cape transformed European theological debates and disputes over church government. The interaction of political and theological questions is scarcely surprising. Christianity provided (and provides) a powerful language of authority. How was that authority to be harnessed, however? What restrictions should be placed on the unrestricted spread of ecstatic news, for example? How were the authority relations implicit in Christianity, and arguably necessary to communal organization, to be balanced against its liberationist potential, and how did both interact with ideas of race in a politically charged environment? Who, more bluntly, owned the gospel? Who spoke for God?

In 1844 it was James Read who looked like the old-fashioned minister, opposed by younger men such as Calderwood, Brownlee, and Birt. These latter men were part of the reformulation of missionary liberalism which would reshape the nineteenth-century missionary drive. The attacks on Read also symbolized, to my mind (whatever else one thinks about the missionary endeavour), a rethinking of the initial promise of an interracial church, with a colour-blind career path for white and black ministers and church officials as well as racially mixed congregations. The disputes of 1844 and 1845 seemed far less significant in the wake of the War of the Axe which erupted in 1846 and the conflagration of 1850–53 which followed. The issues they raised, however, were weighty with implication for the future.

10 Rebellion and Its Aftermath

The 1846–47 War of the Axe proved to be merely one incident in the final war of conquest which raged between the Xhosa and the white colony from 1846 to the catastrophic conclusion to the cattle-killing by the late 1850s. In the wake of victory in 1847, the British annexed a substantial portion of Xhosaland. Under the overall direction of Cape Governor Sir Harry Smith and the local direction of former dissident LMS missionary Henry Calderwood, the colony embarked on a program of forcible Christianization and "civilization." Calderwood finally had his captive audience and a means to salve his wounded pride. The Ngqika Xhosa chiefs were compelled to pay allegiance to Smith, who set himself up as the great chief, as he fondly imagined, over newly subordinate subchiefs. Smith's absurd shenanigans, including an infamous ceremony in which he forced Maqoma and the other Ngqika Xhosa chiefs to kiss his boots, added personal humiliation for the chiefs to the loss of land and autonomy.

By 1850, tension was escalating on both sides. Among the Xhosa, Mlanjeni, a figure of sacred authority, eradicated witches from the community, cleansing the land of *ubuthi*, and strengthened warriors with war magic. "He became so in the eyes of all a wonderman, who could do great things," reported LMS missionary F.G. Kayser.[1] In the meantime, Smith tried to tighten his faltering control over the new territory, and towards the end of the year he sent an ill-advised military patrol into Xhosaland. On Christmas day 1850, Xhosa warriors attacked the military villages which the British had erected in the formerly independent domains of the Ngqika Xhosa. The attackers spared women and children but killed many of the white male settlers. The war announced by this offensive would drag on until 1853, characterized by growing brutality as British troops turned to scorched-earth policies in Xhosa lands to counter the tactics of guerrilla warfare.[2] Although the war was only part of a much longer struggle, it was remarkable because for the first time since the "servants' revolt" of 1799–1803, Khoisan and the formerly enslaved rose in large numbers from within the Cape Colony in support of the Xhosa. For many on both sides, the war became seen as one of "white" against "black."

The internal colonial rebellion has been read as a redemptive moment of subaltern unity in the Cape, whether of class or of race. It has also been seen as a redemptive moment of another sort, the doomed apogee of "Hottentot nationalism." There is much truth to these moving and powerful narratives of redemption. At the same time, there were many shades of grey to this rebellion. For the Khoisan in their then circumstances, it was unwinnable, and therefore tragic, if possibly necessary. Ironically, the war played to the ultimate advantage of wealthy white farmers and land speculators. The Khoisan community was not united behind the rebellion, but deeply divided. The price of this division was that men turned on one another, and male Khoisan loyalists were obliged to hunt down Khoisan rebels. Open military conflict over the meaning of the "Hottentot nation" perhaps in the end meant that nationalism contained the seeds of its own destruction: it was not realizable without more blood than many were willing to shed and without fratricidal division in the name of unity. Furthermore, the rhetoric of sharp ethnic division concealed the interconnection of lives in the Eastern Cape.

At the same time, the rebellion poses many puzzles which are hard to solve. What exactly did "Hottentot nationalism" mean? What was the relative importance of notions of black unity and black consciousness, and of specifically Khoekhoe consciousness? The uprising became a clash of ways of seeing the world, in which fundamental material conflicts were reinterpreted through the prism of narrative. From the cauldron of ethnic conflict arose hardened notions of race and deeper divisions, even as Khoekhoe participants became less able to mobilize politically around the concept of ethnicity. The war is impossible to understand without some account of ambiguity and intertwined lives, although its ironic legacy was an entrenched rhetoric of division.

The rebellion marked a dramatic turning point in a number of the competing narratives which had been told about the so-called "civilized Hottentots" of the Cape Colony, and in particular about Kat River. The aftermath of the rebellion saw the political triumph of the white-settler narrative which rejected the capacity of Africans to become "civilized." This overthrew the central premise of the liberal-humanitarian narrative painstakingly constructed around the notion of Kat River as an exemplary settlement of free blacks, liberated by Christianity, free labour, and access to the marketplace. The triumph of the white-settler narrative both reflected and helped create a developing climate of racial pessimism in Britain, itself increasingly influenced by settler colonialism. At the same time, many rebels used another narrative, about the endurance of the "Hottentot nation." They mobilized "Hottentot" ethnicity to the ends of rebellion and demanded the return of land. Caught in the middle, Khoekhoe loyalists struggled, with great difficulty, to piece back together the "divided self" of colonialism.

THE COURSE OF WAR

Several historians have written compelling accounts of the course of this tragic war which interested readers may wish to consult.[3] The Khoekhoe experience was distinct from that of the Xhosa. In the earliest days of the war, many among the inhabitants of the Kat River settlement and the Eastern Cape mission stations tried to remain neutral except in defence of their own homes. Recruitment officers at Bethelsdorp, for example, were met by a public meeting. Speeches were made in which speakers explained that they had been defrauded of their pay during the last war and had returned to find that their cattle, left without keepers, had been sold at public auction: "On their return home they found themselves *ruined*. They professed the utmost loyalty towards Government and their Queen, but they refused again to serve in the field."[4] Almost the entire white-burgher force of the colony also refused to fight.[5] Afrikaner settlers proved particularly leery of getting involved in a "British" war. Only the so-called "coloured" settlers, however, were accused of rebellion through the very act of not fighting. Neutrality was not an option for the Khoisan.

At least some of the colony had forewarning of the outbreak of war and planned to rebel; how many is hard to judge. On 30 December 1850 Hermanus Matroos, leader of a settlement at Blinkwater in the Kat River, attacked a military post close to Fort Beaufort, and on 1 January 1851 his forces captured the fortified farmhouse of W. Gilbert, a Blinkwater commissioner[6]. Matroos was an ironic leader for a explicitly Khoekhoe or "Hottentot" uprising. He was the son of an escaped slave and a Xhosa woman. In his youth he had worked on a farm in the colony, and at some later point he had been incorporated into the Xhosa Jwara clan.[7] He later served the British government as an interpreter. In exchange, the British had given Matroos territory in the Kat

River settlement, on the western banks of the Blinkwater River. There, by 1842, Matroos had gathered around him a large number of impoverished clients, mostly Xhosa and Mfengu, including forty-eight men and their families; Stockenstrom, who claimed that he was disliked and feared by local Khoekhoe, had reduced his territory in 1836.[8] In the 1846 War of the Axe, Matroos had fought again for the British government. Like so many others, he was defrauded of his pay after the war and nurtured a deep grudge against the British which was further fed by disputes over his tenure of land and by his resentment of illegal taxes levied upon him.[9] Although Matroos would become a nationalist hero, his life story suggests that he was also a would-be client, poorly treated by those with whom he sought to cooperate.

Matroos's group, initially made up mostly of Gonaqua, first attacked local farm houses. Matroos compelled the people of Tidmanton at Kat River, deprived of their guns by nervous white administrators, to join his band.[10] Whether or not these early conscripts were reluctant, the rebellion rapidly spread unaided, gaining adherents as tension escalated during warfare. Farm workers flocked to the rebel standard in large numbers, while inhabitants of the mission stations of Theopolis and Shiloh as well as Kat River residents joined. Women and children went to the rebel camp in large numbers; in many cases, entire families relocated together.

On 8 January 1851 Matroos led an unsuccessful rebel assault on the town of Fort Beaufort. He was shot during the battle, and paid with his life. Willem Uithaalder was chosen "Commandant by general consent" of the rebels to replace Matroos. As Clifton Crais points out, Uithaalder and his brother Frederik were the sons of Philipton erfholder Jan Uithaalder. Both brothers had served in the Cape Mounted Rifles (CMR) and, as Crais surmises, both probably now lacked land.[11] As a former soldier, Uithaalder was also, like Matroos, a man who had cooperated militarily with the British in the past who may well have felt that he had gained little reward in return.

Before the war began, Willem Uithaalder and his brother-in-law Koetgang, another key rebel leader, had travelled from farm to farm seeking support among farm workers. Koetgang and others had held meetings after church services in various parts of the Kat River settlement. Hermanus Matroos, with his many Xhosa links, had himself visited the war prophet Mlanjeni before the outbreak of conflict.[12] The degree of premeditation is difficult to establish, however – especially since settlers sought to exaggerate evidence of premeditation and since, on the other side, denying premeditation became a potentially life-preserving strategy for rebels on trial.[13] A number of people indeed claimed at trial or before subsequent commissions that rebels rounded up civilians and forced them to remain with their forces, and doubtless some were indeed reluctant rebels.

In early 1851 a colonial force led by Colonel Somerset brutally captured the Kat River settlement. Both Mfengu and white members of this force committed atrocities against local inhabitants, including loyalists. Some white settlers paraded through the vallley with a red flag bearing the word "extermination." This was to prove a military watershed, as the colony regained its hold over Kat River. For a number of loyalists, however, the brutalities strained loyalty to the breaking point. Several days thereafter, many of the soldiers in the Cape Corps deserted in order to join the rebels. In late May and June, rebels would be joined by many from the mission station of Theopolis, who subsequently destroyed much of the station.

Rebellion became a place as much as an organized military movement, and it was a place that included many women. As the war settled down into a protracted guerilla conflict, Khoisan rebels lived in separate settlements in the mountain fastnesses of the Amatolas, raiding farm houses and carrying out commando attacks. Although they did not experience clear-cut military defeat, they did not have sufficient resources to hold out for long periods; by 1852, starving women and children were staggering from the rebel camps. Also by 1852, the already fragile alliance with the Xhosa was fracturing. Nonetheless, some rebels would remain in the bush as late as 1858, despite colonial pardons and despite the formal submission of the Xhosa chiefs to the British in 1853.

THE ROOTS OF REBELLION

As we have seen, and as other scholars have observed, there were substantial material causes for the attraction of what might at first glance appear a doomed rebellion.[14] The rise of large-scale capitalist farming, especially sheep farming, for a world commodity market by the 1840s, the corresponding influx of land-hungry white settlers, and the prevalence of land speculation by local white elites placed intense pressure on land in the Eastern Cape. As I argued in chapter 8, white settlers used cattle pounds and boundary disputes to reduce further Khoisan access to land.

Many in the growing community of white British settlers held a market-oriented vision. They saw their land as alienable property and often claimed that they had it through "civilized" economic practices. In contrast, as we have seen, the Khoekhoe had a deeply rooted conviction that the land was theirs by ancestral right. If anything, the political debates of the 1830s onwards may have made the political need for

"Hottentot" unity and pan-Hottentot land claims more obvious. As the rebel Malau Karabana enquired during a visit of Kat River loyalists to the rebel camp in early 1851, "'this land is our land; but what portion of it is in the possession of the Hottentots? Strangers inhabit it, while the real owners have only this ostrich nest, the Kat River; and this is called giving a nation land.'" Tellingly, he then turned and added to the Xhosa in the same rebel camp, "'Don't think that because we are with you against the settlers, we will submit to you; we are ready to fight you at any day if we see that you wish to domineer over us as you did before.'" [15]

Through the 1840s, white settlers tried to tighten once again their control of nonwhite labour, despite Ordinance 50. In 1841 a relatively coercive Masters and Servants Ordinance was introduced, albeit carefully couched in nonracial terms. In the meantime, the metropolitan government sought to devolve more local government to the white-settler colonies in general. By 1850, nonwhites felt a profound sense of vulnerability as they anticipated the inevitable advent of a settler-run parliament which would be vulnerable to control by those they perceived as their enemies. To make matters worse, two months before the outbreak of war, the Legislative Council called for "an Ordinance to facilitate the removal of Squatters from Government land," which appeared to be renewed vagrancy legislation in a different guise. [16] The threat of vagrancy laws unified Khoekhoe and former slaves. Prominent rebel and former slave Koetgang, for example, was a farm worker who rejected his slave name of Africa April. According to evidence at his trial, when the vagrancy law was discussed before the outbreak of rebellion, Koetgang had said that "he was once a slave but before he would again become one it should cost blood." [17]

Against this background of material struggle, many rebels – and probably many who did not take the step of rebellion – mobilized "Hottentot" ethnicity to political ends. This was at least in some respects a defensive reinvention of ethnicity. Nonetheless, a sense of "Hottentot" identity transcended the boundaries of the Cape Colony, since many of the Cape Khoekhoe had personal links with Khoekhoe elsewhere, most importantly among the Griqua in Transorangia. One of the unintended side-effects of Ordinance 50 may in fact have been that it permitted easier back-and-forth intercourse between the colonial Khoisan and Khoisan communities beyond the colonial frontiers, particularly the Griqua. This may have helped consolidate a sense of "pan-Hottentot" identity. Certainly, one should not assume that nationalism was a static given, nor that its nature did not change over time; "nations" are invented as much as they are discovered. For example, contacts between Khoekhoe leaders and white British liberal groups such as the Aborigines Protection Society or the London evangelicals in the 1830s who engineered the 1836 House of Commons Select Committee on Aborigines in no sense created Khoekhoe land claims, but they did provide an audience and a pressure group which made it politically meaningful for Khoekhoe leaders to make public claims to be "aborigines" who were, as a community, the rightful owners of the land.

If these larger material and ideological motivations of the major players guaranteed a conflagration, more local events lit the fuse. The most obvious was the renewed outbreak of war with the Xhosa, which placed severe strain even on those predisposed to be loyal. Kat River had originally been designed as a military buffer zone, and, as we have seen, it had amply fulfilled that function. Indeed, the sense of a contractual obligation to fight as payment for the land persisted in the mind of descendants as late as 1984. In that year the apartheid state moved the last so-called "coloured" inhabitants from the Kat River in what was then the "Homeland" of the Ciskei, part of the forced removals of several million human beings undertaken in the name of apartheid engineering.[18] J.B. Peires recorded the lament of Piet Draghoender, who recalled that his soldier ancestor Isak Draghoender had been awarded a place in Readsdale by Sir Andries Stockenstrom, "'for your dying, for what you gave up to death, to make the place free and you did make it free,'" just as his other ancestors had continued to fight in colonial wars, including world wars.[19] The nineteenth and twentieth centuries merged into one ongoing sacrifice of blood: "This ground was washed clean by blood."[20] After the economic devastation and human cost of the wars of 1835–36 and 1846–47, however, during which nonwhites had essentially been used as unpaid conscript labour, further military support to the colony seemed materially difficult as well as ideologically repugnant to many.

In the run-up to war throughout the 1840s, the feelings of the people were further inflamed by a series of discriminatory measures.[21] From 1847 onwards, a white British official was assigned by the colonial government to work as magistrate of the hitherto self-governing settlement. Magistrates were drawn from the ranks of the local white elite, who maladministered in consequence, despite the strictures of the Cape Town government which recalled two magistrates in four years. The settlement was subjected to a extraordinary degree of insult by all of its putative leaders. The heavy-handed and highly conservative Thomas Biddulph, who saw the inhabitants as "incorrigibly idle" and "thoroughly corrupted," was recalled by the governor, Sir Harry Smith.[22] His replacement, John Mitford Bowker, was another member of the vocal British anti-missionary and pro-war settler lobby centred at Grahamstown. Bowker held beliefs as strong as Biddulph's about the appropriate role of "savages" in the white economy. He believed, for example, that the Xhosa ought to be incorporated as labourers: *"Savages are unfit to be masters in any way,* they must be taught to earn an honest living. They must begin *from the ground,* as herds, as leaders of wagons, as hewers of wood, and drawers of water. If they can rise at any future period *after* having acquired honest and industrious habits, in God's name let them."[23] Bowker infamously believed that certain races were destined to die away as the springbok of South Africa was vanishing from the plains. As he observed in a speech which became notorious: "I said I felt for the spring buck, and who but regrets the waning herds of them? yet the merino (sheep) is far preferable to them. And this extinction of races even amongst men is a palpable fact which we have every day experience of, and *over which we have no control,* and it is well we have not, with our whining nonsense. And Scripture shows, too, in the destruction of the Canaanites, &c., that God at times wills it that one race should *summarily* make room for another."[24]

Bowker's maladministration of the Kat River settlement was much resented. As we saw in chapter 8, however, it was above all his expulsion by fire of the Gqunukhwebe and Mfengu clients of mostly Gonaqua erf-holders of the lower and upper Blinkwater that proved a flashpoint for conflict. The driving of these bijwoner clients back into the hostile arms of the Xhosa was done in the name of civilization, since Bowker claimed that these pastoralists ought to become agriculturalists. By late 1850, as the countdown began to increased local self-government, nerves were stretched to breaking point.

"RACE WARFARE": BRITISH RHETORIC

Once the war had begun, English-speaking whites and nonwhite rebels alike began to use a language about "race warfare." This is particularly clear in white writing in English. Here, at last, was the confrontation colonists had so long feared.

British settlers, particularly those near the frontier, tended to see themselves as surrounded by Africans within and without the colony of whom, on some fundamental level, they were afraid.[25] Whites were about three-fifths of the population within the Cape colony. In 1850 this fed a fertile language in some quarters about fears of being "swamped." The argument was widely used in support of a high-franchise qualification in the projected representative assembly. Paradoxically, frontier conservatives such as Robert Godlonton and Mitford Bowker, passionate supporters of a high-franchise qualification, also claimed that Africans would melt away like native Americans, following the logic of civilization and evolution. This argument tended in turn to serve as a justification for inequitable treatment, including legislative means to compel labour such as vagrancy legislation. As the *Graham's Town Journal*, edited by Robert Godlonton, airily observed in October of 1850, "the colony is growing in wealth, gaining, power and importance, the black man is melting away before the white man," through what appeared to be "a law of nature."[26] In the meantime, more liberal white commentators continued to urge the "civilization" of Africans as a means to permit white and black to live together in southern Africa. In the words of the *Port Elizabeth Mercury* on the eve of the outbreak of war, "there is no possibility of isolation, our vital interests are connected with the social and political condition of our semi-barbarous neighbours."[27] As the war developed, and as a growing number of nonwhite groups joined the Xhosa side, the language of "race warfare" initially adumbrated by conservatives and exemplified in the vituperative outpourings of Godlonton's *Graham's Town Journal* became more widespread. The rhetoric of race warfare would ultimately serve as a cloak in which to wrap the expropriation of many lands in the Kat River settlements, as well, more broadly, masters and servants legislation which would harshen labour relations between white and black.

Clearly, much of the colonial press needed no encouragement to argue that the Xhosa invasion of military villages over Christmas of 1850 was sufficient justification for a war to the finish which would pit white against black. "A war for Life or Death has commenced," claimed the *Port Elizabeth Telegraph* on 1 January 1851. The paper went on to argue for white unity despite previous editorial criticism of controversial Governor Harry Smith: "*Now* that the Kafirs have struck the first blow and deluged the fertile plains and kloofs of their hitherto peaceful country with the blood of the white man, let all Europeans and their descendants combine to support their Governor with hand and heart ... The white man is to be driven into the sea if possible, the lands of the aboriginal inhabitants are to be regained, and the dark reign of barbarism is to succeed the bright dawn of civilization."[28] The high level of participation by African servants and farm workers in the war particularly troubled white commentators. By 1 February 1851, the more moderate *Port Elizabeth Mercury* was horrified at the vision of betrayal from within: "In many a farm house and laager along our border, a man's foes have been those of his own household."

Extreme white rhetoric about race warfare doubtless to some extent created a self-fulfilling prophecy. In the words of James Read Jr, the "position which some of the whites are said to have taken up against the coloured, after the occurrences at lower Blinkwater," including incitements to "bonds, imprisonments, flagellations, and even murders," changed the character of rebels' proceedings "from a rebellion to a war of races, in which the Hottentots and the Kafirs were against the whites."[29] After a white commando looking for rebels killed several loyalists at Kaspar Oliver's camp in the Kat River settlement on 23 January 1851, for example, the mood of loyalists gathered at Fort Armstrong changed dramatically; according to Read, "there seemed to ooze out the premonitions of a war of races, and a threatening of the extermination of whites or blacks."[30] Among the Xhosa, the war was more clearly than it was for many Khoisan one of black against white, although the Xhosa did not presumably share the culturally determined notions of "race" increasingly espoused by many British. As the chief Sandile said in an interview with the Reverend H. Renton on 17 January 1851 (in words translated sentence by sentence by Tiyo Soga and other "native agents" and transcribed by the Reverend J.F. Cumming): "God made a boundary by the sea, and you White Men cross it to rob us of our country. When the Son of God came into the world, you White Men killed Him. It was not Black Men did that; and you White Men are now killing me ..." He insisted that he would fight to the end – "if you kill me my bones will fight, and my bones' bones will fight. I will rise up and fight against the White Man for ever."[31]

SIR HARRY SMITH
AND "HOW TO HANG REBELS"

On the British side, Governor Sir Harry Smith provides an instructive example of the evolution of a patronizing paternalism towards non-white allies to an increasingly open expression of racial hatred in the wake of rebellion. Smith, whose offensive grandstanding so enraged the Xhosa chiefs, appears to have been an unstable man whose blind maladministration infuriated and oppressed Xhosa and Khoisan alike. As commander-in-chief of the army as well as governor of the Cape Colony, he was also enormously powerful – at least until early 1852, when his colonial master, Earl Grey, dismissed him for his inability rapidly to resolve the war. Oddly romantic, Smith appears to have deluded himself that Xhosa and Khoekhoe alike feared and yet in some way loved him. His private letter books from the field between February and April 1851 provide an unusual opportunity to examine his delusions.

In February 1851 Sir Harry Smith was not having a good war. He had been taken off-guard by the Christmas offensive spearheaded by Maqoma against the military villages. In the aftermath of the uprising, he had found himself trapped at Fort Cox, within territory now held by the Ngqika Xhosa, unable to communicate with the colony. Significantly, he had only been able to escape when he disguised himself as a Khoekhoe soldier and fled the fort with an escort of 250 men from the Khoekhoe regiment, the Cape Mounted Rifles).[32] It was an apt symbol of his military dependence on nonwhite soldiers.

By February 1851, Smith, was holed up near the Amatolas, at Fort William, trying to get enough troops to attack the Ngqika Xhosa under Sandile who were using the Waterkloof and the Amatolas as a base of operations against the colony. Yet, fairly quickly, a vicious stalemate of sorts set in. The Xhosa did not possess the military resources to drive the whites from southern Africa completely, however much damage they could inflict in frontier districts, while the colony itself did not possess the troops to subdue the Xhosa, particularly given the guerrilla warfare tactics imposed by the terrain.

From his base at King William's Town, Smith contemplated the fundamental problem of colonial defence which had long informed the British relationship with the Khoekhoe within colonial boundaries. Troops from Britain itself were expensive to maintain. By 1850, as the Colonial Office sought to cut costs in southern Africa, Harry Smith had sent away some 1,500 regular British troops, leaving him with a force of 4,700 soldiers for the entire colony and the frontier zones. Many of these were Khoisan and a smaller number Mfengu, dispossessed refugees from earlier disturbances in the interior, including the events of the "mfecane."[33] Soldiers also included some 400 or so Xhosa men in the "Kaffir Police," created by Smith in a former posting in 1835. In war time, as Smith was in the process of discovering, whites refused to join levies in large numbers. This was particularly true of Dutch-speakers, who distrusted the British and did not wish to become embroiled in British imperial disputes. This left the colony dependent on nonwhite troops, as was the case in other parts of the empire, notably India. In various incarnations, the Khoekhoe regiment based at Cape Town, at this juncture the Cape Mounted Rifles, had provided colonial defence since the end of the VOC period. "Levies" from the "coloured" communities provided the further backbone of the colonial army in times of war. Without nonwhite allies, the colony was powerless until troops could arrive from elsewhere in the empire. The colony also needed noncombatant support: Smith reflected from his fastness at King William's Town that he was utterly dependent on Ndlambe allies keeping the road open between King William's Town and the Cape. From this perspective, the logic of "black" unity was impeccable, even if one could also argue that in 1850 the ability of the British to continue throwing imperial troops at south Africa guaranteed ultimate victory to the British. The logic of unity would have needed to have been applied across the empire as a whole.

Smith had a sentimental attitude to his nonwhite allies. He had been personally responsible for forming the Kaffir Police and was uncomprehending when Xhosa soldiers deserted at the outbreak of war. Despite the injustices Smith had perpetrated towards colonial Khoekhoe and in particular the Kat River settlement, he saw the Khoekhoe as a well-treated group, enjoying the benefits of civilization, as he insisted in both public and private correspondence. "What is the cause of this revolution of Kafirs and Hottentots?" he mused in a letter to Lord FitzRoy Somerset. "I have no reply – They have all been treated with paternal care, and every measure prudence or foresight or judgment can suggest adopted for their improvement. The outbreak has astonished me and *everyone*; it is confidently believed, although as yet I cannot trace it, that some vile agitators within the Colony have excited these Coloured Classes, until a revolution of 'Guerra e Cuchello' to the White Man has burst forth with a fury these wicked Radicals never expected ..."[34] He saw the Khoekhoe as civilized men who had chosen, probably he thought under the influence of the Reads, to rush back to barbarism. Having been, as he saw it, betrayed by the Khoekhoe, Smith now wanted to hang them. He wrote to Andrew Porter in London requesting help with a tribunal to try the rebels after the conclusion of war. "I know what I want to come at, but do not know how to explain myself. I do not want a long and learned discussion, but a practical statement of 'how to hang Rebels by the shortest possible process.'"[35]

The erratic and often irrational Smith comforted himself, however, that the Khoekhoe soldiers in his army and the incoming Khoekhoe levies were loyal. He called them his "Totties" and wrote constantly to his supply officer for soap, coats, and better tobacco for them – "for I can alone rule my Totties through *smoke*"[36] – and for a flow of rations to the wives and children also present in the camp. The CMR were, he declared, "all cheerful and in pluck."

At the end of February, Major-General Somerset conquered the rebels at Kat River, in an engagement in which the leader Hermanus Matroos was killed. Following this victory, many of the Mfengu and British soldiers in Somerset's army brutally looted and burned much of the settlement, including loyalist areas, and shot some loyalists, including children and an elderly woman with leprosy. Smith's letters have nothing about this conduct, which he had probably not yet heard of, unlike his Khoekhoe soldiers who were in contact by letter with both rebels and loyalists in the settlement. Nonetheless, it was with remarkable insensitivity that Smith assembled his Khoekhoe soldiers and read them the news of the taking of Kat River. "I never saw fellows so delighted or heard three more loyal cheers," he recorded.[37] In the meantime, letters were smuggled in from Kat River to the Khoekhoe soldiers; the soldier David Laverlot read a letter out at a putative prayer meeting, for example. Several days later, Smith was asking for thirty or forty gold medals to be made up for his soldiers, and again requesting more coats. By 15 March, forty-six soldiers of the CMR had deserted, and seemingly more would have if given the chance. "They are all men too of a religious turn," commented Smith bemusedly. He cast the desertions in personal language, reminiscent of British school-boy slang: "Poor Somerset is fearfully cut up about it, as are all the Officers." At the same time, he panicked about the racial implications. He described the Khoekhoe rebellion to his colleague Pine in Natal as part of an "infernal coalition" to "immolate the White Man." It was critical to have some demonstration among the "Coloured Classes" of opposition to this coalition; in raising Zulu troops, Pine had accordingly "acted for the great cause, White v. Black, most opportunely & judiciously."

Smith never did hang rebels, since he decided it would be too polit-ically risky. In a bitter dispatch after receiving notice of his dismissal, Smith proclaimed the inherent untrustworthiness of all blacks in south-ern Africa. He flung at Grey the assertion that, with one false step on his part, the whole region would have been plunged into a "chaos of revolution; Her Majesty's troops must have abandoned their advanced positions, and fallen back on Graham's Town; and the T'Slambie tribes would have risen, as well as every curly-headed black from Cape Town to Natal."[39] In this sense, Smith, despite his romanticism and his pater-nalism, provides a case study in the evolution of racial hatred. His let-ters also indicate that remarkable cognitive gulf between Africans and many of their rulers which permitted the rebellion to be read in such inappropriate ways.

REBEL MOTIVATIONS

The conflict was, however, not entirely reducible to race warfare in the sense understood by colonists, nor was it entirely reducible to class struggle, although both were at work and class and race coincided in obvious respects. The landless demonstrated a greater propensity than the landed to rebel; rebels were poorer than loyalists and more likely to be drawn from the ranks of "squatters" and landless labourers. Nonetheless, there were also many "respectable" rebels, as anguished missionaries called them; some 25 per cent of landholders in the Kat River settlement rebelled, for example, with much to lose.

Undergirding economic disputes was a language about honour and shame in a social system that was to some extent shared. At the Cape Colony, as in other slave societies, shame was an important mechanism to justify the oppression of unfree labour. As I have argued throughout this book, white control of the nonwhite body was a critical marker of labour control. Like the bodies of slaves, Khoisan bodies were considered available by many white settlers for sexual exploitation and for the receipt of violence. White defences of vagrancy legislation were couched in terms of the lack of honour of Khoekhoe, and indeed of their lack of their own control over their bodies. Vagrancy legislation, or anti-squatting laws, were couched as means for the state in *locus parentis* to control the dishonourable body of the African.

The many petty insults offered to the Kat River people by many of the English settlers at Grahamstown, through such media as the colonial press, may not have had the same direct impact as the expulsion of Xhosa settlers. Nonetheless, intense colonial criticism recreated the climate of shaming and dishonour which had accompanied de facto slave status.

The assaults of white male comment against nonwhite men, from newspaper editorials to the banner labelled "extermination" carried into the Kat River settlement by white men during the war, might be taken as a form of emasculation. Consider, for example, the particular offence given by an 1850 commission, established to investigate the theft of cattle, which went to every house, putting fingers into cooking pots to discover traces of butcher's meat: this invaded the home, undercutting masculine control of the family. James Read Jr's extended summation of the many material reasons for rebellion ends simply with a weary reference to the power of extended insult to enrage men. Several captured letters from rebels to each other, or to groups that the rebels were attempting to persuade to join, make reference to "manliness." In a parlay with Kat River loyalist leaders and with the missionaries James Read Sr, W. Thomson, and James Read Jr, Uithaalder, for example,

like a naughty child that could not have its own way, threw himself on the ground, and pretended to be much affected while he held his head downwards, saying to Mr. Thomson – "Sir, you and Mr. Read were both young when you came among us, and you are now both old, and klein Mynheer (young Mr. Read) had no beard when he came to Kat River, and he is now getting advanced in years, and yet these oppressions won't cease. The Missionaries have for years written, and their writings won't help. We are now going to stand up for our own affairs. We shall show the settlers that we too are men."[40]

In his stronghold in the Amatolas, Uithaalder set himself up to be respected. He styled himself "koning," had every captain report to him, established a magistrate to administer a written law code he had composed, and insisted that those who waited upon him at dinner wear white gloves. Indeed, Uithaalder's magistrate, Johannes Fortuin, complained after being captured by the British that Uithaalder was becoming increasingly authoritarian, to the dissatisfaction of his fellows.[41] He had glass windows installed in his house. Although he could not read, he displayed his book of laws as a token of his authority. Several years later, he sent a delegation to the British Thembu resident Warner "as a friend." Through this delegation, remaining Khoekhoe in the land of Sarhili explained that to enter service was odious to them and that they required land to live like gentlemen.[42]

The rebel desire to restore honour intersected with the apparent drive of many rebels to reconstitute the shattered "Hottentot" nation. The heterogeneity of Khoekhoe communities by 1850 was not incompatible with a nationalist rhetoric, particularly given the propensity of the Khoekhoe, like other African groups, to incorporate people of other ethnicities. Nonetheless, Khoekhoe identity was under severe threat. The various dialectical variations of Cape Khoekhoe were well on the road to extinction; Dutch had become the lingua franca of the descendants of Khoekhoe and San communities, as of slaves and their descendants. Recall Andries Stoffels's insistence in the 1830s that the Hottentot nation was dying. The term "nation," or *natie*, was widely used in the 1830s to describe what we might now call an ethnic group, without the connotations of late-nineteenth-century cultural nationalism. It clearly already had the sense of the Khoekhoe as a whole, however. Possibly the vicissitudes of common oppression and the emergence of Dutch as a lingua franca in fact helped consolidate a sense of "Hottentot" identity which might earlier have been more fragmented. Be that as it may, in 1851 rebel leader Spielman Kiewit tried to incite a Kat River veldcornet to rebel by appealing directly to notions of the "Hottentot nation": "Our circumstances as the Hottentot nation and other circumstances connected therewith are now become very melancholy, and on this account we have put our hands to a work from which we have no wish to retreat. We have done this without acquainting all of you who belong to our nation, and in this we have acted very improperly ... but with this acknowledgement we take the liberty to acquaint you as our nation, that we have commenced war with the settlers and to call upon you as our nation to assist us ... Arise courageously and work for your motherland and freedom."[43] Willem Uithaalder was equally explicit in a famous letter which sought to win the support of Griqua leader Adam Kok beyond the boundaries of the Cape Colony:

Forasmuch as we the poor oppressed Hottentot race are objects of the present war which is going on here, who have now been for a considerable time oppressed by the unrighteous English settlers, who have so continually petitioned the Government, by memorials, for consent and execution of irregular and oppressive laws, such as vagrant laws, which tend to oppression and complete ruin of the coloured and poor of this land, a land which we, as natives, may justly claim as our mother land, it is my aim and object, by this opportunity esteeming it my duty, owing to all who are there as nation and family of one house (although long delayed and neglected therewith), to give information that this war which is going on here, is declared against us Hottentots because we defend ourselves against above-mentioned laws, or will not let them pass ... Beloved, rise manfully and unanimously as a nation and children of one house to engage yourselves in this important work, a work which concerns your mother country, for not a single person of colour, wherever he may be, will escape this law.[44]

Some Khoekhoe dreamed during the rebellion of establishing a new Khoekhoe territory. Sandile promised the "children of Chama" (described by James Read Jr as "one of the old Hottentot chiefs") that he would restore the "kingdom of Chama"; at a meeting at Soga's place in Xhosaland, Sandile asked assembled Khoekhoe whether they knew of any "heirs of the old Hottentot dynasty" who might be restored to their former position. Read argued that this was "frothy nonsense" but that it was effective in motivating some to rebel.[45] No claimants to an ancient "Hottentot" dynasty were apparently found. This is a significant fact in itself, if true – and reminds us of Uithaalder's comment that the larger "Hottentot" nation had been "long neglected."

One must ask, however, how many might seriously have believed that a "Hottentot" nation might be restored throughout southern Africa, given their knowledge of the entrenchment of British power in the region? It seems even more unlikely that many believed they could expel the British altogether, despite the hysterical fears of settlers. Uithaalder himself affirmed that he was "not against the Queen."[46] There is a fascinating, and not entirely explicable, contradiction between, on the one hand, the reported comments of a number of rebels that they supported Queen Victoria, and, on the other, the rebels' well-documented hatred of English settlers and the stated desire of many to drive them into the sea[47] and the reported desires of others to re-establish a Khoekhoe nation. Did many hope for an independent territory recognized by the queen, removed from settler influence? Arguably, some Khoekhoe were in fact attempting to make a defensive manouvre against white settler aggression by defining themselves as a collectivity and then appealing to the imperial centre in order to assert themselves as a community with a direct relationship to the crown, independent of settler control. In some respects this recalls the Iroquois notion of the "two-row" wampum, important in early nineteenth-century negotiations with the British, and reflects the contemporary strategies of other so-called aboriginal peoples.

The political mobilization of "Hottentot" ethnicity was undertaken in a relatively diverse community in which lives were intertwined and yet which was increasingly fractured by ethnic tension. "You must be cautious with regard to new-comers," Andries Links warned Keivit Pequin of Theopolis, "namely such as emancipated slaves (apprentices) for they are tale-bearers, and they will always be; and you may feel sure that an apprentice will never separate himself from the white man."[48] The Mfengu at Kat River, placed there by government in an unpopular move and later to be the shock troops of the government against the Khoekhoe rebels, were looked down upon and resented by the Khoekhoe, and disliked the Khoekhoe in return. When the colonial commando "relieved" the Kat River settlement, not only most of the English but "the whole of the Fingoes" jeered loyalists coming to meet with General Somerset, "hissing and hooting in derision."[49] Much of the show trial of Gonaqua leader Andries Botha turned around the relationship between Mfengu and Khoekhoe at the Kat River settlement. Mfengu witnesses in the service of the British state gave damning evidence against Botha, while Khoekhoe witnesses defending Botha attested that Botha had fled when the British general Somerset arrived at the settlement, not because he was a rebel but because he feared for his life from Somerset's Mfengu soldiers.[50] Tensions mounted as the war progressed: witnesses at Botha's trial also attested to an incident in which three Mfengu men came close to being lynched by a crowd of enraged Khoekhoe young men.[51] The Mfengu, James Read Jr, observed bitterly in his account of the Kat River Rebellion, were "active but independent factotums and 'footpads'" who "did all the dirty work of their instigators – who uttered all they were told to say, and laid their hands on every thing, animate and inanimate, which came in their way."[52] On 31 May 1851 rebel Khoisan began a revolt at the mission station of Theopolis, some twenty-five miles from Grahamstown, by surrounding the houses of the Mfengu on the station and shooting them as they came out. They shot for about an hour and killed several.[53] The "Kafir Police" who burned out the Blinkwater settlers were also hated, not least because they symbolized the government's willingness to arm defeated Xhosa while taking guns away from the colonial Khoekhoe.

Overriding these tensions, however, was that passionate dislike of the English which would permit Xhosa and Khoisan to make common cause. H. Beich of Kat River, a Khoekhoe witness before the Commission of Inquiry into the Kat River Rebellion, had been "brought up with the Bowkers" and was, according to James Read Jr, "obnoxious to the Hottentot, from being so thoroughly anglasized [sic] in his feelings."[54] It is telling that one of the first demands of rebels was that, except for missionaries, "the English" (including the hapless Beich) leave the settlement: one might see this as a form of purification of the community. The English fled, uncertain of the true feelings even of those who had not rebelled. Ironically, however, the "English" included not only better-off shopkeepers but also, according to James Read Jr, the "many bad English" who sought a "refuge" in Kat River. Some, like Thomas Davis, were married to Khoisan women. Frederick Waddington, in contrast, lived with Matroos Jaris, a Khoekhoe farmer (and former native agent?) at Hartbeestfontein and "kept a young Hottentot female." James Green was a respectable elder in the Philipton Independent church married to a Khoisan woman, whom rebels explicitly permitted to stay in the settlement along with white missionaries; his brother John, however, was, according to Read, a "complete besotted inebriate" who before he became a resident at Kat River had "run his full course of vice" at Bushman's River, "as whites and colored can all testify."[55] This suggests that expelling the English from the settlement may also have been a way of restoring, or perhaps of imagining, a less complicated past of neater ethnic divisions, even though anti-white solidarity between rebels was also an important factor.

A final point to be made about ethnic diversity is the ambivalent relation between Khoekhoe and Xhosa, who had overlapping claims to lands in the Eastern Cape. The Khoekhoe had fought against the Xhosa in previous colonial wars, while Xhosa warriors had twice burnt down much of the Kat River settlement. The war of 1850–53 is rightly considered remarkable because of the mobilization of the concept of blackness by the oppressed of the Eastern Cape to make common cause against colonialism. Nonetheless, the Khoekhoe under Uithaalder defined themselves as "Hottentot" and made it clear to Xhosa groups that the "Hottentots" were fighting their own battles, despite the fact that the Gonaqua in particular tended to speak both the Xhosa and Dutch languages and had a considerable degree of Xhosa ancestry. Indeed, Jacob Peters would later attest during preliminary examinations in the trial of Koetgang that he regretted joining the camp of rebel leader Willem Uithaalder once he realized that Xhosa and Khoekhoe were fighting in the same commandos. "On my return to the Camp I spoke to the prisoner 'Koetgang' respecting the Kaffers and Hottentots and told him if I knew the Kaffers and Hottentots would have joined I would have nothing to do with the war." Koetgang, the former slave for whom black solidarity might well have been a crucial issue, replied "that if he thought that these were my feelings he would shoot me."[56] Late in the war, Uithaalder and his men captured a key Ndlambe chief, Toyise, who had been acting as an informer and supporter to the British. Instead of turning him over to Sandile's men to be put to death, however, they refused to hand him over without a guarantee of a trial and a clear statement of charges and evidence, probably in keeping with Uithaalder's legalistic approach to government and his veneration of the written rule of law. When Sandile refused to guarantee a trial, Uithaalder let Toyise escape – cementing a serious break with Sandile. By the end of the war, ironically, Xhosa chiefs were sending messages to the British asking whether they would be pardoned if they turned in Uithaalder.

In sum, the mobilization of ideas about honour, shame, masculinity, and ethnicity were all important if intangible factors in explaining rebellion. They also, however, point to the ambiguities of intertwined lives in the mid-nineteenth-century south Africa.

CHRISTIANITY AND REBELLION

Furthermore, the conflict cannot fully be understood without consideration of belief in spiritual forces, and debate over them. It is not at all surprising that the Xhosa invasion of their former lands followed a witchcraft-eradication campaign, as the young prophet and spiritual leader Mlanjeni cleansed the land of witches, performed remarkable miracles, and doctored soldiers before battle in order to turn the bullets of the British to water. At the same time, among the Khoekhoe, white missionaries, and perhaps even some Xhosa, the war also became a canvas for debates over the meaning of Christianity. What did Christianity mean politically in the new context of the 1850s? Did it require non-violence? Did it confer worldly power, or the capacity to bear the slings and arrows of the world? Could missionaries themselves be trusted in the wake of the betrayals of Calderwood and others? Khoekhoe rebels implicitly disputed with loyalists the gist of the Christian message as they sought to mobilize Christianity as an instrument of resistance and possibly as a prophylactic to assist in battle. Two further mingled themes, however difficult to recapture at this juncture, were Christian millenarianism and the mutual influence of Xhosa and Christian beliefs.

On 14 January 1851, a delegation of Khoekhoe loyalists, headed by veldcornet Cobus Fourie and including James Read Jr, visited the rebel camp at Blinkwater in order to make known an offer of pardon from General Somerset and to parlay with the rebels. The group was a mixed one of Xhosa and Khoekhoe, who had nonetheless separated themselves into separate camps. Hermanus's followers were there. So, too, were Xhosa former servants, Khoekhoe and Gqunukhwebe from the lower Blinkwater, some Khoekhoe from the upper Blinkwater region of the Kat River settlement, petty tenants who had hired land from Dutch and English farmers, and Khoekhoe former farm workers from the Winterberg district. To the political complaints of rebels were added, according to Read, "a little of *Umlangenism* and a vein of Scripture perversion." Two weeks later, Read, several Khoekhoe loyalists, and a white minister returned to the upper Blinkwater rebel camp on a Sunday to preach. The white minister, W.R. Thomson, went to preach to Uithaalder's people, while James Read went to Hermanus's people and the Gonas, grouped at the settlement of Hendrik Noeka. There, Read found a Xhosa-language church service in progress. At its conclusion, the preacher asked a Xhosa Christian convert named Bozak to pray; "the first part was very good; but we heard him earnestly praying for the great prophet Umlanjeni, and the child of Gaika, Sandilli, on whose head a price had been set." The preacher was Klaas Noeka, whose "clean, orderly and seemingly devout" Xhosa-speaking congregation all broke down at one point in the sermon and wept at Noeka's "torrent of eloquence."[57]

Noeka had been for much of his life a mediator between worlds. He was a Gqunukhwebe Xhosa, born of the admixture of Khoekhoe and Xhosa in the eighteenth century. He had been a guide in the army under Harry Smith and an interpreter in the war of 1835 under Colonel Charles Lennox Stretch, government diplomatic agent in Xhosaland. He had also been a deacon at the London Missionary Society congregation at Tidmanton. In that capacity he had been part of that group of church officials who had insisted the church had the right to call its own ministers, and that the LMS must ordain Arie van Rooyen to be the second nonwhite minister in the colony. He was part of a large family, headed by Hans and Elizabeth Noeka and including four brothers and five sisters, all of whom joined the rebels; Hans Noeka would die during the war in the Waterkloof.[58] Klaas Noeka was clearly a well-connected man of some substance. According to Read, Noeka "had a great deal of intercourse with the elite of Kaffirland and the colony, and was a very intelligent man."[59] He seems to have been adept at cross-cultural communication.

Significantly, Noeka chose to preach on a "subject taken out of Isaiah," although Read did not ask the text. The choice of Isaiah is noteworthy. The prophet Isaiah foretells the suffering of the Israelites at the hands of their enemies, because of their own inequities. God will, however, purify the Israelites through suffering and then overthrow their unrighteous enemies and liberate the land. Indeed, Isaiah is an even more interesting text than might at first appear, because in structure it so closely parallels some of the central beliefs of the millenarian cattle-killing movement that five years later would be the Xhosa response to catastrophic disease among their cattle, the conquest of their lands, and defeat in battle. Obviously, the cattle-killing was driven mostly by the internal belief system of the Xhosa but, as J.B. Peires has shown, with significant Christian admixture nonetheless. Isaiah preaches the wickedness of the people and thus their need for repentance and material suffering as a prerequisite to the intervention of Yahweh. The Israelite will destroy his own vineyard. Most important, the Israelites are portrayed as a colonized people, to whose aid Yahweh will summon distant troops as he punishes the world for its wrongdoing: "On a bare hill hoist a signal, sound the war cry. Beckon them to come to the Nobles' Gate. I, for my part, issue orders to my sacred warriors, I summon my knights to serve my anger, my proud champions. Listen! A rumbling in the mountains like a great crowd ... It is Yahweh Saboath marshalling the troops for battle. They come from a distant country, from the far horizons, Yahweh and the instruments of his fury to lay the whole earth waste" (Isaiah 13:1–5). Is it completely far-fetched to see some significance to a Xhosa congregation weeping over Isaiah five years before the bulk of the Xhosa killed their own cattle, burnt their grain, and ploughed under their grain pits in anticipation of the return of their ancestors, who would return as distant warriors to drive the English into the sea? Be that as it may, Isaiah contained plenty to provide an explanation for suffering and to comfort a colonized community in revolt. James Read Jr knew his Isaiah as well as Noeka. He asked if he could preach at the end of the service and was allowed the courtesy. He chose the vision of peace at the end of Isaiah rather than its violent beginning – chapter 52, verse 7: "How beautiful on the mountains are the feet of one who brings good news, who heralds peace, brings happiness, proclaims salvation, and tells Zion, 'Your God is king.'"[60] This small interchange points to debate over the meaning of the biblical texts which both many loyalists and many rebels held in common. Yet a shared language yielded different readings.

There is other evidence of millenarian belief animating Khoekhoe rebels. After his brief mention of Umlangenism discussed above, Read went on, as we have seen, to describe what he called the "perversion of scripture" among some rebels. "For instance, a man said to me on one occasion, it is written, 'The horse shall walk knee-deep in blood;'

– 'there shall be wars and rumours of wars on the right hand and on the left.' Some pointed to the Sacred Oracles where the punishment of the unbelieving Israelites was predicted, and the destruction of the Canaanites was authorized, and the fate of the human race was foretold. The substance of their remarks was said to have been this, – 'The English must leave the country and go away in the ships.'"[61] Here, too, there are tantalizing echoes of the cattle-killing, whose prophets promised that the English would leave in ships. The reference to "war and rumours of war" is to Jesus's lament over the city of Jerusalem, whose destruction he foresees prior to the end of the world and the day of judgment, when the saved will be placed on God's right hand and the damned on the left. The horse knee-deep in blood is conceivably an oblique reference to the four horses of the apocalypse in Revelation, the rider of one of which unleashes vials of blood upon the earth.

Further tantalizing evidence of Christian millenarianism as a motivating force in the rebellion can be found in Uithaalder's call to the Griqua leaders: "Trust, therefore, in the Lord (whose character is known to be unfriendly to injustice), and undertake your work, and he will give us prosperity – a work for your mother-land and freedom, for it is now the time, yea, the appointed time, and no other."[62] According to the loyalist Moses Jacobs, rebels at Theopolis believed that "it was ordained by Providence that they were to unite with the kafirs and carry the country before them – all the lower country as far as Uitenhage and the Bay." On the other hand, on 6 June 1851, a group of rebels set fire to every building in Theopolis, including the mission chapel. Was this a rejection of missionary authority?

If rebels and loyalists disputed the meaning of biblical texts, they also competed for the righteousness conferred by following Christian practice. When the loyalist Khoekhoe delegation referred to above tried to persuade "Hottentot and Gona chiefs" to make peace, "one of the Noekas" responded with "bitter sarcasm": "'I thought, gentlemen you came to preach. Are you again talking about that matter of making peace with the settlers? We keep the Sabbath, and we don't wish to be troubled about such matters today.'"

One of the key leaders in the defection of the Cape Mounted Rifles was David Laverlot, a man known for his piety who led prayer meetings among the soldiers. He also seems to have been better educated than many other rebels, since he later wrote letters for the illiterate Uithaalder. Bibles were found amid the ruins of the rebel camp at Theopolis, after the British had burned down the mission station. Khoekhoe women sang hymns from hilltops as their men fought below them. One British observer heard one Sunday morning from the rebel camps, "in childlike strains, the glorious morning hymn, 'Awake my soul and with the sun, Thy daily course of duty run.' "[63]

Loyal religious leaders would continue to use pacific biblical texts to urge non-violence and peace. Read himself espoused what he termed the Quaker or "High Tory" vision of "passive obedience" – a concept that is interesting in itself both for its reference to seventeenth-century British history and for its argument that passive obedience was to be embraced, according to high tories, even when governments were odious.

LOYALISTS

As these conflicts over the meaning of Christianity suggest, the war deeply divided the nonwhite communities of the colonial Eastern Cape. Although the bulk of examples suggest that nuclear families went into the bush together, with children, at the most intimate level the war also split many families apart. This was all the more so given the large number of people beyond the nuclear core who were considered to form part of a Khoekhoe family. The most prominent example is that of the veldcornet Andries Botha, whose two sons rebelled. The elder Botha probably remained loyal, even though the colonial state tried to prove otherwise in court – the unproveable charges against Botha, even if true, amounted to at most a few days of flirtation with rebellion. The son was part of Uithaalder's attack on Fort Armstrong, where his father was. The father is said to have said to the son, "I never thought that you, with your gun on your shoulder, would ride up towards your father." Hans replied "something to this effect, 'Father you have bred me up to be a man' (Or, 'Father it is your own bread I have eaten')."[64] "Dela Jaagers" refused to accompany her husband, Klaas; she said that he was "mad for having joined the rebels – I am for the Queen – he may go to Uithaalder." Klaas was shot dead fighting desperately when the British retook Fort Armstrong. His wife didn't learn of his fate until seven years later, when she confronted the colonial state to claim the return of her land at Kat River. Although General Somerset had in 1851 restored her husband's wagon, in 1858 the land remained forfeited for her husband's rebellion.[65] Klaas's kinsman, Andries Jager, schoolmaster and Christian native agent, also rebelled.

The loyalists remained relatively invisible, obscured both by the rebels' rhetorical insistence on "Hottentot" unity and by the desire of white colonists to paint all nonwhites as rebels and thus to justify their wholesale economic expropriation. Charles Lennox Stretch, a former government agent among the Xhosa, commented wearily to a friend in May 1851, "I could enumerate cases how little the life of a Hottentot has been regarded during the [travails?] of men who have no more to do with Rebellions than you have – but he had a Coloured skin and that was sufficient in [?] cases to send him ... to Eternity."[63] During the war, loyalists were endlessly provoked, just as the loyalty of the Khoekhoe had been severely tested during the two previous frontier wars. Ironically, historians, in quest of redemptive narratives in the wake of the horrors of apartheid, have not been much interested in loyalists either. Nonetheless, the majority of inhabitants of the Kat River settlement did not in fact rebel. Indeed, many men, including a number of former rebels, would serve in the colonial levies, fighting against the rebels. Neutrality was impossible; rebellion demanded a life of raiding and killing in the bush; rebellion was also seen by men such as James Read Jr as completely unwinnable. Surely there was a psychological cost.

Take, for example, James Read Jr himself, whose writings on the rebellion form one of our major sources of evidence about it. Read represented in his very body the confusions of identity of the Cape Colony, as the son of a white man and Khoekhoe woman. In conjunction with his father and the radical wing of the LMS he had fought all his life for Christianity, civilization, and the rule of law, which he believed would save the Khoekhoe from degradation and injustice. He had been educated in Scotland and Cape Town, and described himself in the 1830s as a liberal: he believed in the rights of man. He was also a cynical observer of the brutalities of colonial rule. He sat uneasily between white and African society: he was a missionary, and thus at least theoretically respectable, and yet he was of mixed race. The ambivalent position he occupied was summed up by the later Kat River magistrate Louis Meurant, who saw Read as a traitor in a society in which socializing still occurred across the faultlines of race. Read, he complained, was dangerous and untrustworthy, and had betrayed Meurant, despite the fact that Meurant had "taken [Read] by the hand when in Graham's Town, asked [him] to my house there, and walked about with [him], – when almost every inhabitant in the place shunned him – I mean the Rev. James Read – whose half-Hottentot sisters I asked to my house, and who were kindly treated by my wife and grown-up daughter."[67] The Reads were blamed by colonial society and by many imperial officials for the outbreak of war, particularly by those unwilling to accord full agency to the Khoekhoe rebels. At the same time, ironically, the Reads are apparently remembered and blamed in Xhosa oral tradition in the Kat River area for having betrayed troop movements at a critical moment.[68]

Read, I think, tried to work through his own ambivalence and indeed to stave off despair by recording events. He published a series of long letters in the *South African Commercial Advertiser* in which he tried to explain the causes of war, including the injustices to which the Kat River settlement had been subjected, even as he refused to condone rebellion itself. He then revised these letters and published them as a book. He wrote unceasingly to his superiors in London. And in 1853 he kept a notebook as what proved to be an abortive commission of inquiry into the Kat River Rebellion began its work. He attended sessions and took assiduous notes. His notebooks begin with a certain defiant optimism that the truth would out, and even show a biting wit. As the commission proceeded, however, it became clear to Read that local white farmers were using it in an effort to frame him: he had become the primary target of investigation, not colonial injustices. His notes attest to the moral ambiguities of the rebellion. One of Read's principal accusers was a man named John Green, whom Read believed, doubtless correctly, was being used as a tool by the far more respectable Grahamstown wool farmers and land speculators. Green had earlier written a counter-narrative to Read's *The Kat River Settlement in 1851*, also called *The Kat River Settlement in 1851*. He was Read's nemesis: the false recorder, his shadow. Only Green's wife could be found to support his false testimony to the commission. "Poor soul she knows what she has suffered; and what can be expected from a man who is constantly in a state of hallucination who as those intimately conversant with his domestic habits say that when under delerium tremens is constantly seeing the devil waiting for him in the form of a vulture or large black dog or Wolf or follows him in the form of a little hunch-back man from the scenes of his delinquencies in long bush into the Kat River."[69] If Green was the false recorder, Read would devote himself to being the true recorder – and yet within limits. Towards the end of his notebook he comments on the atrocities committed during the war by "Fingoes.and Hottentots and Boers and English on the Caffers and rebels under the British flag." He went on to add: "But we must veil our feelings for it is said the country cannot bear any more excitement – Society must first become more consolidated at present it is ill at ease we must sit & look & take down data if we have nothing better to do & abide the creation of public opinion [...] This is the great lesson taught by the Church the press and the state. Be it so if we can save our consciences and save our country from blood guiltiness."[70] Read retreated into observing. The notion of "blood guiltiness" is a key evangelical concept that has functioned as a leitmotif of this book. When Cain killed Abel, Yahweh said, " 'Now be accursed and driven from the ground that has opened its mouth to receive your brother's blood at your hands.' " "Blood guiltiness" implied that blood would be revenged. Van der Kemp suggested indeed, as I think Read Jr does here as well, that cycles of bloodshed would follow one another. James Read Sr had written that the blood which drenched the soil of South Africa cried to God for vengeance. Piet Dragoender would later describe land washed clean by blood, but his removal underscored that the cycle had not in fact been halted. Read Jr confronted the dilemma: how could members of an oppressed group whose blood had been spilled cease the bloodshed without abandoning the demands of justice?

Read's notebook was not, however, used by LMS. There is an anonymous note on its cover, added in a different hand: "Circular sent out in 1853, *but not* repeated in 1854, on account of the little attention paid to it by some of the Brethren and of its being misunderstood by others." And so James Read Jr stopped writing.

TOWARDS CONCLUSIONS?
ASPECTS OF THE AFTERMATH

The weight of metropolitan British opinion supported the colonists in the war of 1850–53, despite anger at the fiscal irresponsibility of colonists and colonial administrations which embroiled the home country in expensive frontier wars by provoking indigenous peoples and then refusing to fight. Generally, however, much of the British press, as well as leading colonial figures such as the colonial secretary Earl Grey himself, argued that the solution was to force the colony itself to bear the expense of war. As a corollary, colonies should be given more self-government – and thus more rather than less power over local peoples, who tended to be painted as savage, childlike, and irresponsible. For the most part, the war of 1850–53 was thus portrayed in the British press in a pro-colonial light, despite fiscal concerns. The London *Examiner*, for example, deplored "another war with those robust, hardy, warlike, and most truculent savages, the Caffres." "In India we conquer provinces," the editors went on to remark, "at a less cost, of which the yearly revenue equals the cost of suppressing three rebellions at the Cape – such is the wide difference between tame and industrious Hindus and untameable African savages."[71] The Irish nationalist press supported the Xhosa, just as almost fifty years later many Irish nationalists would make common cause with Afrikaners during the South African War of 1899–1902. In Dublin, *The Nation* praised the "heroic cast of the Kaffir's soul," and it hoped in 1852 that the "end of the war and the final triumph of the natives" was "not far off."[72] In England, however, closer to springs of metropolitan power, the *Colonial Intelligencer; or, Aborigine's Friend*, the organ of the Aborigines Protection Society, was a lonely voice outlining Xhosa and Khoisan grievances. More mainstream organs such the *Times* of London published many letters and articles from a white colonial perspective which bitterly reflected on the atrocities committed by Xhosa assailants against whites.

Even the voice of the *Colonial Intelligencer* was equivocal. The APS was in favour of colonization, as long as it took place under the aegis of the rule of law and lands were obtained by treaty and purchase from willing participants. This was a more pro-colonial position than that originally adopted by the moving spirit behind the foundation of the APS, Sir Thomas Buxton, who, despite his later abortive effort to colonize west Africa in an enlightened fashion, in 1835 had pronounced colonialism to be an unmitigated evil. Louis Alexis Chamerovzow and Thomas Hodgkin, secretary and honorary secretary of the APS respectively, thus supported an early version of indirect rule. As they stated in an address to the Colonial Office in 1852, "so far from deposing and trampling on existing native authorities, we would advocate sustaining them as the administrators of an improved code, gradually assimilated to our own, and, as far as possible, connected with our colonial government in its execution." The less radical and more uncertain tone of the APS reflected new colonial realities. As the same address admitted:

if the cause in which we are engaged [advocacy for aborigines], and which we regard as deeply affecting the character of England as a Christian country – as closely connected with her honour amongst civilized nations – as standing in close relation with her influence over those Colonies which regard her as their mother country – and as essentially connected with her commerce and the profitable diffusion of her various manufactures – be surrounded with difficultes; if we have remarked with pain the certain indications that this great cause has in the last few years, somewhat lost ground in the Colonial Office and in Parliament; we are, notwithstanding, unwilling to regard it with discouragement."[73]

The more widespread perception of the war, and specifically of the "Hottentot" rebellion, was that even the assimilated "native" was not to be trusted. In that sense, the reception of the rebellion anticipated reaction to rebellion in India in 1857. It reflected a climate of growing pessimism about the liberal project of assimilation, and a conviction of the inevitability of "racial" conflict.

In the Cape Colony itself, there was enormous settler bitterness against the "Hottentots." In May 1852 the former Kat River veldcornet Andries Botha was tried at Cape Town before the Chief Justice and a jury for the crime of High Treason and condemned to death. As the

Grahamstown Journal editorialized, "the case of 'the Queen versus Andries Botha' is in reality the case of 'The Colonists' versus the Kat River Settlement."[74] If so, the treatment accorded to Botha was symbolically appropriate, since the trial became a political show trial. The main witnesses against Botha, for example, were prisoners who were released after bearing testimony against the elderly official. It is unclear whether or not Botha was actually guilty of rebellion, although I incline to think that he was not, given the vacuity of the specific charges. Be that as it may, Botha's death sentence, although later commuted to one of hard labour, signalled more than the death of one man.[72] The trial was also widely taken as a condemnation of the LMS since it destroyed one of the society's show converts, who had at an earlier stage been a relatively well-off man.

The victory of the white settler narrative was expressed concretely through land confiscations. The initial response of the local state was to dispossess rebels of their land, which was then promptly and efficiently redistributed, mostly to white men. After Hendrick Heyn and Dirk Hatha led a "Hottentot" protest, and Andries Stockenstrom raised the matter in the Legislative Assembly, legislators were compelled to recognize that Roman-Dutch law did not permit the confiscation of land under these circumstances. In consequence, a renewed Kat River commission of inquiry was convened in 1858, this time to hear the requests of the dispossessed for the return of their land at the Kat River. The commissioners decided, however, that while they could scarcely avoid returning land to the few who had clear written title, they would apply to the rest the terms on which land had supposedly been granted in the early period of the settlement: trees must have been planted, grounds enclosed, and brick or stone houses constructed with more than one room and glass windows. The enforcement of this requirement came despite the testimony of many in the settlement that Governor D'Urban had lifted the requirements in the wake of the 1835 devastation of Kat River during war.

And so those who wished the return of land were compelled to describe the state of their house and grounds, as the commissioners sought to demonstrate the quintessential lack of civilization of erfholders without glass windows, brick walls, or more than one room. This lack of civilization in turn justified the colonial rhetoric of "Hottentot" primitiveness and savagery, used for so long to attack the Kat River settlement. In the end, rebels were dispossessed not for the high crime of treason but for the misdemeanour of a lack of glass windows.

One notes, however, an irony. Most Khoekhoe, including veldcornets, were not actually living like middle-class British Victorians. This is particularly clear from the fact that most lived in a single room for the family, and also from the complicated networks of family and dependants revealed by the transmission of land through time. Furthermore, of course, building large houses was clearly not a good investment in a settlement much of which had already been burnt down twice. The records of the 1858 commission reveal, as well, a handful of woman rebels, clearly not punished by the colonial state because viewed as dependants of rebel men. A second gendered aspect also becomes clear: even when women had not rebelled, they bore the brunt of the dispossession of families in the wake of the rebellion of a single male member. Most of the women who requested the return of family land appear to have been forced into domestic service, while men seemingly had more options to regain stock or to emigrate across the Orange River.

The issue of corruption arises around this commission in a triple sense. First, the magistrate Louis Meurant and others were corrupt, colluding to have as much land as possible forfeited. Meurant was clearly engaged in shady practices, such as exploiting the illiteracy of many Kat River settlers to falsify documents. Second, the Kat River settlement was described by settlers as a seat of corruption of the political body – echoing the language once used against the colonial mission station of Bethelsdorp as a seat of venereal disease as well as moral corruption. Third, the rule of law was invoked to dispossess Kat River Khoekhoe: precisely the rule of law upheld by loyalists. One might argue here that the colonial presentation of personal dominion as "law" and as incorruptible in itself was a form of corruption, creating disrespect for the rule of law.[76] Loyalists were left with few places to turn.

After the rebellion, the Khoekhoe were no longer perceived as useful agents of rule by the British state. The government, both colonial and metropolitan, turned firmly to European settlers instead, sought to break up concentrated Khoekhoe settlement as a prophylactic against the formation of "Hottentot" identity, and indeed eschewed the idea of any further "Hottentot" land grants as too politically dangerous. For example, the colonial government refused Uithaalder's offer to create a buffer zone in Sarhili's territory, which the former rebel leader proposed administering under the direct authority of the British monarch. Rather, the lieutenant governor told his subordinate the "Thembu agent" Warner, only Europeans could be trusted and they must be imported in large numbers.[77] This was part of a larger movement across the empire, reflected in other revolts elsewhere, and in the growth of British belief in race. In this context, "Hottentot" identity was no longer politically useful, at least in relations with the colonial state.

A further, and striking, aspect of the aftermath was that many Kat River inhabitants, despite the defeats of the 1850s and the loss of land and status, seem to have become readier to confront the colonial state in more openly critical ways than they had been previously. This seeming shift may be a trick of the archival records. Nonetheless, there is evidence that the anger which led to warfare persisted and led people to be prepared to sound disloyal in public. Large numbers of people openly came forward as former rebels and without apology demanded the return of their lands from the Kat River commission of 1858. Others pursued complaints against the magistrate Meurant. Kaatje N., a former servant of Meurant, presented a memorial to government in 1855 in which she complained that Meurant had promised to give her back the erf which had been taken from her father for rebellion and which adjoined her own small erf (the spelling of her last name is unclear from the archival record; it may be Nieuweld). She claimed that Meurant had then reneged but that the land was hers. In the course of the extended quarrels that ensued among inhabitants of Kat River, the white English speaker Daniel Stewart, to whom Meurant had on paper granted the erf of Nieuweld's father, ploughed under the crops which she had planted. On another occasion, the Dutch-speaking settler Jan Andries Buukkies, who had been given the erf adjoining Nieuweld's, fought with her over the ownership of fruit trees on the boundary line between their properties which she claimed had been planted by her husband when still alive. When Kaatje Nieuweld sent her daughter to gather apples one day, the newcomer Buukkies, who thought the trees were his, demanded of Nieuweld why her child was picking his apples. She replied, "I must not come and speak as they did not belong to me; and swore at me, saying the farmers only came in here to rob the blacks." Infuriated, Buukkies went home and grabbed an axe. He started to cut down the trees – the plaintiff said forty-seven, but Buukkies claimed no more than ten. Nieuweld then asked Saul Solomon and Isak Andries to come and witness Buukkies's actions. "I again told Buukkies that they were my trees, and [he] came towards me and held the axe up to my head in a threatening manner at [the] same time using threatening language towards me." In both instances, Nieuweld accused Meurant of refusing to listen to her complaints or to do her justice. After years of anger, the case finally came before the commissioners of 1858. Predictably, the commissioners ruled in favour of Meurant, leaving the true quarrel unresolved.[78] Tensions were obviously high between black and white at the Kat River settlement, as whites flooded onto hitherto "Hottentot" land. The Khoisan were defeated, but they were by no means cowed.

THE COLOUR GREY

Despite severe racial conflict during the rebellion and its aftermath, this tragic story was not solely one of "black" and "white." It was also one of shades of grey, against a background of violence. The dominant emotions of guilt and fear led to the denial of linkages on all sides. Despite the extreme rhetoric of race warfare, even the Eastern Cape was not in fact entirely divided by race. Before the war, the conniving son of a slave-owner, Louis Meurant, felt obliged to entertain "half-Hottentot" women to his house, no matter how self-conscious and patronizing he felt about the whole thing. Two ministers of colour, Arie van Rooyen and James Read Jr, both preached to whites as well as blacks at the Kat River settlement and had spiritual authority over whites. Veldcornets at the Kat River settlement were Khoekhoe and had jurisdiction over all within their districts.

The aftermath of the rebellion, I suspect, further cast doubt over these types of interactions, as white liberalism retreated yet further to careful social distance from blacks, as whites invaded the Kat River settlement, and as colonial officials disavowed previous alliances with the "Hottentots." On the other hand, what ultimately proved to be a relatively low, colour-blind franchise was designed to soothe Khoisan anger and to provide a voice to individuals, even as the state moved to break up "Hottentot" settlement and identity as much as possible.

Let me return to John Green. Green was a tool of the white capitalist farmers of Grahamstown, and yet he lived in Kat River and, if Read's hints are to be believed, was in fact committing adultery with his Khoekhoe mistress the morning of a crucial battle about which he gave false testimony. And all the while the devil followed and accused him, in the form of a little hunchbacked man. It seems a classic metaphor of ambivalence. The war was driven by extremists on both sides, particularly whites in a climate of anxiety who refused to acknowledge the linkages with nonwhites by which they were surrounded. The notion of ineradicable racial difference gained considerable currency in the wake of the war, discomforting both white liberals at Cape Town and liberal Khoekhoe who had attempted to make bargains with the colonial state in exchange for rights.

There is a letter preserved in the South African Library written to the archivist in 1912 by Mrs T.G. Jones, the last surviving daughter of James Read Jr., in which she requests that he take charge of the Read family papers. She protests that she and the family had met with enormous prejudice as a result of the actions of the James Reads. Just when the reader assumes she is talking about politics she adds, "Was it not better to legally marry them than keep Housekeepers (as is very

often done) .... about a year ago I had occasion to go to Kat River –
the post-cart driver said – Mrs. Jones you don't know me but your late
father knows all about me my father was a magistrate." Jones added,
"No one is more against inter marriage than I am but what is done
can't be undone – & what gain is there to constantly wound others
feelings."[79] The archivist refused to accept the papers of James Read Jr,
the recorder. It seems a fitting image of the denial of history on which
to close a discussion of a rebellion soaked in memory and haunted by
its denial.

11 Conclusions?

The rebellion marked a turning point in the perception of the Khoisan by the British, and of the British by the Khoisan. Indeed, the rebellion was only one of several colonial crises that would cement a new era of pessimism in Great Britain itself from the 1840s onward about the liberal project of the assimilation and westernization of colonized peoples, and about the capacities of the colonized. The Indian Rebellion, the Maori Wars, and the Jamaica uprising would all contribute brutally to a growing discourse about "black" inferiority and ingratitude and the deep difference between "black" and "white." This climate of pessimism nourished racial theory, even as the growing acceptability of racial theory in the metropole further justified the actions of white settlers in the colonies. As Andrew Bank has so trenchantly demonstrated for the Cape Colony in the 1830s, colonial warfare entrenched racial hatreds among white colonists, who in turn relayed back to Britain their concerns about the irreconcilability of black and white.

The rebellion is thus only one example of the complex linkages between the overall history of the British empire, as of the Dutch empire before it, the history of the Eastern Cape, and the history of the British imperial centre (although whether London or the Eastern Cape deserves to be termed the centre or the periphery in this relationship is perhaps a matter for debate). Frontier developments changed the mindset and politics of Khoisan, inhabitants of the United Kingdom, and south African missionaries, settlers, and imperial administrators alike, while these factors influenced frontier developments in their turn.

Ironically, if not surprisingly, the wider use of a language of "race" came at a time at which adherence to Christianity no longer functioned as a key marker of "ethnic" and political status at the Cape. What was at stake in debates over Christianity and its social uses at the Cape shifted over the half-century examined in this book. At the beginning of our period, the close of the eighteenth century, religious difference had long been used at the Cape to draw distinctions between colonizer and colonized. At the same time, Christianity was also used to police the blurred boundaries between "white" and "black." "Mixed-race" children might be incorporated into the "white" or "Christian" community through baptism. Alternatively, the refusal of baptism denied kinship and maintained, for some Christians at least, the economically (and psychologically?) necessary lines between master and servant. Conversion to Christianity by Khoisan people and by the descendants of unions between "white" and "black" parents thus became a means of making local political claims, including kinship claims with the "white" community. Christianity was also seen by "white" and "black" alike as a means of mobilizing power which many in the twentieth century might term "spiritual," but which was thought of at the time as having concrete material implications. God was available to be mobilized for one side or the other in the bitter conflicts that afflicted this contested region. A particular irony in the local Khoisan use of Christianity was that many tried to use mission stations as a means to maintain elements of their ancestors' more nomadic lifestyles, including mobility at will, the gathering of roots, bulbs, and honey, and the accumulation of stock, even as missionaries preached the virtue of an agricultural lifestyle, in accordance with supposedly international and universal norms of "civilization." Others, however, particularly as the century wore on, used a profession of Christianity to proclaim their respectability, whether in terms of the local community or as a larger political claim. This became more frequent from the 1820s on, as LMS missionaries themselves became more "liberal," less millenarian, and more respectable in white terms.

By the end of our period, in the mid-nineteenth century, the Khoisan were largely Christian but Christianity was no longer the key marker of status and identity in colonial society as a whole that it had been in the late eighteenth century. A more explicit language of race, forged in frontier conflict as well as in the academic libraries of Europe, was increasingly widely used instead to maintain boundaries between colonized and colonizers. In this context, ethnic nationalism and the reimagination of community became for many Khoisan converts more potent weapons than loyalist Christianity to wield against the settler state. Nonetheless, this version of nationalism remained heavily tinged with Christianity. Christianity also united relatively diverse groups in rebellion.

At the same time, one notes that by the time of the rebellion many white settlers questioned whether the Khoisan were "truly" Christian. Furthermore, colonial churches, including many LMS-affiliated congregations, were increasingly segregated. Even if Christianity had become a more widely accepted common language, actual religious practice often still divided people. The initial hopes of some Khoisan converts for a common colonial society united by a liberal version of Christianity were certainly not entirely illusory, but remained in important ways unfulfilled.

I have also argued in this book that it mattered that Christianity was a religion of world empire, even as it affected lives in intimate ways. In their struggles in the face of colonialism, Khoisan peoples of southern Africa, long accustomed to long-range contacts, tried to use macrocosmic resources to find solutions to local problems (and sometimes to establish local subimperialisms). Christianity was one such resource, with both local and international implications, "pan-Hottentot" nationalism another. Conversion – or at the least some kind of community alliance with a missionary – permitted entrance into international networks for Africans as well as into transregional diplomatic networks in southern Africa. These networks included contacts with the local colonial administration and (for the extra-colonial Griqua) with other African groups who also had missionaries. Whether or not Christianity also provided an *intellectually* more "macrocosmic" set of beliefs than those of the Khoekhoe before contact with Christianity is a very difficult question to answer. Certainly it appeared more macrocosmic, because it had more adherents in more places. On the other hand, the beliefs of most missionaries, particularly in the early days of the LMS, were far from exemplars of bourgeois rationalism: missionaries brought a universe peopled by the devil and Jesus, fighting a cosmic struggle for the possession of the land and the salvation of souls, a universe in which God's providence might be glimpsed everywhere and which would perhaps sooner than later be brought to a triumphant close with the coming of the millennium. Christianity would cleanse the land, as might an African prophet. James Read was certainly a zealous Christian, but in the end he did not see much structural difference between the beliefs of the Xhosa and those of townsfolk in early-nineteenth-century industrial Britain. Nonetheless, Christianity did provide access to an imperial world beyond the local.

Similarly, missionary networks linked people in Britain, even if only in imagination and often in patronizing ways, to fellow Christians elsewhere in the empire. The language of "darkest Africa" was also reflected in middle-class discourse about the working classes of Britain, since foreign and domestic missionary effort had a mutual influence. Ironically, even as improved communication networks increased the amount of information available about various corners of the world, the missionary movement was also becoming a more important prop of British nationalism and of a more racialized vision of imperialism. Missionary activity ultimately provided an ideological justification for imperial expansion, despite – indeed in many ways because of – the concrete quarrels of individual converts and missionaries in South Africa with white settlers and local administrators, on the one hand, and, on the other, the imaginative empathy with "benighted Africa" created in Britain itself by missionary texts.

In all these ways, Christianity provided points of intersection between the local and the global. Religion, like nationalism, was a point of intersection between the "microcosm" of community and the "macrocosms" of empire, of pan-African connections, of imagined worlds. Andries Stoffels chillingly proclaimed in London in 1835 that the pennies of mission supporters had created him, and "here I am." He was, of course, wrong. South Africa had created Andries Stoffels, including his need to use international resources in his quarrel with local settlers, at the expense of denigrating and denying his past and sometimes his fellows. He was right, however, in a symbolic sense. The pennies of missionary supporters had indeed created an ironic and paradoxical Africa of the imagination, just as an imagined Britain played an important role in Khoisan politics. The local imagination and the harsh realities of global politics shaped one another: they spoke more often than not in the language of religion.

Notes

PRELUDE

1 A veld cornet was an unpaid local militia officer who was responsible for law and order in a given subdivision of a district.
2 Among many possibilities: Desbarats, "Essai sur quelques éléments"; Klein, *Frontiers of Historical Imagination*; Hayden White, *Metahistory*.

INTRODUCTION

1 Among notable recent works: Malherbe, "Cape Khoisan in the Eastern Districts of the Colony"; Penn, "Northern Cape Frontier Zone"; Newton-King, *Masters and Servants*; Elphick and Malherbe, "Khoisan to 1828"; Viljoen, "Moravian Missionaries, Khoisan Labour and the Overberg Colonists"; the articles collected in *Kronos: Journal of Cape History / Tydskrif vir Kaaplandse Geskiedenis*, no. 24, November 1997, including Bank and Minkley, "Reading the Evidence: Implications of the Shift to a Heritage Paradigm in Khoisan Studies," 3–8 and R. Ross, Report on "Khoisan Identities and Cultural Heritage Conference," 154–155. In this latter article, Ross underscores the political implications of contemporary Khoisan identity claims, as well as the resurgent role of history in Khoisan studies. The papers in this issue of *Kronos* were drawn for the most part from the third Khoisan Conference of 1997, on "Khoisan Identities and Cultural Heritage," the proceedings of which illustrate the diversity of new approaches to the nineteenth-century social history of the Khoisan and renewed interest in the subject.

2 A variant of the term San was used by Khoekhoe to describe hunter-gatherers. The term probably had derogatory connotations and so is problematic. As historian Susan Newton-King states, however, "in the absence of a generic term favoured by hunter-gatherers themselves, and given our ignorance of the names assumed by individual hunter-gatherer populations, San (or its western Cape variants 'Soaqua' and 'Sonqua') is probably here to stay." Newton-King, *Masters and Servants*, 28.

3 In addition to works mentioned in note 1 above, see also Newton-King and Malherbe, *Khoikhoi Rebellion in the Eastern Cape* on the eastern Cape "servants' revolt" of 1799 to 1802, and Viljoen, "'Revelation of a Revolution'" on the 1788 western Cape rebellion of Jan Parel, both in illustration of failed attempts at armed resistance at the close of the eighteenth century.

4 Schmidt, et. al., *Das Tagebuch und die Briefe von Georg Schmidt*; Krüger, *Pear Tree Blossoms*, 18–46; Shell, *Children of Bondage*; Gerstner, *Thousand Generation Covenant*.

5 For an overview, see Freund, "Cape Under the Transitional Governments," 324–57.

6 For an overview of missionary activity in the region, see many of the essays in Elphick and Davenport, eds., *Christianity in South Africa*.

7 Among a multitude of important works on the domestic history of the LMS and on the LMS in southern Africa are: de Gruchy, ed., *London Missionary Society in Southern Africa*; Comaroff and Comaroff, *Of Revelation and Revolution*, vols. 1 and 2; Landau, *Realm of the Word*; Ross, *John Philip (1775–1851)*; Stuart, "'Of Savages and Heroes'"; Piggin, *Making Evangelical Missionaries*; Crehan, "Khoi, Boer and Missionary"; Etherington, *Preachers, Peasants and Politics*; Legassick, "The Griqua, the Sotho-Tswana and the Missionaries"; Majeke, *Role of the Missionaries in Conquest*; Macmillan, *Cape Colour Question*; Macmillan, *Bantu, Boer and Britain*; Lovett, *History of the London Missionary Society*.

8 For example: Wilson, *Sense of the People*; Colley, *Britons*; Claydon and McBride, eds., *Protestantism and National Identity*; Davidoff and Hall, *Family Fortunes*.

9 I agree here with the reservations offered by Claydon and McBride about the recent enthusiasm of historians for seeing Protestantism as constitutive of national identity. As they and several authors in their edited collection suggest, and as this book will argue throughout, the degree of consensus about which variant of Protestantism represented the nation must not be overestimated, while the Protestant-nation paradigm proved "ambivalent, flexible and transferable" in practice. In the same collection, Jeremy Black rightly underscores that British Protestantism was subject to international influence and that eighteenth-century European states were

in general more religiously diverse and mutually permeable than a monolithic model of Protestantism as constitutive of "national" identity would
suggest. Claydon and McBride, "Trials of the Chosen Peoples," 21–2;
Black, "Confessional State or Elect Nation?"

10 Comaroff and Comaroff, *Of Revelation and Revolution*, vols. 1 and 2.

11 On evangelical eschatology: Hilton, *Age of Atonement*.

12 Saunders, "Looking Back"; Elphick, "Writing Religion into History"; du
Bruyn and Southey, "Treatment of Christianity and Protestant Missionaries in South African Historiography"; Comaroff and Comaroff, *Of Revelation and Revolution*, vols. 1 and 2; Landau, *Realm of the Word*; Etherington, "Recent Trends"; Elbourne, "Concerning Missionaries."

13 Skinner, "Meaning and Understanding in the History of Ideas"; Skinner,
"Language and Social Change"; and Tully, "Pen is a Mighty Sword."

14 As James Tully puts it: "It is not necessarily or normally the immediate
political struggle, but rather the circulation and adaptation of an ideology
in the stratagems of a wide range of similar struggles that accounts for
ideological entrenchment and hegemony. Tully, "Pen is a Mighty Sword,"
15–16.

15 A particularly powerful case study is Landau, *Realm of the Word*.

16 Jean and John Comaroff, *Of Revelation and Revolution*, vol. 2, 22.

17 Thorne, *Congregational Missions*.

18 Among others, from a variety of ideological perspectives: Gilroy, *The
Black Atlantic*; Stoler and Cooper, *Tensions of Empire*; Bailyn and
Morgan, *Strangers within the Realm*.

19 Setiloane, *African Theology*; Biko, "I Write What I Like" on black theology; Ramphele, "On Being Anglican," on African adjustments within one
"mainstream" mission church. For an East African comparison:
Mugambi, *African Christian Theology*, 39–50, on missions, and Mbiti,
Bible and Theology in African Christianity, 176–227.

20 Elphick, "Introduction: Christianity in South African History," 4.

21 There is a large literature on African Independent Churches as a form of
resistance. See, for example, Comaroff, *Body of Power, Spirit of Resistance*.

CHAPTER ONE

1 On evangelicalism as a marker of middle-class identity, see Hall and
Davidoff, *Family Fortunes*, 73–106 and passim. I do nonetheless find that
Davidoff and Hall exaggerate the degree of consensus excited by evangelicalism in the Victorian middle classes, even as they downplay the extent
of Victorian working-class evangelicalism. Thorne, *Congregational Missions*, 39–43 and passim, convincingly argues that nineteenth-century
middle-class evangelicals used religion to define themselves against

384 Notes to pages 16–33

working-class and aristocratic "others" alike, although she similarly
downplays working-class evangelicalism.

2 For example, Colley, "Britishness and Otherness", especially 316–17, in
which Colley argues that many eighteenth-century British people defined
Britain as a Protestant nation in opposition to a Catholic "other," above
all Catholic France. In support of my broad argument about differentia-
tion within Protestantism, Claydon and McBride, "Trials of the Chosen
People."

3 Hunter, *History of the Missions*, 3–6; Ross, *John Philip (1775–1851)*, 35.

4 Garrett, *Spirit Possession*, 98.

5 Bebbington, *Evangelicalism in Modern Britain*, 3.

6 Prominent among common theological themes was that of the necessity of
a conversion experience of some kind, whether or not the person converted (or literally "turned") to Christ was already a practising Christian;
this was the Wesleyan "New Birth," also known in such terms by the
Calvinist Methodists and by the Lutheran German pietists. Rupp, *Religion in England*, 420; Semmel, *Methodist Revolution*, 37; Ian Bradley,
Call to Seriousness, 21.

7 Martin, *Evangelicals United*, 14.

8 Ibid., especially 40–7 on the interdenominational character of the early
LMS; Lewis, *Lighten Their Darkness*, for a later example of evangelical
interdenominational cooperation.

9 Ward, "Revival and Class Conflict," 285–98; Martin, *Evangelicals
United*.

10 Thomas Haweis, "Autobiography," ML: B1176.

11 Garrett, *Spirit Possession*, 104.

12 Hempton, *Methodism and Politics*, 55–80.

13 Indeed, Ward argues that it was the "torrent" of popular sentiment away
from the establishment in the 1790s that pushed Methodist preachers into
a rapid break with the Church of England. Ward, "Revival and Class
Conflict," 294.

14 Rack, "Survival and Revival," 1–23; Lovegrove, *Established Church*,
passim.

15 Lovegrove, *Established Church*, 14–40, 165. On transformations in the
Baptist "frame of mind," see Ward, "The Baptists and the Transformation of the Church," 167–84, 202–22.

16 Ward, "Revival and Class Conflict," 286, 293; Lovegrove, *Established
Church*.

17 Lovegrove, *Established Church*, 17–22; Martin, *Evangelicals United*,
16–18; Semmel, *Methodist Revolution*, 106–9.

18 CA, A50: James Read to John Philip, 7 March 1846.

19 Fragments of Campbell's correspondence in the National Library of Scotland describe this itinerant activity and the resistance which he and his

companions encountered from local gentry. Unfortunately, this correspondence is quite literally fragmented and therefore unclear, as someone once took scissors to the letters, probably to remove Campbell's autographs. NLS, MS10999.

20 Lovegrove, *Established Church*, 23–5. Henry Foster Burder, *Memoir of the Rev. George Burder*, 23–31, 156–7, 253–5. George Burder, *Village Sermons*. On Eyre's Village Itinerary Association: Dr Williams' Library, London: New College MSS, 41/1-89. On Greatheed: LMS-HO 1/6/A: S. Greatheed to J. Eyre, 13 February 1799; Greatheed, *General Union Recommended to Real Christians*; Lovegrove, *Established Church*, 23–5; Thorne, "'The Conversion of Englishmen.'" I would modify Thorne's argument somewhat, however: language employed in the early "home" missionary movement antedated and influenced that used about the foreign missionary movement, in addition to the converse movement as the century developed.

21 Lovegrove, *Established Church*, 66–87.

22 The term "imagined community" is, of course, from Anderson, *Imagined Communities*. Timothy Hall makes a thought-provoking use of the phrase to describe the notion of an imagined transatlantic community, similarly bound by experience of the true faith: Timothy Hall, *Contested Boundaries*, 4.

23 Edinburgh Missionary Society to John Eyre, 28 December 1802, *Evangelical Magazine*, February 1803, 80–1, 83.

24 LMS, *Reports* vol. 1, 60.

25 Crawford, *Seasons of Grace*, 11.

26 Hobsbawm, *Labouring Men*, 23–33, on radicalism and Methodism as like expressions of more profound changes in British society. Thompson, *Making of the English Working Class*, 385–440, on Methodism as the "chiliasm of despair" among a politically defeated working class. Among responses to Thompson's version of the "Halévy thesis": Jaffe, "The 'Chiliasm of Despair' Reconsidered," 23–42; Laquer, *Religion and Respectability*; Gilbert, "Methodism, Dissent and Political Stability," 381–99. Among considerations of ways in which new religious movements and religious revivalism may have responded to anxieties generated by industrialization, as also to the inability of the established church to cope with burgeoning populations in newly industrialized areas: Crawford, "Origins"; Gilbert, *Religion and Society*.

27 Crawford, "Origins," 364–7; Gilbert, *Religion and Society*, 59-61, 64–7; Kiernan, "Evangelicalism and the French Revolution," 44–5.

28 Crawford, *Seasons of Grace*, 7; Crawford, "Origins," 364–75. John Walsh comments that early Methodism had "the attributes of a *Jugendreligion*; many of its converts were young, and so too were many of their leaders – notably Whitefield, the 'boy preacher.'" Walsh,

"'Methodism' and the Origins of English-Speaking Evangelicalism,"
23.

29 "Memoir of the Late Rev. John Eyre, A.M.," *Evangelical Magazine*, June
1803, 226.

30 LMS-CP, Box 5: E. Evans, Evans to LMS, Chelsea, 7 May 1816.

31 ML B1176: Haweis, "Autobiography."

32 LMS-CP, Box 5, E. Evans: Personal statement of E. Evans, Chelsea, 7 May
1816.

33 ML B1176: Haweis, "Autobiography."

34 Moffat, *Lives of Robert and Mary Moffat*, 4–14.

35 ML B1176: Haweis, "Autobiography."

36 Charles Simeon, "On the New Birth," in A. Pollard (ed.), *Let Wisdom
Judge, University Addresses and Sermon Outlines by Charles Simeon*
(1959), 51, cited in Rosman, *Evangelicals and Culture*, 11–12. Cf. also
Rosman's useful discussion of evangelical conversion. On the pietist/
Moravian debate: Ward, *Protestant Evangelical Awakening*, especially
136–8.

37 Crawford, *Seasons of Grace*, 11–12.

38 Dr Williams' Library, New College MSS 41/40: Thomas Buffrey to John
Eyre, 7 January 1799.

39 For example, Burder, *Memoir of the Rev. George Burder*, 138–9, on
common fears among evangelical Anglicans and Methodists over the
spread of antinomianism.

40 Carey, *Memoir of William Carey*, 14–15.

41 Radford and James, *The Autobiography of the Rev. William Jay*, 18.
Jay's boyhood experiences were, however, quite different from Carey's in
the sense that he had far fewer religious groups to choose from, and religion appears to have been less of a subject for daily dispute: local religious culture varied greatly from place to place.

42 Carey, *Memoir of William Carey*, 16–18.

43 Ibid., 9.

44 Ibid., 13.

45 Ibid., 16-17.

46 Payne, "Introduction," v–viii.

47 Bradley, *Religion, Revolution and English Radicalism*; Stevenson,
"Popular Radicalism and Popular Protest," 68–9.

48 Jay, *Autobiography*, 294.

49 Valenze, *Prophetic Daughters*; Hempton, *Methodism and Politics in
British Society*.

50 The point that Protestant revival had deep roots in the religious forms of
the sixteenth and seventeenth centuries has been made by a number of
American historians – who have collectively spilt a great deal of ink on
Puritanism and evangelicalism and seem to me to be more sensitive to the

history of Protestantism than analogous British historians. Cohen, "Post-Puritan Paradigm of Early American Religious History"; Crawford, *Seasons of Grace*; Westerkamp, *Triumph of the Laity*; Hall, "On Common Ground."

51 In addition to work cited in note 50, above, see among many possibilities: Joutard, *Les Camisards*; Schwartz, *The French Prophets*; Lovejoy, *Religious Enthusiasm*; Walsh, "Origins of the Evangelical Revival"; Ward, *Protestant Evangelical Awakening*; Crawford, "The Origins of Eighteenth-Century Evangelical Revival." On the subject of Methodism before the 1730s, Walsh points out that the patriarch of Welsh Methodism, Griffith Jones of Llandowror, precipitated a small awakening in Carmarthenshire and Pembrokeshire in 1714 which presaged the great Welsh movement of the 1730s; Wesley's preaching was also antedated by that of George Whitefield in England and that of Howell Harris and other revivalists in Wales: Walsh, "Origins of the Evangelical Revival," 133–5.

52 Ward, "Relations of the Enlightenment," 283. Ward argues more broadly here and in other work that the roots of the forms and theology of "revival" must be sought in the reactions of continental Protestantism to the political crises of the late seventeenth and early eighteenth centuries. Ward, "Power and Piety," 231–52; Ward, *Religion and Society*, 1–53.

53 Ward, *Protestant Evangelical Awakening*, especially 54–240.

54 For example, Westerkamp, *Triumph of the Laity*, 13–14 and passim.

55 For example, Butler, "Enthusiasm Described and Decried." I am more convinced by Crawford's rebuttal: Crawford, "Origins," 362.

56 "Memoir of the Late Rev. John Erskine, D.D.," *Evangelical Magazine*, August 1803, 320–1.

57 LMS, *Memoir of the Late Reverend*, 11.

58 O'Brien, "Eighteenth-century Publishing," 38–57; Ward, *Protestant Evangelical Awakening*, 1–13.

59 For example, Rev. Josiah Pratt to missionaries at Liverpool, 30 January 1806, cited in Josiah and John Henry Pratt, *Memoir*, 34–5; here, Pratt pleads with Berlin seminarians en route to Africa through Liverpool not to preach in English, for fear of revealing themselves as dissenting ministers. Elbourne, "Anglican Missionary Impulse."

60 Erskine, *Signs of the Times*, iii, cited in Ward, *Protestant Evangelical Awakening*, 337.

61 Walsh, "Methodism and the Origins of English-Speaking Evangelicalism," 21.

62 As Ruth Bloch observes, for both Baptists and Congregationalists in the United States, "the consciousness of being part of an international movement was vital to their own sense of purpose": Bloch, *Visionary Republic*, 217–22; quote, 221.

63 LMS, *Reports*, vol. 1, 16.

64 LMS, "Report ... at the Second General Meeting," *Reports*, vol. 1, 39.

65 LMS, "Report ... at the Third General Meeting," *Reports*, vol. 1, 74.

66 *Missionary Magazine* 5, no.47 (21 April 1800): 151; Thomas Haweis, *History of the Church*.

67 Edwards, *Humble Attempt*.

68 Ibid., 365–73.

69 Martin, *Evangelicals United*, 23.

70 Edwards, *Humble Attempt*, 361.

71 LMS-HO 1/1/A: W. Lambert to J. Eyre, 6 August 1799.

72 Burder, *Memoir*, 157.

73 LMS, "First Report, respecting the Formation of the Missionary Society," *Reports I*, 7.

74 Bebbington, *Evangelicalism*, 10–12; Bloch, *Visionary Republic*, 18; Spadafora, *Idea of Progress*, 250–2.

75 A similar point is made by Bloch about Jonathan Edwards and New Light millennialism in the United States: *Visionary Republic*, 18.

76 Payne, "Introduction," iii.

77 Ryland Sr, *Overthrow of Popery Predicted*. This edition was a reprint; internal evidence dates the original text to 1779 or shortly thereafter.

78 Ibid., 21.

79 *Evangelical Magazine*, January 1795, reproduced in LMS *Reports I*, 8.

80 Circular letter, 27 January 1795, reproduced in LMS *Reports I*, 10.

81 Oliver, *Prophets and Millennialists*, 40; Hilton, *Age of Atonement*.

82 Hopkins, *Woman to Deliver*; Harrison, *Second Coming*; Oliver, *Prophets and Millennialists*, 14–15, 42–67.

83 LMS-SA 4/1/A: Joseph Hardcastle to Van der Kemp, 3 February 1809.

84 T. Charles, "The Yoke of Bondage," 46.

85 CMS, G/AC3: T. Robinson to T. Scott, Leicester, 11 February 1801.

86 NLS, MS10999: Thomas Scott to John Campbell, 9 August 1794.

87 LMS, "Report ... to the Twelfth General Meeting," *Four Sermons*, 31.

88 Cited by Latrobe, *Select Narratives*, 126–7.

89 NLS, MS10999: Thomas Scott to John Campbell, 9 August 1794.

90 *Report of the Formation of the Cambridge Auxiliary Bible Society*, cited in *Report of the Committee ... May 19, 1812*, 437–8.

91 Crawford, *Seasons of Grace*, 20–1.

92 Hilton, *Age of Atonement*.

93 LMS, "Report ... at the Third General Meeting," 63, and "Report ... at the Fourth General Meeting," 65–73, both in *Reports I*.

94 "The Report ... at the Fourth General Meeting, May 9, 1798," LMS *Reports I*, 74.

95 Charles, "The Yoke of Bondage," 46.

96 De Jong, *As the Waters Cover the Sea*, especially 182–8 on the LMS.

97 Gidney, *History of the London Society*.

98 Perry, "American Board of Commissioners," 126–7.
99 On the forging of a specifically British Protestant nationalism over the course of a century of warfare with France, see Colley, *Britons*.
100 On differential rates of literacy among class groups in villages: Reay, "The Context and Meaning of Popular Literacy," 93–100, 125–7. On the growth of the reading public and the explosion in publishing through the latter half of the eighteenth century: Golby and Purdue, *Civilization of the Crowd* 32–5, 125–35.
101 Marshall and Williams, *Great Map of Mankind*; Adams, *Travel Literature*; Mackay, *In the Wake of Cook*, 193.
102 Carey, *Memoir*, 18. On Cook's influence: Marshall and Williams, *Great Map of Mankind*, 258; Wilson, "Island race."
103 Percy, "Language of Captain James Cook," 4.
104 Haweis, *Travel and Talk*, 194; Radford and James, *Autobiography*, 476.
105 LMS, *Memoir of ... Van der Kemp*, 16; Schoeman, *J.J. Kicherer*, 14, citing "Berichten medegedeeld door den zendeling-broder J.J. Kicherer en van ekders opgezameld ten dienste van het Zendeling-genootschap te Rotterdam, betreffende den toestand en de betrekkingen der zendelingen in 't zuiden van Africa met het begin der 19de eeuw" (1803), MS, Hendrik Kramer Institut, iii–iv.
106 Ryland, *Work of Faith*, 239.
107 Payne, "Introduction," v.
108 Carey, *An Enquiry*, 62–3.
109 Ward, "The Baptists," 205.
110 *Missionary Register for MDCCCXVI*, vol. 1 (London, 1816), 481.
111 Carey, *An Enquiry*, 11–12.
112 Edwards, *Account of the Life ... David Brainerd*; Horne, *Letters on Missions*. On the influence of Horne's work on several LMS founders: Martin, *Evangelicals United*, 41–2.
113 Walls, "A Christian Experiment," 107 ff.
114 *Evangelical Magazine*, July 1803, 280.
115 *Missionary Magazine*, 1 (London, 1796), t.p.
116 *Missionary Magazine*, 2 (London, 1797), iii.
117 Hall, in *Contested Boundaries*, makes a similar point about the challenge of revivalist itinerancy to the established religious, social, and political order in the eighteenth-century American colonies.
118 Bogue and Bennett, *History of Dissenters*, 189–95.
119 Martin, *Evangelicals United*, 28.
120 For example, many historians have explored the authorization given by ecstatic religious experience to women to become prophets and vehicles for the voice of God. Garrett, *Spirit Possesssion*, 21–2, 142; Hopkins, *Woman to Deliver Her People*; Valenze, *Prophetic Daughters*; Niccoli, "End of Prophecy."

121 Hunter, *History of the Missions*, 3–6; Ross, *John Philip*, 35.

122 Thomas Scott to "A Friend in Scotland," 2 July 1796. In Scott, *Letters and Papers*, 184–5.

123 For example, "On the Probable Design of Providence in Subjecting India to Great Britain," *Christian Observer*, February 1809, 221.

124 LMS-SA 1/3/A: Wilks to Van der Kemp, 10 May 10 1800.

125 LMS-HO, 1/6/A: Samuel Greatheed to John Eyre, 13 February 1799; Ward, *Religion and Society*, 47–53. For a list of pan-evangelical county unions and itinerant societies apparently founded by members of the LMS, see Martin, "Pan-Evangelical Impulse," appendix A, 371–2.

126 Methodist Church Archives, Tyerman MSS.iii. fo.79, cited in Ward, *Religion and Society*, 52–3.

127 For example, *Anti-Jacobin Review*, vol. 2, 361–71.

128 *Christian Observer*, March 1802, 179–84; *Cobbett's Annual Register*, vol. 1, 20–7 February 1802, 173; Brown, *Fathers of the Victorians*, 187–233.

129 On problems encountered by some CMS founders suspected of Methodism: CMS, Acc. 81, F5: Henry Venn, "Memoirs of the Red. John Venn – Period first from Birth to College"; Berridge to John Thornton, 24 November 1781, cited in Venn, *Annals of a Clerical Family*, 102; Scott, *Life of the Reverend Thomas Scott*, 30; John Pratt, *Eclectic Notes*, 22; Goode, *Memoir of … Rev. William Goode*, 4; Hole, *Early History*, 635.

130 Bodl., MSS Wilberforce, c.51, fo.30: Thornton to Wilberforce, 21 November 1804.

131 CMS, G/AC3, I: T. Robinson to T. Scott, 26 April 1802.

132 Pratt, *Eclectic Notes*, 13–6.

133 "Prospectus," *Christian Observer*, vol. 1.

134 Ian Bradley, *Call to Seriousness*, 20–1.

135 Rosman, *Evangelicals and Culture*, 12–13.

136 Zinzendorf, *An Exposition*, 26.

137 Latrobe, *Select Narratives*, especially 126–31 on the diaspora church.

138 Oussoren, *William Carey*, 224, 236.

139 Rupp, *Religion in England*, 336.

140 Society for the Furtherance of the Gospel, *Periodical Accounts relating to the Missions of the Church of the United Brethren, established among the Heathen*; La Trobe, *Succinct View*, 8–27; Crantz, *History of Greenland* ; Crantz, *Letter to a Friend*; Loskiel, *History of the Mission*.

141 Martin, *Evangelicals United*, 31–2.

142 ML B1176: Haweis, "Autobiography". Cf. also Reynolds, *Evangelicals at Oxford*, 28.

143 E.M.C., *Short Sketch*.

144 Carey, *Enquiry*, 11; Oussoren, *William Carey*, 33.

145 Richard Cecil, *Memoirs of the Rev. John Newton*, 47–50; *Evangelical Magazine*, January 1803, 35–7.

146 Scott, *Life of the Rev. Thomas Scott*, 311: Scott to Ryland, 24 April 1793.

147 Scott, *Letters and Papers*, 254: Scott to Ryland, 3 December 1814.

148 Payne, "Introduction," iii; Ryland, *Work of Faith*, 242–3. The "acount of the Pellow Islands" was probably Keate, *Account of the Pelew Islands*.

149 "Laws and Regulations of the Society," In *Report of the Glasgow Missionary Society for 1822* (Glasgow, 1822), 5.

150 GMS *Report*, 1822, 7–10.

151 H.F. Burder, *Memoir of the Rev. George Burder*, 156–7; Pratt, *Eclectic Notes*; Horne, *Story of the London Missionary Society*, 4.

152 Resolution from a meeting held to establish the *Evangelical Magazine*, cited by Horne, *Story of the LMS*, 4.

153 Haweis, *Travel and Talk*, 192.

154 Gunson, *Messengers of Grace*, 9; Haweis, *Travel and Talk*, 198–200.

155 Robert Hodgson, *Life of the Right Reverend Beilby Porteus*, 239–40.

156 Seventeen years later, Porteus created a minor furore by refusing to allow Dr Draper, a former preacher for the Countess of Huntingdon and president of one of her colleges, to use his pulpit. Lambeth Palace Library, Porteus Papers, MS2104: Porteus to Cromwell, Fulham House, 2 August 1808.

157 Haweis, *Travel and Talk*, 199: Wilberforce to Haweis, 15 June 1791.

158 Ibid., 200: Wilberforce to Haweis, 20 June 1793.

159 Horne, *Story of the LMS*, 5; Haweis, *Travel and Talk*, 217.

160 LMS "First Report," *Reports I*, 2.

161 Ibid., 3–4.

162 Ibid., 3.

163 *Evangelical Magazine*, October 1795, 421.

164 CMS, Acc. 81, Venn MSS, c.68: Henry Thornton to John Venn, London, 25 September 1795.

165 LMS, "Report ... at the Second General Meeting," *Reports I*, 32–6.

166 For a more extended discussion, see Elbourne, "Foundation of the Church Missionary Society," 247–64.

167 Martin, "Pan-evangelical Impulse," 93; Pratt, *Eclectic Notes*. Nine of the founders of the CMS had been at Oxford, at a time in which the evangelicals at Oxford were a relatively small and persecuted group with an emerging sense of group identity: Reynolds, *Evangelicals at Oxford*, 68.

168 LMS, Acc.81, C.68: "Extract from the will of the late John Thornton Esqr of Clapham in the county of Surrey Dated 2 Apr 1790"; Hole, *Early History*, 621, 635; Venn, *Annals of a Clerical Family*, 127.

169 Innes, "Politics and Morals"; Brown, *Fathers of the Victorians*, especially 83–91 and 317–60.

170 On Sierra Leone and the Claphamites: Curtin, *Image of Africa*; Wilson, *Loyal Blacks*. On India and the Claphamites, Marshall, *Problems of Empire*.

171 Looking back later, CMS secretary Thomas Scott would write to John Ryland: "You will remember our conversations on the subject of missions at Northampton; and now, I think, the close of my life is likely to be especially devoted to promote that object, respecting which we then conversed and prayed."

172 Thomas Scott to "A Friend in Scotland," Chapel Street, 2 July 1796, in Scott, *Letters and Papers*, 185.

173 Pratt, *Eclectic Notes*, 13–16.

174 For statements of their desire for a middle way, by Jowett, Simeon, and Newton respectively: CMS, Acc.81, c.19: Jowett to Venn, 6 May 1795; Carus, *Memoirs of ... Rev. Charles Simeon*, 563; Cecil, *Memoirs of the Rev. John Newton*, 403.

175 Semmel, *Methodist Revolution*, 109.

176 For example, Goode, *A Memoir*, 4.

177 The following draws on Hilton, *Age of Atonement*, 14–19.

178 For example, *Christian Observer*, March 1802, 202.

179 Pratt, *Eclectic Notes*, 96.

180 CMS, G/C1, vol. 1: Committee Minutes, 12 April 1799; CMS, G/CA3: Venn to Archbishop Moore, London, 1 July 1799; CMS, G/AC3: Wilberforce to Venn, 24 July 1800.

181 LPL, Fulham Papers: Porteus Papers, XXXVII.

182 Elbourne, "Foundation of the Church Missionary Society," 259–61. For an example of this process, CMS, G/AC3: Mayor to Scott, 22 January 1800 about a young man whom the Rev. J. Mayor had hoped to tempt to mission work but who became an itinerant Wesleyan minister instead.

183 The CMS 1802 directors' report opined that it was difficult to find missionaries for Sierra Leone: "Perhaps without sufficient foundations," Africa was reputed to be unhealthy and wholly "rude and barbarous in its manners." Society for Missions to Africa and the East (SMAE), "Report of the Directors," 1802, in *Proceedings I*, 137–8. The CMS used this title initially before bowing to popular usage and adopting the name Church Missionary Society.

184 G/AC3, 140(41): Smith to Macaulay, 26 November 1800.

185 CMS, G/AC3: Smith to Macaulay, 29 November 1800.

186 CMS, G/AC3: P.Shurr to Pratt, 8 July 1812.

187 Cnattingius, *Bishops and Societies*, 41–8.

188 Scott, 1801 Anniversary Sermon, in SMAE *Proceedings I*, 44.

189 Kopf, *British Orientalism*, 129–44.

190 For one overview of debates on India from the perspective of the *Christian Observer*: "Review of Buchanan on Christianity in India," April 1813, 239–53.

191 "Religious Intelligence – Christianity in India," *Christian Observer*, April 1813, 263.

192 In opposition: Thomas, *An Address to a Meeting*.

193 Semmel, *Methodist Revolution*, 152.

194 The *Quarterly Papers* were intended to convey "in plain language, intelligence of the Proceedings of the Society, with Engraved representations and Printed Accounts of the ignorance and miseries of the unhappy objects of their kind solicitude. By this means, it was believed, the well-disposed among the Labouring Classes would be enabled to aid in the work of Evangelizing the World, a Missionary Spirit would be more largely excited and cherished, and a considerable addition made to the Funds of the Society." Advertisement in *The First Ten Years' Quarterly Papers of the Church Missionary Society; to which is prefixed a Brief View of the Society*.

195 For example, Bodl. MSS Wilberforce, C.3.: Burder to Wilberforce, 10 February 1818.

CHAPTER TWO

1 Alan Barnard, *Hunters and Herders* 11–12.

2 Elphick, *Khoikhoi and the Founding*, xvi–xvii, 18–22.

3 Barnard, *Hunters and Herders*, 7.

4 Wells, "Eva's Men," 417–37. The *-na* is a common-gender plural suffix. The first VOC governor, Jan van Riebeeck, first recorded the term Khoe as *Quena*. Barnard, *Hunters and Herders*, 7; Monica Wilson, "Notes on the Nomenclature," 252.

5 Barnard, *Hunters and Herders*, 20–7; Elphick and Malherbe, "The Khoisan to 1828," 4–5.

6 For an overview of possible means to classify Khoisan groups and some political connotations of naming, Barnard, *Hunters and Herders*, 7–11, 16–36.

7 Marks, "Khoisan Resistance," 55–80.

8 Elphick, *Khoikhoi and the Founding*, 23–30.

9 "Introduction," Penn, "Northern Cape Frontier Zone"; Newton-King, *Masters and Servants*, 28–9, 59–62.

10 Newton-King, *Masters and Servants*, 28–9, 116–34, 59–62.

11 I use the spelling "Khoisan" here rather than "Khoesen," since the term is, in Alan Barnard's words, reiterated by Susan Newton-King, an "artificial compound" which is "distinctly European" and not Khoisan. Barnard, *Hunters and Herders*, 7; Newton-King, *Masters and Servants*, 250n.25.

12 Alan Barnard makes a case for overall structural similarities, despite
   regional variation, between Khoisan groups across southern Africa:
   "In spite of differences associated with their subsistence pursuits, many
   otherwise diverse Khoisan peoples share a great number of common
   features of territorial organization, gender relations, kinship, ritual, and
   cosmology. These features are not randomly distributed; nor have they
   simply diffused from one group to another as single cultural traits. They
   represent elements of structures held in common across economic, cultural, linguistic and 'racial' boundaries." Barnard, *Hunters and Herders*,
   3.
13 Elphick, *Khoikhoi and the Founding*, 62–3.
14 A late-nineteenth-century ethnographic account in the South African
   Library describes the construction of Khoekhoe homes. "The huts of the
   Hottentots are half-round, 10 to 12 feet diameter and 4 feet high and
   look like big beehives; on one side is a small opening, through which one
   has to crawl, and in the middle is the fire-place. The hut consists of a
   frame of bent tree-branches, which is put together like a cage and can be
   taken to pieces again. This frame is either fastened over with skins and
   mats or covered with dry bushes ... [to make the mats they] take the inner
   skin of a mimosa-species which is gathered and dried in large quantities.
   When they commence making mats, it is first put in hot water and made
   flexible, all members of the family set to work now to prepare it for plaiting by chewing it and rolling it on their legs into strings, then the strings
   are spread on the floor in parallel rows, and by means of counter-strings,
   which are pulled through with pointed bones or thorns, are made into a
   loose fabric. Such a mat answers its purpose perfectly. Whilst on account
   of the loose fabric it allows the air to pass through in the hot season, in
   the rainy season the several strings swell out and make a thick fabric,
   which affords ample protection against rain and storm." SAL: MSB594,
   1(i): "Ethnographic description," n.d.
15 Schapera, "General Introduction," vi–vii.
16 SAL: MSB594, 1 (i): "Ethnographic Observations," n.d.
17 Elphick and Malherbe, "The Khoisan to 1828," 6; Barnard, *Hunters
   and Herders*, 160–1; Schapera, *Early Cape Hottentots*, vii–viii; Rhyne,
   Short Account, 143.
18 Chidester, *Savage Systems*, 71; Landau, "'Religion' and Christian Conversion," 8–30.
19 LMS-SA 23/3/A: James Read Sr and Jr to LMS, Kat River, 12 November
   1847.
20 On resistance: Marks, "Khoisan Resistance," 55–80. Solway and Lee,
   "Foragers, Geniune or Spurious," use the early-modern history of the
   Kalahari San to underscore the complexity of Khoisan interactions with
   other groups and to argue against any monocausal discussion of the fate

of forager and hunter-gatherer groups in contact with European and Nguni intruders. On dispossession: Newton-King, *Masters and Servants*; Elphick and Malherbe, "The Khoisan to 1828," 3–65; Elphick, *Khoikhoi and the Founding*; Marais, *Cape Coloured People*.

21 SAL, MSB594, 1(3): Theophilus Hahn, Stellenbosch, 8 October 1879.

22 Crehan, "Khoi, Boer and Missionary," 113.

23 Elphick, *Khoikhoi and the Founding*, passim, including xvii on clientage and the Khoekhoe propensity to acculturation. Giliomee, "Eastern Frontier," 430.

24 Newton-King, *Masters and Servants*, 44–5 and passim.

25 Work on the eighteenth-century interaction between colonists and Khoisan on colonial frontiers includes Elphick, *Khoikhoi and the Founding*; Newton-King, *Masters and Servants*; Penn, "Northern Cape Frontier Zone"; Legassick, "The Griqua"; Elphick and Giliomee, *Shaping*, including Elphick and Malherbe, "The Khoisan to 1828," Giliomee, "The Eastern Frontier," and other key essays; Marks, "Khoisan Resistance"; R. Ross, "Changing Legal Position," 166–80.

26 Marais, *Maynier*, 1; Keegan, *Colonial South Africa*, 25.

27 Newton-King, *Masters and Servants*.

28 Ibid.

29 R. Ross, "Capitalism," 220–1; R. Ross, "Developmental Spiral," 138–51.

30 Guelke and Shell, "Landscape of Conquest," 803–24.

31 LMS missionary J.T. van der Kemp testified in a 1799 letter to his nephew, for example, to the dearth of opportunities for services, or preaching, and the great desire of the inhabitants of the eastern frontier zones for teachers and ministers. HK: Brieven van J.T. v.d. Kemp, 1780–81, Kast 61, Doos 1: no.53, J.T. van der Kemp, banks of the Tarka River, 4 August 1799 and following.

32 On frontier farmers' control of the commando after 1740 in the northern frontier zone, Penn, "Northern Frontier Zone," 138.

33 Two useful recent surveys of the historiography of the frontier in South African history are Penn, "Northern Cape Frontier Zone," 3–29, and Keegan, *Colonial South Africa*, 1–14. See also Saunders, *Making of the South African Past*; Legassick, "Frontier Tradition."

34 Giliomee, "Processes in the Development."

35 Ismail Rachid usefully raised this point during a workshop at McGill University, February 1998, on the comparative historiography of imperial frontiers, for which I would like to thank him.

36 Newton-King, "Enemy within"; Newton-King, "Labour Market"; Elbourne, "Freedom at Issue," 114–50.

37 Newton-King, "Labour Market," 171–205.

38 Katzen, "White Settlers," 227; Giliomee, "Eastern Frontier," 422.

39 The 1798 opgaaf returns cited by John Barrow in the second volume of his travel account list 4,262 "Christians", 964 "slaves" and 8,947 "Hottentots": Barrow, *Account of Travels*, vol. 2, 377–8. William Freund has argued convincingly, however, that this total of 14,173 must be a significant underestimate, since the indigenous population was probably counted only when in orderly service on white farms. A more realistic figure, he suggests, would be between 25 and 30,000, if not more, with the bulk of the shortfall presumably going to raise the Khoekhoe total to upwards of 25,000. Sheila Patterson estimates, on the basis of British census statistics, that in 1807 there were 25,614 whites in the Cape Colony as a whole, 1,204 "free blacks," 29,303 slaves, and 17,431 Khoisan and "Bastards" – again, probably an underestimate of the Khoisan population. All early figures must, however, be treated with some caution, at least as far as the frontier districts are concerned: in 1797 Barrow observed that the new administration at the Cape was not sure how far away the Graaf-Reinet district was, let alone how many inhabitants it contained. Freund, *Society and Government*, 24–7, 434; Patterson, "Some Speculations," 172.
40 Giliomee, "Eastern Frontier," 428–9.
41 On the Khoisan loss of political and economic power, see Elphick and Malherbe, "The Khoisan to 1828," 28–43, 50–52.
42 Giliomee, "Eastern Frontier," 423–4, 427.
43 Peires, *House of Phalo*, 18–19, 22.
44 J. Hodgson, *God of the Xhosa*, 6–13.
45 Newton-King, *Masters and Servants*, 112.
46 Ibid., 116–20.
47 Giliomee, "Eastern Frontier," 425–6, 429.
48 Ibid., 433.
49 Newton-King, *Masters and Servants*, 146; Marais, *Maynier*, 62–3.
50 Marais, *Maynier*; Elphick and Malherbe, "Khoisan to 1828"; Giliomee, "Eastern Frontier"; and Schutte, "Company and Colonists," 29–30, 439–41, 309–15 respectively; Trapido, "Paternalism to Liberalism," 80–1; A.M. Lewis Robinson, "Introduction," 1; Harlow, "The British Occupations"; Walker, *History of South Africa* 125–8; Newton-King, *Masters and Servants*, 144–7.
51 Malherbe, "Hermanus," 189–202.
52 Barrow, *Account of Travels*, vol. 1, 143–4. Barrow adds that there are in Graaff-Reinet "perhaps not a score of individuals who are not actually in the service of the Dutch" (144). In the light of V.C. Malherbe's work on Khoisan bandit groups in the early nineteenth century, however, it seems unlikely that there were not also groups living in the bush in the eighteenth century, more or less on the run but still independent: presumably what they could not do was live in open independence from the Dutch.

53 Evidence of "Andrew Stoffel" *SCA*, vol. I, 584.

54 Malherbe, "Khoi Captains," 75.

55 Barrow, *Account of Travels*, vol. 2, 93–4.

56 Ibid., 110–11.

57 Newton-King, "Rebellion of the Khoi," 14–29 and passim; Malherbe, "Khoi Captains," 74–5 and passim.

58 Rho, MSS.Afr.s.1, fo.8: Andrew Barnard to Governor Dundas, 20 October 1799. Barrow, *Account of Travels*, vol. 2, 111–13, 127–30, on conflict between the British and Chungwa, described by Barrow as provoked by the Xhosa following misunderstandings and misleading information from local farmers.

59 On the early recruitment policy of the LMS, and change over time towards a greater emphasis on education: Piggin, *Making Evangelical Missionaries*.

60 Haweis, thanksgiving sermon preached at Zion Chapel, 6 August 1798, LMS *Missionary Sermons*, vol. 2, 57.

61 Schoeman, *J.J. Kicherer*, 24.

62 LMS-SA: Haweis to Van der Kemp, 22 February 1799; also cited by Schoeman, *J.J. Kicherer*, 24.

63 Edmond seems to have spelt his name at different times as Edmond and as Edmonds, as Schoeman points out, *J.J. Kicherer*, 256, n.19; this in itself hints at a relatively low level of education.

64 LMS-SA, Candidates Papers, box 9, John Edmond to LMS directors, July 1798.

65 Stuart, "Of Savages and Heroes."

66 LMS, *Memoir of ... Van der Kemp*, 15.

67 Schoeman, *J.J. Kicherer*, 13–15.

68 Ibid., 14–15.

69 Enklaar, *Life and Work*, 57, 65; Schoeman, *J.J. Kicherer*, 13, 16.

70 There is an English translation of Van der Kemp's autobiography in the LMS archives at the School of African and Oriental Studies, London: LMS-Odds, box 8, Vanderkemp papers, item 1. The translation was probably made by Walter Hooper, missionary at Bethelsdorp. The autobiography does not, however, extend beyond Van der Kemp's arrival at the Cape. The Dutch original is lost, according to Enklaar, *Life and Work*, 221. The direct quotations below are from the London version of the manuscript autobiography. This copy is missing the first ten pages and is obscured in places by water-blots. Enklaar has drawn on a better version in the archives of the Nederduitse Gereformeerde Kerk, Cape Town, and I have accordingly used his account of its first few pages. The best biography of Van der Kemp is Enklaar's *Life and Work*. An earlier Dutch version covers Van der Kemp's life until 1799: Enklaar, *De levens-*

geschiedenis van Johannes. See also Freund, "Career of Johannes," 376–90; A.D. Martin, *Dr. Vanderkemp*; Elbourne, "Concerning Missionaries," 153–64.

71 Enklaar, *Life and Work*, 1.
72 On François Adriaan van der Kemp's life: Van der Kemp, *Francis Adrian van der Kemp*.
73 Ibid., 101–5.
74 Simon Schama cites a sermon of F.A. van der Kemp's: "In America, a holy sun has risen and it will shine on us if we so will it ... America can teach us how to fight against the degeneration of our national character; the debasement of our soul, the corruption of its will to resist ... how to throttle tyranny and how to restore to health the all but moribund corpse of freedom." Cited in Schama, *Patriots and Liberators*, 60; cited in turn from Hartog, "Een Heftig Patriot," 58.
75 Van der Kemp, *Francis Adrian van der Kemp*, 7; Enklaar, *Life and Work*, 12.
76 Letter from F.A. van der Kemp to Lincklaen, 8 April 1816, cited in Van der Kemp, *Francis Adrian van der Kemp*, 22.
77 LMS-Odds, box 8: J.T. Van der Kemp, Autobiography.
78 LMS-SA 1/1/A: Van der Kemp to LMS, 26 July 1797.
79 Enklaar, *Life and Works*, 1–40; LMS-SA, Odds: box 8, Van der Kemp, Autobiography.
80 LMS-SA, Odds: box 8, Van der Kemp, Autobiography. Van der Kemp's "intimate friend" Edmund Goodwyn, with whom Van der Kemp carried out experiments in drowning animals, went on to become a medical writer whose most important works included his dissertation, *Dissertatio Medico de morte Submersorum* (Edinburgh, 1786) and its English translation, *The Connexion of Life with Respiration; or an Experimental Enquiry into the Effects of Submersion, Strangulation, and several kinds of Noxious Airs on Living Animals ... and the most effectual means of cure* (London, 1788): *Dictionary of National Biography*. Van der Kemp's own dissertation, presented in 1782, was entitled *Dissertatio Medica exhibens Cogitationes Physiologicas de Vita et vivificatione materiae humanum corpus constituentis.*
81 LMS-SA, Odds, box 8: Van der Kemp, Autobiography, 93.
82 LMS, *Memoir of ... Van der Kemp*, 17.
83 Schama, *Patriots and Liberators*, 64–74.
84 Ibid., 74.
85 LMS-SA, Odds: box 8, Van der Kemp, Autobiography.
86 Letters cited in Enklaar, *Life and Work*, 6.
87 LMS-Odds, box 8, Cornelius Boem to LMS directors, 10 June 1797.
88 LMS-SA, Odds: box 8, Van der Kemp, Autobiography.
89 LMS-SA, Odds: box 8, Van der Kemp, Autobiography.

90 Enklaar, *Life and Work*, 9-12; LMS-Odds: box 8, Van der Kemp, Autobiography.

91 Hilton, *Age of Atonement*, 14.

92 LMS-SA, Odds: box 8, Van der Kemp, Autobiography.

93 LMS-Odds: box 8, Van der Kemp, Autobiography. Van der Kemp explained that this was so clear, it did not require divine revelation: Adam had been a test case which "disqualified" man, as one sour glass of beer from a barrel discredits nine others.

94 Ibid.

95 Enklaar, *Life and Work*, 132.

96 Van der Kemp, Autobiography, 2nd translation (the second translator clearly had a sounder grasp of technical terms in philosophy than the first; thus, some elements of the first translation are actually not comprehensible).

97 Spinoza, *Improvement of the Understanding*, 1–6; Descartes, *Discours de la méthode*.

98 Van der Kemp, *Francis Adrian van der Kemp*, 18.

99 Contrast Spinoza, *Ethics*, Part V, "On the Power of the Understanding, or Of Human Freedom": "Blessedness [love of God in the sense outlined above] is not the reward of virtue, but virtue itself; neither do we rejoice therein, because we control our lusts, but, contrariwise, because we rejoice therein, we are able to control our lusts." Spinoza comments with regard to this proposition, "How potent is the wise man, and how much he surpasses the ignorant man, who is driven only by his lusts." Spinoza, *Ethics*, 270.

100 LMS-SA, Odds: box 8, Van der Kemp to LMS directors.

101 Said, *Orientalism*; Comaroff and Comaroff, *Of Revelation and Revolution*; Stuart, "Of Savages and Heroes"; M.L. Pratt, "Scratches on the Face." For a critique (with which I agree) of Pratt's depiction of John Barrow's views of the San, however, see Penn, "Northern Cape Frontier Zone," 390, n.12.

102 For example, O. Dapper, "Kaffrarie," and Rhyne, "Schediasma de promontorio Bonae Spei (Schaffhausen, 1686)," both reprinted and translated into English in Schapera, *Early Cape Hottentots*.

103 HK, Dag Verhaal J.T. van der Kemp uit Zuid Afrika 1798, 1801–1805: Van der Kemp to LMS directors, 26 May 1798; Enklaar, *Life and Work*, 61.

104 Curtin, *Image of Africa*.

105 *Missionary Magazine*, vol. 6, 19 December 1796, 282.

106 Newton-King, "Enemy within"; Eldredge and Morton, *Slavery in South Africa*, including Eldredge, "Slave Raiding Across the Frontier," and Eldredge, "Delagoa Bay and the Hinterland," 93–165. The extent and regional impact of the covert internal slave trade is a critical issue in current heated debates among historians on the roots and impact of the

so-called mfecane, as well as the very validity of the concept of mfecane; although the debate is far from closed, it has at the very least brought into focus the extent of regional slaving. Hamilton, *Mfecane Aftermath*; Cobbing, "The Mfecane as Alibi."

107 LMS-Odds, box 8, Van der Kemp: items 4–5, "Extracts from a Biography." These extracts contain more material on slavery than does the primary translation.

108 For a discussion of European sources of information about Africa, focusing on West Africa: Curtin, *Image of Africa*, 9–27.

109 Kolbe, *Present State*.

110 *New General Collection of Voyages and Travels*, vol. 3, v–vi.

111 According to Johannes Wilhelm de Grevenbroek, Van Riebeeck Society, vol. 14, 173 and 175, cited by Elphick, *Khoikhoi and the Founding*. Elphick's discussion, "The White Man's Image of the 'Hottentot,'" found on 193–200, is useful.

112 *Modern Part of an Universal History, from the Earliest Accounts to the Present Time*, xxxvii, 166.

113 *New General Collection*, 349.

114 Rousseau, *Discours sur l'origine*, 164–5, n.1; original mention of Rousseau from Elphick, *Khoikhoi and the Founding*, 195, note 9.

115 Merians, "What They Are, Who We Are."

116 Cited Elphick, *Khoikhoi and the Founding*, xv.

117 Penn, "Reflections on Rereading of Peter Kolb," 43.

118 Marsden, *History of Sumatra*, 169–70; cited in Marshall and Williams, *Great Map of Mankind*, 134.

119 *Modern Part of Universal History*, 165–6. This was probably based on the real story of Doman: personal communication, Richard Elphick.

120 *New General Collection*, 348.

121 Sparrman, *Voyage to the Cape*, vol. 1, 201–2. On the thesis that the views of observers as to whether or not Africans possessed a "religion" fluctuated according to frontier conflicts: Chidester, *Savage Systems*.

122 Krüger, *Pear Tree Blossoms*; Schmidt, *Das Tagebuch*.

123 "Account of the Voyage of Brother George Schmidt to the Cape of Good Hope, and of his Abode there from 1736 to 1744. Written by himself," in United Brethren, *Periodical Accounts*, vol. 1, 170–1.

124 *Periodical Accounts*, vol. 1, 286.

125 LMS-SA, 1/2/C: Hardcastle and Eyre to Van der Kemp, London, *c.* end of 1799.

126 Hallett, *African Association*, especially "Introduction," 10–13.

127 LMS-SA 1/1/D: Hardcastle to Van der Kemp, 8 March 1799. A letter from George Burder to Banks inserted into a British Library copy of a memoir of Van der Kemp testifies that the LMS directors sent Banks the pamphlet in thanks "for your numerous and useful exertions in their favour."

Burder to Banks, 4 April 1812, attached to BL copy of *Memoir of ... Van der Kemp*, shelfmark B.702(13). Note that Hawkesworth's 1773 account of voyages to the South Seas was drawn up partially from the papers of Banks, in addition to those of several commanders of voyages (see chapter 2, above), and Banks's prestige dated from the sensational success of this collection. Hallett, *African Association*, 10–11.

128 LMS-SA 1/C/2: Hardcastle and Eyre to Van der Kemp, London, *c.* end of 1799.
129 LMS-SA 1/2/B: Van der Kemp to LMS directors, *c.* August 1799.
130 Hill, *Turbulent, Seditious and Factious*, 378–9.
131 *Evangelical Magazine*, March 1823, 132.
132 LMS-SA 1/2/B: Van der Kemp to Haweis, 12 August 1799.
133 LMS-SA 1/2/B: Hardcastle to Van der Kemp, London, 24 July 1799.
134 Diary of George Barker, reproduced in appendix, Currie, "The History of Theopolis Mission," 28 February and 3 March 1815.

CHAPTER THREE

1 Although many scholars disagree on the nature, extent, and significance of adherence to Calvinism among Dutch-speaking white settlers before the early nineteenth century, as also on the question of how easy it was for non-whites to become Christians, historians do broadly agree that those who would later be termed "whites" were generally labelled "Christians" in official records before the nineteenth century, and that whites tried to obtain the tokens of belonging to the Christian community through such means as seeking baptism for their children even at the cost of a long and arduous journey to a distant minister – albeit often long past the birth of the child. Thus, although Robert Ross, D. van Arkel, and G.C. Quispel argue that Dutch settlers before the late eighteenth century were not particularly pious nor indeed necessarily Calvinist, and did not rigidly exclude nonwhites from the Christian church, they nonetheless underscore that for European settlers "Christianity was the sign of their culture, of their civilization," and that "however low the enthusiasm for the performance of their Christian duties may have been ... the Europeans were conscious and proud of their status as Christians." R. Ross, Van Arkel, and Quispel, "Going beyond the Pale," 79. For a stronger statement of the importance of Christianity in general, and Calvinism in particular, for the sense of identity of early settlers, Gerstner, *Thousand Generation Covenant*. For a skeptical view of the Calvinist origins of Afrikaner nationalism and the centrality of Calvinism for early settlers, Du Toit, "No Chosen People," 920–52. On the ramifications of baptism in theological, legal and popular practice at the Cape: Shell, *Children of Bondage*, 330–70. On covenant theology, Akenson, *God's Peoples*.

2 This was according to Van der Kemp; translation problems should not be ignored of course. HK: *Dag Verhaal J.T. Van der Kemp*, 1801.

3 HK: Kas 61, Doos 1, *Brieven van J.T. van der Kemp*: 53, Van der Kemp to his nephew, banks of the Tarka River, 4 August (and following) 1799. LMS-SA 1/2/B: Van der Kemp to Thomas Haweis, Great Fish River, 16 July 1799. As Van der Kemp wrote to his nephew, "Ik heb overal door dit geheele land van het Roodezand af tot aan graaff [sic] Reinet en achter het Sneeuwgebergen tot over de groote vischrivier gepredikt, en zoo ik vertrouw met aanmerkelijk zegen de begeerte om Gods woord te hooren is alhier onbegrijpelijk groot ..." [I have preached through this entire land from the Roodezand to Graaff Reinet and behind the Snowy Mountains to over the Great Fish River, and so I trust with considerable blessing, the desire to hear God's word is incredibly great ...].

4 Kicherer, *Mr. Kicherer's Narrative*, 3.

5 Burgher petition to the Dutch Chamber of Seventeen, 9 October 1779, in Du Toit and Giliomee, *Afrikaner Political Thought*, 39; *Memorie gedaan Vergadering van Zeventienen door Kapsche Vrijburgers*, translated by the authors from *Kaapsche Geschillen*, Amsterdam 1785, Cape Archives C742.

6 "Petition from some inhabitants to the governor and Political Council of the Cape, 17 February 1784," in Du Toit and Giliomee, *Afrikaner Political Thought*, 43; for commentary on this document, 29–30.

7 R. Ross, "White Population," 125–37, especially 126, 136–7.

8 Shell, *Children of Bondage*, 333, citing Hendrik Kaajan, *De Pro-Acta der Dordtsche Synode* (Rotterdam: T. de Vries 1914), 224.

9 Shell, *Children of Bondage*, 334–48, 350–6, 362–5; n.355.

10 Ross, Van Arkel, and Quispel, "Going beyond the Pale," 78; Schoeman, *J.J. Kicherer*, 17–18; Vos, *Merkwaardig Verhaal*. On female piety and female religious writing at the Cape: Schoeman, "Vroeë Geskrifte," 24–47; Landman, *Piety of Afrikaans Women*.

11 Landman, *Piety of Afrikaans Women*, 19–35, including 20–1 on the engagement. Catharina van Lier's diary and letters were published as Catharina Allegonda van Lier, *Dagboek, gemeenzame brieven en eenzame overdenkingen*, ed. J.J. Kicherer (Utrecht, 1804).

12 Landman, *Piety of Afrikaans Women*, 24.

13 Vos, *Merkwaardig Verhaal*, 115. I follow Jonathan Gerstner's use of the term "Continuing Reformation." Gerstner argues that the Continuing Reformation movement in the Netherlands was not coincidental with pietism, although scholars often confuse the two, Continuing Reformation leaders engaged in theological polemics, in contrast to pietism's opposition to doctrine which was divisive across denominational boundaries; and the Continuing Reformation tradition tried to transform society, unlike pietism, which focused the individual's attention on his or

her inner life. Gerstner, *Thousand Generation Covenant*, 75–6. On Smith: Philip, *Memoir of Mrs. Matilda Smith*; Landman, *Piety of Afrikaans Women*, 48–59.

14 Vos, *Merkwaardig Verhaal*, 1; Schoeman, "Vroeë Geskrifte deur Suid-Afrikaanse Vroue," 28. On the greater importance given by eighteenth-century Cape society to status over "race," and the use of baptism as an admission criterion to "white" society: R. Ross, Van Arkel, and Quispel, "Going beyond the Pale," 69–90.

15 Du Plessis, *History of Christian Missions*, 91–8. On the fact that most of the early directors and leading players in the South African Missionary Society were among the better-off of the white community of Cape Town and Stellenbosch, Schoeman, *J.J. Kicherer*, 19.

16 R. Ross, "White Population," 132.

17 Shell, *Children of Bondage*, 363; R. Ross, "Developmental Spiral," 138–51. Shell cites Andries Sparrman, who noted that illegitimate children by autochthonous women were rarely baptized, "except in case that any one should present himself as the father, and make a point of the child's being baptized, and thus give the infant the right of inheritance." Sparrman, *Voyage to the Cape*, 263–4.

18 Shell, *Children of Bondage*, 364.

19 LMS-SA, 1/2/D: Van der Kemp to LMS, Cape of Good Hope, 13 May 1799. Nigel Penn observes that Floris Visser wrote in the letter describing the dispatch of these captains that their names were Vigiland, Orlam, and Platje, and it is unclear whether Platje and Slaparm were in fact the same person. Penn, "Northern Cape Frontier Zone," 412.

20 "Oorlam" was used to describe Khoisan who now used guns and horses, had a degree of white ancestry, and were moving northwards and subjugating local Khoekhoe groups through this period. Penn points out that Slaparm could have meant literally "weak arm" or "lame arm," but the /Xam also used the term for someone who didn't share meat equally. "A *k"waken //kung* (decayed arm) was someone who was ungenerous about food." Penn, "Northern Cape Frontier Zone," 412 and n.4.

21 Ibid., 392–410.

22 LMS-SA 1/2/D: Van der Kemp to LMS directors, Cape of Good Hope, 13 May 1799.

23 Anne Barnard, *Cape Journals*, 187–8.

24 Kicherer, *Mr. Kicherer's Narrative*, 2–3.

25 LMS, *Transactions* I, 372–3.

26 Kicherer, *Mr. Kicherer's Narrative*, 3; Penn, "Northern Cape Frontier Zone," 417.

27 Kicherer, *Mr Kicherer's Narrative*, 2–3.

28 LMS, *Memoir of ... Van der Kemp*, 21.

29 In early 1801 Edwards went to Cape Town to accuse Kicherer of sleeping

with the wife of J. de Preez and with the widow Olivier. Kicherer was found not guilty by the South African Missionary Society, and Edwards shortly thereafter left the LMS payroll although he continued to work as a missionary among Tswana and Griqua groups. Penn, "Northern Cape Frontier Zone," 426, n.59. Penn cites P.S. de Jongh, "Sendingwerk in Die Landdrosdistrikte Stellenbosch En Tulbagh (Sedert 1822 Worcester)" (MA, Stellenbosch, 1968), 261–2.

30 Edwards wrote to the LMS on 22 November 1803 complaining of his dismissal, adding darkly: "You was in the whole misinformed in respect of Mr. Kicherer, and was you present, you would have an other Idea." LMS-SA 2/3/C: Edwards to LMS, 22 November 1803. This dismissal occurred before Kicherer's departure for Europe (which I discuss below), as is clear from LMS-SA 2/2/C: V.A. Schoonberg to Hardcastle, Cape Town, 15 September 1802.

31 Penn, "Northern Cape Frontier Zone," 419, 422–3.

32 Kicherer, *Mr Kicherer's Narrative*, .3.

33 "The colonists give an excellent character to the Caffres [Xhosa], but on account of the war, and being very ill-used, they are exasperated against the English and Dutch colonists. I hope however that both soon may be disposed to a friendly agreement." LMS-SA 1/2/B: Van der Kemp to Haweis, 16 July 1799. Evidently this was a somewhat naive assessment. Note that at this stage the colonists spoke highly of the Xhosa, in contrast to more extreme racialized language by the early nineteenth century.

34 Marais, *Maynier*, 109–10. "Wij ... hebben op onzen geheelen tocht 2700 osschen en ruim 20000 schaapen verlooren." HK: Brieven van J.T. van der Kemp, Kas 61, Doos 1: J.T. van der Kemp to his nephew, 4 August 1799, banks of the Tarka River.

35 HK: Brieven van J.T. van der Kemp, Kas 61, Doos 1: Van der Kemp to nephew, banks of the Tarka, 4 August 1799 and following. Marais, *Maynier*, 94, n.7, on Van der Walt's opposition to a commando whose organizers wished to capture San children.

36 "4 zoogenaamde christenen 2 Vrouwen 2 Kinderen 13 Bastaard kinderen, Een Kaffersch man en vrouw twee Kaffersche meisjes 4 Hottentotten 6 Hottentottinnen, omtrent 15 Hottentsche Kinderen, Een Jongen van de Tambouchische Natie , 5 Engelsche Deserteurs Een Hoog duitschen en Een Slaaf." HK: Van der Kemp, *Dag Verhaal*, 1801.

37 Schoeman, *J.J. Kicherer*; Penn, "Northern Cape Frontier Zone"; J. Hodgson, "Do We Hear You Nyengana?"; Enklaar, *Life and Work*.

38 Penn, "Northern Cape Frontier Zone," 424–6. The quote comes from a report made by Gerrit Maritz to the landdrost: "toen ik hun vraag wat oorsaaken hy sulks deet heeft hy my geantwoort wat af de sendelingen in syn lant maakt waroom dat sullij niet byde andere duys volk blief dat hy

het et kon verdragen dat de duys volk in syn lant woon" [sic]. Cited by
Penn, 425, from CA10/150, Maritz to landdrost, 30 March 1800.

39 HK: Van der Kemp to nephew, 4 August 1799 and following, banks of
Tarka River.

40 LMS-SA 1/3/C: Van der Kemp, "Journal of the Caffre Mission," 2 July–
28 September 1800.

41 LMS-SA 1/3/C: Van der Kemp, "Journal of the Caffre Mission," 2 July–
28 September 1800, 19 August 1800.

42 LMS-SA 1/3/C: Van der Kemp to LMS, 28 December 1800, "Quakoubi in
Kaffraria."

43 LMS-SA 1/3/C: Van der Kemp to LMS directors, "Quakoubui in Kaffraria,"
28 December 1800.

44 On Xhosa religious beliefs and on the "battle for sacred power" involved
in the mission, J. Hodgson, "Battle for Sacred Power," 69–71; J.
Hodgson, *God of the Xhosa*; Chidester, *Religions of South Africa*, 1–34.
Ibid., 39–41, on competition over rainmaking between missionaries and
African spiritual specialists, and for later examples, Comaroff and
Comaroff, *Of Revelation and Revolution*, vol. 1; Grove, "Scottish Mis-
sionaries," 163–87.

45 "De Satan schijnt dies met geweld ons den ingangin in Kafferland te bes-
tuisten, maar wij hebben eenen machtiger beschermer dan hij ..." HK,
Brieven van J.T. v.d.Kemp, Kas 61, Doos 1: Van der Kemp to nephew,
banks of Tarka, 4 August 1799 and following.

46 HK: Van der Kemp, *Dag Verhaal*, 1801.

47 LMS-SA 1/3/A: Edmond to ?, Cape Town, 20 February 1800; LMS-SA 1/3/A:
Edmond to Rev. Wilks, 1 March 1800.

48 LMS-SA 1/3/A: Edmond to LMS, Cape Town, 20 February 1800.

49 LMS-SA 1/3/A: Edmond to Rev. Wilks, 1 March 1800.

50 LMS-SA 2/3/A, T.N. Desch to LMS directors, 15 February 1803. Report by
Kicherer in *Gedenkschriften van het Nederlandsch Zendeling-
Genootschap*, vol. 2, 1805, 277–86, reproduced in R. Ross, "Bevreesd
naar het land van hun gebieders," in "Terug in de tijd: tussen liefde en
haat," in *Amandla: tijdschrift over zuidelijk-afrika*, November/December
1996, 28–9. My thanks to Robert Ross for his help.

51 LMS-SA 2/3/A, T.N. Desch to LMS directors, 15 February 1803; Kicherer,
Mr Kicherer's Narrative, 43–4.

52 Ibid., 43–4.

53 Ibid., 43.

54 Letters from J. Kicherer in *Gedenkschriften van het Nederlandsch Zendeling-
Genootschap*, vol. 2, 277–86, reproduced in R. Ross, "Bevreesd naar het
land van hun gebieders," 28.

55 Schoeman, *J.J. Kicherer*, 143.

56 Kicherer in Ross, "Bevreesd naar het land," 28.

57 Kicherer, *Mr Kicherer's Narrative*, 43.

58 Kicherer in Ross, "Bevreesd naar het land," 28. V.A. Schoonberg of the South African Missionary Society commented that Kicherer had gone to Europe "to have his baptised Bastard ... taught how to win more souls with the view to his being employed in that work among the Heathen." LMS-SA 2/2/C: V.A. Schoonberg to LMS directors, 15 October 1802. There is a word after "Bastard" that I cannot read but may be "slave."

59 Armstrong and Worden, "Slaves," 153; Kicherer in Ross, "Bevreesd naar het land," 28.

60 Stuart, "Savages and Heroes," 77.

61 LMS-SA 2/2/C: V.A. Schoonberg to Hardcastle, Cape Town, 15 September 1802.

62 Stuart, "Savages and Heroes," 76–7.

63 When George Barker's request for leave in Britain was turned down, he complained revealingly that the society lost great advantages in both Britain and South Africa by not permitting home visits to cheer the faithful. He claimed that no missionary had been allowed home for a visit in thirty-five years, despite some exceptions that proved the rule: "Mr. Ebner went home under peculiar circumstances, Mr. Evans a dying man & Mr. Foster because his stipulated time was expired, not one has returned to cheer the half worn out and drooping spirits of his brethren by a rehearsal of the interest taken in our labours by the directors & the public. I except Mr. Kicherer, he being a Dutch missionary, but I refer you to the effect his visit produced." This underscores how relatively rare it was for the early-nineteenth-century British to encounter LMS missionaries from south Africa, let alone actual converts; the atmosphere of exceptionalism that surrounded such visits must partly be explained by their rarity. LMS-SA: George Barker to William Ellis, Theopolis, 17 April 1835.

64 LMS-SA 2/3/A: T.N. Desch to LMS directors, Stellenbosch, 15 February 1803.

65 LMS-SA: J. Kicherer to LMS directors, the Hague, Holland, 19 August 1803.

66 Stuart "Savages and Heroes," 75–7; Elbourne, "To Colonize the Mind." 132–5. Karel Schoeman has a similarly negative view of the power relations revealed by this exercise; I share his negative view for the most part but nonetheless want to underscore that Arendse and the van Rooijs may also have had their own interests and agendas. Schoeman, *J.J. Kicherer*, 143–4.

67 LMS-SA 2/2/C: V.A. Schoonberg to LMS directors, 15 October 1802.

68 Kicherer in Ross, "Bevreesd naar het land," 29.

69 Stuart, "Savages and Heroes," 76.

70 "In eene gedwongene dienstbaarheid, niet veel van daadelijke slavernij verschillende": Kicherer in Ross, "Bevrees naar het land," 28.

71 *Evangelical Magazine*, December 1803, 591.

72 Kicherer, *Mr Kicherer's Narrative*, 8.

73 *Evangelical Magazine*, January 1804, vi–vii.

74 For example, LMS-SA 2/3/C: Haweis to J.T. Van der Kemp, 6 December 1803.

75 Kicherer, *Mr Kicherer's Narrative*, 40.

76 On female preaching among the Primitive Methodists, Valenze, *Prophetic Sons and Daughters*.

77 Burchell, *Travels in the Interior*, vol. 2,110.

78 Ibid., 111.

79 Ibid., 164. Schoeman observes that this "Hottentot" language was probably Xiri, the language spoken by the people of the Koks, later to be part of the Griqua polity. Schoeman, *J.J. Kicherer*, 276, n.85, and 238–9, on Burchell's interaction with Goieman and van Rooij.

80 Burchell, *Travels in the Interior*, vol. 2, 204, 330, 332.

81 Sales, *Mission Stations*.

82 SAL: Diary of John Campbell (transcript of manuscript, vol. 2), 4 July 1818.

83 Newton-King, "Rebellion of the Khoi," 22.

84 HK: Kas 61, Doos 1, Brieven van J.T. van der Kemp, 53, Van der Kemp to nephew, banks of Tarka, 4 August 1799 and following; LMS-SA 1/2: Dr. Vanderkemp's journal, 30 July 1799; Newton- King, "Rebellion of the Khoi," 24.

85 LMS-SA 1/2: Dr. Vanderkemp's journal, 29 August 1799; Newton-King, "Rebellion of the Khoi," 24.

86 Gerstner, *Thousand Generation Covenant*.

87 HK: Van der Kemp, *Dag Verhaal*, 1801.

88 The other two were the Englishman William Anderson and the Dutchman Bastiaan Tromp.

89 Newton-King, "Rebellion of the Khoi," 32–5; Enklaar, *Life and Work*, 111.

90 Ibid., 118. HK: Van der Kemp, *Dag Verhaal*, 1801.

91 Ibid.,112.

92 HK: Van der Kemp, *Dag Verhaal*, 1801; Enklaar, *Life and Work*, 113.

93 LMS-SA 2/1: Van der Lingen to LMS and Rotterdam Missionary Society directors, Graaff-Reinet, 5 February 1802.

94 HK: Van der Kemp, *Dag Verhaal*, 1801.

95 Schama, *Embarrassment of Riches*, 93–125.

96 *HP*, clxic–clxv: Van der Kemp to Fiscaal, Bota's Place, 19 July 1802.

97 LMS-SA 4/3/A: Read to Langton.

98 Enklaar, *Life and Work*, 117; HK: Van der Kemp, *Dag Verhaal*, 1801.

99 HK: Van der Kemp, *Dag Verhaal*, 1801.

100 Enklaar, *Life and Work*, 114.

101 HK: Van der Kemp, *Dag Verhaal*, 1801. "Een touw t geen een arm Zondaar uitwerpt, en waar meede Hijn zich aan den Hemels [Heavens] vast maakt."

102 HK: Van der Kemp, *Dag Verhaal*, 1801. "Met verscheiden Heidenen, om met hun over den weg ten leeven te spreeken en te bidden."

103 HK: Van der Kemp, *Dag Verhaal*, 1801. "Een kind, wanneer het pas gebooren is, koomt in een nieuw leeven, en als in een nieuwe wereld, te voeren was het in het duister maar nu in het licht, Echter zoo lang het nog niet gewassen is, is het bedekt met de vuiligheid van zyne voorige verblijfplaats en het ziet er walglijk uijt. Ik ben gebooren maar niet gewassen! Doch Christus kan mij door zijnen H. Geist van mijn vuil waschen en mijn klip steenen hart doen Smelten."

104 Enklaar, *Life and Work*, 116.

105 LMS-SA 1/4/E: Van der Kemp to Dundas, 11 November 1801.

106 Newton-King, "Rebellion of the Khoi," 40.

107 Ibid., 38; Van der Kemp to Dundas, Graaff-Reinet, 11 November 1801, cited in Enklaar, *Life and Work*, 119.

108 HP: Van der Kemp to Fiscal, Graaff-Reinet, 25 December 1801, in *HP*, cxxxvi–cxxxvii.

109 HK: Van der Kemp, *Dag Verhaal*, 1801.

110 J. Philip, *Researches in South Africa*, 76; Enklaar, *Life and Work*, 122.

111 LMS-SA 2/2/D: Read to LMS directors, Botha's Place, 18 March 1802.

112 HK: Van der Kemp, *Dag Verhaal*, 1802.

113 Saxe Bannister, *Humane Policy* (hereafter HP), cxxxvii: Van der Kemp to F. Dundas, Bota's Place, 18 March, 1802.

114 HK: Van der Kemp, *Dag Verhaal*, 1801.

115 LMS-SA 2/2/D: Van der Kemp to LMS directors, 1802 Annual Report.

116 Genesis, 34:30–31; 35:1–11. *The Jerusalem Bible*.

117 LMS-SA 2/3/D: Van der Kemp to LMS directors, 1803 Bethelsdorp Annual Report.

118 HP: cxli: Van der Kemp to fiscaal, 18 March 1802. HK: Van der Kemp, *Dag Verhaal*, 1802.

119 HK: Van der Kemp, *Dag Verhaal*, 1802. Cf. also LMS-SA 2/2/D: Van der Kemp to LMS directors, 1802 Bethelsdorp Annual Report, and HP, cxxxix–cxli: Van der Kemp to fiscaal, 18 March 1802.

120 HK: Van der Kemp, *Dag Verhaal*, 1802.

121 LMS-SA 2/2/D: Read to LMS directors, Botha's Place, 18 March 1802.

122 HK: Van der Kemp, *Dag Verhaal*, 1802; Enklaar, *Life and Work*, 124–5.

124 HK: Van der Kemp, *Dag Verhaal*, 1803.

125 Ibid., 1804.

126 Ibid., 1803.

127 HP, cxxxix: Van der Kemp to fiscaal, Bota's Place, 18 March 1802.

128 HP, clxi: Van der Kemp to fiscaal, Bota's Place, 1 July 1802.

129 LMS-SA 2/2/D: 1802 Annual Report. HK: Van der Kemp, *Dag Verhaal*, 1802; Enklaar, *Life and Work*, 126–7.

130 HK: Van der Kemp, *Dag Verhaal*, 1802.

131 Ibid., 1803.

132 Ibid.

133 Paravicini di Capelli, *Reize in de Binnen-Landen*, 98–100, 242–3.

134 Newton-King, "Rebellion of the Khoi," 56.

135 HP, clxxxii–iv: Janssens to Van der Kemp, 3 May 1805; Malherbe, "Khoi Captains," 133.

136 Malherbe, "Khoi Captains," 128–9

137 LMS-SA 2/2/D: 1802 Bethelsdorp Annual Report.

138 Peires, "Xhosa Expansion"; Giliomee, "Eastern Frontier," 430.

139 Malherbe, "Khoi Captains," 130.

140 Newton-King, "Rebellion of the Khoi," 39.

141 Malherbe, "Khoi Captains," 132–3.

142 Malherbe, "David Stuurman."

143 LMS-SA 3/4/D: Read to David Langton, 1 October 1807, LMS-SA 3/4/D; Sales, *Mission Stations*, 67–8, 97. Sales does, however, confuse Jan Boezak, who clearly fought on the side of the Dutch, with his clansman who fought for the rebels: 19, 24, 28.

144 LMS-SA 2/A/2: Read to LMS, Botha's Place, 18 March 1802.

145 "Report of the Commission of Circuit for the Districts of Graaff-Reinet, Uitenhage and George," in RCC, vol. 9, 75.

146 LMS-SA 4/4/A: Read to LMS, Bethelsdorp, 7 January 1811.

147 LMS-SA 5/1/B: "Copy of a letter from Mr. Read to his Excellency Sir John Craddock giving an Account of the origin and present state of Bethelsdorp," 23 January 1812.

148 Read Jr, *Kat River Settlement*, ix.

149 PRO, CO414, 9, 629: Read to Donkin (copy), Bethelsdorp, 22 May 1821.

150 LMS-SA 2/4/C: Van der Kemp to LMS, 29 February 1804.

151 *HP*, clxxxii: Janssens to Van der Kemp, 3 May 1805.

152 LMS-SA 2/4/A: Van der Kemp to LMS, 29 February 1804; *HP*, clxxxiv–v: Janssens to Van der Kemp, 3 May 1805.

153 LMS-SA: Janssens to Van der Kemp, Fort Frederick, Algoa Bay, 31 May 1804: Dutch original and English translation.

154 HK: Van der Kemp, *Dag Verhaal*, 1805.

155 LMS-SA 3/1/A: Janssens to Van der Kemp, Cape of Good Hope, 28 February 1805; Enklaar, *Life and Work*, 154–5.

156 Cited in Sales, *Mission Stations*, 30.

157 For the most comprehensive overview, Enklaar, *Life and Work*, 149–61.

Also, Freund, "Career of Johannes," 376–90; Sales, *Mission Stations,*
21–33.

158 LMS-SA 3/5/B: Read to LMS, 30 August 1808.

159 Janssens to Aziatische Raad, 31 October 1805, Algemeen Rijksarchief,
inventory 86, Aziatishe Raad 311, 547, cited in Freund, "Career of
Johannes," 388.

160 Janssens to Alberti, 25 July 1805, CA, inventory Batavian Republic, 68,
419, cited by Freund, "Career of Johannes," 388.

161 HK: Van der Kemp, *Dag Verhaal,* 1805.

162 Janssens's aide-de-campe, W.B.E. Paravicini di Capelli, records travels in
burned-out lands and encounters with settler refugees, including Susanna
Magdalena du Preez, whose son and husband were murdered before her:
Paravicini di Capelli, *Reize in de Binnen-Landen,* 26–7, 225.

163 HK: Van der Kemp, *Dag Verhaal,* 1805.

164 LMS-SA 4/1/D: James Read to LMS directors, 7 Nov. 1809. Cf. also Paravicini de Capelli, *Reize in de Binnen-Landen,* 3–4, and, for a Dutch
view just after the batavian retreats, Nahuys van Burgst, *Adventures at
the Cape of Good Hope,* 30.

165 *HP,* clxxxii: Janssens to Van der Kemp, 3 May 1805.

166 Alberti, *Account of the Tribal Life,* 113.

167 Ibid., 115.

168 LMS-SA 4/1/E.A: Albrecht, n.d. (c.1810), "Observations made in the
country of the Great Namaqua in the north-western part of South
Africa."

169 *HP,* cliv–v: Van der Kemp to Ross, Botha's place, 17 June 1802.

170 LMS-SA 3/4/D: Van der Kemp to Hardcastle.

171 *HP,* clxxxv–vi: Janssens to Van der Kemp, 3 May 1805.

172 LMS-SA 3/3/D: Bethelsdorp Annual Report, 1806.

173 *HP,* clxxxvii–iii: Janssens to Van der Kemp, Cape Town, 16 May 1805.

174 LMS-SA 3/2/B: Ulbricht to LMS, Bethelsdorp, 29 April 1805–12 March
1806.

175 HK: Van der Kemp, *Dag Verhaal,* 1805.

176 LMS-SA 3/2/B: Van der Kemp to LMS, 13 January 1806.

CHAPTER FOUR

1 LMS-SA 14/2/B: G. Barker to Ellis, Theopolis, 6 October 1834.

2 *British Parliamentary Papers,* H.C., Accounts and Papers (3), Vol. 39,
1835, 330.

3 Marks, "Khoisan Resistance."

4 Newton-King, *Masters and Servants.*

5 Read Sr, *African Witness,* 109.

6 Marks, "Khoisan Resistance," 73; Penn, "The Northern Cape Frontier Zone."

7 Marks, "Khoisan Resistance," 55–74. On hunger among the San, see, for example, Barrow, *Account of Travels*, vol. 1, 224–49; A. Vos to LMS, 15 January 1806, LMS-SA, 3/2/B.

8 Barrow, *Account of Travels*, vol. 1, 242.

9 Cited by Barrow, *Account of Travels*, vol. 1, 381; my translation is from the French.

10 Du Plessis, *History of Christian Missions*, 132.

11 LMS-SA, 3/5/B: James Read to LMS, 30 August 1808.

12 Elbourne, "Concerning Missionaries,"161–4, on the need to take the violence of early south African culture seriously and not to downgrade its prevalence in the name of rebutting the liberal shibboleths of frontier history.

13 Peter Kolbe, who described the ritualistic use of daccha among the Cape Khoekhoe in the seventeenth century, believed that daccha-smoking was confined to ceremonial occasions; nineteenth-century reports indicate, however, that daccha (sometimes described as tobacco) was in constant use. According to a late-nineteenth-century ethnographic account, "the leaves of the wild hemp (Dacha) are generally liked as stimulants, which they smoke either alone or with a mixture of tobacco. The women also particularly use the latter one, and the passion for it is so great, that they exchange for a small quantity a head of cattle." Pipes used were bigger than the European, and smoke was swallowed "by which process they increase considerably the narcotic effect of the weed." Nursing women strengthened themselves by smoking frequently, "and sometimes when the little one becomes restless she lets it taste the sweet weed." SAL: MSB 594, 1(c).

14 But see A.B. Smith, "Khoikhoi susceptibility," 25–6, for the argument that the decline of the Khoekhoe at the Cape was caused more by "increasing usurpation of their pasture land by the colony," and that the "loss of livelihood through livestock epidemics and drought, resulting in their subjugation and a downward cycle of anomie" had a much greater effect than smallpox epidemics. This is a salutary reminder that poverty breeds disease, and likewise that the impact of disease is far greater in conditions of poverty and social breakdown.

15 LMS-SA 23/3/A: James Read Sr and Jr to LMS directors, Kat River, 12 November 1847.

16 For example, Andries Stoffels: Read Sr, *African Witness*, published with Basset, *Life of a Vagrant*, 109; LMS-SA 3/5/A: Read to LMS, David Stuurman's kraal, 30 January 1808.

17 LMS-SA 4/1/E: Annual Report of Bethelsdorp, 1809.

18 LMS-SA 3/1/D: Read to LMS, Cape Town, 7 October 1805; Sales, *Mission Stations*, 72.

19 LMS-SA 2/4/E: Read to LMS, in Annual Report of Bethelsdorp, 1804. See also Malherbe, "Life and Times of Cupido."

20 LMS-SA 2/4/E: Van der Kemp to LMS, 29 February 1804.

21 Viljoen, "Moravian Missionaries," 51–5.

22 Vos, *Merkwaardig*, 115–16.

23 LMS-SA 3/4/C: Cuyler to Castle of Good Hope, Algoa Bay, 8 April 1807.

24 For example, LMS-SA 1/10/E: Richard Miles to LMS, 14 December 1826.

25 Diary of George Barker, 9 January 1816, 7: reproduced in appendix, M. Currie, "History of Theopolis Mission." Henceforth annotated as GB.

26 GB: 25 January 1816, 7.

27 Compare the analysis of conversion among low-caste groups in South Travancore in Kooiman, *Conversion and Social Equality*. Kooiman also comments (p.1) on mass conversions to Islam among *harijan*, at the bottom of the Hindu caste system.

28 Thomas Pringle testified in 1823 before the commissioners of inquiry as to the "general exclusion of the Colour'd race from the rights of proprietors," with the only exception of which he knew being a "free Malay named Fort who was building at Algoa Bay." PRO CO414, 1:21–2.

29 CA, A559: "Missionary Statement of Missionary and Hottentot Grievances."

30 Ibid. On hardships faced by the dependants (including wives) of military conscripts during the 1811–12 war, see LMS-SA 5/3/A: , Read, "Answers upon Mr. Thom's conversations with the Missionaries at Bethelsdorp," Cape Town, 25 January 1814. On the 1818-19 war, see PRO CO414, vol. 9, 610: Philip to Rufane Donkin, 28 April 1821. In the latter case, many men had subsequently to go heavily into debt with farmers, which debts "still keep them in misery and bondage"; twenty-four were forced to join the army.

31 Campbell, *Travels in South Africa*, 89.

32 LMS-SA 5/2/B: Campbell to LMS, Bethelsdorp, 1 April 1813.

33 When James Read was itinerating at David Stuurman's homestead in 1808, for example, an unnamed elderly man, a slave, visited him, saying, "'I have of late heard that I have a soul that must be lost or saved and I wish now to hear if there is no place where my soul can be saved.'" "He had heard of my being here, and with difficulty had got permission to come to hear the word of God. He had asked permission to go to Bethelsdorp for a day or two, but his Mistress had said 'that priviledge shall you never enjoy!'" LMS-SA 3/5/A: Read to LMS, David Stuurman's kraal, 30 January 1808.

34 Col. R. Collins, "Concluding Report," in Moodie, *Record*, part 5.

35 Rho, MSS.Afr.S.1, fo.27: Collins to Caledon, Cape Town, 30 May 1808.

36 LMS-SA 4/3/C: Annual Report of Bethelsdorp, 1810, attests that little attention was paid to the injunction to verify contracts; veldcornets rather did everything to keep the Khoisan in service.

37 Bannister, *Humane Policy*, ccxvii–ccxix: Van der Kemp to Caledon, Bethelsdorp, 4 January 1810.

38 Newton-King, "Labour Market," 174–7.

39 CA, A559: "Missionary Statement of Hottentot and Missionary Grievances"; Newton-King, "Labour Market," 177.

40 Van der Kemp categorized the "Heathens" residing within the colonial boundaries as "Caffrarians, Woodmen, Hottentots and Slaves." LMS-SA 3/D/4: "Yearly Account of Bethelsdorp," 1807.

41 LMS-SA 4/3/C: "Annual Report of Bethelsdorp," 1810.

42 CA, A559: 12 February 1821, "Bethelsdorp: Outgoing Correspondence."

43 GB: 23 December 1818.

44 Sales, *Mission Stations*, 81–2.

45 Ibid., 70.

46 PRO, CO414, IX, 611: Philip "State of Things at Bethelsdorp." I surmise from ancillary comments that the informant was Read.

47 PRO, CO414, IX, 618: "Colonel Cuyler's reply to the State of things at Bethelsdorp, with His Excellency the Acting Governor's observations."

48 PRO, CO414, I, 49.

49 PRO, CO414, I, 67: testimony of Buckenroder.

50 Sales, *Mission Stations*, 82.

51 Newton-King, "Labour Market," 186–7.

52 PRO, CO414, I, 79.

53 PRO, CO414, I, 69.

54 PRO, CO414, IX, 613.

55 For example, J. Philip, *Researches*, vol. 2, 403; CA A559.

56 PRO, CO414, IX, 609: Philip, "State of Things at Bethelsdorp."

57 A leading example cited by Read and Philip in 1821 was that Bethelsdorp men had not only been compelled to dig and clean water channels for Van Rooyen, who was paid to do this by the government and expected to find his own labour, but also made to build him a new house.

58 The Bethelsdorp records are full of such demands; cf., for example, incoming correspondence files, CA A559, vol. 3.

59 On the election of corporals, Cullen Library, University of the Witwatersrand, A.65fo.: James Kitchingman, Diary (1825–26), 4 January 1825. The process of selecting workers was administratively time-consuming, in addition to the problems it posed for the men themselves. For example: "This morning all the men in the institution were called together, in numbers upwards of 20, when the following Hottentots were recommended by the Corporals as being almost the only persons at home qualified for such a service ... These plead that they are unwell, which appears

to be the case. Perhaps some suitable Hottentot may come home this evening." CA, A559, vol. 2, Day Book: J. Kitchingman to J. Cuyler, 3 March 1821.

60 PRO, CO414, IX, 620: "Questions put to Mr. Kitchingman Missionary at Bethelsdorp ...."

61 CA A559, vol. 2, Day Book: J. Kitchingman to J. Cuyler, Bethesldorp, 12 February 1821; J. Kitchingman to J. Cuyler, Bethelsdorp, 3 March, 1821; J. Kitchingman to J. Cuyler, Bethelsdorp, 24 March 1821; J. Kitchingman to J. Cuyler, Bethelsdorp, 26 March 1821; J. Kitchingman to J. Cuyler, Bethelsdorp, 2 April 1821; J. Kitchingman to J. Cuyler, Bethelsdorp, 11 May 1821; J. Kitchingman to J. Cuyler. Bethelsdorp, 14 May 1821; J. Kitchingman to J. Cuyler, Bethelsdorp, 9 June 1821; J. Kitchingman to J. Cuyler, Bethelsdorp, 14 June 1821; J. Kitchingman to J. Cuyler, Bethelsdorp, 21 September 1821; J. Kitchingman to J. Cuyler, Bethelsdorp, 9 October 1821; J. Kitchingman to J. Cuyler, Bethelsdorp, 15 October 1821. CA A559, vol. 3: J. Cuyler to J. Kitchingman, Uitenhage, 23 March 1821; J. Cuyler to J. Kitchingman, Uitenhage, 27 March 1821; J. Cuyler to J. Kitchingman, Uitenhage, 10 May 1821.

62 CA A559: J. Kitchingman to J. Cuyler, 1 March 1821.

63 CA, A768: "Return of the Institution of Bethelsdorp, 29th April 1825" (copy).

64 CA, A559: "Missionary Statement of Missionary and Hottentot Grievances."

65 Ibid. Among numerous possible examples, note CA A559, vol. 2: J. Kitchingman to J. Cuyler, Bethelsdorp, 10 October 1821, in which Kitchingman reports that the old and ill parents of three post riders, Jan Hans, Piet Ruyters, and Mouwer Platjes, have insisted on their return home; Cuyler has permitted their return only if substitutes are found, and the parents of the proposed substitutes, who are also in need of support, wish to know how much the boys will be paid.

66 RCC, VII, 7: Cuyler to Lieut. Col. Collins, Uitenhage, 19 June 1809.

67 PRO, CO414, vol. 9, 610: Philip, "State of things at Bethelsdorp."

68 LeCordeur and Saunders, ed., Kitchingman Papers, 72.

69 Sales, Mission Stations, 88; Philip, Researches, vol. 1, 317.

70 LMS-SA 3/3/A: Van der Kemp to LMS, 10 July 1806.

71 Cullen Library, A65fo.: Diary of James Kitchingman.

72 Robert Ross dissects the ambiguities of respectability and resistance to respectability, including behaviour around drinking, in Status and Respectability. See also Elbourne and R. Ross, "Combatting."

73 Cullen Library, A65fo.: Diary of James Kitchingman, 4 January 1825.

74 "As many of the people of this Institution are continually wandering the country, or hiring themselves without my knowledge, it is impossible for me to know where they are so as to be able to recall them in event of

need," complained George Barker to Cuyler in 1820. CA A559, vol. 2, Day Book: G. Barker to J. Cuyler, 17 November 1820. Barker asked for Cuyler's help in keeping track of Bethelsdorp inhabitants.

75 LMS-SA 8/1/A: F.G. Hooper to LMS, 23 January 1819.

76 LMS-SA 8/1/A: J. George Messer to LMS, 24 January 1819.

77 Campbell, *Travels ... Second Journey*, 321.

78 "The success of Christian missionaries in this country is a matter of history, and whether it be a palatable truth or not we proceed to affirm that the Hottentots within the Colony have all nominally received the gospel and may according to custom be styled Christians." LMS-SA 23/3/A: James Read sr and James Read jr to LMS directors, 12 November 1847.

79 *Inter alia*, Landau, "Religion," 8–30; Van der Veer, *Conversion to Modernities*; Hefner, *Conversion to Christianity*, including Hefner, "Introduction," 3–43, and Ranger, "The Local and the Global," 65–98; Ikenga-Metuh, "The Shattered Microcosm," 11–27; Horton, "African Conversion," 85-108; Horton, "Rationality of Conversion," 219–35, 372–99.

80 LMS-SA 5/1/F: James Read to LMS, Annual Report of Bethelsdorp, 1812.

81 "Report of the Circuit Commissioners," *RCC*, vol. 9, 76–7; Freund, "Cape under the Transitional Governments," 342.

82 The last, unfinished letter Van der Kemp wrote before his death was about the quarrels between the Nama chief Afrikaner and the Nama group gathered around the missionary Albrecht: "I apprehend, that the wandering hordes of Br. Albrecht, abusing his pliable character, have sent him to the Cape as a tool to obtain by his instrumentality as much powder and fire arms as possible to commit more depredations as Afrikaaner ever is said to be guilty of, and that, for this reason they by false or exaggerated representations of imaginary dangers drove my amiable but credulous Brother to the Cape to procure for them these instruments of destruction." LMS-SA 4/5/D: Van der Kemp to LMS, finished by Matilda Smith, Cape Town, December 1811.

83 On Tikkuie: Bredekamp, "Vehettge Tikkuie," 134–41; Swart, "Story of Vehettge Tikkuie,"114–24.

84 GB: 10 February 1816, 8.

85 GB: 11 July 1818.

86 Malherbe, "Life and Times," 365–78. Moffat's book, *Missionary Labours and Scenes in Southern Africa* (London, 1842), became a Victorian missionary classic. The intermediary role of Khoisan evangelists is underestimated in Jean and John Comaroff's analysis of the opening encounters between whites and Tswana: Comaroff and Comaroff, *On Revelation and Revolution*, vol. 1.

87 Schoeman, "Die Londense Sendinggenootskap en die San," 132–52, 221–34; LMS Journals of Erasmus Smit and William Corner for 1815,

reproduced in F.A. Steytler, "Dag Verhaal van Eerw. Erasmus Smit (1815)" and "Journal van William F. Corner (1815)," *Hertzog-Annale van die Suid Afrikaanse Akademie vir Wetenskap en Kuns*, Jaarboek 3, December 1856, 67–103.

88 Compare Tilman Dedering's account of the power of the interpreter in the early-nineteenth-century LMS mission to the Namaqua. Dedering, *Hate the Old*, 95–8.

89 Bredekamp and Plüddemann, *Genadendal Diaries*, vol. 1, 58.

90 Viljoen, "Making Sense," 62–76; quote 68; Viljoen, "Revelation of a Revolution," 3–15; Peires, *Dead Will Arise*.

91 *Periodical Accounts Relating to the Missions of the Church of the United Brethren*, vol. 4, 227.

92 *Periodical Accounts*, vol. 5, 10.

93 LMS-SA 23/3/A: James Read Sr and Jr to LMS directors, Kat River, 12 November 1847.

94 LMS-SA 23/3/A: James Read Sr and Jr to LMS directors, Kat River, 12 Nov 1847.

95 SAL, MSB594.1 (3): Theophilus Hahn to [Kuhle?], Stellenbosch, 8 October 1879.

96 Ibid.

97 Barnard, *Hunters and Herders*. In contrast, Mathias Guenther characterizes "religion as anti- structure" and argues for the extreme idiosyncracy of San beliefs. Barnard finds that Guenther underestimates "the structural uniformity of Khoisan religions when taken collectively and not, as he does, one-by-one." Guenther, "Bushman Religion," 102–32; Barnard, "Structure and Fluidity," 216–36.

98 Hahn, *Tsuni-//Goam*, 122.

99 J. Hodgson, *God of the Xhosa*, 62–3. Both Qamata and Thixo, Xhosa names for God, are loanwords from Khoe; the current-day Xhosa claim that Qamata is of ancient origin, whereas Thixo became widespread only in the nineteenth century. This is the term adopted by missionaries, who, of course, accentuated Khoekhoe influence on the Xhosa through their use of Khoekhoe interpreters and the subsequent prevalence of Khoisan missionaries to the Xhosa.

100 J.T. van der Kemp, "Natural History of Caffraria, by Dr. Vanderkemp," *Missionary Magazine*, 1802, vol. 7, 38.

101 Hahn, *Tsuni-//Goam*, 61–2; Barnard, *Hunters and Herders*, 257–8.

102 Schapera, *Khoisan Peoples*, 385.

103 Barnard, "Structure and Fluidity," 226–7; citation from Schapera, *Khoisan Peoples*, 396.

104 Hodgson, *God of the Xhosa*, 69.

105 Barnard, *Hunters and Herders*, 258. Barnard points out that, for many groups, it is unclear whether similar ancillary figures are aspects of the

two chief divinities or are deities in their own right. They do not, however, possess the same overarching power.

106 Hahn, *Tsuni-//Goam*, 134.

107 Schapera, *Khoisan Peoples*, 385; Schmidt, "Relevance," 102–3.

108 Ibid., 384.

109 Ibid., 372–4, 385–6; Hahn, *Tsuni-//Goam*, 112–3. Authorities differ over whether or not branches were thrown on the graves of ancestors or reserved for the graves of Heitsi-eibib (Schapera, *Khoisan Peoples*, 386). The precise significance of throwing stones on the graves of the deceased, and the overall nature of Khoisan beliefs about the dead, remain somewhat opaque, despite many details, according to Schapera.

110 Campbell, *Travels in South Africa* , 82.

111 SAL: MSB594, 1(c): "Ethnographic description."

112 *Periodical Accounts*, vol. 4, 426.

113 "Account of the Voyage of Brother George Schmidt to the Cape of Good Hope, and of his Abode there from 1736 to 1744. Written by himself," *Periodical Accounts*, vol. 1, 169.

114 "I also asked him, whether they well knew that there was a greater Boss [or master] who gave them their cattle and all that they have. He said: Yes. What do you call the same? He said: Tui'qua. I said: the person they loved, the Tui'qua, this was the Saviour, the maker of blessing. He once became a man and died on the Cross for us men, and wants to make you also a saved people. He said nothing to this." "Kurzer Bericht von Georg Schmidts uber seinen Aufenthalt am Kap, nach seiner Ruckkehr , am 8 September 1744, geschrieben," Schmidt, *Das Tagebuch*, 481.

115 Barrow, *Account of Travels*, vol. 2, 110–11. See chapter 2.

116 *Evangelical Magazine*, December 1803, 595.

117 *Periodical Accounts*, vol. 2, 307.

118 Hodgson, *God of the Xhosa*, 27. "Long before daylight, several go into the woods, where approaching in silence (which our Brother Read did frequently) you may daily hear their fervent prayers." LMS-SA, 2/A/2: Van der Kemp to LMS, 1802 Bethelsdorp Annual Account.

119 Hahn, *Tsuni-//Goam*, 58–9.

120 Schapera, *Khoisan People*, on dreams among the "Cape Bushmen" and Naron, 200–1, and among the Khoekhoe in general, 393. Compare: Fisher, "Dreams and Conversion," on the role of dreams in conversion to Islam in West Africa, and, for Christian comparison, Curley, "Private Dreams," and Charsley, "Dreams in African Churches."

121 For example, Butler, *Awash in a Sea of Faith*, 222–3 and 238–9. Even Anglicans sometimes believed in dreams: John Venn, who helped found the British evangelical Church Missionary Society in 1799, was told of

his mother's death in a dream, while his father, Henry Venn, interrupted
a trip to return to his dying wife's side, again because of a dream.

122 *Periodical Accounts*, vol. 2, 368.

123 Bredekamp and Plüddemann, eds., *Genadendal Diaries*, vol. 1 (11 September 1793), 134.

124 LMS-SA 2/4/E: Van der Kemp to LMS directors, 1804 Bethelsdorp Annual Report.

125 Bredekamp and Plüddemann, *Genadendal Diaries*, 186.

126 Sales, *Mission Stations*, 40–1.

127 LMS-SA 2/4/E: Van der Kemp to LMS, 1804 Bethelsdorp Annual Report; Hoernlé, "Certain Rites of Transition," 57–74; Schapera, *Khoisan Peoples*, 263; Grevenbroek, *Elegant and Accurate Account*, 202–5.

128 Campbell, *Travels in South Africa*, 82.

129 Bredekamp and Plüddemann, *Genadendal Diaries*, 59.

130 *Periodical Accounts*, vol. 4, 423.

131 Schapera, *Khoisan Peoples*, 400–5.

132 LMS-SA 2/4/E: J.Read to LMS directors, 1804 Bethelsdorp Annual Report; also quoted in Elphick and Malherbe, "Khoisan to 1828," 39.

133 LMS-SA 3/5/B: Read to LMS, 30 August 1808.

134 *Missionary Register*, vol. 2, February 1814, 100–1.

135 Although I am convinced by much else in Jonathan's Gerstner's analysis, I differ with him on this issue for this period. Gerstner's examples suggest that "family worship" at which slaves and other farm labourers were present was the norm on the late-eighteenth- and early-nineteenth-century frontier farm. Although joint worship clearly occurred, there are too many counter-examples (including Van der Kemp's aspersions on the exclusion of Khoisan from worship, discussed in chapter 3 above) to admit the generalization until further into the nineteenth century. It is also important that, in the ceremonies witnessed by Lichtenstein and cited by Gerstner, Khoekhoe and slaves were clearly expected to be present but not to participate in the worship; as Gerstner comments, "the Khoi Khoi and slaves were brought to the worship, but not seen as part of God's people." Gerstner, *Thousand Generation Covenant*, 167–170; quote, 169.

136 Shaw, *Memorials of South Africa*, 237–8.

137 LMS-SA 2/4/E: Annual Report of Bethelsdorp, 1804.

138 LMS-SA 4/1/E: Annual Report of Bethelsdorp, 1809.

139 CA, A50: "Minutes of a meeting held at Philipton," 5 August 1834.

140 LMS-SA 4/1/E: Annual Report of Bethelsdorp, 1809.

141 Journal of W. Corner, 28 November 1815, reproduced in Steytler, "'Journal' van William F. Corner," 102.

142 LMS-SA 4/1/E: Annual Report of Bethelsdorp, 1809.

143 LMS-SA 2/4/E: Annual Report of Bethelsdorp, 1804.

144 LMS-SA 4/3/C: Annual Report of Bethelsdorp, 1810.
145 Elphick, "Africans and the Christian Campaign," 300–1.
146 CA, CO291: "Declaration taken at the Native Office, Cape Town, relative to the Murder of the Rev. W. Threlfall," in James Whitworth and Robert Snowdall to Richard Bourke, Wesleyan Mission House, 22 May 1826. It is an illustration both of the greater value placed by the white colony on the life of a white man than that of a native, and of the downgrading by many missionaries of the contributions of indigenous preachers, that this event was reported as the murder of Threlfall, and that the seasoned Links was described by the Wesleyan Methodist Missionary Society as the servant of the inexperienced white missionary. On Links, see also Dedering, *Hate the Old*.
147 Shaw, *Memorials of South Africa*, 100–1.
148 Elphick, "Africans and the Christian Campaign," 300.
149 LMS-SA 11/1/C: Read to Burder, Bethelsdorp, 11 June 1828.
150 GB: 3 and 5 February 1820, 58–9. Deuteronomy 22 lists a series of stern punishments for sexual offences, which are actually quite inappropriate if taken literally: a man who rapes a betrothed virgin must be stoned to death, while one who rapes an unbetrothed virgin must simply be compelled to marry her. Galatians 6:1 reads: "Brothers, if one of you misbehaves, the more spiritual of you who set him right should do so in a spirit of gentleness, not forgetting that you may be tempted yourselves" (New Jerusalem Bible).
151 R. Ross, *Adam Kok's Griquas*.
152 CA, A50, p.5: "Minutes of a meeting held at Philipton."
153 CA A50, "Minutes of a Meeting." This biographical evidence is contained in a speech by Stoffels delivered at least partially in the Khoe language and recorded by Khoekhoe minute-takers (there is a footnote in the text explaining the translation of a particular Khoekhoe word). The only surviving version is in English; the translation was made at the time or immediately afterwards, since the minutes were so rapidly published in the *South African Commercial Advertiser*. Because there is no evidence that Cape Khoe was reduced to writing, beyond Van der Kemp's abortive early effort, the transcribers may also have been translating as they went. Comments by Stoffels from other sources were all both transcribed and translated – obviously a problem for the historian. It is unclear whether Stoffels spoke in Dutch or Khoe in London, but there is a good chance that his translator, the half-Khoekhoe James Read Jr, spoke Khoe.
154 Read Sr, *African Witness*, 109.
155 CA A50, "Minutes of a Meeting."
156 Read Sr, *African Witness*, 109.
157 Ibid., 110–11.

158 *Graham's Town Journal*, 10 April 1834.
159 *Report from the Select Committee on Aborigines*, 588, questions 5058 and 5062.
160 *Missionary Chronicle*, June 1836, 422–4.

CHAPTER FIVE

1 CA, CO2559: Van der Kemp to Baird, January 1806.
2 LMS-SA 3/3/D: 1806 Bethelsdorp Annual Report.
3 LMS-SA 3/4/C: Van der Kemp to Cuyler, 6 April 1807.
4 LMS-SA 3/3/D: 1806 Annual Report of Bethelsdorp.
5 LMS-SA 3/4/C: Van der Kemp to Cuyler, 31 May 1806.
6 LMS-SA 3/5/B: Van der Kemp to Cuyler, 25 May 1808.
7 LMS-SA 3/4/C: Cuyler to Castle of Good Hope, Algoa Bay, 8 April 1807.
8 LMS-Home 1/1/A: W. Lambert to John Eyre, 6 August 1799.
9 LMS-SA 5/3/C: George Thom to George Burder, Cape Town, 16 February 1814.
10 Martin, *Evangelicals United*, 28.
11 LMS-SA 3/5/B: Read to LMS, 30 August 1808.
12 LMS-SA 4/1/D: Read to LMS, Bethelsdorp 7 November 1809.
13 LMS-SA 4/3/C: "Annual Report of Bethesldorp," 1810.
14 LMS-SA 4/3/B: Van der Kemp to LMS, 5 November 1810.
15 Read to Caledon, 19 October 1810. Copy in "Annual Report of Bethelsdorp," 1810, LMS-SA 4/3/C; another copy, *HP*, ccxiv–vi.
16 *HP*, ccxvi–ccxxi: Van der Kemp to Caledon, Bethelsdorp, 4 January 1810; LMS-SA 4/5/A: Van der Kemp to LMS, Cape Town, 25 July 1811. The letter is dated 4 January by Bannister, although Van der Kemp reported to the LMS that he had sent it on 14 January.
17 *HP*, ccxvi.
18 LMS-SA 4/4/B: Colonel Bird to Van der Kemp and Read, 28 February 1811.
19 LMS-SA 4/5/A: Van der Kemp to LMS, Cape Town, 25 July 1811.
20 LMS-SA 4/5/D: "Annual Report of Bethelsdorp," 1811.
21 LMS-SA 4/5/A: Van der Kemp to LMS, Cape Town, 25 July 1811,
22 LMS-SA 4/4/D: Read to LMS, Cape Town, 26 June 1811.
23 LMS-SA 4/4/D: Read to LMS, Cape Town, 26 June 1811; LMS-SA 4/5/A: SAMS directors to LMS directors (translated extracts), 28 June 1811.
24 LMS-SA 4/5/A: Van der Kemp to LMS, Cape Town, 25 July 1811.
25 LMS-SA 5/1/A: LMS directors to Van der Kemp, London, January 1812.
26 For example, Freund, "Cape Under the Transitional Governments," 341; Sales, *Mission Stations* 52–3. Hermann Giliomee is also incorrect that the missionaries alienated potential supporters among "enlightened colonists" because they "sent their complaints of Khoikhoi maltreatment directly to

London and not to the governor in Cape Town." Giliomee, "Eastern Frontier," 454.

27 LMS-SA 5/1/A: LMS directors to Van der Kemp, London, January 1812.

28 Bodl. Wilberforce (Add.), c.46, fos.50–5: Wilberforce to Hardcastle, Kensington, 15 February 1812.

29 LMS-Home 2/5/B: Wilberforce to Burder, Hurstmonceaux, 3 August 1811.

30 Wilberforce to Wellesley, 5 August 1811, in Wilberforce, *Correspondence*, vol. 2, 213–6.

31 Wilberforce to Wesley, 5 August 1811, in Wilberforce, *Correspondence*, vol. 2, 213–216.

32 *RCC*, vol. 7, 133.

33 LMS-SA 4/5/D: "Report of Bethesldorp," 1811; note that this report was written by Michael Wimmer, according to Read to LMS, 9 January 1812, LMS-SA 5/1/A. *HP*, ccxxiii–v: Van der Kemp to Cradock, Cape Town, September 1811.

34 LMS-SA 5/1/F James Read, "Annual Report of the Missionary Institution at Bethelsdorp for the Year 1812." Giliomee states in contrast that the "farmer" force consisted of 900 burgher militia and 700 Khoisan soldiers of the Cape Regiment. Giliomee, "Eastern Frontier," 448.

35 Ibid., 448; Maclennan, *Proper Degree of Terror*.

36 Peires, *House of Phalo*, 142.

37 LMS-SA 4/5/D: "Annual Report of Bethelsdorp," 1811.

38 "Report of the Lieutenant Col. Collins to the Earl of Caledon," 6 August 1809, *RCC*, vol. 7, 106.

39 LMS-SA 5/4/D: "Annual Report of Bethelsdorp," 1811.

40 LMS-SA 5/1/A: Read to LMS, 9 January 1812.

41 LMS-SA 4/5/D: Van der Kemp and Mathilde Smith to LMS, December 1811 and Pacalt to LMS, 16 December 1811.

42 LMS-SA 5/1/E: Read to LMS, Bethelsdorp, 8 August 1812.

43 *RCC*, vol. 7, 385–7; Elphick and Malherbe, "Khoisan to 1828," 41–2; Marais, *Cape Coloured People*, 118–19 and 127–9; W.M. Macmillan, *Cape Colour Question*, 157–70.

44 Even Colonel Collins acknowledged that Khoekhoe children were of little expense to a farmer, and that a Hottentot child "can scarcely crawl before it is turned to some purpose." Collins, "Report," *RCC*, vol. 7, 110–11.

45 CA, A559: Read-Cuyler correspondence, 1812, "Statement of missionary complaints and grievances."

46 LMS-SA 5/1/F: James Read, "Bethelsdorp Annual Report," 1812. I have punctuated the last quote.

47 LMS-SA 5/2/B: Read to LMS, 3 February 1813.

48 Giliomee, "Eastern Frontier," 454.

49 Campbell, *Travels in South Africa*, 344–5.

50 Giliomee, "The Eastern Frontier, 1770–1812," 454.

51 "Report of the Commission of Circuit," *RCC*, vol. 9. Emphasis in original.
52 Hay, "Property, Authority and the Criminal Law"; Langbein, "Albion's Fatal Flaws."
53 "Report of the Commissioners of Circuit," *RCC*, vol. 9, 72, 81.
54 Ibid., 72
55 "Report of the Commissioners of Circuit," *RCC*, vol. 9, 74–5.
56 Douglas, *Purity and Danger*, 2–4.
57 "I am nevertheless convinced that the Hottentots are more cold and moderate in their desires of a certain nature than many other nations; qualities which are the natural consequence of the dull, inactive, and I had almost said, entirely listless disposition, which is the leading characteristic of their minds." Sparrman, *Voyage to the Cape of Good Hope*, vol. 1, 201–2.
58 Gilman, *Difference and Pathology*, 83, on the support given to polygenetic views by claims of profound differences in sexual characteristics between the "Hottentot" and Europeans. Gordon, "The Venal Hottentot," 185–201; Shire, *Digging through Darkness*, 175–8.
59 Potgieter, *Encyclopedia of South Africa*, vol. 2, 297.
60 February, *Mind Your Colour*.
61 Crehan, "Khoi, Boer and Missionary," 127–40, 148–9.
62 LMS-SA 7/2/V: "A Copy of the Original Minutes of the Missionary Deputies Held in the Orphan House, Cape of Good Hope," 9, 39-40.
63 LMS-SA 7/1/A: F. Hooper to LMS, 4 January 1817, cited in Stuart, "O That We Had Wings," 7.
64 Journal of William F. Corner, 1816, in F.A. Steytler, "'Journal' van William F. Corner, *Hertzog-Annale, Jaarboek*, vol. 3 (December 1956), 95–6.
65 Lichtenstein, *Travels in Southern Africa*, vol. 1, 292.
66 LMS-SA 5/2/D: Read to Hardcastle, Klaar Water, 29 July 1813.
67 *Evangelical Magazine* and *Missionary Chronicle*, vol. 14, September 1836, 424.
68 Compare Etherington, "Standard of Living Question."
69 LMS-SA 3/4/D: Read to Mrs Whitaker, 2 October 1807.
70 LMS-SA 5/3/C: George Thom to Burder, Cape of Good Hope, 30 April 1814.
71 Lichtenstein, *Travels in Southern Africa*, vol. 1, 290–6.
72 Latrobe, *Journal of a Visit to South Africa*, 206.
73 Ibid., 207.
74 LMS-SA 5/3/A: Read, "Answers upon Mr. Thom's Conversations with the Missionaries at Bethelsdorp. 1st and 2nd December 1813"; LMS-SA 5/2/B: John Campbell to LMS, Bethelsdorp, 1 April 1813.
75 LMS-SA 5/2/F: "Minutes of the First Conference held by the African Missionaries at Graaff Reinet in August 1814." Also reproduced in F.A.

Skeytler, "Minutes of the First Conference Held by the African Missionaries at Graaff Reinet (1814)," *Hertzog-Annale, Jaarboek*, vol. 3 (December 1956), 104–17.

76 "Minutes of the First Conference."

77 J. Marshall, *Where Are the Ju/wasi of NyaeNyae?* 58–66, 79.

78 Stuart, "Savages and Heroes"; Stuart, "O That We Had Wings"; Stuart, "Wicked Christians."

79 LMS-SA 4/1/C: Pacalt to LMS, Cape Town, 18 September 1809.

80 Schoeman, "The Wife of Dr. Van der Kemp," 189–97; Stuart, "Savages and Heroes," 236.

81 LMS-SA 3/3/D: Schoonberg to Missionary Society of Rotterdam, Cape Town, 31 December 1806.

82 Schoeman, "The Wife of Dr. Van der Kemp," 191.

83 For a summary of different historians' views: Enklaar, *Life and Work*, 204–6.

84 LMS-SA 4/5/C: Van der Kemp to LMS, Cape Town, 30 October 1811.

85 As Hooper attested in his notes on Van der Kemp's autobiography: LMS-Odds, box 8, Vanderkemp.

86 The LMS paid 600 rixdollars for Verhoogd's freedom and Van der Kemp an additional 73 rixdollars; Verhoogd agreed either to work for the society for six years as an evangelist or to repay the proportionate amount should he leave earlier. LMS-SA 4/4/A: Van der Kemp to LMS, Bethelsdorp, 8 January 1811; LMS-SA 4/5/A: Van der Kemp to LMS, Cape Town, 25 July 1811. On Verhoogd's life: Schoeman, "Maart van Mosambiek," 140–9.

87 L.C.H. Strubberg to Henry Lichtenstein, Cape Town, 9 November 1806, in Lichtenstein, *Reizen*, vol. 2, xxixf, cited by Enklaar, *Life and Work*, 205–6.

88 LMS-SA 5/3/C: George Thom to George Burder, Cape Town, 16 February 1814. For further allegations, Stuart, "O That We Had Wings," 12.

89 LMS-SA 3/4/A, Read to LMS, Bethelsdorp, 23 January 1807; LMS-SA 3/3/D: Schoonberg to Rotterdam Missionary Society (copy), 31 December 1806.

90 LMS, *Memoir of ... Van der Kemp*, 37.

91 Stuart, "Wicked Christians"; On Corner, "A Brother of Colour ... a Native of Demerara": *Missionary Magazine*, 11 August 1811, 303.

92 LMS-SA 8/3/A: J. Campbell, Rama Mission Station, Bushmen Country, n.d. [1820], cited in Stuart, "Savages and Heroes," 237, n.28; LMS-SA 7/2/C: "Copy of the Original Minutes of the Missionary Deputies Held in the Orphan House, Cape of Good Hope," August 1817; LMS-SA: Evan Evans to George Burder, Bethelsdorp, 20 May 1817; Stuart, "Wicked Christians," 8.

93 LMS-SA 5/2/D: Read to Hardcastle, Klaar Water, 29 July 1813.

94 LMS-SA 3/D/4: "Yearly Account of Bethelsdorp," 1807.

95 LMS-SA 3/3/B: Read to LMS, 2 August 1806.

96 LMS-SA 8/2/B: Read to Mrs Hamilton, Kuruman, 6 April 1819, enclosed in Mrs Hamilton to directors, Kuruman, 20 April 1819.

97 LMS-SA 5/2/B: Michael Wimmer to LMS, Bethelsdorp, 2 February 1813.

98 Read to Mrs Hamilton, Kuruman, 6 April 1819, enclosed in Mrs Hamilton to LMS, Kuruman, 20 April 1819, LMS-SA 8/2/B.

99 LMS-SA: Evan Evans to George Burder, Bethelsdorp, 20 May 1817.

100 Malherbe, "Pretorius, Andries"; Stuart, "O That We Had Wings," 15–18.

101 Stuart, "O That We Had Wings," 16–18.

102 LMS-SA 8/2/B: Mrs Hamilton to LMS, Kuruman, 20 April 1819.

103 LMS-SA 7/2/C: "Minutes of the Missionary Deputies," August 1817.

104 Ibid.

105 Ibid.

106 Stuart, "Wicked Christians," 5–6; LMS-SA 7/2/C: "Minutes of the Missionary Deputies," August 1817, 17–20. For the best account of the affair: Stuart, "O That We Had Wings." Stuart's title is drawn from Wimmer's memorable phrase in a letter on the subject: "O that we had wings that we might fly over the mountains and live among the heathen."

107 LMS-SA 5/2/C: Campbell to Burder, Graaff-Reinet, 5 May 1813.

108 LMS-SA 5/2/B: Campbell to LMS, Bethesldorp, 1 April 1813.

109 LMS-SA 5/1/F: Bethelsdorp Annual Report, 1812.

110 LMS-SA 5/2/C: Campbell to Burder, Graaff-Reinet, 5 May 1813.

111 LMS-SA 5/1/A: Corner to Hardcastle, Cape Town, 28 January 1812.

112 LMS-SA 5/2/C: Campbell to W. Tracey, 7 April 1813.

113 LMS-SA 5/2/F: "Minutes of the First conference," August 1814.

114 LMS-SA: William Corner to LMS, Bethelsdorp, 26 July 1817.

115 LMS-SA 5/2/E: George Thom to Hardcastle, Cape Town, 27 October 1813.

116 Thom to LMS, Cape Town, 23 May 1813.

117 Pacalt objected to the lack of an altar cloth and proper communion vessels: Sales, *Mission Stations*, 69.

118 LMS-SA 5/2/E: Thom to Hardcastle, Cape Town, 27 October 1813.

119 LMS-SA 4/5/A: Van der Kemp to LMS, Cape Town, 25 July 1811.

120 LMS-SA 4/4/A: Pacalt to LMS, Bethelsdorp, 19 February 1811.

121 LMS-SA 7/2/C: "Minutes of the Missionary Deputies." Stuart, "Savages and Heroes," 273–85.

122 Cited by Stuart, "Savages and Heroes," 234.

123 R. Philip, *Life ... of Rev. John Campbell*, 519–20.

CHAPTER SIX

1 As Andrew Bank has convincingly argued in his magisterial thesis, "Liberals and Their Enemies," especially 82–148. On humanitarian liberalism, see also Keegan, *Colonial South Africa*, 75–82.

2 A. Ross, *John Philip*, 52–76; Keegan, *Colonial South Africa*, 88–92; W.M. Macmillan, *Cape Colour Question*, 95–102.

3 Brent, *Liberal Anglican Politics*, 252–5.

4 Trapido, "Paternalism to Liberalism," 76–104; Peires, "British and the Cape," 472–518.

5 Bourke to Spring Rice, 4 November 1827, Bourke papers, Rhodes House, Oxford, I, fo.52, cited in Hazel King, *Richard Bourke*, 87.

6 Keegan, *Colonial South Africa*, 45–7, 61–74; I. Edwards, *1820 Settlers*.

7 Peires, "British and the Cape," 472.

8 William Hankey, then the LMS secretary, had clearly disapproved of Mrs Van der Kemp's actions: she acknowledges the justice of his strictures but pleads that she thought she was dying. LMS-SA, 10/3/C: Sara van der Kemp to W.A. Hankey, 17 January 1826. This letter is unsigned.

9 LMS-SA 10/3/C: Cornelius van der Kemp to William Hankey, Bethelsdorp, 28 December 1827.

10 LMS-SA 11/4/A: Philip to Orme, Cape Town, 18 November 1829.

11 LMS-SA 14/1/C: Philip to Thomas Wilson, 19 June 1834.

12 LMS-SA 11/2/D: Robson to LMS directors, Bethelsdorp, 31 December 1828.

13 LMS-SA 10/C/1: William Foster to George Burder, Bethelsdorp, 17 June 1826.

14 All land was, strictly speaking, government land; consequently, this ruling actually outlaws such activities altogether.

15 SCA II, 750: "Legislative Council, Sitting, No.22 – Monday 25 August 1834,"; "Papers referred to in Evidence of the Rev. J. Philip, D.D., 11 July 1836."

16 "Letter from Dr. Philip, on the Second Ordinance," "Papers referred to in Evidence of the Rev. J. Philip, D.D. 11 July 1836," SCA, 760.

17 Although in the end it was Matiwane's Ngwane who were attacked and routed by the colonial forces. L. Thompson, "Co-operation and Conflict," 349–50.

18 LMS-SA 11/2/D: A. Robson to LMS, Bethelsdorp, 31 December 1828.

19 Bank, "Liberals and Their Enemies," 189–243. The fundraising brochure *Report of the Committee of the Society for the Relief of the Distressed Settlers at the Cape of Good Hope with Letters and Other Documents Illustrative of Their Present Condition* (London, 1824) reproduces a speech by Philip in support of distressed settlers.

20 Bank, "Liberals and Their Enemies," 121 and passim.

21 On the growing conservatism of parliamentary evangelicals and the decline of the cross-party Claphamite lobby: Brent, *Liberal Anglican Politics*, 272–4; Rosman, *Evangelicals and Culture*, 33–7. "The carrying of the slavery bill in 1833," Rosman comments, "was both the greatest triumph of the older evangelicalism and a mark of its increasing debility:

in his attempt to achieve a more absolute emancipation than the government was prepared to grant, Buxton was supported by fewer than half the evangelical M.P.s." Rosman, 34.

22 On the changing social background of missionaries through the nineteenth century: Piggin, *Making Evangelical Missionaries*; Potter, "Social Origins."

23 Bodl, MSS Wilberforce, c.3: Burder to Wilberforce, 10 February 1818.

24 LMS-SA 10/1/C: Foster to Burder, Bethelsdorp, 17 June 1826.

25 Elbourne, "Domesticity and Dispossession"; Bank, "Liberals and Their Enemies," 118–19, 122–8.

26 Philip, *Researches in South Africa*, vol. 1, 213.

27 P. Anderson, "No-Man's Land." Kate Crehan discusses the missionary effort to eradicate African-style housing. She argues that the square stone or brick house enshrined capitalist values, since it permitted family privacy, fostered individualism, provided evidence for the industriousness, or otherwise, of the inhabitants, allowed possessions to be shown off, and embodied "a clear sense of social order and hierarchy." Crehan, "Khoi, Boer and Missionary," 134–40. Jean and John Comaroff also have an excellent discussion of housing in *Of Revelation and Revolution*, vol. 2.

28 Philip, *Researches in South Africa*, vol. 1, 209.

29 Ibid., 209–10.

30 Erlank, "Jane and John Philips," 86–93.

31 Shops at Bethelsdorp and Theopolis were quickly successful: Ebenezer Kemp's store at Bethelsdorp sold 20,000 rixdollars worth of goods in 1822. Elphick and Malherbe, "Khoisan to 1828," 45.

32 Philip to Kitchingman, Cape Town, 24 October 1823, in Le Cordeur and Saunders, ed., *Kitchingham Papers*, 68.

33 Macmillan, *Bantu, Boer and Briton*, 16.

34 King, *Richard Bourke*, 120.

35 LMS-SA 10/3/C: Cornelius van der Kemp to William Hankey, Bethelsdorp, 28 December 1827; LMS-SA 10/1/C: William Foster to George Burder, Bethelsdorp, 17 June 1826,

36 *Evangelical Magazine* and *Missionary Chronicle*, August 1828, 361.

37 LMS-HO 5/7/A: Hankey to Arundel, 24 November 1831; Hankey to LMS directors, 11 February 1832; John Crisp to LMS directors, 12 November 1832; T. Fiddian to LMS directors, n.d. On the growing radicalism and independence of the nonconformist provincial anti-slavery societies during the 1830s: Brent, *Liberal Anglican Politics*, 276–7.

38 *Missionary Chronicle*, August 1828, 361.

39 LMS-HO 5/2/A: Hay to Hankey, Downing Street, 22 February 1827.

40 Thomas Fowell Buxton Papers (hereafter TFB), vol. 13, 107–10: "Priscilla Buxton's Account of the Liberation of the Hottentots."

41 TFB, vol. 13, 154–6: Philip to T.F. Buxton, August 1834.

42 Macmillan, *Cape Colour Question*, 216.

43 Helly, *Livingstone's Legacy*.

44 Comaroff, "Images of Empire," 665–6.

45 Hilton, *Age of Atonement*, 1–7.

46 LMS-Odds, box 8, Vanderkemp Papers: Autobiography (1).

47 Beattie, *Crime and the Courts*; Foucault, *Surveiller et punir*; Ignatieff, *Just Measure of Pain*. I find Beattie's work more convincing in its historical detail than that of Foucault, but the importance of Foucault's broad ideas to discussions of changing notions of crime and punishment is obviously critical.

48 Buxton, *Enquiry* 15, cited in "Prison Discipline," *Edinburgh Review*, vol. 30, no. 60 (September 1818), 472.

49 H.G. Bennett, *Letter to the Common Council*, cited in ibid., 484.

50 Philip, *Researches* II, 356.

51 Campbell, *Travels in South Africa*, 279.

52 Ibid., 170.

53 CA A50: James Read to John Fairbairn, Philipton, Kat River, 12 April 1833. Andrew Bank cites the example of a rare favourable comment by Fairbairn about the social function of witchcraft: Bank, "Liberals and Their Enemies,"137–8.

54 LMS-SA 14/4/A: John Ross to John Philip, 6 June 1833 (copy).

55 Jagger Manuscript Room, University of Cape Town, BCZA54: John Philip to Jane Ross, 30 March 1808.

56 Hilton, *Age of Atonement*, especially "Preface," vii–x.

57 J.L. Comaroff, "Images of Empire"; Crehan, *Khoi, Boer and Missionary*, 118–60.

58 LMS-SA 14/1/C: John Philip, Memorial, Cape Town, 2 June 1834.

59 *Anti-Slavery Reporter*, reproduced in the *Christian Observer*, vol. 27 (April 1827), 227.

60 Colquhoun, *Treatise on the Wealth*, 392.

61 J. Philip, *Researches*, vol. 1, xi.

62 R. Philip, *Life, Times, and Missionary Enterprises*, 420.

63 J. Philip, *Researches*, vol. 1, 1.

64 LMS-Philip, box 3, cited in Macmillan, *Cape Colour Question*, 218.

65 Le Cordeur and Saunders, eds., *Kitchingman Papers*, 97: John Philip to James Kitchingman, 18 July 1828.

66 *Missionary Chronicle*, August 1828, 362.

67 *Missionary Chronicle*, September 1829.

68 Bank, "Liberals and Their Enemies," 128–9.

69 Peires, "British and the Cape," 486.

70 Ibid., 500–1.

71 Galbraith, *Reluctant Empire*, 83. The two letters in the Bourke papers cited by Galbraith as crucial to indicating Bourke's independence on the

issue are not, however, as illuminating as Galbraith suggests: Bourke to Truter, 22 June 1828, shows merely that Bourke sent a draft copy of the ordinance to Truter for advice, whereas Stockenstrom to Bourke, 21 June 1828, if anything suggests that London was well ahead of colonial opinion and thus that Philip was more important than Galbraith allows.

72 Galbraith, *Reluctant Empire*, 65.

73 Elphick and Malherbe, "Khoisan to 1828," 43–8; Peires, "British and the Cape," 490–9; King, *Richard Bourke*, 109–22; Trapido, "Paternalism to Liberalism," 76–104.

74 Rhodes House, Bourke papers, vol.7, fo.136–7: Stockenstrom to Bourke, 21 June 1828.

75 "Resolutions of the Council, relating to the Moral and Religious Instruction of the Hottentots and other free People of Colour; the Appropriation of Lands for the Benefit of the same; the Subdividing of the Districts of Worcester and Graaf Reinet, and of various Field-cornetcies; the Repeal of the 2d Section of the 50th Ordinance, and of all existing Laws for the Prevention or Punishment of Vagrancy; and praying His Majesty's Government to allow the Vagrant Ordinance," in "Papers referred to in Evidence of the Rev. J. Philip, D.D. 11 July 1836," *SCA*, 755–7.

76 Manifesto of Piet Retief, quoted in Peires, "British and the Cape," 500.

CHAPTER SEVEN

1 James Read to James Kitchingman, Bethelsdorp, August 26, 1828, in Saunders and LeCordeur, eds., *Kitchingman Papers*.

2 Malherbe, "Cape Khoisan in the Eastern Districts," 127–78 and passim; Crais, *White Supremacy and Black Resistance*, 73–6; Duly, "A Revisit with the Cape's Hottentot Ordinance of 1828," 34–46; Elphick and Malherbe, "The Khoisan to 1828," 48.

3 LMS-SA 14/1/C: John Philip, Memorial, Cape Town, 2 June 1834.

4 LMS-SA 11/2/D: Adam Robson to LMS directors, Bethelsdorp, 31 December 1828.

5 LMS-SA 11/3/C: Edwards to Orme, Theopolis, 20 May 1829.

6 LMS-SA 14/2/B: Barker to Ellis, Theopolis, 6 October 1834.

7 Elphick and Malherbe, "Khoisan to 1828," 46.

8 CA CO323: Richard Miles to Sir Richard Plasket, Cape Town, 24 July 1827, and LMS-SA 10/2/D: collected correspondence.

9 Malherbe, "Colonial Justice and the Khoisan," 77–90.

10 Ibid., 86. Malherbe draws the comment of Andries Stoffels from CA, CO2713.

11 CA CO362: Incoming Correspondence, Agents and Missionaries in the Interior.

12 *South African Commercial Advertiser*, 25 June 1834, letter from "A Hottentot."

13 CA A50: J. Read to J. Philip, Kat River, 1 April 1833. "All the chiefs know of the transaction was that Geika [Ngqika] proposed to them that that part of the country should be neutral, and that soldiers should be stationed in the neighbourhood till Slambie [Ndlambie] was reconciled and Peace restored – but by no means finally to lose their country."

14 Anderson, "No-Man's Land: Landscaping Neutrality on the Cape Frontier."

15 Peires, *House of Phalo*, 89; A. Stockenstrom to L. Cole, Cape Town, 6 February 1829, in Stockenstrom (ed. Hutton), *Autobiography of the late Sir Andries Stockenstrom, Bart*, 305–11; evidence of Andries Stockenstrom, SCA, vol. 1, 82, question 965; LMS-SA 11/3/D: Read to W. Orme, Bethelsdorp, 30 July 1829; Stockenstrom, *Light and Shade*, 2; Mostert, *Frontiers*, 618.

16 Evidence of Stockenstrom, SCA, vol. 1, 81, question 965.

17 Glasgow Missionary Society, *Quarterly Papers*, vol. 5, 1–2.

18 Glasgow Missionary Society, *Quarterly Papers*, vol. 6, 11.

19 Andries Stockenstrom, "Hints for the Consideration of the Secretary to Government," 17 April 1829, reproduced in Stockenstrom, *Light and Shade*, 3.

20 Ibid., 4.

21 Ibid., 5.

22 LMS-SA 11/3/C: Barker to Mrs.Thomas, Theopolis, 4 June 1829.

23 Ibid. In a memorial to the government of 17 April 1829 urging the establishment of a Hottentot settlement on the government, Stockenstrom wrote: "No other class of people in the Colony can be brought together in the proposed manner, and no other set of men can be rendered more efficient auxiliaries towards the object in view." Stockenstrom (ed. Hutton), *Autobiography of the late Sir Andries Stockenstrom*, 357.

24 Innes, "Memorandum on the Kat River Settlement," in Read, *Kat River Settlement*, v. According to Innes, the government originally planned a mixed settlement, without racial restrictions on land ownership, but abandoned it in light of these considerations.

25 LMS-SA 11/3/D: Read to Orme, Bethelsdorp, 30 July 1829.

26 Innes, "Memorandum on the Kat River Settlement," in Read, *Kat River Settlement*, iv.

27 CA A50, 7: "Report of a Meeting held at Philipton."

28 CA A50: James Read to John Philip, Philipton, 1 April 1833. The famous "myth of the empty land" reflects ongoing beliefs about the nullity, the non-being, of the Khoikhoi.

29 Mostert, *Frontiers*, 619–21.

430 Notes to pages 266–7

30 Rho, MSS. Africana s.4, fo.175–6: James Read Sr to Miss Hillyard, Philipton, Kat River, 15 March 1839; LMS-SA 11/3/D: Read to Orme, Bethelsdorp, 30 July 1829.

31 Anonymous, "Notes, on the formation of the Kat River settlement in the year 1828, and some of the subsequent events. Compiled from the most authentic sources," in L. Meurant to Southey, Eland's Post, 6 March 1856, CA, LG590, "Formation of the Kat River Settlement in 1828, 1856 Memorandum."

32 LMS-SA 14/1/C: Read to LMS, Philipton, Kat River, 3 July 1834; Evidence of the Rev. James Read, SCA, vol 1, item 5235, 600.

33 The government initially installed Thomson as government agent and forbade missionaries to live in the settlement. The Khoisan resisted, in large part because they wanted schools. "Mr.T. is to have one schoolmaster, suppose he has in his school 150, what is to become of the rest? – well let them remain ignorant rather than be taught by Missionaries ... Capt. Stockenstrom has been preaching to them that they will be now real Christemenschen, all our people from Theopolis and Bethelsdorp stood and insisted upon having a missionary but he was enraged, said they could have no choice, this is strange, that they must now become Dutch Christians or nothing." J. Read to Fairbairn, Kat River, 13 July 1830.

34 LMS-SA 14/1/C: Read to LMS directors, Philipton, Kat River, 3 July 1834.

35 Evidence of James Read, SCA, vol. 1, item 5325, p.600; "Evidence of Mr. James Read," SCA I, item 5156, 592.

36 Kirk, "Progress and Decline in the Kat River Settlement," 412–13.

37 Evidence of Captain A. Stockenstrom, SCA, vol. 1, item 1387, 153; Evidence of Rev. James Read, SCA, vol. 1, item 5235, 599. According to Read, "After the plan was proposed to government, even the governor and many others were of opinion that only persons of property should get land. I urged the example of the British settlers, who, without exception, got lands allotted to them, and liberty to do with them as they chose, by sale, &c Captain Stockenstrom yielded, saying that it was a fact that he, as landdrost, had given hundreds of places to boors and settlers that they had never cultivated, but sold or neglected, and he thought that the Hottentots might have the same trial, and he himself sent in from different parts of the colony very many that had nothing whatever, and the most unlikely persons to succeed."

38 LMS-SA 14/1/B, Philip to LMS directors, Cape Town, July 10 1834. The discrimination in material aid afforded to white and nonwhite farmers was a leading grievance cited at a Philipton meeting against vagrancy legislation in 1834. "Report of a Meeting Held at Philipton – August 5th 1834," CA A50.

39 Evidence of Captain A. Stockenstrom, SCA, vol. 1, item 1387, 154.

40 CA A50, 7: "Report of a Meeting Held at Philipton."
41 Evidence of Rev. James Read, *SCA*, vol. 1, item 5235, 599.
42 Kirk, "Progress and Decline in the Kat River Settlement," 416.
43 Evidence of Rev. James Read, *SCA*, vol. 1, item 5235, 599.
44 CA A50, 6. A sambok is a type of whip.
45 Cf., for example, the testimonies collected by Thomas Pringle in his *Narrative of a Residence in South Africa*, 274–9.
46 Rose Innes, "Memorandum," in Read, *Kat River Settlement*, vi.
47 Evidence of Captain Spiller, *SCA*, vol. 1, item 860, 72.
48 Rose Innes, "Memorandum," in Read, *Kat River Settlement*, vi; Read, ibid., xi. Interestingly, the 1834 figures showing an increase in stock also indicate a decline in wheat and barley cultivated. This may have been due to external problems, such as drought and crop disease; it is still worth speculating, however, that these figures indicate a preference for the accumulation of stock rather than land in times of prosperity. Kirk points out such a pattern among the more recently pastoralist Gonaqua from Xhosaland in Kirk, "Progress and Decline," 416–7.
49 Rose Innes, "Memorandum,"in Read, *Kat River Settlement*, vii; Kirk, "Progress and Decline in the Kat River Settlement," 418.
50 Rose Innes, "Memorandum," in Read, *Kat River Settlement*, vii. This quote was an extract from his private journal on visiting the settlement in 1839.
51 CA 1/UIT 14/37, Kat River Commission of Inquiry (1858).
52 CA LG590, "Notes on the formation of the Kat River Settlement ...," in L. Meurant to Southey, 6 March 1856, 134. Clifton Crais confirms in his detailed analysis that relatively wealthy and westernized "Bastaard Clients" such as Christian Groepe, Klaas Eckert, and Jacob de Clerq "dominated the settlement in the eyes of European admirers" but were not typical of a generally much poorer community. Crais, *White Supremacy and Black Resistance*, 80–82.
53 CA LG590: "Notes on the formation of the Kat River Settlement ...," in L. Meurant to Southey, 6 March 1856, 134–5.
54 LMS-SA 10/1/C: Adam Robson to George Burder, Bethelsdorp, 25 May 1826.
55 LMS-SA 14/2/B: G. Barker to W. Ellis, Theopolis, October 6 1834. The occasion was a meeting held to oppose the Vagrancy Act.
56 LMS-SA 11/1/C: J. Read to G. Burder, Bethelsdorp, June 11 1828.
57 LMS-SA 11/2/D: Bethelsdorp Annual Report, 1828.
58 CA A50, 5: Philipton meeting.
59 LMS-SA 14/2/B: G. Barker to W. Ellis, Theopolis, 6 October 1834.
60 Rose Innes, "Memorandum," in Read, *Kat River Settlement*, vii; extract from journal of 1839.
61 Evidence of Rev. John Philip, D.D., 11 July 1836, SCA, vol. 1, item 5433, 644.

62 J. Read J, to J. Philip, Bethelsdorp, 16 November 1835, in Le Cordeur and Saunders, eds., *Kitchingman Papers*, 159.

63 Ibid., 157.

64 Newspaper clipping, speech by K. Pinney at Weymouth nomination meeting, in TFB, vol. 13, 291.

65 For example, TFB, vol. 14, 176–85, T.F. Buxton to Z. Macaulay, 4 December 1835, describing how a meeting of anti-slavery leaders had decided that a further motion in parliament against the apprenticeship system was injudicious: "The danger in my opinion, and it was not contradicted, lies more in some Vagrancy Law which shall perpetualise slavery under another name."

66 Ross argues that in 1828 "Buxton may well have realized that the cause of the Khoikhoi could perhaps be used to extract statements of principle from the British parliament which could later be used in the West Indies, without the planter interest being aroused." Ross, "James Cropper, John Philip and the Researches in South Africa," 147.

67 TFB, vol. 13, 125–45: Priscilla Buxton to John Philip, 20 September–17 December 1833.

68 Ibid.

69 *Edinburgh Review*, vol.58, January 1834, 363.

70 He means literally the formation of temperance societies and self-conscious abstention from brandy which characterized many early Kat River settlers.

71 Pringle, *Narrative of a Residence in South Africa*, 279–80.

72 SCA, vol. 1, 244–6.

73 Brundage, *Making of the New Poor Law*, 76–7; Davis, *Slavery and Human Progress*, 122–3. Cf. also Keegan, *Colonial South Africa*, 323, 172.

74 Davis, *Slavery and Human Progress*, 122.

75 Elbourne, "Freedom at Issue," 114–50; Crais, *White Supremacy and Black Resistance*, 139–140; Keegan, *Colonial South Africa*, 119; Ross, *John Philip*, 113–15; Marais, *Cape Coloured People*, 180–3.

76 Peires, "Piet Dragenhoeder's Lament," for the use of "blank verse" by the remnants of Kat River settlers in the 1980s.

77 LMS-SA 14/2/B: George Barker to William Ellis, Theopolis, 6 October 1834.

78 LMS-SA 14/2/B: Zwartbooy Ruiters, in G. Barker to W. Ellis, Theopolis, 6 October 1834.

79 CA A50, 3.

80 Ibid., 8.

81 Letter from "Niet een van de tagtig," original version *South African Commercial Advertiser*, 24 September 1834; English translation, 4 October 1834.

82 LMS-SA 14/2/B: G. Barker to LMS, Theopolis, 6 October 1834.

83 LMS-SA 14/2/A: Barker to John Campbell, Theopolis, 2 October 1834.

84 SCA, vol. 1, item 5075, 589.

85 Read Jr, Kat River Settlement, x.

86 Peires, "The British and the Cape"; Thompson, A History of South Africa, 87–8 (for a figure of 6,000); Worden, Making of Modern South Africa, 12 (for 15,000); Crais, White Supremacy and Black Resistance, gives 4,000 but he does not appear to be counting children.

87 Keegan, Colonial South Africa, 139.

88 Williams, When Races Meet. W.R. Thomson's letter of resignation as government agent stressed "the difficult and precarious nature of my situation, in the double capacity of a Christian minister and as resident Agent for Government in Kaffraria, owing to jealousies existing against myself and hostile feelings against the people of the Institution, which I attributed to the connection I had with Government." CA CO362/2, W.R. Thomson to acting colonial secretary, 13 January 1829. Cf. also CA CO360/21, Thomson to acting colonial secretary, 29 October 1828.

89 CA LG590: Anonymous, "Notes on the formation of the Kat River settlement," in L. Meurant to Southey, 6 March 1856.

90 LMS-SA 14/1/C: J. Read to LMS, Philipton, Kat River, 3 July 1834.

91 Ross, John Philip, 120–3.

92 "Evidence of Mr. James Read [Jr]," SCA, vol. 1, item 5190, 595.

93 HK: Van der Kemp, Dag Verhaal.

94 CA 1480: Read to Philip, Philipton, 12 April 1834.

95 CA A50: J. Read to J. Fairbairn, Kat River, 12 April 1833.

96 Peires, House of Phalo, 90; SCA, vol. 1; "Evidence of James Read [Jr]," item 5173, 593–4.

97 Ibid., item 5184, 594.

98 Evidence of the Rev. John Philip, D.D., SCA, vol. 1, items 4509–21, 561–2.

99 CA 1480: Maqomo to J. Philip, Banks of the Keiskama, 18 November 1833.

100 TFB, 12: Priscilla Buxton to J. Philip, 20 September–17 December 1833.

101 Keegan, Colonial South Africa, 140.

102 As Ross argues, in Ross, John Philip, 134. Ross also points out that Tshatshu would later insist before the Select Committee on Aborigines that the wounding of the chief Xo-Xo by a colonial patrol would have been seen as a declaration of war.

103 TFB, vol. 14, 73c–f, 26 July 1835.

104 On the death of Hintsa, see also Mostert, Frontiers, 715–26; Peires, House of Phalo 115; Galbraith, Reluctant Empire, chapter 7; W.M. Macmillan, Bantu, Boer and Briton, chapter 11, especially 132. Macmillan and Galbraith's more optimistic accounts of Hintsa's death and its significance have not been upheld by more recent research.

105 TFB, vol. 2, 81–5: T. Buxton to A. Gurney, 24 November 1835.

106 Cullen Library, University of the Witswatersrand, A85 2.ALS: T. Pringle to J. Philip, Highgate, 23 August 1834.

107 In much the same fashion as the conceptual categories "third world" and "developing societies" give additional clout to the development and aid lobbies today which in so many ways have taken over the functions of the missionaries.

108 TFB, vol. 13, 212: T. Buxton to J. Philip, 16 September 1834.

109 TFB, vol. 15, 71: Upcher to S. Gurney, London, 19 July 1836.

110 Personal communication, John Walsh.

111 *Missionary Chronicle*, June 1836, 550–2.

112 Ibid., 422. "To stand up" or to "stand forward" for something valuable are characteristic expressions used by both Xhosa and Khoisan orators during the period. The ending "I have done," or "I will say no more," was also the usual conclusion to a piece of rhetorical oratory in a public meeting.

113 Ibid., 422–4.

114 Keegan, *Colonial South Africa*, 149–51.

115 Read Sr, *African Witness*.

CHAPTER EIGHT

1 On the issue of Khoisan notions of collective restitution, in contrast with the British state's putatively individualist conception (despite its favourable treatment of white settlers as collectivities), Malherbe, "The Cape Khoisan," 201–6.

2 On the movement towards towns, Malherbe, "Cape Khoisan," 208–16; Crais, *White Supremacy and Black Resistance*, 75.

3 Sales, *Mission Stations*, 121.

4 Sales, *Mission Stations*, 88; Malherbe, "Cape Khoisan," 145–6, 250–6.

5 LMS-SA 16/1/A: John Melvill to LMS directors, Paarl, 1 March 1838.

6 LMS-SA 16/1/A: John Melvill to LMS directors, Paarl, 1 March 1838.

7 Sales, *Mission Stations*, 121.

8 LMS-SA 16/1/A: John Melvill to LMS directors, Paarl, 1 March 1838.

9 Letters from J.G. Messer to John Philip, 29 April and 9 May, 1831, cited in Philip to James Kitchingman, Cape Town, 19 May 1831, in Le Cordeur and Saunders, eds., *Kitchingman Papers*, 107–9. Philip's tone in this letter suggests that he had hoped to remove Messer.

10 LMS-SA, 12/4/E: J. Kitchingman and J. Melvill, n.d., "Report of the Missionary Institution Hankey for 1831." Kitchingman and Melvill observed judiciously that "whilst the prospects of getting a livelihood by cultivating the soil has doubtless influenced many to settle here, others it is believed have been influenced by a sincere desire for religious instruction."

11 Sales, *Mission Sations*, 121–7.

12 Sales, *Mission Stations*, 121.

13 LMS-SA 16/1/A: Melvill to LMS directors, Paarl, 1 March 1838.

14 "Resolutions of 29 January 1833 at a 'Meeting of the Subscribers for the Place called Hankey' held at Bethelsdorp," in LMS-SA 16/1/A: Melvill to LMS directors, Paarl, 1 March 1838.

15 LMS-SA 16/1/B: Williams to LMS directors, Hankey, 23 April 1838.

16 LMS-SA 16/1/A: J. Melvill to LMS directors, Paarl, 1 March 1838.

17 LMS-SA 16/1/A: J. Melvill to LMS directors, 1 March 1838.

18 LMS-SA, 16/1/B: E. Williams to LMS directors, 23 April 1838.

19 Comaroff and Comaroff, *Of Revelation and Revolution*, vols. 1 and 2.

20 LMS-SA 12/4/E: J. Kitchingman and J. Melvill, n.d., "Report of the Missionary Institution Hankey for 1831." Compare Brett Christophers's discussion of the Anglican missionary John Booth Good's attempts to control the morality and space simultaneously of the Nlha7kápmx in late-nineteenth-century British Columbia by persuading semi-nomadic groups to adopt agriculture: Christophers, *Positioning the Missionary*, 82–91.

21 *Evangelical Magazine*, 1856, 497, discussing the situation in the 1830s and 1840s; cited by Sales, *Mission Stations*, 125–6.

22 LMS-SA, 19/2/D: E. Williams to LMS directors, Algoa Bay, November 1843; also cited in Sales, *Mission Stations*, 124.

23 LMS-SA 18/5/C: William Philip to LMS directors, Hankey, 3 January 1843, 1842 annual report for Hankey. Also cited in Sales, *Mission Stations*, 125.

24 CA A1415, William Philip to John Philip, Hankey, 28 September 1842, 64. Page numbers here and in subsequent notes refer to the edited typescript made of these family letters by a descendant of the Philip family and deposited in the Cape Archives.

25 LMS-SA, 18/5/C: William Philip to LMS directors, Hankey, 3 January 1843, 1842 annual report for Hankey. "In the extremity of scareness," Philip wrote, "the people have been almost constantly among the farmers where the smallness of their wages barely permits them to supply with food that part of their families who remain on the station."

26 CA A1415, William Philip to John Philip, Hankey, 25 May 1843, 75.

27 CA A1415, William Philip to Jane Philip, Hankey, 17 November 1843, 88.

28 LMS-SA, 19/2/D: Williams to LMS directors, Algoa Bay, November 1843.

29 LMS-SA 18/5/C: William Philip to LMS directors, Hankey, 3 January 1843, 1842 annual report.

30 CA A1415, William Philip to Jane Philip, Hankey, 17 December 1842, 65.

31 On buildings and supplies: CA A1415, William Philip to Jane Philip, Hankey, 17 November 1843, 88; on Mrs. Kelly, William Philip to John Philip, Hankey, 25 May 1843, 76.

32 CA A1415, William Philip to John Philip, Hankey, 21 April 1843, 71.

33 CA A1415, William Philip to John Philip, Hankey, 25 May 1843, 76.

34 CA A1415, William Philip to Jane Philip, Hankey 17 December 1842, 65; William Philip to John Philip, Hankey, 21 April 1843, 71–2. Cf. also LMS-SA 18/5/C: William Philip to LMS directors, Hankey, 3 January 1843, 1842 annual report for Hankey.

35 LMS-SA 12/4/E: J. Kitchingman and J. Melvill, n.d., "Report of the Missionary Institution Hankey for 1831."

36 CA A1415, William Philip to Jane Philip, Hankey, 17 December 1842, 66.

37 LMS-SA, 16/1/A: E. Williams to LMS directors, Hankey, 29 January 1831; LMS-SA, 16/1/B: E. Williams to LMS directors, Hankey, 23 April 1838. Quotations are from the latter letter.

38 CA A1415, Anon. [Durant Philip], "The Reverend William Philip." In CA A1415, William Philip to Jane Philip, Hankey n.d. (September 1843?), 81, Philip describes his successful treatment with internal homeopathic medicines of an individual who had fallen from a great height and suffered concussions and bodily fractures. In a letter to his then fiancée in 1839 William relates that he had been introduced to homeopathic doctors in Paris and had acquired introductions to "two or three of the most eminent Homeopathists in London," although he does not yet seem to have been completely convinced. Philip met Lord Elgin in Paris, who related his own case and placed in Philip's hands a paper Elgin had written "on the formation of the Homeopathic medicaments." At that stage, however, Philip was "determined not to implicate myself in any incautious reception of a new theory, and did not call again or give any other opinion than that it was very *plausible* which I have no doubt His Lordship thought was very cold." CA A1415, William Philip to Alison Bell, 4 October 1839, 33.

39 In CA A1415, William Philip to Jane Philip, Hankey, 7 February 1845, William advises his mother to take "Rhus tox:, Arsenic, Sachesis, Mix bon: Sulph: Mercury" for an erruption on her hands.

40 CA A1415, William Philip to Jane Philip, Hankey, n.d. (September 1843?), 81.

41 CA A1415, William Philip to John Philip, Hankey, 25 May 1843, 75.

42 Report of LMS deputation of 1855, cited by Sales, *Mission Stations*, 129.

43 Sales, *Mission Stations*, 133.

44 Malherbe, *Cape Khoisan*, 165–74. On the land issue, Macmillan, *Cape Colour Question*, 226–30; Crais, *White Supremacy and Black Resistance*, 153. As Malherbe points out (*Cape Khoisan*, 169), Theopolis historian Marion Currie disagrees with Macmillan's assessment of who was at fault in the Theopolis land dispute: Currie, "The History of Theopolis Mission, 1814–1851," vol. 1, 204.

45 Macmillan, *Cape Coloured Question*, 279–80.
46 Sales, *Mission Stations*, 140.
47 Salt prices fluctuated. Martha Kitchingman commented in 1844, for example, that her father did not expect to get much money from the auxiliary missionary society: "The people put off paying their subscriptions when salt fetched a high price and now though many of them have a mind they have not the means to do so." University of Cape Town, BC 612, Kitchingman family papers, Martha Kitchingman to Sarah Merrington, Bethelsdorp, 26 October 1844.
48 LMS-SA 20/3/C: J. Kitchingman to Tidman and Freeman, 31 December 1844, cited in Crais, *White Supremacy*, 152.
49 Sales, *Mission Stations*, 138; Crais, *White Supremacy*, 152. Citation in Crais from LMS-SA 20/3/C: J. Kitchingman to Tidman and Freeman, 31 December 1844.
50 Malherbe, *Cape Khoisan*, 259–64.
51 LMS-SA, 19/2/D: J.G. Messer to LMS directors, George Town, 27 December 1843.
52 On the movement in Grahamstown from a relatively "easy non-racialism" in worship to separate congregations divided by language and skin colour between the 1820s and 1840s, Ross, "Congregations, Missionaries and the Grahamstown Schism of 1842–3."
53 Ross, *John Philip*, 186.
54 On social stratification at the Kat River settlement, Crais, *White Supremacy*, 81–2, 159, 161.
55 *South African Commercial Advertiser*, 10 September 1834. V.C. Malherbe cites the telling example from the 1834 Philipton anti-vagrancy meeting of the testimony of David Jantje that he would lose all his property should the vagrancy law pass, "owing to the many poor Hottentot friends that would flee into the Kat-river, and he could not allow his poor relatives to be taken ... and given to the Boers": Malherbe, *Colonial Khoisan*, 376.
56 On overcrowding and clientage relationships, Kirk, "Progress and Decline."
57 CA 1/UIT 14/37: Kat River Commission of Inquiry 1858, notebook 1, 95–9.
58 Legassick, "The Griqua, the Sotho-Tswana and the Missionaries," 346–7; Keegan, *Colonial South Africa*, 175–6.
59 CA 1/UIT 14/37: Kat River Commission of Inquiry 1858, vol. 1, 154–155.
60 Ibid., 142–144.
61 Malherbe, *Colonial Khoisan*, 363 and n.195, 363.
62 Kirk, "Kat River Settlement," 420–1.
63 Kirk, "Kat River Settlement," 422.

64 Sales, *Mission Stations*, 135–6. On Dirk Hartha at the Fish River, Le
Cordeur and Saunders, *Kitchingman Papers*, 207, n.70.

65 Crais *White Supremacy*, 161, also observes the disparity between fathers
and sons. I would add only that this was also true for daughters and
widows.

66 This pattern emerges clearly from the 1858 Commission of Inquiry at Kat
River which, as we shall see, examined the claims of those who felt they
had been unjustly deprived of their lands in the aftermath of the 1850–53
rebellion. Many bore witness to adult family members living together on
land originally allocated to one man. CA I/UIT [Uitenhage district] 14/37:
Kat River Commission of Inquiry, 1858.

67 Malherbe, "Colonial Khoisan."

68 Report of Cobus Fourie, Fort Armstrong, 15 January 1851, in Read, *Kat
River Settlement*, 30, and Stockenstrom, *Light and Shade*, 86.

69 Crais, *White Supremacy*, 162; Stockenstrom, *Light and Shade*, 14; Peires,
House of Phalo, 16.

70 CA LG 592: J. Borcherds to Martin West, Fort Beaufort, 10 February
1842. Crais, *White Supremacy*, 160.

71 CA LG 592, "Inquiry regarding the Fingoes in Kat River settlement," in J.
Borcherds to Martin West, Fort Beaufort, 10 February 1842.

72 J. Read Sr to James Kitchingman, Bethelsdorp [Philipton?], 22 October
1842, in Le Cordeur and Saunders, eds., *Kitchingman Papers*, 228. On
Read's enthusiasm for working among the Mfengu and government
concern to reduce their numbers, see also the editors' comments,
189–90.

73 Ibid., 190.

74 Crais, *White Supremacy*, 163.

75 Wool exports from the Cape showed a cumulative annual growth rate
between 1833 and 1851 of 24 per cent. Kirk, "Cape Economy," 229.

76 Kirk, "Cape Economy," 238–40.

77 Struggles over land between Dutch-speakers and English-speakers, especially land speculators, were, of course, a major contributing factor to the
Great Trek, on which the historiography is voluminous. For one recent
statement of position, Keegan, *Colonial South Africa*, 184–96.

78 LMS-SA 14/4/C: J. Melvill to John Philip, 15 July 1835.

79 James Read Jr, LMS-SA 26/4/A, n.d. The document is a statement of the
position of the Kat River Loyal Burghers' Association, signed by James
Read, in response to a letter of complaint from Major-General Somerset
to the missionaries William Thomson and James Read Sr; it may be an
early draft of Read's published letters on the Kat River rebellion.

80 Report of Veldcornet Fourie in Read Jr, *Kat River Settlement*, 31.

81 Ibid., 31–2.

82 James Read jnr., LMS-SA 26/4/A, n.d.

83 Cape Archives, UIT 1/14/37, Kat River Commission of Inquiry, notebooks
   1–3, 1858.

CHAPTER NINE

1 I am not sure that Maqoma's complicated and long-standing relationship
  with missionaries, especially James Read, has ever been satisfactorily
  explored, although existing sources make it difficult to be confident about
  Maqoma's views at various points. J.B. Peires raises seminal points about
  Christian influences on the Xhosa cattle-killing of 1856–57, but it is not
  part of his book's mandate to examine Maqoma's earlier contacts with
  missionaries in detail, while Timothy Stapleton seems to me unduly dis-
  missive of the notion that Maqoma took religious ideas seriously in any
  form. I suspect that Maqoma was ambivalent about Christianity but
  nonetheless interested in it as a possible source of spiritual and material
  authority, and I do not think that he saw Read as a fool, as Stapleton
  argues. Peires, *The Dead Will Arise*; Stapleton, *Maqoma*; Stapleton,
  "Reluctant Slaughter."
2 Helly, *Livingstone's Legacy*.
3 Peter Hinchliff, "Voluntary Absolutism: British Missionary Societies in
  the Nineteenth Century," in which Hinchliff argues that "enthusiasm for
  missions began in the late eighteenth century: the missionary *movement*
  did not become really significant until the 1840s" (363). On Colenso,
  Guy, *The Heretic*.
5 Ross, *John Philip*, 159–84.
6 LMS-SA 19/2/D: W. Elliot to LMS, Uitenhage, 14 November 1843.
7 Ibid.
8 LMS-SA, 19/2/D: Messer to LMS directors, George Town, 27 December
  1847.
9 UCT, BC 612 B1, Kitchingman family papers: James Kitchingman to his
  children, Bethelsdorp, 8 November 1842.
10 de Gruchy, "Alleged Political Conservatism," 17–36.
11 Ross, "Congregations, Missionaries and the Grahamstown Church
   Schism of 1842–3."
12 I agree with Ross's assessment here that Locke concentrated more on his
   white congregation than on the black: Ross, "Congregations, Missionaries and the Grahamstown Church Schism," 124. Locke himself did not
   agree: "Our charge, as you are aware," he wrote to the LMS directors in
   early 1843, "comprises an English and a Native Congregation, to whom
   as much attention is devoted as time and strength will admit." LMS-SA,
   19/1/C: J. Locke to LMS directors, Grahamstown, 4 March 1843.
13 LMS-SA 19/C/1: John Locke to LMS directors, Grahamstown, 4 March
   1843. The price tag of the church had obviously risen slightly, as is the

way of such things, between this 1843 letter from Locke (which asked the directors to stir up financial support in Britain for paying off the loan), and the 1840 *Grahamstown Journal* article cited by Ross.

14 *The Graham's Town Journal*, 15 December 1840, cited by Ross, "Congregations, Missionaries and the Grahamstown Church Schism," 124.

15 Ibid. Smit described his work in LMS-SA 19/3/A: Nicolas Smit to John Philip, Grahamstown, 13 January 1843.

16 Elbourne and Ross, "Combatting Spiritual and Social Bondage"; Ross, "Congregations, Missionaries and the Grahamstown Church Schism."

17 LMS-SA 19/3/A: Nicolas Smit to J. Philip, Grahamstown, 16 December 1842.

18 LMS-SA 19/1/C: Subscribers and deacons to LMS directors, Grahamstown, n.d. The other signatories were Dirk Cole, Adrian Vandervent, Christian Slinger, Ary Pietersson, Cobus Vriel, John William, William October, Seedras Daniels, Jacob [Hatha?], Philip Boosman, and Klaas Hendrik.

19 Ross, "Congregations, Missionaries and the Grahamstown Schism."

20 Brown, "The Ten Years' Conflict and the Disruption of 1843," 1–27.

21 Le Cordeur and Saunders, eds., *The Kitchingman Papers*, 191–2; Ross, *John Philip*, 178.

22 As the infamous battle of Dithakong demonstrates, whatever else it may or may not prove. Some have argued that this battle shows the involvement of Moffat and other missionaries along with Griqua allies in slave-raiding and trading on a large scale, in a manner that launched, in conjunction with Portuguese and (covert) Cape Colony slaving, the cycles of regional disruptions more traditonally ascribed to the military expansion of the Zulu empire. This is an enormously complicated debate, with many facets. Despite the many criticisms one might make of Moffat, however, nothing in his private papers – nor, perhaps more significantly, in the papers of his many and vitriolic enemies – suggests that he was involved in organized slave-trading on a large scale, although he did send several survivors of the Battle of Dithakong to the colony to work as servants and he did incorporate women from this battle into his own household. Many private references to the battle suggest that the military stakes were real – many years later, to take just one example, Moffat would describe in a private letter to his wife meeting a Ndebele warrior who had also participated in the battle and sharing war memories. Furthermore, Philip and his allies privately berated Moffat for ingratitude to Waterboer, as I suggest. I find it unbelievable that, had Moffat been a slave-trader, no one would have turned him in to the society, given that this would have been an instant cause for dismissal, and given that many, including many Griqua, hated him passionately and needed him out of the way. Moffat and Waterboer's Griqua are also unlikely allies. This is not to rule out slave-raiding by some Griqua and even by some rogue missionaries – but

not, I suspect, on the massively organized and disruptive scale suggested by Cobbing, and certainly not by Moffat. Cobbing, "The Mfecane as Alibi: Thoughts on Dithakong and Mbolompo," 487–519. Guy Hartley is critical of Cobbing's interpretation of Dithakong: Hartley, "The Battle of Dithakong and 'Mfecane' Theory." I agree broadly with the criticisms made by Timothy Keegan of Cobbing's view of Dithakong and of Moffat: Keegan, *Colonial South Africa*, 337–8, n.27.

23 Ross, *Adam Kok's Griquas*, 44–5; Legassick, "The Northern Frontier to c. 1840," especially 402–3 and 419, n.206; Legassick, "The Griqua, the Sotho Tswana and the Missionaries"; Elbourne and Ross, "Combatting Spiritual and Social Bondage," 39–40.

24 J. Read Sr to James Kitchingman, Bethelsdorp, 22 January 1844, *Kitchingman Papers*, 242.

25 As argued in LMS-SA 20/3/A: John Brownlee, F.G. Kayser, Merrington, John Locke, Richard Birt, Henry Calderwood, and Joseph Gill to LMS directors, Umxelo, 10 October 1844.

26 On John Philip's involvement in the politics of Transorangia, Ross, *John Philip*, 159–184; Keegan, *Colonial South Africa*, 180–4, 248–51.

27 In making this broad point, Legassick cites the words of Nicholas Kruger to LMS missionary Roger Edwards in 1838, as he threatened Edwards with expulsion from Kuruman: "Look at the American nation, what a powerful (or able) people they are and if our first teachers had done their duty, we should have been as advanced in civilization and knowledge as they, for our nation began to receive the gospel at the very same time the colonization of America commenced ... but now we have able teachers who teach us and we also are now able to teach the inhabitants of the whole country including the Bechuana tribes." When Edwards's wife said that Kuruman was not Griqua territory, Kruger added, "It is my country. My mother was a Mochuana. I shall go and put them to rights. They are all in ignorance. They must hear or obey me." Legassick, "Northern Frontier," 403, citing LMS-SA, Edwards, "Notes of Events at Daniels Kuil," 10 March 1838. On Griqua uses of Christianity as an instrument of regional hegemony, Keegan, *Colonial South Africa*, 170–84, and sources cited in n.23 above.

28 Saunders, "James Read: Towards a Reassessment," 19–25.

29 Many of the pertinent documents are reproduced in Schapera (ed.), *Apprenticeship at Kuruman*. On Moffat's desire to see Read dismissed and efforts to ensure that, see also LMS-SA 8/2/D: R. Moffat to LMS, Griqua Town, 19 September 1820. On Moffat as an authoritarian: Schoeman, *A Thorn Bush Grows in the Path*, for Moffat's treatment of Ann Hamilton; Comaroff and Comaroff, *Of Revelation and Revolution*, vol. 1. On Read and the Tswana mission: du Bruyn, "James Read en die Tlhaping, 1816–1820," 23–38. Stuart, "Of Savages and Heroes,"

disagrees with me on the role of Khoekhoe evangelists at Moffat's station of Kuruman.

30 UCT, BC612 B1, Kitchingman family letters: James Kitchingman to his children, Bethelsdorp, 21 March 1843.

31 Moffat, *Missionary Labours and Scenes in Southern Africa*.

32 Ross, *John Philip (1775–1851)*, 218–19.

33 LMS-SA 16/1/C: J. Philip to William Ellis, Cape Town, 29 July 1838.

34 In 1818 Moffat observed that Bartlett "is happy as the day is long, has a good wife and a sweet child, [and] has his house as clean as any Englishman or woman. He is in this respect an *example*." Robert Moffat to James Kitchingman, Pella, 13 January 1818, Le Cordeur and Saunders, eds., *Kitchingman Papers*, 53.

35 LMS-SA, 16/1/B: J. Philip to W. Ellis, 4 April 1838.

36 J.A. Kolbe to J. Bartlett, n.d., and R. Hamilton, R. Moffat, and R. Edwards to J. Bartlett, Kuruman, 9 January 1834, both enclosed in LMS-SA 16/1/B: J. Philip to W. Ellis, Cape Town, 4 April 1838.

37 Of compensation for his house and 365 rixdollars a year. LMS-SA 16/1/: J. Philip to W. Ellis, Cape Town, 4 April 1838.

38 Written deposition of John Bartlett, in evidence collected by Donald Moodie, Campbell's Dorp, enclosed in LMS-SA 16/1/B: J. Philip to LMS, Cape Town, 4 April, 1838.

39 Testimony of Hendrick Nero and written deposition of John Bartlett before Donald Moodie, Campbell's Dorp, 1834; enclosed in LMS-SA 16/1/B: J.Philip to W. Ellis, Cape Town, 4 April 1838.

40 Testimony of Hannah Goodman before Donald Moodie, Campbell's Dorp, 27 May 1834, enclosed in LMS-SA 16/1/A: J. Philip to W. Ellis, Cape Town, 4 April 1838.

41 Cornelis Kok to Donald Moodie, Campbell, 30 May 1836, enclosed in LMS-SA 16/1/B: J. Philip to W. Ellis, Cape Town, 4 April 1838.

42 LMS-SA 16/1/A: Wright to W. Ellis, Griqua Town, 5 March 1838.

43 LMS-SA 16/1/A: Peter Wright to Ellis, Griqua Town, 5 March 1838.

44 They would send a letter reiterating their case against Philip in the same package as their documents against the Reads. LMS-SA 20/2/D: H. Calderwood and Richard Birt to LMS directors, Umxelo, 26 September 1844. This letter was signed on behalf of Brownlee, Kayser, Locke, Calderwood, Merrington, Gill, and Birt, who had attended the meeting which gave rise to these sentiments.

45 Ross, *John Philip (1775–1851)*, 178.

46 I have a lengthier discussion of the Block Drift affair in de Gruchy, ed., *Sent from London*, on which part of this chapter is based.

47 LMS-SA 22/2/D: Henry Calderwood to LMS, King William's Town, 23 December 1846, announces his appointment.

48 LMS-SA 20/3/A, James Read Jr to John Philip, 13 May 1844, enclosed in J. Philip to Tidman, Cape Town, 10 October 1844, There is a valuable discussion of the affair in Hummel, *Rev. F.G. Kayser*, xx–xxiv; Hummel also reproduces a number of key LMS documents, 164–76.

49 Williams, *When Races Meet*, 137.

50 Brown, "Ten Years Conflict," 136–7.

51 I describe the details of this dispute in more detail in Elbourne, "Who Owns the Gospel?"

52 LMS-SA 20/3/A, Charles Lennox Stretch [presumably to John Philip], "Caffraria," 24 June 1844, enclosed in Philip to A. Tidman, 10 October 1844.

53 LMS-SA 20/3/A, J. Read Jr to J. Philip, 13 May 1844, enclosed in J. Philip to A. Tidman, Cape Town, 10 October 1844.

54 LMS-SA 20/3/A, J. Read Jr to J. Philip, 13 May 1844, and J. Read Sr to Rev. Struthers, Kat River, 22 February 1844, both enclosed in Philip to Tidman, Cape Town, 10 October 1844; J. Read Sr to James Kitchingman, Philipton, 1 July 1844, in le Cordeur and Saunders, eds., *Kitchingman Papers*, 249–51.

55 LMS-SA 20/3/A, J. Read Sr to Rev. Struthers, Kat River, 22 February 1844, in Philip to Tidman, Cape Town, 10 October 1844.

56 Read Sr mentioned his letter to Cumming of the GAMS; Cumming then told his fellow GAMS missionary Thomas Campbell, who in turn, while at dinner at Frederick Gottleib Kayser's house, informed the aged LMS missionary to the Xhosa that someone at the Block Drift meeting, whom Campbell refused to name, was opposed to their proceedings and had written to Glasgow. The "old German Gentleman," in the words of Xhosa diplomatic agent and Calderwood foe Charles Lennox Stretch, "asserted there was 'Treason' and putting his own construction on the case wrote to *his* friends from whom have emanated documents which for their own sake I wish had never existed."Charles Lennox Stretch [presumably to John Philip], "Caffraria," 24 June 1844, enclosed in LMS-SA 20/3/A, J. Philip to A. Tidman, 10 October 1844. Stretch was also John Pringle's brother-in-law.

57 LMS-SA 20/3/A, "Duplicate – Copy of a document signed by the Missionaries" [dated, on internal evidence, 1 May 1844], enclosed in J. Philip to A. Tidman, 10 October 1844. The other missionaries who signed were John Brownlee, F.G. Kayser, John Ross, Alexander McDiarmid, William Govan, W.R. Thomson, John Bennie, James Laing, and John Weir.

58 LMS-SA, 20/3/A, Robert Niven to C.L. Stretch, n.d., enclosed in Philip to Tidman, 10 October 1844.

59 J. Read Sr to James Kitchingman, Philipton, 1 July 1844, in le Cordeur and Saunders, eds., *Kitchingman Papers*, 249.

60 For example, LMS-SA 20/3/A, John Cumming to J. Read Sr, 11 May 1844, and Thomas Campbell to J. Read Sr, 30 May 1844, both enclosed in J. Philip to A. Tidman, 10 October 1844.

61 LMS-SA 21/1/C, William Govan to John Cumming, Lovedale, 10 December 1844, enclosed in J. Philip to LMS directors, 10 February 1845.

62 LMS-SA 21/1/C, John Cumming to William Govan, Iggibigha, 10 December 1844, enclosed in J. Philip to LMS directors, 10 February 1845.

63 Another GMS missionary, William Chalmers, later swore in the presence of all the missionaries who had signed the letter which the Reads would not sign that Cumming had told Chalmers that when he (Cumming) had visited Philipton after the Block Drift meeting, Read Sr asked for Struthers's address because he was "*much dissatisfied* with what was done at said meeting and he meant to write his own explanation or account." "Statement of the Messrs Read relative to the case pending between themselves and the Caffre land Brethren," enclosed in LMS-SA 21/2/A, J. Philip to LMS, 28 February 1845.

64 LMS-SA 20/2/D, "Notes on Revd J. Read's letter to his of Mr. Calderwood's people and the Reads' explanations," enclosed in H. Calderwood and R. Brit to LMS board, 26 September 1844.

65 LMS-SA 20/2/D, James Read Jr to Arie van Rooyen and Valentyn Jacobs, "Mr. Read's letter," enclosed in H. Calderwood and R. Brit to LMS board, 26 September 1844. The letter was written in Dutch and sent to the UK with an English translation. "Ik geef geen dubbeltjie" was Read's original comment on Calderwood's opinion.

66 LMS-SA 22/2/D: H. Calderwood to W. Ellis, King Williams Town, 23 Decmber 1846.

67 LMS-SA 21/1/C, William Govan to John Cumming, Lovedale, 14 December 1844, enclosed in J. Philip to LMS directors, 10 February 1845.

68 LMS-SA 20/2/D, James Read Sr and others to LMS directors, Uitenhage, 24 September 1844, enclosed in W. Elliot to A. Tidman and J.J. Freeman.

69 LMS-SA 20/3/A, Brownlee, Kayser, Merrington, Locke, Birt, Calderwood, and Gill to LMS, Umxelo, 10 October 1844.

70 J. Read Sr to J. Kitchingman, Philipton, 22 January 1844, in Le Cordeur and Saunders, ed., *Kitchingham Papers*, 242–3.

71 The final dispute arose when the British government supported the Court of Sessions' rejection through a series of court cases of the 1834 Veto Act (in itself a political compromise) which had given male heads of families the right to veto the choice of minister imposed upon a congregation by the patronage of the member of the landed gentry, or the burgh, in whose gift the parish was. Brown, "Ten Years' Conflict," 1–27.

72 James Read Sr to James Kitchingman, Philipton, 22 January 1844, in le Cordeur and Saunders, eds., *Kitchingman Papers*, 243.

73 Ultimately bequeathing, so Andrew Ross argues, a more conservative version of evangelicalism to the Dutch Reformed Church and to some at least of the Scottish mission stations than that of Wilberforce, Philip, and Read. Ross, "The Dutch Reformed Church of South Africa: A Product of the Disruption?"

74 Smith, *Passive Obedience and Prophetic Protest*, 52–3.

75 Smith, *Passive Obedience and Prophetic Protest*, 93–186.

76 Read Jr, *Kat River Settlement in 1851*; Ross, *Adam Kok's Griquas*; Ross, *John Philip*, 159–84.

77 LMS-SA 20/2/D, "Notes on Revd J. Read's letter to his to Mr. Calderwood's people and the Reads' explanations ...," enclosed in H. Calderwood and R. Brit to LMS directors, 26 September 1844.

78 LMS-SA 20/2/D, J. Read Jr to H. Calderwood, Philipton, 17 September 1844, enclosed in H.Calderwood and R. Birt to LMS directors, 26 September 1844.

79 LMS-SA 20/3/A, Kayser, Merrington, Locke, Birt, Calderwood, and Gill, to LMS, 10 October 1844.

80 LMS-SA 20/2/D, Locke to LMS directors, Grahamstown, 25 September 1844.

81 LMS-SA 20/2/D, Calderwood and Birt to LMS directors, Umxelo, 26 September 1844.

82 LMS-SA 20/3/A, J. Read senior to A. Tidman, Philipton, 2 October 1844.

83 McKay, *Reminiscences of the Last Kafir War*, 206. McKay also considered that the slovenly wives of sergeants in the British army were not ladies either, nor indeed were the majority of white colonial wives; the instinctive laughter of the troops at the idea of Khoekhoe ladies is nonetheless revealing.

84 Ross, "The Etiquette of Race," 111–21. Pos continued, "Whoever does not want to be considered impolite must always have his hand ready to extend it to every white whom he meets": cited in Ross, 119.

85 "Let me beseech of you, Mr. Calderwood, just to reach back to an incident in your history at Blinkwater which happened a few years ago on Sunday morning, and think seriously of the injurious [influence?] which that single circumstance was calculated to exert over the minds of the people – Perhaps you are not aware that we (who are now charged with having attempted more than once to injure you in the dark) exerted ourselves in your behalf, and did all we could to counteract that influence." LMS-SA 20/2/D, James Read Jr to H. Calderwood, Philipton, 17 September 1844, enclosed in H. Calderwood and R. Birt to LMS directors, Umxelo, 26 September 1844.

86 This, of course, implied that there was a "native character" and that the Reads were familiar with it. "Statement of the Messrs. Read relative to

446 Notes to pages 335–41

the case pending between themselves and the Caffre land Brethren," enclosed in LMS-SA 21/2/A, J. Philip to LMS directors, 28 February 1845.

87 Hodgson, "A Battle for Sacred Power," 68–88; Williams, *When Races Meet*; Chidester, *Religions of South Africa*; Peires, *Dead Will Arise*.

88 Erlank, "Re-examining initial encounters."

89 Ross, *John Philip*, 185–6.

90 LMS-SA 21/2, J. Philip to A. Tidman, 11 March 1845; cited in Ross, *John Philip*, 185.

91 Calderwood, *Caffres and Caffre Missions*, 65–75.

92 Hummel, *Rev. F.G. Kayser*, xix–xx.

93 Calderwood, *Caffres and Caffre Missions*, 17–30.

94 Freeman, *A Tour in South Africa*, 49.

95 Calderwood, *Caffres and Caffre Missions*, 114–16.

96 LMS-SA 19/2/D: H. Helm to Tidman, Caledon Institution, 10 November 1843.

97 On Helm's opposition to district committees, James Read Sr to James Kitchingman, Philipton, 15 April 1844, in Le Cordeur and Saunders, eds., *Kitchingman Papers*, 248.

98 James Read Sr to James Kitchingman, Philipton, 25 March 1844, in le Cordeur and Saunders, eds., *Kitchingman Papers*, 245.

99 James Read Sr to James Kitchingman, Philipton, 11 March 1839, in le Cordeur and Saunders, eds., *Kitchingman Papers*, 206. Just before referring to this figure, Read commented "We have our own plans and we execute them. If the Doctor [Philip] will give us any assistance we take it, otherwise we get on without it as well as we can, but we cannot be waiting the decisions of Church Square. I would rather, as Matthew Wilks said, sell my shirt than the work should stand still, but my visit to England has assisted."

100 James Read senior to James Kitchingman, Philipton, 25 March 1844, in le Cordeur and Saunders, eds., *Kitchingman Papers*, 245.

101 "Account of the Labours &c of Native Teachers supported by private Individuals and churches in England in connection with Philipton Congregation Kat River." LMS-SA 20/1/C, James Read senior, Philipton 17 April 1844.

102 Ibid.

103 Ibid.

104 Saunders, "Madolo: a Bushman life," *African Studies*, 145–54; le Cordeur and Saunders, eds., *Kitchingman Papers*, 189–91. The "Bushman station," later Freemanton, saw disastrous military conflict between Mfengu, Mpondomise, San, and Thembu groups but survived to *c.* 1853.

105 Landau, *Realm of the Word*, xxviii.

106 All quotations from LMS-SA 19/2/A, J. Read to LMS directors, Philipton, 3 June 1843.

107 Ibid.

108 Read Jr, *Kat River Settlement*, 47.

109 Freeman, *A Tour*, 163–6. The deacons were Klaas and Hans Noeka, Christian van Staade, H. Jonker, Base Barze, and Hans Zeilvoort.

CHAPTER TEN

1 LMS-SA: F.G. Kayser to Freeman, Bethelsdorp, 2 April 1851.

2 Among key works on nineteenth-century warfare between the Xhosa and the Cape Colony, Crais, *White Supremacy and Black Resistance*, especially 173–88; Peires, *The Dead Will Arise*, 1–44; Mostert, *Frontiers*; Peires, *House of Phalo*; Stapleton, *Maqoma: Xhosa Resistance*; Keegan, *Colonial South Africa*.

3 See the sources cited in n.2 above as well as Ross, "The Kat River Settlement in the Frontier Wars."

4 Port Elizabeth Telegraph, 23 January 1851: clipping in LMS-SA 26/1/A.

5 Kirk, "Kat River Settlement," 424.

6 Ross, "The Kat River Settlement in the Frontier Wars," 40.

7 Crais, *White Supremacy and Black Resistance*, 162; Peires, *House of Phalo*, 16; Ross, "The Kat River Settlement in the Frontier Wars," 29.

8 Crais, *White Supremacy*, 162; Stockenstrom, *Light and Shade*, 14.

9 Stockenstrom, *Light and Shade*, 22.

10 LMS-SA: Read Sr to Freeman, Philipton, Kat River, 13 April 1851.

11 Crais, *White Supremacy*, 182–3. On the selection of Uithaalder, CA AG2798, evidence of Petersi, 18 September 1852.

12 CA, 1/FBF/1/1/1/2: Declaration of Jan Windvogel, Fort Beaufort, 28 July 1851. CA, AG2798: evidence of John Martin and Jacob Peters, "preliminary examination in case of the Queen against Africa April alias Koetgang and Christian Peters charged with treason & rebellion."

13 Ross, "The Kat River Settlement in the Frontier Wars."

14 Crais, *White Supremacy and Black Resistance*, 147–72; Kirk, "Cape economy, 226–46; Kirk, "Progress and Decline"; Robert Ross "Kat River Rebellion," 91–105.

15 Report of Cobus Fourie, Fort Armstrong, 15 January 1851, in Read, *Kat River Settlement*, 30, and Stockenstrom, *Light and Shade*, 86.

16 Crais, *White Supremacy*, 142–3; Kirk, "Cape Economy," 241.

17 CA AG758: Preliminary Examinations, 2, The Queen against Africa April, alias Koetgang and Christian Peters, evidence of John Martin.

18 Peires, "Piet Draghoender," 6–15. On forced removals more broadly, see Platzky and Walker, *The Surplus People*.

19 Ibid., 9.

20 Ibid., 11.
21 Kirk, "Progress and Decline," 418–24; Kirk, "Cape Economy," 226–43.
22 Crais, *White Supremacy, Black Resistance*, 165, citing Marais, *The Cape Coloured People*, 233.
23 Bowker to "C__," Camp on the lower Koonap, 19 August 1846, in Bowker, *Speeches, Letters and Selections*, 243.
24 Bowker to "C__," Camp on the Koonap, 5 September 1846, in Bowker, *Speeches, Letters and Selections*, 249.
25 On fear in the Western Cape, Bradlow, "The 'Great Fear' at the Cape of Good Hope."
26 "Departure of His Excellency the Governor," Grahamstown Journal, 19 October 1850. James Read Jr would later cite this passage as a particularly egregious example of the inflammatory comments which infuriated Kat River inhabitants; he also objected to the use of "black" as a "generic" term: James Read Jr, *Kat River Settlement*, 72.
27 Port Elizabeth Mercury, 21 December 1850.
28 Telegraph, 1 January 1851.
29 Read, *Kat River Settlement*, 102.
30 Ibid., 48
31 "Rev. H. Renton's Interview with Sandili," *The Colonial Intelligencer; or, Aborigines' Friend*, nos. 3 and 4, January–July 1852, 86–7.
32 Mostert, *Frontiers*, 1070.
33 Ibid., 979.
34 PRO, WO135 (2), Harry Smith to Lord FitzRoy Somerset, King William's Town, 13 February 1851.
35 PRO, WO135 (2), Smith to A. Porter, King William's Town, 17 February 1851.
36 PRO, WO135 (2), Smith to W. Miller, King William's Town, 22 February 1851.
37 PRO, WO135 (2), Smith to Montagu, King William's Town, 1 March 1851.
38 PRO, WO135 (2): Smith to Pine, King William's Town, 9 April 1851.
39 BPP, 1852–53 [1635], vol. 66, 73: Sir H. Smith to Earl Grey, King William's Town, 7 April 1852.
40 Read, *Kat River Settlement*, 47.
41 Testimony of Johannes Fortuin, cited in Green, *Kat River Settlement*, 25–31; Mostert, *Frontiers*, 1152.
42 CA LG 592: "Hottentots in Kreli's country."
43 BPP1635, 143 (281): Translation of a letter sent by the rebel leader Speelman Kiewit to one of the veldcornets of Kat River, 10 January 1851.
44 BPP1428, vol. 33 (1852), 152: W. Uithaalder to A. Kok and H. Hendriks.
45 Read, *Kat River Settlement*, 41.
46 Ibid., 47.
47 *Trial of Andries Botha*, 126.

449 Notes to pages 361–70

48 BPP1428, vol. 33 (1852), 51: Andries Lings (Links?) to Keivit Pequin, Blauw Kraatz, 15 April 1851.

49 Read, *Kat River Settlement*, 80.

50 Jan Fourie simply answered "yes" to the question "Amongst the Hottentots at Fort Armstrong, was there a great hatred to the Fingoes?" *Trial of Andries Botha*, 95.

51 Frederick Jordaan described this incident which took place at Fort Armstrong; the Khoekhoe men had not joined the rebellion, although at least some later would, but they threatened the Mfengu men and said that they were the people who shot their friends at the Blinkwater and at Fort Beaufort. *Trial of Andries Botha*, 105–9.

52 Read, *Kat River Settlement*, 85.

53 BPP1428, vol. 33 (1852), 43–55: Sir H. Smith to Earl Grey, King William's Town, 14 June 1851, and enclosures: "Deposition of Hendrik Jack"; Field-Cornet Gray to Mr. Hudson, Southwell, 31 May 1851; Major-General Somerset to Sir H. Smith, Lombard's Post, Kasouga River, 8 June 1851; "Statement of Moses Jacobs," Lombard's Post, 6 June 1851.

54 LMS-SA 27/4/C: Read Jr, notebook, 1852.

55 Ibid.

56 CA AG 2798: Testimony of Jacob Peters, preliminary examinations of Africa April, alias Koetgan, and Christopher Peters.

57 Read, *Kat River Settlement*, 64.

58 CA I/UIT 14/37: Kat River Commission of Inquiry, 1858, notebook 2, cases nos. 121–3 (Cobus, Jan and Baruis Noeka), 43–6.

59 Read, *Kat River Settlement*, 64.

60 Ibid.

61 Ibid., 35.

62 BPP1428, vol. 33 (1852), 51: Willem Uithaalder to Adam Kok and H. Hendriks, Amatola, 11 June 1851.

63 Mackay, *Reminiscences of the Last Kafir War*; Mostert, *Frontiers*, 1120. Unfortunately, Mostert does not provide a reference for "Awake my soul."

64 Testimony of Commandant Groepe, *Trial of Andries Botha*, 138.

65 CA I/UIT 14/37: Kat River Commission of Inquiry, 1858, notebook 1, 70–1.

66 LMS-SA, 26/1/D: C. Stretch, Glen Avon, May 24, 1851.

67 CA LG 590: L.H. Meurant to Southey, Eland's Post, 6 March 1856, in "Formation of the Kat River Settlement in 1828, 1856 Memorandum," 126.

68 Personal communication, Archie Crail.

69 LMS-SA, 27/4/C: James Read Jr, 1852, *Extract from a Notebook*.

70 Ibid.

71 "The new Caffre war," *The Examiner*, 15 March 1851.

72 "The Kaffirs," *The Nation*, 7 February 1852, 361; "How the Kaffirs were stirred up and why the Kaffirs can't be put down," *The Nation*, 14 August 1852, 793.

73 Address to Sir John Somerset Parkington, principal secretary of state for the Colonial Department, London 24 April 1852, reproduced in the *Colonial Intelligencer; or, Aborigines' Friend*, nos. 1 and 2, April and May 1852, 54.

74 Grahamstown Journal, 29 May 1852.

75 *Trial of Andries Botha*; Marais, *Cape Coloured*, 243–4.

76 A process for which Mahmood Mamdani argues in his *Citizen and Subject*.

77 CA LG 590, "Hottentots in Kreli's Country."

78 CA 1/UIT 14/37: Kat River Commission of Inquiry, 1858, notebook 2, "Special Report, Monday 17 May 1850."

79 SAL MSB858, box 2 (B): Mrs. T.G. Jones, 19 April 1912.

Bibliography

ABBREVIATIONS

Bodl.   Bodleian Library, Oxford University
BPP   British Parliamentary Papers
CA   Cape Archives, Cape Town
CMS   Church Missionary Society archives, University of
        Birmingham
HK   Hendrik Kramer Institute, Leiden
LPL   Lambeth Palace Library, London
LMS   London Missionary Society papers, Council for World
        Mission Archives, School of Oriental and African studies,
        London
            LMS-CP: Candidates' Papers
            LMS-HO: Home Office
            LMS-SA: South African Correspondence
ML   Mitchell Library, Sydney
NLS   National Library of Scotland, Edinburgh
PRO   Public Record Office, London
RCC   G.M. Theal (ed.), *Records of the Cape Colony*
RHO   Rhodes House Library, Oxford University
SAL   South African Library, Cape Town

PRIMARY SOURCES

Archival Records

BODLEIAN LIBRARY, OXFORD
MSS Wilberforce

CAPE ARCHIVES, CAPE TOWN, SOUTH AFRICA
1480
A50: W. R. Morrison Collection
A559: Bethelsdorp Correspondence
A768: Return of the Institution of Bethelsdorp
A1415: Philip Family Papers
AG: Attorney General Papers
    758
    2798: Preliminary Investigations
1/AY 9/23: Albany
3/AY 1/1/1/3: Albany 1/BDP 1/1/2/1/1/1: Burgersdorp
1/CDC/1/6: Craddock
CO: Colonial Office Correspondence (British administration): Selected Files
CSC 1/2/1/49–1/2/1/51: Cape Supreme Court, "Records and Proceedings"
EC3: Executive Council
1/FBF 6/1/3/1/1: Fort Beaufort
1/FBF 1/1/1/2: Fort Beaufort
GH: Government House
    20/23
    28/64
LG: Lieutenant Governor Papers
    151
    590: "Formation of the Kat River Settlement"
    592: "Hottentots in Kreli's Country"
SSE 8/89: Somerset East
    1/2: "Records and Proceedings in Criminal Cases, 1850–8"
UIT/14/37: Kat River Commission of Inquiry, 1858

DR WILLIAMS' LIBRARY, LONDON
New College MSS 41

HENDRIK KRAEMER INSTITUUT, OEGSTGEEST, NETHERLANDS
J.T. van der Kemp: *Brieven*
J.T. van der Kemp: *Dag Verhaal*

LAMBETH PALACE LIBRARY, LONDON
Fulham Papers: Porteus Papers
John Newton Papers

MITCHELL LIBRARY, SYDNEY, AUSTRALIA
B1176: Thomas Haweis, "Autobiography."

NATIONAL LIBRARY OF SCOTLAND, EDINBURGH
John Campbell correspondence

PUBLIC RECORD OFFICE, LONDON
CO48 series (Colonial Office correspondence with South Africa): Selected
   files
CO414: Commission of Eastern Inquiry, Cape of Good Hope
WO135(2): War Office. Letterbook of Sir Harry Smith, 1851.

RHODES HOUSE LIBRARY, OXFORD
MSS Afr.t.7
Bourke Papers
MSS.Afr.s.1: Cape Colony letters
MSS.Afr.s.4
MSS.Brit.Emp.s.444
Thomas Fowell Buxton Papers

RHODES UNIVERSITY, GRAHAMSTOWN, SOUTH AFRICA
Foulger Correspondence
Glasgow Missionary Society Presbytery Minutes, 1824–1830

SCHOOL OF ORIENTAL AND AFRICAN STUDIES, LONDON
Council for World Mission Archives, London Missionary Society
   series:
Candidates' Papers, 1795–1837
Home Office, 1795–1837
Odds, Box 8: Vanderkemp papers
Philip papers
South African Correspondence, 1799–1858

SOUTH AFRICAN LIBRARY, CAPE TOWN
Journals of John Campbell
MSB594
MSB858

UNIVERSITY OF BIRMINGHAM
Church Missionary Society Archives
G/C1: Committee Minutes
G/CA3: Home Correspondence
Acc.54–55
Acc.81: Venn MSS

UNIVERSITY OF CAPE TOWN, JAEGGER LIBRARY, SOUTH AFRICA
BCZA: Philip-Ross correspondence
BC612: Kitchingman family papers

UNIVERSITY OF THE WITWATERSRAND, JOHANNESBURG,
SOUTH AFRICA
A65f: Diary of James Kitchingman, 1825–26
A85: Philip papers

Periodicals

Anti-Jacobin Review
Christian Observer
Cobbett's Annual Register
Colonial Intelligencer
Edinburgh Review
Evangelical Magazine
Examiner (London)
Frontier Times
Grahamstown *Journal*
Missionary Chronicle
Missionary Magazine
Missionary Register
The Nation (Dublin)
*Periodical Accounts Relating to the Missions of the Church of the United
    Brethren, Established among the Heathen*
Port Elizabeth *Mercury*
Port Elizabeth *Telegraph*
Punch
Quarterly Papers of the Church Missionary Society
Quarterly Register
Quarterly Reports of the Glasgow Missionary Society
South African Commercial Advertiser
Times (London)

Government Publications

Great Britain. *Report from the Select Committee on Aborigines (British Settlements) With the Minutes of Evidence, Appendix and Index: Imperial Blue Book*, 538 of 1836.

United Kingdom. Parliament. *Report of the Commissioners of Inquiry upon the Trade of the Cape of Good Hope, the Navigation of the Coast, and the Improvement of the Harbours of that Colony*. London: HMSO 1829 (Command Paper 300).

– *Reports of the Royal Commissions of Inquiry relating to the Condition of the Hottentots, Bushmen, Caffres, and Other Native Tribes of South Africa; the System of Policy Pursued towards Them by the Local Government and by the Colonists, Especially on the Frontiers, [and] the Progress among them of Christian Missions and of Civilization*. London: HMSO 1830 (Command Paper 1595).

– *Papers relative to the Condition and Treatment of the Native Inhabitants of Southern Africa, within the Colony of the Cape of Good Hope, or beyond the Frontiers of that Colony. Part I. Hottentots and Bosjesmen; Caffres; Griquas*. London: HMSO 1835 (Command Paper 50).

– *Further Papers relative to the Condition and Treatment of the Native Inhabitants of Southern Africa, within the Colony of the Cape of Good Hope, or beyond the Frontier of that Colony. Part II*. London: HMSO 1835 (Command Paper 252).

– *Papers in Explanation of the Measures Adopted by His Majesty's Government, for Giving Effect to the Act for the Abolition of Slavery throughout the British Colonies. Part II*. London: HMSO 1835 (Command Paper 278–II).

– *Papers relative to the Late Caffre War, and to the Death of Hintza*. London: HMSO 1836 (Command Paper 279).

– *Correspondence with the Governor of the Cape of Good Hope, relative to the State of the Kafir Tribes on the Eastern Frontier of the Colony*. London: HMSO 1848 (Command Papers 912, 969).

– *Correspondence with the Governor of the Cape of Good Hope relative to the State of the Kafir Tribes, and to the Recent Outbreak on the Eastern Frontier of the Colony*. London: HMSO 1851 (Command Papers 1334, 1352, 1380).

– *Report from the Select Committee on the Kafir Tribes, with Proceedings, Minutes of Evidence, Appendix and Index*. London: HMSO 1851 (Command Paper 635).

– *Correspondence with the Governor of the Cape of Good Hope relative to the State of the Kafir Tribes, and to the Recent Outbreak on the Eastern Frontier of the Colony*. London: HMSO 1852 (Command Paper 1428).

– *Ordinances Which Have Been Passed by the Legislative Council of the Cape of Good Hope since Its Recent Reconstruction.* London: HMSO 1852 (Command Paper 57).
– *Return of the White and Coloured Population of the Colony of the Cape of Good Hope, in the Several Districts of the Eastern and Western Divisions, and also of British Kaffraria, according to the Latest Returns Received at the Colonial Office.* London: HMSO 1852 (Command Paper 124).
– *Correspondence with the Governor of the Cape of Good Hope Relative to the State of the Kafir Tribes, and to the Recent Outbreak on the Eastern Frontier of the Colony.* London: HMSO 1853 (Command Paper 1635).

PUBLISHED SOURCES

Acherley, John ·Hawksey. *The Preface to a Little Pamphlet, Entitled The Bible Society and Its Branch, Called the Church Missionary Society, Against the Ancient Institution for the Promotion of Christian Knowledge.* Bath, 1818.
Adams, Percy Guy. *Travel Literature and the Evolution of the Novel.* Lexington: University Press of Kentucky 1983.
Akenson, Donald H. *God's Peoples: Covenant and Land in South Africa, Israel, and Ulster.* Montreal: McGill-Queens University Press 1992.
Alberti, Ludwig. *Account of the Tribal Life of the Xhosa in 1807. Translated by Dr. William Fehr from the Original Manuscript in German of the Kafirs of the South Coast of Africa.* Cape Town: A.A. Balkema 1968.
Anderson, Benedict. *Imagined Communities: Reflections on the Origin and Spread of Nationalism.* London: Verso 1983.
Anderson, Peter. "No-Man's Land: Landscaping Neutrality on the Cape Frontier." Paper given at African Research Seminar, Oxford University, 11 June 1991.
Andrew, Donna T. *Philanthropy and Police: London Charity in the Eighteenth Century.* Princeton, N.J.: Princeton University Press 1989.
Annan, Noel. "The Intellectual Aristocracy." In *Studies in Social History: A Tribute to G.M. Trevelyan,* edited by J.H. Plumb. London: Longmans, Green 1955.
Anon. *Remarks on the Protest of the Reverend Archdeacon Thomas, and the Defence of the Missionary Society; by the Rev. Daniel Wilson; by a Country Vicar.* Bath, 1818.
– *A Second Protest against the Church Missionary Society Addressed to Lord James O'Brien, Chairman of the Committee of the Bath Missionary Association.* Bath, 1818.
Anstey, Roger T. *The Atlantic Slave Trade and British Abolition, 1769–1810.* London: Macmillan 1975.
– and P.E.H. Hair, eds. *Liverpool: The African Slave Trade and Abolition.* Liverpool: Historical Society of Lancashire and Cheshire 1976.

Arblaster, Anthony. *The Rise and Decline of Western Liberalism*. Oxford, U.K.: B. Blackwell 1984.

Armstrong, James, and Nigel Worden. "The Slaves, 1652–1834." In *The Shaping of South African Society, 1652–1840*, edited by Richard Elphick and Hermann Giliomee. Middletown, Conn.: Wesleyan University Press 1988.

Association for Promoting the Discovery of the Interior Parts of Africa. *Records of the African Association, 1788–1831*. London: Nelson 1964.

Bailyn, Bernard, and Philip D. Morgan, eds. *Strangers within the Realm: Cultural Margins of the First British Empire*. Chapel Hill, N.C.: Institute of Early American History and Culture 1991.

Baker, Derek, ed. *Reformation and Reform: England and the Continent c. 1500–c. 1750*. London: Published for the Ecclesiastical Historical Society by B. Blackwell 1979.

Bank, Andrew. "Liberals and their Enemies: Racial Ideology at the Cape of Good Hope, 1820 to 1850." PHD thesis, Cambridge University 1995.

– and Gary Minkley. "Reading the Evidence: Implications of the Shift to a Heritage Paradigm in Khoisan Studies." *Kronos: Journal of Cape History/ Tydskrif vir Kaaplandse Geskiedenis* 24 (November 1997): 3–8.

Bannister, Saxe. *Humane Policy, or Justice to the Aborigines of New Settlements Essential to a Due Expenditure of British Money, and to the Best Interests of the Settlers, with Suggestions How to Civilise the Natives by an Improved Administration of Existing Means*. London: Dawsons 1968.

Barnard, Alan. *Hunters and Herders of Southern Africa: A Comparative Ethnography of the Khoisan Peoples*. Cambridge, U.K.: Cambridge University Press 1992.

– "Structure and Fluidity in Khoisan Religious Ideas." *Journal of Religion in Africa* 18, no. 3 (1988): 216–36.

Barnard, Anne. *The Cape Journals of Lady Anne Barnard, 1797–1798*. Cape Town: Van Riebeeck Society 1994.

– *The Letters of Lady Anne Barnard to Henry Dundas from the Cape and Elsewhere, 1793–1803*. Cape Town: A.A. Balkema 1973.

Barrow, John. *An Account of Travels into the Interior of Southern Africa in the Years 1797 and 1798*. London: Cadell and Davies 1801.

Basset, Josiah. *The Life of a Vagrant, or the Testimony of an Outcast*. London 1850.

Bayly, C.A. *Imperial Meridian: The British Empire and the World, 1780–1830*. London: Longman 1989.

Beattie, John. *Crime and the Courts, 1660–1815*. Princeton, N.J.: Princeton University Press 1985.

Bebbington, D.W. *Evangelicalism in Modern Britain: A History from the 1730s to the 1980s*. London: Unwin Hyman 1989.

Bellamy, Richard, ed. *Victorian Liberalism: Nineteenth-Century Political Thought and Practice.* London: Routledge 1990.

Bennett, G.V., and John Walsh, eds. *Essays in Modern English Church History.* London: Black 1966.

Bennett, Henry Grey. *A Letter to the Common Council and Livery of the City of London: on the Abuses Existing in Newgate: Showing the Necessity of an Immediate Reform in the Management of That Prison.* London, 1818.

Biko, Steve. "I Write What I Like (The Church as Seen by a Young Layman)." In *I Write What I Like: A Selection of His Writings*, edited with a Personal Memoir by Aelred Stubbs. London: Bowerdean Press 1978.

Black, Jeremy. "Confessional State or Elect Nation? Religion and Identity in Eighteenth-century England." In Tony Claydon and Ian McBride, eds. *Protestantism and National Identity: Britain and Ireland, c. 1650–c. 1850.* Cambridge: Cambridge University Press, 1998: 53–74.

Blackburn, Robin. *The Overthrow of Colonial Slavery, 1776–1848.* London: Verso 1988.

Bloch, Ruth. *Visionary Republic: Millenial Themes in American Thought, 1756–1800.* Cambridge, U.K.: Cambridge University Press, 1985.

Boëseken, Anna J. "The Meaning, Origin and Use of the Terms Khoikhoi, San and Khoisan." *Cabo* 1(1) (August 1972): 5–10; 2(2) (January 1974): 8–10.

Bogue, David, and James Bennett. *History of Dissenters, from the Revolution in 1688, to the Year 1808.* London, 1808–12.

Bowie, Fiona, Deborah Kirkwood, and Shirley Ardener, eds. *Women and Missions: Past and Present: Anthropological and Historical Perceptions.* Providence, R.I.; Oxford: Berg 1993.

Bowker, John, ed. *Speeches, Letters and Selections from the Important Papers, of the Late John Mitford Bowker, Some Years Resident and Diplomatic Agent with Certain Kafir and Fingo Tribes.* Grahamstown, S.A., Godlonton and Richards 1864.

Bradley, Ian. *The Call to Seriousness: The Evangelical Impact on the Victorians.* New York: Macmillan 1976.

Bradley, James E. *Religion, Revolution and English Radicalism: Nonconformity in Eighteenth- Century Politics and Society.* Cambridge: Cambridge University Press 1990.

Bradlow, Edna. "The 'Great Fear' at the Cape of Good Hope, 1851–52." *The International Journal of African Historical Studies* 22, no.3 (1989): 401–21.

Bredekamp, H.C. "Vehettge Tikkuie, alias Moeder Lena van Genadendal, 1739–1800." *Quarterly Bulletin of the South African Library* 41, no.4 (June 1987): 131–41.

Bredekamp, H.C., and H.E.F. Plüddemann, eds. *The Genadendal Diaries: Diaries of the Herrnhut Missionaries H. Marsveld, D. Schwinn and J.C. Kuhnel.* Bellville, S.A.: University of the Western Cape Institute for Historical Research 1992.

Bredekamp, H.C., and Robert Ross. *Missions and Christianity in South African History*. Johannesburg: University of the Witwatersrand Press 1995.

Brent, Richard. *Liberal Anglican Politics: Whiggery, Religion and Reform 1830–1841*. Oxford, U.K.: Clarendon Press 1987.

Brewer, John. *Party Ideology and Popular Politics at the Accession of George III*. Cambridge, U.K.: Cambridge University Press 1976.

Bridgman, F.B. *Report of the Proceedings of the First General Missionary Conference Held at Johannesburg*. Johannesburg, 1905.

Brown, Ford K. *Fathers of the Victorians; the Age of Wilberforce*. Cambridge, U.K.: Cambridge University Press 1961.

Brown, Stewart J. "The Ten Years Conflict and the Disruption of 1843." In *Scotland in the Age of the Disruption*, edited by Stewart J. Brown and Michael Fry. Edinburgh: Edinburgh University Press 1993.

Brown, Stewart J., and Michael Fry, eds. *Scotland in the Age of the Disruption*. Edinburgh: Edinburgh University Press 1993.

Burchell, William J. *Travels in the Interior of Southern Africa*. London: Longman, Hurst, Rees, Orme and Brown 1822–24.

Burder, George. *Village Sermons; or, Plain and Short Discourses on the Principal Doctrines of the Gospel Intended for the Use of Families, Sunday-Schools, or Companies Assembled for Religious Instruction in Country Villages*. London, 1798–1816.

Burder, Henry Foster. *Memoir of the Rev. George Burder*. London: Frederick Westley and A. H. Davis 1833.

Butler, Jon. *Awash in a Sea of Faith: Christianizing the American People*. Cambridge, Mass.; London: Harvard University Press 1990.

– "Enthusiasm Described and Decried: The Great Awakening as Interpretive Fiction." *Journal of American History* 69, no.2 (1982): 305–25.

Buxton, Thomas Fowell. *An Inquiry, Whether Crime and Misery Are Produced or Prevented, by Our Present System of Prison Discipline*. London: J. and A. Arch 1818.

Calderwood, Henry. *Caffres and Caffre Missions; with Preliminary Chapters on the Cape Colony as a Field for Emigration and Basis of Military Operation*. London: James Nisbet 1858.

Campbell, John. *Travels in South Africa*. London, 1815.

– *Travels in South Africa, Undertaken at the Request of the London Missionary Society; Being a Narrative of a Second Journey in the Interior of that Country*. London: F. Westley 1822.

Carey, Eustace. *Memoir of William Carey, D.D. Late Missionary to Bengal; Professor of Oriental Languages in the College of Fort William, Calcutta*. London: Jackson and Walford 1836.

Carey, William. *An Enquiry into the Obligation of Christians, to Use Means for the Conversion of the Heathens*. Leicester, 1792.

Carus, William. *Memoirs of the Life of the Rev. Charles Simeon, M.A.: with a*

Selection from His Writings and Correspondence. London: J. Hatchard 1847.

Cecil, Richard. *Memoirs of the Rev. John Newton, Late Rector of the United Parishes of St. Mary Woolnoth and St. Mary Woolchurch ... with General Remarks on His Life, Connexions and Character.* Edinburgh, 1836.

Cecil, Richard, ed. *The Select Works of the Rev. John Newton: to Which Are Prefixed Memoirs of His Life.* Edinburgh: P. Brown and T. Nelson 1830.

Charles, T. "The Yoke of Bondage Destroyed by Christ. A Sermon Preached before The Missionary Society. At Surry Chapel, Wednesday Morning, May 14, 1806." In *Four Sermons, Preached in London, at the Twelfth General Meeting of the Missionary Society, May 10, 11, 12 1806,* by the London Missionary Society. London: Printed for T. Williams by S. Hollingsworth 1806.

Charsley, S. "Dreams in African Churches." In *Dreaming, Religion and Society in Africa,* edited by M.C. Jedrej and Rosalind Shaw. Leiden; New York: E.J. Brill 1992.

Chidester, David. *Religions of South Africa.* London; New York: Routledge 1992.

– *Savage Systems: Colonialism and Comparative Religion in Southern Africa.* Charlottesville: University of Virginia Press 1996.

Chidester, David, Judy Tobler, and Darrel Wratten. *Christianity in South Africa: An Annotated Bibliography.* Westport, Conn.: Greenwood Press 1997.

Christophers, Brett. *Positioning the Missionary: John Booth Good and the Confluence of Cultures in Nineteenth-Century British Columbia.* Vancouver: University of British Columbia Press 1998.

Church Missionary Society. *The First Ten Years' Quarterly Papers of the Church Missionary Society; to Which is Prefixed a Brief View of the Society.* London, 1826.

Clark, J.C.D. *English Society, 1688–1832.* Cambridge, U.K.: Cambridge University Press 1985.

Claydon, Tony, and Ian McBride, eds. *Protestantism and National Identity: Britain and Ireland, c. 1650–c. 1850.* Cambridge, U.K.: Cambridge University Press 1998.

Claydon, Tony, and Ian McBride, "The Trials of the Chosen Peoples: Recent Interpretations of Protestantism and National Identity in Britain and Ireland." In Tony Claydon and Ian McBride, eds., *Protestantism and National Identity: Britain and Ireland, c. 1650–c. 1850.* Cambridge, U.K.: Cambridge University Press 1998: 3–29.

Cnattingius, Hans. *Bishops and Societies: A Study of Anglican Colonial and Missionary Expansion 1698–1850.* London: Society for the Propagation of Christian Knowledge 1952.

Cobbing, Julian. "The Mfecane as Alibi: Thoughts on Dithakong and Mbolompo." *Journal of African History* 29, no.3 (1988): 487–519.

Cochrane, J.S. *Servants of Power: The Role of English Speaking Churches in South Africa, 1903–1930*. Johannesburg: Raven Press 1987.

Cohen, Charles L. "The Post-Puritan Paradigm of Early American Religious History." *William and Mary Quarterly* 54, no.4 (October 1997): 695–722.

Collected Seminar Papers of the Societies of Southern Africa in the 19th and 20th Centuries. London: University of London, Institute of Commonwealth Studies 1976.

Colley, Linda. "Britishness and Otherness: An Argument." *Journal of British Studies* 31 (October 1992): 309–29.

– *Britons: Forging the Nation 1707–1837*. New Haven, Conn: Yale University Press 1992.

Colquhoun, Patrick. *Treatise on the Wealth, Power and Resources of the British Empire, in Every Quarter of the World, Including the East Indies: The Rise and Progress of the Funding System Explained*. London: Printed for J. Mawman 1815.

Comaroff, Jean. *Body of Power, Spirit of Resistance: The Culture and History of a South African People*. Chicago; London: University of Chicago Press 1985.

Comaroff, Jean, and John L. Comaroff. *Of Revelation and Revolution: Christianity, Colonialism, and Consciousness in South Africa*. Chicago; London: University of Chicago Press 1991.

– *Of Revelation and Revolution: The Dialectics of Modernity on a South African Frontier*. Chicago: University of Chicago Press 1997

– "Through the Looking Glass: Colonial Encounters of the First Kind." *Journal of Historical Sociology* 1, no.1 (1988): 6–32.

Comaroff, John L. "Images of Empire, Contests of Conscience: Models of Colonial Domination in South Africa." *American Ethnologist*. 16, no.4 (November 1989): 665–85.

Cook, James. *A Voyage to the Pacific Ocean Undertaken by Command of His Majesty for Making Discoveries in the Northern Hemisphere, Performed under the Direction of Captains Cook, Clerke, and Gore, in H.M. Ships "Resolution" and "Discovery" in the Years 1776–80*. London: Published by Order of the Lords Commissioners of the Admiralty, G. Nicol and T. Cadell 1784.

Crais, Clifton. *White Supremacy and Black Resistance in Pre-industrial South Africa: The Making of the Colonial Order in the Eastern Cape, 1770–1865*. Cambridge, U.K.: Cambridge University Press 1992.

Crantz, David. *The History of Greenland, Containing a Description of the Country and Its Inhabitants; and Particularly, a Relation of the Mission Carried on for above These Thirty Years by the Unitas Fratrum at the New Hernhuth and Lichtenfels in That Country*. London: Printed for the Brethren's Society for the Furtherance of the Gospel among the Heathen 1767.

- *A Letter to a Friend in Which Some Account is Given of the Brethren's Society for the Furtherance of the Gospel among the Heathen.* London, 1769.

Crawford, Michael J. "Origins of the Eighteenth Century Evangelical Revival: England and New England Compared." *Journal of British Studies* 26, no.4 (1987): 361–97.

- *Seasons of Grace: Colonial New England's Revival Tradition in Its British Context.* Oxford; New York: Oxford University Press 1991.

Crehan, Kate. "Ideology and Practice, A Missionary Case: The London Missionary Society and the Cape Frontier 1799–1850." In *Centre for African Studies, Collected Papers*, vol.4 (1979).

- "Khoi, Boer and Missionary: An Anthropological Study of the Role of the Missionaries on the Cape Frontier 1799–1850." MA thesis, University of Manchester 1978.

Cuming, G.J., ed. *The Mission of the Church and the Propagation of the Faith; Papers Read at the Seventh Summer Meeting and Eighth Winter Meeting of the Ecclesiastical History Society.* London: Cambridge University Press 1970.

Curley, R. "Private Dreams and Public Knowledge in a Camerounian Independent Church." In *Dreaming, Religion and Society in Africa*, edited by M.C. Jedrej and Rosalind Shaw. Leiden; New York: E.J. Brill 1992.

Currie, Marion. "The History of Theopolis Mission." MA thesis, Rhodes University, Grahamstown, S.A., 1986.

Currie, Robert, Alan Gilbert, and Lee Horsley. *Churches and Churchgoers: Patterns of Church Growth in the British Isles since 1700.* Oxford, U.K.: Clarendon Press 1977.

Curtin, Philip. *The Image of Africa: British Ideas and Action. 1780–1850.* Madison: University of Wisconsin Press 1964.

Cuthbertson, Greg. "The English-speaking Churches and Colonialism." In *Theology and Violence: The South-African Debate*, edited by Charles Villa-Vicencio. Johannesburg: Skotaville 1987.

Daniell, Samuel. *Sketches Representing the Native Tribes, Animals, and Scenery of Southern Africa, from Drawings Made by the Late Mr Samuel Daniell.* London: William Daniell 1820.

Dapper, Olfert. "Kaffrarie, of Land der Hottentots." In *The Early Cape Hottentots, Described in the Writings of Olfert Dapper (1688), Willem ten Rhyne (1686) and Johannes Gulielmus de Grevenbroek (1695)*, edited by Isaac Schapera. Westport, Conn.: Greenwood Press 1970.

Davenport, T.R.H. "The Consolidation of a New Society: The Cape Colony." In *The Oxford History of South Africa: South Africa to 1870*, edited by Monica Wilson and Leonard Thompson. Oxford, U.K.: Oxford University Press 1969.

Davies, Rupert, A. Raymond George, and Gordon Rupp, eds. *A History of the Methodist Church in Great Britain.* London, 1978.

Davis, David Brion. *The Problem of Slavery in the Age of Revolution, 1770–1823*. Ithaca, N.Y.: Cornell University Press 1975.

– *Slavery and Human Progress*. Oxford: Oxford University Press 1984.

Deacon, Janette, and Thomas A. Dowson, eds. *Voices from the Past: /Xam Bushmen and the Bleek and Lloyd Collection*. Johannesburg: Witwatersrand Press 1996.

Dedering, Tilman. *Hate the Old and Follow the New: Khoekhoe and Missionaries in Early Nineteenth-Century Namibia*. Stuttgart, Germany: Franz Steiner 1997.

De Gruchy, John, ed. *The London Missionary Society in Southern Africa: Historical Essays in Celebration of the Bicentenary of the LMS in Southern Africa 1799–1999*. Cape Town: David Philip 1999.

de Gruchy, Steve. "The Alleged Political Conservatism of Robert Moffat." In John de Gruchy, ed., *The London Missionary Society in Southern Africa: Historical Essays in Celebration of the Bicentenary of the LMS in Southern Africa 1799–1999*. Cape Town: David Philip 1999: 17–36.

De Jong, J.A. *As the Waters Cover the Sea: Millenial Expectations in the Rise of Anglo-American Missions, 1640–1810*. Kampen, Netherlands: Kok 1970.

De Mist, J.A. *The Memorandum of Commissary J.A. de Mist*. Cape Town: Van Riebeeck Society 1920.

Denbow, James R. "Prehistoric Herders and Foragers of the Kalahari: The Evidence for 1500 Years of Interaction." In *Past and Present in Hunter Gatherer Studies*, edited by Carmel Schrire. London: Orlando, Fla.: Academic Press 1984.

Desbarats, Catherine. "Essai sur quelques éléments de l'histoire amérindienne." *Revue de l'histoire de l'Amérique francaise*, 2000: 491–520.

Descartes, René. *Discours de la méthode*. Paris: Urin, 1966.

De Villiers, Marq. *White Tribe Dreaming: Apartheid's Bitter Roots as Witnessed by Eight Generations of an Afrikaner Family*. London: Viking, 1987.

Dickinson, H.T., ed. *Britain and the French Revolution 1789-1815*. Basingstoke, U.K.: Macmillan Education 1989.

Douglas, Mary. *Purity and Danger: An Analysis of the Concepts of Pollution and Taboo*. London: Routledge and Kegan Paul 1966.

Drescher, Seymour. "Capitalism and Abolition: Values and Forces in Britain, 1783–1814." In *Liverpool: The African Slave Trade and Abolition*, edited by Roger Anstey and P.E.H. Hair. Liverpool, U.K.: Historical Society of Lancashire and Cheshire 1976.

– *Capitalism and Antislavery: British Mobilization in Comparative Perspective*. London: Macmillan 1986.

DuBruyn, Johannes. "James Read en die Thlaping, 1816–1820." *Historia* 35, no.1 (1990): 23–38.

DuBruyn, Johannes and Nicholas Southey. "The Treatment of Christianity and Protestant Missionaries in South African Historiography." In *Missions and*

Christianity in South African History, edited by Henry Bredekamp and Robert Ross. Johannesburg: University of the Witwatersrand Press 1995: 26–47.

Duly, Leslie Clement. "A Revisit with the Cape's Hottentot Ordinance of 1828." In *Studies in Economics and Economic History; Essays in Honour of Professor H.M. Robertson*, edited by M. Kooy. London: Macmillan 1972.

Du Plessis, Johannes Christiaan. *A History of Christian Missions in South Africa*. Cape Town: C. Struik 1965.

Du Toit, André. "No Chosen People: The Myth of the Calvinist Origins of Afrikaner Nationalism and Racial Ideology." *American Historical Review* 88 (October 1983): 920–52.

Du Toit, André, and Hermann Giliomee, eds. *Afrikaner Political Thought: Analysis and Documents*. Berkeley: University of California Press 1983.

Edwards, Isobel. *The 1820 Settlers in South Africa: A Study in British Colonial Policy*. London; New York: Published for the Royal Society by Longmans, Green 1934.

Edwards, Jonathan. *An Account of the Life of the Late Reverend Mr. David Brainerd, Minister of the Gospel, Missionary to the Indians from the Honourable Society in Scotland, for the Propagation of Christian Knowledge, and Pastor of a Church of Christian Indians in New-Jersey: Who Died at Northampton in New-England, October 9th, 1747, in the 30th Year of His Age; Chiefly Taken from His Own Diary and Other Private Writings, Written for His Own Use*. Boston: D. Henchman 1749.

– *An Humble Attempt to Promote Explicit Agreement and Visible Union of God's People in Extraordinary Prayer for the Revival of Religion and the Advancement of Christ's Kingdom on Earth, Pursuant to Scripture Promises and Prophesies concerning the Last Time*. Worcester, Mass., 1808.

Elbourne, Elizabeth. "To Colonize the Mind: Evangelicalism in Britain and the Eastern Cape 1799–1837." DPHIL, Oxford University 1992.

– "Concerning Missionaries: The Case of Van der Kemp." *Journal of Southern African Studies* 17, no.1 (March 1991): 153–64.

– "Domesticity and Dispossession: British Ideologies of 'Home' and the Primitive at Work in the Early Nineteenth-Century Cape," in Wendy Woodward, Patricia Hayes, and Gary Minkley, eds., *Deep Histories: Gender and Colonialism in Southern Africa*. Amsterdam: Rodopi 2002.

– "Early Khoisan Uses of Mission Christianity." In *Missions and Christianity in South African History*, edited by H.C. Bredekamp and Robert Ross. Johannesburg: University of the Witwatersrand Press 1995.

– "The Foundation of the Church Missionary Society: The Anglican Missionary Impulse." In *The Church of England c. 1689–c. 1833: From Toleration to Tractarianism*, edited by John Walsh, Colin Haydon, and Stephen Taylor. Cambridge, U.K.: Cambridge University Press 1993.

— "Freedom at Issue: Vagrancy Legislation and the Meaning of Freedom in

Britain and the Cape Colony, 1799-1842." *Slavery and Abolition*, special issue on "Unfree Labour in the Development of the Atlantic World" 15, no.2 (August 1994): 114–50. Also published in *Unfree Labour in the Development of the Atlantic World*, edited by Nicholas Rogers and Paul E. Lovejoy. London: Frank Cass 1995.

- "A Question of Identity: Evangelical Culture and Khoisan Politics in the Early Nineteenth-Century Eastern Cape." Collected Seminar Papers, 44, University of London: Institute of Commonwealth Studies 1992.
- "Race, Warfare and Religion in Mid-Nineteenth Century Southern Africa: The Khoikhoi Rebellion against the Cape Colony and Its Uses, 1850–58." *Journal of African Cultural Studies* 13(1), 2000, 17–42.
- "Who Owns the Gospel? Conflict in the LMS in the 1840s." In *The London Missionary Society in Southern Africa: Historical Essays in Celebration of the Bicentenary of the LMS in Southern Africa 1799–1999*, edited by John de Gruchy. Cape Town: David Philip 1999.

Elbourne, Elizabeth, and Robert Ross. "Combatting Spiritual and Social Bondage: Early Missions in the Cape Colony." In *Christianity in South Africa: A Political, Social and Cultural History*, edited by Richard Elphick and Rodney Davenport. Berkeley; Los Angeles: University of California Press 1997.

Eldredge, Elizabeth. "Delagoa Bay and the Hinterland in the Early Nineteenth Century: Politics, Trade, Slaves and Slave Raiding." In *Slavery in South Africa: Captive Labour on the Dutch Frontier*, edited by Elizabeth Eldredge and Fred Morton. Boulder, Colo.: Westview Press; Pietermaritzburg, S.A.: University of Natal Press 1994.

- "Slave Raiding across the Frontier." In *Slavery in South Africa: Captive Labour on the Dutch Frontier*, edited by Elizabeth Eldredge and Fred Morton. Boulder, Colo.: Westview Press; Pietermaritzburg, S.A.: University of Natal Press 1994.

Eldredge, Elizabeth, and Fred Morton, eds. *Slavery in South Africa: Captive Labour on the Dutch Frontier*. Boulder, Colo.: Westview Press; Pietermaritzburg, S.A.: University of Natal Press 1994.

Elphick, Richard. "Africans and the Christian Campaign in Southern Africa." In *The Frontier in History: North America and South Africa Compared*, edited by Howard Lamar and Leonard Thompson. New Haven; London: Yale University Press 1981.

- "Conversion and Its Effects in Nineteenth-Century South Africa." Paper presented to Davis Center Seminar, Princeton University, 13 December 1991.
- *Khoikhoi and the Founding of White South Africa*. Johannesburg: Raven Press 1985.
- *Kraal and Castle: Khoekhoe and the Founding of White South Africa*. New Haven: Yale University Press 1977.
- "Writing Religion into History: The Case of South African Christianity." In

Missions and Christianity in South African History, edited by H.C. Bredekamp and Robert Ross. Johannesburg: University of Witwatersrand Press 1995: 11–26.

Elphick, Richard, and Hermann Giliomee, eds. "The Origins and Entrenchment of European Dominance at the Cape, 1652–c.1840." In *The Shaping of South African Society, 1652–1840*, edited by Richard Elphick and Hermann Giliomee. Middletown, Conn.: Wesleyan University Press 1988.

– *The Shaping of South African Society, 1652–1840*. Middletown, Conn.: Wesleyan University Press 1988.

Elphick, Richard, and Rodney Davenport, eds. *Christianity in South Africa: A Political, Social and Cultural History*. Berkeley; Los Angeles: University of California Press 1997.

Elphick, Richard, and V.C. Malherbe. "The Khoisan to 1828." *In The Shaping of South African Society, 1652–1840*, edited by Richard Elphick and Hermann Giliomee. Middletown, Conn.: Wesleyan University Press 1988.

E.M.C. [full name unknown], *A Short Sketch of the work carried on by the Ancient Protestant Episcopal Moravian Church (Dr. 'Unitas Fratrum' – 'United Brethren') in Northamptonshire*. London and Aylesbury, 1886.

England, Frank, and Torquil Paterson, eds. *Bounty in Bondage: The Anglican Church in Southern Africa*. Johannesburg: Raven Press 1989.

Enklaar, Ido H. *De Levensgeschiedenis van Johannes Theodorus van der Kemp, tot zijn aankomst aan de Kaap in 1799*. Wageningen, 1972.

– *Life and Work of Dr. J. Th. van der Kemp, 1747–1811: Missionary, Pioneer and Protagonist of Racial Equality in South Africa*. Cape Town and Rotterdam: A.A. Balkema 1988.

Erlank, Natasha. "Jane and John Philip: Partnership, Usefulness and Sexuality in the Service of God." In John de Gruchy, ed., *The London Missionary Society in Southern Africa: Historical Essays in Celebration of the Bicentenary of the LMS in Southern Africa 1799–1999*. Cape Town: David Philip 1999: 82–98.

– "Re-examining Initial Encounters between Christian missionaries and the Xhosa, 1820–1850: The Scottish case," *Kleio*, 31 (1999).

Erskine, John. *The Signs of the Times Considered*. Edinburgh, 1742.

Etherington, Norman. *Preachers, Peasants and Politics in Southeast Africa, 1835–1880: African Christian Communities in Natal, Pondoland and Zululand*. London: Royal Historical Society 1978.

– "Recent Trends in the Historiography of Christianity in Southern Africa." *Journal of Southern African Studies* 22, no.2 (June 1996): 201–19.

– "The Standard of Living Question in Nineteenth-Century Missions in KwaZulu-Natal." In John de Gruchy, ed, *The London Missionary Society in Southern Africa: Historical Essays in Celebration of the Bicentenary of the LMS in Southern Africa 1799–1999*. Cape Town: David Philip 1999: 156–65.

February, Vernon A. *Mind Your Colour: The 'Coloured' Stereotype in South African Literature*. London: Kegan Paul International 1981.

Field, Clive D. "The Social Structure of English Methodism: Eighteenth–Twentieth Centuries." *British Journal of Sociology* 28, no.2 (1977): 199–225.

Fisher, H.J. "Dreams and Conversion in Black Africa." In *Conversion to Islam*, edited by Nehemia Levtzion. New York: Holmes and Meier 1979.

Fortes, Meyer, and Sheila Patterson, eds. *Studies in African Social Anthropology*. London: Academic Press 1975.

Foucault, Michel. *Histoire de la folie à l'âge classique*. Paris: Gallimand 1961.

– *Surveiller et Punir: Naissance de la prison*. Paris: Gallimand 1975.

Freeman, J.J. *A Tour in South Africa: with Notices of Natal, Mauritius, Madagascar, Ceylon, Egypt, and Palestine*. London: J. Snow 1851.

Freund, W.M. "The Cape under the Transitional Governments, 1795–1814." In *The Shaping of South African Society, 1652–1840*, edited by Richard Elphick and Hermann Giliomee. Middletown, Conn: Wesleyan University Press 1988.

– "The Career of Johannes Theodorus van der Kemp and His Role in the History of South Africa." *Tijdschrift voor Geschiedenis* 86, no.3 (1973): 376–80.

– "Society and Government in Dutch South Africa: The Cape and the Batavians, 1803-1806." PHD thesis, Yale University 1972.

Fuller, Andrew. *The Calvinistic and Socinian Systems Examined and Compared, as to Their Moral Tendency; in a Series of Letters Addressed to the Friends of Vital and Practical Religion, Especially Those amongst Protestant Dissenters*. Market Harborough, 1793.

Funani, Lumka Sheila. *Circumcision Among the Ama-Xhosa – A Medical Investigation*. Braamfontein, South Africa: Skotaville Publishers 1990.

Galbraith, John S. *Reluctant Empire: British Policy on the South Africa Frontier 1834–1854*. Berkeley, Calif.: Berkeley University Press 1963.

Garrett, Clarke. *Spirit Possession and Popular Religion from the Camisards to the Shakers*. Baltimore, Md.; London: Johns Hopkins University Press 1987.

Gates, Henry Louis Jr, ed. *"Race," Writing and Difference*. Chicago: Chicago University Press 1986.

Gerstner, Jonathan. *The Thousand Generation Covenant: Dutch Reformed Covenant Theology and Group Identity in Colonial South Africa 1652–1814*. Leiden; New York: E.J. Brill 1991.

Gidney, William Thomas. *The History of the London Society for Promoting Christianity amongst the Jews from 1809 to 1908*. London: London Society for Promoting Christianity Amongst the Jews 1908.

Gilbert, Alan Dean. "Methodism, Dissent and Political Stability in Early Industrial England." *Journal of Religious History* 10, no.4 (1978–9): 381–99.

– *Religion and Society in Industrial England: Church, Chapel and Social Change, 1740–1914.* London: Longman 1976.

Giliomee, Hermann. "The Eastern Frontier, 1770–1812." In *The Shaping of South African Society, 1652–1840,* edited by Richard Elphick and Hermann Giliomee. Middletown, Conn.: Wesleyan University Press 1988.

– "Processes in the Development of the Southern African Frontier." In *The Frontier in History: North America and South Africa Compared,* edited by Howard Lamar and Leonard Thompson. New Haven, Conn.; London: Yale University Press.

Gilman, Sander L. "Black Bodies, White Bodies: Toward an Iconography of Female Sexuality in Late Nineteenth Century Art, Medicine and Literature." *Critical Inquiry* 12, no.1 (1985): 204–42.

– *Difference and Pathology: Stereotypes of Sexuality, Race and Madness.* Ithaca, N.Y.: Cornell University Press 1985.

Gilroy, Paul. *The Black Atlantic: Modernity and Double Consciousness.* Cambridge, Mass.: Harvard University Press 1993.

Glasgow Missionary Society. *Report of the Glasgow Missionary Society for 1822.* Glasgow, 1822.

Glinker, Roy Richard, and Christopher B. Steiner, eds. Perspectives on Africa: A Reader in Culture, History, and Representation. Cambridge, Mass.: Blackwell 1997.

Golby, J.M., and A.W. Purdue. *The Civilisation of the Crowd: Popular Culture in England, 1750–1900.* London: Batsford Academic and Educational 1984.

Goode, William. *A Memoir of the late Rev. William Goode, MA.* London: Seeley and Burnside 1828.

– *A Sermon Preached ... on Tuesday ... In Whitsun Week, May 19, Before the Society for Missions to Africa and the East.* London, 1812.

Gordon, R.J. "The Venal Hottentot Venus and the Great Chain of Being." *African Studies* 51, no.2 (1992): 185–201.

Greatheed, Samuel. *General Union Recommended to Real Christians in a Sermon Preached at Bedford, October 31, 1797. With an Introductory Account of an Union of Christians of Various Denominations, Which Was Then Instituted to Promote the Knowledge of the Gospel; Including a Plan for a Universal Union in the Genuine Church of Christ.* London, 1798.

Green, John. *The Kat River Settlement in 1851, Containing the Substance of Evidence, Given before the Commission for Investigating the Rebellion.* Graham's Town, 1852.

Grevenbroek, J.C. *An Elegant and Accurate Account of the African Race Living Round the Cape of Good Hope, Commonly Called Hottentots.* Cape Town, 1993

Grove, Richard. "Scottish Missionaries, Evangelical Discourses, and the Origins of Conservation Thinking in Southern Africa 1820–1900." *Journal of Southern African Studies* 15, no.2 (January 1989): 163–87.

Guelke, Leonard, and Robert Shell. "Landscape of Conquest: Frontier Water Alienation and Khoikhoi Strategies of Survival, 1652–1780." *Journal of Southern African Studies* 18, no.4 (1992): 803–24.

Guenther, Mathias. "Bushman Religion and the (Non)sense of Anthropological Theory of Religion." *Sociologicus* 29 (1979): 102–32.

Gunson, Neil. *Messengers of Grace: Evangelical Missionaries in the South Seas 1797–1860.* Melbourne: Oxford University Press 1978.

Guy, Jeff. *The Heretic: a Study of the Life of John William Colenso, 1814–1883.* Johannesburg: Raven Press; Pietermaritzburg, S.A.: University of Natal Press 1983.

Hahn, T. *Tsuni-//Goam, The Supreme Being of the Khoi-khoi.* London: Trubner 1881.

Halevy, Elie. *History of the English People in the Nineteenth Century: England in 1815.* London: Benn 1960.

Hall, David D. "On Common Ground: The Coherence of American Puritan Studies." *William and Mary Quarterly,* 44, no.2 (April 1987): 193–229.

Hall, Timothy. *Contested Boundaries: Itinerancy and the Reshaping of the Colonial American Religious World.* Durham, N.C.: Duke University Press 1994.

Hallett, Robin, ed. *Records of the African Association 1788–1831.* London; New York: Nelson 1964.

Hamilton, Carolyn. *The Mfecane Aftermath: Reconstructive Debates in Southern African History.* Johannesburg: University of Witwatersrand; Pietermaritzburg, S.A.: University of Natal Press 1995.

Harlow, Vincent. "The British Occupations 1795–1806." In *Cambridge History of the British Empire; South Africa, Rhodesia and the High Commission Territories.* Cambridge, U.K.: Cambridge University Press 1963.

Harries, Patrick. "Exclusion, Classification and Internal Colonialism: The Emergence of Ethnicity among the Tsonga-Speakers of South Africa." In The Creation of Tribalism in South Africa, edited by Leroy Vail. London: Currey 1989.

Harrison, J.F.C. *The Second Coming: Popular Millenarianism 1780–1850.* New Brunswick, N.J.: Rutgers University Press 1979.

Hartley, Guy. "The Battle of Dithakong and 'Mfecane' Theory." In *The Mfecane Aftermath: Reconstructive Debates in Southern African History,* edited by Caroline Hamilton. Johannesburg: University of Witwatersrand; Pietermaritzburg, S.A.: University of Natal 1995.

Haskell, Thomas. "Capitalism and the Origins of Humanitarian Sensibility: Some Analytic Considerations. part 1." *American Historical Review* 90, no.2 (1985): 339–61.

Haweis, Hugh Reginald. *Travel and Talk 1885–93–95: My Hundred Thousand Miles of Travel Through America, Canada, Australia, New Zealand,*

Tasmania, Ceylon, and the Paradises of the Pacific. London: Chatto and Windus 1896.

Haweis, Thomas. *History of the Church of Christ; from the Days of the Apostles, till the Famous Disputation between Luther and Miltitz, in 1520.* London, 1800.

Hawkesworth, John. *An Account of the Voyages Undertaken by the Order of his Present Majesty for Making Discoveries in the Southern Hemisphere.* London: W. Strahon and T. Cabell 1773.

Hay, Douglas. "Property, Authority and the Criminal Law." In *Albion's Fatal Tree: Crime and Society in Eighteenth-Century England*, by Douglas Hay and E.P. Thompson. London: Allen Lane 1975.

Hay, Douglas, and E.P. Thompson. *Albion's Fatal Tree: Crime and Society in Eighteenth-Century England.* London: Allan Lane 1975.

Hefner, Robert, ed. *Conversion to Christianity: Historical and Anthropological Perspectives on a Great Transformation.* Berkeley: University of California Press 1993.

Hellmuth, Eckhart, ed. *The Transformation of Political Culture: England and Germany in the Late Eighteenth Century.* Oxford: Oxford University Press for the German Historical Institute 1990

Helly, Dorothy. *Livingstone's Legacy: Horace Waller and Victorian Mythmaking.* Athens, Ohio: Ohio University Press 1987.

Hempton, David. *Methodism and Politics in British Society: 1750–1850.* London: Hutchinson 1984.

Hill, Christopher. *A Turbulent, Seditious and Factious People: John Bunyan and his Church.* Oxford, U.K.: Oxford University Press 1988.

Hilton, Boyd. *The Age of Atonement: The Influence of Evangelicalism on Social and Economic Thought, 1785–1865.* Oxford, U.K.: Clarendon Press 1988.

Hinchliff, Peter. "Voluntary Absolutism: British Missionary Societies in the Nineteenth Century." In *Voluntary Religion*, edited by W.J. Sheils and Diana Wood. Oxford, U.K.: Blackwell 1986.

Hobsbawm, Eric J. *Labouring Men: Studies in the History of Labour.* London: Weidenfeld and Nicolson 1964.

Hodgson, Janet. "A Battle for Sacred Power: Christian Beginnings among the Xhosa." In *Christianity in South Africa: A Political, Social and Cultural History*, edited by Richard Elphick and Rodney Davenport. Berkeley: University of California Press 1997.

– "Do We Hear You Nyengana? Dr. J.T. Vanderkemp and the First Mission to the Xhosa." *Religion in Southern Africa* 5, no.1 (January 1984): 3–47.

– *The God of the Xhosa: A Study of the Origins and Developments of the Traditional Concepts of the Supreme Being.* Cape Town: Oxford University Press 1982.

Hodgson, Robert. *The Life of the Right Reverend Beilby Porteus, D.D. Late Bishop of London.* London: T. Cadell and W. Davies 1811.

Hoernlé, Winnifred. "Certain Rites of Transition and the Conception of !Nau among the Hottentots." In *The Social Organization of the Nama and Other Essays by Winnifred Hoernlé: Centenary Volume*, by Winnifred Hoernlé. Johannesburg: Witwatersrand University Press 1985.

– *The Social Organization of the Nama and Other Essays by Winnifred Hoernlé: Centenary Volume*. Johannesburg: Witwatersrand University Press 1985.

Hofmeyr, Isobel. "Jonah and the Swallowing Whale: Orality and Literacy on a Berlin Mission Station in the Transvaal." Paper presented to the Societies of Southern Africa Seminar, Institute of Commonwealth Studies, London 1991.

Hole, Charles. *Early History of the Church Missionary Society for Africa and the East to the End of A.D. 1814*. London: Church Missionary Society 1896.

Holst Petersen, K., ed. *Religion, Development and African Identity*. Uppsala, Sweden: Scandinavian Institute of African Studies 1987.

Hopkins, James. *A Woman to Deliver Her People: Joanna Southcott and English Millenarianism in an Era of Revolution*. Austin: University of Texas Press 1982.

Horne, Melvill. *Letters on Missions: Addressed to the Protestant Ministers of British Churches*. Bristol, U.K.: Bulgin and Rosser 1794.

Horne, Sylvester. *The Story of the London Missionary Society 1795–1895*. London: London Missionary Society 1894.

Horton, Robin. "African Conversion." *Africa* 41, no.2 (April 1979): 85–108.

– "On the Rationality of Conversion." *Africa* 45, no.3 (1975): 219–35.

– "On the Rationality of Conversion." *Africa* 45, no.4 (1975): 372–99.

Houlihan, Mark. "Writing the Apocalypse." PHD thesis, University of Toronto, 1991.

Hunter, Robert. *History of the Missions of the Free Church of Scotland in India and Africa*. London and New York: T. Nelson 1873.

Ignatieff, Michael. *A Just Measure of Pain: The Penitentiary in the Industrial Revolution, 1750–1850*. New York: Pantheon Books 1978.

Ikenga-Metuh, Emefie. "The Shattered Microcosm: A Critical Survey of Explanations of Conversion in Africa." In *Religion, Development and African Identity*, edited by K. Holst Petersen. Uppsala, Sweden: Scandinavian Institute of African Studies 1987

Innes, Joanna. "Politics and Morals: The Reformation of Manners Movement in Later Eighteenth-Century England." In *The Transformation of Political Culture: England and Germany in the Eighteenth Centruy*, edited by Eskhart Hellmuth. Oxford, U.K.: Oxford University Press for the German Historical Institute 1990.

Jaffe, J.A. "The 'Chiliasm of Despair' Reconsidered: Revivalism and Working Class Agitation in County Durham." *Journal of British Studies* 28, no.1 (January 1989): 23–42.

James, C.L.R. *The Black Jacobins: Toussaint L'Ouverture and the San Domingo Revolution.* New York: Vintage Books 1963.

Jedrej, M.C., and Rosalind Shaw, eds. *Dreaming, Religion, and Society in Africa.* Leiden; New York: E.J. Brill 1992.

Joutard, Pierre. *Les Camisards.* Paris: Gallimard/Julliard 1976.

Katzen, M.F. "White Settlers and the Origin of a New Society, 1652–1778." In *The Oxford History of South Africa: South Africa to 1870,* edited by Monica Wilson and Leonard Thompson. Oxford, U.K.: Oxford University Press 1969.

Kayser, F.G. *Rev. F.G. Kayser: Journal and Letters.* Edited by H.C. Hummel. Grahamstown, S.A.: 1990.

Keate, George. *An Account of the Pelew Islands, Situated in the Western Part of the Pacific Ocean, and Communications of Henry Wilson and Some of His Officers Who, in August 1783, Were There Shipwrecked in the Antelope, a Packet Belonging to the Honourable East India Company.* London: Printed for G. Nicol 1788.

Keegan, Timothy. *Colonial South Africa and the Origins of the Racial Order.* Charlottesville: University Press of Virginia 1996.

Kicherer, J.J. *From the Rev. Mr. Kicherer's Narrative of His Mission in South Africa; together with a Scetch of the Public Conference with the Hottentots in London, Nov. 21, 1803.* Wiscasset, Maine: Babson and Rust 1805.

Kiernan, V. "Evangelicalism and the French Revolution." *Past and Present* 1, no.1 (Fébuary 1952): 44–56.

King, Hazel. *Richard Bourke.* Melbourne: Oxford University Press 1971.

Kirk, Tony. "The Cape Economy and the Expropriation of the Kat River Settlement, 1846–1853." In *Economy and Society in Pre-Industrial South Africa,* edited by Shula Marks and Anthony Atmore. London: Longman 1980.

– "Progress and Decline in the Kat River Settlement, 1829–1854." *Journal of African History* 14, no.3 (1973): 411–28.

Kolb, Peter. *The Present State of the Cape of Good Hope.* London: Printed for W. Innys and R. Manby 1731.

Kooiman, Dick. *Conversion and Social Equality in India: The London Missionary Society in South Travancore in the 19th Century.* New Delhi: Manohar Publications 1989.

Kooy, Marcelle, ed. *Studies in Economics and Economic History: Essays in Honour of Professor H.M. Robertson.* London: Macmillan 1972.

Kopf, David. *British Orientalism and the Bengal Renaissance: The Dynamics of Indian Modernization, 1773–1835.* Berkeley: University of California Press 1969.

Krikler, Jeremy. "William MacMillan and the Working Class." In *Africa and Empire: W.M. MacMillan, Historian and Social Critic,* edited by Hugh MacMillan and Shula Marks. Aldershot, U.K.: Published for the Institute of Commonwealth Studies by Temple Smith 1989.

Krüger, Bernhard. *The Pear Tree Blossoms: A History of the Moravian Mission Stations in South Africa, 1737–1869*. Genadendal: The Provincial Board of the Moravian Church in South Africa 1966.

Labode, Modupe. "From Heathen Kraal to Christian Home: Anglican Mission Education and African Christian Girls, 1850–1900." In *Women and Missions: Past and Present: Anthropological and Historical Perceptions*, edited by Fiona Bowie, Deborah Kirkwood, and Shirley Ardener. Providence, R.I.; Oxford, U.K.: Berg 1993.

Lamar, Howard, and Leonard Thompson, eds. *The Frontier in History: North America and South Africa Compared*. New Haven, Conn.: Yale University Press 1981.

Landau, Paul. *The Realm of the Word: Language, Gender and Christianity in a Southern African Kingdom*. Portsmouth, N.H.: Heinemann 1995.

– "'Religion' and Christian Conversion in African History: A New Model." *The Journal of Religious History* 23, no.1 (February 1999): 8–30.

Landman, Christina. *The Piety of Afrikaans Women: Diaries of Guilt*. Koedoespoort, S.A.: Sigma Press, for the University of South Africa 1994.

Laqueur, Thomas. *Religion and Respectability: Sunday Schools and Working Class Culture, 1780–1850*. New Haven, Conn.: Yale University Press 1976.

Larson, Pier M. "'Capacities and Modes of Thinking': Intellectual Engagements and Subaltern Hegemony in the Early History of Malagasy Christianity." *American Historical Review* 102, no.4 (October 1997): 968–1002.

La Trobe, Benjamin. *A Succinct View of the Missions Established among the Heathen by the Church of the Brethren, or Unitas Fratrum. In a Letter to a Friend*. London: M. Lewis 1771.

Latrobe, C.I. *Journal of a Visit to South Africa in 1815 and 1816 with Some Account of the Missionary Settlements of the United Brethren, Near the Cape of Good Hope*. Cape Town: C. Struik 1969.

– *Select Narratives Extracted from the History of the Church by the Name of Unitas Fratrum; or United Brethren. Chronologically Arranged. Part I. Containing the Ancient History*. London, 1806.

LeCordeur, Basil, and Christopher Saunders, eds. *The Kitchingman Papers: Missionary Letters and Journals, 1817–1848 from the Brenthurst Collection, Johannesburg*. Johannesburg: Brenthurst Press 1976.

Legassick, Martin. "The Frontier Tradition in South African Historiography." In *Economy and Society in Pre-industrial South Africa*, edited by Shula Marks and Anthony Atmore. London: Longman 1980.

– "The Griqua, the Sotho Tswana and the Missionaries, 1780–1880: The Politics of a Frontier Zone." PHD thesis, University of California 1969.

– "The Northern Frontier to c. 1840: The Rise and Decline of the Griqua People." In *The Shaping of South African Society, 1652–1840*, edited by Richard Elphick and Hermann Giliomee. Middletown, Conn.: Wesleyan University Press 1988.

Le Vaillant, F. *New Travels into the Interior Parts of Africa by Way of the Cape of Good Hope in the Years 1783, 1784 and 1785*. London: G.G. and J. Robinson 1796.

Levtzion, Nehemia, ed. *Conversion to Islam*. New York: Holmes and Meier 1979.

Lewis, Donald M. *Lighten Their Darkness: The Evangelical Mission to Working Class London, 1828–1860*. New York: Greenwood Press 1986.

Lichtenstein, Henry. *Travels in Southern Africa in the Years 1803, 1804, 1805 and 1806*. Cape Town: Van Riebeeck Society 1928–30.

London Missionary Society. *Four Sermons, Preached in London, at the Twelfth General Meeting of the Missionary Society, May 10, 11, 12 1806*. London: Printed for T. Williams by S. Hollingsworth 1806.

– "The London Missionary Game" (board game). London, 1836.

– *Memoir of the Late Reverend J.T. Van der Kemp, M.D., Missionary in South Africa*. London, 1812.

– *Missionary Sermons*. London, 1799.

– *Reports of the Missionary Society, From Its Formation in the Years 1795 to 1814, Inclusive. Reprinted from the Original Reports. Volume the First*. London, 1815.

– *Sermons Preached in London at the Formation of the Missionary Society*. London, 1797.

Loskiel, George Henry. *History of the Mission of the United Brethren among the Indians in North America*. London: The Brethren's Society for the Furtherance of the Gospel 1794.

Lovegrove, Deryck. *Established Church, Sectarian People: Itinerancy and the Transformation of English Dissent, 1780–1830*. Cambridge, U.K.: Cambridge University Press 1988.

Lovejoy, David S. *Religious Enthusiasm in the New World: Heresy to Revolution*. Cambridge, Mass.: Harvard University Press 1985.

Lovett, Richard. *The History of the LMS, 1795–1895*. 2 vols. London: H. Frowde 1899.

Macartney, George. *An Embassy to China: Being the Journal Kept by Lord Macartney during His Embassy to the Emperor Chïen-lung, 1793–1794*. London: Longmans 1962.

Mackay, David. *In the Wake of Cook: Exploration, Science and Empire, 1780–1801*. London: Croom Helm 1985.

McKay, James. *Reminiscences of the Last Kaffir War, Illustrated with Numerous Anecdotes*. Cape Town, 1970.

– *The Modern Part of an Universal History, from the Earliest Accounts to the Present Time*. London, 1783.

Macllennan, B. *A Proper Degree of Terror; John Graham and the Cape's Eastern Frontier*. Johannesburg: Raven Press 1986.

MacMillan, Hugh, and Shula Marks, eds. *Africa and Empire: W.M. MacMillan, Historian and Social Critic.* Aldershot, U.K.: Published for the Institute of Commonwealth Studies by Temple Smith 1989.

MacMillan, W.M. *Bantu, Boer and Briton: The Making of the South African Native Policy.* London: Faber and Grwyer 1923.

– *The Cape Colour Question: A Historical Survey.* London: Faber and Gwyer 1927.

Majeke, Nosipho [Dora Taylor]. *The Role of the Missionaries in Contest.* Johannesburg: Society of Young Africa 1952.

Malherbe, V.C. "The Cape Khoisan in the Eastern Districts of the Colony before and after Ordinance 50 of 1828." PHD thesis, University of Cape Town 1997.

– "Colonial Justice and the Khoisan in the Immediate Aftermath of Ordinance 50 of 1828: Denouement at Uitenhage." *Kronos: Journal of Cape History/ Tydskrif vir Kaaplandse Geskiedenis* no.24 (November 1997): 77–90.

– "David Stuurman: 'Last Chief of the Hottentots.'" *African Studies* 39, 1 (1980): 47–64.

– "Hermanus and His Sons: Khoi Bandits and Conspirators in the Post-Rebellion Period (1803–1818)." *African Studies* 41, no.2 (1982): 189–202.

– "The Khoi Captains in the Third Frontier War." In *The Khoikhoi Rebellion in the Eastern Cape (1799ᵃ1803),* edited by Susan Newton-King and V.C. Malherbe. Cape Town: Centre for African Studies, University of Cape Town 1981.

– "The Life and Times of Cupido Kakkerlak." *Journal of African History* 20, no.3 (1979): 365–378.

– "Pretorius, Andries." In *Dictionary of South African Biography.* Pretoria: National Boekhandel (forthcoming).

Mamdani, Mahmood. *Citizen and Subject: Contemporary Africa and the Legacy of Late Colonialism.* Princeton, N.J.: Princeton University Press 1997.

Marais, Johannes. S. *The Cape Coloured People 1652–1937.* Johannesburg: Witwatersrand University Press 1957.

– *Maynier and the First Boer Republic.* Cape Town: Maskew Miller 1944.

Marks, Shula. "Khoisan Resistance to the Dutch in the Seventeenth and Eighteenth Centuries." *Journal of South African History* 13, no.1 (1972): 55–80.

Marks, Shula, and Anthony Atmore, eds. *Economy and Society in Pre-industrial South Africa.* London: Longman 1980.

Marsden, William. *The History of Sumatra (1783).* New York: Oxford University Press 1966.

Marshall, John. *Where Are the Juǀwasi of Nyae Nyae? Changes in a Bushman Society, 1958–1981.* Rondebosch, S.A.: Centre for African Studies, University of Cape Town 1984.

Marshall, P.J. *Problems of Empire: Britain and India 1757–1813.* London: Allen and Unwin 1968.

Marshall, P.J., and Glyndwr Williams. *The Great Map of Mankind: Perceptions of New Worlds in the Age of Enlightenment*. Cambridge, Mass.: Harvard University Press 1982.

Martin, A.D. *Dr Vanderkemp*. London, 1931.

Martin, Roger H. *Evangelicals United: Ecumenical Stirrings in Pre-Victorian Britain, 1795–1830*. Metuchen, N.J.: Scarecrow Press 1983.

– "The Pan-Evangelical Impulse in Britain 1795–1830: With Special Reference to Four London Societies." DPHIL thesis, University of Oxford 1974.

Martinson, Paul Varo. *A Theology of World Religions: Interpreting God, Self and World in Semitic, Indian and Chinese Thought*. Minneapolis: Augsberg Publishing House 1987.

Mason, John Edwin. "Paternalism under Siege: Slavery in Theory and Practice during the Era of Reform, c. 1825 through Emancipation." In Nigel Worden and Clifton Crais, eds., *Breaking the Chains: Slavery and Its Legacy in the Nineteenth-Century Cape Colony*. Johannesburg: Witwatersrand University Press 1994: 45–77.

Mason, John Jr. "'Fit for Freedom': The Slaves, Slavery and Emancipation in the Cape Colony, South Africa, 1806 to 1842." PHD dissertation, Yale University 1992.

Mbiti, J.S. *Bible and Theology in African Christianity*. Nairobi: Oxford University Press 1986.

Merians, Linda E. "What They Are, Who We Are: Representations of the Hottentot in Eighteenth-Century Britain," *Eighteenth-Century Life*, 17, 3 (November 1993): 14–39.

Midgley, Clare. *Women Against Slavery: The British Campaigns, 1780–1870*. London and New York: Routledge 1992.

Moffat, John S. *The Lives of Robert and Mary Moffat*. New York: C.A. Armstrong and Son 1886.

Moffat, Robert. *Missionary Labours and Scenes in Southern Africa*. London: J. Snow 1842.

Moodie, Donald, ed. *The Record: or a Series of Official Papers relative to the Condition and Treatment of Native Tribes of South Africa*. Cape Town: A.A. Balkema 1960.

Mostert, Noël. *Frontiers: The Epic of South Africa's Creation and the Tragedy of the Xhosa People*. London: Jonathan Cape 1992.

Mphahlele, Ezekiel. *The African Image*. London: International Publication Service 1962.

Mudimbe, V.Y. *The Invention of Africa: Gnosis, Philosophy, and the Order of Knowledge*. Bloomington: Indiana University Press 1988.

Mugambi, J.N.K. *African Christian Theology: An Introduction*. Nairobi: Heinemann Kenya 1989.

Nahuys van Burgst, Hubert Gerard. *Adventures at the Cape of Good Hope in 1806*. Translated and edited by M.A. Bax-Botha. Cape Town: Friends of the South African Library 1993.

A New General Collection of Voyages and Travels, Consisting of the Most Es-teemed Relations Which Have Hitherto Published in Any Language Com-prehending Everything Remarkable in Its Kind in Europe, Asia, Africa, and America. Collected by Thomas Astley. London: Printed for Thomas Astley 1747.

Newton-King, Susan. "The Enemy within: The Struggle for Ascendancy on the Cape Eastern Frontier 1760–1799." PHD thesis, School of Oriental and African Studies, University of London 1992.

– "The Labour Market of the Cape Colony." In *Economy and Society in Pre-industrial South Africa*, edited by Shula Marks and Anthony Atmore. London: Longman 1980.

– *Masters and Servants on the Cape Eastern Frontier 1760–1803.* Cambridge, U.K.: Cambridge University Press 1999

– "The Rebellion of the Khoi in Graaf-Reinet: 1799 to 1803." In *The Khoikhoi Rebellion in the Eastern Cape (1799–1803)*, edited by Susan Newton-King and V.C. Malherbe. Rondebosch, S.A.: Centre for African Studies, University of Cape Town 1981.

Newton-King, Susan, and V.C. Malherbe, eds. *The Khoikhoi Rebellion in the Eastern Cape (1799-1803).* Rondebosch, S.A.: Centre for African Studies, University of Cape Town 1981.

Niccoli, Ottavia. "The End of Prophecy." *Journal of Modern History* 61 (1989): 667–82.

Noll, Mark A., David W. Bebbington, and George A. Rawlyk, eds. *Evangeli-calism: Comparative Studies of Popular Protestantism in North America, the British Isles and Beyond, 1700–1990.* New York: Oxford University Press 1994.

O'Brien, Susan. "Eighteenth-Century Publishing Networks in the First Years of Transatlantic Evangelicalism." In *Evangelicalism: Comparative Studies of Popular Protestantism in North America, the British Isles and Beyond, 1700–1990*, edited by Mark A. Noll, David W. Bebbington, and George A. Rawlyk. New York: Oxford University Press 1994.

Oliver, William H. *Prophets and Millennialists: The Uses of Biblical Prophecy in England from the 1790s to the 1840s.* Auckland: Auckland University Press; Oxford, U.K.: Oxford University Press 1978.

Oussoren, Aalbertinus Heiman. *William Carey, Especially His Missionary Principles.* Leiden: A.W. Sijthoff 1945.

Paravicini di Capelli, W.B.E. *Reize in de Binnen-Landen van Zuid-Africa.* Edited, with an English summary, by W.J. de Kock. Cape Town: Van Riebeeck Society 1965.

Paterson, William. *A Narrative of Four Journeys into the Country of the Hot-tentots and Caffraria: in the Years One Thousand Seven Hundred and Seventy-Seven, Eight and Nine.* London: J. Johnson 1789.

Patterson, Sheila. "Some Speculations on the Status and Role of the Free People of Colour in the Western Cape." In *Studies in African Social Anthro-*

pology, edited by Meyer Fortes and Sheila Patterson. London; New York; San Francisco: Academic Press 1975.

Payne, Ernest A. "Introduction." In *An Enquiry into the Obligation of Christians, to Use Means for the Conversion of the Heathens*, by William Carey. London: Carey Kingsgate Press 1961.

Peires, J.B. "The British and the Cape, 1814–1834." In *The Shaping of South African Society, 1652–1840*, edited by Richard Elphick and Hermann Giliomee. Middletown, Conn.: Wesleyan University Press 1988.

– *The Dead Will Arise: Nongqawuse and the Great Khosa Cattle-Killing Movement of 1856–7*. Johannesburg: Raven Press 1989.

– *The House of Phalo: A History of the Xhosa People in the Days of their Independence*. Johannesburg: Raven Press 1981.

– "Piet Dragenhoeder's Lament." *Social Dynamics*, 14 (1989): 6–15.

– "Xhosa Expansion before 1800." In *Collected Seminar Papers of the Societies of Southern Africa in the 19th and 20th Centuries*. London: University of London, Institute of Commonwealth Studies 1976.

Penn, Nigel. "The Northern Cape Frontier Zone, 1700–c.1815." PHD thesis, University of Cape Town 1995.

– "The Orange River Frontier Zone, c. 1700–1805." In Andrew B. Smith, ed., *Einiqualand: Studies of the Orange River Frontier*. Cape Town: UCT Press 1995.

– "Reflections on Rereading Peter Kolb with Regard to the Cultural Heritage of the Khoisan." *Kronos: Journal of Cape History/ Tydskrif vir Kaaplandse Geskiedenis* 24 (November 1997): 30–40.

Percy, Carol. "The Language of Captain James Cook: Some Aspects of the Syntax and Morphology of the 'Endeavour' Journal, 1768–1771." DPHIL thesis, Oxford University 1990.

Perry, Alan Frederick. "The American Board of Commissioners for Foreign Missions and the London Missionary Society in the Nineteenth Century: A Study of Ideas." PHD thesis, Washington University 1974.

Philip, John. *Memoir of Mrs. Matilda Smith, Late of Cape Town, Cape of Good Hope*. London, 1824.

– *Researches in South Africa Illustrating the Civil, Moral, and Religious Condition of Native Tribes*. London: James Duncan 1828.

Philip, Robert. *The Life, Times and Missionary Enterprises of the Rev. John Campbell*. London: J. Snow 1841.

Piggin, Stuart. *Making Evangelical Missionaries 1789–1858: The Social Background, Motives and Training of the British Protestant Missionaries to India*. Abingdon: Suttan Courtenav Press 1984.

Platzky, Laurine, and Cherryl Walker. *The Surplus People: Forced Removals in South Africa*. Johannesburg: Ravan Press 1985.

Plumb, J.H., ed. *Studies in Social History: A Tribute to G.M. Trevelyan*. London: Longsman, Green 1955.

Podmore, C.J. "The Bishops and the Brethren: Anglican Attitudes to the Moravians in the Mid-Eighteenth Century." *Journal of Ecclesiastical History* 41, no.4 (1990): 622–646.

– "The Fetter Lane Society, 1738." *Proceedings of the Wesley Historical Society*, vol.47, 1990.

– "The Fetter Lane Society, 1739–1740." *Proceedings of the Wesley Historical Society*, vol.47, 1990.

Porter, Andrew. "Religion and Empire: British Expansion in the Long Nineteenth Century." *Journal of Imperial and Commonwealth History* 20, no.3 (September 1992): 370–90.

Potgieter, ed. *Standard Encyclopedia of Southern Africa*. Cape Town: NASOU, 1970–76.

Potter, Sarah. *The Social Origins and Recruitment of English Protestant Missionaries to India*. PHD THESIS, University of London 1974.

Pratt, Henry. *Memoir of the Rev. Josiah Pratt B.D.: Late Vicar of St. Stephen's, Coleman Street, and for Twenty-One Years Secretary of the Church Missionary Society*. London: Seeleys 1849

Pratt, John H., ed. *Eclectic Notes; or Notes of Discussions on Religious Topics at the Meetings of the Eclectic Society, London, during the Years 1798–1814*. London: J. Nisbet 1856.

Pratt, Mary Louise. "Scratches on the Face of the Country; or, What Mr. Barrow Saw in the Land of the Bushmen." In *"Race," Writing and Difference*, edited by Henry Louis Gates. Chicago: Chicago University Press 1986.

Pringle, Thomas. *Narrative of a Residence in South Africa*. London: Moxon 1835.

Prochaska, F.K. *Women and Philanthropy in Nineteenth-Century England*. Oxford: Oxford University Press 1980.

Rack, Henry D. "Survival and Revival: John Bennett, Methodism, and the Old Dissent." In *Protestant Evangelicalism: Britain, Ireland, Germany and America c.1750–c.1950. Essays in Honour of W.R. Ward*, edited by Keith Robbins. Oxford, U.K.: Published for the Ecclesiastical Society by B. Blackwell 1990.

Ramphele, Mamphela. "On Being Anglican: The Pain and the Privilege." In *Bounty in Bondage: The Anglican Church in Southern Africa*, edited by Frank England and Torquil Paterson. Johannesburg: Raven Press 1989.

Ranger, Terence. "The Local and the Global in Southern African Religious History." In Robert Hefner, ed., *Conversion to Christianity: Historical and Anthropological Perspectives on a Great Transformation*. Berkeley, Calif.: University of California Press 1993.

– "Missionaries, Migrants and the Manyika: The Invention of Ethnicity in Zimbabwe." In *The Creation of Tribalism in Southern Africa*, edited by Leroy Vail. London: Currey 1989.

Read, James Jr. *The Kat River Settlement in 1851: Described in a Series of*

Letters Published in the South African Commercial Adviser. Cape Town, 1852.

Read, James Sr. *The African Witness: or, a Short Account of the Life of Andries Stoffles; Published with Josiah Basset, The Life of a Vagrant, or the Testimony of an Outcast.* London, 1850.

Reay, Barry. "The Context and Meaning of Popular Literacy: Some Evidence from Nineteenth-Century Rural England." *Past and Present* 131 (May 1991): 89–129.

Redford, George, and John Angell James, eds. *The Autobiography of the Rev. William Jay; with Reminiscences of Some Distinguished Contemporaries, Selections from His Correspondence, etc.* London: Hamilton, Adams 1855.

Reynolds, John Stewart. *The Evangelicals at Oxford 1753–1871: A Record of an Unchronicled Movement.* Appleford, U.K.: Marcham Manor Press 1975.

Rhyne, William ten. "A Short Account of the Cape of Good Hope and of the Hottentots Who Inhabit That Region (1686)." In *The Early Cape Hottentots, Described in the Writings of Olfert Dapper (1688), Willem ten Rhyne (1686) and Johannes Gulielmus de Grevenbroek (1695),* edited by Isaac Schapera. Westport, Conn.: Greenwood Press 1970.

Robbins, Keith. "On Prophecy and Politics: Some Pragmatic Reflections." In *Protestant Evangelicalism: Britain, Ireland, Germany and America c.1750–c.1950. Essays in Honour of W.R. Ward,* edited by Keith Robbins. Oxford, U.K.: Published for the Ecclesiastical Society by B. Blackwell 1990.

Robbins, Keith, ed. *Protestant Evangelicalism: Britain, Ireland, Germany and America c.1750–c.1950. Essays in Honour of W.R. Ward.* Oxford, U.K.: Published for the Ecclesiastical Society by B. Blackwell 1990.

Robertson, Roland. *The Sociological Interpretation of Religion.* Oxford, U.K.: Blackwell 1972.

Robinson, A.M. Lewis. "Introduction." In *The Letters of Lady Anne Barnard to Henry Dundas from the Cape and Elsewhere, 1793–1803.* Cape Town: A.A. Balkema 1973.

Rosman, Doreen. *Evangelicals and Culture.* London: Croom Helm 1984.

Ross, Andrew. "The Dutch Reformed Church of South Africa: A Product of the Disruption?" In *Scotland in the Age of Disruption,* edited by Stewart J. Brown and Michael Fry. Edinburgh: Edinburgh University Press 1993.

– *John Philip (1775–1851): Missions, Race and Politics in South Africa.* Aberdeen: Aberdeen University Press 1985.

Ross, Robert. *Adam Kok's Griquas: a Study in the Development of Stratification in South Africa.* Cambridge, U.K.: Cambridge University Press 1976.

– "Bevreesd naar het land van hun gebieder." Amandla: Tijdschrift over zuidelijk-afrika, (November/December 1996): 28–30.

– *Beyond the Pale: Essays on the History of Colonial South Africa.* Middletown, Conn.; Hanover, N.H.: Wesleyan University, published by University Press of New England 1993.

– "Capitalism, Expansion and Incorporation of the South African Frontier."
In *The Frontier in History: North America and South Africa Compared*,
edited by Howard Lamar and Leonard Thompson. New Haven, Conn.: Yale
University Press 1981.

– "The Changing Legal Position of the Khoisan in the Cape Colony." In
Beyond the Pale: Essays on the History of Colonial South Africa. Middle-
town, Conn.; Hanover, N.H.: Wesleyan University, published by University
Press of New England 1993.

– "Congregations, Missionaries and the Grahamstown Church Schism of
1842–3." In *The London Missionary Society in Southern Africa: Historical
Essays in Celebration of the Bicentenary of the LMS in Southern Africa
1799–1999*, edited by John de Gruchy. Cape Town: David Philip 1999.

– "James Cropper, John Philip and the Researches in South Africa." In *Africa
and Empire: W.M. MacMillan, Historian and Social Critic*, edited by Hugh
MacMillan and Shula Marks. Aldershot, U.K.: Published for the Institute of
Commonwealth Studies by Temple Smith 1989.

– "The Kat River Rebellion and Khoikhoi Nationalism: The Fate of an Ethnic
Identification." *Kronos: Journal of Cape History/ Tydskrif vir Kaaplandse
Geskiedenis* 24 (November 1997): 91–105.

– "The Kat River Settlement in the Frontier Wars, 1835–1853: Hintsa's War,
the War of the Axe and Mlanjeni's War." Unpublished paper presented to
conference on War and Violence in Africa at Siegburg, Germany, February
2000.

– "Report on Khoisan Identities and Cultural Heritage Conference." *Kronos:
Journal of Cape History/ Tydskrif vir Kaaplandse Geskiedenis* 24 (November 1997): 154–5.

Ross, Robert, D. van Arkel, and G.C. Quispel. "Going beyond the Pale: On
the Roots of White Supremacy in South Africa." In *Beyond the Pale: Essays
on the History of Colonial South Africa*, by Robert Ross. Middletown,
Conn.; Hanover, N.H.: Wesleyan University, published by University Press
of New England 1993.

Rousseau, Jean-Jacques. *Discours sur l'origine et les fondements de l'inégalité
parmi les hommes*. Paris, 1971.

Rupp, Gordon. *Religion in England 1688–1791*. Oxford, U.K.: Clarendon
Press 1986.

Ryland, John Jr. *The Work of Faith, the Labour of Love, and the Patience of
Hope Illustrated; in the Life and Death of the Reverend Andrew Fuller, Late
Pastor of the Baptist Church at Kettering, and Secretary to the Baptist Missionary Society, from Its Commencement in 1792*. London: Button and Son
1816.

Ryland, John Sr. *The Overthrow of Popery Predicted. The Book of Revelation
Explained*. London, 1850.

Said, Edward. *Orientalism*. London: Routledge and Kegan Paul 1978.

Sales, Jane. *Mission Stations and the Coloured Communities of the Eastern Cape 1800–1852*. Cape Town and Rotterdam: Balkema 1974.

Sanneh, Lamin. *Translating the Message: The Missionary Impact on Culture.* Maryknoll, N.Y.: Orbis Books 1989.

Saunders, Christopher. "Looking Back: 170 Years of Historical Writing on the LMS in South Africa." In *Sent from London: Essays on the London Missionary Society in Southern Africa: Historical Essays in Celebration of the Bicentenary of the LMS in Southern Africa 1799–1999*, edited by John de Gruchy. Cape Town: David Philip 1999

– "Madolo: An African Life." *African Studies* 36, no.2 (1977): 145–54.

– *The Making of the South African Past: Major Historians on Race and Class.* Cape Town: David Philip 1988.

– "Tile and the Thembu Church: Politics and Independence on the Cape Eastern Frontier in the Late Nineteenth Century." *Journal of African History* 11, no.4 (1970): 553–570.

Schama, Simon. *The Embarassment of Riches: An Interpretation of Dutch Culture in the Golden Age*. Berkeley: University of California Press 1988.

– *Patriots and Liberators: Revolution in the Netherlands 1780–1813*. London: Collins 1977.

Schapera, Isaac. *The Khoisan Peoples of South Africa: Bushmen and Hottentots.* London: Routledge and Paul 1951.

– *Apprenticeship at Kuruman: Being the Journals and Letters of Robert and Mary Moffat, 1820–1828*. London: Chatto and Windus 1951.

– *The Early Cape Hottentots, Described in the Writings of Olfert Dapper (1688), Willem ten Rhyne (1686) and Johannes Gulielmus de Grevenbroek (1695)*. Westport, Conn.: Greenwood Press 1970.

– "General Introduction." In *The Early Cape Hottentots, Described in the Writings of Olfert Dapper (1688), Willem ten Rhyne (1686) and Johannes Gulielmus de Grevenbroek (1695)*, edited by Isaac Schapera. Westport, Conn.: Greenwood Press 1970.

Schmidt, Georg, H.C. Bredekamp, and J.L. Hattingh, eds. *Das Tagebuch und die Briefe von Georg Schmidt, dem ersten Missionar in Sudafrika (1737–1744) / Dagboek en Briewe van George Schmidt, Eerste sendeling in Suid-Afrika (1737–1744)*. Bellville, Cape Town: Die Wes-Kaaplandse Institut vir Historiese Navorsing 1981.

Schmidt, Sigrid. "The Relevance of the Bleek/Lloyd Folktales to the General Khoisan Traditions." In Janette Deacon and Thomas A. Dowson, eds., *Voices from the Past: /Xam Bushmen and the Bleek and Lloyd Collection*. Johannesburg: Witwatersrand University Press 1996.

Schoeman, Karel. "Die Londense Sendinggenootskap en die San: Die Stasies Ramah, Konnah en Philippolis, 1816–1828." *South African Historical Journal/ Suid-Afrikaanse Historiese Joernaal* 29 (1993): 132–52.

- "Die Londense Sendinggenootskap en die San: Die Stasies Toornberg en Hephzibah, 1814–1818." *South African Historical Journal/ Suid-Afrikaanse Historiese Joernaal* 28 (1993): 221–34.
- J.J. *Kicherer en die Vroeë Sending, 1799–1806.* Cape Town: 1996.
- "'Maart van Mosambiek': Andries Verhoogd, A Slave in the Service of the London Missionary Society." *Quarterly Bulletin of the South African Library* 49, no.3 (1995): 140–9.
- '*A Thorn Bush That Grows in the Path*': The Missionary Career of Ann Hamilton, 1815–1823. Cape Town: South African Library 1995.
- "Vroeë Geskrifte deur Suid-Afrikaanse Vroue, 1749–1865." *South African Historical Journal/ Suid-Afrikaanse Historiese Joernaal* 36 (1997): 24–47.
- "The Wife of Dr. Van der Kemp: The Life of Sara Janse (1792–1861)." *Quarterly Bulletin of the South African Library* 49, no.4 (1995): 189–97.
Schoffeleers, Matthew. "Ritual Healing and Political Acquiescence: The Case of the Zionist Churches in Southern Africa." *Africa* 61, no.1 (1991): 1–25.
Schrire, Carmel. *Digging Through Darkness: Chronicles of an Archaeologist.* Charlottesville: University Press of Virginia, 1995.
Schrire, Carmel, ed. *Past and Present in Hunter Gatherer Studies.* Orlando, Fla.: Academic Press 1984.
Schutte, Gerrit. "Company and Colonists at the Cape, 1652–1795." In *The Shaping of South African Society, 1652–1840,* edited by Richard Elphick and Hermann Giliomee. Middletown, Conn.: Wesleyan University Press 1988.
Schwartz, Hillel. *The French Prophets: The History of a Millenarian Group in Eighteenth- Century England.* Berkeley: University of California Press 1980.
Scott, John. *The Life of the Rev. Thomas Scott, Rector of Aston Sandford; Including a Narrative Drawn up by Himself and Copious Extracts of His Letters.* London: Printed for L.B. Seeley 1822.
Scott, John, ed. *Letters and Papers of the Late Reverend Thomas Scott; Never Before Published; with Occasional Observations.* London: L.B. Seeley 1824.
Semmel, Bernard. *The Methodist Revolution.* London: Heinemann 1973.
Setiloane, Gabriel M. *African Theology: An Introduction.* Johannesburg: Skotaville Publishers 1986.
Shaw, Barnabas. *Memorials of South Africa.* London: J. Mason, Hamilton, Adams 1841.
Sheils, W.J., and Diana Wood, eds. *Voluntary Religion.* Oxford, U.K.: Blackwell 1986.
Shell, Robert Carl-Heinz. *Children of Bondage: A Social History of the Slave Society at the Cape of Good Hope, 1652–1838.* Hanover and London: Wesleyan University Press, published by University Press of New England 1994
Simeon, Charles. "On the New Birth." In *Let Wisdom Judge: University Addresses and Sermon Outlines.* London: Inter-varsity Fellowship 1959.
Skinner, Quentin. "Language and Social Change." In *Meaning and Context:*

Quentin Skinner and His Critics, edited by James Tully. Cambridge, U.K.: Polity 1988.

– "Meaning and Understanding in the History of Ideas." In *Meaning and Context: Quentin Skinner and His Critics*, edited by James Tully. Cambridge, U.K.: Polity 1988.

Smith, A.B. (ed). *Einiqualand: Studies of the Orange River Frontier*. Cape Town: UCT Press 1995.

Smith, A.B. "Khoikhoi Susceptibility to Virgin Soil Epidemics in the 18th Century." *South African Medical Journal* 75 (January 1989): 25–6.

Smith, Donald C. *Passive Obedience and Prophetic Protest: Social Criticism in the Scottish Church 1830–1945*. New York: P. Lang 1987.

Smith, Sydney. *The Works of Rev. Sydney Smith*. London: Longman, Brown, Green, Longmans and Roberts 1859.

Society for Missions to Africa and the East. *Proceedings of the Church Missionary Society for Africa and the East*. London, 1801–10.

– *Report of the Committee Delivered to the Annual Meeting, Held May 19, 1812, at the New London Tavern, Cheapside*. London, 1812.

Solway, Jaqueline S., and Richard B. Lee. "Foragers, Genuine or Spurious? Situating the Kalahari San in History." *Current Anthropology* 31, no.2 (1990): 109–46.

Spadafora, David. *The Idea of Progress in Eighteenth-Century Britain*. New Haven, Conn.: Yale University Press 1990.

Sparks, Allister. *The Mind of South Africa: The Story of the Rise and Fall of Apartheid*. London: Heinemann 1990.

Sparrman, Anders. *A Voyage to the Cape of Good Hope Towards the Antarctic Polar Circle Round the World to the Country of the Hottentots and the Caffres from the Year 1772–1776*. Cape Town: Van Riebeeck Society 1975.

Spinoza, Baruch. *The Ethics* (trans. and ed. R.H.M. Elwes). New York: Dover 1955.

– *On the Improvement of the Understanding* (trans. R.H.M. Elwes). London and Toronto, n.d.

Stapleton, Timothy J. *Maqoma: Xhosa Resistance to Colonial Advance, 1798–1873*. Johannesburg: Jonathan Ball Publishers 1994.

– "Reluctant Slaughter: Rethinking Maqoma's Role in the Xhosa Cattle-Killing (1853–1857)." *International Journal of African Historical Studies* 26, no.2 (1992): 345–69.

Stevenson, John. "Popular Radicalism and Popular Protest 1789–1815." In *Britain and the French Revolution 1789–1815*, edited by H.T. Dickinson. Basingstoke, U.K.: Macmillan Education 1989.

Steytler, F.A. "Journal Van William F. Corner," *Hertzog-Annale van die Suid-Afrikaanse Akademie vir Wetenskop en kuns, Jaarboek* III (December 1956): 69–89.

Stockenstrom, Andries. *The Autobiography of the Late Sir Andries Stocken-*

strom, Bart, Sometime Lieutenant Governor of the Eastern Province of the Colony of the Cape of Good Hope. Cape Town: J.C. Juta 1887.

– Light and Shade: As Shown in the Character of the Hottentots of the Kat River Settlement and in the Conduct of the Colonial Government Towards Them: Being the Substance of a Speech by the Hon'ble Sir Andries Stockenstrom, Bart, M.L.C. in the Legislative Council of the Cape of Good Hope. Cape Town, 1854.

Stoler, Ann Laura and Frederick Cooper, eds. "Between Metropole and Colony: Rethinking a Research Agenda." In Tensions of Empire: Colonial Cultures in a Bourgeois World, edited by Ann Laura Stoler and Frederick Cooper. Berkeley: University of California Press 1997.

– Tensions of Empire: Colonial Cultures in a Bourgeois World. Berkeley: University of California Press 1997.

Stuart, Doug. "'Of Savages and Heroes': Discourses of Race, Nation and Gender in the Evangelical Missions to Southern Africa in the Nineteenth Century." PHD thesis, Institute of Commonwealth Studies, University of London 1994.

– "'O That We Had Wings' – Race, Sexual Politics and the Missionaries." Paper presented to seminar on Imperial History, Institute of Historical Research, London, 29 October 1990.

– "The 'Wicked Christians' and the 'Children of the Mist' – Missionary and Khoi Interactions at the Cape in the Early Nineteenth Century." Paper presented to seminar on the Societies of Southern Africa in the 19th and 20th Centuries, Institute of Commonwealth Studies, London, 23 November 1990.

Swart, Angela. "The Story of Vehettge Tikkuie." In Digging up Our Foremothers: Stories of Women in Africa, edited by Christina Landman. Pretoria: University of South Africa 1997.

Theal, George McCall. Records of the Cape Colony: from February 1793 to April 1831. Cape Town: Printed for the Government of the Cape Colony 1897–1905.

Thomas, Josiah. An Address to a Meeting Holden at the Town-hall, in the City of Bath ... for the Purpose of Forming a Church Missionary Society in That City. Bath: Meyler and Son 1818.

Thompson, E.P. The Making of the English Working Class. London: Gollancz 1968.

Thompson, Leonard. "Cooperation and Conflict: The Zulu Kingdom and Natal." In The Oxford History of South Africa: South Africa to 1870, edited by Monica Wilson and Leonard Thompson. Oxford, U.K.: Oxford University Press 1969.

– The Political Mythology of Apartheid. New Haven, Conn.: Yale University Press 1985.

Thorne, Susan. Congregational Missions and the Making of an Imperial

Culture in 19ᵗʰ-Century England. Stanford, Calif.: Stanford University Press 1999.

– "The Conversion of Englishmen and the Conversion of the World Inseparable: Missionary Imperialism and the Language of Class in Early Industrial Britain." In *Tensions of Empire: Colonial Cultures in a Bourgeois World*, edited by Ann Laura Stoler and Frederick Cooper. Berkeley: University of California Press 1997.

Tolmie, Murray. *The Triumph of the Saints: The Separate Churches of London, 1616–1649*. Cambridge, U.K.: Cambridge University Press 1977.

Trapido, Stanley. "'The Friends of the Natives': Merchants, Peasants and the Political and Ideological Structure of Liberalism in the Cape, 1854–1910." In *Economy and Society in Pre-industrial South Africa*, edited by Shula Marks and Anthony Atmore. London: Longman 1980.

– "From Paternalism to Liberalism: The Cape Colony, 1800–1834." *The International History Review* 12, no.1 (February 1990): 76–104.

Trial of Andries Botha, Field-Cornet of the Upper Blinkwater, in the Kat River Settlement, for High Treason in the Supreme Court of the Colony of the Cape of Good Hope, on the 12th May, 1852, and Subsequent Days with a Topographical Sketch of the Kat River Settlement and Adjacent Country. Cape Town: S. Solomon 1969.

Tully, James. "The Pen Is a Mighty Sword." In *Meaning and Context: Quentin Skinner and His Critics*, edited by James Tully. Cambridge, U.K.: Polity 1988.

Tully, James, ed. *Meaning and Context: Quentin Skinner and His Critics*. Cambridge, U.K.: Polity 1988.

Turner, Harold W. *Religious Innovation in Africa: Collected Essays on New Religious Movements*. Boston: G.K. Hall 1979.

Turner, Mary. *Slaves and Missionaries: The Disintegration of Jamaican Slave Society, 1787–1834*. Urbana, Ill.: University of Illinois Press 1982.

Vail, Leroy, ed. *The Creation of Tribalism in Southern Africa*. London: Currey 1989.

Valenze, Deborah. *Prophetic Sons and Daughters: Female Preaching and Popular Religion in Industrial England*. Princeton, N.J.: Princeton University Press 1985.

van der Kemp, Francis Adrian [François Adriaan]. *Francis Adrian van der Kemp, 1752–1829: An Autobiography together with Extracts from His Correspondence*. New York; London, 1903.

van der Veer, Peter, ed. *Conversion to Modernities: The Globalization of Christianity*. New York: Routledge 1996.

Venn, John. *Annals of a Clerical Family, Being Some Account of the Family and Descendants of William Venn, Vicar of Otterton, Devon, 1600–1621*. London; New York: Macmillan 1904.

Viljoen, Russell. "Making Sense of the Khoikhoi Cattle-Killing of 1788: An

Episode of Millenarianism in Khoikhoi Society." *Kronos: Journal of Cape History/ Tydskrif vir Kaaplandse Geskiedenis* 24 (November 1997): 62–76.

– "Moravian Missionaries, Khoisan Labour and the Overberg Colonists at the End of the VOC Era, 1792–95." In *Missions and Christianity in South African History*, edited by H.C. Bredekamp and Robert Ross. Johannesburg: University of the Witwatersrand Press 1995.

– "'Revelation of a Revolution': The Prophecies of Jan Parel alias Onse Liewe Heer." *Kronos: Journal of Cape History/ Tydskrif vir Kaaplandse Geskiedenis* 21 (November 1994): 3–15.

Villa-Vicencio, Charles, ed. *Theology and Violence: The South-African Debate.* Johannesburg: Skotaville 1987.

Vos, Michiel Christiaan. *Merkwaardig verhaal aangaande het leven en de lotgevallen van Michiel Christiaan Vos.* Amsterdam: H. Hoveker 1850.

Walker, Eric A. *A History of South Africa.* London: Longmans, Green 1928.

Wallis, J.P.R., ed. *The Matabele Journals of Robert Moffat, 1829–1860.* 2 vols. London: Chatto and Windus 1945.

Walls, A.F. "A Christian Experiment: The Sierra Leone Colony." In *The Mission of the Church and the Propagation of the Faith: Papers Read at the Seventh Summer and the Eighth Winter Meeting of the Ecclesiastical History Society*, edited by G.J. Cuming. Cambridge, U.K.: Cambridge University Press 1970.

Walsh, John "'Methodism' and the Origins of English-Speaking Evangelicalism." In *Evangelicalism: Comparative Studies of Popular Protestantism in North America, the British Isles, and Beyond, 1700–1990*, edited by Mark A. Noll, David W. Bebbington, and George A. Rawlyk. New York: Oxford University Press 1994.

– "Origins of the Evangelical Revival." In *Essays in Modern English Church History*, edited by G.V. Bennett and John Walsh. London: Black 1966.

Walsh, John, Stephen Taylor and Colin Haydon, eds. *The Church of England c.1689–c.1833; from Toleration to Tractarianism.* Cambridge, U.K.: Cambridge University Press 1992.

Walshe, Peter. *Church versus State in South Africa: The Case of the Christian Institute.* London: C. Hurst and Company 1983.

Ward, Kerry. "Links in the Chain: Community, Identity and Migration in Mamre, 1838 to 1938," in Nigel Worden and Clifton Crais, eds., *Breaking the Chains: Slavery and Its Legacy in the Nineteenth-Century Cape Colony.* Johannesburg: Witwatersrand University Press 1994: 313–33.

Ward, W.R. "The Baptists and the Transformation of the Church, 1780–1830." In *Faith and Faction*, edited by W.R. Ward. London: Epworth Press 1993; first published in *Baptist Quarterly* 25, no.4 (1973): 167–84.

– *Faith and Faction.* London: Epworth Press 1993.

– "Power and Piety: The Origins of Religious Revival in the Early Eighteenth

Century." *Bulletin of the John Rylands University Library of Manchester* 63, no.1 (1980): 231–52.

– *The Protestant Evangelical Awakening.* Cambridge: Cambridge University Press 1992.

– "Relations of the Enlightenment and Religious Revival in Central Europe and the English-speaking World." In *Reformation and Reform: England and the Continent c 1500–c 1750*, edited by Derek Baker. London: Published for the Ecclesiastical Historical Society by B. Blackwell 1972.

– *Religion and Society in England 1790–1850.* London: Batsford 1972.

– "Revival and Class Conflict in Early Nineteenth-century Britain." In *Faith and Faction*, edited by W.R. Ward. London: Epworth Press 1993.

Weber, Max. *The Protestant Ethic and the Spirit of Capitalism* (trans. T. Parsons). London: Allen and Unwin 1958.

Wells, Julia. "Eva's Men: Gender and Power." *Journal of African History* 39, no. 3 (1998): 417-37.

Wesley Historical Society. *Proceedings of the Wesley Historical Society.* Helston, U.K.: The Society 1896/97–.

Westerkamp, Marilyn J. *Triumph of the Laity: Scots-Irish Piety and the Great Awakening, 1625–1760.* New York: Oxford University Press 1988.

Whisson, M.G. "Khoi and San – What's in a Name?" Unpublished paper, Rhodes University, Grahamstown, S.A.

Whitehead, William Bailey. *A Letter to the Rev. Daniel Wilson, AM, Minister of St. John's Chapel, Bedford-Row, London, in Reply to His Defence of the Church Missionary Society, and in Vindication of the Rev. the Archdeacon of Bath, Against the Censures Contained in That Publication.* London, 1818.

Wilberforce, William. *The Correspondence of William Wilberforce.* London: J. Murray 1840.

Wilkinson, J.T. "The Rise of Other Methodist Traditions." In *A History of the Methodist Church in Great Britain*, edited by Rupert Davies, A. Raymond George, and Gordon Rupp. London: Epworth Press 1978.

Williams, Donovan. *When Races Meet: The Life and Times of William Ritchie Thomson, Glasgow Society Missionary, Government Agent and Dutch Reformed Church Minister, 1794–1891.* Johannesburg: A.P.B. Publishers 1967.

Williams, Eric. *Capitalism and Slavery.* Chapel Hill: University of North Carolina Press 1944.

Wilmson, Edwin N. *Land Filled with Flies: A Political Economy of the Kalahari.* Chicago: University of Chicago Press 1989.

Wilson, Daniel. *A Defence of the Church Missionary Society against the Objections of the Rev. Josiah Thomas, MA, Archdeacon of Bath.* London, 1818.

Wilson, Ellen Gibson. *The Loyal Blacks.* New York: Capricorn Books 1976.

Wilson, Kathleen. "The Island Race: Captain Cook, Protestant Evangelicalism and the Construction of English National Identity, 1760–1800." In Tony Claydon and Ian McBride, eds., *Protestantism and National Identity: Britain and Ireland, c. 1650–c. 1850.* Cambridge, U.K.: Cambridge University Press 1998: 265–90.

Wilson, M.L. "By Any Other Name: The Nomenclature of the Khoisan." Unpublished paper, South African Museum, Cape Town.

Wilson, Monica. "Notes on the Nomenclature of the Khoisan." *Annals of the South African Museum* 97, no.8 (August 1986): 251–66.

Wilson, Monica, and Leonard Thompson, eds. *The Oxford History of South Africa: South Africa to 1870.* Oxford, U.K.: Oxford University Press 1969.

Woodward, Wendy. "The Petticoat and the Kaross: Missionary Bodies and the Feminine in the London Missionary Society, 1816–1828." Kronos: *Journal of Cape History/Tydskrif vir Kaaplandse Geskiedenis* (November 1996): 91–107.

Woodward, Wendy, Patricia Hayes, and Gary Minkley, eds. *Deep Histories: Gender and Colonialism in Southern Africa.* Amsterdam: Rodopi 2002.

Worden, Nigel, and Clifton Crais, eds. *Breaking the Chains: Slavery and Its Legacy in the Nineteenth-Century Cape Colony.* Johannesburg: Witwatersrand University Press 1994.

Zinzendorf, Nicolaus Ludwig graf von. *An Exposition of the True State, of the Matters Objected in England to the People Known by the Name of Unitas Fratrum.* London, 1755.

Index